Blackstone's

International Human Rights Documents

13th edition

edited by

Alison Bisset

Associate Professor in International Human Rights Law at the University of Reading

OXFORD
UNIVERSITY PRESS

OXFORD
UNIVERSITY PRESS

Great Clarendon Street, Oxford, OX2 6DP,
United Kingdom

Oxford University Press is a department of the University of Oxford.
It furthers the University's objective of excellence in research, scholarship,
and education by publishing worldwide. Oxford is a registered trade mark of
Oxford University Press in the UK and in certain other countries

Published in the United States of America by Oxford University Press
198 Madison Avenue, New York, NY 10016, United States of America

British Library Cataloguing in Publication Data
Data available

ISBN 978–0–19–285853–5

Printed in the UK by
Bell & Bain Ltd., Glasgow

Contents

Alphabetical contents   *vi*
Chronological contents   *viii*
Editor's preface to the thirteenth edition   *x*
New to this edition   *x*

Part I	**International Instruments**	**1**

1919	Covenant of the League of Nations	1
1945	Human Rights Clauses of the Charter of the United Nations	2
1948	Convention on the Prevention and Punishment of the Crime of Genocide	7
1948	Universal Declaration of Human Rights	10
1951	Convention Relating to the Status of Refugees	13
1967	Protocol Relating to the Status of Refugees	23
1965	International Convention on the Elimination of All Forms of Racial Discrimination	25
1966	International Covenant on Civil and Political Rights	33
1966	(First) Optional Protocol to the International Covenant on Civil and Political Rights	45
1990	Second Optional Protocol to the International Covenant on Civil and Political Rights, Aiming at the Abolition of the Death Penalty	47
1966	International Covenant on Economic, Social and Cultural Rights	49
2008	Optional Protocol to the International Covenant on Economic, Social and Cultural Rights	56
1979	Convention on the Elimination of All Forms of Discrimination against Women	61
1999	Optional Protocol to the Convention on the Elimination of All Forms of Discrimination against Women	69
1981	Declaration on the Elimination of All Forms of Intolerance and of Discrimination Based on Religion or Belief	73
1984	Convention against Torture and Other Cruel, Inhuman or Degrading Treatment or Punishment	75
2002	Optional Protocol to the Convention against Torture and Other Cruel, Inhuman or Degrading Treatment or Punishment	84
1986	Declaration on the Right to Development	92
1989	Convention on the Rights of the Child	95
2000	Optional Protocol to the Convention on the Rights of the Child on the Involvement of Children in Armed Conflict	108
2000	Optional Protocol to the Convention on the Rights of the Child on the Sale of Children, Child Prostitution and Child Pornography	111
2011	Optional Protocol to the Convention on the Rights of the Child on a Communications Procedure	117
1990	International Convention on the Protection of the Rights of All Migrant Workers and Members of Their Families	122

1992 Declaration on the Rights of Persons Belonging to National
      or Ethnic, Religious and Linguistic Minorities   147
1998 Guiding Principles on Internal Displacement   149
1998 Rome Statute of the International Criminal Court   155
2006 Convention on the Rights of Persons with Disabilities   198
2006   Optional Protocol to the Convention on the Rights of Persons
          with Disabilities   215
2006 International Convention for the Protection of All Persons from
      Enforced Disappearance   218
2007 United Nations Declaration on the Rights of Indigenous Peoples   230
2011 United Nations Guiding Principles on Business and
      Human Rights   237
2018 United Nations Declaration on the Rights of Peasants and
      Other People Working in Rural Areas   243
2019 ILC Draft Articles on Prevention and Punishment of Crimes Against
      Humanity   255

Part II   UN Human Rights Council   264

2006 General Assembly Resolution 60/251: Human Rights Council   264
2007 Human Rights Council Resolution 5/1: Institution-building
      of the United Nations Human Rights Council   267

Part III   Regional Instruments   285

A. Europe   285

1950 Convention for the Protection of Human Rights and
      Fundamental Freedoms, as amended by Protocols No. 11, 14 and 15   285
1952   First Protocol   295
1963   Fourth Protocol   296
1983   Sixth Protocol   298
1984   Seventh Protocol   299
2000   Twelfth Protocol   301
2002   Thirteenth Protocol   302
2013   Sixteenth Protocol   304
1961 European Social Charter   306
1988   Additional Protocol to the European Social Charter   317
1991   Protocol Amending the European Social Charter   322
1995   Additional Protocol to the European Social Charter Providing
          for a System of Collective Complaints   325
1996   European Social Charter (Revised)   328
1987 European Convention for the Prevention of Torture and
      Inhuman or Degrading Treatment or Punishment   346
1993   First Protocol   350
1993   Second Protocol   351
1992 European Charter for Regional or Minority Languages   352
1995 Framework Convention for the Protection of National Minorities   362

B. European Union   368

2007 Charter of Fundamental Rights of the European Union   368

C. America   **375**

1948 American Declaration of the Rights and Duties of Man   375
1969 American Convention on Human Rights
      ('Pact of San José, Costa Rica')   379
1988   Additional Protocol to the American Convention on Human Rights
         in the Area of Economic, Social and Cultural Rights
         ('Protocol of San Salvador')   394
1990   Protocol to the American Convention on Human Rights
         to Abolish the Death Penalty   400
1984 Cartagena Declaration on Refugees   401
1985 Inter-American Convention to Prevent and Punish Torture   405
1994 Inter-American Convention on the Forced Disappearance
      of Persons   409
1994 Inter-American Convention on the Prevention,
      Punishment and Eradication of Violence against Women
      ('Convention of Belém Do Para')   413

D. Africa   **418**

1969 OAU Convention Governing the Specific Aspects of Refugee Problems in
      Africa   418
1981 African Charter on Human and Peoples' Rights   422
2003   Protocol to the African Charter on Human and Peoples' Rights on the
         Rights of Women in Africa   432
2008   Protocol on the Statute of the African Court of Justice and
         Human Rights   441
1990 African Charter on the Rights and Welfare of the Child   454

E. Arab States   **465**

2004 Arab Charter on Human Rights   465
2014 Gulf Cooperation Council Human Rights Declaration   475

**Part IV   United Nations World Conferences on Human
            Rights**   **480**

1968 Proclamation of Teheran   480
1993 Vienna Declaration and Programme of Action   482

      Index   *501*

Alphabetical contents

A African Charter on Human and Peoples' Rights 1981...422

Protocol to the African Charter on Human and Peoples' Rights on the Rights of Women in Africa 2003...432

Protocol on the Statute of the African Court of Justice and Human Rights 2008...441

African Charter on the Rights and Welfare of the Child 1990...454

American Convention on Human Rights ('Pact of San José, Costa Rica') 1969...379

Additional Protocol to the American Convention on Human Rights in the Area of Economic, Social and Cultural Rights ('Protocol of San Salvador') 1988...394

Protocol to the American Convention on Human Rights to Abolish the Death Penalty 1990...400

American Declaration of the Rights and Duties of Man 1948...375

Arab Charter on Human Rights 2004...465

C Cartagena Declaration on Refugees 1984...401

Charter of Fundamental Rights of the European Union 2007...368

Convention against Torture and Other Cruel, Inhuman or Degrading Treatment or Punishment 1984...75

Optional Protocol to the Convention against Torture and Other Cruel, Inhuman or Degrading Treatment or Punishment 2002...84

Convention for the Protection of Human Rights and Fundamental Freedoms 1950, as amended by Protocols No. 11, 14 and 15...285

First Protocol 1952...295

Fourth Protocol 1963...296

Sixth Protocol 1983...298

Seventh Protocol 1984...299

Twelfth Protocol 2000...301

Thirteenth Protocol 2002...302

Sixteenth Protocol 2013...304

Convention on the Elimination of All Forms of Discrimination against Women 1979...61

Optional Protocol to the Convention on the Elimination of All Forms of Discrimination against Women 1999...69

Convention on the Prevention and Punishment of the Crime of Genocide 1948...7

Convention on the Rights of Persons with Disabilities 2006...198

Optional Protocol to the Convention on the Rights of Persons with Disabilities 2006...215

Convention on the Rights of the Child 1989...95

Optional Protocol to the Convention on the Rights of the Child on the Involvement of Children in Armed Conflict 2000...108

Optional Protocol to the Convention on the Rights of the Child on the Sale of Children, Child Prostitution and Child Pornography 2000...111

Optional Protocol to the Convention on the Rights of the Child on a Communications Procedure 2011...117

Convention Relating to the Status of Refugees 1951...13

Protocol Relating to the Status of Refugees 1967...23

D Declaration on the Elimination of All Forms of Intolerance and of Discrimination Based on Religion or Belief 1981...73

Declaration on the Right to Development 1986...92

Declaration on the Rights of Persons Belonging to National or Ethnic, Religious and Linguistic Minorities 1992...147

E European Charter for Regional or Minority Languages 1992...352

European Convention for the Prevention of Torture and Inhuman or Degrading Treatment or Punishment 1987...346

First Protocol 1993...350

Second Protocol 1993...351

European Social Charter 1961...306

Additional Protocol to the European Social Charter 1988...317

Protocol Amending the European Social Charter 1991...322

Additional Protocol to the European
Social Charter Providing for a System of
Collective Complaints 1995...325

European Social Charter
(Revised) 1996...328

F Framework Convention for the Protection of
National Minorities 1995...362

G General Assembly Resolution 60/251: Human
Rights Council 2006...264

Guiding Principles on Internal
Displacement 1998...149

Gulf Cooperation Council Human Rights
Declaration 2014...475

H Human Rights Clauses of the Charter of the
United Nations 1945...2

Human Rights Council Resolution 5/1:
Institution-building of the United Nations
Human Rights Council 2007...267

Human Rights Provisions of the Covenant of
the League of Nations 1919...1

I ILC Draft Articles on Prevention and Punishment
of Crimes Against Humanity 2019...255

Inter-American Convention on the Forced
Disappearance of Persons 1994...409

Inter-American Convention on the Prevention,
Punishment and Eradication of Violence
against Women ('Convention of Belém Do
Para') 1994...413

Inter-American Convention to Prevent and
Punish Torture 1985...405

International Convention for the
Protection of All Persons from
Enforced Disappearance 2006...218

International Convention on the
Elimination of All Forms of Racial
Discrimination 1965...25

International Convention on the
Protection of the Rights of All Migrant
Workers and Members of Their
Families 1990...122

International Covenant on Civil and Political
Rights 1966...33

(First) Optional Protocol to the
International Covenant on Civil and
Political Rights 1966...45

Second Optional Protocol to the
International Covenant on Civil and
Political Rights, Aiming at the Abolition
of the Death Penalty 1990...47

International Covenant on Economic, Social
and Cultural Rights 1966...49

Optional Protocol to the International
Covenant on Economic, Social and
Cultural Rights 2008...56

O OAU Convention Governing the Specific
Aspects of Refugee Problems in
Africa 1969...418

P Proclamation of Teheran 1968...480

R Rome Statute of the International Criminal
Court 1998...155

U United Nations Declaration on the Rights of
Indigenous Peoples 2007...230

United Nations Declaration on the Rights of
Peasants and Other People Working in
Rural Areas 2018...243

United Nations Guiding Principles on Business
and Human Rights 2011...237

Universal Declaration of Human Rights
1948...10

V Vienna Declaration and Programme of
Action 1993...482

Chronological contents

1919 Human Rights Provisions of the Covenant of the League of Nations...1

1945 Human Rights Clauses of the Charter of the United Nations...2

1948 American Declaration of the Rights and Duties of Man...375

Convention on the Prevention and Punishment of the Crime of Genocide...7

Universal Declaration of Human Rights...10

1950 Convention for the Protection of Human Rights and Fundamental Freedoms, as amended by Protocols No. 11, 14 and 15...285

First Protocol 1952...295

Fourth Protocol 1963...296

Sixth Protocol 1983...298

Seventh Protocol 1984...299

Twelfth Protocol 2000...301

Thirteenth Protocol 2002...302

Sixteenth Protocol 2013...304

1951 Convention Relating to the Status of Refugees...13

Protocol Relating to the Status of Refugees 1967...23

1961 European Social Charter...306

Additional Protocol to the European Social Charter 1988...317

Protocol Amending the European Social Charter 1991...322

Additional Protocol to the European Social Charter Providing for a System of Collective Complaints 1995...325

European Social Charter (Revised) 1996...328

1965 International Convention on the Elimination of All Forms of Racial Discrimination...25

1966 International Covenant on Civil and Political Rights...33

(First) Optional Protocol to the International Covenant on Civil and Political Rights 1966...45

Second Optional Protocol to the International Covenant on Civil and Political Rights, Aiming at the Abolition of the Death Penalty 1990...47

International Covenant on Economic, Social and Cultural Rights...49

Optional Protocol to the International Covenant on Economic, Social and Cultural Rights 2008...56

1968 Proclamation of Teheran...480

1969 American Convention on Human Rights ('Pact of San José, Costa Rica')...379

Additional Protocol to the American Convention on Human Rights in the Area of Economic, Social and Cultural Rights ('Protocol of San Salvador') 1988...394

Protocol to the American Convention on Human Rights to Abolish the Death Penalty 1990...400

OAU Convention Governing the Specific Aspects of Refugee Problems in Africa...418

1979 Convention on the Elimination of All Forms of Discrimination against Women...61

Optional Protocol to the Convention on the Elimination of All Forms of Discrimination against Women 1999...69

1981 African Charter on Human and Peoples' Rights...422

Protocol to the African Charter on Human and Peoples' Rights on the Rights of Women in Africa 2003...432

Protocol on the Statute of the African Court of Justice and Human Rights 2008...441

Declaration on the Elimination of All Forms of Intolerance and of Discrimination Based on Religion or Belief...73

1984 Cartagena Declaration on Refugees...401

Convention against Torture and Other Cruel, Inhuman or Degrading Treatment or Punishment...75

Optional Protocol to the Convention against Torture and Other Cruel, Inhuman or Degrading Treatment or Punishment 2002...84

1985 Inter-American Convention to Prevent and
       Punish Torture...405
1986 Declaration on the Right to
       Development...92
1987 European Convention for the Prevention
       of Torture and Inhuman or Degrading
       Treatment or Punishment...346
       First Protocol 1993...350
       Second Protocol 1993...351
1989 Convention on the Rights of the Child...95
       Optional Protocol to the
          Convention on the Rights of the
          Child on the Involvement of Children in
          Armed Conflict 2000...108
       Optional Protocol to the Convention on
          the Rights of the Child on the Sale of
          Children, Child Prostitution and Child
          Pornography 2000...111
       Optional Protocol to the Convention
          on the Rights of the Child on a
          Communications Procedure
          2011...117
1990 African Charter on the
       Rights and Welfare of the Child...454
       International Convention on the
          Protection of the Rights of All Migrant
          Workers and Members of Their
          Families...122
1992 Declaration on the Rights of Persons
       Belonging to National or Ethnic,
       Religious and Linguistic
       Minorities...147
       European Charter for Regional or Minority
          Languages...352
1993 Vienna Declaration and Programme of
       Action...482
1994 Inter-American Convention on the Forced
       Disappearance of Persons...409

       Inter-American Convention on the
          Prevention, Punishment and Eradication
          of Violence against Women ('Convention
          of Belém Do Para')...413
1995 Framework Convention for the Protection of
       National Minorities...362
1998 Guiding Principles on Internal
       Displacement...149
       Rome Statute of the International Criminal
          Court...155
2004 Arab Charter on Human Rights...465
2006 Convention on the Rights of Persons with
       Disabilities...198
       Optional Protocol to the Convention on
          the Rights of Persons with Disabilities
          2006...215
       General Assembly Resolution 60/251:
          Human Rights Council...264
       International Convention for the
          Protection of All Persons from Enforced
          Disappearance...218
2007 Charter of Fundamental Rights of the
       European Union...368
       Human Rights Council Resolution 5/1:
          Institution-building of the United Nations
          Human Rights Council...267
       United Nations Declaration on the Rights of
          Indigenous Peoples...230
2011 United Nations Guiding Principles on
       Business and Human Rights...237
2014 Gulf Cooperation Council Human Rights
       Declaration...475
2018 United Nations Declaration on the Rights
       of Peasants and Other People Working in
       Rural Areas 2018...243
2019 ILC Draft Articles on Prevention and
       Punishment of Crimes Against
       Humanity...255

Editor's preface to the thirteenth edition

I am delighted to have edited this thirteenth edition of *Blackstone's International Human Rights Documents*. As ever, I hope it provides students of international human rights law with an accessible resource covering the core international and regional instruments.

Many thanks to those who gave their time to review the twelfth edition, and for the very helpful suggestions on what might be considered for inclusion. As with previous editions, decisions on what to include and what to remove have not been easy, particularly as there appears to be a high degree of satisfaction with the content currently covered. The changes for this edition are, therefore, modest. The ILC's important work on the Draft Articles on Prevention and Punishment of Crimes Against Humanity, 2019, has been added to Part I. In order to better balance regional instruments in Part III, the GCC Human Rights Declaration of 2014 has been added. The ECHR has been amended in light of the changes introduced by Protocol No. 15, which came into force in 2021. To accommodate these changes, the Council of Europe Convention on Action Against Trafficking in Human Beings, 2005, has been removed. This brings parity to Parts I and III as it is now some years since the Palermo Protocol was removed from Part I.

Once again, I would like to extend my thanks to the team at OUP for their invaluable guidance and assistance in producing this thirteenth edition.

Alison Bisset
March 2023

New to this edition

The thirteenth edition of *Blackstone's International Human Rights Documents* has been fully revised and updated to incorporate all relevant legislation through to March 2023, and now includes:

- The ILC Draft Articles on Prevention and Punishment of Crimes Against Humanity 2019
- The Gulf Cooperation Council Human Rights Declaration 2014
- The European Convention on Human Rights as amended by Protocol No. 15 (CETS No. 213) as from its entry into force on 1 August 2021.

Blackstone's Statutes
Unsurpassed in authority, reliability, and accuracy

The titles in the Blackstone's Statutes series are collections of carefully reviewed and selected unannotated legislative material and official documents.

We make every effort to ensure titles in the series meet the needs of their target market. They are reviewed by lecturers to match university courses closely and are expertly edited to be manageable in size, whilst retaining their comprehensive coverage.

The editors only include material from legislation that will be valuable to students and lecturers and it is therefore abridged where necessary.

Part I

International Instruments

Covenant of the League of Nations (1919)

The High Contracting Parties,

In order to promote international co-operation and to achieve international peace and security

by the acceptance of obligations not to resort to war,

by the prescription of open, just and honourable relations between nations,

by the firm establishment of the understandings of international law as the actual rule of conduct among Governments, and

by the maintenance of justice and a scrupulous respect for all treaty obligations in the dealings of organised peoples with one another,

Agree to this Covenant of the League of Nations.

Article 22

1. To those colonies and territories which as a consequence of the late war have ceased to be under the sovereignty of the States which formerly governed them and which are inhabited by peoples not yet able to stand by themselves under the strenuous conditions of the modern world, there should be applied the principle that the well-being and development of such peoples form a sacred trust of civilisation and that securities for the performance of this trust should be embodied in this Covenant.

2. The best method of giving practical effect to this principle is that the tutelage of such peoples should be entrusted to advanced nations who by reason of their resources, their experience or their geographical position can best undertake this responsibility, and who are willing to accept it, and that this tutelage should be exercised by them as Mandatories on behalf of the League.

3. The character of the mandate must differ according to the stage of the development of the people, the geographical situation of the territory, its economic conditions and other similar circumstances.

4. Certain communities formerly belonging to the Turkish Empire have reached a stage of development where their existence as independent nations can be provisionally recognised subject to the rendering of administrative advice and assistance by a Mandatory until such time as they are able to stand alone. The wishes of these communities must be a principal consideration in the selection of the Mandatory.

5. Other peoples, especially those of Central Africa, are at such a stage that the Mandatory must be responsible for the administration of the territory under conditions which will guarantee freedom of conscience and religion, subject only to the maintenance of public order and morals, the prohibition of abuses such as the slave trade, the arms traffic and the liquor traffic, and the prevention of the establishment of fortifications or military and naval bases and of military training of the natives for other than police purposes and the defence of territory, and will also secure equal opportunities for the trade and commerce of other Members of the League.

6. There are territories, such as South-West Africa and certain of the South Pacific Islands, which, owing to the sparseness of their population, or their small size, or their remoteness from the centres of civilisation, or their geographical contiguity to the territory of the Mandatory, and other circumstances, can be best administered under the laws of the Mandatory as integral portions of its territory, subject to the safeguards above mentioned in the interests of the indigenous population.

7. In every case of mandate, the Mandatory shall render to the Council an annual report in reference to the territory committed to its charge.

8. The degree of authority, control, or administration to be exercised by the Mandatory shall, if not previously agreed upon by the Members of the League, be explicitly defined in each case by the Council.

9. A permanent Commission shall be constituted to receive and examine the annual reports of the Mandatories and to advise the Council on all matters relating to the observance of the mandates.

Article 23

Subject to and in accordance with the provisions of international conventions existing or hereafter to be agreed upon, the Members of the League:

(a) will endeavour to secure and maintain fair and humane conditions of labour for men, women, and children, both in their own countries and in all countries to which their commercial and industrial relations extend, and for that purpose will establish and maintain the necessary international organisations;

(b) undertake to secure just treatment of the native inhabitants of territories under their control;

(c) will entrust the League with the general supervision over the execution of agreements with regard to the traffic in women and children, and the traffic in opium and other dangerous drugs;

(d) will entrust the League with the general supervision of the trade in arms and ammunition with the countries in which the control of this traffic is necessary in the common interest;

(e) will make provision to secure and maintain freedom of communications and of transit and equitable treatment for the commerce of all Members of the League. In this connection the special necessities of the regions devastated during the war of 1914–1918 shall be borne in mind;

(f) will endeavour to take steps in matters of international concern for the prevention and control of disease.

Article 25

The Members of the League agree to encourage and promote the establishment and cooperation of duly authorised voluntary national Red Cross organisations having as purposes the improvement of health, the prevention of disease and the mitigation of suffering throughout the world.

Charter of the United Nations (1945)*

WE THE PEOPLES OF THE UNITED NATIONS DETERMINED,

to save succeeding generations from the scourge of war, which twice in our lifetime has brought untold sorrow to mankind, and

to reaffirm faith in fundamental human rights, in the dignity and worth of the human person, in the equal rights of men and women and of nations large and small, and

to establish conditions under which justice and respect for the obligations arising from treaties and other sources of international law can be maintained, and

---

to promote social progress and better standards of life in larger freedom,

AND FOR THESE ENDS

to practise tolerance and live together in peace with one another as good neighbours, and to unite our strength to maintain international peace and security, and

to ensure, by the acceptance of principles and the institution of methods, that armed force shall not be used, save in the common interest, and

to employ international machinery for the promotion of the economic and social advancement of all peoples,

HAVE RESOLVED TO COMBINE OUR EFFORTS TO ACCOMPLISH THESE AIMS.

Accordingly, our respective Governments, through representatives assembled in the City of San Francisco, who have exhibited their full powers found to be in good and due form, have agreed to the present Charter of the United Nations and do hereby establish an international organization to be known as the United Nations.

Chapter I Purposes and Principles

Article 1
The Purposes of the United Nations are:

1. To maintain international peace and security, and to that end: to take effective collective measures for the prevention and removal of threats to the peace, and for the suppression of acts of aggression or other breaches of the peace, and to bring about by peaceful means, and in conformity with the principles of justice and international law, adjustment or settlement of international disputes or situations which might lead to a breach of the peace;

2. To develop friendly relations among nations based on respect for the principle of equal rights and self-determination of peoples, and to take other appropriate measures to strengthen universal peace;

3. To achieve international co-operation in solving international problems of an economic, social, cultural or humanitarian character, and in promoting and encouraging respect for human rights and for fundamental freedoms for all without distinction as to race, sex, language, or religion; and

4. To be a centre for harmonizing the actions of nations in the attainment of these common ends.

Article 2
The Organization and its Members, in pursuit of the Purposes stated in Article 1, shall act in accordance with the following Principles:

1. The Organization is based on the principle of the sovereign equality of all its Members.

2. All Members, in order to ensure to all of them the rights and benefits resulting from membership, shall fulfil in good faith the obligations assumed by them in accordance with the present Charter.

3. All Members shall settle their international disputes by peaceful means in such a manner that international peace and security, and justice, are not endangered.

4. All Members shall refrain in their international relations from the threat or use of force against the territorial integrity or political independence of any State, or in any other manner inconsistent with the Purposes of the United Nations.

5. All Members shall give the United Nations every assistance in any action it takes in accordance with the present Charter, and shall refrain from giving assistance to any State against which the United Nations is taking preventive or enforcement action.

6. The Organization shall ensure that States which are not Members of the United Nations act in accordance with these Principles so far as may be necessary for the maintenance of international peace and security.

7. Nothing contained in the present Charter shall authorize the United Nations to intervene in matters which are essentially within the domestic jurisdiction of any State or shall require the Members to submit such matters to settlement under the present Charter; but this principle shall not prejudice the application of enforcement measures under Chapter VII.

Chapter IV The General Assembly

Functions and Powers

Article 10
The General Assembly may discuss any questions or any matters within the scope of the present Charter or relating to the powers and functions of any organs provided for in the present Charter, and, except as provided in Article 12, may make recommendations to the Members of the United Nations or to the Security Council or to both on any such questions or matters.

Article 12
1. While the Security Council is exercising in respect of any dispute or situation the functions assigned to it in the present Charter, the General Assembly shall not make any recommendation with regard to that dispute or situation unless the Security Council so requests.

2. The Secretary-General, with the consent of the Security Council, shall notify the General Assembly at each session of any matters relative to the maintenance of international peace and security which are being dealt with by the Security Council and shall similarly notify the General Assembly, or the Members of the United Nations if the General Assembly is not in session, immediately the Security Council ceases to deal with such matters.

Article 13
1. The General Assembly shall initiate studies and make recommendations for the purpose of:
    (a) promoting international co-operation in the political field and encouraging the progressive development of international law and its codification;
    (b) promoting international co-operation in the economic, social, cultural, educational, and health fields, and assisting in the realization of human rights and fundamental freedoms for all without distinction as to race, sex, language, or religion.

2. The further responsibilities, functions, and powers of the General Assembly with respect to matters mentioned in paragraph 1(b) above are set forth in Chapters IX and X.

Article 14
Subject to the provisions of Article 12, the General Assembly may recommend measures for the peaceful adjustment of any situation, regardless of origin, which it deems likely to impair the general welfare or friendly relations among nations, including situations resulting from a violation of the provisions of the present Charter setting forth the Purposes and Principles of the United Nations.

Article 16
The General Assembly shall perform such functions with respect to the international trusteeship system as are assigned to it under Chapters XII and XIII, including the approval of the trusteeship agreements for areas not designated as strategic.

Chapter IX International Economic and Social Co-operation

Article 55
With a view to the creation of conditions of stability and well-being which are necessary for peaceful and friendly relations among nations based on respect for the principle of equal rights and self-determination of peoples, the United Nations shall promote:
    (a) higher standards of living, full employment, and conditions of economic and social progress and development;

(b) solutions of international economic, social, health, and related problems; and international cultural and educational co-operation; and

(c) universal respect for, and observance of, human rights and fundamental freedoms for all without distinction as to race, sex, language, or religion.

Article 56

All Members pledge themselves to take joint and separate action in co-operation with the Organization for the achievement of the purposes set forth in Article 55.

Article 60

Responsibility for the discharge of the functions of the Organization set forth in this Chapter shall be vested in the General Assembly and, under the authority of the General Assembly, in the Economic and Social Council, which shall have for this purpose the powers set forth in Chapter X.

Chapter X The Economic and Social Council

Composition

Article 61

1. The Economic and Social Council shall consist of fifty-four* Members of the United Nations elected by the General Assembly.

2. Subject to the provisions of paragraph 3, eighteen members of the Economic and Social Council shall be elected each year for a term of three years. A retiring member shall be eligible for immediate re-election.

3. At the first election after the increase in the membership of the Economic and Social Council from twenty-seven to fifty-four members, in addition to the members elected in place of the nine members whose term of office expires at the end of that year, twenty-seven additional members shall be elected. Of these twenty-seven additional members, the term of office of nine members so elected shall expire at the end of one year, and of nine other members at the end of two years, in accordance with arrangements made by the General Assembly.

4. Each member of the Economic and Social Council shall have one representative.

Functions and powers

Article 62

1. The Economic and Social Council may make or initiate studies and reports with respect to international economic, social, cultural, educational, health, and related matters and may make recommendations with respect to any such matters to the General Assembly, to the Members of the United Nations, and to the specialized agencies concerned.

2. It may make recommendations for the purpose of promoting respect for, and observance of, human rights and fundamental freedoms for all.

3. It may prepare draft conventions for submission to the General Assembly, with respect to matters falling within its competence.

4. It may call, in accordance with the rules prescribed by the United Nations, international conferences on matters falling within its competence.

Article 65

The Economic and Social Council may furnish information to the Security Council and shall assist the Security Council upon its request.

---

* **Editor's Note:** Originally eighteen, increased to twenty-seven (1965).

Article 66

1. The Economic and Social Council shall perform such functions as fall within its competence in connection with the carrying out of the recommendations of the General Assembly.

2. It may, with the approval of the General Assembly, perform services at the request of Members of the United Nations and at the request of specialized agencies.

3. It shall perform such other functions as are specified elsewhere in the present Charter or as may be assigned to it by the General Assembly.

Procedure

Article 68

The Economic and Social Council shall set up Commissions in economic and social fields and for the promotion of human rights, and such other commissions as may be required for the performance of its functions.

Chapter XI Declaration Regarding Non-Self-Governing Territories

Article 73

Members of the United Nations which have or assume responsibilities for the administration of territories whose peoples have not yet attained a full measure of self-government recognize the principle that the interests of the inhabitants of these territories are paramount, and accept as a sacred trust the obligation to promote to the utmost, within the system of international peace and security established by the present Charter, the well-being of the inhabitants of these territories, and to this end:

    (a) to ensure, with due respect for the culture of the peoples concerned, their political, economic, social and educational advancement, their just treatment, and their protection against abuses;

    (b) to develop self-government, to take due account of the political aspirations of the peoples, and to assist them in the progressive development of their free political institutions, according to the particular circumstances of each territory and its peoples and their varying stages of advancement;

    (c) to further international peace and security;

    (d) to promote constructive measures of development, to encourage research, and to co-operate with one another and, when and where appropriate, with specialized international bodies with a view to the practical achievement of the social, economic, and scientific purposes set forth in this Article; and

    (e) to transmit regularly to the Secretary-General for information purposes, subject to such limitation as security and constitutional considerations may require, statistical and other information of a technical nature relating to economic, social, and educational conditions in the territories for which they are respectively responsible other than those territories to which Chapters XII and XIII apply.

Chapter XII International Trusteeship System

Article 75

The United Nations shall establish under its authority an international trusteeship system for the administration and supervision of such territories as may be placed thereunder by subsequent individual agreements. These territories are hereinafter referred to as trust territories.

Article 76

The basic objectives of the trusteeship system, in accordance with the Purposes of the United Nations laid down in Article 1 of the present Charter, shall be:

    (a) to further international peace and security;

(b) to promote the political, economic, social, and educational advancement of the inhabitants of the trust territories, and their progressive development towards self-government or independence as may be appropriate to the particular circumstances of each territory and its peoples and the freely expressed wishes of the people concerned, and as may be provided by the terms of each trusteeship agreement;

(c) to encourage respect for human rights and for fundamental freedoms for all without distinction as to race, sex, language, or religion, and to encourage recognition of the interdependence of the peoples of the world; and

(d) to ensure equal treatment in social, economic and commercial matters for all Members of the United Nations and their nationals, and also equal treatment for the latter in the administration of justice, without prejudice to the attainment of the foregoing objectives and subject to the provisions of Article 80.

Article 77

1. The trusteeship system shall apply to such territories in the following categories as may be placed thereunder by means of trusteeship agreements:

(a) territories now held under mandate;

(b) territories which may be detached from enemy States as a result of the Second World War; and

(c) territories voluntarily placed under the system by States responsible for their administration.

2. It will be a matter for subsequent agreement as to which territories in the foregoing categories will be brought under the trusteeship system and upon what terms.

Article 78

The trusteeship system shall not apply to territories which have become Members of the United Nations, relationship among which shall be based on respect for the principle of sovereign equality.

Convention on the Prevention and Punishment of the Crime of Genocide (1948)*

The Contracting Parties,

Having considered the declaration made by the General Assembly of the United Nations in its resolution 96 (I) dated 11 December 1946 that genocide is a crime under international law, contrary to the spirit and aims of the United Nations and condemned by the civilized world;

Recognizing that at all periods of history genocide has inflicted great losses on humanity; and

Being convinced that, in order to liberate mankind from such an odious scourge, international co-operation is required:

Hereby agree as hereinafter provided:

Article I

The Contracting Parties confirm that genocide, whether committed in time of peace or in time of war, is a crime under international law which they undertake to prevent and to punish.

Article II

In the present Convention, genocide means any of the following acts committed with intent to destroy, in whole or in part, a national, ethnical, racial or religious groups, as such:

(a) killing members of the group;

(b) causing serious bodily or mental harm to members of the group;

(c) deliberately inflicting on the group conditions of life calculated to bring about its physical destruction in whole or in part,

(d) imposing measures intended to prevent births within the group;

(e) forcibly transferring children of the group to another group.

Article III
The following acts shall be punishable:
> (a) genocide;
> (b) conspiracy to commit genocide;
> (c) direct and public incitement to commit genocide;
> (d) attempt to commit genocide;
> (e) complicity in genocide.

Article IV
Persons committing genocide or any of the other acts enumerated in Article III shall be punished, whether they are constitutionally responsible rulers, public officials or private individuals.

Article V
The Contracting Parties undertake to enact, in accordance with their respective Constitutions, the necessary legislation to give effect to the provisions of the present Convention and, in particular, to provide effective penalties for persons guilty of genocide or of any of the other acts enumerated in Article III.

Article VI
Persons charged with genocide or any of the other acts enumerated in Article III shall be tried by a competent tribunal of the State in the territory of which the act was committed, or by such international penal tribunal as may have jurisdiction with respect to those Contracting Parties which shall have accepted its jurisdiction.

Article VII
Genocide and the other acts enumerated in Article III shall not be considered as political crimes for the purpose of extradition.

The Contracting Parties pledge themselves in such cases to grant extradition in accordance with their laws and treaties in force.

Article VIII
Any Contracting Party may call upon the competent organs of the United Nations to take such action under the Charter of the United Nations as they consider appropriate for the prevention and suppression of acts of genocide or any of the other acts enumerated in Article III.

Article IX
Disputes between the Contracting Parties relating to the interpretation, application or fulfilment of the present Convention, including those relating to the responsibility of a State for genocide or for any of the other acts enumerated in Article III, shall be submitted to the International Court of Justice at the request of any of the parties to the dispute.

Article X
The present Convention, of which the Chinese, English, French, Russian and Spanish texts are equally authentic, shall bear the date of 9 December 1948.

Article XI
The present Convention shall be open until 31 December 1949 for signature on behalf of any Member of the United Nations and of any non-member State to which an invitation to sign has been addressed by the General Assembly.

The present Convention shall be ratified, and the instruments of ratification shall be deposited with the Secretary-General of the United Nations.

After 1 January 1950 the present Convention may be acceded to on behalf of any Member of the United Nations and of any non-member State which has received an invitation as aforesaid.

Instruments of accession shall be deposited with the Secretary-General of the United Nations.

Article XII

Any Contracting Party may at any time, by notification addressed to the Secretary-General of the United Nations, extend the application of the present Convention to all or any of the territories for the conduct of whose foreign relations that Contracting Party is responsible.

Article XIII

On the day when the first twenty instruments of ratification or accession have been deposited, the Secretary-General shall draw up a *procès-verbal* and transmit a copy thereof to each Member of the United Nations and to each of the non-member States contemplated in Article XI.

   The present Convention shall come into force on the ninetieth day following the date of deposit of the twentieth instrument of ratification or accession.

   Any ratification or accession effected subsequent to the latter date shall become effective on the ninetieth day following the deposit of the instrument of ratification or accession.

Article XIV

The present Convention shall remain in effect for a period of ten years as from the date of its coming into force.

   It shall thereafter remain in force for successive periods of five years for such Contracting Parties as have not denounced it at least six months before the expiration of the current period.

   Denunciation shall be effected by a written notification addressed to the Secretary-General of the United Nations.

Article XV

If, as a result of denunciations, the number of Parties to the present Convention should become less than sixteen, the Convention shall cease to be in force as from the date on which the last of these denunciations shall become effective.

Article XVI

A request for the revision of the present Convention may be made at any time by any Contracting Party by means of a notification in writing addressed to the Secretary-General.

   The General Assembly shall decide upon the steps, if any, to be taken in respect of such request.

Article XVII

The Secretary-General of the United Nations shall notify all Members of the United Nations and the non-member States contemplated in Article XI of the following:

      (a) signatures, ratifications and accessions received in accordance with Article XI;

      (b) notifications received in accordance with Article XII;

      (c) the date upon which the present Convention comes into force in accordance with Article XIII;

      (d) denunciations received in accordance with Article XIV;

      (e) the abrogation of the Convention in accordance with Article XV;

      (f) notifications received in accordance with Article XVI.

Article XVIII

The original of the present Convention shall be deposited in the archives of the United Nations.

   A certified copy of the Convention shall be transmitted to each Member of the United Nations and to each of the non-member States contemplated in Article XI.

Article XIX

The present Convention shall be registered by the Secretary-General of the United Nations on the date of its coming into force.

Universal Declaration of Human Rights (1948)*

PREAMBLE

Whereas recognition of the inherent dignity and of the equal and inalienable rights of all members of the human family is the foundation of freedom, justice and peace in the world,

Whereas disregard and contempt for human rights have resulted in barbarous acts which have outraged the conscience of mankind, and the advent of a world in which human beings shall enjoy freedom of speech and belief and freedom from fear and want has been proclaimed as the highest aspiration of the common people,

Whereas it is essential, if man is not to be compelled to have recourse, as a last resort, to rebellion against tyranny and oppression, that human rights should be protected by the rule of law,

Whereas it is essential to promote the development of friendly relations between nations,

Whereas the peoples of the United Nations have in the Charter reaffirmed their faith in fundamental human rights, in the dignity and worth of the human person and in the equal rights of men and women and have determined to promote social progress and better standards of life in larger freedom,

Whereas Member States have pledged themselves to achieve, in co-operation with the United Nations, the promotion of universal respect for and observance of human rights and fundamental freedoms,

Whereas a common understanding of these rights and freedoms is of the greatest importance for the full realization of this pledge,

Now, therefore, THE GENERAL ASSEMBLY *proclaims*

This Universal Declaration of Human Rights as a common standard of achievement for all peoples and all nations, to the end that every individual and every organ of society, keeping this Declaration constantly in mind, shall strive by teaching and education to promote respect for these rights and freedoms and by progressive measures, national and international, to secure their universal and effective recognition and observance, both among the peoples of Member States themselves and among the peoples of territories under their jurisdiction.

Article 1

All human beings are born free and equal in dignity and rights. They are endowed with reason and conscience and should act towards one another in a spirit of brotherhood.

Article 2

Everyone is entitled to all the rights and freedoms set forth in this Declaration, without distinction of any kind, such as race, colour, sex, language, religion, political or other opinion, national or social origin, property, birth or other status.

Furthermore, no distinction shall be made on the basis of the political, jurisdictional or international status of the country or territory to which a person belongs, whether it be independent, trust, non-self-governing or under any other limitation of sovereignty.

Article 3

Everyone has the right to life, liberty and the security of person.

Article 4

No one shall be held in slavery or servitude; slavery and the slave trade shall be prohibited in all their forms.

Article 5

No one shall be subjected to torture or to cruel, inhuman or degrading treatment or punishment.

Article 6

Everyone has the right to recognition everywhere as a person before the law.

Article 7

All are equal before the law and are entitled without any discrimination to equal protection of the law. All are entitled to equal protection against any discrimination in violation of this Declaration and against any incitement to such discrimination.

Article 8

Everyone has the right to an effective remedy by the competent national tribunals for acts violating the fundamental rights granted him by the constitution or by law.

Article 9

No one shall be subjected to arbitrary arrest, detention or exile.

Article 10

Everyone is entitled in full equality to a fair and public hearing by an independent and impartial tribunal, in the determination of his rights and obligations and of any criminal charge against him.

Article 11

1. Everyone charged with a penal offence has the right to be presumed innocent until proved guilty according to law in a public trial at which he has had all the guarantees necessary for his defence.

2. No one shall be held guilty of any penal offence on account of any act or omission which did not constitute a penal offence, under national or international law, at the time when it was committed. Nor shall a heavier penalty be imposed than the one that was applicable at the time the penal offence was committed.

Article 12

No one shall be subjected to arbitrary interference with his privacy, family, home or correspondence, nor to attacks upon his honour and reputation. Everyone has the right to the protection of the law against such interference or attacks.

Article 13

1. Everyone has the right to freedom of movement and residence within the borders of each State.

2. Everyone has the right to leave any country, including his own, and to return to his country.

Article 14

1. Everyone has the right to seek and to enjoy in other countries asylum from persecution.

2. This right may not be invoked in the case of prosecutions genuinely arising from non-political crimes or from acts contrary to the purposes and principles of the United Nations.

Article 15

1. Everyone has the right to a nationality.

2. No one shall be arbitrarily deprived of his nationality nor denied the right to change his nationality.

Article 16

1. Men and women of full age, without any limitation due to race, nationality or religion, have the right to marry and to found a family. They are entitled to equal rights as to marriage, during marriage and at its dissolution.

2. Marriage shall be entered into only with the free and full consent of the intending spouses.

3. The family is the natural and fundamental group unit of society and is entitled to protection by society and the State.

Article 17

1. Everyone has the right to own property alone as well as in association with others.

2. No one shall be arbitrarily deprived of his property.

Article 18
Everyone has the right to freedom of thought, conscience and religion; this right includes freedom to change his religion or belief, and freedom, either alone or in community with others and in public or private, to manifest his religion or belief in teaching, practice, worship and observance.

Article 19
Everyone has the right to freedom of opinion and expression; this right includes freedom to hold opinions without interference and to seek, receive and impart information and ideas through any media and regardless of frontiers.

Article 20
1. Everyone has the right to freedom of peaceful assembly and association.
2. No one may be compelled to belong to an association.

Article 21
1. Everyone has the right to take part in the government of his country, directly or through freely chosen representatives.
2. Everyone has the right of equal access to public service in his country.
3. The will of the people shall be the basis of the authority of government; this will shall be expressed in periodic and genuine elections which shall be by universal and equal suffrage and shall be held by secret vote or by equivalent free voting procedures.

Article 22
Everyone, as a member of society, has the right to social security and is entitled to realization, through national effort and international co-operation and in accordance with the organization and resources of each State, of the economic, social and cultural rights indispensable for his dignity and the free development of his personality.

Article 23
1. Everyone has the right to work, to free choice of employment, to just and favourable conditions of work and to protection against unemployment.
2. Everyone, without any discrimination, has the right to equal pay for equal work.
3. Everyone who works has the right to just and favourable remuneration ensuring for himself and his family an existence worthy of human dignity, and supplemented, if necessary, by other means of social protection.
4. Everyone has the right to form and to join trade unions for the protection of his interests.

Article 24
Everyone has the right to rest and leisure, including reasonable limitation of working hours and periodic holidays with pay.

Article 25
1. Everyone has the right to a standard of living adequate for the health and well-being of himself and of his family, including food, clothing, housing and medical care and necessary social services, and the right to security in the event of unemployment, sickness, disability, widowhood, old age or other lack of livelihood in circumstances beyond his control.
2. Motherhood and childhood are entitled to special care and assistance. All children, whether born in or out of wedlock, shall enjoy the same social protection.

Article 26
1. Everyone has the right to education. Education shall be free, at least in the elementary and fundamental stages. Elementary education shall be compulsory. Technical and professional education shall be made generally available and higher education shall be equally accessible to all on the basis of merit.
2. Education shall be directed to the full development of the human personality and to the strengthening of respect for human rights and fundamental freedoms. It shall promote understanding,

tolerance and friendship among all nations, racial or religious groups, and shall further the activities of the United Nations for the maintenance of peace.

3. Parents have a prior right to choose the kind of education that shall be given to their children.

Article 27

1. Everyone has the right freely to participate in the cultural life of the community, to enjoy the arts and to share in scientific advancement and its benefits.

2. Everyone has the right to the protection of the moral and material interests resulting from any scientific, literary or artistic production of which he is the author.

Article 28

Everyone is entitled to a social and international order in which the rights and freedoms set forth in this Declaration can be fully realized.

Article 29

1. Everyone has duties to the community in which alone the free and full development of his personality is possible.

2. In the exercise of his rights and freedoms, everyone shall be subject only to such limitations as are determined by law solely for the purpose of securing due recognition and respect for the rights and freedoms of others and of meeting the just requirements of morality, public order and the general welfare in a democratic society.

3. These rights and freedoms may in no case be exercised contrary to the purposes and principles of the United Nations.

Article 30

Nothing in this Declaration may be interpreted as implying for any State, group or person any right to engage in any activity or to perform any act aimed at the destruction of any of the rights and freedoms set forth herein.

Convention Relating to the Status of Refugees (1951)*

PREAMBLE

The High Contracting Parties,

Considering that the Charter of the United Nations and the Universal Declaration of Human Rights approved on 10 December 1948 by the General Assembly have affirmed the principle that human beings shall enjoy fundamental rights and freedoms without discrimination,

Considering that the United Nations has, on various occasions, manifested its profound concern for refugees and endeavoured to assure refugees the widest possible exercise of these fundamental rights and freedoms,

Considering that it is desirable to revise and consolidate previous international agreements relating to the status of refugees and to extend the scope of and the protection accorded by such instruments by means of a new agreement,

Considering that the grant of asylum may place unduly heavy burdens on certain countries, and that a satisfactory solution of a problem of which the United Nations has recognized the international scope and nature cannot therefore be achieved without international cooperation,

Expressing the wish that all States, recognising the social and humanitarian nature of the problem of refugees, will do everything within their power to prevent this problem from becoming a cause of tension between States,

Noting that the United Nations High Commissioner for Refugees is charged with the task of supervising international conventions providing for the protection of refugees, and recognizing

---

that the effective coordination of measures taken to deal with this problem will depend upon the cooperation of States with the High Commission,

Have agreed as follows:

Chapter I General Provisions

Article 1 Definition of the term 'refugee'

A. For the purposes of the present Convention, the term 'refugee' shall apply to any person who:

(1) Has been considered a refugee under the Arrangements of 12 May 1926 and 30 June 1928 or under the Conventions of 28 October 1933 and 10 February 1938, the Protocol of 14 September 1939 or the Constitution of the International Refugee Organization;

Decisions of non-eligibility taken by the International Refugee Organization during the period of its activities shall not prevent the status of refugee being accorded to persons who fulfil the conditions of paragraph 2 of this section;

(2) As a result of events occurring before 1 January 1951 and owing to well-founded fear of being persecuted for reasons of race, religion, nationality, membership of a particular social group or political opinion, is outside the country of his nationality and is unable, or owing to such fear, is unwilling to avail himself of the protection of that country; or who, not having a nationality and being outside the country of his former habitual residence as a result of such events, is unable or, owing to such fear, is unwilling to return to it.

In the case of a person who has more than one nationality, the term 'the country of his nationality' shall mean each of the countries of which he is a national, and a person shall not be deemed to be lacking the protection of the country of his nationality if, without any valid reason based on well-founded fear, he has not availed himself of the protection of one of the countries of which he is a national.

B. (1) For the purposes of this Convention, the words 'events occurring before 1 January 1951' in article 1, section A, shall be understood to mean either (a) 'events occurring in Europe before 1 January 1951'; or (b) 'events occurring in Europe or elsewhere before 1 January 1951'; and each Contracting State shall make a declaration at the time of signature, ratification or accession, specifying which of these meanings it applies for the purpose of its obligations under this Convention.

(2) Any Contracting State which has adopted alternative (a) may at any time extend its obligations by adopting alternative (b) by means of a notification addressed to the Secretary-General of the United Nations.

C. This Convention shall cease to apply to any person falling under the terms of section A if:

(1) He has voluntarily re-availed himself of the protection of the country of his nationality; or

(2) Having lost his nationality, he has voluntarily reacquired it; or

(3) He has acquired a new nationality, and enjoys the protection of the country of his new nationality; or

(4) He has voluntarily re-established himself in the country which he left or outside which he remained owing to fear of persecution; or

(5) He can no longer, because the circumstances in connection with which he has been recognized as a refugee have ceased to exist, continue to refuse to avail himself of the protection of the country of his nationality;

Provided that this paragraph shall not apply to a refugee falling under section A(1) of this article who is able to invoke compelling reasons arising out of previous persecution for refusing to avail himself of the protection of the country of nationality;

(6) Being a person who has no nationality he is, because the circumstances in connection with which he has been recognized as a refugee have ceased to exist, able to return to the country of his former habitual residence;

Provided that this paragraph shall not apply to a refugee falling under section A(1) of this article who is able to invoke compelling reasons arising out of previous persecution for refusing to return to the country of his former habitual residence.

D. This Convention shall not apply to persons who are at present receiving from organs or agencies of the United Nations other than the United Nations High Commissioner for Refugees protection or assistance.

When such protection or assistance has ceased for any reason, without the position of such persons being definitively settled in accordance with the relevant resolutions adopted by the General Assembly of the United Nations, these persons shall *ipso facto* be entitled to the benefits of this Convention.

E. This Convention shall not apply to a person who is recognized by the competent authorities of the country in which he has taken residence as having the rights and obligations which are attached to the possession of the nationality of that country.

F. The provisions of this Convention shall not apply to any person with respect to whom there are serious reasons for considering that:

(a) He has committed a crime against peace, a war crime, or a crime against humanity, as defined in the international instruments drawn up to make provision in respect of such crimes;

(b) He has committed a serious non-political crime outside the country of refuge prior to his admission to that country as a refugee;

(c) He has been guilty of acts contrary to the purposes and principles of the United Nations.

Article 2   General obligations
Every refugee has duties to the country in which he finds himself which require in particular that he conform to its laws and regulations as well as to measures taken for the maintenance of public order.

Article 3   Non-discrimination
The Contracting States shall apply the provisions of this Convention to refugees without discrimination as to race, religion or country of origin.

Article 4   Religion
The Contracting States shall accord to refugees within their territories treatment at least as favourable as that accorded to their nationals with respect to freedom to practise their religion and freedom as regards the religious education of their children.

Article 5   Rights granted apart from this Convention
Nothing in this Convention shall be deemed to impair any rights and benefits granted by a Contracting State to refugees apart from this Convention.

Article 6   The term 'in the same circumstances'
For the purposes of this Convention, the term 'in the same circumstances' implies that any requirements (including requirements as to length and conditions of sojourn or residence) which the particular individual would have to fulfil for the enjoyment of the right in question, if he were not a refugee, must be fulfilled by him, with the exception of requirements which by their nature a refugee is incapable of fulfilling.

Article 7   Exemption from reciprocity
1. Except where this Convention contains more favourable provisions, a Contracting State shall accord to refugees the same treatment as is accorded to aliens generally.

2. After a period of three years' residence, all refugees shall enjoy exemption from legislative reciprocity in the territory of the Contracting States.

3. Each Contracting State shall continue to accord to refugees the rights and benefits to which they were already entitled, in the absence of reciprocity, at the date of entry into force of this Convention for that State.

4. The Contracting States shall consider favourably the possibility of according to refugees, in the absence of reciprocity, rights and benefits beyond those to which they are entitled according to paragraphs 2 and 3, and to extending exemption from reciprocity to refugees who do not fulfil the conditions provided for in paragraphs 2 and 3.

5. The provisions of paragraphs 2 and 3 apply both to the rights and benefits referred to in articles 13, 18, 19, 21 and 22 of this Convention and to rights and benefits for which this Convention does not provide.

Article 8   Exemption from exceptional measures

With regard to exceptional measures which may be taken against the person, property or interests of nationals of a foreign State, the Contracting States shall not apply such measures to a refugee who is formally a national of the said State solely on account of such nationality. Contracting States which, under their legislation, are prevented from applying the general principle expressed in this article, shall, in appropriate cases, grant exemptions in favour of such refugees.

Article 9   Provisional measures

Nothing in this Convention shall prevent a Contracting State, in time of war or other grave and exceptional circumstances, from taking provisionally measures which it considers to be essential to the national security in the case of a particular person, pending a determination by the Contracting State that that person is in fact a refugee and that the continuance of such measures is necessary in his case in the interests of national security.

Article 10   Continuity of residence

1. Where a refugee has been forcibly displaced during the Second World War and removed to the territory of a Contracting State, and is resident there, the period of such enforced sojourn shall be considered to have been lawful residence within that territory.

2. Where a refugee has been forcibly displaced during the Second World War from the territory of a Contracting State and has, prior to the date of entry into force of this Convention, returned there for the purpose of taking up residence, the period of residence before and after such enforced displacement shall be regarded as one uninterrupted period for any purposes for which uninterrupted residence is required.

Article 11   Refugee seamen

In the case of refugees regularly serving as crew members on board a ship flying the flag of a Contracting State, that State shall give sympathetic consideration to their establishment on its territory and the issue of travel documents to them or their temporary admission to its territory particularly with a view to facilitating their establishment in another country.

Chapter II Juridical Status

Article 12   Personal status

1. The personal status of a refugee shall be governed by the law of the country of his domicile or, if he has no domicile, by the law of the country of his residence.

2. Rights previously acquired by a refugee and dependent on personal status, more particularly rights attaching to marriage, shall be respected by a Contracting State, subject to compliance, if this be necessary, with the formalities required by the law of that State, provided that the right in question is one which would have been recognized by the law of that State had he not become a refugee.

Article 13   Movable and immovable property

The Contracting States shall accord to a refugee treatment as favourable as possible and, in any event, not less favourable than that accorded to aliens generally in the same circumstances, as regards the acquisition of movable and immovable property and other rights pertaining thereto, and to leases and other contracts relating to movable and immovable property.

Article 14   Artistic rights and industrial property

In respect of the protection of industrial property, such as inventions, designs or models, trade marks, trade names, and of rights in literary, artistic and scientific works, a refugee shall be accorded in the country in which he has his habitual residence the same protection as is accorded to nationals of that country. In the territory of any other Contracting States, he shall be accorded the same protection as is accorded in that territory to nationals of the country in which he has his habitual residence.

Article 15   Right of association
As regards non-political and non-profit-making associations and trade unions the Contracting States shall accord to refugees lawfully staying in their territory the most favourable treatment accorded to nationals of a foreign country, in the same circumstances.

Article 16   Access to courts
1. A refugee shall have free access to the courts of law on the territory of all Contracting States.
2. A refugee shall enjoy in the Contracting State in which he has his habitual residence the same treatment as a national in matters pertaining to access to the courts, including legal assistance and exemption from *cautio judicatum solvi*.
3. A refugee shall be accorded in the matters referred to in paragraph 2 in countries other than that in which he has his habitual residence the treatment granted to a national of the country of his habitual residence.

Chapter III Gainful Employment

Article 17   Wage-earning employment
1. The Contracting States shall accord to refugees lawfully staying in their territory the most favourable treatment accorded to nationals of a foreign country in the same circumstances, as regards the right to engage in wage-earning employment.
2. In any case, restrictive measures imposed on aliens or the employment of aliens for the protection of the national labour market shall not be applied to a refugee who was already exempt from them at the date of entry into force of this Convention for the Contracting State concerned, or who fulfils one of the following conditions:
    (a) He has completed three years' residence in the country;
    (b) He has a spouse possessing the nationality of the country of residence. A refugee may not invoke the benefit of this provision if he has abandoned his spouse;
    (c) He has one or more children possessing the nationality of the country of residence.
3. The Contracting States shall give sympathetic consideration to assimilating the rights of all refugees with regard to wage-earning employment to those of nationals, and in particular of those refugees who have entered their territory pursuant to programmes of labour recruitment or under immigration schemes.

Article 18   Self-employment
The Contracting States shall accord to a refugee lawfully in their territory treatment as favourable as possible and, in any event, not less favourable than that accorded to aliens generally in the same circumstances, as regards the right to engage on his own account in agriculture, industry, handicrafts and commerce and to establish commercial and industrial companies.

Article 19   Liberal professions
1. Each Contracting State shall accord to refugees lawfully staying in their territory who hold diplomas recognized by the competent authorities of that State, and who are desirous of practising a liberal profession, treatment as favourable as possible and, in any event, not less favourable than that accorded to aliens generally in the same circumstances.
2. The Contracting States shall use their best endeavours consistently with their laws and constitutions to secure the settlement of such refugees in the territories, other than the metropolitan territory, for whose international relations they are responsible.

Chapter IV Welfare

Article 20   Rationing

Where a rationing system exists, which applies to the population at large and regulates the general distribution of products in short supply, refugees shall be accorded the same treatment as nationals.

Article 21   Housing

As regards housing, the Contracting States, in so far as the matter is regulated by laws or regulations or is subject to the control of public authorities, shall accord to refugees lawfully staying in their territory treatment as favourable as possible and, in any event, not less favourable than that accorded to aliens generally in the same circumstances.

Article 22   Public education

1. The Contracting States shall accord to refugees the same treatment as is accorded to nationals with respect to elementary education.

2. The Contracting States shall accord to refugees treatment as favourable as possible, and, in any event, not less favourable than that accorded to aliens generally in the same circumstances, with respect to education other than elementary education and, in particular, as regards access to studies, the recognition of foreign school certificates, diplomas and degrees, the remission of fees and charges and the award of scholarships.

Article 23   Public relief

The Contracting States shall accord to refugees lawfully staying in their territory the same treatment with respect to public relief and assistance as is accorded to their nationals.

Article 24   Labour legislation and social security

1. The Contracting States shall accord to refugees lawfully staying in their territory the same treatment as is accorded to nationals in respect of the following matters:

    (a) In so far as such matters are governed by laws or regulations or are subject to the control of administrative authorities: remuneration, including family allowances where these form part of remuneration, hours of work, overtime arrangements, holidays with pay, restrictions on home work, minimum age of employment, apprenticeship and training, women's work and the work of young persons, and the enjoyment of the benefits of collective bargaining;

    (b) Social security (legal provisions in respect of employment injury, occupational diseases, maternity, sickness, disability, old age, death, unemployment, family responsibilities and any other contingency which, according to national laws or regulations, is covered by a social security scheme), subject to the following limitations:

        (i)   There may be appropriate arrangements for the maintenance of acquired rights and rights in course of acquisition;

        (ii) National laws or regulations of the country of residence may prescribe special arrangements concerning benefits or portions of benefits which are payable wholly out of public funds, and concerning allowances paid to persons who do not fulfil the contribution conditions prescribed for the award of a normal pension.

2. The right to compensation for the death of a refugee resulting from employment injury or from occupational disease shall not be affected by the fact that the residence of the beneficiary is outside the territory of the Contracting State.

3. The Contracting States shall extend to refugees the benefits of agreements concluded between them, or which may be concluded between them in the future, concerning the maintenance of acquired rights and rights in the process of acquisition in regard to social security, subject only to the conditions which apply to nationals of the States signatory to the agreements in question.

4. The Contracting States will give sympathetic consideration to extending to refugees so far as possible the benefits of similar agreements which may at any time be in force between such Contracting States and non-contracting States.

Chapter V Administrative Measures

Article 25   Administrative assistance

1. When the exercise of a right by a refugee would normally require the assistance of authorities of a foreign country to whom he cannot have recourse, the Contracting States in whose territory he is residing shall arrange that such assistance be afforded to him by their own authorities or by an international authority.

2. The authority or authorities mentioned in paragraph 1 shall deliver or cause to be delivered under their supervision to refugees such documents or certifications as would normally be delivered to aliens by or through their national authorities.

3. Documents or certificates so delivered shall stand in the stead of the official instruments delivered to aliens by or through their national authorities, and shall be given credence in the absence of proof to the contrary.

4. Subject to such exceptional treatment as may be granted to indigent persons, fees may be charged for the services mentioned herein, but such fees shall be moderate and commensurate with those charged to nationals for similar services.

5. The provisions of this article shall be without prejudice to articles 27 and 28.

Article 26   Freedom of movement

Each Contracting State shall accord to refugees lawfully in its territory the right to choose their place of residence and to move freely within its territory subject to any regulations applicable to aliens generally in the same circumstances.

Article 27   Identity papers

The Contracting States shall issue identity papers to any refugee in their territory who does not possess a valid travel document.

Article 28   Travel documents

1. The Contracting States shall issue to refugees lawfully staying in their territory travel documents for the purpose of travel outside their territory, unless compelling reasons of national security or public order otherwise require, and the provisions of the Schedule to this Convention shall apply with respect to such documents. The Contracting States may issue such a travel document to any other refugee in their territory; they shall in particular give sympathetic consideration to the issue of such a travel document to refugees in their territory who are unable to obtain a travel document from the country of their lawful residence.

2. Travel documents issued to refugees under previous international agreements by Parties thereto shall be recognized and treated by the Contracting States in the same way as if they had been issued pursuant to this article.

Article 29   Fiscal charges

1. The Contracting States shall not impose upon refugees duties, charges or taxes of any description whatsoever, other or higher than those which are or may be levied on their nationals in similar situations.

2. Nothing in the above paragraph shall prevent the application to refugees of the laws and regulations concerning charges in respect of the issue to aliens of administrative documents including identity papers.

Article 30   Transfer of assets

1. A Contracting State shall, in conformity with its laws and regulations, permit refugees to transfer assets which they have brought into its territory, to another country where they have been admitted for the purposes of resettlement.

2. A Contracting State shall give sympathetic consideration to the application of refugees for permission to transfer assets wherever they may be and which are necessary for their resettlement in another country to which they have been admitted.

Article 31   Refugees unlawfully in the country of refuge

1. The Contracting States shall not impose penalties, on account of their illegal entry or presence, on refugees who, coming directly from a territory where their life or freedom was threatened in the sense of article 1, enter or are present in their territory without authorization, provided they present themselves without delay to the authorities and show good cause for their illegal entry or presence.

2. The Contracting States shall not apply to the movements of such refugees restrictions other than those which are necessary and such restrictions shall only be applied until their status in the country is regularised or they obtain admission into another country. The Contracting States shall allow such refugees a reasonable period and all the necessary facilities to obtain admission into another country.

Article 32   Expulsion

1. The Contracting States shall not expel a refugee lawfully in their territory save on grounds of national security or public order.

2. The expulsion of such a refugee shall be only in pursuance of a decision reached in accordance with due process of law. Except where compelling reasons of national security otherwise require, the refugee shall be allowed to submit evidence to clear himself, and to appeal to and be represented for the purpose before competent authority or a person or persons specially designated by the competent authority.

3. The Contracting States shall allow such a refugee a reasonable period within which to seek legal admission into another country. The Contracting States reserve the right to apply during that period such internal measures as they may deem necessary.

Article 33   Prohibition of expulsion or return ('refoulement')

1. No Contracting State shall expel or return ('refouler') a refugee in any manner whatsoever to the frontiers of territories where his life or freedom would be threatened on account of his race, religion, nationality, membership of a particular social group or political opinion.

2. The benefit of the present provision may not, however, be claimed by a refugee whom there are reasonable grounds for regarding as a danger to the security of the country in which he is, or who, having been convicted by a final judgement of a particularly serious crime, constitutes a danger to the community of that country.

Article 34   Naturalization

The Contracting States shall as far as possible facilitate the assimilation and naturalization of refugees. They shall in particular make every effort to expedite naturalization proceedings and to reduce as far as possible the charges and costs of such proceedings.

Chapter VI Executory and Transitory Provisions

Article 35   Cooperation of the national authorities with the United Nations

1. The Contracting States undertake to cooperate with the Office of the United Nations High Commissioner for Refugees, or any other agency of the United Nations which may succeed it, in the exercise of its functions, and shall in particular facilitate its duty of supervising the application of the provisions of this Convention.

2. In order to enable the Office of the High Commissioner or any other agency of the United Nations which may succeed it, to make reports to the competent organs of the United Nations, the

Contracting States undertake to provide them in the appropriate form with information and statistical data requested concerning:

(a) The condition of refugees;

(b) The implementation of this Convention;

(c) Laws, regulations and decrees which are, or may hereafter be, in force relating to refugees.

Article 36   Information on national legislation

The Contracting States shall communicate to the Secretary-General of the United Nations the laws and regulations which they may adopt to ensure the application of this Convention.

Article 37   Relation to previous conventions

Without prejudice to article 28, paragraph 2, of this Convention, this Convention replaces, as between Parties to it, the Arrangements of 5 July 1922, 31 May 1924, 12 May 1926, 30 June 1928 and 30 July 1935, the Conventions of 28 October 1933 and 10 February 1938, the Protocol of 14 September 1939 and the Agreement of 15 October 1946.

Chapter VII Final Clauses

Article 38   Settlement of disputes and accession

Any dispute between Parties to this Convention relating to its interpretation or application, which cannot be settled by other means, shall be referred to the International Court of Justice at the request of any one of the parties to the dispute.

Article 39   Signature, ratification and accession

1. This Convention shall be opened for signature at Geneva on 28 July 1951 and shall thereafter be deposited with the Secretary-General of the United Nations. It shall be open for signature at the European Office of the United Nations from 28 July to 31 August 1951 and shall be re-opened for signature at the Headquarters of the United Nations from 17 September 1951 to 31 December 1952.

2. This Convention shall be open for signature on behalf of all States Members of the United Nations, and also on behalf of any other State invited to attend the Conference of Plenipotentiaries on the Status of Refugees and Stateless Persons or to which an invitation to sign will have been addressed by the General Assembly. It shall be ratified and the instruments of ratification shall be deposited with the Secretary-General of the United Nations.

3. This Convention shall be open from 28 July 1951 for accession by the States referred to in paragraph 2 of this article. Accession shall be effected by the deposit of an instrument of accession with the Secretary-General of the United Nations.

Article 40   Territorial application clause

1. Any State may, at the time of signature, ratification or accession, declare that this Convention shall extend to all or any of the territories for the international relations of which it is responsible. Such a declaration shall take effect when the Convention enters into force for the State concerned.

2. At any time thereafter any such extension shall be made by notification addressed to the Secretary-General of the United Nations and shall take effect as from the ninetieth day after the day of receipt by the Secretary-General of the United Nations of this notification, or as from the date of entry into force of the Convention for the State concerned, whichever is the later.

3. With respect to those territories to which this Convention is not extended at the time of signature, ratification or accession, each State concerned shall consider the possibility of taking the necessary steps in order to extend the application of this Convention to such territories, subject, where necessary for constitutional reasons, to the consent of the Governments of such territories.

Article 41   Federal clause

In the case of a Federal or non-unitary State, the following provisions shall apply:

(a) With respect to those articles of this Convention that come within the legislative jurisdiction of the federal legislative authority, the obligations of the Federal Government shall to this extent be the same as those of parties which are not Federal States;

(b) With respect to those articles of this Convention that come within the legislative jurisdiction of constituent States, provinces or cantons which are not, under the constitutional system of the Federation, bound to take legislative action, the Federal Government shall bring such articles with a favourable recommendation to the notice of the appropriate authorities of States, provinces or cantons at the earliest possible moment;

(c) A Federal State Party to this Convention shall, at the request of any other Contracting State transmitted through the Secretary-General of the United Nations, supply a statement of the law and practice of the Federation and its constituent units in regard to any particular provision of the Convention showing the extent to which effect has been given to that provision by legislative or other action.

Article 42   Reservations

1. At the time of signature, ratification or accession, any State may make reservations to articles of the Convention other than to articles 1, 3, 4, 16(1), 33, 36–46 inclusive.

2. Any State making a reservation in accordance with paragraph 1 of this article may at any time withdraw the reservation by a communication to that effect addressed to the Secretary-General of the United Nations.

Article 43   Entry into force

1. This Convention shall come into force on the ninetieth day following the day of deposit of the sixth instrument of ratification or accession.

2. For each State ratifying or acceding to the Convention after the deposit of the sixth instrument of ratification or accession, the Convention shall enter into force on the ninetieth day following the date of deposit by such State of its instrument of ratification or accession.

Article 44   Denunciation

1. Any Contracting State may denounce this Convention at any time by a notification addressed to the Secretary-General of the United Nations.

2. Such denunciation shall take effect for the Contracting State concerned one year from the date upon which it is received by the Secretary-General of the United Nations.

3. Any State which has made a declaration or notification under article 40 may, at any time thereafter, by a notification to the Secretary-General of the United Nations, declare that the Convention shall cease to extend to such territory one year after the date of receipt of the notification by the Secretary-General.

Article 45   Revision

1. Any Contracting State may request revision of this Convention at any time by a notification addressed to the Secretary-General of the United Nations.

2. The General Assembly of the United Nations shall recommend the steps, if any, to be taken in respect of such request.

Article 46   Notifications by the Secretary-General of the United Nations

The Secretary-General of the United Nations shall inform all Members of the United Nations and non-member States referred to in article 39:

(a) Of declarations and notifications in accordance with section B of article 1;

(b) Of signatures, ratifications and accessions in accordance with article 39;

(c) Of declarations and notifications in accordance with article 40;

(d) Of reservations and withdrawals in accordance with article 42;

(e) Of the date on which this Convention will come into force in accordance with article 43;

(f) Of denunciations and notifications in accordance with article 44;

(g) Of requests for revision in accordance with article 45.

IN FAITH WHEREOF the undersigned, duly authorized, have signed this Convention on behalf of their respective Governments.

DONE at Geneva, this twenty-eighth day of July, one thousand nine hundred and fifty-one, in a single copy, of which the English and French texts are equally authentic and which shall remain deposited in the archives of the United Nations, and certified true copies of which shall be delivered to all Members of the United Nations and to the non-member States referred to in article 39.

Protocol Relating to the Status of Refugees (1967)*

The States Parties to the present Protocol,

Considering that the Convention relating to the Status of Refugees done at Geneva on 28 July 1951 (hereinafter referred to as the Convention) covers only those persons who have become refugees as a result of events occurring before 1 January 1951,

Considering that new refugee situations have arisen since the Convention was adopted and that the refugees concerned may therefore not fall within the scope of the Convention,

Considering that it is desirable that equal status should be enjoyed by all refugees covered by the definition in the Convention irrespective of the dateline 1 January 1951,

Have agreed as follows:

Article I   General provision

1. The States Parties to the present Protocol undertake to apply articles 2 to 34 inclusive of the Convention to refugees as hereinafter defined.

2. For the purpose of the present Protocol, the term 'refugee' shall, except as regards the application of paragraph 3 of this article, mean any person within the definition of article 1 of the Convention as if the words 'As a result of events occurring before 1 January 1951 and…' and the words '…as a result of such events', in article 1A(2) were omitted.

3. The present Protocol shall be applied by the States Parties hereto without any geographic limitation, save that existing declarations made by States already Parties to the Convention in accordance with article 1B(1)(a) of the Convention, shall, unless extended under article 1B(2) thereof, apply also under the present Protocol.

Article II   Cooperation of the national authorities with the United Nations

1. The States Parties to the present Protocol undertake to cooperate with the Office of the United Nations High Commissioner for Refugees, or any other agency of the United Nations which may succeed it, in the exercise of its functions, and shall in particular facilitate its duty of supervising the application of the provisions of the present Protocol.

2. In order to enable the Office of the High Commissioner or any other agency of the United Nations which may succeed it, to make reports to the competent organs of the United Nations, the States Parties to the present Protocol undertake to provide them with the information and statistical data requested, in the appropriate form, concerning:

(a) The condition of refugees;

(b) The implementation of the present Protocol;

(c) Laws, regulations and decrees which are, or may hereafter be, in force relating to refugees.

Article III   Information on national legislation

The States Parties to the present Protocol shall communicate to the Secretary-General of the United Nations the laws and regulations which they may adopt to ensure the application of the present Protocol.

Article IV   Settlement of disputes

Any dispute between States Parties to the present Protocol which relates to its interpretation or application and which cannot be settled by other means shall be referred to the International Court of Justice at the request of any one of the parties to the dispute.

Article V   Accession

The present Protocol shall be open for accession on behalf of all States Parties to the Convention and of any other State Member of the United Nations or member of any of the specialized agencies or to which an invitation to accede may have been addressed by the General Assembly of the United Nations. Accession shall be effected by the deposit of an instrument of accession with the Secretary-General of the United Nations.

Article VI   Federal clause

In the case of a Federal or non-unitary State, the following provisions shall apply:

    (a) With respect to those articles of the Convention to be applied in accordance with article I, paragraph 1, of the present Protocol that come within the legislative jurisdiction of the federal legislative authority, the obligations of the Federal Government shall to this extent be the same as those of States Parties which are not Federal States;

    (b) With respect to those articles of the Convention to be applied in accordance with article I, paragraph 1, of the present Protocol that come within the legislative jurisdiction of constituent States, provinces or cantons which are not, under the constitutional system of the Federation, bound to take legislative action, the Federal Government shall bring such articles with a favourable recommendation to the notice of the appropriate authorities of States, provinces or cantons at the earliest possible moment;

    (c) A Federal State Party to the present Protocol shall, at the request of any other State Party hereto transmitted through the Secretary-General of the United Nations supply a statement of the law and practice of the Federation and its constituent units in regard to any particular provision of the Convention to be applied in accordance with article I, paragraph 1, of the present Protocol, showing the extent to which effect has been given to that provision by legislative or other action.

Article VII   Reservations and declarations

1. At the time of accession, any State may make reservations in respect of article IV of the present Protocol and in respect of the application in accordance with article I of the present Protocol of any provisions of the Convention other than those contained in articles 1, 3, 4, 16(1) and 33 thereof, provided that in the case of a State Party to the Convention reservations made under this article shall not extend to refugees in respect of whom the Convention applies.

2. Reservations made by States Parties to the Convention in accordance with article 42 thereof shall, unless withdrawn, be applicable in relation to their obligations under the present Protocol.

3. Any State making a reservation in accordance with paragraph 1 of this article may at any time withdraw such reservation by a communication to that effect addressed to the Secretary-General of the United Nations.

4. Declarations made under article 40, paragraphs 1 and 2, of the Convention by a State Party thereto which accedes to the present Protocol shall be deemed to apply in respect of the present Protocol, unless upon accession a notification to the contrary is addressed by the State Party concerned to the Secretary-General of the United Nations. The provisions of article 40, paragraphs 2 and 3, and of article 44, paragraph 3, of the Convention shall be deemed to apply *mutatis mutandis* to the present Protocol.

Article VIII   Entry into force

1. The present Protocol shall come into force on the day of deposit of the sixth instrument of accession.

2. For each State acceding to the Protocol after the deposit of the sixth instrument of accession, the Protocol shall come into force on the date of deposit by such State of its instrument of accession.

Article IX   Denunciation

1. Any State Party hereto may denounce this Protocol at any time by a notification addressed to the Secretary-General of the United Nations.

2. Such denunciation shall take effect for the State Party concerned one year from the date on which it is received by the Secretary-General of the United Nations.

Article X   Notifications by the Secretary-General of the United Nations

The Secretary-General of the United Nations shall inform the States referred to in article V above of the date of entry into force, accessions, reservations and withdrawals of reservations to and denunciations of the present Protocol, and of declarations and notifications relating hereto.

Article XI   Deposit in the archives of the Secretariat of the United Nations

A copy of the present Protocol, of which the Chinese, English, French, Russian and Spanish texts are equally authentic, signed by the President of the General Assembly and by the Secretary-General of the United Nations, shall be deposited in the archives of the Secretariat of the United Nations. The Secretary-General will transmit certified copies thereof to all State Members of the United Nations and to the other States referred to in article V above.

International Convention on the Elimination of All Forms of Racial Discrimination (1965)*

The States Parties to this Convention,

Considering that the Charter of the United Nations is based on the principles of the dignity and equality inherent in all human beings, and that all Member States have pledged themselves to take joint and separate action, in co-operation with the Organization, for the achievement of one of the purposes of the United Nations which is to promote and encourage universal respect for and observance of human rights and fundamental freedoms for all, without distinction as to race, sex, language or religion,

Considering that the Universal Declaration of Human Rights proclaims that all human beings are born free and equal in dignity and rights and that everyone is entitled to all the rights and freedoms set out therein, without distinction of any kind, in particular as to race, colour or national origin,

Considering that all human beings are equal before the law and are entitled to equal protection of the law against any discrimination and against any incitement to discrimination,

Considering that the United Nations has condemned colonialism and all practices of segregation and discrimination associated therewith, in whatever form and wherever they exist, and that the Declaration on the Granting of Independence to Colonial Countries and Peoples of 14 December 1960 (General Assembly resolution 1514 (XV)) has affirmed and solemnly proclaimed the necessity of bringing them to a speedy and unconditional end,

Considering that the United Nations Declaration on the Elimination of All Forms of Racial Discrimination of 20 November 1963 (General Assembly resolution 1904 (XVIII)) solemnly affirms the necessity of speedily eliminating racial discrimination throughout the world in all its forms and manifestations and of securing understanding of and respect for the dignity of the human person,

Convinced that any doctrine of superiority based on racial differentiation is scientifically false, morally condemnable, socially unjust and dangerous, and that there is no justification for racial discrimination, in theory or in practice, anywhere,

Reaffirming that discrimination between human beings on the grounds of race, colour or ethnic origin is an obstacle to friendly and peaceful relations among nations and is capable of disturbing peace and security among peoples and the harmony of persons living side by side even within one and the same State,

Convinced that the existence of racial barriers is repugnant to the ideals of any human society,

Alarmed by manifestations of racial discrimination still in evidence in some areas of the world and by governmental policies based on racial superiority or hatred, such as policies of *apartheid*, segregation or separation,

Resolved to adopt all necessary measures for speedily eliminating racial discrimination in all its forms and manifestations, and to prevent and combat racist doctrines and practices in order to promote understanding between races and to build an international community free from all forms of racial segregation and racial discrimination,

Bearing in mind the Convention concerning Discrimination in respect of Employment and Occupation adopted by the International Labour Organization in 1958, and the Convention against Discrimination in Education adopted by the United Nations Educational, Scientific, and Cultural Organization in 1960,

Desiring to implement the principles embodied in the United Nations Declaration on the Elimination of All Forms of Racial Discrimination and to secure the earliest adoption of practical measures to that end,

Have agreed as follows:

PART I

Article 1

1. In this Convention, the term 'racial discrimination' shall mean any distinction, exclusion, restriction or preference based on race, colour, descent, or national or ethnic origin which has the purpose or effect of nullifying or impairing the recognition, enjoyment or exercise, on an equal footing, of human rights and fundamental freedoms in the political, economic, social, cultural or any other field of public life.

2. This Convention shall not apply to distinctions, exclusions, restrictions or preferences made by a State Party to this Convention between citizens and noncitizens.

3. Nothing in this Convention may be interpreted as affecting in any way the legal provisions of States Parties concerning nationality, citizenship or naturalization, provided that such provisions do not discriminate against any particular nationality.

4. Special measures taken for the sole purpose of securing adequate advancement of certain racial or ethnic groups or individuals requiring such protection as may be necessary in order to ensure such groups or individuals equal enjoyment or exercise of human rights and fundamental freedoms shall not be deemed racial discrimination, provided, however, that such measures do not, as a consequence, lead to the maintenance of separate rights for different racial groups and that they shall not be continued after the objectives for which they were taken have been achieved.

Article 2

1. States Parties condemn racial discrimination and undertake to pursue by all appropriate means and without delay a policy of eliminating racial discrimination in all its forms and promoting understanding among all races, and, to this end:

    (a) each State Party undertakes to engage in no act or practice of racial discrimination against persons, groups of persons or institutions and to ensure that all public authorities and public institutions, national and local, shall act in conformity with this obligation;

    (b) each State Party undertakes not to sponsor, defend or support racial discrimination by any persons or organizations;

    (c) each State Party shall take effective measures to review governmental, national and local policies, and to amend, rescind or nullify any laws and regulations which have the effect of creating or perpetuating racial discrimination wherever it exists;

    (d) each State Party shall prohibit and bring to an end, by all appropriate means, including legislation as required by circumstances, racial discrimination by any persons, group or organization;

(e) each State Party undertakes to encourage, where appropriate, integrationist multi-racial organizations and movements and other means of eliminating barriers between races, and to discourage anything which tends to strengthen racial division.

2. States Parties shall, when the circumstances so warrant, take, in the social, economic, cultural and other fields, special and concrete measures to ensure the adequate development and protection of certain racial groups or individuals belonging to them, for the purpose of guaranteeing them the full and equal enjoyment of human rights and fundamental freedoms. These measures shall in no case entail as a consequence the maintenance of unequal or separate rights for different racial groups after the objectives for which they were taken have been achieved.

Article 3
States Parties particularly condemn racial segregation and *apartheid* and undertake to prevent, prohibit and eradicate all practices of this nature in territories under their jurisdiction.

Article 4
States Parties condemn all propaganda and all organizations which are based on ideas or theories of superiority of one race or group of persons of one colour or ethnic origin, or which attempt to justify or promote racial hatred and discrimination in any form, and undertake to adopt immediate and positive measures designed to eradicate all incitement to, or acts of, such discrimination and, to this end, with due regard to the principles embodied in the Universal Declaration of Human Rights and the rights expressly set forth in Article 5 of this Convention, *inter alia:*

(a) shall declare an offence punishable by law all dissemination of ideas based on racial superiority or hatred, incitement to racial discrimination, as well as all acts of violence or incitement to such acts against any race or group of persons of another colour or ethnic origin, and also the provision of any assistance to racist activities, including the financing thereof;

(b) shall declare illegal and prohibit organizations, and also organized and all other propaganda activities, which promote and incite racial discrimination, and shall recognize participation in such organizations or activities as an offence punishable by law;

(c) shall not permit public authorities or public institutions, national or local, to promote or incite racial discrimination.

Article 5
In compliance with the fundamental obligations laid down in Article 2 of this Convention, States Parties undertake to prohibit and to eliminate racial discrimination in all its forms and to guarantee the right of everyone, without distinction as to race, colour, or national or ethnic origin, to equality before the law, notably in the enjoyment of the following rights:

(a) the right to equal treatment before the tribunals and all other organs administering justice;

(b) the right to security of person and protection by the State against violence or bodily harm, whether inflicted by government officials or by any individual, group or institution;

(c) political rights, in particular the rights to participate in elections—to vote and to stand for election—on the basis of universal and equal suffrage, to take part in the Government as well as in the conduct of public affairs at any level and to have equal access to public service;

(d) other civil rights, in particular:

   (i) the right to freedom of movement and residence within the border of the State;

   (ii) the right to leave any country, including one's own, and to return to one's country;

   (iii) the right to nationality;

   (iv) the right to marriage and choice of spouse;

   (v) the right to own property alone as well as in association with others;

   (vi) the right to inherit;

   (vii) the right to freedom of thought, conscience and religion;

   (viii) the right to freedom of opinion and expression;

   (ix) the right to freedom of peaceful assembly and association;

(e) economic, social and cultural rights, in particular:
   (i)   the rights to work, to free choice of employment, to just and favourable conditions of work, to protection against unemployment, to equal pay for equal work, to just and favourable remuneration;
   (ii) the right to form and join trade unions;
   (iii) the right to housing;
   (iv) the right to public health, medical care, social security and social services;
   (v) the right to education and training;
   (vi) the right to equal participation in cultural activities;
(f) the right of access to any place or service intended for use by the general public, such as transport, hotels, restaurants, cafés, theatres and parks.

Article 6

States Parties shall assure to everyone within their jurisdiction effective protection and remedies, through the competent national tribunals and other State institutions, against any acts of racial discrimination which violate his human rights and fundamental freedoms contrary to this Convention, as well as the right to seek from such tribunals just and adequate reparation or satisfaction for any damage suffered as a result of such discrimination.

Article 7

States Parties undertake to adopt immediate and effective measures, particularly in the fields of teaching, education, culture and information, with a view to combating prejudices which lead to racial discrimination and to promoting understanding, tolerance and friendship among nations and racial or ethnical groups, as well as to propagating the purposes and principles of the Charter of the United Nations, the Universal Declaration of Human Rights, the United Nations Declaration on the Elimination of All Forms of Racial Discrimination, and this Convention.

PART II

Article 8

1. There shall be established a Committee on the Elimination of Racial Discrimination (hereinafter referred to as the Committee) consisting of eighteen experts of high moral standing and acknowledged impartiality elected by States Parties from among their nationals, who shall serve in their personal capacity, consideration being given to equitable geographical distribution and to the representation of the different forms of civilization as well as of the principal legal systems.

2. The members of the Committee shall be elected by secret ballot from a list of persons nominated by the States Parties. Each State Party may nominate one person from among its own nationals.

3. The initial election shall be held six months after the date of the entry into force of this Convention. At least three months before the date of each election the Secretary-General of the United Nations shall address a letter to the States Parties inviting them to submit their nominations within two months. The Secretary-General shall prepare a list in alphabetical order of all persons thus nominated, indicating the States Parties which have nominated them, and shall submit it to the States Parties.

4. Elections of the members of the Committee shall be held at a meeting of States Parties convened by the Secretary-General at United Nations Headquarters. At that meeting, for which two-thirds of the States Parties shall constitute a quorum, the persons elected to the Committee shall be those nominees who obtain the largest number of votes and an absolute majority of the votes of the representatives of States Parties present and voting.

5. (a) The members of the Committee shall be elected for a term of four years. However, the terms of nine of the members elected at the first election shall expire at the end of two years; immediately after the first election the names of these nine members shall be chosen by lot by the Chairman of the Committee.

(b) For the filling of casual vacancies, the State Party whose expert has ceased to function as a member of the Committee shall appoint another expert from among its nationals, subject to the approval of the Committee.

6. States Parties shall be responsible for the expenses of the members of the Committee while they are in performance of Committee duties.

Article 9

1. States Parties undertake to submit to the Secretary-General of the United Nations, for consideration by the Committee, a report on the legislative, judicial, administrative or other measures which they have adopted and which give effect to the provisions of this Convention:

(a) within one year after the entry into force of the Convention for the State concerned; and

(b) thereafter every two years and whenever the Committee so requests. The Committee may request further information from the States Parties.

2. The Committee shall report annually, through the Secretary-General, to the General Assembly of the United Nations on its activities and may make suggestions and general recommendations based on the examination of the reports and information received from the States Parties. Such suggestions and general recommendations shall be reported to the General Assembly together with comments, if any, from States Parties.

Article 10

1. The Committee shall adopt its own rules of procedure.

2. The Committee shall elect its officers for a term of two years.

3. The secretariat of the Committee shall be provided by the Secretary-General of the United Nations.

4. The meetings of the Committee shall normally be held at United Nations Headquarters.

Article 11

1. If a State Party considers that another State Party is not giving effect to the provisions of this Convention, it may bring the matter to the attention of the Committee. The Committee shall then transmit the communication to the State Party concerned. Within three months, the receiving State shall submit to the Committee written explanations or statements clarifying the matter and the remedy, if any, that may have been taken by that State.

2. If the matter is not adjusted to the satisfaction of both parties, either by bilateral negotiations or by any other procedure open to them, within six months after the receipt by the receiving State of the initial communication, either State shall have the right to refer the matter again to the Committee by notifying the Committee and also the other State.

3. The Committee shall deal with a matter referred to it in accordance with paragraph 2 of this Article after it has ascertained that all available domestic remedies have been invoked and exhausted in the case, in conformity with the generally recognized principles of international law. This shall not be the rule where the application of the remedies is unreasonably prolonged.

4. In any matter referred to it, the Committee may call upon the States Parties concerned to supply any other relevant information.

5. When any matter arising out of this article is being considered by the Committee, the States Parties concerned shall be entitled to send a representative to take part in the proceedings of the Committee, without voting rights, while the matter is under consideration.

Article 12

1. (a) After the Committee has obtained and collated all the information it deems necessary, the Chairman shall appoint an *ad hoc* Conciliation Commission (hereinafter referred to as the Commission) comprising five persons who may or may not be members of the Committee. The members of the Commission shall be appointed with the unanimous consent of the parties to the dispute, and its good offices shall be made available to the States concerned with a view to an amicable solution of the matter on the basis of respect for this Convention.

(b) If the States Parties to the dispute fail to reach agreement within three months on all or part of the composition of the Commission, the members of the Commission not agreed upon by the States Parties to the dispute shall be elected by secret ballot by a two-thirds majority vote of the Committee from among its own members.

2. The members of the Commission shall serve in their personal capacity. They shall not be nationals of the States Parties to the dispute or of a State not Party to this Convention.

3. The Commission shall elect its own Chairman and adopt its own rules of procedure.

4. The meetings of the Commission shall normally be held at United Nations Headquarters or at any other convenient place as determined by the Commission.

5. The secretariat provided in accordance with Article 10, paragraph 3, of this Convention shall also service the Commission whenever a dispute among States Parties brings the Commission into being.

6. The States Parties to the dispute shall share equally all the expenses of the members of the Commission in accordance with estimates to be provided by the Secretary-General of the United Nations.

7. The Secretary-General shall be empowered to pay the expenses of the members of the Commission, if necessary, before reimbursement by the States Parties to the dispute in accordance with paragraph 6 of this Article.

8. The information obtained and collated by the Committee shall be made available to the Commission, and the Commission may call upon the States concerned to supply any other relevant information.

Article 13

1. When the Commission has fully considered the matter, it shall prepare and submit to the Chairman of the Committee a report embodying its findings on all questions of fact relevant to the issue between the parties and containing such recommendations as it may think proper for the amicable solution of the dispute.

2. The Chairman of the Committee shall communicate the report of the Commission to each of the States Parties to the dispute. These States shall, within three months, inform the Chairman of the Committee whether or not they accept the recommendations contained in the report of the Commission.

3. After the period provided for in paragraph 2 of this Article, the Chairman of the Committee shall communicate the report of the Commission and the declarations of the States Parties concerned to the other States Parties to this Convention.

Article 14

1. A State Party may at any time declare that it recognizes the competence of the Committee to receive and consider communications from individuals or groups of individuals within its jurisdiction claiming to be victims of a violation by that State Party of any of the rights set forth in this Convention. No communication shall be received by the Committee if it concerns a State Party which has not made such a declaration.

2. Any State Party which makes a declaration as provided for in paragraph 1 of this Article may establish or indicate a body within its national legal order which shall be competent to receive and consider petitions from individuals and groups of individuals within its jurisdiction who claim to be victims of a violation of any of the rights set forth in this Convention and who have exhausted other available local remedies.

3. A declaration made in accordance with paragraph 1 of this Article and the name of any body established or indicated in accordance with paragraph 2 of this Article shall be deposited by the State Party concerned with the Secretary-General of the United Nations, who shall transmit copies thereof to the other States Parties. A declaration may be withdrawn at any time by notification to the Secretary-General, but such a withdrawal shall not affect communications pending before the Committee.

4. A register of petitions shall be kept by the body established or indicated in accordance with paragraph 2 of this Article, and certified copies of the register shall be filed annually through appropriate channels with the Secretary-General on the understanding that the contents shall not be publicly disclosed.

5. In the event of failure to obtain satisfaction from the body established or indicated in accordance with paragraph 2 of this Article, the petitioner shall have the right to communicate the matter to the Committee within six months.

6. (a) The Committee shall confidentially bring any communication referred to it to the attention of the State Party alleged to be violating any provision of this Convention, but the identity of the individual or groups of individuals concerned shall not be revealed without his or their express consent. The Committee shall not receive anonymous communications.

   (b) Within three months, the receiving State shall submit to the Committee written explanations or statements clarifying the matter and the remedy, if any, that may have been taken by that State.

7. (a) The Committee shall consider communications in the light of all information made available to it by the State Party concerned and by the petitioner. The Committee shall not consider any communication from a petitioner unless it has ascertained that the petitioner has exhausted all available domestic remedies. However, this shall not be the rule where the application of the remedies is unreasonably prolonged.

   (b) The Committee shall forward its suggestions and recommendations, if any, to the State Party concerned and to the petitioner.

8. The Committee shall include in its annual report a summary of such communications and, where appropriate, a summary of the explanations and statements of the States Parties concerned and of its own suggestions and recommendations.

9. The Committee shall be competent to exercise the functions provided for in this Article only when at least ten States Parties to this Convention are bound by declarations in accordance with paragraph 1 of this Article.

Article 15

1. Pending the achievement of the objectives of the Declaration on the Granting of Independence to Colonial Countries and Peoples, contained in General Assembly resolution 1514 (XV) of 14 December 1960, the provisions of this Convention shall in no way limit the right of petition granted to these peoples by other international instruments or by the United Nations and its specialized agencies.

2. (a) The Committee established under Article 8, paragraph 1, of this Convention shall receive copies of the petitions from, and submit expressions of opinion and recommendations on these petitions to, the bodies of the United Nations which deal with matters directly related to the principles and objectives of this Convention in their consideration of petitions from the inhabitants of Trust and Non-Self-Governing Territories and all other territories to which General Assembly resolution 1514 (XV) applies, relating to matters covered by this Convention which are before these bodies.

   (b) The Committee shall receive from the competent bodies of the United Nations copies of the reports concerning the legislative, judicial, administrative or other measures directly related to the principles and objectives of this Convention applied by the administering Powers within the Territories mentioned in subparagraph (a) of this paragraph, and shall express opinions and make recommendations to these bodies.

3. The Committee shall include in its report to the General Assembly a summary of the petitions and reports it has received from United Nations bodies, and the expressions of opinion and recommendations of the Committee relating to the said petitions and reports.

4. The Committee shall request from the Secretary-General of the United Nations all information relevant to the objectives of this Convention and available to him regarding the Territories mentioned in paragraph 2(a) of this Article.

Article 16

The provisions of this Convention concerning the settlement of disputes or complaints shall be applied without prejudice to other procedures for settling disputes or complaints in the field of discrimination laid down in the constituent instruments of, or in conventions adopted by, the United Nations and its specialized agencies, and shall not prevent the States Parties from having recourse to other procedures for settling a dispute in accordance with general or special international agreements in force between them.

PART III

Article 17

1. This Convention is open for signature by any State Member of the United Nations or member of any of its specialized agencies, by any State Party to the Statute of the International Court of Justice, and by any other State which has been invited by the General Assembly of the United Nations to become a Party to this Convention.

2. This Convention is subject to ratification. Instruments of ratification shall be deposited with the Secretary-General of the United Nations.

Article 18

1. This Convention shall be open to accession by any State referred to in Article 17, paragraph 1, of the Convention.

2. Accession shall be effected by the deposit of an instrument of accession with the Secretary-General of the United Nations.

Article 19

1. This Convention shall enter into force on the thirtieth day after the date of the deposit with the Secretary-General of the United Nations of the twenty-seventh instrument of ratification or instrument of accession.

2. For each State ratifying this Convention or acceding to it after the deposit of the twenty-seventh instrument of ratification or instrument of accession, the Convention shall enter into force on the thirtieth day after the date of the deposit of its own instrument of ratification or instrument of accession.

Article 20

1. The Secretary-General of the United Nations shall receive and circulate to all States which are or may become Parties to this Convention reservations made by States at the time of ratification or accession. Any State which objects to the reservation shall, within a period of ninety days from the date of the said communication, notify the Secretary-General that it does not accept it.

2. A reservation incompatible with the object and purpose of this Convention shall not be permitted, nor shall a reservation the effect of which would inhibit the operation of any of the bodies established by this Convention be allowed. A reservation shall be considered incompatible or inhibitive if at least two-thirds of the States Parties to this Convention object to it.

3. Reservations may be withdrawn at any time by notification to this effect addressed to the Secretary-General. Such notification shall take effect on the date on which it is received.

Article 21

A State Party may denounce this Convention by written notification to the Secretary-General of the United Nations. Denunciation shall take effect one year after the date of receipt of the notification by the Secretary-General.

Article 22

Any dispute between two or more States Parties with respect to the interpretation or application of this Convention, which is not settled by negotiation or by the procedures expressly provided for in this Convention, shall, at the request of any of the parties to the dispute, be referred to the International Court of Justice for decision, unless the disputants agree to another mode of settlement.

Article 23

1. A request for the revision of this Convention may be made at any time by any State Party by means of a notification in writing addressed to the Secretary-General of the United Nations.

2. The General Assembly of the United Nations shall decide upon the steps, if any, to be taken in respect of such a request.

Article 24

The Secretary-General of the United Nations shall inform all States referred to in Article 17, paragraph 1, of this Convention of the following particulars:

    (a) signatures, ratifications and accessions under Articles 17 and 18;

    (b) the date of entry into force of this Convention under Article 19;

    (c) communications and declarations received under Articles 14, 20 and 23;

    (d) denunciations under Article 21.

Article 25

1. This Convention, of which the Chinese, English, French, Russian and Spanish texts are equally authentic, shall be deposited in the archives of the United Nations.

2. The Secretary-General of the United Nations shall transmit certified copies of this Convention to all States belonging to any of the categories mentioned in Article 17, paragraph 1, of the Convention.

In faith whereof the undersigned, being duly authorized thereto by their respective Governments, have signed the present Convention, opened for signature at New York, on the seventh day of March, one thousand nine hundred and sixty-six.

International Covenant on Civil and Political Rights (1966)*

PREAMBLE

The States Parties to the Present Covenant,

    Considering that, in accordance with the principles proclaimed in the Charter of the United Nations, recognition of the inherent dignity and of the equal and inalienable rights of all members of the human family is the foundation of freedom, justice and peace in the world,

    Recognizing that these rights derive from the inherent dignity of the human person,

    Recognizing that, in accordance with the Universal Declaration of Human Rights, the ideal of free human beings enjoying civil and political freedom and freedom from fear and want can only be achieved if conditions are created whereby everyone may enjoy his civil and political rights, as well as his economic, social and cultural rights,

    Considering the obligation of States under the Charter of the United Nations to promote universal respect for, and observance of, human rights and freedoms,

    Realizing that the individual, having duties to other individuals and to the community to which he belongs, is under a responsibility to strive for the promotion and observance of the rights recognized in the present Covenant,

    Agree upon the following articles:

PART I

Article 1

1. All peoples have the right of self-determination. By virtue of that right they freely determine their political status and freely pursue their economic, social and cultural development.

2. All peoples may, for their own ends, freely dispose of their natural wealth and resources without prejudice to any obligations arising out of international economic cooperation, based upon

the principle of mutual benefit, and international law. In no case may a people be deprived of its own means of subsistence.

3. The States Parties to the present Covenant, including those having responsibility for the administration of Non-Self-Governing and Trust Territories, shall promote the realization of the right of self-determination, and shall respect that right, in conformity with the provisions of the Charter of the United Nations.

PART II

Article 2

1. Each State Party to the present Covenant undertakes to respect and to ensure to all individuals within its territory and subject to its jurisdiction the rights recognized in the present Covenant, without distinction of any kind, such as race, colour, sex, language, religion, political or other opinion, national or social origin, property, birth or other status.

2. Where not already provided for by existing legislative or other measures, each State Party to the present Covenant undertakes to take the necessary steps, in accordance with its constitutional processes and with the provisions of the present Covenant, to adopt such legislative or other measures as may be necessary to give effect to the rights recognized in the present Covenant.

3. Each State Party to the present Covenant undertakes:

   (a) to ensure that any person whose rights or freedoms as herein recognized are violated shall have an effective remedy, notwithstanding that the violation has been committed by persons acting in an official capacity;

   (b) to ensure that any person claiming such a remedy shall have his right thereto determined by competent judicial, administrative or legislative authorities, or by any other competent authority provided for by the legal system of the State, and to develop the possibilities of judicial remedy;

   (c) to ensure that the competent authorities shall enforce such remedies when granted.

Article 3

The States Parties to the present Covenant undertake to ensure the equal right of men and women to the enjoyment of all civil and political rights set forth in the present Covenant.

Article 4

1. In time of public emergency which threatens the life of the nation and the existence of which is officially proclaimed, the States Parties to the present Covenant may take measures derogating from their obligations under the present Covenant to the extent strictly required by the exigencies of the situation, provided that such measures are not inconsistent with their other obligations under international law and do not involve discrimination solely on the ground of race, colour, sex, language, religion or social origin.

2. No derogation from articles 6, 7, 8 (paragraphs 1 and 2), 11, 15, 16 and 18 may be made under this provision.

3. Any State Party to the present Covenant availing itself of the right of derogation shall immediately inform the other States Parties to the present Covenant, through the intermediary of the Secretary-General of the United Nations, of the provisions from which it has derogated and of the reasons by which it was actuated. A further communication shall be made, through the same intermediary, on the date on which it terminates such derogation.

Article 5

1. Nothing in the present Covenant may be interpreted as implying for any State, group or person any right to engage in any activity or perform any act aimed at the destruction of any of the rights and freedoms recognized herein or at their limitation to a greater extent than is provided for in the present Covenant.

2. There shall be no restriction upon or derogation from any of the fundamental human rights recognized or existing in any State Party to the present Covenant pursuant to law, conventions, regulations or custom on the pretext that the present Covenant does not recognize such rights or that it recognizes them to a lesser extent.

PART III

Article 6
1. Every human being has the inherent right to life. This right shall be protected by law. No one shall be arbitrarily deprived of his life.

2. In countries which have not abolished the death penalty, sentence of death may be imposed only for the most serious crimes in accordance with the law in force at the time of the commission of the crime and not contrary to the provisions of the present Covenant and to the Convention on the Prevention and Punishment of the Crime of Genocide. This penalty can only be carried out pursuant to a final judgement rendered by a competent court.

3. When deprivation of life constitutes the crime of genocide, it is understood that nothing in this article shall authorize any State Party to the present Covenant to derogate in any way from any obligation assumed under the provisions of the Convention on the Prevention and Punishment of the Crime of Genocide.

4. Anyone sentenced to death shall have the right to seek pardon or commutation of the sentence. Amnesty, pardon or commutation of the sentence of death may be granted in all cases.

5. Sentence of death shall not be imposed for crimes committed by persons below eighteen years of age and shall not be carried out on pregnant women.

6. Nothing in this article shall be invoked to delay or to prevent the abolition of capital punishment by any State Party to the present Covenant.

Article 7
No one shall be subjected to torture or to cruel, inhuman or degrading treatment or punishment. In particular, no one shall be subjected without his free consent to medical or scientific experimentation.

Article 8
1. No one shall be held in slavery; slavery and the slave-trade in all their forms shall be prohibited.
2. No one shall be held in servitude.
3. (a) No one shall be required to perform forced or compulsory labour;
   (b) Paragraph 3(a) shall not be held to preclude, in countries where imprisonment with hard labour may be imposed as a punishment for a crime, the performance of hard labour in pursuance of a sentence to such punishment by a competent court;
   (c) For the purpose of this paragraph the term 'forced or compulsory labour' shall not include:
      (i) any work or service, not referred to in subparagraph (b), normally required of a person who is under detention in consequence of a lawful order of a court, or of a person during conditional release from such detention;
      (ii) any service of a military character and, in countries where conscientious objection is recognized, any national service required by law of conscientious objectors;
      (iii) any service exacted in cases of emergency or calamity threatening the life or well-being of the community;
      (iv) any work or service which forms part of normal civil obligations.

Article 9
1. Everyone has the right to liberty and security of person. No one shall be subjected to arbitrary arrest or detention. No one shall be deprived of his liberty except on such grounds and in accordance with such procedures as are established by law.

2. Anyone who is arrested shall be informed, at the time of arrest, of the reasons for his arrest and shall be promptly informed of any charges against him.

3. Anyone arrested or detained on a criminal charge shall be brought promptly before a judge or other officer authorized by law to exercise judicial power and shall be entitled to trial within a reasonable time or to release. It shall not be the general rule that persons awaiting trial shall be detained in custody, but release may be subject to guarantees to appear for trial, at any other stage of the judicial proceedings, and, should occasion arise, for execution of the judgement.

4. Anyone who is deprived of his liberty by arrest or detention shall be entitled to take proceedings before a court, in order that that court may decide without delay on the lawfulness of his detention and order his release if the detention is not lawful.

5. Anyone who has been the victim of unlawful arrest or detention shall have an enforceable right to compensation.

Article 10

1. All persons deprived of their liberty shall be treated with humanity and with respect for the inherent dignity of the human person.

2. (a) Accused persons shall, save in exceptional circumstances, be segregated from convicted persons and shall be subject to separate treatment appropriate to their status as unconvicted persons;

(d) Accused juvenile persons shall be separated from adults and brought as speedily as possible for adjudication.

3. The penitentiary system shall comprise treatment of prisoners the essential aim of which shall be their reformation and social rehabilitation. Juvenile offenders shall be segregated from adults and be accorded treatment appropriate to their age and legal status.

Article 11

No one shall be imprisoned merely on the ground of inability to fulfil a contractual obligation.

Article 12

1. Everyone lawfully within the territory of a State shall, within that territory, have the right to liberty of movement and freedom to choose his residence.

2. Everyone shall be free to leave any country, including his own.

3. The above-mentioned rights shall not be subject to any restrictions except those which are provided by law, are necessary to protect national security, public order (*ordre public*), public health or morals or the rights and freedoms of others, and are consistent with the other rights recognized in the present Covenant.

4. No one shall be arbitrarily deprived of the right to enter his own country.

Article 13

An alien lawfully in the territory of a State Party to the present Covenant may be expelled therefrom only in pursuance of a decision reached in accordance with law and shall, except where compelling reasons of national security otherwise require, be allowed to submit the reasons against his expulsion and to have his case reviewed by, and be represented for the purpose before, the competent authority or a person or persons especially designated by the competent authority.

Article 14

1. All persons shall be equal before the courts and tribunals. In the determination of any criminal charge against him, or of his rights and obligations in a suit at law, everyone shall be entitled to a fair and public hearing by a competent, independent and impartial tribunal established by law. The Press and the public may be excluded from all or part of a trial for reasons of morals, public order (*ordre public*) or national security in a democratic society, or when the interest of the private lives of the parties so requires, or to the extent strictly necessary in the opinion of the court in special circumstances where publicity would prejudice the interests of justice; but any judgement rendered in a criminal

case or in a suit at law shall be made public except where the interest of juvenile persons otherwise requires or the proceedings concern matrimonial disputes or the guardianship of children.

2. Everyone charged with a criminal offence shall have the right to be presumed innocent until proved guilty according to law.

3. In the determination of any criminal charge against him, everyone shall be entitled to the following minimum guarantees, in full equality:

    (a) to be informed promptly and in detail in a language which he understands of the nature and cause of the charge against him;

    (b) to have adequate time and facilities for the preparation of his defence and to communicate with counsel of his own choosing;

    (c) to be tried without undue delay;

    (d) to be tried in his presence, and to defend himself in person or through legal assistance of his own choosing; to be informed, if he does not have legal assistance, of this right; and to have legal assistance assigned to him, in any case where the interests of justice so require, and without payment by him in any such case if he does not have sufficient means to pay for it;

    (e) to examine, or have examined, the witnesses against him and to obtain the attendance and examination of witnesses on his behalf under the same conditions as witnesses against him;

    (f) to have the free assistance of an interpreter if he cannot understand or speak the language used in court;

    (g) not to be compelled to testify against himself or to confess guilt.

4. In the case of juvenile persons, the procedure shall be such as will take account of their age and the desirability of promoting their rehabilitation.

5. Everyone convicted of a crime shall have the right to his conviction and sentence being reviewed by a higher tribunal according to law.

6. When a person has by a final decision been convicted of a criminal offence and when subsequently his conviction has been reversed or he has been pardoned on the ground that a new or newly discovered fact shows conclusively that there has been a miscarriage of justice, the person who has suffered punishment as a result of such conviction shall be compensated according to law, unless it is proved that the non-disclosure of the unknown fact in time is wholly or partly attributable to him.

7. No one shall be liable to be tried or punished again for an offence for which he has already been finally convicted or acquitted in accordance with the law and penal procedure of each country.

Article 15

1. No one shall be held guilty of any criminal offence on account of any act or omission which did not constitute a criminal offence, under national or international law, at the time when it was committed. Nor shall a heavier penalty be imposed than the one that was applicable at the time when the criminal offence was committed. If, subsequent to the commission of the offence, provision is made by law for the imposition of a lighter penalty, the offender shall benefit thereby.

2. Nothing in this article shall prejudice the trial and punishment of any person for any act or omission which, at the time when it was committed, was criminal according to the general principles of law recognized by the community of nations.

Article 16

Everyone shall have the right to recognition everywhere as a person before the law.

Article 17

1. No one shall be subjected to arbitrary or unlawful interference with his privacy, family, home or correspondence, nor to unlawful attacks on his honour and reputation.

2. Everyone has the right to the protection of the law against such interference or attacks.

Article 18

1. Everyone shall have the right to freedom of thought, conscience and religion. This right shall include freedom to have or to adopt a religion or belief of his choice, and freedom, either individually or in community with others and in public or private, to manifest his religion or belief in worship, observance, practice and teaching.

2. No one shall be subject to coercion which would impair his freedom to have or to adopt a religion or belief of his choice.

3. Freedom to manifest one's religion or beliefs may be subject only to such limitations as are prescribed by law and are necessary to protect public safety, order, health, or morals or the fundamental rights and freedoms of others.

4. The States Parties to the present Covenant undertake to have respect for the liberty of parents and, when applicable, legal guardians to ensure the religious and moral education of their children in conformity with their own convictions.

Article 19

1. Everyone shall have the right to hold opinions without interference.

2. Everyone shall have the right to freedom of expression; this right shall include freedom to seek, receive and impart information and ideas of all kinds, regardless of frontiers, either orally, in writing or in print, in the form of art, or through any other media of his choice.

3. The exercise of the rights provided for in paragraph 2 of this article carries with it special duties and responsibilities. It may therefore be subject to certain restrictions, but these shall only be such as are provided by law and are necessary:

   (a) for respect of the rights or reputations of others;
   (b) for the protection of national security or of public order (*ordre public*), or of public health or morals.

Article 20

1. Any propaganda for war shall be prohibited by law.

2. Any advocacy of national, racial or religious hatred that constitutes incitement to discrimination, hostility or violence shall be prohibited by law.

Article 21

The right of peaceful assembly shall be recognized. No restrictions may be placed on the exercise of this right other than those imposed in conformity with the law and which are necessary in a democratic society in the interests of national security or public safety, public order (*ordre public*), the protection of public health or morals or the protection of the rights and freedoms of others.

Article 22

1. Everyone shall have the right to freedom of association with others, including the right to form and join trade unions for the protection of his interests.

2. No restrictions may be placed on the exercise of this right other than those which are prescribed by law and which are necessary in a democratic society in the interests of national security or public safety, public order (*ordre public*), the protection of public health or morals or the protection of the rights and freedoms of others. This article shall not prevent the imposition of lawful restrictions on members of the armed forces and of the police in their exercise of this right.

3. Nothing in this article shall authorize States Parties to the International Labour Organisation Convention of 1948 concerning Freedom of Association and Protection of the Right to Organise to take legislative measures which would prejudice, or to apply the law in such a manner as to prejudice, the guarantees provided for in that Convention.

Article 23

1. The family is the natural and fundamental group unit of society and is entitled to protection by society and the State.

2. The right of men and women of marriageable age to marry and to found a family shall be recognized.

3. No marriage shall be entered into without the free and full consent of the intending spouses.

4. States Parties to the present Covenant shall take appropriate steps to ensure equality of rights and responsibilities of spouses as to marriage, during marriage and at its dissolution. In the case of dissolution, provision shall be made for the necessary protection of any children.

Article 24

1. Every child shall have, without any discrimination as to race, colour, sex, language, religion, national or social origin, property or birth, the right to such measures of protection as are required by his status as a minor, on the part of his family, society and the State.

2. Every child shall be registered immediately after birth and shall have a name.

3. Every child has the right to acquire a nationality.

Article 25

Every citizen shall have the right and the opportunity, without any of the distinctions mentioned in article 2 and without unreasonable restrictions:

(a) to take part in the conduct of public affairs, directly or through freely chosen representatives;

(b) to vote and to be elected at genuine periodic elections which shall be by universal and equal suffrage and shall be held by secret ballot, guaranteeing the free expression of the will of the electors;

(c) to have access, on general terms of equality, to public service in his country.

Article 26

All persons are equal before the law and are entitled without any discrimination to the equal protection of the law. In this respect, the law shall prohibit any discrimination and guarantee to all persons equal and effective protection against discrimination on any ground such as race, colour, sex, language, religion, political or other opinion, national or social origin, property, birth or other status.

Article 27

In those States in which ethnic, religious or linguistic minorities exist, persons belonging to such minorities shall not be denied the right, in community with the other members of their group, to enjoy their own culture, to profess and practise their own religion, or to use their own language.

PART IV

Article 28

1. There shall be established a Human Rights Committee (hereafter referred to in the present Covenant as the Committee). It shall consist of eighteen members and shall carry out the functions hereinafter provided.

2. The Committee shall be composed of nationals of the States Parties to the present Covenant who shall be persons of high moral character and recognized competence in the field of human rights, consideration being given to the usefulness of the participation of some persons having legal experience.

3. The members of the Committee shall be elected and shall serve in their personal capacity.

Article 29

1. The members of the Committee shall be elected by secret ballot from a list of persons possessing the qualifications prescribed in article 28 and nominated for the purpose by the States Parties to the present Covenant.

2. Each State Party to the present Covenant may nominate not more than two persons. These persons shall be nationals of the nominating State.

3. A person shall be eligible for renomination.

Article 30

1. The initial election shall be held no later than six months after the date of the entry into force of the present Covenant.

2. At least four months before the date of each election to the Committee, other than an election to fill a vacancy declared in accordance with article 34, the Secretary-General of the United Nations shall address a written invitation to the States Parties to the present Covenant to submit their nominations for membership of the Committee within three months.

3. The Secretary-General of the United Nations shall prepare a list in alphabetical order of all the persons thus nominated, with an indication of the States Parties which have nominated them, and shall submit it to the States Parties to the present Covenant no later than one month before the date of each election.

4. Elections of the members of the Committee shall be held at a meeting of the States Parties to the present Covenant convened by the Secretary-General of the United Nations at the Headquarters of the United Nations. At that meeting, for which two thirds of the States Parties to the present Covenant shall constitute a quorum, the persons elected to the Committee shall be those nominees who obtain the largest number of votes and an absolute majority of the votes of the representatives of States Parties present and voting.

Article 31

1. The Committee may not include more than one national of the same State.

2. In the election of the Committee, consideration shall be given to equitable geographical distribution of membership and to the representation of the different forms of civilization and of the principal legal systems.

Article 32

1. The members of the Committee shall be elected for a term of four years. They shall be eligible for re-election if renominated. However, the terms of nine of the members elected at the first election shall expire at the end of two years; immediately after the first election, the names of these nine members shall be chosen by lot by the Chairman of the meeting referred to in article 30, paragraph 4.

2. Elections at the expiry of office shall be held in accordance with the preceding articles of this part of the present Covenant.

Article 33

1. If, in the unanimous opinion of the other members, a member of the Committee has ceased to carry out his functions for any cause other than absence of a temporary character, the Chairman of the Committee shall notify the Secretary-General of the United Nations, who shall then declare the seat of that member to be vacant.

2. In the event of the death or the resignation of a member of the Committee, the Chairman shall immediately notify the Secretary-General of the United Nations, who shall declare the seat vacant from the date of death or the date on which the resignation takes effect.

Article 34

1. When a vacancy is declared in accordance with article 33 and if the term of office of the member to be replaced does not expire within six months of the declaration of the vacancy, the Secretary-General of the United Nations shall notify each of the States Parties to the present Covenant, which may within two months submit nominations in accordance with article 29 for the purpose of filling the vacancy.

2. The Secretary-General of the United Nations shall prepare a list in alphabetical order of the persons thus nominated and shall submit it to the States Parties to the present Covenant. The election to fill the vacancy shall then take place in accordance with the relevant provisions of this part of the present Covenant.

3. A member of the Committee elected to fill a vacancy declared in accordance with article 33 shall hold office for the remainder of the term of the member who vacated the seat on the Committee under the provisions of that article.

Article 35

The members of the Committee shall, with the approval of the General Assembly of the United Nations, receive emoluments from United Nations resources on such terms and conditions as the General Assembly may decide, having regard to the importance of the Committee's responsibilities.

Article 36

The Secretary-General of the United Nations shall provide the necessary staff and facilities for the effective performance of the functions of the Committee under the present Covenant.

Article 37

1. The Secretary-General of the United Nations shall convene the initial meeting of the Committee at the Headquarters of the United Nations.

2. After its initial meeting, the Committee shall meet at such times as shall be provided in its rules of procedure.

3. The Committee shall normally meet at the Headquarters of the United Nations or at the United Nations Office at Geneva.

Article 38

Every member of the Committee shall, before taking up his duties, make a solemn declaration in open committee that he will perform his functions impartially and conscientiously.

Article 39

1. The Committee shall elect its officers for a term of two years. They may be re-elected.

2. The Committee shall establish its own rules of procedure, but these rules shall provide, *inter alia*, that:

    (a) twelve members shall constitute a quorum;

    (b) decisions of the Committee shall be made by a majority vote of the members present.

Article 40

1. The States Parties to the present Covenant undertake to submit reports on the measures they have adopted which give effect to the rights recognized herein and on the progress made in the enjoyment of those rights:

    (a) within one year of the entry into force of the present Covenant for the States Parties concerned;

    (b) thereafter whenever the Committee so requests.

2. All reports shall be submitted to the Secretary-General of the United Nations, who shall transmit them to the Committee for consideration. Reports shall indicate the factors and difficulties, if any, affecting the implementation of the present Covenant.

3. The Secretary-General of the United Nations may, after consultation with the Committee, transmit to the specialized agencies concerned copies of such parts of the reports as may fall within their field of competence.

4. The Committee shall study the reports submitted by the States Parties to the present Covenant. It shall transmit its reports, and such general comments as it may consider appropriate, to the States Parties. The Committee may also transmit to the Economic and Social Council these comments along with the copies of the reports it has received from States Parties to the present Covenant.

5. The States Parties to the present Covenant may submit to the Committee observations on any comments that may be made in accordance with paragraph 4 of this article.

Article 41

1. A State Party to the present Covenant may at any time declare under this article that it recognizes the competence of the Committee to receive and consider communications to the effect that a State Party claims that another State Party is not fulfilling its obligations under the present Covenant. Communications under this article may be received and considered only if submitted by a State Party which has made a declaration recognizing in regard to itself the competence of the Committee. No

communication shall be received by the Committee if it concerns a State Party which has not made such a declaration. Communications received under this article shall be dealt with in accordance with the following procedure:

(a) If a State Party to the present Covenant considers that another State Party is not giving effect to the provisions of the present Covenant, it may, by written communication, bring the matter to the attention of that State Party. Within three months after the receipt of the communication, the receiving State shall afford the State which sent the communication an explanation or any other statement in writing clarifying the matter, which should include, to the extent possible and pertinent, reference to domestic procedures and remedies taken, pending, or available in the matter.

(b) If the matter is not adjusted to the satisfaction of both States Parties concerned within six months after the receipt by the receiving State of the initial communication, either State shall have the right to refer the matter to the Committee, by notice given to the Committee and to the other State.

(c) The Committee shall deal with a matter referred to it only after it has ascertained that all available domestic remedies have been invoked and exhausted in the matter, in conformity with the generally recognized principles of international law. This shall not be the rule where the application of the remedies is unreasonably prolonged.

(d) The Committee shall hold closed meetings when examining communications under this article.

(e) Subject to the provisions of subparagraph (c), the Committee shall make available its good offices to the States Parties concerned with a view to a friendly solution of the matter on the basis of respect for human rights and fundamental freedoms as recognized in the present Covenant.

(f) In any matter referred to it, the Committee may call upon the States Parties concerned, referred to in subparagraph (b), to supply any relevant information.

(g) The States Parties concerned, referred to in subparagraph (b), shall have the right to be represented when the matter is being considered in the Committee and to make submissions orally and/or in writing.

(h) The Committee shall, within twelve months after the date of receipt of notice under subparagraph (b), submit a report:

(i) if a solution within the terms of subparagraph (e) is reached, the Committee shall confine its report to a brief statement of the facts and of the solution reached;

(ii) if a solution within the terms of subparagraph (e) is not reached, the Committee shall confine its report to a brief statement of the facts; the written submissions and record of the oral submissions made by the States Parties concerned shall be attached to the report.

In every matter, the report shall be communicated to the States Parties concerned.

2. The provisions of this article shall come into force when ten States Parties to the present Covenant have made declarations under paragraph 1 of this article. Such declarations shall be deposited by the States Parties with the Secretary-General of the United Nations, who shall transmit copies thereof to the other States Parties. A declaration may be withdrawn at any time by notification to the Secretary-General. Such a withdrawal shall not prejudice the consideration of any matter which is the subject of a communication already transmitted under this article; no further communication by any State Party shall be received after the notification of withdrawal of the declaration has been received by the Secretary-General, unless the State Party concerned has made a new declaration.

Article 42

1. (a) If a matter referred to the Committee in accordance with article 41 is not resolved to the satisfaction of the States Parties concerned, the Committee may, with the prior consent of the States Parties concerned, appoint an *ad hoc* Conciliation Commission (hereinafter

referred to as the Commission). The good offices of the Commission shall be made available to the States Parties concerned with a view to an amicable solution of the matter on the basis of respect for the present Covenant;

    (b) The Commission shall consist of five persons acceptable to the States Parties concerned. If the States Parties concerned fail to reach agreement within three months on all or part of the composition of the Commission, the members of the Commission concerning whom no agreement has been reached shall be elected by secret ballot by a two-thirds majority vote of the Committee from among its members.

2. The members of the Commission shall serve in their personal capacity. They shall not be nationals of the States Parties concerned, or of a State not party to the present Covenant, or of a State Party which has not made a declaration under article 41.

3. The Commission shall elect its own Chairman and adopt its own rules of procedure.

4. The meetings of the Commission shall normally be held at the Headquarters of the United Nations or at the United Nations Office at Geneva. However, they may be held at such other convenient places as the Commission may determine in consultation with the Secretary-General of the United Nations and the States Parties concerned.

5. The secretariat provided in accordance with article 36 shall also service the commissions appointed under this article.

6. The information received and collated by the Committee shall be made available to the Commission and the Commission may call upon the States Parties concerned to supply any other relevant information.

7. When the Commission has fully considered the matter, but in any event not later than twelve months after having been seized of the matter, it shall submit to the Chairman of the Committee a report for communication to the States Parties concerned:

    (a) if the Commission is unable to complete its consideration of the matter within twelve months, it shall confine its report to a brief statement of the status of its consideration of the matter;

    (b) if an amicable solution to the matter on the basis of respect for human rights as recognized in the present Covenant is reached, the Commission shall confine its report to a brief statement of the facts and of the solution reached;

    (c) if a solution within the terms of subparagraph (b) is not reached, the Commission's report shall embody its findings on all questions of fact relevant to the issues between the States Parties concerned, and its views on the possibilities of an amicable solution of the matter. This report shall also contain the written submissions and a record of the oral submissions made by the States Parties concerned;

    (d) if the Commission's report is submitted under subparagraph (c), the States Parties concerned shall, within three months of the receipt of the report, notify the Chairman of the Committee whether or not they accept the contents of the report of the Commission.

8. The provisions of this article are without prejudice to the responsibilities of the Committee under article 41.

9. The States Parties concerned shall share equally all the expenses of the members of the Commission in accordance with estimates to be provided by the Secretary-General of the United Nations.

10. The Secretary-General of the United Nations shall be empowered to pay the expenses of the members of the Commission, if necessary, before reimbursement by the States Parties concerned, in accordance with paragraph 9 of this article.

Article 43

The members of the Committee, and of the *ad hoc* conciliation commissions which may be appointed under article 42, shall be entitled to the facilities, privileges and immunities of experts on mission for the United Nations as laid down in the relevant sections of the Convention on the Privileges and Immunities of the United Nations.

Article 44

The provisions for the implementation of the present Covenant shall apply without prejudice to the procedures prescribed in the field of human rights by or under the constituent instruments and the conventions of the United Nations and of the specialized agencies and shall not prevent the States Parties to the present Covenant from having recourse to other procedures for settling a dispute in accordance with general or special international agreements in force between them.

Article 45

The Committee shall submit to the General Assembly of the United Nations, through the Economic and Social Council, an annual report on its activities.

PART V

Article 46

Nothing in the present Covenant shall be interpreted as impairing the provisions of the Charter of the United Nations and of the constitutions of the specialized agencies which define the respective responsibilities of the various organs of the United Nations and of the specialized agencies in regard to the matters dealt with in the present Covenant.

Article 47

Nothing in the present Covenant shall be interpreted as impairing the inherent right of all peoples to enjoy and utilize fully and freely their natural wealth and resources.

PART VI

Article 48

1. The present Covenant is open for signature by any State Member of the United Nations or member of any of its specialized agencies, by any State Party to the Statute of the International Court of Justice, and by any other State which has been invited by the General Assembly of the United Nations to become a party to the present Covenant.

2. The present Covenant is subject to ratification. Instruments of ratification shall be deposited with the Secretary-General of the United Nations.

3. The present Covenant shall be open to accession by any State referred to in paragraph 1 of this article.

4. Accession shall be effected by the deposit of an instrument of accession with the Secretary-General of the United Nations.

5. The Secretary-General of the United Nations shall inform all States which have signed this Covenant or acceded to it of the deposit of each instrument of ratification or accession.

Article 49

1. The present Covenant shall enter into force three months after the date of the deposit with the Secretary-General of the United Nations of the thirty-fifth instrument of ratification or instrument of accession.

2. For each State ratifying the present Covenant or acceding to it after the deposit of the thirty-fifth instrument of ratification or instrument of accession, the present Covenant shall enter into force three months after the date of the deposit of its own instrument of ratification or instrument of accession.

Article 50

The provisions of the present Covenant shall extend to all parts of federal States without any limitations or exceptions.

Article 51

1. Any State Party to the present Covenant may propose an amendment and file it with the Secretary-General of the United Nations. The Secretary-General of the United Nations shall thereupon communicate any proposed amendments to the States Parties to the present Covenant with

a request that they notify him whether they favour a conference of States Parties for the purpose of considering and voting upon the proposals. In the event that at least one third of the States Parties favours such a conference, the Secretary-General shall convene the conference under the auspices of the United Nations. Any amendment adopted by a majority of the States Parties present and voting at the conference shall be submitted to the General Assembly of the United Nations for approval.

2. Amendments shall come into force when they have been approved by the General Assembly of the United Nations and accepted by a two-thirds majority of the States Parties to the present Covenant in accordance with their respective constitutional processes.

3. When amendments come into force, they shall be binding on those States Parties which have accepted them, other States Parties still being bound by the provisions of the present Covenant and any earlier amendment which they have accepted.

Article 52

Irrespective of the notifications made under article 48, paragraph 5, the Secretary-General of the United Nations shall inform all States referred to in paragraph 1 of the same article of the following particulars:

(a) signatures, ratifications and accessions under article 48;

(b) the date of the entry into force of the present Covenant under article 49 and the date of the entry into force of any amendments under article 51.

Article 53

1. The present Covenant, of which the Chinese, English, French, Russian and Spanish texts are equally authentic, shall be deposited in the archives of the United Nations.

2. The Secretary-General of the United Nations shall transmit certified copies of the present Covenant to all States referred to in article 48.

(First) Optional Protocol to the International Covenant on Civil and Political Rights (1966)*

The States Parties to the present Protocol,

Considering that in order further to achieve the purposes of the Covenant on Civil and Political Rights (hereinafter referred to as the Covenant) and the implementation of its provisions it would be appropriate to enable the Human Rights Committee set up in part IV of the Covenant (hereinafter referred to as the Committee) to receive and consider, as provided in the present Protocol, communications from individuals claiming to be victims of violations of any of the rights set forth in the Covenant,

Have agreed as follows:

Article 1

A State Party to the Covenant that becomes a party to the present Protocol recognizes the competence of the Committee to receive and consider communications from individuals subject to its jurisdiction who claim to be victims of a violation by that State Party of any of the rights set forth in the Covenant. No communication shall be received by the Committee if it concerns a State Party to the Covenant which is not a party to the present Protocol.

Article 2

Subject to the provisions of article 1, individuals who claim that any of their rights enumerated in the Covenant have been violated and who have exhausted all available domestic remedies may submit a written communication to the Committee for consideration.

Article 3

The Committee shall consider inadmissible any communication under the present Protocol which is anonymous, or which it considers to be an abuse of the right of submission of such communications or to be incompatible with the provisions of the Covenant.

Article 4

1. Subject to the provisions of article 3, the Committee shall bring any communications submitted to it under the present Protocol to the attention of the State Party to the present Protocol alleged to be violating any provision of the Covenant.

2. Within six months, the receiving State shall submit to the Committee written explanations or statements clarifying the matter and the remedy, if any, that may have been taken by that State.

Article 5

1. The Committee shall consider communications received under the present Protocol in the light of all written information made available to it by the individual and by the State Party concerned.

2. The Committee shall not consider any communication from an individual unless it has ascertained that:

    (a) the same matter is not being examined under another procedure of international investigation or settlement;

    (b) the individual has exhausted all available domestic remedies. This shall not be the rule where the application of the remedies is unreasonably prolonged.

3. The Committee shall hold closed meetings when examining communications under the present Protocol.

4. The Committee shall forward its views to the State Party concerned and to the individual.

Article 6

The Committee shall include in its annual report under article 45 of the Covenant a summary of its activities under the present Protocol.

Article 7

Pending the achievement of the objectives of resolution 1514(XV) adopted by the General Assembly of the United Nations on 14 December 1960 concerning the Declaration on the Granting of Independence to Colonial Countries and Peoples, the provisions of the present Protocol shall in no way limit the right of petition granted to these peoples by the Charter of the United Nations and other international conventions and instruments under the United Nations and its specialized agencies.

Article 8

1. The present Protocol is open for signature by any State which has signed the Covenant.

2. The present Protocol is subject to ratification by any State which has ratified or acceded to the Covenant. Instruments of ratification shall be deposited with the Secretary-General of the United Nations.

3. The present Protocol shall be open to accession by any State which has ratified or acceded to the Covenant.

4. Accession shall be effected by the deposit of an instrument of accession with the Secretary-General of the United Nations.

5. The Secretary-General of the United Nations shall inform all States which have signed the present Protocol or acceded to it of the deposit of each instrument of ratification or accession.

Article 9

1. Subject to the entry into force of the Covenant, the present Protocol shall enter into force three months after the date of the deposit with the Secretary-General of the United Nations of the tenth instrument of ratification or instrument of accession.

2. For each State ratifying the present Protocol or acceding to it after the deposit of the tenth instrument of ratification or instrument of accession, the present Protocol shall enter into force three months after the date of the deposit of its own instrument of ratification or instrument of accession.

Article 10

The provisions of the present Protocol shall extend to all parts of federal States without any limitations or exceptions.

Article 11

1. Any State Party to the present Protocol may propose an amendment and file it with the Secretary-General of the United Nations. The Secretary-General shall thereupon communicate any proposed amendments to the States Parties to the present Protocol with a request that they notify him whether they favour a conference of States Parties for the purpose of considering and voting upon the proposal. In the event that at least one third of the States Parties favours such a conference, the Secretary-General shall convene the conference under the auspices of the United Nations. Any amendment adopted by a majority of the States Parties present and voting at the conference shall be submitted to the General Assembly of the United Nations for approval.

2. Amendments shall come into force when they have been approved by the General Assembly of the United Nations and accepted by a two-thirds majority of the States Parties to the present Protocol in accordance with their respective constitutional processes.

3. When amendments come into force, they shall be binding on those States Parties which have accepted them, other States Parties still being bound by the provisions of the present Protocol and any earlier amendment which they have accepted.

Article 12

1. Any State Party may denounce the present Protocol at any time by written notification addressed to the Secretary-General of the United Nations. Denunciation shall take effect three months after the date of receipt of the notification by the Secretary-General.

2. Denunciation shall be without prejudice to the continued application of the provisions of the present Protocol to any communication submitted under article 2 before the effective date of denunciation.

Article 13

Irrespective of the notifications made under article 8, paragraph 5, of the present Protocol, the Secretary-General of the United Nations shall inform all States referred to in article 48, paragraph 1, of the Covenant of the following particulars:

(a) signatures, ratifications and accessions under article 8;

(b) the date of the entry into force of the present Protocol under article 9 and the date of the entry into force of any amendments under article 11;

(c) denunciations under article 12.

Article 14

1. The present Protocol, of which the Chinese, English, French, Russian and Spanish texts are equally authentic, shall be deposited in the archives of the United Nations.

2. The Secretary-General of the United Nations shall transmit certified copies of the present Protocol to all States referred to in article 48 of the Covenant.

Second Optional Protocol to the International Covenant on Civil and Political Rights, Aiming at the Abolition of the Death Penalty (1990)*

The States Parties to the present Protocol,

Believing that abolition of the death penalty contributes to enhancement of human dignity and progressive development of human rights,

Recalling article 3 of the Universal Declaration of Human Rights adopted on 10 December 1948 and article 6 of the International Covenant on Civil and Political Rights adopted on 16 December 1966,

Noting that article 6 of the International Covenant on Civil and Political Rights refers to abolition of the death penalty in terms that strongly suggest that abolition is desirable,

Convinced that all measures of abolition of the death penalty should be considered as progress in the enjoyment of the right to life,

Desirous to undertake hereby an international commitment to abolish the death penalty,

Have agreed as follows:

Article 1

1. No one within the jurisdiction of a State Party to the present Optional Protocol shall be executed.

2. Each State Party shall take all necessary measures to abolish the death penalty within its jurisdiction.

Article 2

1. No reservation is admissible to the present Protocol, except for a reservation made at the time of ratification or accession that provides for the application of the death penalty in time of war pursuant to a conviction for a most serious crime of a military nature committed during wartime.

2. The State Party making such a reservation shall at the time of ratification or accession communicate to the Secretary-General of the United Nations the relevant provisions of its national legislation applicable during wartime.

3. The State Party having made such a reservation shall notify the Secretary-General of the United Nations of any beginning or ending of a state of war applicable to its territory.

Article 3

The States Parties to the present Protocol shall include in the reports they submit to the Human Rights Committee, in accordance with article 40 of the Covenant, information on the measures that they have adopted to give effect to the present Protocol.

Article 4

With respect to the States Parties to the Covenant that have made a declaration under article 41, the competence of the Human Rights Committee to receive and consider communications when a State Party claims that another State Party is not fulfilling its obligations shall extend to the provisions of the present Protocol, unless the State Party concerned has made a statement to the contrary at the moment of ratification or accession.

Article 5

With respect to the States Parties to the (First) Optional Protocol to the International Covenant on Civil and Political Rights adopted on 16 December 1966, the competence of the Human Rights Committee to receive and consider communications from individuals subject to its jurisdiction shall extend to the provisions of the present Protocol, unless the State Party concerned has made a statement to the contrary at the moment of ratification or accession.

Article 6

1. The provisions of the present Protocol shall apply as additional provisions to the Covenant.

2. Without prejudice to the possibility of a reservation under article 2 of the present Protocol, the right guaranteed in article 1, paragraph 1, of the present Protocol shall not be subject to any derogation under article 4 of the Covenant.

Article 7

1. The present Protocol is open for signature by any State that has signed the Covenant.

2. The present Protocol is subject to ratification by any State that has ratified the Covenant or acceded to it. Instruments of ratification shall be deposited with the Secretary-General of the United Nations.

3. The present Protocol shall be open to accession by any State that has ratified the Covenant or acceded to it.

4. Accession shall be effected by the deposit of an instrument of accession with the Secretary-General of the United Nations.

5. The Secretary-General of the United Nations shall inform all States that have signed the present Protocol or acceded to it of the deposit of each instrument of ratification or accession.

Article 8

1. The present Protocol shall enter into force three months after the date of the deposit with the Secretary-General of the United Nations of the tenth instrument of ratification or accession.

2. For each State ratifying the present Protocol or acceding to it after the deposit of the tenth instrument of ratification or accession, the present Protocol shall enter into force three months after the date of the deposit of its own instrument of ratification or accession.

Article 9

The provisions of the present Protocol shall extend to all parts of federal States without any limitations or exceptions.

Article 10

The Secretary-General of the United Nations shall inform all States referred to in article 48, paragraph 1, of the Covenant of the following particulars:

    (a) reservations, communications and notifications under article 2 of the present Protocol;

    (b) statements made under its articles 4 or 5;

    (c) signatures, ratifications and accessions under its article 7;

    (d) the date of the entry into force of the present Protocol under its article 8.

Article 11

1. The present Protocol, of which the Arabic, Chinese, English, French, Russian and Spanish texts are equally authentic, shall be deposited in the archives of the United Nations.

2. The Secretary-General of the United Nations shall transmit certified copies of the present Protocol to all States referred to in article 48 of the Covenant.

International Covenant on Economic, Social and Cultural Rights (1966)*

PREAMBLE

The States Parties to the present Covenant,

    Considering that, in accordance with the principles proclaimed in the Charter of the United Nations, recognition of the inherent dignity and of the equal and inalienable rights of all members of the human family is the foundation of freedom, justice and peace in the world,

    Recognizing that these rights derive from the inherent dignity of the human person,

    Recognizing that, in accordance with the Universal Declaration of Human Rights, the ideal of free human beings enjoying freedom from fear and want can only be achieved if conditions are created whereby everyone may enjoy his economic, social and cultural rights, as well as his civil and political rights,

    Considering the obligation of States under the Charter of the United Nations to promote universal respect for, and observance of, human rights and freedoms,

    Realizing that the individual, having duties to other individuals and to the community to which he belongs, is under a responsibility to strive for the promotion and observance of the rights recognized in the present Covenant,

    Agree upon the following articles:

PART I

Article 1

1. All peoples have the right of self-determination. By virtue of that right they freely determine their political status and freely pursue their economic, social and cultural development.

2. All peoples may, for their own ends, freely dispose of their natural wealth and resources without prejudice to any obligations arising out of international economic cooperation, based upon the principle of mutual benefit, and international law. In no case may a people be deprived of its own means of subsistence.

3. The States Parties to the present Covenant, including those having responsibility for the administration of Non-Self-Governing and Trust Territories, shall promote the realization of the right of self-determination, and shall respect that right, in conformity with the provisions of the Charter of the United Nations.

PART II

Article 2

1. Each State Party to the present Covenant undertakes to take steps, individually and through international assistance and co-operation, especially economic and technical, to the maximum of its available resources, with a view to achieving progressively the full realization of the rights recognized in the present Covenant by all appropriate means, including particularly the adoption of legislative measures.

2. The States Parties to the present Covenant undertake to guarantee that the rights enunciated in the present Covenant will be exercised without discrimination of any kind as to race, colour, sex, language, religion, political or other opinion, national or social origin, property, birth or other status.

3. Developing countries, with due regard to human rights and their national economy, may determine to what extent they would guarantee the economic rights recognized in the present Covenant to non-nationals.

Article 3

The States Parties to the present Covenant undertake to ensure the equal right of men and women to the enjoyment of all economic, social and cultural rights set forth in the present Covenant.

Article 4

The States Parties to the present Covenant recognize that, in the enjoyment of those rights provided by the State in conformity with the present Covenant, the State may subject such rights only to such limitations as are determined by law only in so far as this may be compatible with the nature of these rights and solely for the purpose of promoting the general welfare in a democratic society.

Article 5

1. Nothing in the present Covenant may be interpreted as implying for any State, group or person any right to engage in any activity or to perform any act aimed at the destruction of any of the rights or freedoms recognized herein, or at their limitation to a greater extent than is provided for in the present Covenant.

2. No restriction upon or derogation from any of the fundamental human rights recognized or existing in any country in virtue of law, conventions, regulations or custom shall be admitted on the pretext that the present Covenant does not recognize such rights or that it recognizes them to a lesser extent.

PART III

Article 6

1. The States Parties to the present Covenant recognize the right to work, which includes the right of everyone to the opportunity to gain his living by work which he freely chooses or accepts, and will take appropriate steps to safeguard this right.

2. The steps to be taken by a State Party to the present Covenant to achieve the full realization of this right shall include technical and vocational guidance and training programmes, policies and techniques to achieve steady economic, social and cultural development and full and productive employment under conditions safeguarding fundamental political and economic freedoms to the individual.

Article 7

The States Parties to the present Covenant recognize the right of everyone to the enjoyment of just and favourable conditions of work which ensure, in particular:

(a) remuneration which provides all workers, as a minimum, with:

    (i) fair wages and equal remuneration for work of equal value without distinction of any kind, in particular women being guaranteed conditions of work not inferior to those enjoyed by men, with equal pay for equal work;

    (ii) a decent living for themselves and their families in accordance with the provisions of the present Covenant;

(b) safe and healthy working conditions;

(c) equal opportunity for everyone to be promoted in his employment to an appropriate higher level, subject to no considerations other than those of seniority and competence;

(d) rest, leisure and reasonable limitation of working hours and periodic holidays with pay, as well as remuneration for public holidays.

Article 8

1. The States Parties to the present Covenant undertake to ensure:

(a) the right of everyone to form trade unions and join the trade union of his choice, subject only to the rules of the organization concerned, for the promotion and protection of his economic and social interests. No restrictions may be placed on the exercise of this right other than those prescribed by law and which are necessary in a democratic society in the interests of national security or public order or for the protection of the rights and freedoms of others;

(b) the right of trade unions to establish national federations or confederations and the right of the latter to form or join international trade-union organizations;

(c) the right of trade unions to function freely subject to no limitations other than those prescribed by law and which are necessary in a democratic society in the interests of national security or public order or for the protection of the rights and freedoms of others;

(d) the right to strike, provided that it is exercised in conformity with the laws of the particular country.

2. This article shall not prevent the imposition of lawful restrictions on the exercise of these rights by members of the armed forces or of the police or of the administration of the State.

3. Nothing in this article shall authorize States Parties to the International Labour Organisation Convention of 1948 concerning Freedom of Association and Protection of the Right to Organise to take legislative measures which would prejudice, or apply the law in such a manner as would prejudice, the guarantees provided for in that Convention.

Article 9

The States Parties to the present Covenant recognize the right of everyone to social security, including social insurance.

Article 10

The States Parties to the present Covenant recognize that:

1. The widest possible protection and assistance should be accorded to the family, which is the natural and fundamental group unit of society, particularly for its establishment and while it is responsible for the care and education of dependent children. Marriage must be entered into with the free consent of the intending spouses.

2. Special protection should be accorded to mothers during a reasonable period before and after childbirth. During such period working mothers should be accorded paid leave or leave with adequate social security benefits.

3. Special measures of protection and assistance should be taken on behalf of all children and young persons without any discrimination for reasons of parentage or other conditions. Children and young persons should be protected from economic and social exploitation. Their employment in work harmful to their morals or health or dangerous to life or likely to hamper their normal development should be punishable by law. States should also set age limits below which the paid employment of child labour should be prohibited and punishable by law.

Article 11

1. The States Parties to the present Covenant recognize the right of everyone to an adequate standard of living for himself and his family, including adequate food, clothing and housing, and to the continuous improvement of living conditions. The States Parties will take appropriate steps to ensure the realization of this right, recognizing to this effect the essential importance of international co-operation based on free consent.

2. The States Parties to the present Covenant, recognizing the fundamental right of everyone to be free from hunger, shall take, individually and through international co-operation, the measures, including specific programmes, which are needed:

    (a) to improve methods of production, conservation and distribution of food by making full use of technical and scientific knowledge, by disseminating knowledge of the principles of nutrition and by developing or reforming agrarian systems in such a way as to achieve the most efficient development and utilization of natural resources;

    (b) taking into account the problems of both food-importing and food-exporting countries, to ensure an equitable distribution of world food supplies in relation to need.

Article 12

1. The States Parties to the present Covenant recognize the right of everyone to the enjoyment of the highest attainable standard of physical and mental health.

2. The steps to be taken by the States Parties to the present Covenant to achieve the full realization of this right shall include those necessary for:

    (a) the provision for the reduction of the stillbirth-rate and of infant mortality and for the healthy development of the child;

    (b) the improvement of all aspects of environmental and industrial hygiene;

    (c) the prevention, treatment and control of epidemic, endemic, occupational and other diseases;

    (d) the creation of conditions which would assure to all medical service and medical attention in the event of sickness.

Article 13

1. The States Parties to the present Covenant recognize the right of everyone to education. They agree that education shall be directed to the full development of the human personality and the sense of its dignity, and shall strengthen the respect for human rights and fundamental freedoms. They further agree that education shall enable all persons to participate effectively in a free society, promote understanding, tolerance and friendship among all nations and all racial, ethnic or religious groups, and further the activities of the United Nations for the maintenance of peace.

2. The States Parties to the present Covenant recognize that, with a view to achieving the full realization of this right:

    (a) primary education shall be compulsory and available free to all;

    (b) secondary education in its different forms, including technical and vocational secondary education, shall be made generally available and accessible to all by every appropriate means, and in particular by the progressive introduction of free education;

(c) higher education shall be made equally accessible to all, on the basis of capacity, by every appropriate means, and in particular by the progressive introduction of free education;

(d) fundamental education shall be encouraged or intensified as far as possible for those persons who have not received or completed the whole period of their primary education;

(e) the development of a system of schools at all levels shall be actively pursued, an adequate fellowship system shall be established, and the material conditions of teaching staff shall be continuously improved.

3. The States Parties to the present Covenant undertake to have respect for the liberty of parents and, when applicable, legal guardians to choose for their children schools, other than those established by the public authorities, which conform to such minimum educational standards as may be laid down or approved by the State and to ensure the religious and moral education of their children in conformity with their own convictions.

4. No part of this article shall be construed so as to interfere with the liberty of individuals and bodies to establish and direct educational institutions, subject always to the observance of the principles set forth in paragraph 1 of this article and to the requirement that the education given in such institutions shall conform to such minimum standards as may be laid down by the State.

Article 14

Each State Party to the present Covenant which, at the time of becoming a Party, has not been able to secure in its metropolitan territory or other territories under its jurisdiction compulsory primary education, free of charge, undertakes, within two years, to work out and adopt a detailed plan of action for the progressive implementation, within a reasonable number of years, to be fixed in the plan, of the principle of compulsory education free of charge for all.

Article 15

1. The States Parties to the present Covenant recognize the right of everyone:
    (a) to take part in cultural life;
    (b) to enjoy the benefits of scientific progress and its applications;
    (c) to benefit from the protection of the moral and material interests resulting from any scientific, literary or artistic production of which he is the author.

2. The steps to be taken by the States Parties to the present Covenant to achieve the full realization of this right shall include those necessary for the conservation, the development and the diffusion of science and culture.

3. The States Parties to the present Covenant undertake to respect the freedom indispensable for scientific research and creative activity.

4. The States Parties to the present Covenant recognize the benefits to be derived from the encouragement and development of international contacts and co-operation in the scientific and cultural fields.

PART IV

Article 16

1. The States Parties to the present Covenant undertake to submit in conformity with this part of the Covenant reports on the measures which they have adopted and the progress made in achieving the observance of the rights recognized herein.

2. (a) All reports shall be submitted to the Secretary-General of the United Nations, who shall transmit copies to the Economic and Social Council for consideration in accordance with the provisions of the present Covenant;

    (b) The Secretary-General of the United Nations shall also transmit to the specialized agencies copies of the reports, or any relevant parts therefrom, from States Parties to the present

Covenant which are also members of these specialized agencies in so far as these reports, or parts therefrom, relate to any matters which fall within the responsibilities of the said agencies in accordance with their constitutional instruments.

Article 17

1. The States Parties to the present Covenant shall furnish their reports in stages, in accordance with a programme to be established by the Economic and Social Council within one year of the entry into force of the present Covenant after consultation with the States Parties and the specialized agencies concerned.

2. Reports may indicate factors and difficulties affecting the degree of fulfilment of obligations under the present Covenant.

3. Where relevant information has previously been furnished to the United Nations or to any specialized agency by any State Party to the present Covenant, it will not be necessary to reproduce that information, but a precise reference to the information so furnished will suffice.

Article 18

Pursuant to its responsibilities under the Charter of the United Nations in the field of human rights and fundamental freedoms, the Economic and Social Council may make arrangements with the specialized agencies in respect of their reporting to it on the progress made in achieving the observance of the provisions of the present Covenant falling within the scope of their activities. These reports may include particulars of decisions and recommendations on such implementation adopted by their competent organs.

Article 19

The Economic and Social Council may transmit to the Commission on Human Rights for study and general recommendation or, as appropriate, for information the reports concerning human rights submitted by States in accordance with articles 16 and 17, and those concerning human rights submitted by the specialized agencies in accordance with article 18.

Article 20

The States Parties to the present Covenant and the specialized agencies concerned may submit comments to the Economic and Social Council on any general recommendation under article 19 or reference to such general recommendation in any report of the Commission on Human Rights or any documentation referred to therein.

Article 21

The Economic and Social Council may submit from time to time to the General Assembly reports with recommendations of a general nature and a summary of the information received from the States Parties to the present Covenant and the specialized agencies on the measures taken and the progress made in achieving general observance of the rights recognized in the present Covenant.

Article 22

The Economic and Social Council may bring to the attention of other organs of the United Nations, their subsidiary organs and specialized agencies concerned with furnishing technical assistance any matters arising out of the reports referred to in this part of the present Covenant which may assist such bodies in deciding, each within its field of competence, on the advisability of international measures likely to contribute to the effective progressive implementation of the present Covenant.

Article 23

The States Parties to the present Covenant agree that international action for the achievement of the rights recognized in the present Covenant includes such methods as the conclusion of conventions, the adoption of recommendations, the furnishing of technical assistance and the holding of regional meetings and technical meetings for the purpose of consultation and study organized in conjunction with the Governments concerned.

Article 24

Nothing in the present Covenant shall be interpreted as impairing the provisions of the Charter of the United Nations and of the constitutions of the specialized agencies which define the respective responsibilities of the various organs of the United Nations and of the specialized agencies in regard to the matters dealt with in the present Covenant.

Article 25

Nothing in the present Covenant shall be interpreted as impairing the inherent right of all peoples to enjoy and utilize fully and freely their natural wealth and resources.

PART V

Article 26

1. The present Covenant is open for signature by any State Member of the United Nations or member of any of its specialized agencies, by any State Party to the Statute of the International Court of Justice, and by any other State which has been invited by the General Assembly of the United Nations to become a party to the present Covenant.

2. The present Covenant is subject to ratification. Instruments of ratification shall be deposited with the Secretary-General of the United Nations.

3. The present Covenant shall be open to accession by any State referred to in paragraph 1 of this article.

4. Accession shall be effected by the deposit of an instrument of accession with the Secretary-General of the United Nations.

5. The Secretary-General of the United Nations shall inform all States which have signed the present Covenant or acceded to it of the deposit of each instrument of ratification or accession.

Article 27

1. The present Covenant shall enter into force three months after the date of the deposit with the Secretary-General of the United Nations of the thirty-fifth instrument of ratification or instrument of accession.

2. For each State ratifying the present Covenant or acceding to it after the deposit of the thirty-fifth instrument of ratification or instrument of accession, the present Covenant shall enter into force three months after the date of the deposit of its own instrument of ratification or instrument of accession.

Article 28

The provisions of the present Covenant shall extend to all parts of federal States without any limitations or exceptions.

Article 29

1. Any State Party to the present Covenant may propose an amendment and file it with the Secretary-General of the United Nations. The Secretary-General shall thereupon communicate any proposed amendments to the States Parties to the present Covenant with a request that they notify him whether they favour a conference of States Parties for the purpose of considering and voting upon the proposals. In the event that at least one third of the States Parties favours such a conference, the Secretary-General shall convene the conference under the auspices of the United Nations. Any amendment adopted by a majority of the States Parties present and voting at the conference shall be submitted to the General Assembly of the United Nations for approval.

2. Amendments shall come into force when they have been approved by the General Assembly of the United Nations and accepted by a two-thirds majority of the States Parties to the present Covenant in accordance with their respective constitutional processes.

3. When amendments come into force they shall be binding on those States Parties which have accepted them, other States Parties still being bound by the provisions of the present Covenant and any earlier amendment which they have accepted.

Article 30
Irrespective of the notifications made under article 26, paragraph 5, the Secretary-General of the United Nations shall inform all States referred to in paragraph 1 of the same article of the following particulars:
    (a) signatures, ratifications and accessions under article 26;
    (b) the date of the entry into force of the present Covenant under article 27 and the date of the entry into force of any amendments under article 29.

Article 31
1. The present Covenant, of which the Chinese, English, French, Russian and Spanish texts are equally authentic, shall be deposited in the archives of the United Nations.

2. The Secretary-General of the United Nations shall transmit certified copies of the present Covenant to all States referred to in article 26.

Optional Protocol to the International Covenant on Economic, Social and Cultural Rights (2008)*

PREAMBLE

The States Parties to the present Protocol,

Considering that, in accordance with the principles proclaimed in the Charter of the United Nations, recognition of the inherent dignity and of the equal and inalienable rights of all members of the human family is the foundation of freedom, justice and peace in the world,

Noting that the Universal Declaration of Human Rights proclaims that all human beings are born free and equal in dignity and rights and that everyone is entitled to all the rights and freedoms set forth therein, without distinction of any kind, such as race, colour, sex, language, religion, political or other opinion, national or social origin, property, birth or other status,

Recalling that the Universal Declaration of Human Rights and the International Covenants on Human Rights recognize that the ideal of free human beings enjoying freedom from fear and want can only be achieved if conditions are created whereby everyone may enjoy civil, cultural, economic, political and social rights,

Reaffirming the universality, indivisibility, interdependence and interrelatedness of all human rights and fundamental freedoms,

Recalling that each State Party to the International Covenant on Economic, Social and Cultural Rights (hereinafter referred to as the Covenant) undertakes to take steps, individually and through international assistance and cooperation, especially economic and technical, to the maximum of its available resources, with a view to achieving progressively the full realization of the rights recognized in the Covenant by all appropriate means, including particularly the adoption of legislative measures,

Considering that, in order further to achieve the purposes of the Covenant and the implementation of its provisions, it would be appropriate to enable the Committee on Economic, Social and Cultural Rights (hereinafter referred to as the Committee) to carry out the functions provided for in the present Protocol,

Have agreed as follows:

Article 1   Competence of the Committee to receive and consider communications
1. A State Party to the Covenant that becomes a Party to the present Protocol recognizes the competence of the Committee to receive and consider communications as provided for by the provisions of the present Protocol.

* From Optional Protocol to the International Covenant on Economic, Social and Cultural Rights, by Office of the United Nations High Commissioner for Human Rights (OHCHR), © 2008 United Nations. Reprinted with the permission of the United Nations.

2. No communication shall be received by the Committee if it concerns a State Party to the Covenant which is not a Party to the present Protocol.

Article 2   Communications

Communications may be submitted by or on behalf of individuals or groups of individuals, under the jurisdiction of a State Party, claiming to be victims of a violation of any of the economic, social and cultural rights set forth in the Covenant by that State Party. Where a communication is submitted on behalf of individuals or groups of individuals, this shall be with their consent unless the author can justify acting on their behalf without such consent.

Article 3   Admissibility

1. The Committee shall not consider a communication unless it has ascertained that all available domestic remedies have been exhausted. This shall not be the rule where the application of such remedies is unreasonably prolonged.

2. The Committee shall declare a communication inadmissible when:

   (a) It is not submitted within one year after the exhaustion of domestic remedies, except in cases where the author can demonstrate that it had not been possible to submit the communication within that time limit;

   (b) The facts that are the subject of the communication occurred prior to the entry into force of the present Protocol for the State Party concerned unless those facts continued after that date;

   (c) The same matter has already been examined by the Committee or has been or is being examined under another procedure of international investigation or settlement;

   (d) It is incompatible with the provisions of the Covenant;

   (e) It is manifestly ill-founded, not sufficiently substantiated or exclusively based on reports disseminated by mass media;

   (f) It is an abuse of the right to submit a communication; or when

   (g) It is anonymous or not in writing.

Article 4   Communications not revealing a clear disadvantage

The Committee may, if necessary, decline to consider a communication where it does not reveal that the author has suffered a clear disadvantage, unless the Committee considers that the communication raises a serious issue of general importance.

Article 5   Interim measures

1. At any time after the receipt of a communication and before a determination on the merits has been reached, the Committee may transmit to the State Party concerned for its urgent consideration a request that the State Party take such interim measures as may be necessary in exceptional circumstances to avoid possible irreparable damage to the victim or victims of the alleged violations.

2. Where the Committee exercises its discretion under paragraph 1 of the present article, this does not imply a determination on admissibility or on the merits of the communication.

Article 6   Transmission of the communication

1. Unless the Committee considers a communication inadmissible without reference to the State Party concerned, the Committee shall bring any communication submitted to it under the present Protocol confidentially to the attention of the State Party concerned.

2. Within six months, the receiving State Party shall submit to the Committee written explanations or statements clarifying the matter and the remedy, if any, that may have been provided by that State Party.

Article 7   Friendly settlement

1. The Committee shall make available its good offices to the parties concerned with a view to reaching a friendly settlement of the matter on the basis of the respect for the obligations set forth in the Covenant.

2. An agreement on a friendly settlement closes consideration of the communication under the present Protocol.

Article 8 Examination of communications

1. The Committee shall examine communications received under article 2 of the present Protocol in the light of all documentation submitted to it, provided that this documentation is transmitted to the parties concerned.

2. The Committee shall hold closed meetings when examining communications under the present Protocol.

3. When examining a communication under the present Protocol, the Committee may consult, as appropriate, relevant documentation emanating from other United Nations bodies, specialized agencies, funds, programmes and mechanisms, and other international organizations, including from regional human rights systems, and any observations or comments by the State Party concerned.

4. When examining communications under the present Protocol, the Committee shall consider the reasonableness of the steps taken by the State Party in accordance with part II of the Covenant. In doing so, the Committee shall bear in mind that the State Party may adopt a range of possible policy measures for the implementation of the rights set forth in the Covenant.

Article 9 Follow-up to the views of the Committee

1. After examining a communication, the Committee shall transmit its views on the communication, together with its recommendations, if any, to the parties concerned.

2. The State Party shall give due consideration to the views of the Committee, together with its recommendations, if any, and shall submit to the Committee, within six months, a written response, including information on any action taken in the light of the views and recommendations of the Committee.

3. The Committee may invite the State Party to submit further information about any measures the State Party has taken in response to its views or recommendations, if any, including as deemed appropriate by the Committee, in the State Party's subsequent reports under articles 16 and 17 of the Covenant.

Article 10 Inter-State communications

1. A State Party to the present Protocol may at any time declare under the present article that it recognizes the competence of the Committee to receive and consider communications to the effect that a State Party claims that another State Party is not fulfilling its obligations under the Covenant. Communications under the present article may be received and considered only if submitted by a State Party that has made a declaration recognizing in regard to itself the competence of the Committee. No communication shall be received by the Committee if it concerns a State Party which has not made such a declaration. Communications received under the present article shall be dealt with in accordance with the following procedure:

    (a) If a State Party to the present Protocol considers that another State Party is not fulfilling its obligations under the Covenant, it may, by written communication, bring the matter to the attention of that State Party. The State Party may also inform the Committee of the matter. Within three months after the receipt of the communication the receiving State shall afford the State that sent the communication an explanation, or any other statement in writing clarifying the matter, which should include, to the extent possible and pertinent, reference to domestic procedures and remedies taken, pending or available in the matter;

    (b) If the matter is not settled to the satisfaction of both States Parties concerned within six months after the receipt by the receiving State of the initial communication, either State shall have the right to refer the matter to the Committee, by notice given to the Committee and to the other State;

    (c) The Committee shall deal with a matter referred to it only after it has ascertained that all available domestic remedies have been invoked and exhausted in the matter. This shall not be the rule where the application of the remedies is unreasonably prolonged;

(d) Subject to the provisions of subparagraph (c) of the present paragraph the Committee shall make available its good offices to the States Parties concerned with a view to a friendly solution of the matter on the basis of the respect for the obligations set forth in the Covenant;

(e) The Committee shall hold closed meetings when examining communications under the present article;

(f) In any matter referred to it in accordance with subparagraph (b) of the present paragraph, the Committee may call upon the States Parties concerned, referred to in subparagraph (b), to supply any relevant information;

(g) The States Parties concerned, referred to in subparagraph (b) of the present paragraph, shall have the right to be represented when the matter is being considered by the Committee and to make submissions orally and/or in writing;

(h) The Committee shall, with all due expediency after the date of receipt of notice under subparagraph (b) of the present paragraph, submit a report, as follows:

  (i) If a solution within the terms of subparagraph (d) of the present paragraph is reached, the Committee shall confine its report to a brief statement of the facts and of the solution reached;

  (ii) If a solution within the terms of subparagraph (d) is not reached, the Committee shall, in its report, set forth the relevant facts concerning the issue between the States Parties concerned. The written submissions and record of the oral submissions made by the States Parties concerned shall be attached to the report. The Committee may also communicate only to the States Parties concerned any views that it may consider relevant to the issue between them.

In every matter, the report shall be communicated to the States Parties concerned.

2. A declaration under paragraph 1 of the present article shall be deposited by the States Parties with the Secretary-General of the United Nations, who shall transmit copies thereof to the other States Parties. A declaration may be withdrawn at any time by notification to the Secretary-General. Such a withdrawal shall not prejudice the consideration of any matter that is the subject of a communication already transmitted under the present article; no further communication by any State Party shall be received under the present article after the notification of withdrawal of the declaration has been received by the Secretary-General, unless the State Party concerned has made a new declaration.

Article 11   Inquiry procedure

1. A State Party to the present Protocol may at any time declare that it recognizes the competence of the Committee provided for under the present article.

2. If the Committee receives reliable information indicating grave or systematic violations by a State Party of any of the economic, social and cultural rights set forth in the Covenant, the Committee shall invite that State Party to cooperate in the examination of the information and to this end to submit observations with regard to the information concerned.

3. Taking into account any observations that may have been submitted by the State Party concerned as well as any other reliable information available to it, the Committee may designate one or more of its members to conduct an inquiry and to report urgently to the Committee. Where warranted and with the consent of the State Party, the inquiry may include a visit to its territory.

4. Such an inquiry shall be conducted confidentially and the cooperation of the State Party shall be sought at all stages of the proceedings.

5. After examining the findings of such an inquiry, the Committee shall transmit these findings to the State Party concerned together with any comments and recommendations.

6. The State Party concerned shall, within six months of receiving the findings, comments and recommendations transmitted by the Committee, submit its observations to the Committee.

7. After such proceedings have been completed with regard to an inquiry made in accordance with paragraph 2 of the present article, the Committee may, after consultations with the State Party concerned, decide to include a summary account of the results of the proceedings in its annual report provided for in article 15 of the present Protocol.

8. Any State Party having made a declaration in accordance with paragraph 1 of the present article may, at any time, withdraw this declaration by notification to the Secretary-General.

Article 12   Follow-up to the inquiry procedure

1. The Committee may invite the State Party concerned to include in its report under articles 16 and 17 of the Covenant details of any measures taken in response to an inquiry conducted under article 11 of the present Protocol.

2. The Committee may, if necessary, after the end of the period of six months referred to in article 11, paragraph 6, invite the State Party concerned to inform it of the measures taken in response to such an inquiry.

Article 13   Protection measures

A State Party shall take all appropriate measures to ensure that individuals under its jurisdiction are not subjected to any form of ill-treatment or intimidation as a consequence of communicating with the Committee pursuant to the present Protocol.

Article 14   International assistance and cooperation

1. The Committee shall transmit, as it may consider appropriate, and with the consent of the State Party concerned, to United Nations specialized agencies, funds and programmes and other competent bodies, its views or recommendations concerning communications and inquiries that indicate a need for technical advice or assistance, along with the State Party's observations and suggestions, if any, on these views or recommendations.

2. The Committee may also bring to the attention of such bodies, with the consent of the State Party concerned, any matter arising out of communications considered under the present Protocol which may assist them in deciding, each within its field of competence, on the advisability of international measures likely to contribute to assisting States Parties in achieving progress in implementation of the rights recognized in the Covenant.

3. A trust fund shall be established in accordance with the relevant procedures of the General Assembly, to be administered in accordance with the financial regulations and rules of the United Nations, with a view to providing expert and technical assistance to States Parties, with the consent of the State Party concerned, for the enhanced implementation of the rights contained in the Covenant, thus contributing to building national capacities in the area of economic, social and cultural rights in the context of the present Protocol.

4. The provisions of the present article are without prejudice to the obligations of each State Party to fulfil its obligations under the Covenant.

Article 15   Annual report

The Committee shall include in its annual report a summary of its activities under the present Protocol.

Article 16   Dissemination and information

Each State Party undertakes to make widely known and to disseminate the Covenant and the present Protocol and to facilitate access to information about the views and recommendations of the Committee, in particular, on matters involving that State Party, and to do so in accessible formats for persons with disabilities.

Article 17   Signature, ratification and accession

1. The present Protocol is open for signature by any State that has signed, ratified or acceded to the Covenant.

2. The present Protocol is subject to ratification by any State that has ratified or acceded to the Covenant. Instruments of ratification shall be deposited with the Secretary-General of the United Nations.

3. The present Protocol shall be open to accession by any State that has ratified or acceded to the Covenant.

4. Accession shall be effected by the deposit of an instrument of accession with the Secretary-General of the United Nations.

Article 18   Entry into force

1. The present Protocol shall enter into force three months after the date of the deposit with the Secretary-General of the United Nations of the tenth instrument of ratification or accession.

2. For each State ratifying or acceding to the present Protocol, after the deposit of the tenth instrument of ratification or accession, the Protocol shall enter into force three months after the date of the deposit of its instrument of ratification or accession.

Article 19   Amendments

1. Any State Party may propose an amendment to the present Protocol and submit it to the Secretary-General of the United Nations. The Secretary-General shall communicate any proposed amendments to States Parties, with a request to be notified whether they favour a meeting of States Parties for the purpose of considering and deciding upon the proposals. In the event that, within four months from the date of such communication, at least one third of the States Parties favour such a meeting, the Secretary-General shall convene the meeting under the auspices of the United Nations. Any amendment adopted by a majority of two thirds of the States Parties present and voting shall be submitted by the Secretary-General to the General Assembly for approval and thereafter to all States Parties for acceptance.

2. An amendment adopted and approved in accordance with paragraph 1 of the present article shall enter into force on the thirtieth day after the number of instruments of acceptance deposited reaches two thirds of the number of States Parties at the date of adoption of the amendment. Thereafter, the amendment shall enter into force for any State Party on the thirtieth day following the deposit of its own instrument of acceptance. An amendment shall be binding only on those States Parties which have accepted it.

Article 20   Denunciation

1. Any State Party may denounce the present Protocol at any time by written notification addressed to the Secretary-General of the United Nations. Denunciation shall take effect six months after the date of receipt of the notification by the Secretary-General.

2. Denunciation shall be without prejudice to the continued application of the provisions of the present Protocol to any communication submitted under articles 2 and 10 or to any procedure initiated under article 11 before the effective date of denunciation.

Article 21   Notification by the Secretary-General

The Secretary-General of the United Nations shall notify all States referred to in article 26, paragraph 1, of the Covenant of the following particulars:

(a) Signatures, ratifications and accessions under the present Protocol;

(b) The date of entry into force of the present Protocol and of any amendment under article 19;

(c) Any denunciation under article 20.

Article 22   Official languages

1. The present Protocol, of which the Arabic, Chinese, English, French, Russian and Spanish texts are equally authentic, shall be deposited in the archives of the United Nations.

2. The Secretary-General of the United Nations shall transmit certified copies of the present Protocol to all States referred to in article 26 of the Covenant.

Convention on the Elimination of All Forms of Discrimination against Women (1979)*

The States Parties to the present Convention,

Noting that the Charter of the United Nations reaffirms faith in fundamental human rights, in the dignity and worth of the human person and in the equal rights of men and women,

Noting that the Universal Declaration of Human Rights affirms the principle of the inadmissibility of discrimination and proclaims that all human beings are born free and equal in dignity and rights and that everyone is entitled to all the rights and freedoms set forth therein, without distinction of any kind, including distinction based on sex,

Noting that the States Parties to the International Covenants on Human Rights have the obligation to ensure the equal right of men and women to enjoy all economic, social, cultural, civil and political rights,

Considering the international conventions concluded under the auspices of the United Nations and the specialized agencies promoting equality of rights of men and women,

Noting also the resolutions, declarations and recommendations adopted by the United Nations and the specialized agencies promoting equality of rights of men and women,

Concerned, however, that despite these various instruments extensive discrimination against women continues to exist,

Recalling that discrimination against women violates the principles of equality of rights and respect for human dignity, is an obstacle to the participation of women, on equal terms with men, in the political, social, economic and cultural life of their countries, hampers the growth of the prosperity of society and the family and makes more difficult the full development of the potentialities of women in the service of their countries and of humanity,

Concerned that in situations of poverty women have the least access to food, health, education, training and opportunities for employment and other needs,

Convinced that the establishment of the new international economic order based on equity and justice will contribute significantly towards the promotion of equality between men and women,

Emphasizing that the eradication of *apartheid,* of all forms of racism, racial discrimination, colonialism, neo-colonialism, aggression, foreign occupation and domination and interference in the internal affairs of States is essential to the full enjoyment of the rights of men and women,

Affirming that the strengthening of international peace and security, relaxation of international tension, mutual co-operation among all States irrespective of their social and economic systems, general and complete disarmament, and in particular nuclear disarmament under strict and effective international control, the affirmation of the principles of justice, equality and mutual benefit in relations among countries and the realization of the right of peoples under alien and colonial domination and foreign occupation to self-determination and independence, as well as respect for national sovereignty and territorial integrity, will promote social progress and development and as a consequence will contribute to the attainment of full equality between men and women,

Convinced that the full and complete development of a country, the welfare of the world and the cause of peace require the maximum participation of women on equal terms with men in all fields,

Bearing in mind the great contribution of women to the welfare of the family and to the development of society, so far not fully recognized, the social significance of maternity and the role of both parents in the family and in the upbringing of children, and aware that the role of women in procreation should not be a basis for discrimination but that the upbringing of children requires a sharing of responsibility between men and women and society as a whole,

Aware that a change in the traditional role of men as well as the role of women in society and in the family is needed to achieve full equality between men and women,

Determined to implement the principles set forth in the Declaration on the Elimination of Discrimination against Women and, for that purpose, to adopt the measures required for the elimination of such discrimination in all its forms and manifestations,

Have agreed on the following:

PART I

Article 1

For the purposes of the present Convention, the term 'discrimination against women' shall mean any distinction, exclusion or restriction made on the basis of sex which has the effect or purpose of impairing or nullifying the recognition, enjoyment or exercise by women, irrespective of their marital status, on a basis of equality of men and women, of human rights and fundamental freedoms in the political, economic, social, cultural, civil or any other field.

Article 2
States Parties condemn discrimination against women in all its forms, agree to pursue by all appropriate means and without delay a policy of eliminating discrimination against women and, to this end, undertake:

(a) To embody the principle of the equality of men and women in their national constitutions or other appropriate legislation if not yet incorporated therein and to ensure, through law and other appropriate means, the practical realization of this principle;

(b) To adopt appropriate legislative and other measures, including sanctions where appropriate, prohibiting all discrimination against women;

(c) To establish legal protection of the rights of women on an equal basis with men and to ensure through competent national tribunals and other public institutions the effective protection of women against any act of discrimination;

(d) To refrain from engaging in any act or practice of discrimination against women and to ensure that public authorities and institutions shall act in conformity with this obligation;

(e) To take all appropriate measures to eliminate discrimination against women by any person, organization or enterprise;

(f) To take all appropriate measures, including legislation, to modify or abolish existing laws, regulations, customs and practices which constitute discrimination against women;

(g) To repeal all national penal provisions which constitute discrimination against women.

Article 3
States Parties shall take in all fields, in particular in the political, social, economic and cultural fields, all appropriate measures, including legislation, to ensure the full development and advancement of women, for the purpose of guaranteeing them the exercise and enjoyment of human rights and fundamental freedoms on a basis of equality with men.

Article 4
1. Adoption by States Parties of temporary special measures aimed at accelerating *de facto* equality between men and women shall not be considered discrimination as defined in the present Convention, but shall in no way entail as a consequence the maintenance of unequal or separate standards; these measures shall be discontinued when the objectives of equality of opportunity and treatment have been achieved.

2. Adoption by States Parties of special measures, including those measures contained in the present Convention, aimed at protecting maternity shall not be considered discriminatory.

Article 5
States Parties shall take all appropriate measures:

(a) To modify the social and cultural patterns of conduct of men and women, with a view to achieving the elimination of prejudices and customary and all other practices which are based on the idea of the inferiority or the superiority of either of the sexes or on stereotyped roles for men and women;

(b) To ensure that family education includes a proper understanding of maternity as a social function and the recognition of the common responsibility of men and women in the upbringing and development of their children, it being understood that the interest of the children is the primordial consideration in all cases.

Article 6
States Parties shall take all appropriate measures, including legislation, to suppress all forms of traffic in women and exploitation of prostitution of women.

PART II

Article 7

States Parties shall take all appropriate measures to eliminate discrimination against women in the political and public life of the country and, in particular, shall ensure to women, on equal terms with men, the right:

    (a) To vote in all elections and public referenda and to be eligible for election to all publicly elected bodies;

    (b) To participate in the formulation of government policy and the implementation thereof and to hold public office and perform all public functions at all levels of government;

    (c) To participate in non-governmental organizations and associations concerned with the public and political life of the country.

Article 8

States Parties shall take all appropriate measures to ensure to women, on equal terms with men and without any discrimination, the opportunity to represent their Governments at the international level and to participate in the work of international organizations.

Article 9

    1. States Parties shall grant women equal rights with men to acquire, change or retain their nationality. They shall ensure in particular that neither marriage to an alien nor change of nationality by the husband during marriage shall automatically change the nationality of the wife, render her stateless or force upon her the nationality of the husband.

    2. States Parties shall grant women equal rights with men with respect to the nationality of their children.

PART III

Article 10

States Parties shall take all appropriate measures to eliminate discrimination against women in order to ensure to them equal rights with men in the field of education and in particular to ensure, on a basis of equality of men and women:

    (a) The same conditions for career and vocational guidance, for access to studies and for the achievement of diplomas in educational establishments of all categories in rural as well as in urban areas; this equality shall be ensured in pre-school, general, technical, professional and higher technical education, as well as in all types of vocational training;

    (b) Access to the same curricula, the same examinations, teaching staff with qualifications of the same standard and school premises and equipment of the same quality;

    (c) The elimination of any stereotyped concept of the roles of men and women at all levels and in all forms of education by encouraging coeducation and other types of education which will help to achieve this aim and, in particular, by the revision of textbooks and school programmes and the adaptation of teaching methods;

    (d) The same opportunities to benefit from scholarships and other study grants;

    (e) The same opportunities for access to programmes of continuing education, including adult and functional literacy programmes, particularly those aimed at reducing, at the earliest possible time, any gap in education existing between men and women;

    (f) The reduction of female student drop-out rates and the organization of programmes for girls and women who have left school prematurely;

    (g) The same opportunities to participate actively in sports and physical education;

    (h) Access to specific educational information to help to ensure the health and well-being of families, including information and advice on family planning.

Article 11

1. States Parties shall take all appropriate measures to eliminate discrimination against women in the field of employment in order to ensure, on a basis of equality of men and women, the same rights, in particular:

    (a) The right to work as an inalienable right of all human beings;

    (b) The right to the same employment opportunities, including the application of the same criteria for selection in matters of employment;

    (c) The right to free choice of profession and employment, the right to promotion, job security and all benefits and conditions of service and the right to receive vocational training and retraining, including apprenticeships, advanced vocational training and recurrent training;

    (d) The right to equal remuneration, including benefits, and to equal treatment in respect of work of equal value, as well as equality of treatment in the evaluation of the quality of work;

    (e) The right to social security, particularly in cases of retirement, unemployment, sickness, invalidity and old age and other incapacity to work, as well as the right to paid leave;

    (f) The right to protection of health and to safety in working conditions, including the safeguarding of the function of reproduction.

2. In order to prevent discrimination against women on the grounds of marriage or maternity and to ensure their effective right to work, States Parties shall take appropriate measures:

    (a) To prohibit, subject to the imposition of sanctions, dismissal on the grounds of pregnancy or of maternity leave and discrimination in dismissals on the basis of marital status;

    (b) To introduce maternity leave with pay or with comparable social benefits without loss of former employment, seniority or social allowances;

    (c) To encourage the provision of the necessary supporting social services to enable parents to combine family obligations with work responsibilities and participation in public life, in particular through promoting the establishment and development of a network of child-care facilities;

    (d) To provide special protection to women during pregnancy in types of work proved to be harmful to them.

3. Protective legislation relating to matters covered in this article shall be reviewed periodically in the light of scientific and technological knowledge and shall be revised, repealed or extended as necessary.

Article 12

1. States Parties shall take all appropriate measures to eliminate discrimination against women in the field of health care in order to ensure, on a basis of equality of men and women, access to health care services, including those related to family planning.

2. Notwithstanding the provisions of paragraph 1 of this article, States Parties shall ensure to women appropriate services in connection with pregnancy, confinement and the post-natal period, granting free services where necessary, as well as adequate nutrition during pregnancy and lactation.

Article 13

States Parties shall take all appropriate measures to eliminate discrimination against women in other areas of economic and social life in order to ensure, on a basis of equality of men and women, the same rights, in particular:

    (a) The right to family benefits;

    (b) The right to bank loans, mortgages and other forms of financial credit;

    (c) The right to participate in recreational activities, sports and all aspects of cultural life.

Article 14

1. States Parties shall take into account the particular problems faced by rural women and the significant roles which rural women play in the economic survival of their families, including their work in the non-monetized sectors of the economy, and shall take all appropriate measures to ensure the application of the provisions of this Convention to women in rural areas.

2. States Parties shall take all appropriate measures to eliminate discrimination against women in rural areas in order to ensure, on a basis of equality of men and women, that they participate in and benefit from rural development and, in particular, shall ensure to such women the right:

    (a) To participate in the elaboration and implementation of development planning at all levels;

    (b) To have access to adequate health care facilities, including information, counselling and services in family planning;

    (c) To benefit directly from social security programmes;

    (d) To obtain all types of training and education, formal and non-formal, including that relating to functional literacy, as well as, *inter alia,* the benefit of all community and extension services, in order to increase their technical proficiency;

    (e) To organize self-help groups and co-operatives in order to obtain equal access to economic opportunities through employment or self-employment;

    (f) To participate in all community activities;

    (g) To have access to agricultural credit and loans, marketing facilities, appropriate technology and equal treatment in land and agrarian reform as well as in land resettlement schemes;

    (h) To enjoy adequate living conditions, particularly in relation to housing, sanitation, electricity and water supply, transport and communications.

PART IV

Article 15

1. States Parties shall accord to women equality with men before the law.

2. States Parties shall accord to women, in civil matters, a legal capacity identical to that of men and the same opportunities to exercise that capacity. In particular, they shall give women equal rights to conclude contracts and to administer property and shall treat them equally in all stages of procedure in courts and tribunals.

3. States Parties agree that all contracts and all other private instruments of any kind with a legal effect which is directed at restricting the legal capacity of women shall be deemed null and void.

4. States Parties shall accord to men and women the same rights with regard to the law relating to the movement of persons and the freedom to choose their residence and domicile.

Article 16

1. States Parties shall take all appropriate measures to eliminate discrimination against women in all matters relating to marriage and family relations and in particular shall ensure, on a basis of equality of men and women:

    (a) The same right to enter into marriage;

    (b) The same right freely to choose a spouse and to enter into marriage only with their free and full consent;

    (c) The same rights and responsibilities during marriage and at its dissolution;

    (d) The same rights and responsibilities as parents, irrespective of their marital status, in matters relating to their children; in all cases the interests of the children shall be paramount;

    (e) The same rights to decide freely and responsibly on the number and spacing of their children and to have access to the information, education and means to enable them to exercise these rights;

    (f) The same rights and responsibilities with regard to guardianship, wardship, trusteeship and adoption of children, or similar institutions where these concepts exist in national legislation; in all cases the interests of the children shall be paramount;

    (g) The same personal rights as husband and wife, including the right to choose a family name, a profession and an occupation;

(h) The same rights for both spouses in respect of the ownership, acquisition, management, administration, enjoyment and disposition of property, whether free of charge or for a valuable consideration.

2. The betrothal and the marriage of a child shall have no legal effect, and all necessary action, including legislation, shall be taken to specify a minimum age for marriage and to make the registration of marriages in an official registry compulsory.

PART V

Article 17

1. For the purpose of considering the progress made in the implementation of the present Convention, there shall be established a Committee on the Elimination of Discrimination against Women (hereinafter referred to as the, Committee) consisting, at the time of entry into force of the Convention, of eighteen and, after ratification of or accession to the Convention by the thirty-fifth State Party, of twenty-three experts of high moral standing and competence in the field covered by the Convention. The experts shall be elected by States Parties from among their nationals and shall serve in their personal capacity, consideration being given to equitable geographical distribution and to the representation of the different forms of civilization as well as the principal legal systems.

2. The members of the Committee shall be elected by secret ballot from a list of persons nominated by States Parties. Each State Party may nominate one person from among its own nationals.

3. The initial election shall be held six months after the date of the entry into force of the present Convention. At least three months before the date of each election the Secretary-General of the United Nations shall address a letter to the States Parties inviting them to submit their nominations within two months. The Secretary-General shall prepare a list in alphabetical order of all persons thus nominated, indicating the States Parties which have nominated them, and shall submit it to the States Parties.

4. Elections of the members of the Committee shall be held at a meeting of States Parties convened by the Secretary-General at United Nations Headquarters. At that meeting, for which two thirds of the States Parties shall constitute a quorum, the persons elected to the Committee shall be those nominees who obtain the largest number of votes and an absolute majority of the votes of the representatives of States Parties present and voting.

5. The members of the Committee shall be elected for a term of four years. However, the terms of nine of the members elected at the first election shall expire at the end of two years; immediately after the first election the names of these nine members shall be chosen by lot by the Chairman of the Committee.

6. The election of the five additional members of the Committee shall be held in accordance with the provisions of paragraphs 2, 3 and 4 of this article, following the thirty-fifth ratification or accession. The terms of two of the additional members elected on this occasion shall expire at the end of two years, the names of these two members having been chosen by lot by the Chairman of the Committee.

7. For the filling of casual vacancies, the State Party whose expert has ceased to function as a member of the Committee shall appoint another expert from among its nationals, subject to the approval of the Committee.

8. The members of the Committee shall, with the approval of the General Assembly, receive emoluments from United Nations resources on such terms and conditions as the Assembly may decide, having regard to the importance of the Committee's responsibilities.

9. The Secretary-General of the United Nations shall provide the necessary staff and facilities for the effective performance of the functions of the Committee under the present Convention.

Article 18

1. States Parties undertake to submit to the Secretary-General of the United Nations, for consideration by the Committee, a report on the legislative, judicial, administrative or other measures which

they have adopted to give effect to the provisions of the present Convention and on the progress made in this respect:

    (a) Within one year after the entry into force for the State concerned; and

    (b) Thereafter at least every four years and further whenever the Committee so requests.

    2. Reports may indicate factors and difficulties affecting the degree of fulfilment of obligations under the present Convention.

Article 19

    1. The Committee shall adopt its own rules of procedure.

    2. The Committee shall elect its officers for a term of two years.

Article 20

    1. The Committee shall normally meet for a period of not more than two weeks annually in order to consider the reports submitted in accordance with article 18 of the present Convention.

    2. The meetings of the Committee shall normally be held at United Nations Headquarters or at any other convenient place as determined by the Committee.

Article 21

    1. The Committee shall, through the Economic and Social Council, report annually to the General Assembly of the United Nations on its activities and may make suggestions and general recommendations based on the examination of reports and information received from the States Parties. Such suggestions and general recommendations shall be included in the report of the Committee together with comments, if any, from States Parties.

    2. The Secretary-General shall transmit the reports of the Committee to the Commission on the Status of Women for its information.

Article 22

The specialized agencies shall be entitled to be represented at the consideration of the implementation of such provisions of the present Convention as fall within the scope of their activities. The Committee may invite the specialized agencies to submit reports on the implementation of the Convention in areas falling within the scope of their activities.

PART VI

Article 23

Nothing in this Convention shall affect any provisions that are more conducive to the achievement of equality between men and women which may be contained:

    (a) In the legislation of a State Party; or

    (b) In any other international convention, treaty or agreement in force for that State.

Article 24

States Parties undertake to adopt all necessary measures at the national level aimed at achieving the full realization of the rights recognized in the present Convention.

Article 25

    1. The present Convention shall be open for signature by all States.

    2. The Secretary-General of the United Nations is designated as the depositary of the present Convention.

    3. The present Convention is subject to ratification. Instruments of ratification shall be deposited with the Secretary-General of the United Nations.

    4. The present Convention shall be open to accession by all States. Accession shall be effected by the deposit of an instrument of accession with the Secretary-General of the United Nations.

Article 26

1. A request for the revision of the present Convention may be made at any time by any State Party by means of a notification in writing addressed to the Secretary-General of the United Nations.

2. The General Assembly of the United Nations shall decide upon the steps, if any, to be taken in respect of such a request.

Article 27

1. The present Convention shall enter into force on the thirtieth day after the date of deposit with the Secretary-General of the United Nations of the twentieth instrument of ratification or accession.

2. For each State ratifying the present Convention or acceding to it after the deposit of the twentieth instrument of ratification or accession, the Convention shall enter into force on the thirtieth day after the date of the deposit of its own instrument of ratification or accession.

Article 28

1. The Secretary-General of the United Nations shall receive and circulate to all States the text of reservations made by States at the time of ratification or accession.

2. A reservation incompatible with the object and purpose of the present Convention shall not be permitted.

3. Reservations may be withdrawn at any time by notification to this effect addressed to the Secretary-General of the United Nations, who shall then inform all States thereof. Such notification shall take effect on the date on which it is received.

Article 29

1. Any dispute between two or more States Parties concerning the interpretation or application of the present Convention which is not settled by negotiation shall, at the request of one of them, be submitted to arbitration. If within six months from the date of the request for arbitration the parties are unable to agree on the organization of the arbitration, any one of those parties may refer the dispute to the International Court of Justice by request in conformity with the Statute of the Court.

2. Each State Party may at the time of signature or ratification of this Convention or accession thereto declare that it does not consider itself bound by paragraph 1 of this article. The other States Parties shall not be bound by that paragraph with respect to any State Party which has made such a reservation.

3. Any State Party which has made a reservation in accordance with paragraph 2 of this article may at any time withdraw that reservation by notification to the Secretary-General of the United Nations.

Article 30

The present Convention, the Arabic, Chinese, English, French, Russian and Spanish texts of which are equally authentic, shall be deposited with the Secretary-General of the United Nations.

In witness whereof the undersigned, duly authorized, have signed the present Convention.

Optional Protocol to the Convention on the Elimination of All Forms of Discrimination against Women (1999)*

The States Parties to this Protocol,

Noting that the Charter of the United Nations reaffirms faith in fundamental human rights, in the dignity and worth of the human person and in the equal rights of men and women,

Noting that the Universal Declaration of Human Rights proclaims that all human beings are born free and equal in dignity and rights and that everyone is entitled to all the rights and freedoms set forth therein, without distinction of any kind, including distinction based on sex,

Recalling that the International Covenants on Human Rights and other international human rights instruments prohibit discrimination on the basis of sex,

Recalling also the Convention on the Elimination of All Forms of Discrimination against Women ('the Convention'), in which the States Parties thereto condemn discrimination against women in all its forms and agree to pursue by all appropriate means and without delay a policy of eliminating discrimination against women,

Reaffirming their determination to ensure the full and equal enjoyment by women of all human rights and fundamental freedoms and to take effective action to prevent violations of these rights and freedoms,

Have agreed as follows:

Article 1
A State Party to this Protocol ('State Party') recognizes the competence of the Committee on the Elimination of Discrimination against Women ('the Committee') to receive and consider communications submitted in accordance with article 2.

Article 2
Communications may be submitted by or on behalf of individuals or groups of individuals, under the jurisdiction of a State Party, claiming to be victims of a violation of any of the rights set forth in the Convention by that State Party. Where a communication is submitted on behalf of individuals or groups of individuals, this shall be with their consent unless the author can justify acting on their behalf without such consent.

Article 3
Communications shall be in writing and shall not be anonymous. No communication shall be received by the Committee if it concerns a State Party to the Convention that is not a party to this Protocol.

Article 4
1. The Committee shall not consider a communication unless it has ascertained that all available domestic remedies have been exhausted unless the application of such remedies is unreasonably prolonged or unlikely to bring effective relief.
2. The Committee shall declare a communication inadmissible where:
   (a) The same matter has already been examined by the Committee or has been or is being examined under another procedure of international investigation or settlement;
   (b) It is incompatible with the provisions of the Convention;
   (c) It is manifestly ill-founded or not sufficiently substantiated;
   (d) It is an abuse of the right to submit a communication;
   (e) The facts that are the subject of the communication occurred prior to the entry into force of this Protocol for the State Party concerned unless those facts continued after that date.

Article 5
1. At any time after the receipt of a communication and before a determination on the merits has been reached, the Committee may transmit to the State Party concerned for its urgent consideration a request that the State Party take such interim measures as may be necessary to avoid possible irreparable damage to the victim or victims of the alleged violation.
2. Where the Committee exercises its discretion under paragraph 1, this does not imply a determination on admissibility or on the merits of the communication.

Article 6
1. Unless the Committee considers a communication inadmissible without reference to the State Party concerned, and provided that the individual or individuals consent to the disclosure of their identity to that State Party, the Committee shall bring any communication submitted to it under this Protocol confidentially to the attention of the State Party concerned.
2. Within six months, the receiving State Party shall submit to the Committee written explanations or statements clarifying the matter and the remedy, if any, that may have been provided by that State Party.

Article 7

1. The Committee shall consider communications received under this Protocol in the light of all information made available to it by or on behalf of individuals or groups of individuals and by the State Party concerned, provided that this information is transmitted to the parties concerned.

2. The Committee shall hold closed meetings when examining communications under this Protocol.

3. After examining a communication, the Committee shall transmit its views on the communication, together with its recommendations, if any, to the parties concerned.

4. The State Party shall give due consideration to the views of the Committee, together with its recommendations, if any, and shall submit to the Committee, within six months, a written response, including information on any action taken in the light of the views and recommendations of the Committee.

5. The Committee may invite the State Party to submit further information about any measures the State Party has taken in response to its views or recommendations, if any, including as deemed appropriate by the Committee, in the State Party's subsequent reports under article 18 of the Convention.

Article 8

1. If the Committee receives reliable information indicating grave or systematic violations by a State Party of rights set forth in the Convention, the Committee shall invite that State Party to co-operate in the examination of the information and to this end to submit observations with regard to the information concerned.

2. Taking into account any observations that may have been submitted by the State Party concerned as well as any other reliable information available to it, the Committee may designate one or more of its members to conduct an inquiry and to report urgently to the Committee. Where warranted and with the consent of the State Party, the inquiry may include a visit to its territory.

3. After examining the findings of such an inquiry, the Committee shall transmit these findings to the State Party concerned together with any comments and recommendations.

4. The State Party concerned shall, within six months of receiving the findings, comments and recommendations transmitted by the Committee, submit its observations to the Committee.

5. Such an inquiry shall be conducted confidentially and the cooperation of that State Party shall be sought at all stages of the proceedings.

Article 9

1. The Committee may invite the State Party concerned to include in its report under article 18 of the Convention details of any measures taken in response to an inquiry conducted under article 8 of this Protocol.

2. The Committee may, if necessary, after the end of the period of six months referred to in article 8.4, invite the State Party concerned to inform it of the measures taken in response to such an inquiry.

Article 10

1. Each State Party may, at the time of signature or ratification of this Protocol or accession thereto, declare that it does not recognize the competence of the Committee provided for in articles 8 and 9.

2. Any State Party having made a declaration in accordance with paragraph 1 of this article may, at any time, withdraw this declaration by notification to the Secretary-General.

Article 11

A State Party shall take all appropriate steps to ensure that individuals under its jurisdiction are not subjected to ill-treatment or intimidation as a consequence of communicating with the Committee pursuant to this Protocol.

Article 12

The Committee shall include in its annual report under article 21 of the Convention a summary of its activities under this Protocol.

Article 13

Each State Party undertakes to make widely known and to give publicity to the Convention and this Protocol and to facilitate access to information about the views and recommendations of the Committee, in particular, on matters involving that State Party.

Article 14

The Committee shall develop its own rules of procedure to be followed when exercising the functions conferred on it by this Protocol.

Article 15

1. This Protocol shall be open for signature by any State that has signed, ratified or acceded to the Convention.

2. This Protocol shall be subject to ratification by any State that has ratified or acceded to the Convention. Instruments of ratification shall be deposited with the Secretary-General of the United Nations.

3. This Protocol shall be open to accession by any State that has ratified or acceded to the Convention.

4. Accession shall be effected by the deposit of an instrument of accession with the Secretary-General of the United Nations.

Article 16

1. This Protocol shall enter into force three months after the date of the deposit with the Secretary-General of the United Nations of the tenth instrument of ratification or accession.

2. For each State ratifying this Protocol or acceding to it after its entry into force, this Protocol shall enter into force three months after the date of the deposit of its own instrument of ratification or accession.

Article 17

No reservations to this Protocol shall be permitted.

Article 18

1. Any State Party may propose an amendment to this Protocol and file it with the Secretary-General of the United Nations. The Secretary-General shall thereupon communicate any proposed amendments to the States Parties with a request that they notify her/him whether they favour a conference of States Parties for the purpose of considering and voting on the proposal. In the event that at least one third of the States Parties favour such a conference, the Secretary-General shall convene the conference under the auspices of the United Nations. Any amendment adopted by a majority of the States Parties present and voting at the conference shall be submitted to the General Assembly of the United Nations for approval.

2. Amendments shall come into force when they have been approved by the General Assembly of the United Nations and accepted by a two-thirds majority of the States Parties to this Protocol in accordance with their respective constitutional processes.

3. When amendments come into force, they shall be binding on those States Parties that have accepted them, other States Parties still being bound by the provisions of this Protocol and any earlier amendments that they have accepted.

Article 19

1. Any State Party may denounce this Protocol at any time by written notification addressed to the Secretary-General of the United Nations. Denunciation shall take effect six months after the date of receipt of the notification by the Secretary-General.

2. Denunciation shall be without prejudice to the continued application of the provisions of this Protocol to any communication submitted under article 2 or any inquiry initiated under article 8 before the effective date of denunciation.

Article 20
The Secretary-General of the United Nations shall inform all States of:
> (a) Signatures, ratifications and accessions under this Protocol;
> (b) The date of entry into force of this Protocol and of any amendment under article 18;
> (c) Any denunciation under article 19.

Article 21
1. This Protocol, of which the Arabic, Chinese, English, French, Russian and Spanish texts are equally authentic, shall be deposited in the archives of the United Nations.
2. The Secretary-General of the United Nations shall transmit certified copies of this Protocol to all States referred to in article 25 of the Convention.

Declaration on the Elimination of All Forms of Intolerance and of Discrimination Based on Religion or Belief (1981)*

The General Assembly,

Considering that one of the basic principles of the Charter of the United Nations is that of the dignity and equality inherent in all human beings, and that all Member States have pledged themselves to take joint and separate action in co-operation with the Organization to promote and encourage universal respect for and observance of human rights and fundamental freedoms for all, without distinction as to race, sex, language or religion,

Considering that the Universal Declaration of Human Rights and the International Covenants on Human Rights proclaim the principles of non-discrimination and equality before the law and the right to freedom of thought, conscience, religion and belief,

Considering that the disregard and infringement of human rights and fundamental freedoms, in particular of the right to freedom of thought, conscience, religion or whatever belief, have brought, directly or indirectly, wars and great suffering to mankind, especially where they serve as a means of foreign interference in the internal affairs of other States and amount to kindling hatred between peoples and nations,

Considering that religion or belief, for anyone who professes either, is one of the fundamental elements in his conception of life and that freedom of religion or belief should be fully respected and guaranteed,

Considering that it is essential to promote understanding, tolerance and respect in matters relating to freedom of religion and belief and to ensure that the use of religion or belief for ends inconsistent with the Charter of the United Nations, other relevant instruments of the United Nations and the purposes and principles of the present Declaration is inadmissible,

Convinced that freedom of religion and belief should also contribute to the attainment of the goals of world peace, social justice and friendship among peoples and to the elimination of ideologies or practices of colonialism and racial discrimination,

Noting with satisfaction the adoption of several, and the coming into force of some, conventions, under the aegis of the United Nations and of the specialized agencies, for the elimination of various forms of discrimination,

Concerned by manifestations of intolerance and by the existence of discrimination in matters of religion or belief still in evidence in some areas of the world,

Resolved to adopt all necessary measures for the speedy elimination of such intolerance in all its forms and manifestations and to prevent and combat discrimination on the ground of religion or belief,

Proclaims this Declaration on the Elimination of All Forms of Intolerance and of Discrimination Based on Religion or Belief:

Article 1

1. Everyone shall have the right to freedom of thought, conscience and religion. This right shall include freedom to have a religion or whatever belief of his choice, and freedom, either individually or in community with others and in public or private, to manifest his religion or belief in worship, observance, practice and teaching.

2. No one shall be subject to coercion which would impair his freedom to have a religion or belief of his choice.

3. Freedom to manifest one's religion or belief may be subject only to such limitations as are prescribed by law and are necessary to protect public safety, order, health or morals or the fundamental rights and freedoms of others.

Article 2

1. No one shall be subject to discrimination by any State, institution, group of persons, or person on the grounds of religion or other belief.

2. For the purposes of the present Declaration, the expression 'intolerance and discrimination based on religion or belief' means any distinction, exclusion, restriction or preference based on religion or belief and having as its purpose or as its effect nullification or impairment of the recognition, enjoyment or exercise of human rights and fundamental freedoms on an equal basis.

Article 3

Discrimination between human beings on the grounds of religion or belief constitutes an affront to human dignity and a disavowal of the principles of the Charter of the United Nations, and shall be condemned as a violation of the human rights and fundamental freedoms proclaimed in the Universal Declaration of Human Rights and enunciated in detail in the International Covenants on Human Rights, and as an obstacle to friendly and peaceful relations between nations.

Article 4

1. All States shall take effective measures to prevent and eliminate discrimination on the grounds of religion or belief in the recognition, exercise and enjoyment of human rights and fundamental freedoms in all fields of civil, economic, political, social and cultural life.

2. All States shall make all efforts to enact or rescind legislation where necessary to prohibit any such discrimination, and to take all appropriate measures to combat intolerance on the grounds of religion or other beliefs in this matter.

Article 5

1. The parents or, as the case may be, the legal guardians of the child have the right to organize the life within the family in accordance with their religion or belief and bearing in mind the moral education in which they believe the child should be brought up.

2. Every child shall enjoy the right to have access to education in the matter of religion or belief in accordance with the wishes of his parents or, as the case may be, legal guardians, and shall not be compelled to receive teaching on religion or belief against the wishes of his parents or legal guardians, the best interests of the child being the guiding principle.

3. The child shall be protected from any form of discrimination on the ground of religion or belief. He shall be brought up in a spirit of understanding, tolerance, friendship among peoples, peace and universal brotherhood, respect for freedom of religion or belief of others, and in full consciousness that his energy and talents should be devoted to the service of his fellow men.

4. In the case of a child who is not under the care either of his parents or of legal guardians, due account shall be taken of their expressed wishes or of any other proof of their wishes in the matter of religion or belief, the best interests of the child being the guiding principle.

5. Practices of a religion or belief in which a child is brought up must not be injurious to his physical or mental health or to his full development, taking into account article 1, paragraph 3, of the present Declaration.

Article 6
In accordance with article 1 of the present Declaration, and subject to the provisions of article 1, paragraph 3, the right to freedom of thought, conscience, religion or belief shall include, *inter alia*, the following freedoms:
(a) To worship or assemble in connection with a religion or belief, and to establish and maintain places for these purposes;
(b) To establish and maintain appropriate charitable or humanitarian institutions;
(c) To make, acquire and use to an adequate extent the necessary articles and materials related to the rites or customs of a religion or belief;
(d) To write, issue and disseminate relevant publications in these areas;
(e) To teach a religion or belief in places suitable for these purposes;
(f) To solicit and receive voluntary financial and other contributions from individuals and institutions;
(g) To train, appoint, elect or designate by succession appropriate leaders called for by the requirements and standards of any religion or belief;
(h) To observe days of rest and to celebrate holidays and ceremonies in accordance with the precepts of one's religion or belief;
(i) To establish and maintain communications with individuals and communities in matters of religion and belief at the national and international levels.

Article 7
The rights and freedoms set forth in the present Declaration shall be accorded in national legislation in such a manner that everyone shall be able to avail himself of such rights and freedoms in practice.

Article 8
Nothing in the present Declaration shall be construed as restricting or derogating from any right defined in the Universal Declaration of Human Rights and the International Covenants on Human Rights.

Convention against Torture and Other Cruel, Inhuman or Degrading Treatment or Punishment (1984)*

The States Parties to this Convention,
    Considering that, in accordance with the principles proclaimed in the Charter of the United Nations, recognition of the equal and inalienable rights of all members of the human family is the foundation of freedom, justice and peace in the world,
    Recognizing that those rights derive from the inherent dignity of the human person,
    Considering the obligation of States under the Charter, in particular Article 55, to promote universal respect for, and observance of, human rights and fundamental freedoms,
    Having regard to article 5 of the Universal Declaration of Human Rights and article 7 of the International Covenant on Civil and Political Rights, both of which provide that no one shall be subjected to torture or to cruel, inhuman or degrading treatment or punishment,
    Having regard also to the Declaration on the Protection of All Persons from Being Subjected to Torture and Other Cruel, Inhuman or Degrading Treatment or Punishment, adopted by the General Assembly on 9 December 1975,

* From Convention against Torture and Other Cruel, Inhuman or Degrading Treatment or Punishment, © 1984 United Nations. Reprinted with the permission of the United Nations.

Desiring to make more effective the struggle against torture and other cruel, inhuman or degrading treatment or punishment throughout the world,

Have agreed as follows:

PART I

Article 1

1. For the purposes of this Convention, the term 'torture' means any act by which severe pain or suffering, whether physical or mental, is intentionally inflicted on a person for such purposes as obtaining from him or a third person information or a confession, punishing him for an act he or a third person has committed or is suspected of having committed, or intimidating or coercing him or a third person, or for any reason based on discrimination of any kind, when such pain or suffering is inflicted by or at the instigation of or with the consent or acquiescence of a public official or other person acting in an official capacity. It does not include pain or suffering arising only from, inherent in or incidental to lawful sanctions.

2. This article is without prejudice to any international instrument or national legislation which does or may contain provisions of wider application.

Article 2

1. Each State Party shall take effective legislative, administrative, judicial or other measures to prevent acts of torture in any territory under its jurisdiction.

2. No exceptional circumstances whatsoever, whether a state of war or a threat of war, internal political instability or any other public emergency, may be invoked as a justification of torture.

3. An order from a superior officer or a public authority may not be invoked as a justification of torture.

Article 3

1. No State Party shall expel, return ('*refouler*') or extradite a person to another State where there are substantial grounds for believing that he would be in danger of being subjected to torture.

2. For the purpose of determining whether there are such grounds, the competent authorities shall take into account all relevant considerations including, where applicable, the existence in the State concerned of a consistent pattern of gross, flagrant or mass violations of human rights.

Article 4

1. Each State Party shall ensure that all acts of torture are offences under its criminal law. The same shall apply to an attempt to commit torture and to an act by any person which constitutes complicity or participation in torture.

2. Each State Party shall make these offences punishable by appropriate penalties which take into account their grave nature.

Article 5

1. Each State Party shall take such measures as may be necessary to establish its jurisdiction over the offences referred to in article 4 in the following cases:

    (a) when the offences are committed in any territory under its jurisdiction or on board a ship or aircraft registered in that State;

    (b) when the alleged offender is a national of that State;

    (c) when the victim is a national of that State if that State considers it appropriate.

2. Each State Party shall likewise take such measures as may be necessary to establish its jurisdiction over such offences in cases where the alleged offender is present in any territory under its jurisdiction and it does not extradite him pursuant to article 8 to any of the States mentioned in paragraph 1 of this article.

3. This Convention does not exclude any criminal jurisdiction exercised in accordance with internal law.

Article 6

1. Upon being satisfied, after an examination of information available to it, that the circumstances so warrant, any State Party in whose territory a person alleged to have committed any offence referred to in article 4 is present shall take him into custody or take other legal measures to ensure his presence. The custody and other legal measures shall be as provided in the law of that State but may be continued only for such time as is necessary to enable any criminal or extradition proceedings to be instituted.

2. Such State shall immediately make a preliminary inquiry into the facts.

3. Any person in custody pursuant to paragraph 1 of this article shall be assisted in communicating immediately with the nearest appropriate representative of the State of which he is a national, or, if he is a stateless person, with the representative of the State where he usually resides.

4. When a State, pursuant to this article, has taken a person into custody, it shall immediately notify the States referred to in article 5, paragraph 1, of the fact that such person is in custody and of the circumstances which warrant his detention. The State which makes the preliminary inquiry contemplated in paragraph 2 of this article shall promptly report its findings to the said States and shall indicate whether it intends to exercise jurisdiction.

Article 7

1. The State Party in the territory under whose jurisdiction a person alleged to have committed any offence referred to in article 4 is found shall in the cases contemplated in article 5, if it does not extradite him, submit the case to its competent authorities for the purpose of prosecution.

2. These authorities shall take their decision in the same manner as in the case of any ordinary offence of a serious nature under the law of that State. In the cases referred to in article 5, paragraph 2, the standards of evidence required for prosecution and conviction shall in no way be less stringent than those which apply in the cases referred to in article 5, paragraph 1.

3. Any person regarding whom proceedings are brought in connection with any of the offences referred to in article 4 shall be guaranteed fair treatment at all stages of the proceedings.

Article 8

1. The offences referred to in article 4 shall be deemed to be included as extraditable offences in any extradition treaty existing between States Parties. States Parties undertake to include such offences as extraditable offences in every extradition treaty to be concluded between them.

2. If a State Party which makes extradition conditional on the existence of a treaty receives a request for extradition from another State Party with which it has no extradition treaty, it may consider this Convention as the legal basis for extradition in respect of such offences. Extradition shall be subject to the other conditions provided by the law of the requested State.

3. States Parties which do not make extradition conditional on the existence of a treaty shall recognize such offences as extraditable offences between themselves subject to the conditions provided by the law of the requested State.

4. Such offences shall be treated, for the purpose of extradition between States Parties, as if they had been committed not only in the place in which they occurred but also in the territories of the States required to establish their jurisdiction in accordance with article 5, paragraph 1.

Article 9

1. States Parties shall afford one another the greatest measure of assistance in connection with criminal proceedings brought in respect of any of the offences referred to in article 4, including the supply of all evidence at their disposal necessary for the proceedings.

2. States Parties shall carry out their obligations under paragraph 1 of this article in conformity with any treaties on mutual judicial assistance that may exist between them.

Article 10

1. Each State Party shall ensure that education and information regarding the prohibition against torture are fully included in the training of law enforcement personnel, civil or military,

medical personnel, public officials and other persons who may be involved in the custody, interrogation or treatment of any individual subjected to any form of arrest, detention or imprisonment.

2. Each State Party shall include this prohibition in the rules or instructions issued in regard to the duties and functions of any such persons.

Article 11
Each State Party shall keep under systematic review interrogation rules, instructions, methods and practices as well as arrangements for the custody and treatment of persons subjected to any form of arrest, detention or imprisonment in any territory under its jurisdiction, with a view to preventing any cases of torture.

Article 12
Each State Party shall ensure that its competent authorities proceed to a prompt and impartial investigation, wherever there is reasonable ground to believe that an act of torture has been committed in any territory under its jurisdiction.

Article 13
Each State Party shall ensure that any individual who alleges he has been subjected to torture in any territory under its jurisdiction has the right to complain to, and to have his case promptly and impartially examined by, its competent authorities. Steps shall be taken to ensure that the complainant and witnesses are protected against all ill-treatment or intimidation as a consequence of his complaint or any evidence given.

Article 14
1. Each State Party shall ensure in its legal system that the victim of an act of torture obtains redress and has an enforceable right to fair and adequate compensation, including the means for as full rehabilitation as possible. In the event of the death of the victim as a result of an act of torture, his dependants shall be entitled to compensation.

2. Nothing in this article shall affect any right of the victim or other persons to compensation which may exist under national law.

Article 15
Each State Party shall ensure that any statement which is established to have been made as a result of torture shall not be invoked as evidence in any proceedings, except against a person accused of torture as evidence that the statement was made.

Article 16
1. Each State Party shall undertake to prevent in any territory under its jurisdiction other acts of cruel, inhuman or degrading treatment or punishment which do not amount to torture as defined in article 1, when such acts are committed by or at the instigation of or with the consent or acquiescence of a public official or other person acting in an official capacity. In particular, the obligations contained in articles 10, 11, 12 and 13 shall apply with the substitution for references to torture of references to other forms of cruel, inhuman or degrading treatment or punishment.

2. The provisions of this Convention are without prejudice to the provisions of any other international instrument or national law which prohibits cruel, inhuman or degrading treatment or punishment or which relates to extradition or expulsion.

PART II

Article 17
1. There shall be established a Committee against Torture (hereinafter referred to as the Committee) which shall carry out the functions hereinafter provided. The Committee shall consist of ten experts of high moral standing and recognized competence in the field of human rights, who shall serve in their personal capacity. The experts shall be elected by the States Parties, consideration

being given to equitable geographical distribution and to the usefulness of the participation of some persons having legal experience.

2. The members of the Committee shall be elected by secret ballot from a list of persons nominated by States Parties. Each State Party may nominate one person from among its own nationals. States Parties shall bear in mind the usefulness of nominating persons who are also members of the Human Rights Committee established under the International Covenant on Civil and Political Rights and who are willing to serve on the Committee against Torture.

3. Elections of the members of the Committee shall be held at biennial meetings of States Parties convened by the Secretary-General of the United Nations. At those meetings, for which two thirds of the States Parties shall constitute a quorum, the persons elected to the Committee shall be those who obtain the largest number of votes and an absolute majority of the votes of the representatives of States Parties present and voting.

4. The initial election shall be held no later than six months after the date of the entry into force of this Convention. At least four months before the date of each election, the Secretary-General of the United Nations shall address a letter to the States Parties inviting them to submit their nominations within three months. The Secretary-General shall prepare a list in alphabetical order of all persons thus nominated, indicating the States Parties which have nominated them, and shall submit it to the States Parties.

5. The members of the Committee shall be elected for a term of four years. They shall be eligible for re-election if renominated. However, the term of five of the members elected at the first election shall expire at the end of two years; immediately after the first election the names of these five members shall be chosen by lot by the chairman of the meeting referred to in paragraph 3 of this article.

6. If a member of the Committee dies or resigns or for any other cause can no longer perform his Committee duties, the State Party which nominated him shall appoint another expert from among its nationals to serve for the remainder of his term, subject to the approval of the majority of the States Parties. The approval shall be considered given unless half or more of the States Parties respond negatively within six weeks after having been informed by the Secretary-General of the United Nations of the proposed appointment.

7. States Parties shall be responsible for the expenses of the members of the Committee while they are in performance of Committee duties.

Article 18

1. The Committee shall elect its officers for a term of two years. They may be re-elected.

2. The Committee shall establish its own rules of procedure, but these rules shall provide, *inter alia*, that:

    (a) six members shall constitute a quorum;

    (b) decisions of the Committee shall be made by a majority vote of the members present.

3. The Secretary-General of the United Nations shall provide the necessary staff and facilities for the effective performance of the functions of the Committee under this Convention.

4. The Secretary-General of the United Nations shall convene the initial meeting of the Committee. After its initial meeting, the Committee shall meet at such times as shall be provided in its rules of procedure.

5. The States Parties shall be responsible for expenses incurred in connection with the holding of meetings of the States Parties and of the Committee, including reimbursement to the United Nations for any expenses, such as the cost of staff and facilities, incurred by the United Nations pursuant to paragraph 3 of this article.

Article 19

1. The States Parties shall submit to the Committee, through the Secretary-General of the United Nations, reports on the measures they have taken to give effect to their undertakings under this Convention, within one year after the entry into force of the Convention for the State Party

concerned. Thereafter the States Parties shall submit supplementary reports every four years on any new measures taken and such other reports as the Committee may request.

2. The Secretary-General of the United Nations shall transmit the reports to all States Parties.

3. Each report shall be considered by the Committee which may make such general comments on the report as it may consider appropriate and shall forward these to the State Party concerned. That State Party may respond with any observations it chooses to the Committee.

4. The Committee may, at its discretion, decide to include any comments made by it in accordance with paragraph 3 of this article, together with the observations thereon received from the State Party concerned, in its annual report made in accordance with article 24. If so requested by the State Party concerned, the Committee may also include a copy of the report submitted under paragraph 1 of this article.

Article 20

1. If the Committee receives reliable information which appears to it to contain well-founded indications that torture is being systematically practised in the territory of a State Party, the Committee shall invite that State Party to co-operate in the examination of the information and to this end to submit observations with regard to the information concerned.

2. Taking into account any observations which may have been submitted by the State Party concerned, as well as any other relevant information available to it, the Committee may, if it decides that this is warranted, designate one or more of its members to make a confidential inquiry and to report to the Committee urgently.

3. If an inquiry is made in accordance with paragraph 2 of this article, the Committee shall seek the co-operation of the State Party concerned. In agreement with that State Party, such an inquiry may include a visit to its territory.

4. After examining the findings of its member or members submitted in accordance with paragraph 2 of this article, the Committee shall transmit these findings to the State Party concerned together with any comments or suggestions which seem appropriate in view of the situation.

5. All the proceedings of the Committee referred to in paragraphs 1 to 4 of this article shall be confidential, and at all stages of the proceedings the co-operation of the State Party shall be sought. After such proceedings have been completed with regard to an inquiry made in accordance with paragraph 2, the Committee may, after consultations with the State Party concerned, decide to include a summary account of the results of the proceedings in its annual report made in accordance with article 24.

Article 21

1. A State Party to this Convention may at any time declare under this article that it recognizes the competence of the Committee to receive and consider communications to the effect that a State Party claims that another State Party is not fulfilling its obligations under this Convention. Such communications may be received and considered according to the procedures laid down in this article only if submitted by a State Party which has made a declaration recognizing in regard to itself the competence of the Committee. No communication shall be dealt with by the Committee under this article if it concerns a State Party which has not made such a declaration. Communications received under this article shall be dealt with in accordance with the following procedure:

    (a) if a State Party considers that another State Party is not giving effect to the provisions of this Convention, it may, by written communication, bring the matter to the attention of that State Party. Within three months after the receipt of the communication the receiving State shall afford the State which sent the communication an explanation or any other statement in writing clarifying the matter, which should include, to the extent possible and pertinent, reference to domestic procedures and remedies taken, pending or available in the matter;

    (b) if the matter is not adjusted to the satisfaction of both States Parties concerned within six months after the receipt by the receiving State of the initial communication, either State shall have the right to refer the matter to the Committee, by notice given to the Committee and to the other State;

(c) the Committee shall deal with a matter referred to it under this article only after it has ascertained that all domestic remedies have been invoked and exhausted in the matter, in conformity with the generally recognized principles of international law. This shall not be the rule where the application of the remedies is unreasonably prolonged or is unlikely to bring effective relief to the person who is the victim of the violation of this Convention;

(d) the Committee shall hold closed meetings when examining communications under this article;

(e) subject to the provisions of subparagraph (c), the Committee shall make available its good offices to the States Parties concerned with a view to a friendly solution of the matter on the basis of respect for the obligations provided for in this Convention. For this purpose, the Committee may, when appropriate, set up an *ad hoc* conciliation commission;

(f) in any matter referred to it under this article, the Committee may call upon the States Parties concerned, referred to in subparagraph (b), to supply any relevant information;

(g) the States Parties concerned, referred to in subparagraph (b) shall have the right to be represented when the matter is being considered by the Committee and to make submissions orally and/or in writing;

(h) the Committee shall, within twelve months after the date of receipt of notice under subparagraph (b), submit a report:
  (i) if a solution within the terms of subparagraph (e) is reached, the Committee shall confine its report to a brief statement of the facts and of the solution reached;
  (ii) if a solution within the terms of subparagraph (e) is not reached the Committee shall confine its report to a brief statement of the facts; the written submissions and record of the oral submissions made by the States Parties concerned shall be attached to the report.

In every matter, the report shall be communicated to the States Parties concerned.

2. The provisions of this article shall come into force when five States Parties to this Convention have made declarations under paragraph 1 of this article. Such declarations shall be deposited by the States Parties with the Secretary-General of the United Nations, who shall transmit copies thereof to the other States Parties. A declaration may be withdrawn at any time by notification to the Secretary-General. Such a withdrawal shall not prejudice the consideration of any matter which is the subject of a communication already transmitted under this article; no further communication by any State Party shall be received under this article after the notification of withdrawal of the declaration has been received by the Secretary-General, unless the State Party concerned has made a new declaration.

Article 22

1. A State Party to this Convention may at any time declare under this article that it recognizes the competence of the Committee to receive and consider communications from or on behalf of individuals subject to its jurisdiction who claim to be victims of a violation by a State Party of the provisions of the Convention. No communication shall be received by the Committee if it concerns a State Party which has not made such a declaration.

2. The Committee shall consider inadmissible any communication under this article which is anonymous or which it considers to be an abuse of the right of submission of such communications or to be incompatible with the provisions of this Convention.

3. Subject to the provisions of paragraph 2, the Committee shall bring any communications submitted to it under this article to the attention of the State Party to this Convention which has made a declaration under paragraph 1 and is alleged to be violating any provisions of the Convention. Within six months, the receiving State shall submit to the Committee written explanations or statements clarifying the matter and the remedy, if any, that may have been taken by that State.

4. The Committee shall consider communications received under this article in the light of all information made available to it by or on behalf of the individual and by the State Party concerned.

5. The Committee shall not consider any communications from an individual under this article unless it has ascertained that:

    (a) the same matter has not been, and is not being, examined under another procedure of international investigation or settlement;

    (b) the individual has exhausted all available domestic remedies; this shall not be the rule where the application of the remedies is unreasonably prolonged or is unlikely to bring effective relief to the person who is the victim of the violation of this Convention.

6. The Committee shall hold closed meetings when examining communications under this article.

7. The Committee shall forward its views to the State Party concerned and to the individual.

8. The provisions of this article shall come into force when five States Parties to this Convention have made declarations under paragraph 1 of this article. Such declarations shall be deposited by the States Parties with the Secretary-General of the United Nations, who shall transmit copies thereof to the other States Parties. A declaration may be withdrawn at any time by notification to the Secretary-General. Such a withdrawal shall not prejudice the consideration of any matter which is the subject of a communication already transmitted under this article, no further communication by or on behalf of an individual shall be received under this article after the notification of withdrawal of the declaration has been received by the Secretary-General, unless the State Party has made a new declaration.

Article 23

The members of the Committee and of the *ad hoc* conciliation commissions which may be appointed under article 21, paragraph 1(e), shall be entitled to the facilities, privileges and immunities of experts on mission for the United Nations as laid down in the relevant sections of the Convention on the Privileges and Immunities of the United Nations.

Article 24

The Committee shall submit an annual report on its activities under this Convention to the States Parties and to the General Assembly of the United Nations.

PART III

Article 25

1. This Convention is open for signature by all States.

2. This Convention is subject to ratification. Instruments of ratification shall be deposited with the Secretary-General of the United Nations.

Article 26

This Convention is open to accession by all States. Accession shall be effected by the deposit of an instrument of accession with the Secretary-General of the United Nations.

Article 27

1. This Convention shall enter into force on the thirtieth day after the date of the deposit with the Secretary-General of the United Nations of the twentieth instrument of ratification or accession.

2. For each State ratifying this Convention or acceding to it after the deposit of the twentieth instrument of ratification or accession, the Convention shall enter into force on the thirtieth day after the date of the deposit of its own instrument of ratification or accession.

Article 28

1. Each State may, at the time of signature or ratification of this Convention or accession thereto, declare that it does not recognize the competence of the Committee provided for in article 20.

2. Any State Party having made a reservation in accordance with paragraph 1 of this article may, at any time, withdraw this reservation by notification to the Secretary-General of the United Nations.

Article 29

1. Any State Party to this Convention may propose an amendment and file it with the Secretary-General of the United Nations. The Secretary-General shall thereupon communicate the proposed amendment to the States Parties with a request that they notify him whether they favour a conference of States Parties for the purpose of considering and voting upon the proposal. In the event that within four months from the date of such communication at least one third of the States Parties favours such a conference, the Secretary-General shall convene the conference under the auspices of the United Nations. Any amendment adopted by a majority of the States Parties present and voting at the conference shall be submitted by the Secretary-General to all the States Parties for acceptance.

2. An amendment adopted in accordance with paragraph 1 of this article shall enter into force when two thirds of the States Parties to this Convention have notified the Secretary-General of the United Nations that they have accepted it in accordance with their respective constitutional processes.

3. When amendments enter into force, they shall be binding on those States Parties which have accepted them, other States Parties still being bound by the provisions of this Convention and any earlier amendments which they have accepted.

Article 30

1. Any dispute between two or more States Parties concerning the interpretation or application of this Convention which cannot be settled through negotiation shall, at the request of one of them, be submitted to arbitration. If within six months from the date of the request for arbitration the Parties are unable to agree on the organization of the arbitration, any one of those Parties may refer the dispute to the International Court of Justice by request in conformity with the Statute of the Court.

2. Each State may, at the time of signature or ratification of this Convention or accession thereto, declare that it does not consider itself bound by paragraph 1 of this article. The other States Parties shall not be bound by paragraph 1 of this article with respect to any State Party having made such a reservation.

3. Any State Party having made a reservation in accordance with paragraph 2 of this article may at any time withdraw this reservation by notification to the Secretary-General of the United Nations.

Article 31

1. A State Party may denounce this Convention by written notification to the Secretary-General of the United Nations. Denunciation becomes effective one year after the date of receipt of the notification by the Secretary-General.

2. Such a denunciation shall not have the effect of releasing the State Party from its obligations under this Convention in regard to any act or omission which occurs prior to the date at which the denunciation becomes effective, nor shall denunciation prejudice in any way the continued consideration of any matter which is already under consideration by the Committee prior to the date at which the denunciation becomes effective.

3. Following the date at which the denunciation of a State Party becomes effective, the Committee shall not commence consideration of any new matter regarding that State.

Article 32

The Secretary-General of the United Nations shall inform all States Members of the United Nations and all States which have signed this Convention or acceded to it of the following:

    (a) signatures, ratifications and accessions under articles 25 and 26;

    (b) the date of entry into force of this Convention under article 27 and the date of the entry into force of any amendments under article 29;

    (c) denunciations under article 31.

Article 33

1. This Convention, of which the Arabic, Chinese, English, French, Russian and Spanish texts are equally authentic, shall be deposited with the Secretary-General of the United Nations.

2. The Secretary-General of the United Nations shall transmit certified copies of this Convention to all States.

Optional Protocol to the Convention against Torture and Other Cruel, Inhuman or Degrading Treatment or Punishment (2002)*

PREAMBLE

The States Parties to the present Protocol,

Reaffirming that torture and other cruel, inhuman or degrading treatment or punishment are prohibited and constitute serious violations of human rights,

Convinced that further measures are necessary to achieve the purposes of the Convention against Torture and Other Cruel, Inhuman or Degrading Treatment or Punishment (hereinafter referred to as the Convention) and to strengthen the protection of persons deprived of their liberty against torture and other cruel, inhuman or degrading treatment or punishment,

Recalling that articles 2 and 16 of the Convention oblige each State Party to take effective measures to prevent acts of torture and other cruel, inhuman or degrading treatment or punishment in any territory under its jurisdiction,

Recognizing that States have the primary responsibility for implementing those articles, that strengthening the protection of people deprived of their liberty and the full respect for their human rights is a common responsibility shared by all and that international implementing bodies complement and strengthen national measures,

Recalling that the effective prevention of torture and other cruel, inhuman or degrading treatment or punishment requires education and a combination of various legislative, administrative, judicial and other measures,

Recalling also that the World Conference on Human Rights firmly declared that efforts to eradicate torture should first and foremost be concentrated on prevention and called for the adoption of an optional protocol to the Convention, intended to establish a preventive system of regular visits to places of detention,

Convinced that the protection of persons deprived of their liberty against torture and other cruel, inhuman or degrading treatment or punishment can be strengthened by non-judicial means of a preventive nature, based on regular visits to places of detention,

Have agreed as follows:

PART I GENERAL PRINCIPLES

Article 1

The objective of the present Protocol is to establish a system of regular visits undertaken by independent international and national bodies to places where people are deprived of their liberty, in order to prevent torture and other cruel, inhuman or degrading treatment or punishment.

Article 2

1. A Subcommittee on Prevention of Torture and Other Cruel, Inhuman or Degrading Treatment or Punishment of the Committee against Torture (hereinafter referred to as the Subcommittee on Prevention) shall be established and shall carry out the functions laid down in the present Protocol.

---

* From Optional Protocol to the Convention against Torture and Other Cruel, Inhuman or Degrading Treatment or Punishment, by Office of the United Nations High Commissioner for Human Rights (OHCHR), © 2002 United Nations. Reprinted with the permission of the United Nations.

2. The Subcommittee on Prevention shall carry out its work within the framework of the Charter of the United Nations and will be guided by the purposes and principles thereof, as well as the norms of the United Nations concerning the treatment of people deprived of their liberty.

3. Equally, the Subcommittee on Prevention shall be guided by the principles of confidentiality, impartiality, non-selectivity, universality and objectivity.

4. The Subcommittee on Prevention and the States Parties shall cooperate in the implementation of the present Protocol.

Article 3
Each State Party shall set up, designate or maintain at the domestic level one or several visiting bodies for the prevention of torture and other cruel, inhuman or degrading treatment or punishment (hereinafter referred to as the national preventive mechanism).

Article 4
1. Each State Party shall allow visits, in accordance with the present Protocol, by the mechanisms referred to in articles 2 and 3 to any place under its jurisdiction and control where persons are or may be deprived of their liberty, either by virtue of an order given by a public authority or at its instigation or with its consent or acquiescence (hereinafter referred to as places of detention). These visits shall be undertaken with a view to strengthening, if necessary, the protection of these persons against torture and other cruel, inhuman or degrading treatment or punishment.

2. For the purposes of the present Protocol, deprivation of liberty means any form of detention or imprisonment or the placement of a person in a public or private custodial setting which that person is not permitted to leave at will by order of any judicial, administrative or other authority.

PART II SUBCOMMITTEE ON PREVENTION

Article 5
1. The Subcommittee on Prevention shall consist of ten members. After the fiftieth ratification or accession to the present Protocol, the number of the members of the Subcommittee on Prevention shall increase to twenty-five.

2. The members of the Subcommittee shall be chosen from among persons of high moral character, having proven professional experience in the field of the administration of justice, in particular criminal law, prison or police administration, or in the various fields relevant to the treatment of persons deprived of their liberty.

3. In the composition of the Subcommittee due consideration shall be given to equitable geographic distribution and to the representation of different forms of civilization and legal systems of the States Parties.

4. In this composition consideration shall also be given to balanced gender representation on the basis of the principles of equality and non-discrimination.

5. No two members of the Subcommittee may be nationals of the same State.

6. The members of the Subcommittee shall serve in their individual capacity, shall be independent and impartial and shall be available to serve the Subcommittee efficiently.

Article 6
1. Each State Party may nominate, in accordance with paragraph 2 of the present article, up to two candidates possessing the qualifications and meeting the requirements set out in article 5, and in doing so shall provide detailed information on the qualifications of the nominees.

2. (a) The nominees shall have the nationality of a State Party to the present Protocol;
   (b) At least one of the two candidates shall have the nationality of the nominating State Party;
   (c) No more than two nationals of a State Party shall be nominated;
   (d) Before a State Party nominates a national of another State Party, it shall seek and obtain the consent of that State Party.

3. At least five months before the date of the meeting of the States Parties during which the elections will be held, the Secretary-General of the United Nations shall address a letter to the States Parties inviting them to submit their nominations within three months. The Secretary-General shall submit a list, in alphabetical order, of all persons thus nominated, indicating the States Parties that have nominated them.

Article 7

1. The members of the Subcommittee on Prevention shall be elected in the following manner:
    (a) Primary consideration shall be given to the fulfilment of the requirements and criteria of article 5 of the present Protocol;
    (b) The initial election shall be held no later than six months after the entry into force of the present Protocol;
    (c) The States Parties shall elect the members of the Subcommittee by secret ballot;
    (d) Elections of the members of the Subcommittee shall be held at biennial meetings of the States Parties convened by the Secretary-General of the United Nations. At those meetings, for which two thirds of the States Parties shall constitute a quorum, the persons elected to the Subcommittee shall be those who obtain the largest number of votes and an absolute majority of the votes of the representatives of the States Parties present and voting.

2. If during the election process two nationals of a State Party have become eligible to serve as members of the Subcommittee on Prevention, the candidate receiving the higher number of votes shall serve as the member of the Subcommittee. Where nationals have received the same number of votes, the following procedure applies:
    (a) Where only one has been nominated by the State Party of which he or she is a national, that national shall serve as the member of the Subcommittee on Prevention;
    (b) Where both candidates have been nominated by the State Party of which they are nationals, a separate vote by secret ballot shall be held to determine which national shall become member;
    (c) Where neither candidate has been nominated by the State Party of which he or she is a national, a separate vote by secret ballot shall be held to determine which candidate shall be the member.

Article 8

If a member of the Subcommittee on Prevention dies or resigns, or for any cause can no longer perform his or her duties, the State Party that nominated the member shall nominate another eligible person possessing the qualifications and meeting the requirements set out in article 5, taking into account the need for a proper balance among the various fields of competence, to serve until the next meeting of the States Parties, subject to the approval of the majority of the States Parties. The approval shall be considered given unless half or more of the States Parties respond negatively within six weeks after having been informed by the Secretary-General of the United Nations of the proposed appointment.

Article 9

The members of the Subcommittee on Prevention shall be elected for a term of four years. They shall be eligible for re-election once if renominated. The term of half the members elected at the first election shall expire at the end of two years; immediately after the first election the names of those members shall be chosen by lot by the Chairman of the meeting referred to in article 7, paragraph 1(d).

Article 10

1. The Subcommittee on Prevention shall elect its officers for a term of two years. They may be re-elected.

2. The Subcommittee on Prevention shall establish its own rules of procedure. These rules shall provide, *inter alia*, that:
    (a) Half the members plus one shall constitute a quorum;

(b) Decisions of the Subcommittee on Prevention shall be made by a majority vote of the members present;

(c) The Subcommittee on Prevention shall meet in camera.

3. The Secretary-General of the United Nations shall convene the initial meeting of the Subcommittee on Prevention. After its initial meeting, the Subcommittee shall meet at such times as shall be provided by its rules of procedure. The Subcommittee on Prevention and the Committee against Torture shall hold their sessions simultaneously at least once a year.

PART III MANDATE OF THE SUBCOMMITTEE ON PREVENTION

Article 11
The Subcommittee on Prevention shall:

(a) Visit the places referred to in article 4 and make recommendations to States Parties concerning the protection of persons deprived of their liberty against torture and other cruel, inhuman or degrading treatment or punishment;

(b) In regard to the national preventive mechanisms:

    (i) Advise and assist States Parties, when necessary, in their establishment;

    (ii) Maintain direct, and if necessary confidential, contact with the national preventive mechanisms and offer them training and technical assistance with a view to strengthening their capacities;

    (iii) Advise and assist them in the evaluation of the needs and the means necessary to strengthen the protection of persons deprived of their liberty against torture and other cruel, inhuman or degrading treatment or punishment;

    (iv) Make recommendations and observations to the States Parties with a view to strengthening the capacity and the mandate of the national preventive mechanisms for the prevention of torture and other cruel, inhuman or degrading treatment or punishment;

(c) Cooperate, for the prevention of torture in general, with the relevant United Nations organs and mechanisms as well as with the international, regional and national institutions or organizations working towards the strengthening of the protection of all persons against torture and other cruel, inhuman or degrading treatment or punishment.

Article 12
In order to enable the Subcommittee on Prevention to comply with its mandate as laid out in article 11, the States Parties undertake:

(a) To receive the Subcommittee on Prevention in their territory and grant it access to the places of detention as defined in article 4 of the present Protocol;

(b) To provide all relevant information the Subcommittee on Prevention may request to evaluate the needs and measures that should be adopted to strengthen the protection of persons deprived of their liberty against torture and other cruel, inhuman or degrading treatment or punishment;

(c) To encourage and facilitate contacts between the Subcommittee on Prevention and the national preventive mechanisms;

(d) To examine the recommendations of the Subcommittee on Prevention and enter into dialogue with it on possible implementation measures.

Article 13
1. The Subcommittee on Prevention shall establish, at first by lot, a programme of regular visits to the States Parties in order to fulfil its mandate as established in article 11.

2. After consultations, the Subcommittee on Prevention shall notify the States Parties of its programme in order that they may, without delay, make the necessary practical arrangements for the visits to be conducted.

3. The visits shall be conducted by at least two members of the Subcommittee on Prevention. These members may be accompanied, if needed, by experts of demonstrated professional experience and knowledge in the fields covered by the present Protocol who shall be selected from a roster of experts prepared on the basis of proposals made by the States Parties, the Office of the United Nations High Commissioner for Human Rights and the United Nations Centre for International Crime Prevention. In preparing the roster, the States Parties concerned shall propose no more than five national experts. The State Party concerned may oppose the inclusion of a specific expert in the visit, whereupon the Subcommittee on Prevention shall propose another expert.

4. If the Subcommittee on Prevention considers it appropriate, it may propose a short follow-up visit after a regular visit.

Article 14

1. In order to enable the Subcommittee on Prevention to fulfil its mandate, the States Parties to the present Protocol undertake to grant it:

    (a) Unrestricted access to all information concerning the number of persons deprived of their liberty in places of detention as defined in article 4, as well as the number of places and their location;

    (b) Unrestricted access to all information referring to the treatment of those persons as well as their conditions of detention;

    (c) Subject to paragraph 2 below, unrestricted access to all places of detention and their installations and facilities;

    (d) The opportunity to have private interviews with the persons deprived of their liberty without witnesses, either personally or with a translator if deemed necessary, as well as with any other person who the Subcommittee on Prevention believes may supply relevant information;

    (e) The liberty to choose the places it wants to visit and the persons it wants to interview.

2. Objection to a visit to a particular place of detention may be made only on urgent and compelling grounds of national defence, public safety, natural disaster or serious disorder in the place to be visited that temporarily prevent the carrying out of such a visit. The existence of a declared state of emergency as such shall not be invoked by a State Party as a reason to object to a visit.

Article 15

No authority or official shall order, apply, permit or tolerate any sanction against any person or organization for having communicated to the Subcommittee on Prevention or to its delegates any information, whether true or false, and no such person or organization shall be otherwise prejudiced in any way.

Article 16

1. The Subcommittee on Prevention shall communicate its recommendations and observations confidentially to the State Party and, if relevant, to the national preventive mechanism.

2. The Subcommittee on Prevention shall publish its report, together with any comments of the State Party concerned, whenever requested to do so by that State Party. If the State Party makes part of the report public, the Subcommittee on Prevention may publish the report in whole or in part. However, no personal data shall be published without the express consent of the person concerned.

3. The Subcommittee on Prevention shall present a public annual report on its activities to the Committee against Torture.

4. If the State Party refuses to cooperate with the Subcommittee on Prevention according to articles 12 and 14, or to take steps to improve the situation in the light of the Subcommittee's recommendations, the Committee against Torture may, at the request of the Subcommittee on Prevention, decide, by a majority of its members, after the State Party has had an opportunity to make its views known, to make a public statement on the matter or to publish the report of the Subcommittee.

PART IV NATIONAL PREVENTIVE MECHANISMS

Article 17

Each State Party shall maintain, designate or establish, at the latest one year after the entry into force of the present Protocol or of its ratification or accession, one or several independent national preventive mechanisms for the prevention of torture at the domestic level. Mechanisms established by decentralized units may be designated as national preventive mechanisms for the purposes of the present Protocol if they are in conformity with its provisions.

Article 18

1. The States Parties shall guarantee the functional independence of the national preventive mechanisms as well as the independence of their personnel.

2. The States Parties shall take the necessary measures to ensure that the experts of the national preventive mechanism have the required capabilities and professional knowledge. They shall strive for a gender balance and the adequate representation of ethnic and minority groups in the country.

3. The States Parties undertake to make available the necessary resources for the functioning of the national preventive mechanisms.

4. When establishing national preventive mechanisms, States Parties shall give due consideration to the Principles relating to the status of national institutions for the promotion and protection of human rights.

Article 19

The national preventive mechanisms shall be granted at a minimum the power:

(a) To regularly examine the treatment of the persons deprived of their liberty in places of detention as defined in article 4, with a view to strengthening, if necessary, their protection against torture, cruel, inhuman or degrading treatment or punishment;

(b) To make recommendations to the relevant authorities with the aim of improving the treatment and the conditions of the persons deprived of their liberty and to prevent torture and cruel, inhuman or degrading treatment or punishment, taking into consideration the relevant norms of the United Nations;

(c) To submit proposals and observations concerning existing or draft legislation.

Article 20

In order to enable the national preventive mechanisms to fulfil their mandate, the States Parties to the present Protocol undertake to grant them:

(a) Access to all information concerning the number of persons deprived of their liberty in places of detention as defined in article 4, as well as the number of places and their location;

(b) Access to all information referring to the treatment of those persons as well as their conditions of detention;

(c) Access to all places of detention and their installations and facilities;

(d) The opportunity to have private interviews with the persons deprived of their liberty without witnesses, either personally or with a translator if deemed necessary, as well as with any other person who the national preventive mechanism believes may supply relevant information;

(e) The liberty to choose the places they want to visit and the persons they want to interview;

(f) The right to have contacts with the Subcommittee on Prevention, to send it information and to meet with it.

Article 21

1. No authority or official shall order, apply, permit or tolerate any sanction against any person or organization for having communicated to the national preventive mechanism any information, whether true or false, and no such person or organization shall be otherwise prejudiced in any way.

2. Confidential information collected by the national preventive mechanism shall be privileged. No personal data shall be published without the express consent of the person concerned.

Article 22

The competent authorities of the State Party concerned shall examine the recommendations of the national preventive mechanism and enter into a dialogue with it on possible implementation measures.

Article 23

The States Parties to the present Protocol undertake to publish and disseminate the annual reports of the national preventive mechanisms.

PART V DECLARATION

Article 24

1. Upon ratification, States Parties may make a declaration postponing the implementation of their obligations either under part III or under part IV of the present Protocol.

2. This postponement shall be valid for a maximum of three years. After due representations made by the State Party and after consultation with the Subcommittee on Prevention, the Committee against Torture may extend that period for an additional two years.

PART VI FINANCIAL PROVISIONS

Article 25

1. The expenditure incurred by the Subcommittee on Prevention in the implementation of the present Protocol shall be borne by the United Nations.

2. The Secretary-General of the United Nations shall provide the necessary staff and facilities for the effective performance of the functions of the Subcommittee under the present Protocol.

Article 26

1. A Special Fund shall be set up in accordance with the relevant procedures of the General Assembly, to be administered in accordance with the financial regulations and rules of the United Nations, to help finance the implementation of the recommendations made by the Subcommittee on Prevention after a visit to a State Party, as well as education programmes of the national preventive mechanisms.

2. The Special Fund may be financed through voluntary contributions made by Governments, intergovernmental and non-governmental organizations and other private or public entities.

PART VII FINAL PROVISIONS

Article 27

1. The present Protocol is open for signature by any State that has signed the Convention.

2. The present Protocol is subject to ratification by any State that has ratified or acceded to the Convention. Instruments of ratification shall be deposited with the Secretary-General of the United Nations.

3. The present Protocol shall be open to accession by any State that has ratified or acceded to the Convention.

4. Accession shall be effected by the deposit of an instrument of accession with the Secretary-General of the United Nations.

5. The Secretary-General of the United Nations shall inform all States that have signed the present Protocol or acceded to it of the deposit of each instrument of ratification or accession.

Article 28

1. The present Protocol shall enter into force on the thirtieth day after the date of deposit with the Secretary-General of the United Nations of the twentieth instrument of ratification or accession.

2. For each State ratifying the present Protocol or acceding to it after the deposit with the Secretary-General of the United Nations of the twentieth instrument of ratification or accession, the present Protocol shall enter into force on the thirtieth day after the date of deposit of its own instrument of ratification or accession.

Article 29

The provisions of the present Protocol shall extend to all parts of federal States without any limitations or exceptions.

Article 30

No reservations shall be made to the present Protocol.

Article 31

The provisions of the present Protocol shall not affect the obligations of States Parties under any regional convention instituting a system of visits to places of detention. The Subcommittee on Prevention and the bodies established under such regional conventions are encouraged to consult and cooperate with a view to avoiding duplication and promoting effectively the objectives of the present Protocol.

Article 32

The provisions of the present Protocol shall not affect the obligations of States Parties to the four Geneva Conventions of 12 August 1949 and the Additional Protocols thereto of 8 June 1977, nor the opportunity available to any State Party to authorize the International Committee of the Red Cross to visit places of detention in situations not covered by international humanitarian law.

Article 33

1. Any State Party may denounce the present Protocol at any time by written notification addressed to the Secretary-General of the United Nations, who shall thereafter inform the other States Parties to the present Protocol and the Convention. Denunciation shall take effect one year after the date of receipt of the notification by the Secretary-General.

2. Such a denunciation shall not have the effect of releasing the State Party from its obligations under the present Protocol in regard to any act or situation that may occur prior to the date at which the denunciation becomes effective, or to the actions that the Subcommittee on Prevention has decided or may decide to take with respect to the State Party concerned, nor shall denunciation prejudice in any way the continued consideration of any matter already under consideration by the Subcommittee on Prevention prior to the date at which the denunciation becomes effective.

3. Following the date at which the denunciation of the State Party becomes effective, the Subcommittee on Prevention shall not commence consideration of any new matter regarding that State.

Article 34

1. Any State Party to the present Protocol may propose an amendment and file it with the Secretary-General of the United Nations. The Secretary-General shall thereupon communicate the proposed amendment to the States Parties to the present Protocol with a request that they notify him whether they favour a conference of States Parties for the purpose of considering and voting upon the proposal. In the event that within four months from the date of such communication at least one third of the States Parties favour such a conference, the Secretary-General shall convene the conference under the auspices of the United Nations. Any amendment adopted by a majority of two thirds of the States Parties present and voting at the conference shall be submitted by the Secretary-General of the United Nations to all States Parties for acceptance.

2. An amendment adopted in accordance with paragraph 1 of the present article shall come into force when it has been accepted by a two-thirds majority of the States Parties to the present Protocol in accordance with their respective constitutional processes.

3. When amendments come into force, they shall be binding on those States Parties that have accepted them, other States Parties still being bound by the provisions of the present Protocol and any earlier amendment that they have accepted.

Article 35
Members of the Subcommittee on Prevention and of the national preventive mechanisms shall be accorded such privileges and immunities as are necessary for the independent exercise of their functions. Members of the Subcommittee on Prevention shall be accorded the privileges and immunities specified in section 22 of the Convention on Privileges and Immunities of the United Nations of 13 February 1946, subject to the provisions of section 23 of that Convention.

Article 36
When visiting a State Party, the members of the Subcommittee on Prevention shall, without prejudice to the provisions and purposes of the present Protocol and such privileges and immunities as they may enjoy:
    (a) Respect the laws and regulations of the visited State;
    (b) Refrain from any action or activity incompatible with the impartial and international nature of their duties.

Article 37
1. The present Protocol, of which the Arabic, Chinese, English, French, Russian and Spanish texts are equally authentic, shall be deposited with the Secretary-General of the United Nations.

2. The Secretary-General of the United Nations shall transmit certified copies of the present Protocol to all States.

Declaration on the Right to Development (1986)*

The General Assembly,

Bearing in mind the purposes and principles of the Charter of the United Nations relating to the achievement of international co-operation in solving international problems of an economic, social, cultural or humanitarian nature, and in promoting and encouraging respect for human rights and fundamental freedoms for all without distinction as to race, sex, language or religion,

Recognizing that development is a comprehensive economic, social, cultural and political process, which aims at the constant improvement of the well-being of the entire population and of all individuals on the basis of their active, free and meaningful participation in development and in the fair distribution of benefits resulting therefrom,

Considering that under the provisions of the Universal Declaration of Human Rights everyone is entitled to a social and international order in which the rights and freedoms set forth in that Declaration can be fully realized,

Recalling the provisions of the International Covenant on Economic, Social and Cultural Rights and of the International Covenant on Civil and Political Rights,

Recalling further the relevant agreements, conventions, resolutions, recommendations and other instruments of the United Nations and its specialized agencies concerning the integral development of the human being, economic and social progress and development of all peoples, including those instruments concerning decolonization, the prevention of discrimination, respect for and observance of, human rights and fundamental freedoms, the maintenance of international peace and security and the further promotion of friendly relations and co-operation among States in accordance with the Charter,

Recalling the right of peoples to self-determination, by virtue of which they have the right freely to determine their political status and to pursue their economic, social and cultural development,

Recalling also the right of peoples to exercise, subject to the relevant provisions of both International Covenants on Human Rights, full and complete sovereignty over all their natural wealth and resources,

Mindful of the obligation of States under the Charter to promote universal respect for and observance of human rights and fundamental freedoms for all without distinction of any kind such as race, colour, sex, language, religion, political or other opinion, national or social origin, property, birth or other status,

Considering that the elimination of the massive and flagrant violations of the human rights of the peoples and individuals affected by situations such as those resulting from colonialism, neo-colonialism, apartheid, all forms of racism and racial discrimination, foreign domination and occupation, aggression and threats against national sovereignty, national unity and territorial integrity and threats of war would contribute to the establishment of circumstances propitious to the development of a great part of mankind,

Concerned at the existence of serious obstacles to development, as well as to the complete fulfilment of human beings and of peoples, constituted, inter alia, by the denial of civil, political, economic, social and cultural rights, and considering that all human rights and fundamental freedoms are indivisible and interdependent and that, in order to promote development, equal attention and urgent consideration should be given to the implementation, promotion and protection of civil, political, economic, social and cultural rights and that, accordingly, the promotion of, respect for and enjoyment of certain human rights and fundamental freedoms cannot justify the denial of other human rights and fundamental freedoms,

Considering that international peace and security are essential elements for the realization of the right to development,

Reaffirming that there is a close relationship between disarmament and development and that progress in the field of disarmament would considerably promote progress in the field of development and that resources released through disarmament measures should be devoted to the economic and social development and well-being of all peoples and, in particular, those of the developing countries,

Recognizing that the human person is the central subject of the development process and that development policy should therefore make the human being the main participant and beneficiary of development,

Recognizing that the creation of conditions favourable to the development of peoples and individuals is the primary responsibility of their States,

Aware that efforts at the international level to promote and protect human rights should be accompanied by efforts to establish a new international economic order,

Confirming that the right to development is an inalienable human right and that equality of opportunity for development is a prerogative both of nations and of individuals who make up nations,

Proclaims the following Declaration on the Right to Development:

Article 1

1. The right to development is an inalienable human right by virtue of which every human person and all peoples are entitled to participate in, contribute to, and enjoy economic, social, cultural and political development, in which all human rights and fundamental freedoms can be fully realized.

2. The human right to development also implies the full realization of the right of peoples to self-determination, which includes, subject to the relevant provisions of both International Covenants on Human Rights, the exercise of their inalienable right to full sovereignty over all their natural wealth and resources.

Article 2

1. The human person is the central subject of development and should be the active participant and beneficiary of the right to development.

2. All human beings have a responsibility for development, individually and collectively, taking into account the need for full respect for their human rights and fundamental freedoms as well as

their duties to the community, which alone can ensure the free and complete fulfilment of the human being, and they should therefore promote and protect an appropriate political, social and economic order for development.

3. States have the right and the duty to formulate appropriate national development policies that aim at the constant improvement of the well-being of the entire population and of all individuals, on the basis of their active, free and meaningful participation in development and in the fair distribution of the benefits resulting therefrom.

Article 3

1. States have the primary responsibility for the creation of national and international conditions favourable to the realization of the right to development.

2. The realization of the right to development requires full respect for the principles of international law concerning friendly relations and co-operation among States in accordance with the Charter of the United Nations.

3. States have the duty to co-operate with each other in ensuring development and eliminating obstacles to development. States should realize their rights and fulfil their duties in such a manner as to promote a new international economic order based on sovereign equality, interdependence, mutual interest and co-operation among all States, as well as to encourage the observance and realization of human rights.

Article 4

1. States have the duty to take steps, individually and collectively, to formulate international development policies with a view to facilitating the full realization of the right to development.

2. Sustained action is required to promote more rapid development of developing countries. As a complement to the efforts of developing countries, effective international co-operation is essential in providing these countries with appropriate means and facilities to foster their comprehensive development.

Article 5

States shall take resolute steps to eliminate the massive and flagrant violations of the human rights of peoples and human beings affected by situations such as those resulting from apartheid, all forms of racism and racial discrimination, colonialism, foreign domination and occupation, aggression, foreign interference and threats against national sovereignty, national unity and territorial integrity, threats of war and refusal to recognize the fundamental right of peoples to self-determination.

Article 6

1. All States should co-operate with a view to promoting, encouraging and strengthening universal respect for and observance of all human rights and fundamental freedoms for all without any distinction as to race, sex, language or religion.

2. All human rights and fundamental freedoms are indivisible and interdependent; equal attention and urgent consideration should be given to the implementation, promotion and protection of civil, political, economic, social and cultural rights.

3. States should take steps to eliminate obstacles to development resulting from failure to observe civil and political rights, as well as economic, social and cultural rights.

Article 7

All States should promote the establishment, maintenance and strengthening of international peace and security and, to that end, should do their utmost to achieve general and complete disarmament under effective international control, as well as to ensure that the resources released by effective disarmament measures are used for comprehensive development, in particular that of the developing countries.

Article 8

1. States should undertake, at the national level, all necessary measures for the realization of the right to development and shall ensure, inter alia, equality of opportunity for all in their access to basic resources, education, health services, food, housing, employment and the fair distribution of

income. Effective measures should be undertaken to ensure that women have an active role in the development process. Appropriate economic and social reforms should be carried out with a view to eradicating all social injustices.

2. States should encourage popular participation in all spheres as an important factor in development and in the full realization of all human rights.

Article 9

1. All the aspects of the right to development set forth in the present Declaration are indivisible and interdependent and each of them should be considered in the context of the whole.

2. Nothing in the present Declaration shall be construed as being contrary to the purposes and principles of the United Nations, or as implying that any State, group or person has a right to engage in any activity or to perform any act aimed at the violation of the rights set forth in the Universal Declaration of Human Rights and in the International Covenants on Human Rights.

Article 10

Steps should be taken to ensure the full exercise and progressive enhancement of the right to development, including the formulation, adoption and implementation of policy, legislative and other measures at the national and international levels.

Convention on the Rights of the Child (1989)*

PREAMBLE

The States Parties to the present Convention,

Considering that, in accordance with the principles proclaimed in the Charter of the United Nations, recognition of the inherent dignity and of the equal and inalienable rights of all members of the human family is the foundation of freedom, justice and peace in the world,

Bearing in mind that the peoples of the United Nations have, in the Charter, reaffirmed their faith in fundamental human rights and in the dignity and worth of the human person, and have determined to promote social progress and better standards of life in larger freedom,

Recognizing that the United Nations has, in the Universal Declaration of Human Rights and in the International Covenants on Human Rights, proclaimed and agreed that everyone is entitled to all the rights and freedoms set forth therein, without distinction of any kind, such as race, colour, sex, language, religion, political or other opinion, national or social origin, property, birth or other status,

Recalling that, in the Universal Declaration of Human Rights, the United Nations has proclaimed that childhood is entitled to special care and assistance,

Convinced that the family, as the fundamental group of society and the natural environment for the growth and well-being of all its members and particularly children, should be afforded the necessary protection and assistance so that it can fully assume its responsibilities within the community,

Recognizing that the child, for the full and harmonious development of his or her personality, should grow up in a family environment, in an atmosphere of happiness, love and understanding,

Considering that the child should be fully prepared to live an individual life in society, and brought up in the spirit of the ideals proclaimed in the Charter of the United Nations, and in particular in the spirit of peace, dignity, tolerance, freedom, equality and solidarity,

Bearing in mind that the need to extend particular care to the child has been stated in the Geneva Declaration of the Rights of the Child of 1924 and in the Declaration of the Rights of the Child adopted by the General Assembly on 20 November 1959 and recognized in the Universal Declaration of Human

Rights, in the International Covenant on Civil and Political Rights (in particular in articles 23 and 24), in the International Covenant on Economic, Social and Cultural Rights (in particular in article 10) and in the statutes and relevant instruments of specialized agencies and international organizations concerned with the welfare of children,

Bearing in mind that, as indicated in the Declaration of the Rights of the Child, 'the child, by reason of his physical and mental immaturity, needs special safeguards and care, including appropriate legal protection, before as well as after birth',

Recalling the provisions of the Declaration on Social and Legal Principles relating to the Protection and Welfare of Children, with Special Reference to Foster Placement and Adoption Nationally and Internationally; the United Nations Standard Minimum Rules for the Administration of Juvenile Justice (The Beijing Rules); and the Declaration on the Protection of Women and Children in Emergency and Armed Conflict,

Recognizing that, in all countries in the world, there are children living in exceptionally difficult conditions, and that such children need special consideration,

Taking due account of the importance of the traditions and cultural values of each people for the protection and harmonious development of the child,

Recognizing the importance of international co-operation for improving the living conditions of children in every country, in particular in the developing countries,

Have agreed as follows:

PART I

Article 1
For the purposes of the present Convention, a child means every human being below the age of eighteen years unless, under the law applicable to the child, majority is attained earlier.

Article 2
1. States Parties shall respect and ensure the rights set forth in the present Convention to each child within their jurisdiction without discrimination of any kind, irrespective of the child's or his or her parent's or legal guardian's race, colour, sex, language, religion, political or other opinion, national, ethnic or social origin, property, disability, birth or other status.

2. States Parties shall take all appropriate measures to ensure that the child is protected against all forms of discrimination or punishment on the basis of the status, activities, expressed opinions, or beliefs of the child's parents, legal guardians, or family members.

Article 3
1. In all actions concerning children, whether undertaken by public or private social welfare institutions, courts of law, administrative authorities or legislative bodies, the best interests of the child shall be a primary consideration.

2. States Parties undertake to ensure the child such protection and care as is necessary for his or her well-being, taking into account the rights and duties of his or her parents, legal guardians, or other individuals legally responsible for him or her, and, to this end, shall take all appropriate legislative and administrative measures.

3. States Parties shall ensure that the institutions, services and facilities responsible for the care or protection of children shall conform with the standards established by competent authorities, particularly in the areas of safety, health, in the number and suitability of their staff, as well as competent supervision.

Article 4
States Parties shall undertake all appropriate legislative, administrative, and other measures for the implementation of the rights recognized in the present Convention. With regard to economic, social and cultural rights, States Parties shall undertake such measures to the maximum extent of their available resources and, where needed, within the framework of international co-operation.

Article 5

States Parties shall respect the responsibilities, rights and duties of parents or, where applicable, the members of the extended family or community as provided for by local custom, legal guardians or other persons legally responsible for the child, to provide, in a manner consistent with the evolving capacities of the child, appropriate direction and guidance in the exercise by the child of the rights recognized in the present Convention.

Article 6

1. States Parties recognize that every child has the inherent right to life.

2. States Parties shall ensure to the maximum extent possible the survival and development of the child.

Article 7

1. The child shall be registered immediately after birth and shall have the right from birth to a name, the right to acquire a nationality and, as far as possible, the right to know and be cared for by his or her parents.

2. States Parties shall ensure the implementation of these rights in accordance with their national law and their obligations under the relevant international instruments in this field, in particular where the child would otherwise be stateless.

Article 8

1. States Parties undertake to respect the right of the child to preserve his or her identity, including nationality, name and family relations as recognized by law without unlawful interference.

2. Where a child is illegally deprived of some or all of the elements of his or her identity, States Parties shall provide appropriate assistance and protection, with a view to speedily re-establishing his or her identity.

Article 9

1. States Parties shall ensure that a child shall not be separated from his or her parents against their will, except when competent authorities subject to judicial review determine, in accordance with applicable law and procedures, that such separation is necessary for the best interests of the child. Such determination may be necessary in a particular case such as one involving abuse or neglect of the child by the parents, or one where the parents are living separately and a decision must be made as to the child's place of residence.

2. In any proceedings pursuant to paragraph 1 of the present article, all interested parties shall be given an opportunity to participate in the proceedings and make their views known.

3. States Parties shall respect the right of the child who is separated from one or both parents to maintain personal relations and direct contact with both parents on a regular basis, except if it is contrary to the child's best interests.

4. Where such separation results from any action initiated by a State Party, such as the detention, imprisonment, exile, deportation or death (including death arising from any cause while the person is in the custody of the State) of one or both parents or of the child, that State Party shall, upon request, provide the parents, the child or, if appropriate, another member of the family with the essential information concerning the whereabouts of the absent member(s) of the family unless the provision of the information would be detrimental to the well-being of the child. States Parties shall further ensure that the submission of such a request shall of itself entail no adverse consequences for the person(s) concerned.

Article 10

1. In accordance with the obligation of States Parties under article 9, paragraph 1, applications by a child or his or her parents to enter or leave a State Party for the purpose of family reunification shall be dealt with by State Parties in a positive, humane and expeditious manner. States Parties shall further ensure that the submission of such a request shall entail no adverse consequences for the applicants and for the members of their family.

2. A child whose parents reside in different States shall have the right to maintain on a regular basis, save in exceptional circumstances personal relations and direct contacts with both parents. Towards that end and in accordance with the obligation of States Parties under article 9, paragraph 2, States Parties shall respect the right of the child and his or her parents to leave any country, including their own, and to enter their own country. The right to leave any country shall be subject only to such restrictions as are prescribed by law and which are necessary to protect the national security, public order (*ordre public*), public health or morals or the rights and freedoms of others and are consistent with the other rights recognized in the present Convention.

Article 11

1. States Parties shall take measures to combat the illicit transfer and non-return of children abroad.

2. To this end, States Parties shall promote the conclusion of bilateral or multilateral agreements or accession to existing agreements.

Article 12

1. States Parties shall assure to the child who is capable of forming his or her own views the right to express those views freely in all matters affecting the child, the views of the child being given due weight in accordance with the age and maturity of the child.

2. For this purpose, the child shall in particular be provided the opportunity to be heard in any judicial and administrative proceedings affecting the child, either directly, or through a representative or an appropriate body, in a manner consistent with the procedural rules of national law.

Article 13

1. The child shall have the right to freedom of expression; this right shall include freedom to seek, receive and impart information and ideas of all kinds, regardless of frontiers, either orally, in writing or in print, in the form of art, or through any other media of the child's choice.

2. The exercise of this right may be subject to certain restrictions, but these shall only be such as are provided by law and are necessary:

    (a) for respect of the rights or reputations of others; or

    (b) for the protection of national security or of public order (*ordre public*), or of public health or morals.

Article 14

1. States Parties shall respect the right of the child to freedom of thought, conscience and religion.

2. States Parties shall respect the rights and duties of the parents and, when applicable, legal guardians, to provide direction to the child in the exercise of his or her right in a manner consistent with the evolving capacities of the child.

3. Freedom to manifest one's religion or beliefs may be subject only to such limitations as are prescribed by law and are necessary to protect public safety, order, health or morals, or the fundamental rights and freedoms of others.

Article 15

1. States Parties recognize the rights of the child to freedom of association and to freedom of peaceful assembly.

2. No restrictions may be placed on the exercise of these rights other than those imposed in conformity with the law and which are necessary in a democratic society in the interests of national security or public safety, public order (*ordre public*), the protection of public health or morals or the protection of the rights and freedoms of others.

Article 16

1. No child shall be subjected to arbitrary or unlawful interference with his or her privacy, family, home or correspondence, nor to unlawful attacks on his or her honour and reputation.

2. The child has the right to the protection of the law against such interference or attacks.

Article 17

States Parties recognize the important function performed by the mass media and shall ensure that the child has access to information and material from a diversity of national and international sources, especially those aimed at the promotion of his or her social, spiritual and moral well-being and physical and mental health. To this end, States Parties shall:

(a) encourage the mass media to disseminate information and material of social and cultural benefit to the child and in accordance with the spirit of article 29;

(b) encourage international co-operation in the production, exchange and dissemination of such information and material from a diversity of cultural, national and international sources;

(c) encourage the production and dissemination of children's books;

(d) encourage the mass media to have particular regard to the linguistic needs of the child who belongs to a minority group or who is indigenous;

(e) encourage the development of appropriate guidelines for the protection of the child from information and material injurious to his or her well-being, bearing in mind the provisions of articles 13 and 18.

Article 18

1. States Parties shall use their best efforts to ensure recognition of the principle that both parents have common responsibilities for the upbringing and development of the child. Parents or, as the case may be, legal guardians, have the primary responsibility for the upbringing and development of the child. The best interests of the child will be their basic concern.

2. For the purpose of guaranteeing and promoting the rights set forth in the present Convention, States Parties shall render appropriate assistance to parents and legal guardians in the performance of their child-rearing responsibilities and shall ensure the development of institutions, facilities and services for the care of children.

3. States Parties shall take all appropriate measures to ensure that children of working parents have the right to benefit from child-care services and facilities for which they are eligible.

Article 19

1. States Parties shall take all appropriate legislative, administrative, social and educational measures to protect the child from all forms of physical or mental violence, injury or abuse, neglect or negligent treatment, maltreatment or exploitation, including sexual abuse, while in the care of parent(s), legal guardian(s) or any other person who has the care of the child.

2. Such protective measures should, as appropriate, include effective procedures for the establishment of social programmes to provide necessary support for the child and for those who have the care of the child, as well as for other forms of prevention and for identification, reporting, referral, investigation, treatment and follow-up of instances of child maltreatment described heretofore, and, as appropriate, for judicial involvement.

Article 20

1. A child temporarily or permanently deprived of his or her family environment, or in whose own best interests cannot be allowed to remain in that environment, shall be entitled to special protection and assistance provided by the State.

2. States Parties shall in accordance with their national laws ensure alternative care for such a child.

3. Such care could include, *inter alia*, foster placement, *kafalah* of Islamic law, adoption or if necessary placement in suitable institutions for the care of children. When considering solutions, due regard shall be paid to the desirability of continuity in a child's upbringing and to the child's ethnic, religious, cultural and linguistic background.

Article 21

States Parties that recognize and/or permit the system of adoption shall ensure that the best interests of the child shall be the paramount consideration and they shall:

(a) ensure that the adoption of a child is authorized only by competent authorities who determine, in accordance with applicable law and procedures and on the basis of all pertinent and reliable information, that the adoption is permissible in view of the child's status concerning parents, relatives and legal guardians and that, if required, the persons concerned have given their informed consent to the adoption on the basis of such counselling as may be necessary;

(b) recognize that inter-country adoption may be considered as an alternative means of child's care, if the child cannot be placed in a foster or an adoptive family or cannot in any suitable manner be cared for in the child's country of origin;

(c) ensure that the child concerned by inter-country adoption enjoys safeguards and standards equivalent to those existing in the case of national adoption;

(d) take all appropriate measures to ensure that, in inter-country adoption, the placement does not result in improper financial gain for those involved in it;

(e) promote, where appropriate, the objectives of the present article by concluding bilateral or multilateral arrangements or agreements, and endeavour, within this framework, to ensure that the placement of the child in another country is carried out by competent authorities or organs.

Article 22

1. States Parties shall take appropriate measures to ensure that a child who is seeking refugee status or who is considered a refugee in accordance with applicable international or domestic law and procedures shall, whether unaccompanied or accompanied by his or her parents or by any other person, receive appropriate protection and humanitarian assistance in the enjoyment of applicable rights set forth in this Convention and in other international human rights or humanitarian instruments to which the said States are Parties.

2. For this purpose, States Parties shall provide, as they consider appropriate, cooperation in any efforts by the United Nations and other competent intergovernmental organizations or non-governmental organizations co-operating with the United Nations to protect and assist such a child and to trace the parents or other members of the family of any refugee child in order to obtain information necessary for reunification with his or her family. In cases where no parents or other members of the family can be found, the child shall be accorded the same protection as any other child permanently or temporarily deprived of his or her family environment for any reason, as set forth in the present Convention.

Article 23

1. States Parties recognize that a mentally or physically disabled child should enjoy a full and decent life, in conditions which ensure dignity, promote self-reliance and facilitate the child's active participation in the community.

2. States Parties recognize the right of the disabled child to special care and shall encourage and ensure the extension, subject to available resources, to the eligible child and those responsible for his or her care, of assistance for which application is made and which is appropriate to the child's condition and to the circumstances of the parents or others caring for the child.

3. Recognizing the special needs of a disabled child, assistance extended in accordance with paragraph 2 of the present article shall be provided free of charge, whenever possible, taking into account the financial resources of the parents or others caring for the child, and shall be designed to ensure that the disabled child has effective access to and receives education, training, health care services, rehabilitation services, preparation for employment and recreation opportunities in a manner conducive to the child's achieving the fullest possible social integration and individual development, including his or her cultural and spiritual development.

4. States Parties shall promote, in the spirit of international co-operation, the exchange of appropriate information in the field of preventive health care and of medical, psychological and functional treatment of disabled children, including dissemination of and access to information concerning methods of rehabilitation, education and vocational services, with the aim of enabling States Parties

to improve their capabilities and skills and to widen their experience in these areas. In this regard, particular account shall be taken of the needs of developing countries.

Article 24

1. States Parties recognize the right of the child to the enjoyment of the highest attainable standard of health and to facilities for the treatment of illness and rehabilitation of health. States Parties shall strive to ensure that no child is deprived of his or her right of access to such health care services.

2. States Parties shall pursue full implementation of this right and, in particular, shall take appropriate measures:

   (a) to diminish infant and child mortality;
   (b) to ensure the provision of necessary medical assistance and health care to all children with emphasis on the development of primary health care;
   (c) to combat disease and malnutrition, including within the framework of primary health care, through, *inter alia*, the application of readily available technology and through the provision of adequate nutritious foods and clean drinking-water, taking into consideration the dangers and risks of environmental pollution;
   (d) to ensure appropriate prenatal and post-natal health care for mothers;
   (e) to ensure that all segments of society, in particular parents and children, are informed, have access to education and are supported in the use of basic knowledge of child health and nutrition, the advantages of breast-feeding, hygiene and environmental sanitation and the prevention of accidents;
   (f) to develop preventive care, guidance for parents and family planning education and services.

3. States Parties shall take all effective and appropriate measures with a view to abolishing traditional practices prejudicial to the health of children.

4. States Parties undertake to promote and encourage international co-operation with a view to achieving progressively the full realization of the right recognized in the present article. In this regard, particular account shall be taken of the needs of developing countries.

Article 25

States Parties recognize the right of a child who has been placed by the competent authorities for the purposes of care, protection or treatment of his or her physical or mental health, to a periodic review of the treatment provided to the child and all other circumstances relevant to his or her placement.

Article 26

1. States Parties shall recognize for every child the right to benefit from social security, including social insurance, and shall take the necessary measures to achieve the full realization of this right in accordance with their national law.

2. The benefits should, where appropriate, be granted, taking into account the resources and the circumstances of the child and persons having responsibility for the maintenance of the child, as well as any other consideration relevant to an application for benefits made by or on behalf of the child.

Article 27

1. States Parties recognize the right of every child to a standard of living adequate for the child's physical, mental, spiritual, moral and social development.

2. The parent(s) or others responsible for the child have the primary responsibility to secure, within their abilities and financial capacities, the conditions of living necessary for the child's development.

3. States Parties, in accordance with national conditions and within their means, shall take appropriate measures to assist parents and others responsible for the child to implement this right and shall in case of need provide material assistance and support programmes, particularly with regard to nutrition, clothing and housing.

4. States Parties shall take all appropriate measures to secure the recovery of maintenance for the child from the parents or other persons having financial responsibility for the child, both within the State Party and from abroad. In particular, where the person having financial responsibility for the child lives in a State different from that of the child, States Parties shall promote the accession to international agreements or the conclusion of such agreements, as well as the making of other appropriate arrangements.

Article 28

1. States Parties recognize the right of the child to education, and with a view to achieving this right progressively and on the basis of equal opportunity, they shall, in particular:

   (a) make primary education compulsory and available free to all;

   (b) encourage the development of different forms of secondary education, including general and vocational education, make them available and accessible to every child, and take appropriate measures such as the introduction of free education and offering financial assistance in case of need;

   (c) make higher education accessible to all on the basis of capacity by every appropriate means;

   (d) make educational and vocational information and guidance available and accessible to all children;

   (e) take measures to encourage regular attendance at schools and the reduction of drop-out rates.

2. States Parties shall take all appropriate measures to ensure that school discipline is administered in a manner consistent with the child's human dignity and in conformity with the present Convention.

3. States Parties shall promote and encourage international co-operation in matters relating to education, in particular with a view to contributing to the elimination of ignorance and illiteracy throughout the world and facilitating access to scientific and technical knowledge and modern teaching methods. In this regard, particular account shall be taken of the needs of developing countries.

Article 29

1. States Parties agree that the education of the child shall be directed to:

   (a) the development of the child's personality, talents and mental and physical abilities to their fullest potential;

   (b) the development of respect for human rights and fundamental freedoms, and for the principles enshrined in the Charter of the United Nations;

   (c) the development of respect for the child's parents, his or her own cultural identity, language and values, for the national values of the country in which the child is living, the country from which he or she may originate, and for civilizations different from his or her own;

   (d) the preparation of the child for responsible life in a free society, in the spirit of understanding, peace, tolerance, equality of sexes, and friendship among all peoples, ethnic, national and religious groups and persons of indigenous origin;

   (e) the development of respect for the natural environment.

2. No part of the present article or article 28 shall be construed so as to interfere with the liberty of individuals and bodies to establish and direct educational institutions, subject always to the observance of the principles set forth in paragraph 1 of the present article and to the requirements that the education given in such institutions shall conform to such minimum standards as may be laid down by the State.

Article 30

In those States in which ethnic, religious or linguistic minorities or persons of indigenous origin exist, a child belonging to such a minority or who is indigenous shall not be denied the right, in community with other members of his or her group, to enjoy his or her own culture, to profess and practise his or her own religion, or to use his or her own language.

Article 31

1. States Parties recognize the right of the child to rest and leisure, to engage in play and recreational activities appropriate to the age of the child and to participate freely in cultural life and the arts.

2. States Parties shall respect and promote the right of the child to participate fully in cultural and artistic life and shall encourage the provision of appropriate and equal opportunities for cultural, artistic, recreational and leisure activity.

Article 32

1. States Parties recognize the right of the child to be protected from economic exploitation and from performing any work that is likely to be hazardous or to interfere with the child's education, or to be harmful to the child's health or physical, mental, spiritual, moral or social development.

2. States Parties shall take legislative, administrative, social and educational measures to ensure the implementation of the present article. To this end, and having regard to the relevant provisions of other international instruments, States Parties shall in particular:
   (a) provide for a minimum age or minimum ages for admission to employment;
   (b) provide for appropriate regulation of the hours and conditions of employment;
   (c) provide for appropriate penalties or other sanctions to ensure the effective enforcement of the present article.

Article 33

States Parties shall take all appropriate measures, including legislative, administrative, social and educational measures, to protect children from the illicit use of narcotic drugs and psychotropic substances as defined in the relevant international treaties, and to prevent the use of children in the illicit production and trafficking of such substances.

Article 34

States Parties undertake to protect the child from all forms of sexual exploitation and sexual abuse. For these purposes, States Parties shall in particular take all appropriate national, bilateral and multilateral measures to prevent:
   (a) the inducement or coercion of a child to engage in any unlawful sexual activity;
   (b) the exploitative use of children in prostitution or other unlawful sexual practices;
   (c) the exploitative use of children in pornographic performances and materials.

Article 35

States Parties shall take all appropriate national, bilateral and multilateral measures to prevent the abduction of, the sale of or traffic in children for any purpose or in any form.

Article 36

States Parties shall protect the child against all other forms of exploitation prejudicial to any aspects of the child's welfare.

Article 37

States Parties shall ensure that:
   (a) no child shall be subjected to torture or other cruel, inhuman or degrading treatment or punishment. Neither capital punishment nor life imprisonment without possibility of release shall be imposed for offences committed by persons below eighteen years of age;
   (b) no child shall be deprived of his or her liberty unlawfully or arbitrarily. The arrest, detention or imprisonment of a child shall be in conformity with the law and shall be used only as a measure of last resort and for the shortest appropriate period of time;
   (c) every child deprived of liberty shall be treated with humanity and respect for the inherent dignity of the human person, and in a manner which takes into account the needs of persons of his or her age. In particular, every child deprived of liberty shall be separated

from adults unless it is considered in the child's best interest not to do so and shall have the right to maintain contact with his or her family through correspondence and visits, save in exceptional circumstances;

(d) every child deprived of his or her liberty shall have the right to prompt access to legal and other appropriate assistance, as well as the right to challenge the legality of the deprivation of his or her liberty before a court or other competent, independent and impartial authority, and to a prompt decision on any such action.

Article 38

1. States Parties undertake to respect and to ensure respect for rules of international humanitarian law applicable to them in armed conflicts which are relevant to the child.

2. States Parties shall take all feasible measures to ensure that persons who have not attained the age of fifteen years do not take a direct part in hostilities.

3. States Parties shall refrain from recruiting any person who has not attained the age of fifteen years into their armed forces. In recruiting among those persons who have attained the age of fifteen years but who have not attained the age of eighteen years, States Parties shall endeavour to give priority to those who are oldest.

4. In accordance with their obligations under international humanitarian law to protect the civilian population in armed conflicts, States Parties shall take all feasible measures to ensure protection and care of children who are affected by an armed conflict.

Article 39

States Parties shall take all appropriate measures to promote physical and psychological recovery and social reintegration of a child victim of: any form of neglect, exploitation, or abuse; torture or any other form of cruel, inhuman or degrading treatment or punishment; or armed conflicts. Such recovery and reintegration shall take place in an environment which fosters the health, self-respect and dignity of the child.

Article 40

1. States Parties recognize the right of every child alleged as, accused of, or recognized as having infringed the penal law to be treated in a manner consistent with the promotion of the child's sense of dignity and worth, which reinforces the child's respect for the human rights and fundamental freedoms of others and which takes into account the child's age and the desirability of promoting the child's reintegration and the child's assuming a constructive role in society.

2. To this end, and having regard to the relevant provisions of international instruments, States Parties shall, in particular, ensure that:

(a) no child shall be alleged as, be accused of, or recognized as having infringed the penal law by reason of acts or omissions that were not prohibited by national or international law at the time they were committed;

(b) every child alleged as or accused of having infringed the penal law has at least the following guarantees:

(i)   to be presumed innocent until proven guilty according to law;

(ii)   to be informed promptly and directly of the charges against him or her, and, if appropriate, through his or her parents or legal guardians, and to have legal or other appropriate assistance in the preparation and presentation of his or her defence;

(iii) to have the matter determined without delay by a competent, independent and impartial authority or judicial body in a fair hearing according to law, in the presence of legal or other appropriate assistance and, unless it is considered not to be in the best interest of the child, in particular, taking into account his or her age or situation, his or her parents or legal guardians;

(iv)   not to be compelled to give testimony or to confess guilt; to examine or have examined adverse witnesses and to obtain the participation and examination of witnesses on his or her behalf under conditions of equality;

    (v)   if considered to have infringed the penal law, to have this decision and any measures imposed in consequence thereof reviewed by a higher competent, independent and impartial authority or judicial body according to law;

    (vi) to have the free assistance of an interpreter if the child cannot understand or speak the language used;

    (vii) to have his or her privacy fully respected at all stages of the proceedings.

3. States Parties shall seek to promote the establishment of laws, procedures, authorities and institutions specifically applicable to children alleged as, accused of, or recognized as having infringed the penal law, and, in particular:

    (a) the establishment of a minimum age below which children shall be presumed not to have the capacity to infringe the penal law;

    (b) whenever appropriate and desirable, measures for dealing with such children without resorting to judicial proceedings, providing that human rights and legal safeguards are fully respected.

4. A variety of dispositions, such as care, guidance and supervision orders; counselling; probation; foster care; education and vocational training programmes and other alternatives to institutional care shall be available to ensure that children are dealt with in a manner appropriate to their well-being and proportionate both to their circumstances and the offence.

Article 41

Nothing in the present Convention shall affect any provisions which are more conducive to the realization of the rights of the child and which may be contained in:

    (a) the law of a State Party; or

    (b) international law in force for that State.

PART II

Article 42

States Parties undertake to make the principles and provisions of the Convention widely known, by appropriate and active means, to adults and children alike.

Article 43

1. For the purpose of examining the progress made by States Parties in achieving the realization of the obligations undertaken in the present Convention, there shall be established a Committee on the Rights of the Child, which shall carry out the functions hereinafter provided.

2. The Committee shall consist of ten experts of high moral standing and recognized competence in the field covered by this Convention. The members of the Committee shall be elected by States Parties from among their nationals and shall serve in their personal capacity, consideration being given to equitable geographical distribution, as well as to the principal legal systems.

3. The members of the Committee shall be elected by secret ballot from a list of persons nominated by States Parties. Each State Party may nominate one person from among its own nationals.

4. The initial election to the Committee shall be held no later than six months after the date of the entry into force of the present Convention and thereafter every second year. At least four months before the date of each election, the Secretary-General of the United Nations shall address a letter to States Parties inviting them to submit their nominations within two months. The Secretary-General shall subsequently prepare a list in alphabetical order of all persons thus nominated, indicating States Parties which have nominated them, and shall submit it to the States Parties to the present Convention.

5. The elections shall be held at meetings of States Parties convened by the Secretary-General at United Nations Headquarters. At those meetings, for which two thirds of States Parties shall constitute a quorum, the persons elected to the Committee shall be those who obtain the largest number of votes and an absolute majority of the votes of the representatives of States Parties present and voting.

6. The members of the Committee shall be elected for a term of four years. They shall be eligible for re-election if renominated. The term of five of the members elected at the first election shall expire at the end of two years; immediately after the first election, the names of these five members shall be chosen by lot by the Chairman of the meeting.

7. If a member of the Committee dies or resigns or declares that for any other cause he or she can no longer perform the duties of the Committee, the State Party which nominated the member shall appoint another expert from among its nationals to serve for the remainder of the term, subject to the approval of the Committee.

8. The Committee shall establish its own rules of procedure.

9. The Committee shall elect its officers for a period of two years.

10. The meetings of the Committee shall normally be held at United Nations Headquarters or at any other convenient place as determined by the Committee. The Committee shall normally meet annually. The duration of the meetings of the Committee shall be determined, and reviewed, if necessary, by a meeting of the States Parties to the present Convention, subject to the approval of the General Assembly.

11. The Secretary-General of the United Nations shall provide the necessary staff and facilities for the effective performance of the functions of the Committee under the present Convention.

12. With the approval of the General Assembly, the members of the Committee established under the present Convention shall receive emoluments from United Nations resources on such terms and conditions as the Assembly may decide.

Article 44

1. States Parties undertake to submit to the Committee, through the Secretary-General of the United Nations, reports on the measures they have adopted which give effect to the rights recognized herein and on the progress made on the enjoyment of those rights:

(a) within two years of the entry into force of the Convention for the State Party concerned;

(b) thereafter every five years.

2. Reports made under the present article shall indicate factors and difficulties, if any, affecting the degree of fulfilment of the obligations under the present Convention. Reports shall also contain sufficient information to provide the Committee with a comprehensive understanding of the implementation of the Convention in the country concerned.

3. A State Party which has submitted a comprehensive initial report to the Committee need not, in its subsequent reports submitted in accordance with paragraph 1(b) of the present article, repeat basic information previously provided.

4. The Committee may request from States Parties further information relevant to the implementation of the Convention.

5. The Committee shall submit to the General Assembly, through the Economic and Social Council, every two years, reports on its activities.

6. States Parties shall make their reports widely available to the public in their own countries.

Article 45

In order to foster the effective implementation of the Convention and to encourage international co-operation in the field covered by the Convention:

(a) the specialized agencies, the United Nations Children's Fund, and other United Nations organs shall be entitled to be represented at the consideration of the implementation of such provisions of the present Convention as fall within the scope of their mandate. The Committee may invite the specialized agencies, the United Nations Children's Fund and other competent bodies as it may consider appropriate to provide expert advice on the implementation of the Convention in areas falling within the scope of their respective mandates. The Committee may invite the specialized agencies, the United Nations Children's Fund, and other United Nations organs to submit reports on the implementation of the Convention in areas falling within the scope of their activities;

(b) the Committee shall transmit, as it may consider appropriate, to the specialized agencies, the United Nations Children's Fund and other competent bodies, any reports from States Parties that contain a request, or indicate a need, for technical advice or assistance, along with the Committee's observations and suggestions, if any, on these requests or indications;

(c) the Committee may recommend to the General Assembly to request the Secretary-General to undertake on its behalf studies on specific issues relating to the rights of the child;

(d) the Committee may make suggestions and general recommendations based on information received pursuant to articles 44 and 45 of the present Convention. Such suggestions and general recommendations shall be transmitted to any State Party concerned and reported to the General Assembly, together with comments, if any, from States Parties.

PART III

Article 46
The present Convention shall be open for signature by all States.

Article 47
The present Convention is subject to ratification. Instruments of ratification shall be deposited with the Secretary-General of the United Nations.

Article 48
The present Convention shall remain open for accession by any State. The instruments of accession shall be deposited with the Secretary-General of the United Nations.

Article 49
1. The present Convention shall enter into force on the thirtieth day following the date of deposit with the Secretary-General of the United Nations of the twentieth instrument of ratification or accession.

2. For each State ratifying or acceding to the Convention after the deposit of the twentieth instrument of ratification or accession, the Convention shall enter into force on the thirtieth day after the deposit by such State of its instrument of ratification or accession.

Article 50
1. Any State Party may propose an amendment and file it with the Secretary-General of the United Nations. The Secretary-General shall thereupon communicate the proposed amendment to States Parties, with a request that they indicate whether they favour a conference of States Parties for the purpose of considering and voting upon the proposals. In the event that, within four months from the date of such communication, at least one third of the States Parties favour such a conference, the Secretary-General shall convene the conference under the auspices of the United Nations. Any amendment adopted by a majority of States Parties present and voting at the conference shall be submitted to the General Assembly for approval.

2. An amendment adopted in accordance with paragraph 1 of the present article shall enter into force when it has been approved by the General Assembly of the United Nations and accepted by a two-thirds majority of States Parties.

3. When an amendment enters into force, it shall be binding on those States Parties which have accepted it, other States Parties still being bound by the provisions of the present Convention and any earlier amendments which they have accepted.

Article 51
1. The Secretary-General of the United Nations shall receive and circulate to all States the text of reservations made by States at the time of ratification or accession.

2. A reservation incompatible with the object and purpose of the present Convention shall not be permitted.

3. Reservations may be withdrawn at any time by notification to that effect addressed to the Secretary-General of the United Nations, who shall then inform all States. Such notification shall take effect on the date on which it is received by the Secretary-General.

Article 52

A State Party may denounce the present Convention by written notification to the Secretary-General of the United Nations. Denunciation becomes effective one year after the date of receipt of the notification by the Secretary-General.

Article 53

The Secretary-General of the United Nations is designated as the depositary of the present Convention.

Article 54

The original of the present Convention, of which the Arabic, Chinese, English, French, Russian and Spanish texts are equally authentic, shall be deposited with the Secretary-General of the United Nations.

In witness thereof the undersigned plenipotentiaries, being duly authorized thereto by their respective Governments, have signed the present Convention.

Optional Protocol to the Convention on the Rights of the Child on the Involvement of Children in Armed Conflict (2000)*

The States Parties to the present Protocol,

Encouraged by the overwhelming support for the Convention on the Rights of the Child, demonstrating the widespread commitment that exists to strive for the promotion and protection of the rights of the child,

Reaffirming that the rights of children require special protection, and calling for continuous improvement of the situation of children without distinction, as well as for their development and education in conditions of peace and security,

Disturbed by the harmful and widespread impact of armed conflict on children and the long-term consequences it has for durable peace, security and development,

Condemning the targeting of children in situations of armed conflict and direct attacks on objects protected under international law, including places that generally have a significant presence of children, such as schools and hospitals,

Noting the adoption of the Rome Statute of the International Criminal Court, in particular, the inclusion therein as a war crime, of conscripting or enlisting children under the age of 15 years or using them to participate actively in hostilities in both international and non-international armed conflicts,

Considering therefore that to strengthen further the implementation of rights recognized in the Convention on the Rights of the Child there is a need to increase the protection of children from involvement in armed conflict,

Noting that article 1 of the Convention on the Rights of the Child specifies that, for the purposes of that Convention, a child means every human being below the age of 18 years unless, under the law applicable to the child, majority is attained earlier,

Convinced that an optional protocol to the Convention that raises the age of possible recruitment of persons into armed forces and their participation in hostilities will contribute effectively to the implementation of the principle that the best interests of the child are to be a primary consideration in all actions concerning children,

Noting that the twenty-sixth International Conference of the Red Cross and Red Crescent in December 1995 recommended, *inter alia*, that parties to conflict take every feasible step to ensure that children below the age of 18 years do not take part in hostilities,

---

Welcoming the unanimous adoption, in June 1999, of International Labour Organization Convention No. 182 on the Prohibition and Immediate Action for the Elimination of the Worst Forms of Child Labour, which prohibits, *inter alia*, forced or compulsory recruitment of children for use in armed conflict,

Condemning with the gravest concern the recruitment, training and use within and across national borders of children in hostilities by armed groups distinct from the armed forces of a State, and recognizing the responsibility of those who recruit, train and use children in this regard,

Recalling the obligation of each party to an armed conflict to abide by the provisions of international humanitarian law,

Stressing that the present Protocol is without prejudice to the purposes and principles contained in the Charter of the United Nations, including Article 51, and relevant norms of humanitarian law,

Bearing in mind that conditions of peace and security based on full respect of the purposes and principles contained in the Charter and observance of applicable human rights instruments are indispensable for the full protection of children, in particular during armed conflicts and foreign occupation,

Recognizing the special needs of those children who are particularly vulnerable to recruitment or use in hostilities contrary to the present Protocol owing to their economic or social status or gender,

Mindful of the necessity of taking into consideration the economic, social and political root causes of the involvement of children in armed conflicts,

Convinced of the need to strengthen international cooperation in the implementation of the present Protocol, as well as the physical and psychosocial rehabilitation and social reintegration of children who are victims of armed conflict,

Encouraging the participation of the community and, in particular, children and child victims in the dissemination of informational and educational programmes concerning the implementation of the Protocol,

Have agreed as follows:

Article 1

States Parties shall take all feasible measures to ensure that members of their armed forces who have not attained the age of 18 years do not take a direct part in hostilities.

Article 2

States Parties shall ensure that persons who have not attained the age of 18 years are not compulsorily recruited into their armed forces.

Article 3

1. States Parties shall raise the minimum age for the voluntary recruitment of persons into their national armed forces from that set out in article 38, paragraph 3, of the Convention on the Rights of the Child, taking account of the principles contained in that article and recognizing that under the Convention persons under the age of 18 years are entitled to special protection.

2. Each State Party shall deposit a binding declaration upon ratification of or accession to the present Protocol that sets forth the minimum age at which it will permit voluntary recruitment into its national armed forces and a description of the safeguards it has adopted to ensure that such recruitment is not forced or coerced.

3. States Parties that permit voluntary recruitment into their national armed forces under the age of 18 years shall maintain safeguards to ensure, as a minimum, that:

    (a) Such recruitment is genuinely voluntary;

    (b) Such recruitment is carried out with the informed consent of the person's parents or legal guardians;

    (c) Such persons are fully informed of the duties involved in such military service;

    (d) Such persons provide reliable proof of age prior to acceptance into national military service.

4. Each State Party may strengthen its declaration at any time by notification to that effect addressed to the Secretary-General of the United Nations, who shall inform all States Parties. Such notification shall take effect on the date on which it is received by the Secretary-General.

5. The requirement to raise the age in paragraph 1 of the present article does not apply to schools operated by or under the control of the armed forces of the States Parties, in keeping with articles 28 and 29 of the Convention on the Rights of the Child.

Article 4

1. Armed groups that are distinct from the armed forces of a State should not, under any circumstances, recruit or use in hostilities persons under the age of 18 years.

2. States Parties shall take all feasible measures to prevent such recruitment and use, including the adoption of legal measures necessary to prohibit and criminalize such practices.

3. The application of the present article shall not affect the legal status of any party to an armed conflict.

Article 5

Nothing in the present Protocol shall be construed as precluding provision in the law of a State Party or in international instruments and international humanitarian law that are more conducive to the realization of the rights of the child.

Article 6

1. Each State Party shall take all necessary legal, administrative and other measures to ensure the effective implementation and enforcement of the provisions of the present Protocol within its jurisdiction.

2. States Parties undertake to make the principles and provisions of the present Protocol widely known and promoted by appropriate means, to adults and children alike.

3. States Parties shall take all feasible measures to ensure that persons within their jurisdiction recruited or used in hostilities contrary to the present Protocol are demobilized or otherwise released from service. States Parties shall, when necessary, accord to such persons all appropriate assistance for their physical and psychological recovery and their social reintegration.

Article 7

1. States Parties shall cooperate in the implementation of the present Protocol, including in the prevention of any activity contrary thereto and in the rehabilitation and social reintegration of persons who are victims of acts contrary thereto, including through technical cooperation and financial assistance. Such assistance and cooperation will be undertaken in consultation with the States Parties concerned and the relevant international organizations.

2. States Parties in a position to do so shall provide such assistance through existing multilateral, bilateral or other programmes or, *inter alia*, through a voluntary fund established in accordance with the rules of the General Assembly.

Article 8

1. Each State Party shall, within two years following the entry into force of the present Protocol for that State Party, submit a report to the Committee on the Rights of the Child providing comprehensive information on the measures it has taken to implement the provisions of the Protocol, including the measures taken to implement the provisions on participation and recruitment.

2. Following the submission of the comprehensive report, each State Party shall include in the reports it submits to the Committee on the Rights of the Child, in accordance with article 44 of the Convention, any further information with respect to the implementation of the Protocol. Other States Parties to the Protocol shall submit a report every five years.

3. The Committee on the Rights of the Child may request from States Parties further information relevant to the implementation of the present Protocol.

Article 9

1. The present Protocol is open for signature by any State that is a party to the Convention or has signed it.

2. The present Protocol is subject to ratification and is open to accession by any State. Instruments of ratification or accession shall be deposited with the Secretary-General of the United Nations.

3. The Secretary-General, in his capacity as depositary of the Convention and the Protocol, shall inform all States Parties to the Convention and all States that have signed the Convention of each instrument of declaration pursuant to article 3.

Article 10

1. The present Protocol shall enter into force three months after the deposit of the tenth instrument of ratification or accession.

2. For each State ratifying the present Protocol or acceding to it after its entry into force, the Protocol shall enter into force one month after the date of the deposit of its own instrument of ratification or accession.

Article 11

1. Any State Party may denounce the present Protocol at any time by written notification to the Secretary-General of the United Nations, who shall thereafter inform the other States Parties to the Convention and all States that have signed the Convention. The denunciation shall take effect one year after the date of receipt of the notification by the Secretary-General. If, however, on the expiry of that year the denouncing State Party is engaged in armed conflict, the denunciation shall not take effect before the end of the armed conflict.

2. Such a denunciation shall not have the effect of releasing the State Party from its obligations under the present Protocol in regard to any act that occurs prior to the date on which the denunciation becomes effective. Nor shall such a denunciation prejudice in any way the continued consideration of any matter that is already under consideration by the Committee on the Rights of the Child prior to the date on which the denunciation becomes effective.

Article 12

1. Any State Party may propose an amendment and file it with the Secretary-General of the United Nations. The Secretary-General shall thereupon communicate the proposed amendment to States Parties with a request that they indicate whether they favour a conference of States Parties for the purpose of considering and voting upon the proposals. In the event that, within four months from the date of such communication, at least one third of the States Parties favour such a conference, the Secretary-General shall convene the conference under the auspices of the United Nations. Any amendment adopted by a majority of States Parties present and voting at the conference shall be submitted to the General Assembly of the United Nations for approval.

2. An amendment adopted in accordance with paragraph 1 of the present article shall enter into force when it has been approved by the General Assembly and accepted by a two-thirds majority of States Parties.

3. When an amendment enters into force, it shall be binding on those States Parties that have accepted it, other States Parties still being bound by the provisions of the present Protocol and any earlier amendments they have accepted.

Article 13

1. The present Protocol, of which the Arabic, Chinese, English, French, Russian and Spanish texts are equally authentic, shall be deposited in the archives of the United Nations.

2. The Secretary-General of the United Nations shall transmit certified copies of the present Protocol to all States Parties to the Convention and all States that have signed the Convention.

Optional Protocol to the Convention on the Rights of the Child on the Sale of Children, Child Prostitution and Child Pornography (2000)*

The States Parties to the present Protocol,

   Considering that, in order further to achieve the purposes of the Convention on the Rights of the Child and the implementation of its provisions, especially articles 1, 11, 21, 32, 33, 34, 35 and 36, it would be appropriate to extend the measures that States Parties should undertake in order to guarantee the protection of the child from the sale of children, child prostitution and child pornography,

Considering also that the Convention on the Rights of the Child recognizes the right of the child to be protected from economic exploitation and from performing any work that is likely to be hazardous or to interfere with the child's education, or to be harmful to the child's health or physical, mental, spiritual, moral or social development,

Gravely concerned at the significant and increasing international traffic in children for the purpose of the sale of children, child prostitution and child pornography,

Deeply concerned at the widespread and continuing practice of sex tourism, to which children are especially vulnerable, as it directly promotes the sale of children, child prostitution and child pornography,

Recognizing that a number of particularly vulnerable groups, including girl children, are at greater risk of sexual exploitation and that girl children are disproportionately represented among the sexually exploited,

Concerned about the growing availability of child pornography on the Internet and other evolving technologies, and recalling the International Conference on Combating Child Pornography on the Internet, held in Vienna in 1999, in particular its conclusion calling for the worldwide criminalization of the production, distribution, exportation, transmission, importation, intentional possession and advertising of child pornography, and stressing the importance of closer cooperation and partnership between Governments and the Internet industry,

Believing that the elimination of the sale of children, child prostitution and child pornography will be facilitated by adopting a holistic approach, addressing the contributing factors, including underdevelopment, poverty, economic disparities, inequitable socioeconomic structure, dysfunctioning families, lack of education, urban-rural migration, gender discrimination, irresponsible adult sexual behaviour, harmful traditional practices, armed conflicts and trafficking in children,

Believing also that efforts to raise public awareness are needed to reduce consumer demand for the sale of children, child prostitution and child pornography, and believing further in the importance of strengthening global, partnership among all actors and of improving law enforcement at the national level,

Noting the provisions of international legal instruments relevant to the protection of children, including the Hague Convention on Protection of Children and Cooperation in Respect of Intercountry Adoption, the Hague Convention on the Civil Aspects of International Child Abduction, the Hague Convention on Jurisdiction, Applicable Law, Recognition, Enforcement and Cooperation in Respect of Parental Responsibility and Measures for the Protection of Children, and International Labour Organization Convention No. 182 on the Prohibition and Immediate Action for the Elimination of the Worst Forms of Child Labour,

Encouraged by the overwhelming support for the Convention on the Rights of the Child, demonstrating the widespread commitment that exists for the promotion and protection of the rights of the child,

Recognizing the importance of the implementation of the provisions of the Programme of Action for the Prevention of the Sale of Children, Child Prostitution and Child Pornography and the Declaration and Agenda for Action adopted at the World Congress against Commercial Sexual Exploitation of Children, held in Stockholm from 27 to 31 August 1996, and the other relevant decisions and recommendations of pertinent international bodies,

Taking due account of the importance of the traditions and cultural values of each people for the protection and harmonious development of the child,

Have agreed as follows:

Article 1

States Parties shall prohibit the sale of children, child prostitution and child pornography as provided for by the present Protocol.

Article 2

For the purposes of the present Protocol:

(a) Sale of children means any act or transaction whereby a child is transferred by any person or group of persons to another for remuneration or any other consideration;

(b) Child prostitution means the use of a child in sexual activities for remuneration or any other form of consideration;

(c) Child pornography means any representation, by whatever means, of a child engaged in real or simulated explicit sexual activities or any representation of the sexual parts of a child for primarily sexual purposes.

Article 3

1. Each State Party shall ensure that, as a minimum, the following acts and activities are fully covered under its criminal or penal law, whether such offences are committed domestically or transnationally or on an individual or organized basis:

(a) In the context of sale of children as defined in article 2:

(i) Offering, delivering or accepting, by whatever means, a child for the purpose of:

(a) Sexual exploitation of the child;

(b) Transfer of organs of the child for profit;

(c) Engagement of the child in forced labour;

(ii) Improperly inducing consent, as an intermediary, for the adoption of a child in violation of applicable international legal instruments on adoption;

(b) Offering, obtaining, procuring or providing a child for child prostitution, as defined in article 2;

(c) Producing, distributing, disseminating, importing, exporting, offering, selling or possessing for the above purposes child pornography as defined in article 2.

2. Subject to the provisions of the national law of a State Party, the same shall apply to an attempt to commit any of the said acts and to complicity or participation in any of the said acts.

3. Each State Party shall make such offences punishable by appropriate penalties that take into account their grave nature.

4. Subject to the provisions of its national law, each State Party shall take measures, where appropriate, to establish the liability of legal persons for offences established in paragraph 1 of the present article. Subject to the legal principles of the State Party, such liability of legal persons may be criminal, civil or administrative.

5. States Parties shall take all appropriate legal and administrative measures to ensure that all persons involved in the adoption of a child act in conformity with applicable international legal instruments.

Article 4

1. Each State Party shall take such measures as may be necessary to establish its jurisdiction over the offences referred to in article 3, paragraph 1, when the offences are committed in its territory or on board a ship or aircraft registered in that State.

2. Each State Party may take such measures as may be necessary to establish its jurisdiction over the offences referred to in article 3, paragraph 1, in the following cases:

(a) When the alleged offender is a national of that State or a person who has his habitual residence in its territory;

(b) When the victim is a national of that State.

3. Each State Party shall also take such measures as may be necessary to establish its jurisdiction over the aforementioned offences when the alleged offender is present in its territory and it does not extradite him or her to another State Party on the ground that the offence has been committed by one of its nationals.

4. The present Protocol does not exclude any criminal jurisdiction exercised in accordance with internal law.

Article 5

1. The offences referred to in article 3, paragraph 1, shall be deemed to be included as extraditable offences in any extradition treaty existing between States Parties and shall be included as extraditable offences in every extradition treaty subsequently concluded between them, in accordance with the conditions set forth in such treaties.

2. If a State Party that makes extradition conditional on the existence of a treaty receives a request for extradition from another State Party with which it has no extradition treaty, it may consider the present Protocol to be a legal basis for extradition in respect of such offences. Extradition shall be subject to the conditions provided by the law of the requested State.

3. States Parties that do not make extradition conditional on the existence of a treaty shall recognize such offences as extraditable offences between themselves subject to the conditions provided by the law of the requested State.

4. Such offences shall be treated, for the purpose of extradition between States Parties, as if they had been committed not only in the place in which they occurred but also in the territories of the States required to establish their jurisdiction in accordance with article 4.

5. If an extradition request is made with respect to an offence described in article 3, paragraph 1, and the requested State Party does not or will not extradite on the basis of the nationality of the offender, that State shall take suitable measures to submit the case to its competent authorities for the purpose of prosecution.

Article 6

1. States Parties shall afford one another the greatest measure of assistance in connection with investigations or criminal or extradition proceedings brought in respect of the offences set forth in article 3, paragraph 1, including assistance in obtaining evidence at their disposal necessary for the proceedings.

2. States Parties shall carry out their obligations under paragraph 1 of the present article in conformity with any treaties or other arrangements on mutual legal assistance that may exist between them. In the absence of such treaties or arrangements, States Parties shall afford one another assistance in accordance with their domestic law.

Article 7

States Parties shall, subject to the provisions of their national law:

    (a) Take measures to provide for the seizure and confiscation, as appropriate, of:
        (i) Goods, such as materials, assets and other instrumentalities used to commit or facilitate offences under the present protocol;
        (ii) Proceeds derived from such offences;
    (b) Execute requests from another State Party for seizure or confiscation of goods or proceeds referred to in subparagraph (a)(i) and (ii);
    (c) Take measures aimed at closing, on a temporary or definitive basis, premises used to commit such offences.

Article 8

1. States Parties shall adopt appropriate measures to protect the rights and interests of child victims of the practices prohibited under the present Protocol at all stages of the criminal justice process, in particular by:

    (a) Recognizing the vulnerability of child victims and adapting procedures to recognize their special needs, including their special needs as witnesses;
    (b) Informing child victims of their rights, their role and the scope, timing and progress of the proceedings and of the disposition of their cases;
    (c) Allowing the views, needs and concerns of child victims to be presented and considered in proceedings where their personal interests are affected, in a manner consistent with the procedural rules of national law;
    (d) Providing appropriate support services to child victims throughout the legal process;

(e) Protecting, as appropriate, the privacy and identity of child victims and taking measures in accordance with national law to avoid the inappropriate dissemination of information that could lead to the identification of child victims;

(f) Providing, in appropriate cases, for the safety of child victims, as well as that of their families and witnesses on their behalf, from intimidation and retaliation;

(g) Avoiding unnecessary delay in the disposition of cases and the execution of orders or decrees granting compensation to child victims.

2. States Parties shall ensure that uncertainty as to the actual age of the victim shall not prevent the initiation of criminal investigations, including investigations aimed at establishing the age of the victim.

3. States Parties shall ensure that, in the treatment by the criminal justice system of children who are victims of the offences described in the present Protocol, the best interest of the child shall be a primary consideration.

4. States Parties shall take measures to ensure appropriate training, in particular legal and psychological training, for the persons who work with victims of the offences prohibited under the present Protocol.

5. States Parties shall, in appropriate cases, adopt measures in order to protect the safety and integrity of those persons and/or organizations involved in the prevention and/or protection and rehabilitation of victims of such offences.

6. Nothing in the present article shall be construed to be prejudicial to or inconsistent with the rights of the accused to a fair and impartial trial.

Article 9

1. States Parties shall adopt or strengthen, implement and disseminate laws, administrative measures, social policies and programmes to prevent the offences referred to in the present Protocol. Particular attention shall be given to protect children who are especially vulnerable to such practices.

2. States Parties shall promote awareness in the public at large, including children, through information by all appropriate means, education and training, about the preventive measures and harmful effects of the offences referred to in the present Protocol. In fulfilling their obligations under this article, States Parties shall encourage the participation of the community and, in particular, children and child victims, in such information and education and training programmes, including at the international level.

3. States Parties shall take all feasible measures with the aim of ensuring all appropriate assistance to victims of such offences, including their full social reintegration and their full physical and psychological recovery.

4. States Parties shall ensure that all child victims of the offences described in the present Protocol have access to adequate procedures to seek, without discrimination, compensation for damages from those legally responsible.

5. States Parties shall take appropriate measures aimed at effectively prohibiting the production and dissemination of material advertising the offences described in the present Protocol.

Article 10

1. States Parties shall take all necessary steps to strengthen international cooperation by multilateral, regional and bilateral arrangements for the prevention, detection, investigation, prosecution and punishment of those responsible for acts involving the sale of children, child prostitution, child pornography and child sex tourism. States Parties shall also promote international cooperation and coordination between their authorities, national and international non-governmental organizations and international organizations.

2. States Parties shall promote international cooperation to assist child victims in their physical and psychological recovery, social reintegration and repatriation.

3. States Parties shall promote the strengthening of international cooperation in order to address the root causes, such as poverty and underdevelopment, contributing to the vulnerability of children to the sale of children, child prostitution, child pornography and child sex tourism.

4. States Parties in a position to do so shall provide financial, technical or other assistance through existing multilateral, regional, bilateral or other programmes.

Article 11

Nothing in the present Protocol shall affect any provisions that are more conducive to the realization of the rights of the child and that may be contained in:

(a) The law of a State Party;

(b) International law in force for that State.

Article 12

1. Each State Party shall, within two years following the entry into force of the present Protocol for that State Party, submit a report to the Committee on the Rights of the Child providing comprehensive information on the measures it has taken to implement the provisions of the Protocol.

2. Following the submission of the comprehensive report, each State Party shall include in the reports they submit to the Committee on the Rights of the Child, in accordance with article 44 of the Convention, any further information with respect to the implementation of the present Protocol. Other States Parties to the Protocol shall submit a report every five years.

3. The Committee on the Rights of the Child may request from States Parties further information relevant to the implementation of the present Protocol.

Article 13

1. The present Protocol is open for signature by any State that is a party to the Convention or has signed it.

2. The present Protocol is subject to ratification and is open to accession by any State that is a party to the Convention or has signed it. Instruments of ratification or accession shall be deposited with the Secretary-General of the United Nations.

Article 14

1. The present Protocol shall enter into force three months after the deposit of the tenth instrument of ratification or accession.

2. For each State ratifying the present Protocol or acceding to it after its entry into force, the Protocol shall enter into force one month after the date of the deposit of its own instrument of ratification or accession.

Article 15

1. Any State Party may denounce the present Protocol at any time by written notification to the Secretary-General of the United Nations, who shall thereafter inform the other States Parties to the Convention and all States that have signed the Convention. The denunciation shall take effect one year after the date of receipt of the notification by the Secretary-General.

2. Such a denunciation shall not have the effect of releasing the State Party from its obligations under the present Protocol in regard to any offence that occurs prior to the date on which the denunciation becomes effective. Nor shall such a denunciation prejudice in any way the continued consideration of any matter that is already under consideration by the Committee on the Rights of the Child prior to the date on which the denunciation becomes effective.

Article 16

1. Any State Party may propose an amendment and file it with the Secretary-General of the United Nations. The Secretary-General shall thereupon communicate the proposed amendment to States Parties with a request that they indicate whether they favour a conference of States Parties for the purpose of considering and voting upon the proposals. In the event that, within four months from the date of such communication, at least one third of the States Parties favour such a conference, the Secretary-General shall convene the conference under the auspices of the United Nations. Any amendment adopted by a majority of States Parties present and voting at the conference shall be submitted to the General Assembly of the United Nations for approval.

2. An amendment adopted in accordance with paragraph 1 of the present article shall enter into force when it has been approved by the General Assembly and accepted by a two-thirds majority of States Parties.

3. When an amendment enters into force, it shall be binding on those States Parties that have accepted it, other States Parties still being bound by the provisions of the present Protocol and any earlier amendments they have accepted.

Article 17

1. The present Protocol, of which the Arabic, Chinese, English, French, Russian and Spanish texts are equally authentic, shall be deposited in the archives of the United Nations.

2. The Secretary-General of the United Nations shall transmit certified copies of the present Protocol to all States Parties to the Convention and all States that have signed the Convention.

Optional Protocol to the Convention on the Rights of the Child on a Communications Procedure (2011)*

The States parties to the present Protocol,

Considering that, in accordance with the principles proclaimed in the Charter of the United Nations, the recognition of the inherent dignity and the equal and inalienable rights of all members of the human family is the foundation of freedom, justice and peace in the world,

Noting that the States parties to the Convention on the Rights of the Child (hereinafter referred to as 'the Convention') recognize the rights set forth in it to each child within their jurisdiction without discrimination of any kind, irrespective of the child's or his or her parent's or legal guardian's race, colour, sex, language, religion, political or other opinion, national, ethnic or social origin, property, disability, birth or other status,

Reaffirming the universality, indivisibility, interdependence and interrelatedness of all human rights and fundamental freedoms,

Reaffirming also the status of the child as a subject of rights and as a human being with dignity and with evolving capacities,

Recognizing that children's special and dependent status may create real difficulties for them in pursuing remedies for violations of their rights,

Considering that the present Protocol will reinforce and complement national and regional mechanisms allowing children to submit complaints for violations of their rights,

Recognizing that the best interests of the child should be a primary consideration to be respected in pursuing remedies for violations of the rights of the child, and that such remedies should take into account the need for child-sensitive procedures at all levels,

Encouraging States parties to develop appropriate national mechanisms to enable a child whose rights have been violated to have access to effective remedies at the domestic level,

Recalling the important role that national human rights institutions and other relevant specialized institutions, mandated to promote and protect the rights of the child, can play in this regard,

Considering that, in order to reinforce and complement such national mechanisms and to further enhance the implementation of the Convention and, where applicable, the Optional Protocols thereto on the sale of children, child prostitution and child pornography and on the involvement of children in armed conflict, it would be appropriate to enable the Committee on the Rights of the Child (hereinafter referred to as 'the Committee') to carry out the functions provided for in the present Protocol,

Have agreed as follows:

PART I GENERAL PROVISIONS

Article 1   Competence of the Committee on the Rights of the Child

1. A State party to the present Protocol recognizes the competence of the Committee as provided for by the present Protocol.

2. The Committee shall not exercise its competence regarding a State party to the present Protocol on matters concerning violations of rights set forth in an instrument to which that State is not a party.

3. No communication shall be received by the Committee if it concerns a State that is not a party to the present Protocol.

Article 2   General principles guiding the functions of the Committee

In fulfilling the functions conferred on it by the present Protocol, the Committee shall be guided by the principle of the best interests of the child. It shall also have regard for the rights and views of the child, the views of the child being given due weight in accordance with the age and maturity of the child.

Article 3   Rules of procedure

1. The Committee shall adopt rules of procedure to be followed when exercising the functions conferred on it by the present Protocol. In doing so, it shall have regard, in particular, for article 2 of the present Protocol in order to guarantee child-sensitive procedures.

2. The Committee shall include in its rules of procedure safeguards to prevent the manipulation of the child by those acting on his or her behalf and may decline to examine any communication that it considers not to be in the child's best interests.

Article 4   Protection measures

1. A State party shall take all appropriate steps to ensure that individuals under its jurisdiction are not subjected to any human rights violation, ill-treatment or intimidation as a consequence of communications or cooperation with the Committee pursuant to the present Protocol.

2. The identity of any individual or group of individuals concerned shall not be revealed publicly without their express consent.

PART II COMMUNICATIONS PROCEDURE

Article 5   Individual communications

1. Communications may be submitted by or on behalf of an individual or group of individuals, within the jurisdiction of a State party, claiming to be victims of a violation by that State party of any of the rights set forth in any of the following instruments to which that State is a party:

    (a) The Convention;

    (b) The Optional Protocol to the Convention on the sale of children, child prostitution and child pornography;

    (c) The Optional Protocol to the Convention on the involvement of children in armed conflict.

2. Where a communication is submitted on behalf of an individual or group of individuals, this shall be with their consent unless the author can justify acting on their behalf without such consent.

Article 6   Interim measures

1. At any time after the receipt of a communication and before a determination on the merits has been reached, the Committee may transmit to the State party concerned for its urgent consideration a request that the State party take such interim measures as may be necessary in exceptional circumstances to avoid possible irreparable damage to the victim or victims of the alleged violations.

2. Where the Committee exercises its discretion under paragraph 1 of the present article, this does not imply a determination on admissibility or on the merits of the communication.

Article 7   Admissibility

The Committee shall consider a communication inadmissible when:

    (a) The communication is anonymous;

    (b) The communication is not in writing;

    (c) The communication constitutes an abuse of the right of submission of such communications or is incompatible with the provisions of the Convention and/or the Optional Protocols thereto;

(d) The same matter has already been examined by the Committee or has been or is being examined under another procedure of international investigation or settlement;

(e) All available domestic remedies have not been exhausted. This shall not be the rule where the application of the remedies is unreasonably prolonged or unlikely to bring effective relief;

(f) The communication is manifestly ill-founded or not sufficiently substantiated;

(g) The facts that are the subject of the communication occurred prior to the entry into force of the present Protocol for the State party concerned, unless those facts continued after that date;

(h) The communication is not submitted within one year after the exhaustion of domestic remedies, except in cases where the author can demonstrate that it had not been possible to submit the communication within that time limit.

Article 8   Transmission of the communication

1. Unless the Committee considers a communication inadmissible without reference to the State party concerned, the Committee shall bring any communication submitted to it under the present Protocol confidentially to the attention of the State party concerned as soon as possible.

2. The State party shall submit to the Committee written explanations or statements clarifying the matter and the remedy, if any, that it may have provided. The State party shall submit its response as soon as possible and within six months.

Article 9   Friendly settlement

1. The Committee shall make available its good offices to the parties concerned with a view to reaching a friendly settlement of the matter on the basis of respect for the obligations set forth in the Convention and/or the Optional Protocols thereto.

2. An agreement on a friendly settlement reached under the auspices of the Committee closes consideration of the communication under the present Protocol.

Article 10   Consideration of communications

1. The Committee shall consider communications received under the present Protocol as quickly as possible, in the light of all documentation submitted to it, provided that this documentation is transmitted to the parties concerned.

2. The Committee shall hold closed meetings when examining communications received under the present Protocol.

3. Where the Committee has requested interim measures, it shall expedite the consideration of the communication.

4. When examining communications alleging violations of economic, social or cultural rights, the Committee shall consider the reasonableness of the steps taken by the State party in accordance with article 4 of the Convention. In doing so, the Committee shall bear in mind that the State party may adopt a range of possible policy measures for the implementation of the economic, social and cultural rights in the Convention.

5. After examining a communication, the Committee shall, without delay, transmit its views on the communication, together with its recommendations, if any, to the parties concerned.

Article 11   Follow-up

1. The State party shall give due consideration to the views of the Committee, together with its recommendations, if any, and shall submit to the Committee a written response, including information on any action taken and envisaged in the light of the views and recommendations of the Committee. The State party shall submit its response as soon as possible and within six months.

2. The Committee may invite the State party to submit further information about any measures the State party has taken in response to its views or recommendations or implementation of a friendly settlement agreement, if any, including as deemed appropriate by the Committee, in the State party's subsequent reports under article 44 of the Convention, article 12 of the Optional Protocol to the Convention on the sale of children, child prostitution and child pornography or article 8 of the Optional Protocol to the Convention on the involvement of children in armed conflict, where applicable.

Article 12   Inter-State communications

1. A State party to the present Protocol may, at any time, declare that it recognizes the competence of the Committee to receive and consider communications in which a State party claims that another State party is not fulfilling its obligations under any of the following instruments to which the State is a party:

    (a) The Convention;

    (b) The Optional Protocol to the Convention on the sale of children, child prostitution and child pornography;

    (c) The Optional Protocol to the Convention on the involvement of children in armed conflict.

2. The Committee shall not receive communications concerning a State party that has not made such a declaration or communications from a State party that has not made such a declaration.

3. The Committee shall make available its good offices to the States parties concerned with a view to a friendly solution of the matter on the basis of the respect for the obligations set forth in the Convention and the Optional Protocols thereto.

4. A declaration under paragraph 1 of the present article shall be deposited by the States parties with the Secretary-General of the United Nations, who shall transmit copies thereof to the other States parties. A declaration may be withdrawn at any time by notification to the Secretary-General. Such a withdrawal shall not prejudice the consideration of any matter that is the subject of a communication already transmitted under the present article; no further communications by any State party shall be received under the present article after the notification of withdrawal of the declaration has been received by the Secretary-General, unless the State party concerned has made a new declaration.

PART III INQUIRY PROCEDURE

Article 13   Inquiry procedure for grave or systematic violations

1. If the Committee receives reliable information indicating grave or systematic violations by a State party of rights set forth in the Convention or in the Optional Protocols thereto on the sale of children, child prostitution and child pornography or on the involvement of children in armed conflict, the Committee shall invite the State party to cooperate in the examination of the information and, to this end, to submit observations without delay with regard to the information concerned.

2. Taking into account any observations that may have been submitted by the State party concerned, as well as any other reliable information available to it, the Committee may designate one or more of its members to conduct an inquiry and to report urgently to the Committee. Where warranted and with the consent of the State party, the inquiry may include a visit to its territory.

3. Such an inquiry shall be conducted confidentially, and the cooperation of the State party shall be sought at all stages of the proceedings.

4. After examining the findings of such an inquiry, the Committee shall transmit without delay these findings to the State party concerned, together with any comments and recommendations.

5. The State party concerned shall, as soon as possible and within six months of receiving the findings, comments and recommendations transmitted by the Committee, submit its observations to the Committee.

6. After such proceedings have been completed with regard to an inquiry made in accordance with paragraph 2 of the present article, the Committee may, after consultation with the State party concerned, decide to include a summary account of the results of the proceedings in its report provided for in article 16 of the present Protocol.

7. Each State party may, at the time of signature or ratification of the present Protocol or accession thereto, declare that it does not recognize the competence of the Committee provided for in the present article in respect of the rights set forth in some or all of the instruments listed in paragraph 1.

8. Any State party having made a declaration in accordance with paragraph 7 of the present article may, at any time, withdraw this declaration by notification to the Secretary-General of the United Nations.

Article 14   Follow-up to the inquiry procedure

1. The Committee may, if necessary, after the end of the period of six months referred to in article 13, paragraph 5, invite the State party concerned to inform it of the measures taken and envisaged in response to an inquiry conducted under article 13 of the present Protocol.

2. The Committee may invite the State party to submit further information about any measures that the State party has taken in response to an inquiry conducted under article 13, including as deemed appropriate by the Committee, in the State party's subsequent reports under article 44 of the Convention, article 12 of the Optional Protocol to the Convention on the sale of children, child prostitution and child pornography or article 8 of the Optional Protocol to the Convention on the involvement of children in armed conflict, where applicable.

PART IV FINAL PROVISIONS

Article 15   International assistance and cooperation

1. The Committee may transmit, with the consent of the State party concerned, to United Nations specialized agencies, funds and programmes and other competent bodies its views or recommendations concerning communications and inquiries that indicate a need for technical advice or assistance, together with the State party's observations and suggestions, if any, on these views or recommendations.

2. The Committee may also bring to the attention of such bodies, with the consent of the State party concerned, any matter arising out of communications considered under the present Protocol that may assist them in deciding, each within its field of competence, on the advisability of international measures likely to contribute to assisting States parties in achieving progress in the implementation of the rights recognized in the Convention and/or the Optional Protocols thereto.

Article 16   Report to the General Assembly

The Committee shall include in its report submitted every two years to the General Assembly in accordance with article 44, paragraph 5, of the Convention a summary of its activities under the present Protocol.

Article 17   Dissemination of and information on the Optional Protocol

Each State party undertakes to make widely known and to disseminate the present Protocol and to facilitate access to information about the views and recommendations of the Committee, in particular with regard to matters involving the State party, by appropriate and active means and in accessible formats to adults and children alike, including those with disabilities.

Article 18   Signature, ratification and accession

1. The present Protocol is open for signature to any State that has signed, ratified or acceded to the Convention or either of the first two Optional Protocols thereto.

2. The present Protocol is subject to ratification by any State that has ratified or acceded to the Convention or either of the first two Optional Protocols thereto. Instruments of ratification shall be deposited with the Secretary-General of the United Nations.

3. The present Protocol shall be open to accession by any State that has ratified or acceded to the Convention or either of the first two Optional Protocols thereto.

4. Accession shall be effected by the deposit of an instrument of accession with the Secretary-General.

Article 19   Entry into force

1. The present Protocol shall enter into force three months after the deposit of the tenth instrument of ratification or accession.

2. For each State ratifying the present Protocol or acceding to it after the deposit of the tenth instrument of ratification or instrument of accession, the present Protocol shall enter into force three months after the date of the deposit of its own instrument of ratification or accession.

Article 20 Violations occurring after the entry into force

1. The Committee shall have competence solely in respect of violations by the State party of any of the rights set forth in the Convention and/or the first two Optional Protocols thereto occurring after the entry into force of the present Protocol.

2. If a State becomes a party to the present Protocol after its entry into force, the obligations of that State vis-à-vis the Committee shall relate only to violations of the rights set forth in the Convention and/or the first two Optional Protocols thereto occurring after the entry into force of the present Protocol for the State concerned.

Article 21 Amendments

1. Any State party may propose an amendment to the present Protocol and submit it to the Secretary-General of the United Nations. The Secretary-General shall communicate any proposed amendments to States parties with a request to be notified whether they favour a meeting of States parties for the purpose of considering and deciding upon the proposals. In the event that, within four months of the date of such communication, at least one third of the States parties favour such a meeting, the Secretary-General shall convene the meeting under the auspices of the United Nations. Any amendment adopted by a majority of two thirds of the States parties present and voting shall be submitted by the Secretary-General to the General Assembly for approval and, thereafter, to all States parties for acceptance.

2. An amendment adopted and approved in accordance with paragraph 1 of the present article shall enter into force on the thirtieth day after the number of instruments of acceptance deposited reaches two thirds of the number of States parties at the date of adoption of the amendment. Thereafter, the amendment shall enter into force for any State party on the thirtieth day following the deposit of its own instrument of acceptance. An amendment shall be binding only on those States parties that have accepted it.

Article 22 Denunciation

1. Any State party may denounce the present Protocol at any time by written notification to the Secretary-General of the United Nations. The denunciation shall take effect one year after the date of receipt of the notification by the Secretary-General.

2. Denunciation shall be without prejudice to the continued application of the provisions of the present Protocol to any communication submitted under articles 5 or 12 or any inquiry initiated under article 13 before the effective date of denunciation.

Article 23 Depositary and notification by the Secretary-General

1. The Secretary-General of the United Nations shall be the depositary of the present Protocol.

2. The Secretary-General shall inform all States of:
   (a) Signatures, ratifications and accessions under the present Protocol;
   (b) The date of entry into force of the present Protocol and of any amendment thereto under article 21;
   (c) Any denunciation under article 22 of the present Protocol.

Article 24 Languages

1. The present Protocol, of which the Arabic, Chinese, English, French, Russian and Spanish texts are equally authentic, shall be deposited in the archives of the United Nations.

2. The Secretary-General of the United Nations shall transmit certified copies of the present Protocol to all States.

International Convention on the Protection of the Rights of All Migrant Workers and Members of Their Families (1990)*

The States Parties to the present Convention,

   Taking into account the principles embodied in the basic instruments of the United Nations concerning human rights, in particular the Universal Declaration of Human Rights, the International

Covenant on Economic, Social and Cultural Rights, the International Covenant on Civil and Political Rights, the International Convention on the Elimination of All Forms of Racial Discrimination, the Convention on the Elimination of All Forms of Discrimination against Women and the Convention on the Rights of the Child,

Taking into account also the principles and standards set forth in the relevant instruments elaborated within the framework of the International Labour Organisation, especially the Convention concerning Migration for Employment (No. 97), the Convention concerning Migrations in Abusive Conditions and the Promotion of Equality of Opportunity and Treatment of Migrant Workers (No. 143), the Recommendation concerning Migration for Employment (No. 86), the Recommendation concerning Migrant Workers (No. 151), the Convention concerning Forced or Compulsory Labour (No. 29) and the Convention concerning Abolition of Forced Labour (No. 105),

Reaffirming the importance of the principles contained in the Convention against Discrimination in Education of the United Nations Educational, Scientific and Cultural Organization,

Recalling the Convention against Torture and Other Cruel, Inhuman or Degrading Treatment or Punishment, the Declaration of the Fourth United Nations Congress on the Prevention of Crime and the Treatment of Offenders, the Code of Conduct for Law Enforcement Officials, and the Slavery Conventions,

Recalling that one of the objectives of the International Labour Organisation, as stated in its Constitution, is the protection of the interests of workers when employed in countries other than their own, and bearing in mind the expertise and experience of that organization in matters related to migrant workers and members of their families,

Recognizing the importance of the work done in connection with migrant workers and members of their families in various organs of the United Nations, in particular in the Commission on Human Rights and the Commission for Social Development, and in the Food and Agriculture Organization of the United Nations, the United Nations Educational, Scientific and Cultural Organization and the World Health Organization, as well as in other international organizations,

Recognizing also the progress made by certain States on a regional or bilateral basis towards the protection of the rights of migrant workers and members of their families, as well as the importance and usefulness of bilateral and multilateral agreements in this field,

Realizing the importance and extent of the migration phenomenon, which involves millions of people and affects a large number of States in the international community,

Aware of the impact of the flows of migrant workers on States and people concerned, and desiring to establish norms which may contribute to the harmonization of the attitudes of States through the acceptance of basic principles concerning the treatment of migrant workers and members of their families,

Considering the situation of vulnerability in which migrant workers and members of their families frequently find themselves owing, among other things, to their absence from their State of origin and to the difficulties they may encounter arising from their presence in the State of employment,

Convinced that the rights of migrant workers and members of their families have not been sufficiently recognized everywhere and therefore require appropriate international protection,

Taking into account the fact that migration is often the cause of serious problems for the members of the families of migrant workers as well as for the workers themselves, in particular because of the scattering of the family,

Bearing in mind that the human problems involved in migration are even more serious in the case of irregular migration and convinced therefore that appropriate action should be encouraged in order to prevent and eliminate clandestine movements and trafficking in migrant workers, while at the same time assuring the protection of their fundamental human rights,

Considering that workers who are non-documented or in an irregular situation are frequently employed under less favourable conditions of work than other workers and that certain employers find this an inducement to seek such labour in order to reap the benefits of unfair competition,

Considering also that recourse to the employment of migrant workers who are in an irregular situation will be discouraged if the fundamental human rights of all migrant workers are more widely recognized and, moreover, that granting certain additional rights to migrant workers and members of their families in a regular situation will encourage all migrants and employers to respect and comply with the laws and procedures established by the States concerned,

Convinced, therefore, of the need to bring about the international protection of the rights of all migrant workers and members of their families, reaffirming and establishing basic norms in a comprehensive convention which could be applied universally,

Have agreed as follows:

PART I SCOPE AND DEFINITIONS

Article 1

1. The present Convention is applicable, except as otherwise provided hereafter, to all migrant workers and members of their families without distinction of any kind such as sex, race, colour, language, religion or conviction, political or other opinion, national, ethnic or social origin, nationality, age, economic position, property, marital status, birth or other status.

2. The present Convention shall apply during the entire migration process of migrant workers and members of their families, which comprises preparation for migration, departure, transit and the entire period of stay and remunerated activity in the State of employment as well as return to the State of origin or the State of habitual residence.

Article 2

For the purposes of the present Convention:

1. The term 'migrant worker' refers to a person who is to be engaged, is engaged or has been engaged in a remunerated activity in a State of which he or she is not a national.

2. (a) The term 'frontier worker' refers to a migrant worker who retains his or her habitual residence in a neighbouring State to which he or she normally returns every day or at least once a week;

   (b) The term 'seasonal worker' refers to a migrant worker whose work by its character is dependent on seasonal conditions and is performed only during part of the year;

   (c) The term 'seafarer', which includes a fisherman, refers to a migrant worker employed on board a vessel registered in a State of which he or she is not a national;

   (d) The term 'worker on an offshore installation' refers to a migrant worker employed on an offshore installation that is under the jurisdiction of a State of which he or she is not a national;

   (e) The term 'itinerant worker' refers to a migrant worker who, having his or her habitual residence in one State, has to travel to another State or States for short periods, owing to the nature of his or her occupation;

   (f) The term 'project-tied worker' refers to a migrant worker admitted to a State of employment for a defined period to work solely on a specific project being carried out in that State by his or her employer;

   (g) The term 'specified-employment worker' refers to a migrant worker:

      (i) Who has been sent by his or her employer for a restricted and defined period of time to a State of employment to undertake a specific assignment or duty; or

      (ii) Who engages for a restricted and defined period of time in work that requires professional, commercial, technical or other highly specialized skill; or

      (iii) Who, upon the request of his or her employer in the State of employment, engages for a restricted and defined period of time in work whose nature is transitory or brief; and who is required to depart from the State of employment either at the expiration of his or her authorized period of stay, or earlier if he or she no longer undertakes that specific assignment or duty or engages in that work;

(h) The term 'self-employed worker' refers to a migrant worker who is engaged in a remunerated activity otherwise than under a contract of employment and who earns his or her living through this activity normally working alone or together with members of his or her family, and to any other migrant worker recognized as self-employed by applicable legislation of the State of employment or bilateral or multilateral agreements.

Article 3

The present Convention shall not apply to:

(a) Persons sent or employed by international organizations and agencies or persons sent or employed by a State outside its territory to perform official functions, whose admission and status are regulated by general international law or by specific international agreements or conventions;

(b) Persons sent or employed by a State or on its behalf outside its territory who participate in development programmes and other co-operation programmes, whose admission and status are regulated by agreement with the State of employment and who, in accordance with that agreement, are not considered migrant workers;

(c) Persons taking up residence in a State different from their State of origin as investors;

(d) Refugees and stateless persons, unless such application is provided for in the relevant national legislation of, or international instruments in force for, the State Party concerned;

(e) Students and trainees;

(f) Seafarers and workers on an offshore installation who have not been admitted to take up residence and engage in a remunerated activity in the State of employment.

Article 4

For the purposes of the present Convention the term 'members of the family' refers to persons married to migrant workers or having with them a relationship that, according to applicable law, produces effects equivalent to marriage, as well as their dependent children and other dependent persons who are recognized as members of the family by applicable legislation or applicable bilateral or multilateral agreements between the States concerned.

Article 5

For the purposes of the present Convention, migrant workers and members of their families:

(a) Are considered as documented or in a regular situation if they are authorized to enter, to stay and to engage in a remunerated activity in the State of employment pursuant to the law of that State and to international agreements to which that State is a party;

(b) Are considered as non-documented or in an irregular situation if they do not comply with the conditions provided for in subparagraph (a) of the present article.

Article 6

For the purposes of the present Convention:

(a) The term 'State of origin' means the State of which the person concerned is a national;

(b) The term 'State of employment' means a State where the migrant worker is to be engaged, is engaged or has been engaged in a remunerated activity, as the case may be;

(c) The term 'State of transit,' means any State through which the person concerned passes on any journey to the State of employment or from the State of employment to the State of origin or the State of habitual residence.

PART II NON-DISCRIMINATION WITH RESPECT TO RIGHTS

Article 7

States Parties undertake, in accordance with the international instruments concerning human rights, to respect and to ensure to all migrant workers and members of their families within their territory or subject to their jurisdiction the rights provided for in the present Convention without distinction of any kind such as to sex, race, colour, language, religion or conviction, political or other opinion, national, ethnic or social origin, nationality, age, economic position, property, marital status, birth or other status.

PART III HUMAN RIGHTS OF ALL MIGRANT WORKERS AND MEMBERS OF THEIR FAMILIES

Article 8
1. Migrant workers and members of their families shall be free to leave any State, including their State of origin. This right shall not be subject to any restrictions except those that are provided by law, are necessary to protect national security, public order (*ordre public*), public health or morals or the rights and freedoms of others and are consistent with the other rights recognized in the present part of the Convention.

2. Migrant workers and members of their families shall have the right at any time to enter and remain in their State of origin.

Article 9
The right to life of migrant workers and members of their families shall be protected by law.

Article 10
No migrant worker or member of his or her family shall be subjected to torture or to cruel, inhuman or degrading treatment or punishment.

Article 11
1. No migrant worker or member of his or her family shall be held in slavery or servitude.

2. No migrant worker or member of his or her family shall be required to perform forced or compulsory labour.

3. Paragraph 2 of the present article shall not be held to preclude, in States where imprisonment with hard labour may be imposed as a punishment for a crime, the performance of hard labour in pursuance of a sentence to such punishment by a competent court.

4. For the purpose of the present article the term 'forced or compulsory labour' shall not include:
   (a) Any work or service not referred to in paragraph 3 of the present article normally required of a person who is under detention in consequence of a lawful order of a court or of a person during conditional release from such detention;
   (b) Any service exacted in cases of emergency or calamity threatening the life or well-being of the community;
   (c) Any work or service that forms part of normal civil obligations so far as it is imposed also on citizens of the State concerned.

Article 12
1. Migrant workers and members of their families shall have the right to freedom of thought, conscience and religion. This right shall include freedom to have or to adopt a religion or belief of their choice and freedom either individually or in community with others and in public or private to manifest their religion or belief in worship, observance, practice and teaching.

2. Migrant workers and members of their families shall not be subject to coercion that would impair their freedom to have or to adopt a religion or belief of their choice.

3. Freedom to manifest one's religion or belief may be subject only to such limitations as are prescribed by law and are necessary to protect public safety, order, health or morals or the fundamental rights and freedoms of others.

4. States Parties to the present Convention undertake to have respect for the liberty of parents, at least one of whom is a migrant worker, and, when applicable, legal guardians to ensure the religious and moral education of their children in conformity with their own convictions.

Article 13

1. Migrant workers and members of their families shall have the right to hold opinions without interference.

2. Migrant workers and members of their families shall have the right to freedom of expression; this right shall include freedom to seek, receive and impart information and ideas of all kinds, regardless of frontiers, either orally, in writing or in print, in the form of art or through any other media of their choice.

3. The exercise of the right provided for in paragraph 2 of the present article carries with it special duties and responsibilities. It may therefore be subject to certain restrictions, but these shall only be such as are provided by law and are necessary:

(a) For respect of the rights or reputation of others;
(b) For the protection of the national security of the States concerned or of public order (*ordre public*) or of public health or morals;
(c) For the purpose of preventing any propaganda for war;
(d) For the purpose of preventing any advocacy of national, racial or religious hatred that constitutes incitement to discrimination, hostility or violence.

Article 14

No migrant worker or member of his or her family shall be subjected to arbitrary or unlawful interference with his or her privacy, family, home, correspondence or other communications, or to unlawful attacks on his or her honour and reputation. Each migrant worker and member of his or her family shall have the right to the protection of the law against such interference or attacks.

Article 15

No migrant worker or member of his or her family shall be arbitrarily deprived of property, whether owned individually or in association with others. Where, under the legislation in force in the State of employment, the assets of a migrant worker or a member of his or her family are expropriated in whole or in part, the person concerned shall have the right to fair and adequate compensation.

Article 16

1. Migrant workers and members of their families shall have the right to liberty and security of person.

2. Migrant workers and members of their families shall be entitled to effective protection by the State against violence, physical injury, threats and intimidation, whether by public officials or by private individuals, groups or institutions.

3. Any verification by law enforcement officials of the identity of migrant workers or members of their families shall be carried out in accordance with procedure established by law.

4. Migrant workers and members of their families shall not be subjected individually or collectively to arbitrary arrest or detention; they shall not be deprived of their liberty except on such grounds and in accordance with such procedures as are established by law.

5. Migrant workers and members of their families who are arrested shall be informed at the time of arrest as far as possible in a language they understand of the reasons for their arrest and they shall be promptly informed in a language they understand of any charges against them.

6. Migrant workers and members of their families who are arrested or detained on a criminal charge shall be brought promptly before a judge or other officer authorized by law to exercise judicial power and shall be entitled to trial within a reasonable time or to release. It shall not be the general rule that while awaiting trial they shall be detained in custody, but release may be subject to guarantees to appear for trial, at any other stage of the judicial proceedings and, should the occasion arise, for the execution of the judgement.

7. When a migrant worker or a member of his or her family is arrested or committed to prison or custody pending trial or is detained in any other manner:

    (a) The consular or diplomatic authorities of his or her State of origin or of a State representing the interests of that State shall, if he or she so requests, be informed without delay of his or her arrest or detention and of the reasons therefor;

    (b) The person concerned shall have the right to communicate with the said authorities. Any communication by the person concerned to the said authorities shall be forwarded without delay, and he or she shall also have the right to receive communications sent by the said authorities without delay;

    (c) The person concerned shall be informed without delay of this right and of rights deriving from relevant treaties, if any, applicable between the States concerned, to correspond and to meet with representatives of the said authorities and to make arrangements with them for his or her legal representation.

8. Migrant workers and members of their families who are deprived of their liberty by arrest or detention shall be entitled to take proceedings before a court, in order that that court may decide without delay on the lawfulness of their detention and order their release if the detention is not lawful. When they attend such proceedings, they shall have the assistance, if necessary without cost to them, of an interpreter, if they cannot understand or speak the language used.

9. Migrant workers and members of their families who have been victims of unlawful arrest or detention shall have an enforceable right to compensation.

Article 17

1. Migrant workers and members of their families who are deprived of their liberty shall be treated with humanity and with respect for the inherent dignity of the human person and for their cultural identity.

2. Accused migrant workers and members of their families shall, save in exceptional circumstances, be separated from convicted persons and shall be subject to separate treatment appropriate to their status as unconvicted persons. Accused juvenile persons shall be separated from adults and brought as speedily as possible for adjudication.

3. Any migrant worker or member of his or her family who is detained in a State of transit or in a State of employment for violation of provisions relating to migration shall be held, in so far as practicable, separately from convicted persons or persons detained pending trial.

4. During any period of imprisonment in pursuance of a sentence imposed by a court of law, the essential aim of the treatment of a migrant worker or a member of his or her family shall be his or her reformation and social rehabilitation. Juvenile offenders shall be separated from adults and be accorded treatment appropriate to their age and legal status.

5. During detention or imprisonment, migrant workers and members of their families shall enjoy the same rights as nationals to visits by members of their families.

6. Whenever a migrant worker is deprived of his or her liberty, the competent authorities of the State concerned shall pay attention to the problems that may be posed for members of his or her family, in particular for spouses and minor children.

7. Migrant workers and members of their families who are subjected to any form of detention or imprisonment in accordance with the law in force in the State of employment or in the State of transit shall enjoy the same rights as nationals of those States who are in the same situation.

8. If a migrant worker or a member of his or her family is detained for the purpose of verifying any infraction of provisions related to migration, he or she shall not bear any costs arising therefrom.

Article 18

1. Migrant workers and members of their families shall have the right to equality with nationals of the State concerned before the courts and tribunals. In the determination of any criminal charge against them or of their rights and obligations in a suit of law, they shall be entitled to a fair and public hearing by a competent, independent and impartial tribunal established by law.

2. Migrant workers and members of their families who are charged with a criminal offence shall have the right to be presumed innocent until proven guilty according to law.

3. In the determination of any criminal charge against them, migrant workers and members of their families shall be entitled to the following minimum guarantees:

    (a) To be informed promptly and in detail in a language they understand of the nature and cause of the charge against them;

    (b) To have adequate time and facilities for the preparation of their defence and to communicate with counsel of their own choosing;

    (c) To be tried without undue delay;

    (d) To be tried in their presence and to defend themselves in person or through legal assistance of their own choosing; to be informed, if they do not have legal assistance, of this right; and to have legal assistance assigned to them, in any case where the interests of justice so require and without payment by them in any such case if they do not have sufficient means to pay;

    (e) To examine or have examined the witnesses against them and to obtain the attendance and examination of witnesses on their behalf under the same conditions as witnesses against them;

    (f) To have the free assistance of an interpreter if they cannot understand or speak the language used in court;

    (g) Not to be compelled to testify against themselves or to confess guilt.

4. In the case of juvenile persons, the procedure shall be such as will take account of their age and the desirability of promoting their rehabilitation.

5. Migrant workers and members of their families convicted of a crime shall have the right to their conviction and sentence being reviewed by a higher tribunal according to law.

6. When a migrant worker or a member of his or her family has, by a final decision, been convicted of a criminal offence and when subsequently his or her conviction has been reversed or he or she has been pardoned on the ground that a new or newly discovered fact shows conclusively that there has been a miscarriage of justice, the person who has suffered punishment as a result of such conviction shall be compensated according to law, unless it is proved that the non-disclosure of the unknown fact in time is wholly or partly attributable to that person.

7. No migrant worker or member of his or her family shall be liable to be tried or punished again for an offence for which he or she has already been finally convicted or acquitted in accordance with the law and penal procedure of the State concerned.

Article 19

1. No migrant worker or member of his or her family shall be held guilty of any criminal offence on account of any act or omission that did not constitute a criminal offence under national or international law at the time when the criminal offence was committed, nor shall a heavier penalty be imposed than the one that was applicable at the time when it was committed. If, subsequent to the commission of the offence, provision is made by law for the imposition of a lighter penalty, he or she shall benefit thereby.

2. Humanitarian considerations related to the status of a migrant worker, in particular with respect to his or her right of residence or work, should be taken into account in imposing a sentence for a criminal offence committed by a migrant worker or a member of his or her family.

Article 20

1. No migrant worker or member of his or her family shall be imprisoned merely on the ground of failure to fulfil a contractual obligation.

2. No migrant worker or member of his or her family shall be deprived of his or her authorization of residence or work permit or expelled merely on the ground of failure to fulfil an obligation arising out of a work contract unless fulfilment of that obligation constitutes a condition for such authorization or permit.

Article 21

It shall be unlawful for anyone, other than a public official duly authorized by law, to confiscate, destroy or attempt to destroy identity documents, documents authorizing entry to or stay, residence or establishment in the national territory or work permits. No authorized confiscation of such documents shall take place without delivery of a detailed receipt. In no case shall it be permitted to destroy the passport or equivalent document of a migrant worker or a member of his or her family.

Article 22

1. Migrant workers and members of their families shall not be subject to measures of collective expulsion. Each case of expulsion shall be examined and decided individually.

2. Migrant workers and members of their families may be expelled from the territory of a State Party only in pursuance of a decision taken by the competent authority in accordance with law.

3. The decision shall be communicated to them in a language they understand. Upon their request where not otherwise mandatory, the decision shall be communicated to them in writing and, save in exceptional circumstances on account of national security, the reasons for the decision likewise stated. The persons concerned shall be informed of these rights before or at the latest at the time the decision is rendered.

4. Except where a final decision is pronounced by a judicial authority, the person concerned shall have the right to submit the reason he or she should not be expelled and to have his or her case reviewed by the competent authority, unless compelling reasons of national security require otherwise. Pending such review, the person concerned shall have the right to seek a stay of the decision of expulsion.

5. If a decision of expulsion that has already been executed is subsequently annulled, the person concerned shall have the right to seek compensation according to law and the earlier decision shall not be used to prevent him or her from re-entering the State concerned.

6. In case of expulsion, the person concerned shall have a reasonable opportunity before or after departure to settle any claims for wages and other entitlements due to him or her and any pending liabilities.

7. Without prejudice to the execution of a decision of expulsion, a migrant worker or a member of his or her family who is subject to such a decision may seek entry into a State other than his or her State of origin.

8. In case of expulsion of a migrant worker or a member of his or her family the costs of expulsion shall not be borne by him or her. The person concerned may be required to pay his or her own travel costs.

9. Expulsion from the State of employment shall not in itself prejudice any rights of a migrant worker or a member of his or her family acquired in accordance with the law of that State, including the right to receive wages and other entitlements due to him or her.

Article 23

Migrant workers and members of their families shall have the right to have recourse to the protection and assistance of the consular or diplomatic authorities of their State of origin or of a State representing the interests of that State whenever the rights recognized in the present Convention are impaired. In particular, in case of expulsion, the person concerned shall be informed of this right without delay and the authorities of the expelling State shall facilitate the exercise of such right.

Article 24

Every migrant worker and every member of his or her family shall have the right to recognition everywhere as a person before the law.

Article 25

1. Migrant workers shall enjoy treatment not less favourable than that which applies to nationals of the State of employment in respect of remuneration and:

　　(a) Other conditions of work, that is to say, overtime, hours of work, weekly rest, holidays with pay, safety, health, termination of the employment relationship and any other conditions of work which, according to national law and practice, are covered by these terms;

(b) Other terms of employment, that is to say, minimum age of employment, restriction on home work and any other matters which, according to national law and practice, are considered a term of employment.

2. It shall not be lawful to derogate in private contracts of employment from the principle of equality of treatment referred to in paragraph 1 of the present article.

3. States Parties shall take all appropriate measures to ensure that migrant workers are not deprived of any rights derived from this principle by reason of any irregularity in their stay or employment. In particular, employers shall not be relieved of any legal or contractual obligations, nor shall their obligations be limited in any manner by reason of such irregularity.

Article 26

1. States Parties recognize the right of migrant workers and members of their families:

(a) To take part in meetings and activities of trade unions and of any other associations established in accordance with law, with a view to protecting their economic, social, cultural and other interests, subject only to the rules of the organization concerned;

(b) To join freely any trade union and any such association as aforesaid, subject only to the rules of the organization concerned;

(c) To seek the aid and assistance of any trade union and of any such association as aforesaid.

2. No restrictions may be placed on the exercise of these rights other than those that are prescribed by law and which are necessary in a democratic society in the interests of national security, public order (*ordre public*) or the protection of the rights and freedoms of others.

Article 27

1. With respect to social security, migrant workers and members of their families shall enjoy in the State of employment the same treatment granted to nationals in so far as they fulfil the requirements provided for by the applicable legislation of that State and the applicable bilateral and multilateral treaties. The competent authorities of the State of origin and the State of employment can at any time establish the necessary arrangements to determine the modalities of application of this norm.

2. Where the applicable legislation does not allow migrant workers and members of their families a benefit, the States concerned shall examine the possibility of reimbursing interested persons the amount of contributions made by them with respect to that benefit on the basis of the treatment granted to nationals who are in similar circumstances.

Article 28

Migrant workers and members of their families shall have the right to receive any medical care that is urgently required for the preservation of their life or the avoidance of irreparable harm to their health on the basis of equality of treatment with nationals of the State concerned. Such emergency medical care shall not be refused them by reason of any irregularity with regard to stay or employment.

Article 29

Each child of a migrant worker shall have the right to a name, to registration of birth and to a nationality.

Article 30

Each child of a migrant worker shall have the basic right of access to education on the basis of equality of treatment with nationals of the State concerned. Access to public pre-school educational institutions or schools shall not be refused or limited by reason of the irregular situation with respect to stay or employment of either parent or by reason of the irregularity of the child's stay in the State of employment.

Article 31

1. States Parties shall ensure respect for the cultural identity of migrant workers and members of their families and shall not prevent them from maintaining their cultural links with their State of origin.

2. States Parties may take appropriate measures to assist and encourage efforts in this respect.

Article 32

Upon the termination of their stay in the State of employment, migrant workers and members of their families shall have the right to transfer their earnings and savings and, in accordance with the applicable legislation of the States concerned, their personal effects and belongings.

Article 33

1. Migrant workers and members of their families shall have the right to be informed by the State of origin, the State of employment or the State of transit as the case may be concerning:

    (a) Their rights arising out of the present Convention;

    (b) The conditions of their admission, their rights and obligations under the law and practice of the State concerned and such other matters as will enable them to comply with administrative or other formalities in that State.

2. States Parties shall take all measures they deem appropriate to disseminate the said information or to ensure that it is provided by employers, trade unions or other appropriate bodies or institutions. As appropriate, they shall co-operate with other States concerned.

3. Such adequate information shall be provided upon request to migrant workers and members of their families, free of charge, and, as far as possible, in a language they are able to understand.

Article 34

Nothing in the present part of the Convention shall have the effect of relieving migrant workers and the members of their families from either the obligation to comply with the laws and regulations of any State of transit and the State of employment or the obligation to respect the cultural identity of the inhabitants of such States.

Article 35

Nothing in the present part of the Convention shall be interpreted as implying the regularization of the situation of migrant workers or members of their families who are non-documented or in an irregular situation or any right to such regularization of their situation, nor shall it prejudice the measures intended to ensure sound and equitable conditions for international migration as provided in part VI of the present Convention.

PART IV OTHER RIGHTS OF MIGRANT WORKERS AND MEMBERS OF THEIR FAMILIES WHO ARE DOCUMENTED OR IN A REGULAR SITUATION

Article 36

Migrant workers and members of their families who are documented or in a regular situation in the State of employment shall enjoy the rights set forth in the present part of the Convention in addition to those set forth in part III.

Article 37

Before their departure, or at the latest at the time of their admission to the State of employment, migrant workers and members of their families shall have the right to be fully informed by the State of origin or the State of employment, as appropriate, of all conditions applicable to their admission and particularly those concerning their stay and the remunerated activities in which they may engage as well as of the requirements they must satisfy in the State of employment and the authority to which they must address themselves for any modification of those conditions.

Article 38

1. States of employment shall make every effort to authorize migrant workers and members of the families to be temporarily absent without effect upon their authorization to stay or to work, as the case may be. In doing so, States of employment shall take into account the special needs and obligations of migrant workers and members of their families, in particular in their States of origin.

2. Migrant workers and members of their families shall have the right to be fully informed of the terms on which such temporary absences are authorized.

Article 39

1. Migrant workers and members of their families shall have the right to liberty of movement in the territory of the State of employment and freedom to choose their residence there.

2. The rights mentioned in paragraph 1 of the present article shall not be subject to any restrictions except those that are provided by law, are necessary to protect national security, public order (*ordre public*), public health or morals, or the rights and freedoms of others and are consistent with the other rights recognized in the present Convention.

Article 40

1. Migrant workers and members of their families shall have the right to form associations and trade unions in the State of employment for the promotion and protection of their economic, social, cultural and other interests.

2. No restrictions may be placed on the exercise of this right other than those that are prescribed by law and are necessary in a democratic society in the interests of national security, public order (*ordre public*) or the protection of the rights and freedoms of others.

Article 41

1. Migrant workers and members of their families shall have the right to participate in public affairs of their State of origin and to vote and to be elected at elections of that State, in accordance with its legislation.

2. The States concerned shall, as appropriate and in accordance with their legislation, facilitate the exercise of these rights.

Article 42

1. States Parties shall consider the establishment of procedures or institutions through which account may be taken, both in States of origin and in States of employment, of special needs, aspirations and obligations of migrant workers and members of their families and shall envisage, as appropriate, the possibility for migrant workers and members of their families to have their freely chosen representatives in those institutions.

2. States of employment shall facilitate, in accordance with their national legislation, the consultation or participation of migrant workers and members of their families in decisions concerning the life and administration of local communities.

3. Migrant workers may enjoy political rights in the State of employment if that State, in the exercise of its sovereignty, grants them such rights.

Article 43

1. Migrant workers shall enjoy equality of treatment with nationals of the State of employment in relation to:
  (a) Access to educational institutions and services subject to the admission requirements and other regulations of the institutions and services concerned;
  (b) Access to vocational guidance and placement services;
  (c) Access to vocational training and retraining facilities and institutions;
  (d) Access to housing, including social housing schemes, and protection against exploitation in respect of rents;
  (e) Access to social and health services, provided that the requirements for participation in the respective schemes are met;
  (f) Access to co-operatives and self-managed enterprises, which shall not imply a change of their migration status and shall be subject to the rules and regulations of the bodies concerned;
  (g) Access to and participation in cultural life.

2. States Parties shall promote conditions to ensure effective equality of treatment to enable migrant workers to enjoy the rights mentioned in paragraph 1 of the present article whenever the terms of their stay, as authorized by the State of employment, meet the appropriate requirements.

3. States of employment shall not prevent an employer of migrant workers from establishing housing or social or cultural facilities for them. Subject to article 70 of the present Convention, a State of employment may make the establishment of such facilities subject to the requirements generally applied in that State concerning their installation.

Article 44

1. States Parties, recognizing that the family is the natural and fundamental group unit of society and is entitled to protection by society and the State, shall take appropriate measures to ensure the protection of the unity of the families of migrant workers.

2. States Parties shall take measures that they deem appropriate and that fall within their competence to facilitate the reunification of migrant workers with their spouses or persons who have with the migrant worker a relationship that, according to applicable law, produces effects equivalent to marriage, as well as with their minor dependent unmarried children.

3. States of employment, on humanitarian grounds, shall favourably consider granting equal treatment, as set forth in paragraph 2 of the present article, to other family members of migrant workers.

Article 45

1. Members of the families of migrant workers shall, in the State of employment, enjoy equality of treatment with nationals of that State in relation to:
    (a) Access to educational institutions and services, subject to the admission requirements and other regulations of the institutions and services concerned;
    (b) Access to vocational guidance and training institutions and services, provided that requirements for participation are met;
    (c) Access to social and health services, provided that requirements for participation in the respective schemes are met;
    (d) Access to and participation in cultural life.

2. States of employment shall pursue a policy, where appropriate in collaboration with the States of origin, aimed at facilitating the integration of children of migrant workers in the local school system, particularly in respect of teaching them the local language.

3. States of employment shall endeavour to facilitate for the children of migrant workers the teaching of their mother tongue and culture and, in this regard, States of origin shall collaborate whenever appropriate.

4. States of employment may provide special schemes of education in the mother tongue of children of migrant workers, if necessary in collaboration with the States of origin.

Article 46

Migrant workers and members of their families shall, subject to the applicable legislation of the States concerned, as well as relevant international agreements and the obligations of the States concerned arising out of their participation in customs unions, enjoy exemption from import and export duties and taxes in respect of their personal and household effects as well as the equipment necessary to engage in the remunerated activity for which they were admitted to the State of employment:
    (a) Upon departure from the State of origin or State of habitual residence;
    (b) Upon initial admission to the State of employment;
    (c) Upon final departure from the State of employment;
    (d) Upon final return to the State of origin or State of habitual residence.

Article 47

1. Migrant workers shall have the right to transfer their earnings and savings, in particular those funds necessary for the support of their families, from the State of employment to their State of origin

or any other State. Such transfers shall be made in conformity with procedures established by applicable legislation of the State concerned and in conformity with applicable international agreements.

2. States concerned shall take appropriate measures to facilitate such transfers.

Article 48

1. Without prejudice to applicable double taxation agreements, migrant workers and members of their families shall, in the matter of earnings in the State of employment:
    (a) Not be liable to taxes, duties or charges of any description higher or more onerous than those imposed on nationals in similar circumstances;
    (b) Be entitled to deductions or exemptions from taxes of any description and to any tax allowances applicable to nationals in similar circumstances, including tax allowances for dependent members of their families.

2. States Parties shall endeavour to adopt appropriate measures to avoid double taxation of the earnings and savings of migrant workers and members of their families.

Article 49

1. Where separate authorizations to reside and to engage in employment are required by national legislation, the States of employment shall issue to migrant workers authorization of residence for at least the same period of time as their authorization to engage in remunerated activity.

2. Migrant workers who in the State of employment are allowed freely to choose their remunerated activity shall neither be regarded as in an irregular situation nor shall they lose their authorization of residence by the mere fact of the termination of their remunerated activity prior to the expiration of their work permits or similar authorizations.

3. In order to allow migrant workers referred to in paragraph 2 of the present article sufficient time to find alternative remunerated activities, the authorization of residence shall not be withdrawn at least for a period corresponding to that during which they may be entitled to unemployment benefits.

Article 50

1. In the case of death of a migrant worker or dissolution of marriage, the State of employment shall favourably consider granting family members of that migrant worker residing in that State on the basis of family reunion an authorization to stay; the State of employment shall take into account the length of time they have already resided in that State.

2. Members of the family to whom such authorization is not granted shall be allowed before departure a reasonable period of time in order to enable them to settle their affairs in the State of employment.

3. The provisions of paragraphs 1 and 2 of the present article may not be interpreted as adversely affecting any right to stay and work otherwise granted to such family members by the legislation of the State of employment or by bilateral and multilateral treaties applicable to that State.

Article 51

Migrant workers who in the State of employment are not permitted freely to choose their remunerated activity shall neither be regarded as in an irregular situation nor shall they lose their authorization of residence by the mere fact of the termination of their remunerated activity prior to the expiration of their work permit, except where the authorization of residence is expressly dependent upon the specific remunerated activity for which they were admitted. Such migrant workers shall have the right to seek alternative employment, participation in public work schemes and retraining during the remaining period of their authorization to work, subject to such conditions and limitations as are specified in the authorization to work.

Article 52

1. Migrant workers in the State of employment shall have the right freely to choose their remunerated activity, subject to the following restrictions or conditions.

2. For any migrant worker a State of employment may:
    (a) Restrict access to limited categories of employment, functions, services or activities where this is necessary in the interests of this State and provided for by national legislation;
    (b) Restrict free choice of remunerated activity in accordance with its legislation concerning recognition of occupational qualifications acquired outside its territory. However, States Parties concerned shall endeavour to provide for recognition of such qualifications.
3. For migrant workers whose permission to work is limited in time, a State of employment may also:
    (a) Make the right freely to choose their remunerated activities subject to the condition that the migrant worker has resided lawfully in its territory for the purpose of remunerated activity for a period of time prescribed in its national legislation that should not exceed two years;
    (b) Limit access by a migrant worker to remunerated activities in pursuance of a policy of granting priority to its nationals or to persons who are assimilated to them for these purposes by virtue of legislation or bilateral or multilateral agreements. Any such limitation shall cease to apply to a migrant worker who has resided lawfully in its territory for the purpose of remunerated activity for a period of time prescribed in its national legislation that should not exceed five years.
4. States of employment shall prescribe the conditions under which a migrant worker who has been admitted to take up employment may be authorized to engage in work on his or her own account. Account shall be taken of the period during which the worker has already been lawfully in the State of employment.

Article 53

1. Members of a migrant worker's family who have themselves an authorization of residence or admission that is without limit of time or is automatically renewable shall be permitted freely to choose their remunerated activity under the same conditions as are applicable to the said migrant worker in accordance with article 52 of the present Convention.

2. With respect to members of a migrant worker's family who are not permitted freely to choose their remunerated activity, States Parties shall consider favourably granting them priority in obtaining permission to engage in a remunerated activity over other workers who seek admission to the State of employment, subject to applicable bilateral and multilateral agreements.

Article 54

1. Without prejudice to the terms of their authorization of residence or their permission to work and the rights provided for in articles 25 and 27 of the present Convention, migrant workers shall enjoy equality of treatment with nationals of the State of employment in respect of:
    (a) Protection against dismissal;
    (b) Unemployment benefits;
    (c) Access to public work schemes intended to combat unemployment;
    (d) Access to alternative employment in the event of loss of work or termination of other remunerated activity, subject to article 52 of the present Convention.
2. If a migrant worker claims that the terms of his or her work contract have been violated by his or her employer, he or she shall have the right to address his or her case to the competent authorities of the State of employment, on terms provided for in article 18, paragraph 1, of the present Convention.

Article 55

Migrant workers who have been granted permission to engage in a remunerated activity, subject to the conditions attached to such permission, shall be entitled to equality of treatment with nationals of the State of employment in the exercise of that remunerated activity.

Article 56

1. Migrant workers and members of their families referred to in the present part of the Convention may not be expelled from a State of employment, except for reasons defined in the national legislation of that State, and subject to the safeguards established in part III.

2. Expulsion shall not be resorted to for the purpose of depriving a migrant worker or a member of his or her family of the rights arising out of the authorization of residence and the work permit.

3. In considering whether to expel a migrant worker or a member of his or her family, account should be taken of humanitarian considerations and of the length of time that the person concerned has already resided in the State of employment.

PART V PROVISIONS APPLICABLE TO PARTICULAR CATEGORIES OF MIGRANT WORKERS AND OF THEIR FAMILIES

Article 57

The particular categories of migrant workers and members of their families specified in the present part of the Convention who are documented or in a regular situation shall enjoy the rights set forth in part III and, except as modified below, the rights set forth in part IV.

Article 58

1. Frontier workers, as defined in article 2, paragraph 2(a), of the present Convention, shall be entitled to the rights provided for in part IV that can be applied to them by reason of their presence and work in the territory of the State of employment, taking into account that they do not have their habitual residence in that State.

2. States of employment shall consider favourably granting frontier workers the right freely to choose their remunerated activity after a specified period of time. The granting of that right shall not affect their status as frontier workers.

Article 59

1. Seasonal workers, as defined in article 2, paragraph 2(b), of the present Convention, shall be entitled to the rights provided for in part IV that can be applied to them by reason of their presence and work in the territory of the State of employment and that are compatible with their status in that State as seasonal workers, taking into account the fact that they are present in that State for only part of the year.

2. The State of employment shall, subject to paragraph 1 of the present article, consider granting seasonal workers who have been employed in its territory for a significant period of time the possibility of taking up other remunerated activities and giving them priority over other workers who seek admission to that State, subject to applicable bilateral and multilateral agreements.

Article 60

Itinerant workers, as defined in article 2, paragraph 2(A), of the present Convention, shall be entitled to the rights provided for in part IV that can be granted to them by reason of their presence and work in the territory of the State of employment and that are compatible with their status as itinerant workers in that State.

Article 61

1. Project-tied workers, as defined in article 2, paragraph 2 of the present Convention, and members of their families shall be entitled to the rights provided for in part IV except the provisions of article 43, paragraphs 1(b) and(c), article 43, paragraph 1(d), as it pertains to social housing schemes, article 45, paragraph 1(b), and articles 52 to 55.

2. If a project-tied worker claims that the terms of his or her work contract have been violated by his or her employer, he or she shall have the right to address his or her case to the competent authorities of the State which has jurisdiction over that employer, on terms provided for in article 18, paragraph 1, of the present Convention.

3. Subject to bilateral or multilateral agreements in force for them, the States Parties concerned shall endeavour to enable project-tied workers to remain adequately protected by the social security systems of their States of origin or habitual residence during their engagement in the project. States Parties concerned shall take appropriate measures with the aim of avoiding any denial of rights or duplication of payments in this respect.

4. Without prejudice to the provisions of article 47 of the present Convention and to relevant bilateral or multilateral agreements, States Parties concerned shall permit payment of the earnings of project-tied workers in their State of origin or habitual residence.

Article 62

1. Specified-employment workers as defined in article 2, paragraph 2(g), of the present Convention, shall be entitled to the rights provided for in part IV, except the provisions of article 43, paragraphs 1(b) and (c), article 43, paragraph 1(d), as it pertains to social housing schemes, article 52, and article 54, paragraph 1(d).

2. Members of the families of specified-employment workers shall be entitled to the rights relating to family members of migrant workers provided for in part IV of the present Convention, except the provisions of article 53.

Article 63

1. Self-employed workers, as defined in article 2, paragraph 2(h), of the present Convention, shall be entitled to the rights provided for in part IV with the exception of those rights which are exclusively applicable to workers having a contract of employment.

2. Without prejudice to articles 52 and 79 of the present Convention, the termination of the economic activity of the self-employed workers shall not in itself imply the withdrawal of the authorization for them or for the members of their families to stay or to engage in a remunerated activity in the State of employment except where the authorization of residence is expressly dependent upon the specific remunerated activity for which they were admitted.

PART VI PROMOTION OF SOUND, EQUITABLE, HUMANE AND LAWFUL CONDITIONS IN CONNECTION WITH INTERNATIONAL MIGRATION OF WORKERS AND MEMBERS OF THEIR FAMILIES

Article 64

1. Without prejudice to article 79 of the present Convention, the States Parties concerned shall as appropriate consult and co-operate with a view to promoting sound, equitable and humane conditions in connection with international migration of workers and members of their families.

2. In this respect, due regard shall be paid not only to labour needs and resources, but also to the social, economic, cultural and other needs of migrant workers and members of their families involved, as well as to the consequences of such migration for the communities concerned.

Article 65

1. States Parties shall maintain appropriate services to deal with questions concerning international migration of workers and members of their families. Their functions shall include, *inter alia*:

    (a) The formulation and implementation of policies regarding such migration;

    (b) An exchange of information. consultation and co-operation with the competent authorities of other States Parties involved in such migration;

(c) The provision of appropriate information, particularly to employers, workers and their organizations on policies, laws and regulations relating to migration and employment, on agreements concluded with other States concerning migration and on other relevant matters;

(d) The provision of information and appropriate assistance to migrant workers and members of their families regarding requisite authorizations and formalities and arrangements for departure, travel, arrival, stay, remunerated activities, exit and return, as well as on conditions of work and life in the State of employment and on customs, currency, tax and other relevant laws and regulations.

2. States Parties shall facilitate as appropriate the provision of adequate consular and other services that are necessary to meet the social, cultural and other needs of migrant workers and members of their families.

Article 66

1. Subject to paragraph 2 of the present article, the right to undertake operations with a view to the recruitment of workers for employment in another State shall be restricted to:

(a) Public services or bodies of the State in which such operations take place;

(b) Public services or bodies of the State of employment on the basis of agreement between the States concerned;

(c) A body established by virtue of a bilateral or multilateral agreement.

2. Subject to any authorization, approval and supervision by the public authorities of the States Parties concerned as may be established pursuant to the legislation and practice of those States, agencies, prospective employers or persons acting on their behalf may also be permitted to undertake the said operations.

Article 67

1. States Parties concerned shall co-operate as appropriate in the adoption of measures regarding the orderly return of migrant workers and members of their families to the State of origin when they decide to return or their authorization of residence or employment expires or when they are in the State of employment in an irregular situation.

2. Concerning migrant workers and members of their families in a regular situation, States Parties concerned shall co-operate as appropriate, on terms agreed upon by those States, with a view to promoting adequate economic conditions for their resettlement and to facilitating their durable social and cultural reintegration in the State of origin.

Article 68

1. States Parties, including States of transit, shall collaborate with a view to preventing and eliminating illegal or clandestine movements and employment of migrant workers in an irregular situation. The measures to be taken to this end within the jurisdiction of each State concerned shall include:

(a) Appropriate measures against the dissemination of misleading information relating to emigration and immigration;

(b) Measures to detect and eradicate illegal or clandestine movements of migrant workers and members of their families and to impose effective sanctions on persons, groups or entities which organize, operate or assist in organizing or operating such movements;

(c) Measures to impose effective sanctions on persons, groups or entities which use violence, threats or intimidation against migrant workers or members of their families in an irregular situation.

2. States of employment shall take all adequate and effective measures to eliminate employment in their territory of migrant workers in an irregular situation, including, whenever appropriate, sanctions on employers of such workers. The rights of migrant workers vis-à-vis their employer arising from employment shall not be impaired by these measures.

Article 69

1. States Parties shall, when there are migrant workers and members of their families within their territory in an irregular situation, take appropriate measures to ensure that such a situation does not persist.

2. Whenever States Parties concerned consider the possibility of regularizing the situation of such persons in accordance with applicable national legislation and bilateral or multilateral agreements, appropriate account shall be taken of the circumstances of their entry, the duration of their stay in the States of employment and other relevant considerations, in particular those relating to their family situation.

Article 70

States Parties shall take measures not less favourable than those applied to nationals to ensure that working and living conditions of migrant workers and members of their families in a regular situation are in keeping with the standards of fitness, safety, health and principles of human dignity.

Article 71

1. States Parties shall facilitate, whenever necessary, the repatriation to the State of origin of the bodies of deceased migrant workers or members of their families.

2. As regards compensation matters relating to the death of a migrant worker or a member of his or her family, States Parties shall, as appropriate, provide assistance to the persons concerned with a view to the prompt settlement of such matters. Settlement of these matters shall be carried out on the basis of applicable national law in accordance with the provisions of the present Convention and any relevant bilateral or multilateral agreements.

PART VII APPLICATION OF THE CONVENTION

Article 72

1. (a) For the purpose of reviewing the application of the present Convention, there shall be established a Committee on the Protection of the Rights of All Migrant Workers and Members of Their Families (hereinafter referred to as 'the Committee');

   (b) The Committee shall consist, at the time of entry into force of the present Convention, of ten and, after the entry into force of the Convention for the forty-first State Party, of fourteen experts of high moral standing, impartiality and recognized competence in the field covered by the Convention.

2. (a) Members of the Committee shall be elected by secret ballot by the States Parties from a list of persons nominated by the States Parties, due consideration being given to equitable geographical distribution, including both States of origin and States of employment, and to the representation of the principal legal system. Each State Party may nominate one person from among its own nationals;

   (b) Members shall be elected and shall serve in their personal capacity.

3. The initial election shall be held no later than six months after the date of the entry into force of the present Convention and subsequent elections every second year. At least four months before the date of each election, the Secretary-General of the United Nations shall address a letter to all States Parties inviting them to submit their nominations within two months. The Secretary-General shall prepare a list in alphabetical order of all persons thus nominated, indicating the States Parties that have nominated them, and shall submit it to the States Parties not later than one month before the date of the corresponding election, together with the curricula vitae of the persons thus nominated.

4. Elections of members of the Committee shall be held at a meeting of States Parties convened by the Secretary-General at United Nations Headquarters. At that meeting, for which two thirds of the States Parties shall constitute a quorum, the persons elected to the Committee shall be those

nominees who obtain the largest number of votes and an absolute majority of the votes of the States Parties present and voting.

    5. (a) The members of the Committee shall serve for a term of four years. However, the terms of five of the members elected in the first election shall expire at the end of two years; immediately after the first election, the names of these five members shall be chosen by lot by the Chairman of the meeting of States Parties;

     (b) The election of the four additional members of the Committee shall be held in accordance with the provisions of paragraphs 2, 3 and 4 of the present article, following the entry into force of the Convention for the forty-first State Party. The term of two of the additional members elected on this occasion shall expire at the end of two years; the names of these members shall be chosen by lot by the Chairman of the meeting of States Parties;

     (c) The members of the Committee shall be eligible for re-election if renominated.

    6. If a member of the Committee dies or resigns or declares that for any other cause he or she can no longer perform the duties of the Committee, the State Party that nominated the expert shall appoint another expert from among its own nationals for the remaining part of the term. The new appointment is subject to the approval of the Committee.

    7. The Secretary-General of the United Nations shall provide the necessary staff and facilities for the effective performance of the functions of the Committee.

    8. The members of the Committee shall receive emoluments from United Nations resources on such terms and conditions as the General Assembly may decide.

    9. The members of the Committee shall be entitled to the facilities, privileges and immunities of experts on mission for the United Nations as laid down in the relevant sections of the Convention on the Privileges and Immunities of the United Nations.

Article 73

    1. States Parties undertake to submit to the Secretary-General of the United Nations for consideration by the Committee a report on the legislative, judicial, administrative and other measures they have taken to give effect to the provisions of the present Convention:

     (a) Within one year after the entry into force of the Convention for the State Party concerned;

     (b) Thereafter every five years and whenever the Committee so requests.

    2. Reports prepared under the present article shall also indicate factors and difficulties, if any, affecting the implementation of the Convention and shall include information on the characteristics of migration flows in which the State Party concerned is involved.

    3. The Committee shall decide any further guidelines applicable to the content of the reports.

    4. States Parties shall make their reports widely available to the public in their own countries.

Article 74

    1. The Committee shall examine the reports submitted by each State Party and shall transmit such comments as it may consider appropriate to the State Party concerned. This State Party may submit to the Committee observations on any comment made by the Committee in accordance with the present article. The Committee may request supplementary information from States Parties when considering these reports.

    2. The Secretary-General of the United Nations shall, in due time before the opening of each regular session of the Committee, transmit to the Director-General of the International Labour Office copies of the reports submitted by States Parties concerned and information relevant to the consideration of these reports, in order to enable the Office to assist the Committee with the expertise the Office may provide regarding those matters dealt with by the present Convention that fall within the sphere of competence of the International Labour Organisation. The Committee shall consider in its deliberations such comments and materials as the Office may provide.

    3. The Secretary-General of the United Nations may also, after consultation with the Committee, transmit to other specialized agencies as well as to intergovernmental organizations, copies of such parts of these reports as may fall within their competence.

4. The Committee may invite the specialized agencies and organs of the United Nations, as well as intergovernmental organizations and other concerned bodies to submit, for consideration by the Committee, written information on such matters dealt with in the present Convention as fall within the scope of their activities.

5. The International Labour Office shall be invited by the Committee to appoint representatives to participate, in a consultative capacity, in the meetings of the Committee.

6. The Committee may invite representatives of other specialized agencies and organs of the United Nations, as well as of intergovernmental organizations, to be present and to be heard in its meetings whenever matters falling within their field of competence are considered.

7. The Committee shall present an annual report to the General Assembly of the United Nations on the implementation of the present Convention, containing its own considerations and recommendations, based, in particular, on the examination of the reports and any observations presented by States Parties.

8. The Secretary-General of the United Nations shall transmit the annual reports of the Committee to the States Parties to the present Convention, the Economic and Social Council, the Commission on Human Rights of the United Nations, the Director-General of the International Labour Office and other relevant organizations.

Article 75

1. The Committee shall adopt its own rules of procedure.
2. The Committee shall elect its officers for a term of two years.
3. The Committee shall normally meet annually.
4. The meetings of the Committee shall normally be held at United Nations Headquarters.

Article 76

1. A State Party to the present Convention may at any time declare under this article that it recognizes the competence of the Committee to receive and consider communications to the effect that a State Party claims that another State Party is not fulfilling its obligations under the present Convention. Communications under this article may be received and considered only if submitted by a State Party that has made a declaration recognizing in regard to itself the competence of the Committee. No communication shall be received by the Committee if it concerns a State Party which has not made such a declaration. Communications received under this article shall be dealt with in accordance with the following procedure:

  (a) If a State Party to the present Convention considers that another State Party is not ful- filling its obligations under the present Convention, it may, by written communication, bring the matter to the attention of that State Party. The State Party may also inform the Committee of the matter. Within three months after the receipt of the communication the receiving State shall afford the State that sent the communication an explanation, or any other statement in writing clarifying the matter which should include, to the extent possible and pertinent, reference to domestic procedures and remedies taken, pending or available in the matter;

  (b) If the matter is not adjusted to the satisfaction of both States Parties concerned within six months after the receipt by the receiving State of the initial communication, either State shall have the right to refer the matter to the Committee, by notice given to the Committee and to the other State;

  (c) The Committee shall deal with a matter referred to it only after it has ascertained that all available domestic remedies have been invoked and exhausted in the matter, in con- formity with the generally recognized principles of international law. This shall not be the rule where, in the view of the Committee, the application of the remedies is unreasonably prolonged;

  (d) Subject to the provisions of subparagraph (c) of the present paragraph, the Committee shall make available its good offices to the States Parties concerned with a view to a friendly solution of the matter on the basis of the respect for the obligations set forth in the present Convention;

(e) The Committee shall hold closed meetings when examining communications under the present article;

(f) In any matter referred to it in accordance with subparagraph (b) of the present paragraph, the Committee may call upon the States Parties concerned, referred to in subparagraph (b), to supply any relevant information;

(g) The States Parties concerned, referred to in subparagraph (b) of the present paragraph, shall have the right to be represented when the matter is being considered by the Committee and to make submissions orally and/or in writing;

(h) The Committee shall, within twelve months after the date of receipt of notice under subparagraph (b) of the present paragraph, submit a report, as follows:

   (i) If a solution within the terms of subparagraph (d) of the present paragraph is reached, the Committee shall confine its report to a brief statement of the facts and of the solution reached;

   (ii) If a solution within the terms of subparagraph (d) is not reached, the Committee shall, in its report, set forth the relevant facts concerning the issue between the States Parties concerned. The written submissions and record of the oral submissions made by the States Parties concerned shall be attached to the report. The Committee may also communicate only to the States Parties concerned any views that it may consider relevant to the issue between them.

   In every matter, the report shall be communicated to the States Parties concerned.

2. The provisions of the present article shall come into force when ten States Parties to the present Convention have made a declaration under paragraph 1 of the present article. Such declarations shall be deposited by the States Parties with the Secretary-General of the United Nations, who shall transmit copies thereof to the other States Parties. A declaration may be withdrawn at any time by notification to the Secretary-General. Such a withdrawal shall not prejudice the consideration of any matter that is the subject of a communication already transmitted under the present article; no further communication by any State Party shall be received under the present article after the notification of withdrawal of the declaration has been received by the Secretary-General, unless the State Party concerned has made a new declaration.

Article 77

1. A State Party to the present Convention may at any time declare under the present article that it recognizes the competence of the Committee to receive and consider communications from or on behalf of individuals subject to its jurisdiction who claim that their individual rights as established by the present Convention have been violated by that State Party. No communication shall be received by the Committee if it concerns a State Party that has not made such a declaration.

2. The Committee shall consider inadmissible any communication under the present article which is anonymous or which it considers to be an abuse of the right of submission of such communications or to be incompatible with the provisions of the present Convention.

3. The Committee shall not consider any communication from an individual under the present article unless it has ascertained that:

(a) The same matter has not been, and is not being, examined under another procedure of international investigation or settlement;

(b) The individual has exhausted all available domestic remedies; this shall not be the rule where, in the view of the Committee, the application of the remedies is unreasonably prolonged or is unlikely to bring effective relief to that individual.

4. Subject to the provisions of paragraph 2 of the present article, the Committee shall bring any communications submitted to it under this article to the attention of the State Party to the present Convention that has made a declaration under paragraph 1 and is alleged to be violating any

provisions of the Convention. Within six months, the receiving State shall submit to the Committee written explanations or statements clarifying the matter and the remedy, if any, that may have been taken by that State.

5. The Committee shall consider communications received under the present article in the light of all information made available to it by or on behalf of the individual and by the State Party concerned.

6. The Committee shall hold closed meetings when examining communications under the present article.

7. The Committee shall forward its views to the State Party concerned and to the individual.

8. The provisions of the present article shall come into force when ten States Parties to the present Convention have made declarations under paragraph 1 of the present article. Such declarations shall be deposited by the States Parties with the Secretary-General of the United Nations, who shall transmit copies thereof to the other States Parties. A declaration may be withdrawn at any time by notification to the Secretary-General. Such a withdrawal shall not prejudice the consideration of any matter that is the subject of a communication already transmitted under the present article; no further communication by or on behalf of an individual shall be received under the present article after the notification of withdrawal of the declaration has been received by the Secretary-General, unless the State Party has made a new declaration.

Article 78

The provisions of article 76 of the present Convention shall be applied without prejudice to any procedures for settling disputes or complaints in the field covered by the present Convention laid down in the constituent instruments of, or in conventions adopted by, the United Nations and the specialized agencies and shall not prevent the States Parties from having recourse to any procedures for settling a dispute in accordance with international agreements in force between them.

PART VIII GENERAL PROVISIONS

Article 79

Nothing in the present Convention shall affect the right of each State Party to establish the criteria governing admission of migrant workers and members of their families. Concerning other matters related to their legal situation and treatment as migrant workers and members of their families, States Parties shall be subject to the limitations set forth in the present Convention.

Article 80

Nothing in the present Convention shall be interpreted as impairing the provisions of the Charter of the United Nations and of the constitutions of the specialized agencies which define the respective responsibilities of the various organs of the United Nations and of the specialized agencies in regard to the matters dealt with in the present Convention.

Article 81

1. Nothing in the present Convention shall affect more favourable rights or freedoms granted to migrant workers and members of their families by virtue of:

(a) The law or practice of a State Party; or

(b) Any bilateral or multilateral treaty in force for the State Party concerned.

2. Nothing in the present Convention may be interpreted as implying for any State, group or person any right to engage in any activity or perform any act that would impair any of the rights and freedoms as set forth in the present Convention.

Article 82

The rights of migrant workers and members of their families provided for in the present Convention may not be renounced. It shall not be permissible to exert any form of pressure upon migrant workers and members of their families with a view to their relinquishing or foregoing any of the said rights. It shall not be possible to derogate by contract from rights recognized in the present Convention. States Parties shall take appropriate measures to ensure that these principles are respected.

Article 83

Each State Party to the present Convention undertakes:

   (a) To ensure that any person whose rights or freedoms as herein recognized are violated shall have an effective remedy, notwithstanding that the violation has been committed by persons acting in an official capacity;

   (b) To ensure that any persons seeking such a remedy shall have his or her claim reviewed and decided by competent judicial, administrative or legislative authorities, or by any other competent authority provided for by the legal system of the State, and to develop the possibilities of judicial remedy;

   (c) To ensure that the competent authorities shall enforce such remedies when granted.

Article 84

Each State Party undertakes to adopt the legislative and other measures that are necessary to implement the provisions of the present Convention.

PART IX FINAL PROVISIONS

Article 85

The Secretary-General of the United Nations is designated as the depositary of the present Convention.

Article 86

1. The present Convention shall be open for signature by all States. It is subject to ratification.

2. The present Convention shall be open to accession by any State.

3. Instruments of ratification or accession shall be deposited with the Secretary-General of the United Nations.

Article 87

1. The present Convention shall enter into force on the first day of the month following a period of three months after the date of the deposit of the twentieth instrument of ratification or accession.

2. For each State ratifying or acceding to the present Convention after its entry into force, the Convention shall enter into force on the first day of the month following a period of three months after the date of the deposit of its own instrument of ratification or accession.

Article 88

A State ratifying or acceding to the present Convention may not exclude the application of any Part of it, or, without prejudice to article 3, exclude any particular category of migrant workers from its application.

Article 89

1. Any State Party may denounce the present Convention, not earlier than five years after the Convention has entered into force for the State concerned, by means of a notification writing addressed to the Secretary-General of the United Nations.

2. Such denunciation shall become effective on the first day of the month following the expiration of a period of twelve months after the date of the receipt of the notification by the Secretary-General of the United Nations.

3. Such a denunciation shall not have the effect of releasing the State Party from its obligations under the present Convention in regard to any act or omission which occurs prior to the date at which the denunciation becomes effective, nor shall denunciation prejudice in any way the continued

consideration of any matter which is already under consideration by the Committee prior to the date at which the denunciation becomes effective.

4. Following the date at which the denunciation of a State Party becomes effective, the Committee shall not commence consideration of any new matter regarding that State.

Article 90

1. After five years from the entry into force of the Convention a request for the revision of the Convention may be made at any time by any State Party by means of a notification in writing addressed to the Secretary-General of the United Nations. The Secretary-General shall thereupon communicate any proposed amendments to the States Parties with a request that they notify him whether the favour a conference of States Parties for the purpose of considering and voting upon the proposals. In the event that within four months from the date of such communication at least one third of the States Parties favours such a conference, the Secretary-General shall convene the conference under the auspices of the United Nations. Any amendment adopted by a majority of the States Parties present and voting shall be submitted to the General Assembly for approval.

2. Amendments shall come into force when they have been approved by the General Assembly of the United Nations and accepted by a two-thirds majority of the States Parties in accordance with their respective constitutional processes.

3. When amendments come into force, they shall be binding on those States Parties that have accepted them, other States Parties still being bound by the provisions of the present Convention and any earlier amendment that they have accepted.

Article 91

1. The Secretary-General of the United Nations shall receive and circulate to all States the text of reservations made by States at the time of signature, ratification or accession.

2. A reservation incompatible with the object and purpose of the present Convention shall not be permitted.

3. Reservations may be withdrawn at any time by notification to this effect addressed to the Secretary-General of the United Nations, who shall then inform all States thereof. Such notification shall take effect on the date on which it is received.

Article 92

1. Any dispute between two or more States Parties concerning the interpretation or application of the present Convention that is not settled by negotiation shall, at the request of one of them, be submitted to arbitration. If within six months from the date of the request for arbitration the Parties are unable to agree on the organization of the arbitration, any one of those Parties may refer the dispute to the International Court of Justice by request in conformity with the Statute of the Court.

2. Each State Party may at the time of signature or ratification of the present Convention or accession thereto declare that it does not consider itself bound by paragraph 1 of the present article. The other States Parties shall not be bound by that paragraph with respect to any State Party that has made such a declaration.

3. Any State Party that has made a declaration in accordance with paragraph 2 of the present article may at any time withdraw that declaration by notification to the Secretary-General of the United Nations.

Article 93

1. The present Convention, of which the Arabic, Chinese, English, French, Russian and Spanish texts are equally authentic, shall be deposited with the Secretary-General of the United Nations.

2. The Secretary-General of the United Nations shall transmit certified copies of the present Convention to all States.

IN WITNESS WHEREOF the undersigned plenipotentiaries, being duly authorized thereto by their respective Governments, have signed the present Convention.

Declaration on the Rights of Persons Belonging to National or Ethnic, Religious and Linguistic Minorities (1992)*

The General Assembly,

Reaffirming that one of the basic aims of the United Nations, as proclaimed in the Charter, is to promote and encourage respect for human rights and for fundamental freedoms for all, without distinction as to race, sex, language or religion,

Reaffirming faith in fundamental human rights, in the dignity and worth of the human person, in the equal rights of men and women and of nations large and small,

Desiring to promote the realization of the principles contained in the Charter, the Universal Declaration of Human Rights, the Convention on the Prevention and Punishment of the Crime of Genocide, the International Convention on the Elimination of All Forms of Racial Discrimination, the International Covenant on Civil and Political Rights, the International Covenant on Economic, Social and Cultural Rights, the Declaration on the Elimination of All Forms of Intolerance and of Discrimination Based on Religion or Belief, and the Convention on the Rights of the Child, as well as other relevant international instruments that have been adopted at the universal or regional level and those concluded between individual States Members of the United Nations,

Inspired by the provisions of article 27 of the International Covenant on Civil and Political Rights concerning the rights of persons belonging to ethnic, religious or linguistic minorities,

Considering that the promotion and protection of the rights of persons belonging to national or ethnic, religious and linguistic minorities contribute to the political and social stability of States in which they live,

Emphasizing that the constant promotion and realization of the rights of persons belonging to national or ethnic, religious and linguistic minorities, as an integral part of the development of society as a whole and within a democratic framework based on the rule of law, would contribute to the strengthening of friendship and cooperation among peoples and States,

Considering that the United Nations has an important role to play regarding the protection of minorities,

Bearing in mind the work done so far within the United Nations system, in particular by the Commission on Human Rights, the Subcommission on Prevention of Discrimination and Protection of Minorities and the bodies established pursuant to the International Covenants on Human Rights and other relevant international human rights instruments in promoting and protecting the rights of persons belonging to national or ethnic, religious and linguistic minorities,

Taking into account the important work which is done by intergovernmental and nongovernmental organizations in protecting minorities and in promoting and protecting the rights of persons belonging to national or ethnic, religious and linguistic minorities,

Recognizing the need to ensure even more effective implementation of international human rights instruments with regard to the rights of persons belonging to national or ethnic, religious and linguistic minorities,

Proclaims this Declaration on the Rights of Persons Belonging to National or Ethnic, Religious and Linguistic Minorities:

Article 1

1. States shall protect the existence and the national or ethnic, cultural, religious and linguistic identity of minorities within their respective territories and shall encourage conditions for the promotion of that identity.

2. States shall adopt appropriate legislative and other measures to achieve those ends.

Article 2

1. Persons belonging to national or ethnic, religious and linguistic minorities (hereinafter referred to as persons belonging to minorities) have the right to enjoy their own culture, to profess and

practise their own religion, and to use their own language, in private and in public, freely and without interference or any form of discrimination.

2. Persons belonging to minorities have the right to participate effectively in cultural, religious, social, economic and public life.

3. Persons belonging to minorities have the right to participate effectively in decisions on the national and, where appropriate, regional level concerning the minority to which they belong or the regions in which they live, in a manner not incompatible with national legislation.

4. Persons belonging to minorities have the right to establish and maintain their own associations.

5. Persons belonging to minorities have the right to establish and maintain, without any discrimination, free and peaceful contacts with other members of their group and with persons belonging to other minorities, as well as contacts across frontiers with citizens of other States to whom they are related by national or ethnic, religious or linguistic ties.

Article 3

1. Persons belonging to minorities may exercise their rights, including those set forth in the present Declaration, individually as well as in community with other members of their group, without any discrimination.

2. No disadvantage shall result for any person belonging to a minority as the consequence of the exercise or non-exercise of the rights set forth in the present Declaration.

Article 4

1. States shall take measures where required to ensure that persons belonging to minorities may exercise fully and effectively all their human rights and fundamental freedoms without any discrimination and in full equality before the law.

2. States shall take measures to create favourable conditions to enable persons belonging to minorities to express their characteristics and to develop their culture, language, religion, traditions and customs, except where specific practices are in violation of national law and contrary to international standards.

3. States should take appropriate measures so that, wherever possible, persons belonging to minorities may have adequate opportunities to learn their mother tongue or to have instruction in their mother tongue.

4. States should, where appropriate, take measures in the field of education, in order to encourage knowledge of the history, traditions, language and culture of the minorities existing within their territory. Persons belonging to minorities should have adequate opportunities to gain knowledge of the society as a whole.

5. States should consider appropriate measures so that persons belonging to minorities may participate fully in the economic progress and development in their country.

Article 5

1. National policies and programmes shall be planned and implemented with due regard for the legitimate interests of persons belonging to minorities.

2. Programmes of cooperation and assistance among States should be planned and implemented with due regard for the legitimate interests of persons belonging to minorities.

Article 6

States should cooperate on questions relating to persons belonging to minorities, *inter alia,* exchanging information and experiences, in order to promote mutual understanding and confidence.

Article 7

States should cooperate in order to promote respect for the rights set forth in the present Declaration.

Article 8

1. Nothing in the present Declaration shall prevent the fulfilment of international obligations of States in relation to persons belonging to minorities. In particular, States shall fulfil in good faith

the obligations and commitments they have assumed under international treaties and agreements to which they are parties.

2. The exercise of the rights set forth in the present Declaration shall not prejudice the enjoyment by all persons of universally recognized human rights and fundamental freedoms.

3. Measures taken by States to ensure the effective enjoyment of the rights set forth in the present Declaration shall not *prima facie* be considered contrary to the principle of equality contained in the Universal Declaration of Human Rights.

4. Nothing in the present Declaration may be construed as permitting any activity contrary to the purposes and principles of the United Nations, including sovereign equality, territorial integrity and political independence of States.

Article 9

The specialized agencies and other organizations of the United Nations system shall contribute to the full realization of the rights and principles set forth in the present Declaration, within their respective fields of competence.

Guiding Principles on Internal Displacement (1998)*

INTRODUCTION: SCOPE AND PURPOSE

1. These Guiding Principles address the specific needs of internally displaced persons worldwide. They identify rights and guarantees relevant to the protection of persons from forced displacement and to their protection and assistance during displacement as well as during return or resettlement and reintegration.

2. For the purposes of these Principles, internally displaced persons are persons or groups of persons who have been forced or obliged to flee or to leave their homes or places of habitual residence, in particular as a result of or in order to avoid the effects of armed conflict, situations of generalized violence, violations of human rights or natural or human-made disasters, and who have not crossed an internationally recognized State border.

3. These Principles reflect and are consistent with international human rights law and international humanitarian law. They provide guidance to:
    (a) The Representative of the Secretary-General on internally displaced persons in carrying out his mandate;
    (b) States when faced with the phenomenon of internal displacement;
    (c) All other authorities, groups and persons in their relations with internally displaced persons; and
    (d) Intergovernmental and non-governmental organizations when addressing internal displacement.

4. These Guiding Principles should be disseminated and applied as widely as possible.

SECTION I GENERAL PRINCIPLES

Principle 1

1. Internally displaced persons shall enjoy, in full equality, the same rights and freedoms under international and domestic law as do other persons in their country. They shall not be discriminated against in the enjoyment of any rights and freedoms on the ground that they are internally displaced.

2. These Principles are without prejudice to individual criminal responsibility under international law, in particular relating to genocide, crimes against humanity and war crimes.

Principle 2

1. These Principles shall be observed by all authorities, groups and persons irrespective of their legal status and applied without any adverse distinction. The observance of these Principles shall not affect the legal status of any authorities, groups or persons involved.

2. These Principles shall not be interpreted as restricting, modifying or impairing the provisions of any international human rights or international humanitarian law instrument or rights granted to persons under domestic law. In particular, these Principles are without prejudice to the right to seek and enjoy asylum in other countries.

Principle 3

1. National authorities have the primary duty and responsibility to provide protection and humanitarian assistance to internally displaced persons within their jurisdiction.

2. Internally displaced persons have the right to request and to receive protection and humanitarian assistance from these authorities. They shall not be persecuted or punished for making such a request.

Principle 4

1. These Principles shall be applied without discrimination of any kind, such as race, colour, sex, language, religion or belief, political or other opinion, national, ethnic or social origin, legal or social status, age, disability, property, birth, or on any other similar criteria.

2. Certain internally displaced persons, such as children, especially unaccompanied minors, expectant mothers, mothers with young children, female heads of household, persons with disabilities and elderly persons, shall be entitled to protection and assistance required by their condition and to treatment which takes into account their special needs.

SECTION II PRINCIPLES RELATING TO PROTECTION FROM DISPLACEMENT

Principle 5

All authorities and international actors shall respect and ensure respect for their obligations under international law, including human rights and humanitarian law, in all circumstances, so as to prevent and avoid conditions that might lead to displacement of persons.

Principle 6

1. Every human being shall have the right to be protected against being arbitrarily displaced from his or her home or place of habitual residence.

2. The prohibition of arbitrary displacement includes displacement:

   (a) When it is based on policies of apartheid, 'ethnic cleansing' or similar practices aimed at/or resulting in altering the ethnic, religious or racial composition of the affected population;

   (b) In situations of armed conflict, unless the security of the civilians involved or imperative military reasons so demand;

   (c) In cases of large-scale development projects, which are not justified by compelling and overriding public interests;

   (d) In cases of disasters, unless the safety and health of those affected requires their evacuation; and

   (e) When it is used as a collective punishment.

3. Displacement shall last no longer than required by the circumstances.

Principle 7

1. Prior to any decision requiring the displacement of persons, the authorities concerned shall ensure that all feasible alternatives are explored in order to avoid displacement altogether. Where no alternatives exist, all measures shall be taken to minimize displacement and its adverse effects.

2. The authorities undertaking such displacement shall ensure, to the greatest practicable extent, that proper accommodation is provided to the displaced persons, that such displacements are effected in satisfactory conditions of safety, nutrition, health and hygiene, and that members of the same family are not separated.

3. If displacement occurs in situations other than during the emergency stages of armed conflicts and disasters, the following guarantees shall be complied with:

    (a) A specific decision shall be taken by a State authority empowered by law to issue such measures;

    (b) Adequate measures shall be taken to guarantee to those to be displaced full information on the reasons and procedures for their displacement, and, where applicable, on compensation and relocation;

    (c) The free and informed consent of those to be displaced shall be sought;

    (d) The authorities concerned shall endeavor to involve those affected, particularly women, in the planning and management of their relocation;

    (e) Law enforcement measures, where required, shall be carried out by competent legal authorities; and

    (f) The right to an effective remedy, including the review of such decisions by appropriate judicial authorities, shall be respected.

Principle 8

Displacement shall not be carried out in a manner that violates the rights to life, dignity, liberty and security of those affected.

Principle 9

States are under a particular obligation to protect against the displacement of indigenous peoples, minorities, peasants, pastoralists and other groups with a special dependency on and attachment to their lands.

SECTION III PRINCIPLES RELATING TO PROTECTION DURING DISPLACEMENT

Principle 10

1. Every human being has the inherent right to life which shall be protected by law. No one shall be arbitrarily deprived of his or her life. Internally displaced persons shall be protected in particular against:

    (a) Genocide;

    (b) Murder;

    (c) Summary or arbitrary executions; and

    (d) Enforced disappearances, including abduction or unacknowledged detention, threatening or resulting in death.

Threats and incitement to commit any of the foregoing acts shall be prohibited.

2. Attacks or other acts of violence against internally displaced persons who do not or no longer participate in hostilities are prohibited in all circumstances. Internally displaced persons shall be protected, in particular, against:

    (a) Direct or indiscriminate attacks or other acts of violence, including the creation of areas wherein attacks on civilians are permitted;

    (b) Starvation as a method of combat;

    (c) Their use to shield military objectives from attack, or to shield, favour or impede military operations;

    (d) Attacks against their camps or settlements; and

    (e) The use of anti-personnel landmines.

Principle 11

1. Every human being has the right to dignity and physical, mental and moral integrity.

2. Internally displaced persons, whether or not their liberty has been restricted, shall be protected in particular against:

    (a) Rape, mutilation, torture, cruel, inhuman or degrading treatment or punishment, and other outrages upon personal dignity, such as acts of gender-specific violence, forced prostitution and any form of indecent assault;

    (b) Slavery or any contemporary form of slavery, such as sale into marriage, sexual exploitation, or forced labour of children; and

    (c) Acts of violence intended to spread terror among internally displaced persons.

Threats and incitement to commit any of the foregoing acts shall be prohibited.

Principle 12

1. Every human being has the right to liberty and security of person. No one shall be subjected to arbitrary arrest or detention.

2. To give effect to this right for internally displaced persons, they shall not be interned in or confined to a camp. If in exceptional circumstances such internment or confinement is absolutely necessary, it shall not last longer than required by the circumstances.

3. Internally displaced persons shall be protected from discriminatory arrest and detention as a result of their displacement.

4. In no case shall internally displaced persons be taken hostage.

Principle 13

1. In no circumstances shall displaced children be recruited nor be required or permitted to take part in hostilities.

2. Internally displaced persons shall be protected against discriminatory practices of recruitment into any armed forces or groups as a result of their displacement. In particular any cruel, inhuman or degrading practices that compel compliance or punish non-compliance with recruitment are prohibited in all circumstances.

Principle 14

1. Every internally displaced person has the right to liberty of movement and freedom to choose his or her residence.

2. In particular, internally displaced persons have the right to move freely in and out of camps or other settlements.

Principle 15

Internally displaced persons have:

    (a) The right to seek safety in another part of the country;

    (b) The right to leave their country;

    (c) The right to seek asylum in another country; and

    (d) The right to be protected against forcible return to or settlement in any place where their life, safety, liberty and/or health would be at risk.

Principle 16

1. All internally displaced persons have the right to know the fate and whereabouts of missing relatives.

2. The authorities concerned shall endeavour to establish the fate and whereabouts of internally displaced persons reported missing, and cooperate with relevant international organizations engaged in this task. They shall inform the next of kin on the progress of the investigation and notify them of any result.

3. The authorities concerned shall endeavour to collect and identify the mortal remains of those deceased, prevent their despoliation or mutilation, and facilitate the return of those remains to the next of kin or dispose of them respectfully.

4. Grave sites of internally displaced persons should be protected and respected in all circumstances. Internally displaced persons should have the right of access to the grave sites of their deceased relatives.

Principle 17

1. Every human being has the right to respect of his or her family life.

2. To give effect to this right for internally displaced persons, family members who wish to remain together shall be allowed to do so.

3. Families which are separated by displacement should be reunited as quickly as possible. All appropriate steps shall be taken to expedite the reunion of such families, particularly when children are involved. The responsible authorities shall facilitate inquiries made by family members and encourage and cooperate with the work of humanitarian organizations engaged in the task of family reunification.

4. Members of internally displaced families whose personal liberty has been restricted by internment or confinement in camps shall have the right to remain together.

Principle 18

1. All internally displaced persons have the right to an adequate standard of living.

2. At the minimum, regardless of the circumstances, and without discrimination, competent authorities shall provide internally displaced persons with and ensure safe access to:

    (a) Essential food and potable water;

    (b) Basic shelter and housing;

    (c) Appropriate clothing; and

    (d) Essential medical services and sanitation.

3. Special efforts should be made to ensure the full participation of women in the planning and distribution of these basic supplies.

Principle 19

1. All wounded and sick internally displaced persons as well as those with disabilities shall receive to the fullest extent practicable and with the least possible delay, the medical care and attention they require, without distinction on any grounds other than medical ones. When necessary, internally displaced persons shall have access to psychological and social services.

2. Special attention should be paid to the health needs of women, including access to female health care providers and services, such as reproductive health care, as well as appropriate counselling for victims of sexual and other abuses.

3. Special attention should also be given to the prevention of contagious and infectious diseases, including AIDS, among internally displaced persons.

Principle 20

1. Every human being has the right to recognition everywhere as a person before the law.

2. To give effect to this right for internally displaced persons, the authorities concerned shall issue to them all documents necessary for the enjoyment and exercise of their legal rights, such as passports, personal identification documents, birth certificates and marriage certificates. In particular, the authorities shall facilitate the issuance of new documents or the replacement of documents lost in the course of displacement, without imposing unreasonable conditions, such as requiring the return to one's area of habitual residence in order to obtain these or other required documents.

3. Women and men shall have equal rights to obtain such necessary documents and shall have the right to have such documentation issued in their own names.

Principle 21

1. No one shall be arbitrarily deprived of property and possessions.

2. The property and possessions of internally displaced persons shall in all circumstances be protected, in particular, against the following acts:

    (a) Pillage;

    (b) Direct or indiscriminate attacks or other acts of violence;

    (c) Being used to shield military operations or objectives;

(d) Being made the object of reprisal; and

(e) Being destroyed or appropriated as a form of collective punishment.

3. Property and possessions left behind by internally displaced persons should be protected against destruction and arbitrary and illegal appropriation, occupation or use.

Principle 22

1. Internally displaced persons, whether or not they are living in camps, shall not be discriminated against as a result of their displacement in the enjoyment of the following rights;

(a) The rights to freedom of thought, conscience, religion or belief, opinion and expression;

(b) The right to seek freely opportunities for employment and to participate in economic activities;

(c) The right to associate freely and participate equally in community affairs;

(d) The right to vote and to participate in governmental and public affairs, including the right to have access to the means necessary to exercise this right; and

(e) The right to communicate in a language they understand.

Principle 23

1. Every human being has the right to education.

2. To give effect to this right for internally displaced persons, the authorities concerned shall ensure that such persons, in particular displaced children, receive education which shall be free and compulsory at the primary level. Education should respect their cultural identity, language and religion.

3. Special efforts should be made to ensure the full and equal participation of women and girls in educational programmes.

4. Education and training facilities shall be made available to internally displaced persons, in particular adolescents and women, whether or not living in camps, as soon as conditions permit.

SECTION IV PRINCIPLES RELATING TO HUMANITARIAN ASSISTANCE

Principle 24

1. All humanitarian assistance shall be carried out in accordance with the principles of humanity and impartiality and without discrimination.

2. Humanitarian assistance to internally displaced persons shall not be diverted, in particular for political or military reasons.

Principle 25

1. The primary duty and responsibility for providing humanitarian assistance to internally displaced persons lies with national authorities.

2. International humanitarian organizations and other appropriate actors have the right to offer their services in support of the internally displaced. Such an offer shall not be regarded as an unfriendly act or an interference in a State's internal affairs and shall be considered in good faith. Consent thereto shall not be arbitrarily withheld, particularly when authorities concerned are unable or unwilling to provide the required humanitarian assistance.

3. All authorities concerned shall grant and facilitate the free passage of humanitarian assistance and grant persons engaged in the provision of such assistance rapid and unimpeded access to the internally displaced.

Principle 26

Persons engaged in humanitarian assistance, their transport and supplies shall be respected and protected. They shall not be the object of attack or other acts of violence.

Principle 27

1. International humanitarian organizations and other appropriate actors when providing assistance should give due regard to the protection needs and human rights of internally displaced persons

and take appropriate measures in this regard. In so doing, these organizations and actors should respect relevant international standards and codes of conduct.

2. The preceding paragraph is without prejudice to the protection responsibilities of international organizations mandated for this purpose, whose services may be offered or requested by States.

SECTION V PRINCIPLES RELATING TO RETURN, RESETTLEMENT AND REINTEGRATION

Principle 28

1. Competent authorities have the primary duty and responsibility to establish conditions, as well as provide the means, which allow internally displaced persons to return voluntarily, in safety and with dignity, to their homes or places of habitual residence, or to resettle voluntarily in part of the country. Such authorities shall endeavour to facilitate reintegration of returned or resettled internally displaced persons.

2. Special efforts should be made to ensure the full participation of internally displaced persons in the planning and management of their return or resettlement and reintegration.

Principle 29

1. Internally displaced persons who have returned to their homes or places of habitual residence or who have resettled in another part of the country shall not be discriminated against as a result of their having been displaced. They shall have the right to participate fully and equally in public affairs at all levels and have equal access to public services.

2. Competent authorities have the duty and responsibility to assist returned and/or resettled internally displaced persons to recover, to the extent possible, their property and possessions which they left behind or were dispossessed of upon their displacement. When recovery of such property and possessions is not possible, competent authorities shall provide or assist these persons in obtaining appropriate compensation or another form of just reparation.

Principle 30

All authorities concerned shall grant and facilitate for international humanitarian organizations and other appropriate actors, in the exercise of their respective mandates, rapid and unimpeded access to internally displaced persons to assist in their return or resettlement and reintegration.

Rome Statute of the International Criminal Court (1998)*

PREAMBLE

The States Parties to this Statute

Conscious that all peoples are united by common bonds, their cultures pieced together in a shared heritage, and concerned that this delicate mosaic may be shattered at any time,

Mindful that during this century millions of children, women and men have been victims of unimaginable atrocities that deeply shock the conscience of humanity,

Recognizing that such grave crimes threaten the peace, security and well-being of the world,

Affirming that the most serious crimes of concern to the international community as a whole must not go unpunished and that their effective prosecution must be ensured by taking measures at the national level and by enhancing international cooperation,

Determined to put an end to impunity for the perpetrators of these crimes and thus to contribute to the prevention of such crimes,

* **Editor's Note:** As amended by the Resolutions adopted by the Review Conference in June 2010 concerning Article 8 (Res.5) and the crime of aggression (Res.6) and by Resolution ICC-ASP/16/Res.4, adopted by the Assembly of States Parties in December 2017, concerning Article 8. From Rome Statute of the International Criminal Court, by Public Affairs Unit International Criminal Court, © 1998 United Nations. Reprinted with the permission of the United Nations.

Recalling that it is the duty of every State to exercise its criminal jurisdiction over those responsible for international crimes,

Reaffirming the Purposes and Principles of the Charter of the United Nations, and in particular that all States shall refrain from the threat or use of force against the territorial integrity or political independence of any State, or in any other manner inconsistent with the Purposes of the United Nations,

Emphasizing in this connection that nothing in this Statute shall be taken as authorizing any State Party to intervene in an armed conflict in the internal affairs of any State,

Determined to these ends and for the sake of present and future generations, to establish an independent permanent International Criminal Court in relationship with the United Nations system, with jurisdiction over the most serious crimes of concern to the international community as a whole,

Emphasizing that the International Criminal Court established under this Statute shall be complementary to national criminal jurisdictions,

Resolved to guarantee lasting respect for the enforcement of international justice,

Have agreed as follows:

PART 1 ESTABLISHMENT OF THE COURT

Article 1   The Court
An International Criminal Court ('the Court') is hereby established. It shall be a permanent institution and shall have the power to exercise its jurisdiction over persons for the most serious crimes of international concern, as referred to in this Statute, and shall be complementary to national criminal jurisdictions. The jurisdiction and functioning of the Court shall be governed by the provisions of this Statute.

Article 2   Relationship of the Court with the United Nations
The Court shall be brought into relationship with the United Nations through an agreement to be approved by the Assembly of States Parties to this Statute and thereafter concluded by the President of the Court on its behalf.

Article 3   Seat of the Court
1. The seat of the Court shall be established at The Hague in the Netherlands ('the host State').
2. The Court shall enter into a headquarters agreement with the host State, to be approved by the Assembly of States Parties and thereafter concluded by the President of the Court on its behalf.
3. The Court may sit elsewhere, whenever it considers it desirable, as provided in this Statute.

Article 4   Legal status and powers of the Court
1. The Court shall have international legal personality. It shall also have such legal capacity as may be necessary for the exercise of its functions and the fulfilment of its purposes.
2. The Court may exercise its functions and powers, as provided in this Statute, on the territory of any State Party and, by special agreement, on the territory of any other State.

PART 2 JURISDICTION, ADMISSIBILITY AND APPLICABLE LAW

Article 5*   Crimes within the jurisdiction of the Court
The jurisdiction of the Court shall be limited to the most serious crimes of concern to the international community as a whole. The Court has jurisdiction in accordance with this Statute with respect to the following crimes:
   (a) The crime of genocide;
   (b) Crimes against humanity;

---

* **Editor's Note:** Article 5(2) was deleted in accordance with RC/Res.6, annex I, of 11 June 2010.

(c) War crimes;

(d) The crime of aggression.

Article 6 Genocide

For the purpose of this Statute, 'genocide' means any of the following acts committed with intent to destroy, in whole or in part, a national, ethnical, racial or religious group, as such:

(a) Killing members of the group;

(b) Causing serious bodily or mental harm to members of the group;

(c) Deliberately inflicting on the group conditions of life calculated to bring about its physical destruction in whole or in part;

(d) Imposing measures intended to prevent births within the group;

(e) Forcibly transferring children of the group to another group.

Article 7 Crimes against humanity

1. For the purpose of this Statute, 'crime against humanity' means any of the following acts when committed as part of a widespread or systematic attack directed against any civilian population, with knowledge of the attack:

(a) Murder;

(b) Extermination;

(c) Enslavement;

(d) Deportation or forcible transfer of population;

(e) Imprisonment or other severe deprivation of physical liberty in violation of fundamental rules of international law;

(f) Torture;

(g) Rape, sexual slavery, enforced prostitution, forced pregnancy, enforced sterilization, or any other form of sexual violence of comparable gravity;

(h) Persecution against any identifiable group or collectivity on political, racial, national, ethnic, cultural, religious, gender as defined in paragraph 3, or other grounds that are universally recognized as impermissible under international law, in connection with any act referred to in this paragraph or any crime within the jurisdiction of the Court;

(i) Enforced disappearance of persons;

(j) The crime of apartheid;

(k) Other inhumane acts of a similar character intentionally causing great suffering, or serious injury to body or to mental or physical health.

2. For the purpose of paragraph 1:

(a) 'Attack directed against any civilian population' means a course of conduct involving the multiple commission of acts referred to in paragraph 1 against any civilian population, pursuant to or in furtherance of a State or organizational policy to commit such attack;

(b) 'Extermination' includes the intentional infliction of conditions of life, *inter alia* the deprivation of access to food and medicine, calculated to bring about the destruction of part of a population;

(c) 'Enslavement' means the exercise of any or all of the powers attaching to the right of ownership over a person and includes the exercise of such power in the course of trafficking in persons, in particular women and children;

(d) 'Deportation or forcible transfer of population' means forced displacement of the persons concerned by expulsion or other coercive acts from the area in which they are lawfully present, without grounds permitted under international law;

(e) 'Torture' means the intentional infliction of severe pain or suffering, whether physical or mental, upon a person in the custody or under the control of the accused; except that torture shall not include pain or suffering arising only from, inherent in or incidental to, lawful sanctions;

(f) 'Forced pregnancy' means the unlawful confinement, of a woman forcibly made pregnant, with the intent of affecting the ethnic composition of any population or carrying out other grave violations of international law. This definition shall not in any way be interpreted as affecting national laws relating to pregnancy;

(g) 'Persecution' means the intentional and severe deprivation of fundamental rights contrary to international law by reason of the identity of the group or collectivity;

(h) 'The crime of apartheid' means inhumane acts of a character similar to those referred to in paragraph 1, committed in the context of an institutionalized regime of systematic oppression and domination by one racial group over any other racial group or groups and committed with the intention of maintaining that regime;

(i) 'Enforced disappearance of persons' means the arrest, detention or abduction of persons by, or with the authorization, support or acquiescence of, a State or a political organization, followed by a refusal to acknowledge that deprivation of freedom or to give information on the fate or whereabouts of those persons, with the intention of removing them from the protection of the law for a prolonged period of time.

3. For the purpose of this Statute, it is understood that the term 'gender' refers to the two sexes, male and female, within the context of society. The term 'gender' does not indicate any meaning different from the above.

Article 8* War crimes

1. The Court shall have jurisdiction in respect of war crimes in particular when committed as part of a plan or policy or as part of a large-scale commission of such crimes.

2. For the purpose of this Statute, 'war crimes' means:

(a) Grave breaches of the Geneva Conventions of 12 August 1949, namely, any of the following acts against persons or property protected under the provisions of the relevant Geneva Convention:

(i)   Wilful killing;

(ii)   Torture or inhuman treatment, including biological experiments;

(iii)   Wilfully causing great suffering, or serious injury to body or health;

(iv)   Extensive destruction and appropriation of property, not justified by military necessity and carried out unlawfully and wantonly;

(v)   Compelling a prisoner of war or other protected person to serve in the forces of a hostile Power;

(vi)   Wilfully depriving a prisoner of war or other protected person of the rights of fair and regular trial;

(vii)   Unlawful deportation or transfer or unlawful confinement;

(viii) Taking of hostages.

(b) Other serious violations of the laws and customs applicable in international armed conflict, within the established framework of international law, namely, any of the following acts:

(i)   Intentionally directing attacks against the civilian population as such or against individual civilians not taking direct part in hostilities;

(ii)   Intentionally directing attacks against civilian objects, that is, objects which are not military objectives;

(iii)   Intentionally directing attacks against personnel, installations, material, units or vehicles involved in a humanitarian assistance or peacekeeping mission in

---

* **Editor's Note:** Article 8(2)(e)(xiii)–(xv) is added by Resolution RC/Res.5 of 11 June 2010. Article 8(2)(b)(xxvii)–(xxix) and Article 8(2)(e)(xvi)–(xviii) is added by Resolution ICC-ASP/16/Res.4 of 14 December 2017.

accordance with the Charter of the United Nations, as long as they are entitled to the protection given to civilians or civilian objects under the international law of armed conflict;

(iv) Intentionally launching an attack in the knowledge that such attack will cause incidental loss of life or injury to civilians or damage to civilian objects or widespread, long-term and severe damage to the natural environment which would be clearly excessive in relation to the concrete and direct overall military advantage anticipated;

(v) Attacking or bombarding, by whatever means, towns, villages, dwellings or buildings which are undefended and which are not military objectives;

(vi) Killing or wounding a combatant who, having laid down his arms or having no longer means of defence, has surrendered at discretion;

(vii) Making improper use of a flag of truce, of the flag or of the military insignia and uniform of the enemy or of the United Nations, as well as of the distinctive emblems of the Geneva Conventions, resulting in death or serious personal injury;

(viii) The transfer, directly or indirectly, by the Occupying Power of parts of its own civilian population into the territory it occupies, or the deportation or transfer of all or parts of the population of the occupied territory within or outside this territory;

(ix) Intentionally directing attacks against buildings dedicated to religion, education, art, science or charitable purposes, historic monuments, hospitals and places where the sick and wounded are collected, provided they are not military objectives;

(x) Subjecting persons who are in the power of an adverse party to physical mutilation or to medical or scientific experiments of any kind which are neither justified by the medical, dental or hospital treatment of the person concerned nor carried out in his or her interest, and which cause death to or seriously endanger the health of such person or persons;

(xi) Killing or wounding treacherously individuals belonging to the hostile nation or army;

(xii) Declaring that no quarter will be given;

(xiii) Destroying or seizing the enemy's property unless such destruction or seizure be imperatively demanded by the necessities of war;

(xiv) Declaring abolished, suspended or inadmissible in a court of law the rights and actions of the nationals of the hostile party;

(xv) Compelling the nationals of the hostile party to take part in the operations of war directed against their own country, even if they were in the belligerent's service before the commencement of the war;

(xvi) Pillaging a town or place, even when taken by assault;

(xvii) Employing poison or poisoned weapons;

(xviii) Employing asphyxiating, poisonous or other gases, and all analogous liquids, materials or devices;

(xix) Employing bullets which expand or flatten easily in the human body, such as bullets with a hard envelope which does not entirely cover the core or is pierced with incisions;

(xx) Employing weapons, projectiles and material and methods of warfare which are of a nature to cause superfluous injury or unnecessary suffering or which are inherently indiscriminate in violation of the international law of armed conflict, provided that such weapons, projectiles and material and methods of warfare are the subject of a comprehensive prohibition and are included in an annex to this Statute, by an amendment in accordance with the relevant provisions set forth in articles 121 and 123;

(xxi)   Committing outrages upon personal dignity, in particular humiliating and degrading treatment;

(xxii) Committing rape, sexual slavery, enforced prostitution, forced pregnancy, as defined in article 7, paragraph 2(f), enforced sterilization, or any other form of sexual violence also constituting a grave breach of the Geneva Conventions;

(xxiii) Utilizing the presence of a civilian or other protected person to render certain points, areas or military forces immune from military operations;

(xxiv) Intentionally directing attacks against buildings, material, medical units and transport and personnel using the distinctive emblems of the Geneva Conventions in conformity with international law;

(xxv)   Intentionally using starvation of civilians as a method of warfare by depriving them of objects indispensable to their survival, including wilfully impeding relief supplies as provided for under the Geneva Conventions;

(xxvi) Conscripting or enlisting children under the age of fifteen years into the national armed forces or using them to participate actively in hostilities;

(xxvii) Employing weapons, which use microbial or other biological agents, or toxins, whatever their origin or method of production;

(xxviii) Employing weapons the primary effect of which is to injure by fragments which in the human body escape detection by X-rays;

(xxix) Employing laser weapons specifically designed, as their sole combat function or as one of their combat functions, to cause permanent blindness to unenhanced vision, that is to the naked eye or to the eye with corrective eyesight devices;

(c) In the case of an armed conflict not of an international character, serious violations of article 3 common to the four Geneva Conventions of 12 August 1949, namely, any of the following acts committed against persons taking no active part in the hostilities, including members of armed forces who have laid down their arms and those placed hors de combat by sickness, wounds, detention or any other cause:

(i)   Violence to life and person, in particular murder of all kinds, mutilation, cruel treatment and torture;

(ii)   Committing outrages upon personal dignity, in particular humiliating and degrading treatment;

(iii)   Taking of hostages;

(iv)   The passing of sentences and the carrying out of executions without previous judgement pronounced by a regularly constituted court, affording all judicial guarantees which are generally recognized as indispensable.

(d) Paragraph 2(c) applies to armed conflicts not of an international character and thus does not apply to situations of internal disturbances and tensions, such as riots, isolated and sporadic acts of violence or other acts of a similar nature.

(e) Other serious violations of the laws and customs applicable in armed conflicts not of an international character, within the established framework of international law, namely, any of the following acts:

(i)   Intentionally directing attacks against the civilian population as such or against individual civilians not taking direct part in hostilities;

(ii)   Intentionally directing attacks against buildings, material, medical units and transport, and personnel using the distinctive emblems of the Geneva Conventions in conformity with international law;

(iii)   Intentionally directing attacks against personnel, installations, material, units or vehicles involved in a humanitarian assistance or peacekeeping mission in accordance with the Charter of the United Nations, as long as they are entitled to the protection given to civilians or civilian objects under the international law of armed conflict;

(iv)   Intentionally directing attacks against buildings dedicated to religion, education, art, science or charitable purposes, historic monuments, hospitals and places where the sick and wounded are collected, provided they are not military objectives;

(v)   Pillaging a town or place, even when taken by assault;

(vi)   Committing rape, sexual slavery, enforced prostitution, forced pregnancy, as defined in article 7, paragraph 2(f), enforced sterilization, and any other form of sexual violence also constituting a serious violation of article 3 common to the four Geneva Conventions;

(vii) Conscripting or enlisting children under the age of fifteen years into armed forces or groups or using them to participate actively in hostilities;

(viii) Ordering the displacement of the civilian population for reasons related to the conflict, unless the security of the civilians involved or imperative military reasons so demand;

(ix)   Killing or wounding treacherously a combatant adversary;

(x)   Declaring that no quarter will be given;

(xi)   Subjecting persons who are in the power of another party to the conflict to physical mutilation or to medical or scientific experiments of any kind which are neither justified by the medical, dental or hospital treatment of the person concerned nor carried out in his or her interest, and which cause death to or seriously endanger the health of such person or persons;

(xii) Destroying or seizing the property of an adversary unless such destruction or seizure be imperatively demanded by the necessities of the conflict;

(xiii) Employing poison or poisoned weapons;

(xiv) Employing asphyxiating, poisonous or other gases, and all analogous liquids, materials or devices;

(xv)   Employing bullets which expand or flatten easily in the human body, such as bullets with a hard envelope which does not entirely cover the core or is pierced with incisions.

(xvi) Employing weapons, which use microbial or other biological agents, or toxins, whatever their origin or method of production;

(xvii) Employing weapons the primary effect of which is to injure by fragments which in the human body escape detection by X-rays;

(xviii) Employing laser weapons specifically designed, as their sole combat function or as one of their combat functions, to cause permanent blindness to unenhanced vision, that is to the naked eye or to the eye with corrective eyesight devices.

(f) Paragraph 2(e) applies to armed conflicts not of an international character and thus does not apply to situations of internal disturbances and tensions, such as riots, isolated and sporadic acts of violence or other acts of a similar nature. It applies to armed conflicts that take place in the territory of a State when there is protracted armed conflict between governmental authorities and organized armed groups or between such groups.

3. Nothing in paragraphs 2(c) and (e) shall affect the responsibility of a Government to maintain or re-establish law and order in the State or to defend the unity and territorial integrity of the State, by all legitimate means.

Article 8 *bis**   Crime of aggression

1. For the purpose of this Statute, 'crime of aggression' means the planning, preparation, initiation or execution, by a person in a position effectively to exercise control over or to direct the political or military action of a State, of an act of aggression which, by its character, gravity and scale, constitutes a manifest violation of the Charter of the United Nations.

2. For the purpose of paragraph 1, 'act of aggression' means the use of armed force by a State against the sovereignty, territorial integrity or political independence of another State, or in any other manner inconsistent with the Charter of the United Nations. Any of the following acts, regardless of a declaration of war, shall, in accordance with United Nations General Assembly resolution 3314 (XXIX) of 14 December 1974, qualify as an act of aggression:

(a) The invasion or attack by the armed forces of a State of the territory of another State, or any military occupation, however temporary, resulting from such invasion or attack, or any annexation by the use of force of the territory of another State or part thereof;

---

* **Editor's Note:** Article 8 *bis* is added by Resolution RC/Res.6 of 11 June 2010.

(b) Bombardment by the armed forces of a State against the territory of another State or the use of any weapons by a State against the territory of another State;

(c) The blockade of the ports or coasts of a State by the armed forces of another State;

(d) An attack by the armed forces of a State on the land, sea or air forces, or marine and air fleets of another State;

(e) The use of armed forces of one State which are within the territory of another State with the agreement of the receiving State, in contravention of the conditions provided for in the agreement or any extension of their presence in such territory beyond the termination of the agreement;

(f) The action of a State in allowing its territory, which it has placed at the disposal of another State, to be used by that other State for perpetrating an act of aggression against a third State;

(g) The sending by or on behalf of a State of armed bands, groups, irregulars or mercenaries, which carry out acts of armed force against another State of such gravity as to amount to the acts listed above, or its substantial involvement therein.

Article 9* Elements of Crimes

1. Elements of Crimes shall assist the Court in the interpretation and application of articles 6, 7, 8 and 8 *bis*. They shall be adopted by a two-thirds majority of the members of the Assembly of States Parties.

2. Amendments to the Elements of Crimes may be proposed by:

(a) Any State Party;

(b) The judges acting by an absolute majority;

(c) The Prosecutor.

Such amendments shall be adopted by a two-thirds majority of the members of the Assembly of States Parties.

3. The Elements of Crimes and amendments thereto shall be consistent with this Statute.

Article 10

Nothing in this Part shall be interpreted as limiting or prejudicing in any way existing or developing rules of international law for purposes other than this Statute.

Article 11 Jurisdiction *ratione temporis*

1. The Court has jurisdiction only with respect to crimes committed after the entry into force of this Statute.

2. If a State becomes a Party to this Statute after its entry into force, the Court may exercise its jurisdiction only with respect to crimes committed after the entry into force of this Statute for that State, unless that State has made a declaration under article 12, paragraph 3.

Article 12 Preconditions to the exercise of jurisdiction

1. A State which becomes a Party to this Statute thereby accepts the jurisdiction of the Court with respect to the crimes referred to in article 5.

2. In the case of article 13, paragraph (a) or (c), the Court may exercise its jurisdiction if one or more of the following States are Parties to this Statute or have accepted the jurisdiction of the Court in accordance with paragraph 3:

(a) The State on the territory of which the conduct in question occurred or, if the crime was committed on board a vessel or aircraft, the State of registration of that vessel or aircraft;

(b) The State of which the person accused of the crime is a national.

3. If the acceptance of a State which is not a Party to this Statute is required under paragraph 2, that State may, by declaration lodged with the Registrar, accept the exercise of jurisdiction by the Court with respect to the crime in question. The accepting State shall cooperate with the Court without any delay or exception in accordance with Part 9.

---

* **Editor's Note:** Article 9 is amended by Resolution RC/Res.6 of 11 June 2010 to include a reference to Article 8 *bis*.

Article 13   Exercise of jurisdiction

The Court may exercise its jurisdiction with respect to a crime referred to in article 5 in accordance with the provisions of this Statute if:

(a) A situation in which one or more of such crimes appears to have been committed is referred to the Prosecutor by a State Party in accordance with article 14;

(b) A situation in which one or more of such crimes appears to have been committed is referred to the Prosecutor by the Security Council acting under Chapter VII of the Charter of the United Nations; or

(c) The Prosecutor has initiated an investigation in respect of such a crime in accordance with article 15.

Article 14   Referral of a situation by a State Party

1. A State Party may refer to the Prosecutor a situation in which one or more crimes within the jurisdiction of the Court appear to have been committed requesting the Prosecutor to investigate the situation for the purpose of determining whether one or more specific persons should be charged with the commission of such crimes.

2. As far as possible, a referral shall specify the relevant circumstances and be accompanied by such supporting documentation as is available to the State referring the situation.

Article 15   Prosecutor

1. The Prosecutor may initiate investigations *proprio motu* on the basis of information on crimes within the jurisdiction of the Court.

2. The Prosecutor shall analyse the seriousness of the information received. For this purpose, he or she may seek additional information from States, organs of the United Nations, intergovernmental or non-governmental organizations, or other reliable sources that he or she deems appropriate, and may receive written or oral testimony at the seat of the Court.

3. If the Prosecutor concludes that there is a reasonable basis to proceed with an investigation, he or she shall submit to the Pre-Trial Chamber a request for authorization of an investigation, together with any supporting material collected. Victims may make representations to the Pre-Trial Chamber, in accordance with the Rules of Procedure and Evidence.

4. If the Pre-Trial Chamber, upon examination of the request and the supporting material, considers that there is a reasonable basis to proceed with an investigation, and that the case appears to fall within the jurisdiction of the Court, it shall authorize the commencement of the investigation, without prejudice to subsequent determinations by the Court with regard to the jurisdiction and admissibility of a case.

5. The refusal of the Pre-Trial Chamber to authorize the investigation shall not preclude the presentation of a subsequent request by the Prosecutor based on new facts or evidence regarding the same situation.

6. If, after the preliminary examination referred to in paragraphs 1 and 2, the Prosecutor concludes that the information provided does not constitute a reasonable basis for an investigation, he or she shall inform those who provided the information. This shall not preclude the Prosecutor from considering further information submitted to him or her regarding the same situation in the light of new facts or evidence.

Article 15 *bis**   Exercise of jurisdiction over the crime of aggression (State referral, *proprio motu*)

1. The Court may exercise jurisdiction over the crime of aggression in accordance with article 13, paragraphs (a) and (c), subject to the provisions of this article.

2. The Court may exercise jurisdiction only with respect to crimes of aggression committed one year after the ratification or acceptance of the amendments by thirty States Parties.

3. The Court shall exercise jurisdiction over the crime of aggression in accordance with this article, subject to a decision to be taken after 1 January 2017 by the same majority of States Parties as is required for the adoption of an amendment to the Statute.

---

* **Editor's Note:** Article 15 *bis* is added by Resolution RC/Res.6 of 11 June 2010.

4. The Court may, in accordance with article 12, exercise jurisdiction over a crime of aggression, arising from an act of aggression committed by a State Party, unless that State Party has previously declared that it does not accept such jurisdiction by lodging a declaration with the Registrar. The withdrawal of such a declaration may be effected at any time and shall be considered by the State Party within three years.

5. In respect of a State that is not a party to this Statute, the Court shall not exercise its jurisdiction over the crime of aggression when committed by that State's nationals or on its territory.

6. Where the Prosecutor concludes that there is a reasonable basis to proceed with an investigation in respect of a crime of aggression, he or she shall first ascertain whether the Security Council has made a determination of an act of aggression committed by the State concerned. The Prosecutor shall notify the Secretary-General of the United Nations of the situation before the Court, including any relevant information and documents.

7. Where the Security Council has made such a determination, the Prosecutor may proceed with the investigation in respect of a crime of aggression.

8. Where no such determination is made within six months after the date of notification, the Prosecutor may proceed with the investigation in respect of a crime of aggression, provided that the Pre-Trial Division has authorized the commencement of the investigation in respect of a crime of aggression in accordance with the procedure contained in article 15, and the Security Council has not decided otherwise in accordance with article 16.

9. A determination of an act of aggression by an organ outside the Court shall be without prejudice to the Court's own findings under this Statute.

10. This article is without prejudice to the provisions relating to the exercise of jurisdiction with respect to other crimes referred to in article 5.

Article 15 *ter**   Exercise of jurisdiction over the crime of aggression (Security Council referral)

1. The Court may exercise jurisdiction over the crime of aggression in accordance with article 13, paragraph (b), subject to the provisions of this article.

2. The Court may exercise jurisdiction only with respect to crimes of aggression committed one year after the ratification or acceptance of the amendments by thirty States Parties.

3. The Court shall exercise jurisdiction over the crime of aggression in accordance with this article, subject to a decision to be taken after 1 January 2017 by the same majority of States Parties as is required for the adoption of an amendment to the Statute.

4. A determination of an act of aggression by an organ outside the Court shall be without prejudice to the Court's own findings under this Statute.

5. This article is without prejudice to the provisions relating to the exercise of jurisdiction with respect to other crimes referred to in article 5.

Article 16   Deferral of investigation or prosecution

No investigation or prosecution may be commenced or proceeded with under this Statute for a period of 12 months after the Security Council, in a resolution adopted under Chapter VII of the Charter of the United Nations, has requested the Court to that effect; that request may be renewed by the Council under the same conditions.

Article 17   Issues of admissibility

1. Having regard to paragraph 10 of the Preamble and article 1, the Court shall determine that a case is inadmissible where:
  (a) The case is being investigated or prosecuted by a State which has jurisdiction over it, unless the State is unwilling or unable genuinely to carry out the investigation or prosecution;
  (b) The case has been investigated by a State which has jurisdiction over it and the State has decided not to prosecute the person concerned, unless the decision resulted from the unwillingness or inability of the State genuinely to prosecute;

---

* **Editor's Note:** Article 15 *ter* is added by Resolution RC/Res.6 of 11 June 2010.

(c) The person concerned has already been tried for conduct which is the subject of the complaint, and a trial by the Court is not permitted under article 20, paragraph 3;

(d) The case is not of sufficient gravity to justify further action by the Court.

2. In order to determine unwillingness in a particular case, the Court shall consider, having regard to the principles of due process recognized by international law, whether one or more of the following exist, as applicable:

(a) The proceedings were or are being undertaken or the national decision was made for the purpose of shielding the person concerned from criminal responsibility for crimes within the jurisdiction of the Court referred to in article 5;

(b) There has been an unjustified delay in the proceedings which in the circumstances is inconsistent with an intent to bring the person concerned to justice;

(c) The proceedings were not or are not being conducted independently or impartially, and they were or are being conducted in a manner which, in the circumstances, is inconsistent with an intent to bring the person concerned to justice.

3. In order to determine inability in a particular case, the Court shall consider whether, due to a total or substantial collapse or unavailability of its national judicial system, the State is unable to obtain the accused or the necessary evidence and testimony or otherwise unable to carry out its proceedings.

Article 18   Preliminary rulings regarding admissibility

1. When a situation has been referred to the Court pursuant to article 13(a) and the Prosecutor has determined that there would be a reasonable basis to commence an investigation, or the Prosecutor initiates an investigation pursuant to articles 13(c) and 15, the Prosecutor shall notify all States Parties and those States which, taking into account the information available, would normally exercise jurisdiction over the crimes concerned. The Prosecutor may notify such States on a confidential basis and, where the Prosecutor believes it necessary to protect persons, prevent destruction of evidence or prevent the absconding of persons, may limit the scope of the information provided to States.

2. Within one month of receipt of that notice, a State may inform the Court that it is investigating or has investigated its nationals or others within its jurisdiction with respect to criminal acts which may constitute crimes referred to in article 5 and which relate to the information provided in the notification to States. At the request of that State, the Prosecutor shall defer to the State's investigation of those persons unless the Pre-Trial Chamber, on the application of the Prosecutor, decides to authorize the investigation.

3. The Prosecutor's deferral to a State's investigation shall be open to review by the Prosecutor six months after the date of deferral or at any time when there has been a significant change of circumstances based on the State's unwillingness or inability genuinely to carry out the investigation.

4. The State concerned or the Prosecutor may appeal to the Appeals Chamber against a ruling of the Pre-Trial Chamber, in accordance with article 82. The appeal may be heard on an expedited basis.

5. When the Prosecutor has deferred an investigation in accordance with paragraph 2, the Prosecutor may request that the State concerned periodically inform the Prosecutor of the progress of its investigations and any subsequent prosecutions. States Parties shall respond to such requests without undue delay.

6. Pending a ruling by the Pre-Trial Chamber, or at any time when the Prosecutor has deferred an investigation under this article, the Prosecutor may, on an exceptional basis, seek authority from the Pre-Trial Chamber to pursue necessary investigative steps for the purpose of preserving evidence where there is a unique opportunity to obtain important evidence or there is a significant risk that such evidence may not be subsequently available.

7. A State which has challenged a ruling of the Pre-Trial Chamber under this article may challenge the admissibility of a case under article 19 on the grounds of additional significant facts or significant change of circumstances.

Article 19   Challenges to the jurisdiction of the Court or the admissibility of a case

1. The Court shall satisfy itself that it has jurisdiction in any case brought before it. The Court may, on its own motion, determine the admissibility of a case in accordance with article 17.

2. Challenges to the admissibility of a case on the grounds referred to in article 17 or challenges to the jurisdiction of the Court may be made by:

    (a) An accused or a person for whom a warrant of arrest or a summons to appear has been issued under article 58;

    (b) A State which has jurisdiction over a case, on the ground that it is investigating or prosecuting the case or has investigated or prosecuted; or

    (c) A State from which acceptance of jurisdiction is required under article 12.

3. The Prosecutor may seek a ruling from the Court regarding a question of jurisdiction or admissibility. In proceedings with respect to jurisdiction or admissibility, those who have referred the situation under article 13, as well as victims, may also submit observations to the Court.

4. The admissibility of a case or the jurisdiction of the Court may be challenged only once by any person or State referred to in paragraph 2. The challenge shall take place prior to or at the commencement of the trial. In exceptional circumstances, the Court may grant leave for a challenge to be brought more than once or at a time later than the commencement of the trial. Challenges to the admissibility of a case, at the commencement of a trial, or subsequently with the leave of the Court, may be based only on article 17, paragraph 1(c).

5. A State referred to in paragraph 2(b) and (c) shall make a challenge at the earliest opportunity.

6. Prior to the confirmation of the charges, challenges to the admissibility of a case or challenges to the jurisdiction of the Court shall be referred to the Pre-Trial Chamber. After confirmation of the charges, they shall be referred to the Trial Chamber. Decisions with respect to jurisdiction or admissibility may be appealed to the Appeals Chamber in accordance with article 82.

7. If a challenge is made by a State referred to in paragraph 2(b) or (c), the Prosecutor shall suspend the investigation until such time as the Court makes a determination in accordance with article 17.

8. Pending a ruling by the Court, the Prosecutor may seek authority from the Court:

    (a) To pursue necessary investigative steps of the kind referred to in article 18, paragraph 6;

    (b) To take a statement or testimony from a witness or complete the collection and examination of evidence which had begun prior to the making of the challenge; and

    (c) In cooperation with the relevant States, to prevent the absconding of persons in respect of whom the Prosecutor has already requested a warrant of arrest under article 58.

9. The making of a challenge shall not affect the validity of any act performed by the Prosecutor or any order or warrant issued by the Court prior to the making of the challenge.

10. If the Court has decided that a case is inadmissible under article 17, the Prosecutor may submit a request for a review of the decision when he or she is fully satisfied that new facts have arisen which negate the basis on which the case had previously been found inadmissible under article 17.

11. If the Prosecutor, having regard to the matters referred to in article 17, defers an investigation, the Prosecutor may request that the relevant State make available to the Prosecutor information on the proceedings. That information shall, at the request of the State concerned, be confidential. If the Prosecutor thereafter decides to proceed with an investigation, he or she shall notify the State to which deferral of the proceedings has taken place.

Article 20*   *Ne bis in idem*

1. Except as provided in this Statute, no person shall be tried before the Court with respect to conduct which formed the basis of crimes for which the person has been convicted or acquitted by the Court.

---

* **Editor's Note:** Amended by Resolution RC/Res.6 of 11 June 2010 to include a reference to Article 8 *bis*.

2. No person shall be tried by another court for a crime referred to in article 5 for which that person has already been convicted or acquitted by the Court.

3. No person who has been tried by another court for conduct also proscribed under articles 6, 7, 8 or 8 *bis* shall be tried by the Court with respect to the same conduct unless the proceedings in the other court:

    (a) Were for the purpose of shielding the person concerned from criminal responsibility for crimes within the jurisdiction of the Court; or

    (b) Otherwise were not conducted independently or impartially in accordance with the norms of due process recognized by international law and were conducted in a manner which, in the circumstances, was inconsistent with an intent to bring the person concerned to justice.

Article 21   Applicable law

1. The Court shall apply:

    (a) In the first place, this Statute, Elements of Crimes and its Rules of Procedure and Evidence;

    (b) In the second place, where appropriate, applicable treaties and the principles and rules of international law, including the established principles of the international law of armed conflict;

    (c) Failing that, general principles of law derived by the Court from national laws of legal systems of the world including, as appropriate, the national laws of States that would normally exercise jurisdiction over the crime, provided that those principles are not inconsistent with this Statute and with international law and internationally recognized norms and standards.

2. The Court may apply principles and rules of law as interpreted in its previous decisions.

3. The application and interpretation of law pursuant to this article must be consistent with internationally recognized human rights, and be without any adverse distinction founded on grounds such as gender as defined in article 7, paragraph 3, age, race, colour, language, religion or belief, political or other opinion, national, ethnic or social origin, wealth, birth or other status.

PART 3   GENERAL PRINCIPLES OF CRIMINAL LAW

Article 22   *Nullum crimen sine lege*

1. A person shall not be criminally responsible under this Statute unless the conduct in question constitutes, at the time it takes place, a crime within the jurisdiction of the Court.

2. The definition of a crime shall be strictly construed and shall not be extended by analogy. In case of ambiguity, the definition shall be interpreted in favour of the person being investigated, prosecuted or convicted.

3. This article shall not affect the characterization of any conduct as criminal under international law independently of this Statute.

Article 23   *Nulla poena sine lege*

A person convicted by the Court may be punished only in accordance with this Statute.

Article 24   Non-retroactivity *ratione personae*

1. No person shall be criminally responsible under this Statute for conduct prior to the entry into force of the Statute.

2. In the event of a change in the law applicable to a given case prior to a final judgement, the law more favourable to the person being investigated, prosecuted or convicted shall apply.

Article 25*   Individual criminal responsibility

1. The Court shall have jurisdiction over natural persons pursuant to this Statute.

---

* **Editor's Note:** Article 25(3) *bis* is added by Resolution RC/Res.6 of 11 June 2010.

2. A person who commits a crime within the jurisdiction of the Court shall be individually responsible and liable for punishment in accordance with this Statute.

3. In accordance with this Statute, a person shall be criminally responsible and liable for punishment for a crime within the jurisdiction of the Court if that person:

    (a) Commits such a crime, whether as an individual, jointly with another or through another person, regardless of whether that other person is criminally responsible;

    (b) Orders, solicits or induces the commission of such a crime which in fact occurs or is attempted;

    (c) For the purpose of facilitating the commission of such a crime, aids, abets or otherwise assists in its commission or its attempted commission, including providing the means for its commission;

    (d) In any other way contributes to the commission or attempted commission of such a crime by a group of persons acting with a common purpose. Such contribution shall be intentional and shall either:

        (i) Be made with the aim of furthering the criminal activity or criminal purpose of the group, where such activity or purpose involves the commission of a crime within the jurisdiction of the Court; or

        (ii) Be made in the knowledge of the intention of the group to commit the crime;

    (e) In respect of the crime of genocide, directly and publicly incites others to commit genocide;

    (f) Attempts to commit such a crime by taking action that commences its execution by means of a substantial step, but the crime does not occur because of circumstances independent of the person's intentions. However, a person who abandons the effort to commit the crime or otherwise prevents the completion of the crime shall not be liable for punishment under this Statute for the attempt to commit that crime if that person completely and voluntarily gave up the criminal purpose.

3 *bis*. In respect of the crime of aggression, the provisions of this article shall apply only to persons in a position effectively to exercise control over or to direct the political or military action of a State.

4. No provision in this Statute relating to individual criminal responsibility shall affect the responsibility of States under international law.

Article 26   Exclusion of jurisdiction over persons under eighteen

The Court shall have no jurisdiction over any person who was under the age of 18 at the time of the alleged commission of a crime.

Article 27   Irrelevance of official capacity

1. This Statute shall apply equally to all persons without any distinction based on official capacity. In particular, official capacity as a Head of State or Government, a member of a Government or parliament, an elected representative or a government official shall in no case exempt a person from criminal responsibility under this Statute, nor shall it, in and of itself, constitute a ground for reduction of sentence.

2. Immunities or special procedural rules which may attach to the official capacity of a person, whether under national or international law, shall not bar the Court from exercising its jurisdiction over such a person.

Article 28   Responsibility of commanders and other superiors

In addition to other grounds of criminal responsibility under this Statute for crimes within the jurisdiction of the Court:

    (a) A military commander or person effectively acting as a military commander shall be criminally responsible for crimes within the jurisdiction of the Court committed by forces under his or her effective command and control, or effective authority and control as the case may be, as a result of his or her failure to exercise control properly over such forces, where:

     (i)   That military commander or person either knew or, owing to the circumstances at the time, should have known that the forces were committing or about to commit such crimes; and

     (ii) That military commander or person failed to take all necessary and reasonable measures within his or her power to prevent or repress their commission or to submit the matter to the competent authorities for investigation and prosecution.

(b) With respect to superior and subordinate relationships not described in paragraph (a), a superior shall be criminally responsible for crimes within the jurisdiction of the Court committed by subordinates under his or her effective authority and control, as a result of his or her failure to exercise control properly over such subordinates, where:

     (i)   The superior either knew, or consciously disregarded information which clearly indicated, that the subordinates were committing or about to commit such crimes;

     (ii) The crimes concerned activities that were within the effective responsibility and control of the superior; and

     (iii) The superior failed to take all necessary and reasonable measures within his or her power to prevent or repress their commission or to submit the matter to the competent authorities for investigation and prosecution.

Article 29   Non-applicability of statute of limitations

The crimes within the jurisdiction of the Court shall not be subject to any statute of limitations.

Article 30   Mental element

1. Unless otherwise provided, a person shall be criminally responsible and liable for punishment for a crime within the jurisdiction of the Court only if the material elements are committed with intent and knowledge.

2. For the purposes of this article, a person has intent where:

    (a) In relation to conduct, that person means to engage in the conduct;

    (b) In relation to a consequence, that person means to cause that consequence or is aware mat it will occur in the ordinary course of events.

3. For the purposes of this article, 'knowledge' means awareness that a circumstance exists or a consequence will occur in the ordinary course of events. 'Know' and 'knowingly' shall be construed accordingly.

Article 31   Grounds for excluding criminal responsibility

1. In addition to other grounds for excluding criminal responsibility provided for in this Statute, a person shall not be criminally responsible if, at the time of that person's conduct:

    (a) The person suffers from a mental disease or defect that destroys that person's capacity to appreciate the unlawfulness or nature of his or her conduct, or capacity to control his or her conduct to conform to the requirements of law;

    (b) The person is in a state of intoxication that destroys that person's capacity to appreciate the unlawfulness or nature of his or her conduct, or capacity to control his or her conduct to conform to the requirements of law, unless the person has become voluntarily intoxicated under such circumstances that the person knew, or disregarded the risk, that, as a result of the intoxication, he or she was likely to engage in conduct constituting a crime within the jurisdiction of the Court;

    (c) The person acts reasonably to defend himself or herself or another person or, in the case of war crimes, property which is essential for the survival of the person or another person or property which is essential for accomplishing a military mission, against an imminent and unlawful use of force in a manner proportionate to the degree of danger to the person or the other person or property protected. The fact that the person was involved in a defensive operation conducted by forces shall not in itself constitute a ground for excluding criminal responsibility under this subparagraph;

(d) The conduct which is alleged to constitute a crime within the jurisdiction of the Court has been caused by duress resulting from a threat of imminent death or of continuing or imminent serious bodily harm against that person or another person, and the person acts necessarily and reasonably to avoid this threat, provided that the person does not intend to cause a greater harm than the one sought to be avoided. Such a threat may either be:
   (i)   Made by other persons; or
   (ii) Constituted by other circumstances beyond that person's control.

2. The Court shall determine the applicability of the grounds for excluding criminal responsibility provided for in this Statute to the case before it.

3. At trial, the Court may consider a ground for excluding criminal responsibility other than those referred to in paragraph 1 where such a ground is derived from applicable law as set forth in article 21. The procedures relating to the consideration of such a ground shall be provided for in the Rules of Procedure and Evidence.

Article 32   Mistake of fact or mistake of law

1. A mistake of fact shall be a ground for excluding criminal responsibility only if it negates the mental element required by the crime.

2. A mistake of law as to whether a particular type of conduct is a crime within the jurisdiction of the Court shall not be a ground for excluding criminal responsibility. A mistake of law may, however, be a ground for excluding criminal responsibility if it negates the mental element required by such a crime, or as provided for in article 33.

Article 33   Superior orders and prescription of law

1. The fact that a crime within the jurisdiction of the Court has been committed by a person pursuant to an order of a Government or of a superior, whether military or civilian, shall not relieve that person of criminal responsibility unless:
   (a) The person was under a legal obligation to obey orders of the Government or the superior in question;
   (b) The person did not know that the order was unlawful; and
   (c) The order was not manifestly unlawful.

2. For the purposes of this article, orders to commit genocide or crimes against humanity are manifestly unlawful.

PART 4 COMPOSITION AND ADMINISTRATION OF THE COURT

. . .

PART 5 INVESTIGATION AND PROSECUTION

Article 53   Initiation of an investigation

1. The Prosecutor shall, having evaluated the information made available to him or her, initiate an investigation unless he or she determines that there is no reasonable basis to proceed under this Statute. In deciding whether to initiate an investigation, the Prosecutor shall consider whether:
   (a) The information available to the Prosecutor provides a reasonable basis to believe that a crime within the jurisdiction of the Court has been or is being committed;
   (b) The case is or would be admissible under article 17; and
   (c) Taking into account the gravity of the crime and the interests of victims, there are nonetheless substantial reasons to believe that an investigation would not serve the interests of justice.

If the Prosecutor determines that there is no reasonable basis to proceed and his or her determination is based solely on subparagraph (c) above, he or she shall inform the Pre-Trial Chamber.

2. If, upon investigation, the prosecutor concludes that there is not a sufficient basis for a prosecution because:

    (a) There is not a sufficient legal or factual basis to seek a warrant or summons under article 58;

    (b) The case is inadmissible under article 17; or

    (c) A prosecution is not in the interests of justice, taking into account all the circumstances, including the gravity of the crime, the interests of victims and the age or infirmity of the alleged perpetrator, and his or her role in the alleged crime;

the Prosecutor shall inform the Pre-Trial Chamber and the State making a referral under article 14 or the Security Council in a case under article 13, paragraph (b), of his or her conclusion and the reasons for the conclusion.

3. (a) At the request of the State making a referral under article 14 or the Security Council under article 13, paragraph (b) the Pre-Trial Chamber may review a decision of the Prosecutor under paragraph 1 or 2 not to proceed and may request the Prosecutor to reconsider that decision.

    (b) In addition, the Pre-Trial Chamber may, on its own initiative, review a decision of the Prosecutor not to proceed if it is based solely on paragraph 1(c) or 2(c). In such a case, the decision of the Prosecutor shall be effective only if confirmed by the Pre-Trial Chamber.

4. The Prosecutor may, at any time, reconsider a decision whether to initiate an investigation or prosecution based on new facts or information.

Article 54   Duties and powers of the Prosecutor with respect to investigations

1. The Prosecutor shall:

    (a) In order to establish the truth, extend the investigation to cover all facts and evidence relevant to an assessment of whether there is criminal responsibility under this Statute, and, in doing so, investigate incriminating and exonerating circumstances equally;

    (b) Take appropriate measures to ensure the effective investigation and prosecution of crimes within the jurisdiction of the Court, and in doing so respect the interests and personal circumstances of victims and witnesses, including age, gender as defined in article 7, paragraph 3, and health, and take into account the nature of the crime, in particular where it involves sexual violence, gender violence or violence against children; and

    (c) Fully respect the rights of persons arising under this Statute.

2. The Prosecutor may conduct investigations on the territory of a State:

    (a) In accordance with the provisions of Part 9; or

    (b) As authorized by the Pre-Trial Chamber under article 57, paragraph 3(d).

3. The Prosecutor may:

    (a) Collect and examine evidence;

    (b) Request the presence of and question persons being investigated, victims and witnesses;

    (c) Seek the cooperation of any State or intergovernmental organization or arrangement in accordance with its respective competence and/or mandate;

    (d) Enter into such arrangements or agreements, not inconsistent with this Statute, as may be necessary to facilitate the cooperation of a State, intergovernmental organization or person;

    (e) Agree not to disclose, at any stage of the proceedings, documents or information that the Prosecutor obtains on the condition of confidentiality and solely for the purpose of generating new evidence, unless the provider of the information consents; and

    (f) Take necessary measures, or request that necessary measures be taken, to ensure the confidentiality of information, the protection of any person or the preservation of evidence.

Article 55   Rights of persons during an investigation

1. In respect of an investigation under this Statute, a person:
    - (a) Shall not be compelled to incriminate himself or herself or to confess guilt;
    - (b) Shall not be subjected to any form of coercion, duress or threat, to torture or to any other form of cruel, inhuman or degrading treatment or punishment; and
    - (c) Shall, if questioned in a language other than a language the person fully understands and speaks, have, free of any cost, the assistance of a competent interpreter and such translations as are necessary to meet the requirements of fairness;
    - (d) Shall not be subjected to arbitrary arrest or detention, and shall not be deprived of his or her liberty except on such grounds and in accordance with such procedures as are established in this Statute.

2. Where there are grounds to believe that a person has committed a crime within the jurisdiction of the Court and that person is about to be questioned either by the Prosecutor, or by national authorities pursuant to a request made under Part 9 that person shall also have the following rights of which he or she shall be informed prior to being questioned:
    - (a) To be informed, prior to being questioned, that there are grounds to believe that he or she has committed a crime within the jurisdiction of the Court;
    - (b) To remain silent, without such silence being a consideration in the determination of guilt or innocence;
    - (c) To have legal assistance of the person's choosing, or, if the person does not have legal assistance, to have legal assistance assigned to him or her, in any case where the interests of justice so require, and without payment by the person in any such case if the person does not have sufficient means to pay for it;
    - (d) To be questioned in the presence of counsel unless the person has voluntarily waived his or her right to counsel.

Article 56   Role of the Pre-Trial Chamber in relation to a unique investigative opportunity

1. (a) Where the Prosecutor considers an investigation to present a unique opportunity to take testimony or a statement from a witness or to examine, collect or test evidence, which may not be available subsequently for the purposes of a trial, the Prosecutor shall so inform the Pre-Trial Chamber.
    - (b) In that case, the Pre-Trial Chamber may, upon request of the Prosecutor, take such measures as may be necessary to ensure the efficiency and integrity of the proceedings and, in particular, to protect the rights of the defence.
    - (c) Unless the Pre-Trial Chamber orders otherwise, the Prosecutor shall provide the relevant information to the person who has been arrested or appeared in response to a summons in connection with the investigation referred to in subparagraph (a), in order that he or she may be heard on the matter.

2. The measures referred to in paragraph 1(b) may include:
    - (a) Making recommendations or orders regarding procedures to be followed;
    - (b) Directing that a record be made of the proceedings;
    - (c) Appointing an expert to assist;
    - (d) Authorizing counsel or a person who has been arrested, or appeared before the Court in response to a summons, to participate, or where there has not yet been such an arrest or appearance or counsel has not been designated, appointing another counsel to attend and represent the interests of the defence;
    - (e) Naming one of its members or, if necessary, another available judge of the Pre-Trial or Trial Division to observe and make recommendations or orders regarding the collection and preservation of evidence and the questioning of persons;
    - (f) Taking such other action as may be necessary to collect or preserve evidence.

3. (a) Where the Prosecutor has not sought measures pursuant to this article but the Pre-Trial Chamber considers that such measures are required to preserve evidence that it deems would be essential for the defence at trial, it shall consult with the Prosecutor as to whether there is good reason for the Prosecutor's failure to request the measures. If upon consultation, the Pre-Trial Chamber concludes that the Prosecutor's failure to request such measures is unjustified, the Pre-Trial Chamber may take such measures on its own initiative.

(b) A decision of the Pre-Trial Chamber to act on its own initiative under this paragraph may be appealed by the Prosecutor. The appeal shall be heard on an expedited basis.

4. The admissibility of evidence preserved or collected for trial pursuant to this article, or the record thereof, shall be governed at trial by article 69, and given such weight as determined by the Trial Chamber.

Article 57   Functions and powers of the Pre-Trial Chamber

1. Unless otherwise provided in this Statute, the Pre-Trial Chamber shall exercise its functions in accordance with the provisions of this article.

2. (a) Orders or rulings of the Pre-Trial Chamber issued under articles 15, 18, 19, 54, paragraph 2, 61, paragraph 7, and 72 must be concurred in by a majority of its judges.

(b) In all other cases, a single judge of the Pre-Trial Chamber may exercise the functions provided for in this Statute, unless otherwise provided for in the Rules of Procedure and Evidence or by a majority of the Pre-Trial Chamber.

3. In addition to its other functions under this Statute, the Pre-Trial Chamber may:

(a) At the request of the Prosecutor, issue such orders and warrants as may be required for the purposes of an investigation;

(b) Upon the request of a person who has been arrested or has appeared pursuant to a summons under article 58, issue such orders, including measures such as those described in article 56, or seek such cooperation pursuant to Part 9 as may be necessary to assist the person in the preparation of his or her defence;

(c) Where necessary, provide for the protection and privacy of victims and witnesses, the preservation of evidence, the protection of persons who have been arrested or appeared in response to a summons, and the protection of national security information;

(d) Authorize the Prosecutor to take specific investigative steps within the territory of a State Party without having secured the cooperation of that State under Part 9 if, whenever possible having regard to the views of the State concerned, the Pre-Trial Chamber has determined in that case that the State is clearly unable to execute a request for cooperation due to the unavailability of any authority or any component of its judicial system competent to execute the request for cooperation under Part 9.

(e) Where a warrant of arrest or a summons has been issued under article 58, and having due regard to the strength of the evidence and the rights of the parties concerned, as provided for in this Statute and the Rules of Procedure and Evidence, seek the cooperation of States pursuant to article 93, paragraph 1(j), to take protective measures for the purpose of forfeiture, in particular for the ultimate benefit of victims.

Article 58   Issuance by the Pre-Trial Chamber of a warrant of arrest or a summons to appear

1. At any time after the initiation of an investigation, the Pre-Trial Chamber shall, on the application of the Prosecutor, issue a warrant of arrest of a person if, having examined the application and the evidence or other information submitted by the Prosecutor, it is satisfied that:

(a) There are reasonable grounds to believe that the person has committed a crime within the jurisdiction of the Court; and

(b) The arrest of the person appears necessary:

    (c) To ensure the person's appearance at trial,

      (i) To ensure that the person does not obstruct or endanger the investigation or the court proceedings, or

      (ii) Where applicable, to prevent the person from continuing with the commission of that crime or a related crime which is within the jurisdiction of the Court and which arises out of the same circumstances.

2. The application of the Prosecutor shall contain:

    (a) The name of the person and any other relevant identifying information;

    (b) A specific reference to the crimes within the jurisdiction of the Court which the person is alleged to have committed;

    (c) A concise statement of the facts which are alleged to constitute those crimes;

    (d) A summary of the evidence and any other information which establish reasonable grounds to believe that the person committed those crimes; and

    (e) The reason why the Prosecutor believes that the arrest of the person is necessary.

3. The warrant of arrest shall contain:

    (a) The name of the person and any other relevant identifying information;

    (b) A specific reference to the crimes within the jurisdiction of the Court for which the person's arrest is sought; and

    (c) A concise statement of the facts which are alleged to constitute those crimes.

4. The warrant of arrest shall remain in effect until otherwise ordered by the Court.

5. On the basis of the warrant of arrest, the Court may request the provisional arrest or the arrest and surrender of the person under Part 9.

6. The Prosecutor may request the Pre-Trial Chamber to amend the warrant of arrest by modifying or adding to the crimes specified therein. The Pre-Trial Chamber shall so amend the warrant if it is satisfied that there are reasonable grounds to believe that the person committed the modified or additional crimes.

7. As an alternative to seeking a warrant of arrest, the Prosecutor may submit an application requesting that the Pre-Trial Chamber issue a summons for the person to appear. If the Pre-Trial Chamber is satisfied that there are reasonable grounds to believe that the person committed the crime alleged and that a summons is sufficient to ensure the person's appearance, it shall issue the summons, with or without conditions restricting liberty (other than detention) if provided for by national law, for the person to appear. The summons shall contain:

    (a) The name of the person and any other relevant identifying information;

    (b) The specified date on which the person is to appear;

    (c) A specific reference to the crimes within the jurisdiction of the Court which the person is alleged to have committed; and

    (d) A concise statement of the facts which are alleged to constitute the crime. The summons shall be served on the person.

Article 59   Arrest proceedings in the custodial State

1. A State Party which has received a request for provisional arrest or for arrest and surrender shall immediately take steps to arrest the person in question in accordance with its laws and the provisions of Part 9.

2. A person arrested shall be brought promptly before the competent judicial authority in the custodial State which shall determine, in accordance with the law of that State, that:

    (a) The warrant applies to that person;

    (b) The person has been arrested in accordance with the proper process; and

    (c) The person's rights have been respected.

3. The person arrested shall have the right to apply to the competent authority in the custodial State for interim release pending surrender.

4. In reaching a decision on any such application, the competent authority in the custodial State shall consider whether, given the gravity of the alleged crimes, there are urgent and exceptional

circumstances to justify interim release and whether necessary safeguards exist to ensure that the custodial State can fulfil its duty to surrender the person to the Court. It shall not be open to the competent authority of the custodial State to consider whether the warrant of arrest was properly issued in accordance with article 58, paragraph 1(a) and (b).

5. The Pre-Trial Chamber shall be notified of any request for interim release and shall make recommendations to the competent authority in the custodial State. The competent authority in the custodial State shall give full consideration to such recommendations, including any recommendations on measures to prevent the escape of the person, before rendering its decision.

6. If the person is granted interim release, the Pre-Trial Chamber may request periodic reports on the status of the interim release.

7. Once ordered to be surrendered by the custodial State, the person shall be delivered to the Court as soon as possible.

Article 60   Initial proceedings before the Court

1. Upon the surrender of the person to the Court, or the person's appearance before the Court voluntarily or pursuant to a summons, the Pre-Trial Chamber shall satisfy itself that the person has been informed of the crimes which he or she is alleged to have committed, and of his or her rights under this Statute, including the right to apply for interim release pending trial.

2. A person subject to a warrant of arrest may apply for interim release pending trial. If the Pre-Trial Chamber is satisfied that the conditions set forth in article 58, paragraph 1, are met, the person shall continue to be detained. If it is not so satisfied, the Pre-Trial Chamber shall release the person, with or without conditions.

3. The Pre-Trial Chamber shall periodically review its ruling on the release or detention of the person, and may do so at any time on the request of the Prosecutor or the person. Upon such review, it may modify its ruling as to detention, release or conditions of release, if it is satisfied that changed circumstances so require.

4. The Pre-Trial Chamber shall ensure that a person is not detained for an unreasonable period prior to trial due to inexcusable delay by the Prosecutor. If such delay occurs, the Court shall consider releasing the person, with or without conditions.

5. If necessary, the Pre-Trial Chamber may issue a warrant of arrest to secure the presence of a person who has been released.

Article 61   Confirmation of the charges before trial

1. Subject to the provisions of paragraph 2, within a reasonable time after the person's surrender or voluntary appearance before the Court, the Pre-Trial Chamber shall hold a hearing to confirm the charges on which the Prosecutor intends to seek trial. The hearing shall be held in the presence of the Prosecutor and the person charged, as well as his or her counsel.

2. The Pre-Trial Chamber may, upon request of the Prosecutor or on its own motion, hold a hearing in the absence of the person charged to confirm the charges on which the Prosecutor intends to seek trial when the person has:

(a) Waived his or her right to be present; or

(b) Fled or cannot be found and all reasonable steps have been taken to secure his or her appearance before the Court and to inform the person of the charges and that a hearing to confirm those charges will be held. In that case, the person shall be represented by counsel where the Pre-Trial Chamber determines that it is in the interests of justice.

3. Within a reasonable time before the hearing, the person shall:

(a) Be provided with a copy of the document containing the charges on which the Prosecutor intends to bring the person to trial; and

(b) Be informed of the evidence on which the Prosecutor intends to rely at the hearing. The Pre-Trial Chamber may issue orders regarding the disclosure of information for the purposes of the hearing.

4. Before the hearing, the Prosecutor may continue the investigation and may amend or withdraw any charges. The person shall be given reasonable notice before the hearing of any amendment

to or withdrawal of charges. In case of a withdrawal of charges, the Prosecutor shall notify the Pre-Trial Chamber of the reasons for the withdrawal.

5. At the hearing, the Prosecutor shall support each charge with sufficient evidence to establish substantial grounds to believe that the person committed the crime charged. The Prosecutor may rely on documentary or summary evidence and need not call the witnesses expected to testify at the trial.

6. At the hearing, the person may:

(a) Object to the charges;

(b) Challenge the evidence presented by the Prosecutor; and

(c) Present evidence.

7. The Pre-Trial Chamber shall, on the basis of the hearing, determine whether there is sufficient evidence to establish substantial grounds to believe that the person committed each of the crimes charged. Based on its determination, the Pre-Trial Chamber shall:

(a) Confirm those charges in relation to which it has determined that there is sufficient evidence, and commit the person to a Trial Chamber for trial on the charges as confirmed;

(b) Decline to confirm those charges in relation to which it has determined that there is insufficient evidence;

(c) Adjourn the hearing and request the Prosecutor to consider:

(i) Providing further evidence or conducting further investigation with respect to a particular charge; or

(ii) Amending a charge because the evidence submitted appears to establish a different crime within the jurisdiction of the Court.

8. Where the Pre-Trial Chamber declines to confirm a charge, the Prosecutor shall not be precluded from subsequently requesting its confirmation if the request is supported by additional evidence.

9. After the charges are confirmed and before the trial has begun, the Prosecutor may, with the permission of the Pre-Trial Chamber and after notice to the accused, amend the charges. If the Prosecutor seeks to add additional charges or to substitute more serious charges, a hearing under this article to confirm those charges must be held. After commencement of the trial, the Prosecutor may, with the permission of the Trial Chamber, withdraw the charges.

10. Any warrant previously issued shall cease to have effect with respect to any charges which have not been confirmed by the Pre-Trial Chamber or which have been withdrawn by the Prosecutor.

11. Once the charges have been confirmed, in accordance with this article, the Presidency shall constitute a Trial Chamber which, subject to paragraph 8 and to article 64, paragraph 4, shall be responsible for the conduct of subsequent proceedings and may exercise any function of the Pre-Trial Chamber that is relevant and capable of application in those proceedings.

PART 6   THE TRIAL

Article 62   Place of trial
Unless otherwise decided, the place of the trial shall be the seat of the Court.

Article 63   Trial in the presence of the accused
1. The accused shall be present during the trial.

2. If the accused, being present before the Court, continues to disrupt the trial, the Trial Chamber may remove the accused and shall make provision for him or her to observe the trial and instruct counsel from outside the courtroom, through the use of communications technology, if required. Such measures shall be taken only in exceptional circumstances after other reasonable alternatives have proved inadequate, and only for such duration as is strictly required.

Article 64   Functions and powers of the Trial Chamber
1. The functions and powers of the Trial Chamber set out in this article shall be exercised in accordance with this Statute and the Rules of Procedure and Evidence.

2. The Trial Chamber shall ensure that a trial is fair and expeditious and is conducted with full respect for the rights of the accused and due regard for the protection of victims and witnesses.

3. Upon assignment of a case for trial in accordance with this Statute, the Trial Chamber assigned to deal with the case shall:

(a) Confer with the parties and adopt such procedures as are necessary to facilitate the fair and expeditious conduct of the proceedings;

(b) Determine the language or languages to be used at trial; and

(c) Subject to any other relevant provisions of this Statute, provide for disclosure of documents or information not previously disclosed, sufficiently in advance of the commencement of the trial to enable adequate preparation for trial.

4. The Trial Chamber may, if necessary for its effective and fair functioning, refer preliminary issues to the Pre-Trial Chamber or, if necessary, to another available judge of the Pre-Trial Division.

5. Upon notice to the parties, the Trial Chamber may, as appropriate, direct that there be joinder or severance in respect of charges against more than one accused.

6. In performing its functions prior to trial or during the course of a trial, the Trial Chamber may, as necessary:

(a) Exercise any functions of the Pre-Trial Chamber referred to in article 61, paragraph 11;

(b) Require the attendance and testimony of witnesses and production of documents and other evidence by obtaining, if necessary, the assistance of States as provided in this Statute;

(c) Provide for the protection of confidential information;

(d) Order the production of evidence in addition to that already collected prior to the trial or presented during the trial by the parties;

(e) Provide for the protection of the accused, witnesses and victims; and

(f) Rule on any other relevant matters.

7. The trial shall be held in public. The Trial Chamber may, however, determine that special circumstances require that certain proceedings be in closed session for the purposes set forth in article 68, or to protect confidential or sensitive information to be given in evidence.

8. (a) At the commencement of the trial, the Trial Chamber shall have read to the accused the charges previously confirmed by the Pre-Trial Chamber. The Trial Chamber shall satisfy itself that the accused understands the nature of the charges. It shall afford him or her the opportunity to make an admission of guilt in accordance with article 65 or to plead not guilty.

(b) At the trial, the presiding judge may give directions for the conduct of proceedings, including to ensure that they are conducted in a fair and impartial manner. Subject to any directions of the presiding judge, the parties may submit evidence in accordance with the provisions of this Statute.

9. The Trial Chamber shall have, *inter alia*, the power on application of a party or on its own motion to:

(a) Rule on the admissibility or relevance of evidence; and

(b) Take all necessary steps to maintain order in the course of a hearing.

10. The Trial Chamber shall ensure that a complete record of the trial, which accurately reflects the proceedings, is made and that it is maintained and preserved by the Registrar.

Article 65   Proceedings on an admission of guilt

1. Where the accused makes an admission of guilt pursuant to article 64, paragraph 8(a), the Trial Chamber shall determine whether:

(a) The accused understands the nature and consequences of the admission of guilt;

(b) The admission is voluntarily made by the accused after sufficient consultation with defence counsel; and

(c) The admission of guilt is supported by the facts of the case that are contained in:

(i)   The charges brought by the Prosecutor and admitted by the accused;

(ii) Any materials presented by the Prosecutor which supplement the charges and which the accused accepts; and

(iii) Any other evidence, such as the testimony of witnesses, presented by the Prosecutor or the accused.

2. Where the Trial Chamber is satisfied that the matters referred to in paragraph 1 are established, it shall consider the admission of guilt, together with any additional evidence presented, as establishing all the essential facts that are required to prove the crime to which the admission of guilt relates, and may convict the accused of that crime.

3. Where the Trial Chamber is not satisfied that the matters referred to in paragraph 1 are established, it shall consider the admission of guilt as not having been made, in which case it shall order that the trial be continued under the ordinary trial procedures provided by this Statute and may remit the case to another Trial Chamber.

4. Where the Trial Chamber is of the opinion that a more complete presentation of the facts of the case is required in the interests of justice, in particular the interests of the victims, the Trial Chamber may:

(a) Request the Prosecutor to present additional evidence, including the testimony of witnesses; or

(b) Order that the trial be continued under the ordinary trial procedures provided by this Statute, in which case it shall consider the admission of guilt as not having been made and may remit the case to another Trial Chamber.

5. Any discussions between the Prosecutor and the defence regarding modification of the charges, the admission of guilt or the penalty to be imposed shall not be binding on the Court.

Article 66   Presumption of innocence

1. Everyone shall be presumed innocent until proved guilty before the Court in accordance with the applicable law.

2. The onus is on the Prosecutor to prove the guilt of the accused.

3. In order to convict the accused, the Court must be convinced of the guilt of the accused beyond reasonable doubt.

Article 67   Rights of the accused

1. In the determination of any charge, the accused shall be entitled to a public hearing, having regard to the provisions of this Statute, to a fair hearing conducted impartially, and to the following minimum guarantees, in full equality:

(a) To be informed promptly and in detail of the nature, cause and content of the charge, in a language which the accused fully understands and speaks;

(b) To have adequate time and facilities for the preparation of the defence and to communicate freely with counsel of the accused's choosing in confidence;

(c) To be tried without undue delay;

(d) Subject to article 63, paragraph 2, to be present at the trial, to conduct the defence in person or through legal assistance of the accused's choosing, to be informed, if the accused does not have legal assistance, of this right and to have legal assistance assigned by the Court in any case where the interests of justice so require, and without payment if the accused lacks sufficient means to pay for it;

(e) To examine, or have examined, the witnesses against him or her and to obtain the attendance and examination of witnesses on his or her behalf under the same conditions as witnesses against him or her. The accused shall also be entitled to raise defences and to present other evidence admissible under this Statute;

(f) To have, free of any cost, the assistance of a competent interpreter and such translations as are necessary to meet the requirements of fairness, if any of the proceedings of or documents presented to the Court are not in a language which the accused fully understands and speaks;

(g) Not to be compelled to testify or to confess guilt and to remain silent, without such silence being a consideration in the determination of guilt or innocence;

(h) To make an unsworn oral or written statement in his or her defence; and

(i) Not to have imposed on him or her any reversal of the burden of proof or any onus of rebuttal.

2. In addition to any other disclosure provided for in this Statute, the Prosecutor shall, as soon as practicable, disclose to the defence evidence in the Prosecutor's possession or control which he or she believes shows or tends to show the innocence of the accused, or to mitigate the guilt of the accused, or which may affect the credibility of prosecution evidence. In case of doubt as to the application of this paragraph, the Court shall decide.

Article 68   Protection of the victims and witnesses and their participation in the proceedings

1. The Court shall take appropriate measures to protect the safety, physical and psychological well-being, dignity and privacy of victims and witnesses. In so doing, the Court shall have regard to all relevant factors, including age, gender as defined in article 7, paragraph 3, and health, and the nature of the crime, in particular, but not limited to, where the crime involves sexual or gender violence or violence against children. The Prosecutor shall take such measures particularly during the investigation and prosecution of such crimes. These measures shall not be prejudicial to or inconsistent with the rights of the accused and a fair and impartial trial.

2. As an exception to the principle of public hearings provided for in article 67, the Chambers of the Court may, to protect victims and witnesses or an accused, conduct any part of the proceedings in camera or allow the presentation of evidence by electronic or other special means. In particular, such measures shall be implemented in the case of a victim of sexual violence or a child who is a victim or a witness, unless otherwise ordered by the Court, having regard to all the circumstances, particularly the views of the victim or witness.

3. Where the personal interests of the victims are affected, the Court shall permit their views and concerns to be presented and considered at stages of the proceedings determined to be appropriate by the Court and in a manner which is not prejudicial to or inconsistent with the rights of the accused and a fair and impartial trial. Such views and concerns may be presented by the legal representatives of the victims where the Court considers it appropriate, in accordance with the Rules of Procedure and Evidence.

4. The Victims and Witnesses Unit may advise the Prosecutor and the Court on appropriate protective measures, security arrangements, counselling and assistance as referred to in article 43, paragraph 6.

5. Where the disclosure of evidence or information pursuant to this Statute may lead to the grave endangerment of the security of a witness or his or her family, the Prosecutor may, for the purposes of any proceedings conducted prior to the commencement of the trial, withhold such evidence or information and instead submit a summary thereof. Such measures shall be exercised in a manner which is not prejudicial to or inconsistent with the rights of the accused and a fair and impartial trial.

6. A State may make an application for necessary measures to be taken in respect of the protection of its servants or agents and the protection of confidential or sensitive information.

Article 69   Evidence

1. Before testifying, each witness shall, in accordance with the Rules of Procedure and Evidence, give an undertaking as to the truthfulness of the evidence to be given by that witness.

2. The testimony of a witness at trial shall be given in person, except to the extent provided by the measures set forth in article 68 or in the Rules of Procedure and Evidence. The Court may also permit the giving of viva voce (oral) or recorded testimony of a witness by means of video or audio technology, as well as the introduction of documents or written transcripts, subject to this Statute and in accordance with the Rules of Procedure and Evidence. These measures shall not be prejudicial to or inconsistent with the rights of the accused.

3. The parties may submit evidence relevant to the case, in accordance with article 64. The Court shall have the authority to request the submission of all evidence that it considers necessary for the determination of the truth.

4. The Court may rule on the relevance or admissibility of any evidence, taking into account, *inter alia*, the probative value of the evidence and any prejudice that such evidence may cause to a fair trial or to a fair evaluation of the testimony of a witness, in accordance with the Rules of Procedure and Evidence.

5. The Court shall respect and observe privileges on confidentiality as provided for in the Rules of Procedure and Evidence.

6. The Court shall not require proof of facts of common knowledge but may take judicial notice of them.

7. Evidence obtained by means of a violation of this Statute or internationally recognized human rights shall not be admissible if:

    (a) The violation casts substantial doubt on the reliability of the evidence; or

    (b) The admission of the evidence would be antithetical to and would seriously damage the integrity of the proceedings.

8. When deciding on the relevance or admissibility of evidence collected by a State, the Court shall not rule on the application of the State's national law.

Article 70   Offences against the administration of justice

1. The Court shall have jurisdiction over the following offences against its administration of justice when committed intentionally:

    (a) Giving false testimony when under an obligation pursuant to article 69, paragraph 1, to tell the truth;

    (b) Presenting evidence that the party knows is false or forged;

    (c) Corruptly influencing a witness, obstructing or interfering with the attendance or testimony of a witness, retaliating against a witness for giving testimony or destroying, tampering with or interfering with the collection of evidence;

    (d) Impeding, intimidating or corruptly influencing an official of the Court for the purpose of forcing or persuading the official not to perform, or to perform improperly, his or her duties;

    (e) Retaliating against an official of the Court on account of duties performed by that or another official;

    (f) Soliciting or accepting a bribe as an official of the Court in conjunction with his or her official duties.

2. The principles and procedures governing the Court's exercise of jurisdiction over offences under this article shall be those provided for in the Rules of Procedure and Evidence. The conditions for providing international cooperation to the Court with respect to its proceedings under this article shall be governed by the domestic laws of the requested State.

3. In the event of conviction, the Court may impose a term of imprisonment not exceeding five years, or a fine in accordance with the Rules of Procedure and Evidence, or both.

4. (a) Each State Party shall extend its criminal laws penalizing offences against the integrity of its own investigative or judicial process to offences against the administration of justice referred to in this article, committed on its territory, or by one of its nationals;

    (b) Upon request by the Court, whenever it deems it proper, the State Party shall submit the case to its competent authorities for the purpose of prosecution. Those authorities shall treat such cases with diligence and devote sufficient resources to enable them to be conducted effectively.

Article 71   Sanctions for misconduct before the Court

1. The Court may sanction persons present before it who commit misconduct, including disruption of its proceedings or deliberate refusal to comply with its directions, by administrative measures

other than imprisonment, such as temporary or permanent removal from the courtroom, a fine or other similar measures provided for in the Rules of Procedure and Evidence.

2. The procedures governing the imposition of the measures set forth in paragraph 1 shall be those provided for in the Rules of Procedure and Evidence.

Article 72   Protection of national security information

1. This article applies in any case where the disclosure of the information or documents of a State would, in the opinion of that State, prejudice its national security interests. Such cases include those falling within the scope of article 56, paragraphs 2 and 3, article 61, paragraph 3, article 64, paragraph 3, article 67, paragraph 2, article 68, paragraph 6, article 87, paragraph 6 and article 93, as well as cases arising at any other stage of the proceedings where such disclosure may be at issue.

2. This article shall also apply when a person who has been requested to give information or evidence has refused to do so or has referred the matter to the State on the ground that disclosure would prejudice the national security interests of a State and the State concerned confirms that it is of the opinion that disclosure would prejudice its national security interests.

3. Nothing in this article shall prejudice the requirements of confidentiality applicable under article 54, paragraph 3(e) and (f), or the application of article 73.

4. If a State learns that information or documents of the State are being, or are likely to be, disclosed at any stage of the proceedings, and it is of the opinion that disclosure would prejudice its national security interests, that State shall have the right to intervene in order to obtain resolution of the issue in accordance with this article.

5. If, in the opinion of a State, disclosure of information would prejudice its national security interests, all reasonable steps will be taken by the State, acting in conjunction with the Prosecutor, the defence or the Pre-Trial Chamber or Trial Chamber, as the case may be, to seek to resolve the matter by cooperative means. Such steps may include:

(a) Modification or clarification of the request;

(b) A determination by the Court regarding the relevance of the information or evidence sought, or a determination as to whether the evidence, though relevant, could be or has been obtained from a source other than the requested State;

(c) Obtaining the information or evidence from a different source or in a different form; or

(d) Agreement on conditions under which the assistance could be provided including, among other things, providing summaries or redactions, limitations on disclosure, use of *in camera* or *ex parte* proceedings, or other protective measures permissible under the Statute and the Rules.

6. Once all reasonable steps have been taken to resolve the matter through cooperative means, and if the State considers that there are no means or conditions under which the information or documents could be provided or disclosed without prejudice to its national security interests, it shall so notify the Prosecutor or the Court of the specific reasons for its decision, unless a specific description of the reasons would itself necessarily result in such prejudice to the State's national security interests.

7. Thereafter, if the Court determines that the evidence is relevant and necessary for the establishment of the guilt or innocence of the accused, the Court may undertake the following actions:

(a) Where disclosure of the information or document is sought pursuant to a request for cooperation under Part 9 or the circumstances described in paragraph 2, and the State has invoked the ground for refusal referred to in article 93, paragraph 4:

(i) The Court may, before making any conclusion referred to in subparagraph 7(a)(ii), request further consultations for the purpose of considering the State's representations, which may include, as appropriate, hearings *in camera* and *ex parte*;

(ii) If the Court concludes that, by invoking the ground for refusal under article 93, paragraph 4, in the circumstances of the case, the requested State is not acting in accordance with its obligations under this Statute, the Court may refer the matter in accordance with article 87, paragraph 7, specifying the reasons for its conclusion; and

    (iii) The Court may make such inference in the trial of the accused as to the existence or non-existence of a fact, as may be appropriate in the circumstances; or

  (b) In all other circumstances:

    (i) Order disclosure; or

    (ii) To the extent it does not order disclosure, make such inference in the trial of the accused as to the existence or non-existence of a fact, as may be appropriate in the circumstances.

Article 73   Third-party information or documents

If a State Party is requested by the Court to provide a document or information in its custody, possession or control, which was disclosed to it in confidence by a State, intergovernmental organization or international organization, it shall seek the consent of the originator to disclose that document or information. If the originator is a State Party, it shall either consent to disclosure of the information or document or undertake to resolve the issue of disclosure with the Court, subject to the provisions of article 72. If the originator is not a State Party and refuses to consent to disclosure, the requested State shall inform the Court that it is unable to provide the document or information because of a pre-existing obligation of confidentiality to the originator.

Article 74   Requirements for the decision

1. All the judges of the Trial Chamber shall be present at each stage of the trial and throughout their deliberations. The Presidency may, on a case-by-case basis, designate, as available, one or more alternate judges to be present at each stage of the trial and to replace a member of the Trial Chamber if that member is unable to continue attending.

2. The Trial Chamber's decision shall be based on its evaluation of the evidence and the entire proceedings. The decision shall not exceed the facts and circumstances described in the charges and any amendments to the charges. The Court may base its decision only on evidence submitted and discussed before it at the trial.

3. The judges shall attempt to achieve unanimity in their decision, failing which the decision shall be taken by a majority of the judges.

4. The deliberations of the Trial Chamber shall remain secret.

5. The decision shall be in writing and shall contain a full and reasoned statement of the Trial Chamber's findings on the evidence and conclusions. The Trial Chamber shall issue one decision. When there is no unanimity, the Trial Chamber's decision shall contain the views of the majority and the minority. The decision or a summary thereof shall be delivered in open court.

Article 75   Reparations to victims

1. The Court shall establish principles relating to reparations to, or in respect of, victims, including restitution, compensation and rehabilitation. On this basis, in its decision the Court may, either upon request or on its own motion in exceptional circumstances, determine the scope and extent of any damage, loss and injury to, or in respect of, victims and will state the principles on which it is acting.

2. The Court may make an order directly against a convicted person specifying appropriate reparations to, or in respect of, victims, including restitution, compensation and rehabilitation. Where appropriate, the Court may order that the award for reparations be made through the Trust Fund provided for in article 79.

3. Before making an order under this article, the Court may invite and shall take account of representations from or on behalf of the convicted person, victims, other interested persons or interested States.

4. In exercising its power under this article, the Court may, after a person is convicted of a crime within the jurisdiction of the Court, determine whether, in order to give effect to an order which it may make under this article, it is necessary to seek measures under article 93, paragraph 1.

5. A State Party shall give effect to a decision under this article as if the provisions of article 109 were applicable to this article.

6. Nothing in this article shall be interpreted as prejudicing the rights of victims under national or international law.

Article 76   Sentencing

1. In the event of a conviction, the Trial Chamber shall consider the appropriate sentence to be imposed and shall take into account the evidence presented and submissions made during the trial that are relevant to the sentence.

2. Except where article 65 applies and before the completion of the trial, the Trial Chamber may on its own motion and shall, at the request of the Prosecutor or the accused, hold a further hearing to hear any additional evidence or submissions relevant to the sentence, in accordance with the Rules of Procedure and Evidence.

3. Where paragraph 2 applies, any representations under article 75 shall be heard during the further hearing referred to in paragraph 2 and, if necessary, during any additional hearing.

4. The sentence shall be pronounced in public and, wherever possible, in the presence of the accused.

PART 7   PENALTIES

Article 77   Applicable penalties

1. Subject to article 110, the Court may impose one of the following penalties on a person convicted of a crime referred to in article 5 of this Statute:
   (a) Imprisonment for a specified number of years, which may not exceed a maximum of 30 years; or
   (b) A term of life imprisonment when justified by the extreme gravity of the crime and the individual circumstances of the convicted person.

2. In addition to imprisonment, the Court may order:
   (a) A fine under the criteria provided for in the Rules of Procedure and Evidence;
   (b) A forfeiture of proceeds, property and assets derived directly or indirectly from that crime, without prejudice to the rights of bona fide third parties.

Article 78   Determination of the sentence

1. In determining the sentence, the Court shall, in accordance with the Rules of Procedure and Evidence, take into account such factors as the gravity of the crime and the individual circumstances of the convicted person.

2. In imposing a sentence of imprisonment, the Court shall deduct the time, if any, previously spent in detention in accordance with an order of the Court. The Court may deduct any time otherwise spent in detention in connection with conduct underlying the crime.

3. When a person has been convicted of more than one crime, the Court shall pronounce a sentence for each crime and a joint sentence specifying the total period of imprisonment. This period shall be no less than the highest individual sentence pronounced and shall not exceed 30 years' imprisonment or a sentence of life imprisonment in conformity with article 77, paragraph 1(b).

Article 79   Trust Fund

1. A Trust Fund shall be established by decision of the Assembly of States Parties for the benefit of victims of crimes within the jurisdiction of the Court, and of the families of such victims.

2. The Court may order money and other property collected through fines or forfeiture to be transferred, by order of the Court, to the Trust Fund.

3. The Trust Fund shall be managed according to criteria to be determined by the Assembly of States Parties.

Article 80   Non-prejudice to national application of penalties and national laws

Nothing in this Part affects the application by States of penalties prescribed by their national law, nor the law of States which do not provide for penalties prescribed in this Part.

PART 8 APPEAL AND REVISION

Article 81   Appeal against decision of acquittal or conviction or against sentence

1. A decision under article 74 may be appealed in accordance with the Rules of Procedure and Evidence as follows:
   (a) The Prosecutor may make an appeal on any of the following grounds:
       (i) Procedural error,
       (ii) Error of fact, or
       (iii) Error of law;
   (b) The convicted person, or the Prosecutor on that person's behalf, may make an appeal on any of the following grounds:
       (i) Procedural error,
       (ii) Error of fact,
       (iii) Error of law, or
       (iv) Any other ground that affects the fairness or reliability of the proceedings or decision.
2. (a) A sentence may be appealed, in accordance with the Rules of Procedure and Evidence, by the Prosecutor or the convicted person on the ground of disproportion between the crime and the sentence;
   (b) If on an appeal against sentence the Court considers that there are grounds on which the conviction might be set aside, wholly or in part, it may invite the Prosecutor and the convicted person to submit grounds under article 81, paragraph 1(a) or (b), and may render a decision on conviction in accordance with article 83;
   (c) The same procedure applies when the Court, on an appeal against conviction only, considers that there are grounds to reduce the sentence under paragraph 2(a).
3. (a) Unless the Trial Chamber orders otherwise, a convicted person shall remain in custody pending an appeal;
   (b) When a convicted person's time in custody exceeds the sentence of imprisonment imposed, that person shall be released, except that if the Prosecutor is also appealing, the release may be subject to the conditions under subparagraph (c) below;
   (c) In case of an acquittal, the accused shall be released immediately, subject to the following:
       (i) Under exceptional circumstances, and having regard, *inter alia*, to the concrete risk of flight, the seriousness of the offence charged and the probability of success on appeal, the Trial Chamber, at the request of the Prosecutor, may maintain the detention of the person pending appeal;
       (ii) A decision by the Trial Chamber under subparagraph (c)(i) may be appealed in accordance with the Rules of Procedure and Evidence.
4. Subject to the provisions of paragraph 3(a) and (b), execution of the decision or sentence shall be suspended during the period allowed for appeal and for the duration of the appeal proceedings.

Article 82   Appeal against other decisions

1. Either party may appeal any of the following decisions in accordance with the Rules of Procedure and Evidence:
   (a) A decision with respect to jurisdiction or admissibility;

(b) A decision granting or denying release of the person being investigated or prosecuted;

(c) A decision of the Pre-Trial Chamber to act on its own initiative under article 56, paragraph 3;

(d) A decision that involves an issue that would significantly affect the fair and expeditious conduct of the proceedings or the outcome of the trial, and for which, in the opinion of the Pre-Trial or Trial Chamber, an immediate resolution by the Appeals Chamber may materially advance the proceedings.

2. A decision of the Pre-Trial Chamber under article 57, paragraph 3(d), may be appealed against by the State concerned or by the Prosecutor, with the leave of the Pre-Trial Chamber. The appeal shall be heard on an expedited basis.

3. An appeal shall not of itself have suspensive effect unless the Appeals Chamber so orders, upon request, in accordance with the Rules of Procedure and Evidence.

4. A legal representative of the victims, the convicted person or a bona fide owner of property adversely affected by an order under article 75 may appeal against the order for reparations, as provided in the Rules of Procedure and Evidence.

Article 83   Proceedings on appeal

1. For the purposes of proceedings under article 81 and this article, the Appeals Chamber shall have all the powers of the Trial Chamber.

2. If the Appeals Chamber finds that the proceedings appealed from were unfair in a way that affected the reliability of the decision or sentence, or that the decision or sentence appealed from was materially affected by error of fact or law or procedural error, it may:

(a) Reverse or amend the decision or sentence; or

(b) Order a new trial before a different Trial Chamber.

For these purposes, the Appeals Chamber may remand a factual issue to the original Trial Chamber for it to determine the issue and to report back accordingly, or may itself call evidence to determine the issue. When the decision or sentence has been appealed only by the person convicted, or the Prosecutor on that person's behalf, it cannot be amended to his or her detriment.

3. If in an appeal against sentence the Appeals Chamber finds that the sentence is disproportionate to the crime, it may vary the sentence in accordance with Part 7.

4. The judgment of the Appeals Chamber shall be taken by a majority of the judges and shall be delivered in open court. The judgment shall state the reasons on which it is based. When there is no unanimity, the judgment of the Appeals Chamber shall contain the views of the majority and the minority, but a judge may deliver a separate or dissenting opinion on a question of law.

5. The Appeals Chamber may deliver its judgement in the absence of the person acquitted or convicted.

Article 84   Revision of conviction or sentence

1. The convicted person or, after death, spouses, children, parents or one person alive at the time of the accused's death who has been given express written instructions from the accused to bring such a claim, or the Prosecutor on the person's behalf, may apply to the Appeals Chamber to revise the final judgement of conviction or sentence on the grounds that:

(a) New evidence has been discovered that:

(i) Was not available at the time of trial, and such unavailability was not wholly or partially attributable to the party making application; and

(ii) Is sufficiently important that had it been proved at trial it would have been likely to have resulted in a different verdict;

(b) It has been newly discovered that decisive evidence, taken into account at trial and upon which the conviction depends, was false, forged or falsified;

(c) One or more of the judges who participated in conviction or confirmation of the charges has committed, in that case, an act of serious misconduct or serious breach of duty of sufficient gravity to justify the removal of that judge or those judges from office under article 46.

2. The Appeals Chamber shall reject the application if it considers it to be unfounded. If it determines that the application is meritorious, it may, as appropriate:

  (a) Reconvene the original Trial Chamber;

  (b) Constitute a new Trial Chamber; or

  (c) Retain jurisdiction over the matter,

with a view to, after hearing the parties in the manner set forth in the Rules of Procedure and Evidence, arriving at a determination on whether the judgement should be revised.

Article 85   Compensation to an arrested or convicted person

1. Anyone who has been the victim of unlawful arrest or detention shall have an enforceable right to compensation.

2. When a person has by a final decision been convicted of a criminal offence, and when subsequently his or her conviction has been reversed on the ground that a new or newly discovered fact shows conclusively that there has been a miscarriage of justice, the person who has suffered punishment as a result of such conviction shall be compensated according to law, unless it is proved that the non-disclosure of the unknown fact in time is wholly or partly attributable to him or her.

3. In exceptional circumstances, where the Court finds conclusive facts showing that there has been a grave and manifest miscarriage of justice, it may in its discretion award compensation, according to the criteria provided in the Rules of Procedure and Evidence, to a person who has been released from detention following a final decision of acquittal or a termination of the proceedings for that reason.

PART 9 INTERNATIONAL COOPERATION AND JUDICIAL ASSISTANCE

Article 86   General obligation to cooperate

States Parties shall, in accordance with the provisions of this Statute, cooperate fully with the Court in its investigation and prosecution of crimes within the jurisdiction of the Court.

Article 87   Requests for cooperation: general provisions

1. (a) The Court shall have the authority to make requests to States Parties for cooperation. The requests shall be transmitted through the diplomatic channel or any other appropriate channel as may be designated by each State Party upon ratification, acceptance, approval or accession. Subsequent changes to the designation shall be made by each State Party in accordance with the Rules of Procedure and Evidence.

  (b) When appropriate, without prejudice to the provisions of subparagraph (a), requests may also be transmitted through the International Criminal Police Organization or any appropriate regional organization.

2. Requests for cooperation and any documents supporting the request shall either be in or be accompanied by a translation into an official language of the requested State or in one of the working languages of the Court, in accordance with the choice made by that State upon ratification, acceptance, approval or accession. Subsequent changes to this choice shall be made in accordance with the Rules of Procedure and Evidence.

3. The requested State shall keep confidential a request for cooperation and any documents supporting the request, except to the extent that the disclosure is necessary for execution of the request.

4. In relation to any request for assistance presented under Part 9, the Court may take such measures, including measures related to the protection of information, as may be necessary to ensure the safety or physical or psychological well-being of any victims, potential witnesses and their families. The Court may request that any information that is made available under Part 9 shall be provided and handled in a manner that protects the safety and physical or psychological well-being of any victims, potential witnesses and their families.

5. (a) The Court may invite any State not party to this Statute to provide assistance under this Part on the basis of an ad hoc arrangement, an agreement with such State or any other appropriate basis.

   (b) Where a State not party to this Statute, which has entered into an ad hoc arrangement or an agreement with the Court, fails to cooperate with requests pursuant to any such arrangement or agreement, the Court may so inform the Assembly of States Parties or, where the Security Council referred the matter to the Court, the Security Council.

6. The Court may ask any intergovernmental organization to provide information or documents. The Court may also ask for other forms of cooperation and assistance which may be agreed upon with such an organization and which are in accordance with its competence or mandate.

7. Where a State Party fails to comply with a request to cooperate by the Court contrary to the provisions of this Statute, thereby preventing the Court from exercising its functions and powers under this Statute, the Court may make a finding to that effect and refer the matter to the Assembly of States Parties or, where the Security Council referred the matter to the Court, to the Security Council.

Article 88   Availability of procedures under national law

States Parties shall ensure that there are procedures available under their national law for all of the forms of cooperation which are specified under this Part.

Article 89   Surrender of persons to the Court

1. The Court may transmit a request for the arrest and surrender of a person, together with the material supporting the request outlined in article 91, to any State on the territory of which that person may be found and shall request the cooperation of that State in the arrest and surrender of such a person. States Parties shall, in accordance with the provisions of this Part and the procedure under their national law, comply with requests for arrest and surrender.

2. Where the person sought for surrender brings a challenge before a national court on the basis of the principle of *ne bis in idem* as provided in article 20, the requested State shall immediately consult with the Court to determine if there has been a relevant ruling on admissibility. If the case is admissible, the requested State shall proceed with the execution of the request. If an admissibility ruling is pending, the requested State may postpone the execution of the request for surrender of the person until the Court makes a determination on admissibility.

3. (a) A State Party shall authorize, in accordance with its national procedural law, transportation through its territory of a person being surrendered to the Court by another State, except where transit through that State would impede or delay the surrender.

   (b) A request by the Court for transit shall be transmitted in accordance with article 87. The request for transit shall contain:

      (i)   A description of the person being transported;

      (ii) A brief statement of the facts of the case and their legal characterization; and

      (iii) The warrant for arrest and surrender;

   (c) A person being transported shall be detained in custody during the period of transit;

   (d) No authorization is required if the person is transported by air and no landing is scheduled on the territory of the transit State;

   (e) If an unscheduled landing occurs on the territory of the transit State, that State may require a request for transit from the Court as provided for in subparagraph (b). The transit State shall detain the person being transported until the request for transit is received and the transit is effected, provided that detention for purposes of this subparagraph may not be extended beyond 96 hours from the unscheduled landing unless the request is received within that time.

4. If the person sought is being proceeded against or is serving a sentence in the requested State for a crime different from that for which surrender to the Court is sought, the requested State, after making its decision to grant the request, shall consult with the Court.

Article 90 Competing requests

1. A State Party which receives a request from the Court for the surrender of a person under article 89 shall, if it also receives a request from any other State for the extradition of the same person for the same conduct which forms the basis of the crime for which the Court seeks the person's surrender, notify the Court and the requesting State of that fact.

2. Where the requesting State is a State Party, the requested State shall give priority to the request from the Court if:

   (a) The Court has, pursuant to articles 18 and 19, made a determination that the case in respect of which surrender is sought is admissible and that determination takes into account the investigation or prosecution conducted by the requesting State in respect of its request for extradition; or

   (b) The Court makes the determination described in subparagraph (a) pursuant to the requested State's notification under paragraph 1.

3. Where a determination under paragraph 2(a) has not been made, the requested State may, at its discretion, pending the determination of the Court under paragraph 2(b), proceed to deal with the request for extradition from the requesting State but shall not extradite the person until the Court has determined that the case is inadmissible. The Court's determination shall be made on an expedited basis.

4. If the requesting State is a State not Party to this Statute the requested State, if it is not under an international obligation to extradite the person to the requesting State, shall give priority to the request for surrender from the Court, if the Court has determined that the case is admissible.

5. Where a case under paragraph 4 has not been determined to be admissible by the Court, the requested State may, at its discretion, proceed to deal with the request for extradition from the requesting State.

6. In cases where paragraph 4 applies except that the requested State is under an existing international obligation to extradite the person to the requesting State not Party to this Statute, the requested State shall determine whether to surrender the person to the Court or extradite the person to the requesting State. In making its decision, the requested State shall consider all the relevant factors, including but not limited to:

   (a) The respective dates of the requests;

   (b) The interests of the requesting State including, where relevant, whether the crime was committed in its territory and the nationality of the victims and of the person sought; and

   (c) The possibility of subsequent surrender between the Court and the requesting State.

7. Where a State Party which receives a request from the Court for the surrender of a person also receives a request from any State for the extradition of the same person for conduct other than that which constitutes the crime for which the Court seeks the person's surrender:

   (a) The requested State shall, if it is not under an existing international obligation to extradite the person to the requesting State, give priority to the request from the Court;

   (b) The requested State shall, if it is under an existing international obligation to extradite the person to the requesting State, determine whether to surrender the person to the Court or to extradite the person to the requesting State. In making its decision, the requested State shall consider all the relevant factors, including but not limited to those set out in paragraph 6, but shall give special consideration to the relative nature and gravity of the conduct in question.

8. Where pursuant to a notification under this article, the Court has determined a case to be inadmissible, and subsequently extradition to the requesting State is refused, the requested State shall notify the Court of this decision.

Article 91 Contents of request for arrest and surrender

1. A request for arrest and surrender shall be made in writing. In urgent cases, a request may be made by any medium capable of delivering a written record, provided that the request shall be confirmed through the channel provided for in article 87, paragraph 1(a).

2. In the case of a request for the arrest and surrender of a person for whom a warrant of arrest has been issued by the Pre-Trial Chamber under article 58, the request shall contain or be supported by:

    (a) Information describing the person sought, sufficient to identify the person, and information as to that person's probable location;

    (b) A copy of the warrant of arrest; and

    (c) Such documents, statements or information as may be necessary to meet the requirements for the surrender process in the requested State, except that those requirements should not be more burdensome than those applicable to requests for extradition pursuant to treaties or arrangements between the requested State and other States and should, if possible, be less burdensome, taking into account the distinct nature of the Court.

3. In the case of a request for the arrest and surrender of a person already convicted, the request shall contain or be supported by:

    (a) A copy of any warrant of arrest for that person;

    (b) A copy of the judgement of conviction;

    (c) Information to demonstrate that the person sought is the one referred to in the judgement of conviction; and

    (d) If the person sought has been sentenced, a copy of the sentence imposed and, in the case of a sentence for imprisonment, a statement of anytime already served and the time remaining to be served.

4. Upon the request of the Court, a State Party shall consult with the Court, either generally or with respect to a specific matter, regarding any requirements under its national law that may apply under paragraph 2(c). During the consultations, the State Party shall advise the Court of the specific requirements of its national law.

Article 92   Provisional arrest

1. In urgent cases, the Court may request the provisional arrest of the person sought, pending presentation of the request for surrender and the documents supporting the request as specified in article 91.

2. The request for provisional arrest shall be made by any medium capable of delivering a written record and shall contain:

    (a) Information describing the person sought, sufficient to identify the person, and information as to that person's probable location;

    (b) A concise statement of the crimes for which the person's arrest is sought and of the facts which are alleged to constitute those crimes, including, where possible, the date and location of the crime;

    (c) A statement of the existence of a warrant of arrest or a judgement of conviction against the person sought; and

    (d) A statement that a request for surrender of the person sought will follow.

3. A person who is provisionally arrested may be released from custody if the requested State has not received the request for surrender and the documents supporting the request as specified in article 91 within the time limits specified in the Rules of Procedure and Evidence. However, the person may consent to surrender before the expiration of this period if permitted by the law of the requested State. In such a case, the requested State shall proceed to surrender the person to the Court as soon as possible.

4. The fact that the person sought has been released from custody pursuant to paragraph 3 shall not prejudice the subsequent arrest and surrender of that person if the request for surrender and the documents supporting the request are delivered at a later date.

Article 93   Other forms of cooperation

1. States Parties shall, in accordance with the provisions of this Part and under procedures of national law, comply with requests by the Court to provide the following assistance in relation to investigations or prosecutions:

    (a) The identification and whereabouts of persons or the location of items;

    (b) The taking of evidence, including testimony under oath, and the production of evidence, including expert opinions and reports necessary to the Court;

    (c) The questioning of any person being investigated or prosecuted;

    (d) The service of documents, including judicial documents;

    (e) Facilitating the voluntary appearance of persons as witnesses or experts before the Court;

    (f) The temporary transfer of persons as provided in paragraph 7;

    (g) The examination of places or sites, including the exhumation and examination of grave sites;

    (h) The execution of searches and seizures;

    (i) The provision of records and documents, including official records and documents;

    (j) The protection of victims and witnesses and the preservation of evidence;

    (k) The identification, tracing and freezing or seizure of proceeds, property and assets and instrumentalities of crimes for the purpose of eventual forfeiture, without prejudice to the rights of bona fide third parties; and

    (l) Any other type of assistance which is not prohibited by the law of the requested State, with a view to facilitating the investigation and prosecution of crimes within the jurisdiction of the Court.

2. The Court shall have the authority to provide an assurance to a witness or an expert appearing before the Court that he or she will not be prosecuted, detained or subjected to any restriction of personal freedom by the Court in respect of any act or omission that preceded the departure of that person from the requested State.

3. Where execution of a particular measure of assistance detailed in a request presented under paragraph 1, is prohibited in the requested State on the basis of an existing fundamental legal principle of general application, the requested State shall promptly consult with the Court to try to resolve the matter. In the consultations, consideration should be given to whether the assistance can be rendered in another manner or subject to conditions. If after consultations the matter cannot be resolved, the Court shall modify the request as necessary.

4. In accordance with article 72, a State Party may deny a request for assistance, in whole or in part, only if the request concerns the production of any documents or disclosure of evidence which relates to its national security.

5. Before denying a request for assistance under paragraph 1(1), the requested State shall consider whether the assistance can be provided subject to specified conditions, or whether the assistance can be provided at a later date or in an alternative manner, provided that if the Court or the Prosecutor accepts the assistance subject to conditions, the Court or the Prosecutor shall abide by them.

6. If a request for assistance is denied, the requested State Party shall promptly inform the Court or the Prosecutor of the reasons for such denial.

7. (a) The Court may request the temporary transfer of a person in custody for purposes of identification or for obtaining testimony or other assistance. The person may be transferred if the following conditions are fulfilled:

    (i) The person freely gives his or her informed consent to the transfer; and

    (ii) The requested State agrees to the transfer, subject to such conditions as that State and the Court may agree.

    (b) The person being transferred shall remain in custody. When the purposes of the transfer have been fulfilled, the Court shall return the person without delay to the requested State.

8. (a) The Court shall ensure the confidentiality of documents and information, except as required for the investigation and proceedings described in the request.

    (b) The requested State may, when necessary, transmit documents or information to the Prosecutor on a confidential basis. The Prosecutor may then use them solely for the purpose of generating new evidence;

(c) The requested State may, on its own motion or at the request of the Prosecutor, subsequently consent to the disclosure of such documents or information. They may then be used as evidence pursuant to the provisions of Parts 5 and 6 and in accordance with the Rules of Procedure and Evidence.

9. (a) (i) In the event that a State Party receives competing requests other than for surrender or extradition, from the Court and from another State pursuant to an international obligation, the State Party shall endeavour, in consultation with the Court and the other State, to meet both requests, if necessary by postponing or attaching conditions to one or the other request.

   (ii) Failing that, competing requests shall be resolved in accordance with the principles established in article 90.

   (b) Where, however, the request from the Court concerns information, property or persons which are subject to the control of a third State or an international organization by virtue of an international agreement, the requested States shall so inform the Court and the Court shall direct its request to the third State or international organization.

10. (a) The Court may, upon request, cooperate with and provide assistance to a State Party conducting an investigation into or trial in respect of conduct which constitutes a crime within the jurisdiction of the Court or which constitutes a serious crime under the national law of the requesting State.

    (b) (i) The assistance provided under subparagraph (a) shall include, *inter alia*:

       (a) The transmission of statements, documents or other types of evidence obtained in the course of an investigation or a trial conducted by the Court; and

       (b) The questioning of any person detained by order of the Court;

    (ii) In the case of assistance under subparagraph (b)(i)(a):

       (a) If the documents or other types of evidence have been obtained with the assistance of a State, such transmission shall require the consent of that State;

       (b) If the statements, documents or other types of evidence have been provided by a witness or expert, such transmission shall be subject to the provisions of article 68.

    (c) The Court may, under the conditions set out in this paragraph, grant a request for assistance under this paragraph from a State which is not a Party to this Statute.

Article 94   Postponement of execution of a request in respect of ongoing investigation or prosecution

1. If the immediate execution of a request would interfere with an ongoing investigation or prosecution of a case different from that to which the request relates, the requested State may postpone the execution of the request for a period of time agreed upon with the Court. However, the postponement shall be no longer than is necessary to complete the relevant investigation or prosecution in the requested State. Before making a decision to postpone, the requested State should consider whether the assistance may be immediately provided subject to certain conditions.

2. If a decision to postpone is taken pursuant to paragraph 1, the Prosecutor may, however, seek measures to preserve evidence, pursuant to article 93, paragraph 1(j).

Article 95   Postponement of execution of a request in respect of an admissibility challenge

Without prejudice to article 53, paragraph 2, where there is an admissibility challenge under consideration by the Court pursuant to articles 18 or 19, the requested State may postpone the execution of a request under this Part pending a determination by the Court, unless the Court has specifically ordered that the Prosecutor may pursue the collection of such evidence pursuant to articles 18 or 19.

Article 96   Contents of request for other forms of assistance under article 93

1. A request for other forms of assistance referred to in article 93 shall be made in writing. In urgent cases, a request may be made by any medium capable of delivering a written record, provided that the request shall be confirmed through the channel provided for in article 87, paragraph 1(a).

2. The request shall, as applicable, contain or be supported by the following:

    (a) A concise statement of the purpose of the request and the assistance sought, including the legal basis and the grounds for the request;

    (b) As much detailed information as possible about the location or identification of any person or place that must be found or identified in order for the assistance sought to be provided;

    (c) A concise statement of the essential facts underlying the request;

    (d) The reasons for and details of any procedure or requirement to be followed;

    (e) Such information as may be required under the law of the requested State in order to execute the request; and

    (f) Any other information relevant in order for the assistance sought to be provided.

3. Upon the request of the Court, a State Party shall consult with the Court, either generally or with respect to a specific matter, regarding any requirements under its national law that may apply under paragraph 2(e). During the consultations, the State Party shall advise the Court of the specific requirements of its national law.

4. The provisions of this article shall, where applicable, also apply in respect of a request for assistance made to the Court.

Article 97   Consultations

Where a State Party receives a request under this Part in relation to which it identifies problems which may impede or prevent the execution of the request, that State shall consult with the Court without delay in order to resolve the matter. Such problems may include, *inter alia*:

    (a) Insufficient information to execute the request;

    (b) In the case of a request for surrender, the fact that despite best efforts, the person sought cannot be located or that the investigation conducted has determined that the person in the requested State is clearly not the person named in the warrant; or

    (c) The fact that execution of the request in its current form would require the requested State to breach a pre-existing treaty obligation undertaken with respect to another State.

Article 98   Cooperation with respect to waiver of immunity and consent to surrender

1. The Court may not proceed with a request for surrender or assistance which would require the requested State to act inconsistently with its obligations under international law with respect to the State or diplomatic immunity of a person or property of a third State, unless the Court can first obtain the cooperation of that third State for the waiver of the immunity.

2. The Court may not proceed with a request for surrender which would require the requested State to act inconsistently with its obligations under international agreements pursuant to which the consent of a sending State is required to surrender a person of that State to the Court, unless the Court can first obtain the cooperation of the sending State for the giving of consent for the surrender.

Article 99   Execution of requests under articles 93 and 96

1. Requests for assistance shall be executed in accordance with the relevant procedure under the law of the requested State and, unless prohibited by such law, in the manner specified in the request, including following any procedure outlined therein or permitting persons specified in the request to be present at and assist in the execution process.

2. In the case of an urgent request, the documents or evidence produced in response shall, at the request of the Court, be sent urgently.

3. Replies from the requested State shall be transmitted in their original language and form.

4. Without prejudice to other articles in this Part, where it is necessary for the successful execution of a request which can be executed without any compulsory measures, including specifically the interview of or taking evidence from a person on a voluntary basis, including doing so without the presence of the authorities of the requested State Party if it is essential for the request to be executed, and the examination without modification of a public site or other public place, the Prosecutor may execute such request directly on the territory of a State as follows:

(a) When the State Party requested is a State on the territory of which the crime is alleged to have been committed, and there has been a determination of admissibility pursuant to articles 18 or 19, the Prosecutor may directly execute such request following all possible consultations with the requested State Party;

(b) In other cases, the Prosecutor may execute such request following consultations with the requested State Party and subject to any reasonable conditions or concerns raised by that State Party. Where the requested State Party identifies problems with the execution of a request pursuant to this subparagraph it shall, without delay, consult with the Court to resolve the matter.

5. Provisions allowing a person heard or examined by the Court under article 72 to invoke restrictions designed to prevent disclosure of confidential information connected with national defence or security shall also apply to the execution of requests for assistance under this article.

Article 100   Costs

1. The ordinary costs for execution of requests in the territory of the requested State shall be borne by that State, except for the following, which shall be borne by the Court:

(a) Costs associated with the travel and security of witnesses and experts or the transfer under article 93 of persons in custody;

(b) Costs of translation, interpretation and transcription;

(c) Travel and subsistence costs of the judges, the Prosecutor, the Deputy Prosecutors, the Registrar, the Deputy Registrar and staff of any organ of the Court;

(d) Costs of any expert opinion or report requested by the Court;

(e) Costs associated with the transport of a person being surrendered to the Court by a custodial State; and

(f) Following consultations, any extraordinary costs that may result from the execution of a request.

2. The provisions of paragraph 1 shall, as appropriate, apply to requests from States Parties to the Court. In that case, the Court shall bear the ordinary costs of execution.

Article 101   Rule of speciality

1. A person surrendered to the Court under this Statute shall not be proceeded against, punished or detained for any conduct committed prior to surrender, other than the conduct or course of conduct which forms the basis of the crimes for which that person has been surrendered.

2. The Court may request a waiver of the requirements of paragraph 1 from the State which surrendered the person to the Court and, if necessary, the Court shall provide additional information in accordance with article 91. States Parties shall have the authority to provide a waiver to the Court and should endeavour to do so.

Article 102   Use of terms

For the purposes of this Statute:

(a) 'surrender' means the delivering up of a person by a State to the Court, pursuant to this Statute.

(b) 'extradition' means the delivering up of a person by one State to another as provided by treaty, convention or national legislation.

PART 10 ENFORCEMENT

Article 103   Role of States in enforcement of sentences of imprisonment

1. (a) A sentence of imprisonment shall be served in a State designated by the Court from a list of States which have indicated to the Court their willingness to accept sentenced persons.

    (b) At the time of declaring its willingness to accept sentenced persons, a State may attach conditions to its acceptance as agreed by the Court and in accordance with this Part.

    (c) A State designated in a particular case shall promptly inform the Court whether it accepts the Court's designation.

2. (a) The State of enforcement shall notify the Court of any circumstances, including the exercise of any conditions agreed under paragraph 1, which could materially affect the terms or extent of the imprisonment. The Court shall be given at least 45 days' notice of any such known or foreseeable circumstances. During this period, the State of enforcement shall take no action that might prejudice its obligations under article 110.

    (b) Where the Court cannot agree to the circumstances referred to in subparagraph (a), it shall notify the State of enforcement and proceed in accordance with article 104, paragraph 1.

3. In exercising its discretion to make a designation under paragraph 1, the Court shall take into account the following:

    (a) The principle that States Parties should share the responsibility for enforcing sentences of imprisonment, in accordance with principles of equitable distribution, as provided in the Rules of Procedure and Evidence;

    (b) The application of widely accepted international treaty standards governing the treatment of prisoners;

    (c) The views of the sentenced person;

    (d) The nationality of the sentenced person;

    (e) Such other factors regarding the circumstances of the crime or the person sentenced, or the effective enforcement of the sentence, as may be appropriate in designating the State of enforcement.

4. If no State is designated under paragraph 1, the sentence of imprisonment shall be served in a prison facility made available by the host State, in accordance with the conditions set out in the headquarters agreement referred to in article 3, paragraph 2. In such a case, the costs arising out of the enforcement of a sentence of imprisonment shall be borne by the Court.

Article 104   Change in designation of State of enforcement

1. The Court may, at any time, decide to transfer a sentenced person to a prison of another State.

2. A sentenced person may, at any time, apply to the Court to be transferred from the State of enforcement.

Article 105   Enforcement of the sentence

1. Subject to conditions which a State may have specified in accordance with article 103, paragraph 1(b), the sentence of imprisonment shall be binding on the States Parties, which shall in no case modify it.

2. The Court alone shall have the right to decide any application for appeal and revision. The State of enforcement shall not impede the making of any such application by a sentenced person.

Article 106   Supervision of enforcement of sentences and conditions of imprisonment

1. The enforcement of a sentence of imprisonment shall be subject to the supervision of the Court and shall be consistent with widely accepted international treaty standards governing treatment of prisoners.

2. The conditions of imprisonment shall be governed by the law of the State of enforcement and shall be consistent with widely accepted international treaty standards governing treatment of prisoners; in no case shall such conditions be more or less favourable than those available to prisoners convicted of similar offences in the State of enforcement.

3. Communications between a sentenced person and the Court shall be unimpeded and confidential.

Article 107   Transfer of the person upon completion of sentence

1. Following completion of the sentence, a person who is not a national of the State of enforcement may, in accordance with the law of the State of enforcement, be transferred to a State which is obliged to receive him or her, or to another State which agrees to receive him or her, taking into account any wishes of the person to be transferred to that State, unless the State of enforcement authorizes the person to remain in its territory.

2. If no State bears the costs arising out of transferring the person to another State pursuant to paragraph 1, such costs shall be borne by the Court.

3. Subject to the provisions of article 108, the State of enforcement may also, in accordance with its national law, extradite or otherwise surrender the person to the State which has requested the extradition or surrender of the person for purposes of trial or enforcement of a sentence.

Article 108   Limitation on the prosecution or punishment of other offences

1. A sentenced person in the custody of the State of enforcement shall not be subject to prosecution or punishment or to extradition to a third State for any conduct engaged in prior to that person's delivery to the State of enforcement, unless such prosecution, punishment or extradition has been approved by the Court at the request of the State of enforcement.

2. The Court shall decide the matter after having heard the views of the sentenced person.

3. Paragraph 1 shall cease to apply if the sentenced person remains voluntarily for more than 30 days in the territory of the State of enforcement after having served the full sentence imposed by the Court, or returns to the territory of that State after having left it.

Article 109   Enforcement of fines and forfeiture measures

1. States Parties shall give effect to fines or forfeitures ordered by the Court under Part 7, without prejudice to the rights of *bona fide* third parties, and in accordance with the procedure of their national law.

2. If a State Party is unable to give effect to an order for forfeiture, it shall take measures to recover the value of the proceeds, property or assets ordered by the Court to be forfeited, without prejudice to the rights of *bona fide* third parties.

3. Property, or the proceeds of the sale of real property or, where appropriate, the sale of other property, which is obtained by a State Party as a result of its enforcement of a judgement of the Court shall be transferred to the Court.

Article 110   Review by the Court concerning reduction of sentence

1. The State of enforcement shall not release the person before expiry of the sentence pronounced by the Court.

2. The Court alone shall have the right to decide any reduction of sentence, and shall rule on the matter after having heard the person.

3. When the person has served two thirds of the sentence, or 25 years in the case of life imprisonment, the Court shall review the sentence to determine whether it should be reduced. Such a review shall not be conducted before that time.

4. In its review under paragraph 3, the Court may reduce the sentence if it finds that one or more of the following factors are present:

    (a) The early and continuing willingness of the person to cooperate with the Court in its investigations and prosecutions;

(b) The voluntary assistance of the person in enabling the enforcement of the judgements and orders of the Court in other cases, and in particular providing assistance in locating assets subject to orders of fine, forfeiture or reparation which may be used for the benefit of victims; or

(c) Other factors establishing a clear and significant change of circumstances sufficient to justify the reduction of sentence, as provided in the Rules of Procedure and Evidence.

5. If the Court determines in its initial review under paragraph 3 that it is not appropriate to reduce the sentence, it shall thereafter review the question of reduction of sentence at such intervals and applying such criteria as provided for in the Rules of Procedure and Evidence.

Article 111   Escape

If a convicted person escapes from custody and flees the State of enforcement, that State may, after consultation with the Court, request the person's surrender from the State in which the person is located pursuant to existing bilateral or multilateral arrangements, or may request that the Court seek the person's surrender. It may direct that the person be delivered to the State in which he or she was serving the sentence or to another State designated by the Court.

PART 11 ASSEMBLY OF STATES PARTIES

. . .

PART 12 FINANCING

. . .

PART 13 FINAL CLAUSES

Article 119   Settlement of disputes

1. Any dispute concerning the judicial functions of the Court shall be settled by the decision of the Court.

2. Any other dispute between two or more States Parties relating to the interpretation or application of this Statute which is not settled through negotiations within three months of their commencement shall be referred to the Assembly of States Parties. The Assembly may itself seek to settle the dispute or may make recommendations on further means of settlement of the dispute, including referral to the International Court of Justice in conformity with the Statute of that Court.

Article 120   Reservations

No reservations may be made to this Statute.

Article 121   Amendments

1. After the expiry of seven years from the entry into force of this Statute, any State Party may propose amendments thereto. The text of any proposed amendment shall be submitted to the Secretary-General of the United Nations, who shall promptly circulate it to all States Parties.

2. No sooner than three months from the date of notification, the next Assembly of States Parties shall, by a majority of those present and voting, decide whether to take up the proposal. The Assembly may deal with the proposal directly or convene a Review Conference if the issue involved so warrants.

3. The adoption of an amendment at a meeting of the Assembly of States Parties or at a Review Conference on which consensus cannot be reached shall require a two-thirds majority of States Parties.

4. Except as provided in paragraph 5, an amendment shall enter into force for all States Parties one year after instruments of ratification or acceptance have been deposited with the Secretary-General of the United Nations by seven-eighths of them.

5. Any amendment to articles 5, 6, 7 and 8 of this Statute shall enter into force for those States Parties which have accepted the amendment one year after the deposit of their instruments of ratification or acceptance. In respect of a State Party which has not accepted the amendment, the Court shall not exercise its jurisdiction regarding a crime covered by the amendment when committed by that State Party's nationals or on its territory.

6. If an amendment has been accepted by seven-eighths of States Parties in accordance with paragraph 4, any State Party which has not accepted the amendment may withdraw from the Statute with immediate effect, notwithstanding article 127, paragraph 1 but subject to article 127, paragraph 2, by giving notice no later than one year after the entry into force of such amendment.

7. The Secretary-General of the United Nations shall circulate to all States Parties any amendment adopted at a meeting of the Assembly of States Parties or at a Review Conference.

Article 122   Amendments to provisions of an institutional nature

1. Amendments to provisions of this Statute which are of an exclusively institutional nature, namely, article 35, article 36, paragraphs 8 and 9, article 37, article 38, article 39, paragraphs 1 (first two sentences), 2 and 4, article 42, paragraphs 4 to 9, article 43, paragraphs 2 and 3, and articles 44, 46, 47 and 49, may be proposed at any time, notwithstanding article 121, paragraph 1, by any State Party. The text of any proposed amendment shall be submitted to the Secretary-General of the United Nations or such other person designated by the Assembly of States Parties who shall promptly circulate it to all States Parties and to others participating in the Assembly.

2. Amendments under this article on which consensus cannot be reached shall be adopted by the Assembly of States Parties or by a Review Conference, by a two-thirds majority of States Parties. Such amendments shall enter into force for all States Parties six months after their adoption by the Assembly or, as the case may be, by the Conference.

Article 123   Review of the Statute

1. Seven years after the entry into force of this Statute the Secretary-General of the United Nations shall convene a Review Conference to consider any amendments to this Statute. Such review may include, but is not limited to, the list of crimes contained in article 5. The Conference shall be open to those participating in the Assembly of States Parties and on the same conditions.

2. At any time thereafter, at the request of a State Party and for the purposes set out in paragraph 1, the Secretary-General of the United Nations shall, upon approval by a majority of States Parties, convene a Review Conference.

3. The provisions of article 121, paragraphs 3 to 7, shall apply to the adoption and entry into force of any amendment to the Statute considered at a Review Conference.

Article 124   Transitional provision

Notwithstanding article 12, paragraphs 1 and 2, a State, on becoming a party to this Statute, may declare that for a period of seven years after the entry into force of this Statute for the State concerned, it does not accept the jurisdiction of the Court with respect to the category of crimes referred to in article 8 when a crime is alleged to have been committed by its nationals or on its territory. A declaration under this article may be withdrawn at any time. The provisions of this article shall be reviewed at the Review Conference convened in accordance with article 123, paragraph 1.

Article 125   Signature, ratification, acceptance, approval or accession

1. This Statute shall be open for signature by all States in Rome, at the headquarters of the Food and Agriculture Organization of the United Nations, on 17 July 1998. Thereafter, it shall remain open

for signature in Rome at the Ministry of Foreign Affairs of Italy until 17 October 1998. After that date, the Statute shall remain open for signature in New York, at United Nations Headquarters, until 31 December 2000.

2. This Statute is subject to ratification, acceptance or approval by signatory States. Instruments of ratification, acceptance or approval shall be deposited with the Secretary-General of the United Nations.

3. This Statute shall be open to accession by all States. Instruments of accession shall be deposited with the Secretary-General of the United Nations.

Article 126   Entry into force

1. This Statute shall enter into force on the first day of the month after the 60th day following the date of the deposit of the 60th instrument of ratification, acceptance, approval or accession with the Secretary-General of the United Nations.

2. For each State ratifying, accepting, approving or acceding to this Statute after the deposit of the 60th instrument of ratification, acceptance, approval or accession, the Statute shall enter into force on the first day of the month after the 60th day following the deposit by such State of its instrument of ratification, acceptance, approval or accession.

Article 127   Withdrawal

1. A State Party may, by written notification addressed to the Secretary-General of the United Nations, withdraw from this Statute. The withdrawal shall take effect one year after the date of receipt of the notification, unless the notification specifies a later date.

2. A State shall not be discharged, by reason of its withdrawal, from the obligations arising from this Statute while it was a Party to the Statute, including any financial obligations which may have accrued. Its withdrawal shall not affect any cooperation with the Court in connection with criminal investigations and proceedings in relation to which the withdrawing State had a duty to cooperate and which were commenced prior to the date on which the withdrawal became effective, nor shall it prejudice in any way the continued consideration of any matter which was already under consideration by the Court prior to the date on which the withdrawal became effective.

Article 128   Authentic texts

The original of this Statute, of which the Arabic, Chinese, English, French, Russian and Spanish texts are equally authentic, shall be deposited with the Secretary-General of the United Nations, who shall send certified copies thereof to all States.

In witness whereof, the undersigned, being duly authorized thereto by their respective Governments, have signed this Statute.

Done at Rome, this 17th day of July 1998.

Convention on the Rights of Persons with Disabilities (2006)*

PREAMBLE

The States Parties to the present Convention,

(a) *Recalling* the principles proclaimed in the Charter of the United Nations which recognize the inherent dignity and worth and the equal and inalienable rights of all members of the human family as the foundation of freedom, justice and peace in the world,

(b) *Recognizing* that the United Nations, in the Universal Declaration of Human Rights and in the International Covenants on Human Rights, has proclaimed and agreed that everyone is entitled to all the rights and freedoms set forth therein, without distinction of any kind,

(c) *Reaffirming* the universality, indivisibility, interdependence and interrelatedness of all human rights and fundamental freedoms and the need for persons with disabilities to be guaranteed their full enjoyment without discrimination,

(d) *Recalling* the International Covenant on Economic, Social and Cultural Rights, the International Covenant on Civil and Political Rights, the International Convention on the Elimination of All Forms of Racial Discrimination, the Convention on the Elimination of All Forms of Discrimination against Women, the Convention against Torture and Other Cruel, Inhuman or Degrading Treatment or Punishment, the Convention on the Rights of the Child, and the International Convention on the Protection of the Rights of All Migrant Workers and Members of Their Families,

(e) *Recognizing* that disability is an evolving concept and that disability results from the interaction between persons with impairments and attitudinal and environmental barriers that hinders their full and effective participation in society on an equal basis with others,

(f) *Recognizing* the importance of the principles and policy guidelines contained in the World Programme of Action concerning Disabled Persons and in the Standard Rules on the Equalization of Opportunities for Persons with Disabilities in influencing the promotion, formulation and evaluation of the policies, plans, programmes and actions at the national, regional and international levels to further equalize opportunities for persons with disabilities,

(g) *Emphasizing* the importance of mainstreaming disability issues as an integral part of relevant strategies of sustainable development,

(h) *Recognizing* also that discrimination against any person on the basis of disability is a violation of the inherent dignity and worth of the human person,

(i) *Recognizing* further the diversity of persons with disabilities,

(j) *Recognizing* the need to promote and protect the human rights of all persons with disabilities, including those who require more intensive support,

(k) *Concerned* that, despite these various instruments and undertakings, persons with disabilities continue to face barriers in their participation as equal members of society and violations of their human rights in all parts of the world,

(l) *Recognizing* the importance of international cooperation for improving the living conditions of persons with disabilities in every country, particularly in developing countries,

(m) *Recognizing* the valued existing and potential contributions made by persons with disabilities to the overall well-being and diversity of their communities, and that the promotion of the full enjoyment by persons with disabilities of their human rights and fundamental freedoms and of full participation by persons with disabilities will result in their enhanced sense of belonging and in significant advances in the human, social and economic development of society and the eradication of poverty,

(n) *Recognizing* the importance for persons with disabilities of their individual autonomy and independence, including the freedom to make their own choices,

(o) *Considering* that persons with disabilities should have the opportunity to be actively involved in decision-making processes about policies and programmes, including those directly concerning them,

(p) *Concerned* about the difficult conditions faced by persons with disabilities who are subject to multiple or aggravated forms of discrimination on the basis of race, colour, sex, language, religion, political or other opinion, national, ethnic, indigenous or social origin, property, birth, age or other status,

(q) *Recognizing* that women and girls with disabilities are often at greater risk, both within and outside the home, of violence, injury or abuse, neglect or negligent treatment, maltreatment or exploitation,

(r) *Recognizing* that children with disabilities should have full enjoyment of all human rights and fundamental freedoms on an equal basis with other children, and recalling obligations to that end undertaken by States Parties to the Convention on the Rights of the Child,

(s) *Emphasizing* the need to incorporate a gender perspective in all efforts to promote the full enjoyment of human rights and fundamental freedoms by persons with disabilities,

(t) *Highlighting* the fact that the majority of persons with disabilities live in conditions of poverty, and in this regard recognizing the critical need to address the negative impact of poverty on persons with disabilities,

(u) *Bearing in mind* that conditions of peace and security based on full respect for the purposes and principles contained in the Charter of the United Nations and observance of applicable human rights instruments are indispensable for the full protection of persons with disabilities, in particular during armed conflicts and foreign occupation,

(v) *Recognizing* the importance of accessibility to the physical, social, economic and cultural environment, to health and education and to information and communication, in enabling persons with disabilities to fully enjoy all human rights and fundamental freedoms,

(w) *Realizing* that the individual, having duties to other individuals and to the community to which he or she belongs, is under a responsibility to strive for the promotion and observance of the rights recognized in the International Bill of Human Rights,

(x) *Convinced* that the family is the natural and fundamental group unit of society and is entitled to protection by society and the State, and that persons with disabilities and their family members should receive the necessary protection and assistance to enable families to contribute towards the full and equal enjoyment of the rights of persons with disabilities,

(y) *Convinced* that a comprehensive and integral international convention to promote and protect the rights and dignity of persons with disabilities will make a significant contribution to redressing the profound social disadvantage of persons with disabilities and promote their participation in the civil, political, economic, social and cultural spheres with equal opportunities, in both developing and developed countries,

Have agreed as follows:

Article 1   Purpose

The purpose of the present Convention is to promote, protect and ensure the full and equal enjoyment of all human rights and fundamental freedoms by all persons with disabilities, and to promote respect for their inherent dignity.

Persons with disabilities include those who have long-term physical, mental, intellectual or sensory impairments which in interaction with various barriers may hinder their full and effective participation in society on an equal basis with others.

Article 2   Definitions

For the purposes of the present Convention:

'Communication' includes languages, display of text, Braille, tactile communication, large print, accessible multimedia as well as written, audio, plain-language, human-reader and augmentative and alternative modes, means and formats of communication, including accessible information and communication technology;

'Language' includes spoken and signed languages and other forms of non-spoken languages;

'Discrimination on the basis of disability' means any distinction, exclusion or restriction on the basis of disability which has the purpose or effect of impairing or nullifying the recognition, enjoyment or exercise, on an equal basis with others, of all human rights and fundamental freedoms in the political, economic, social, cultural, civil or any other field. It includes all forms of discrimination, including denial of reasonable accommodation;

'Reasonable accommodation' means necessary and appropriate modification and adjustments not imposing a disproportionate or undue burden, where needed in a particular case, to ensure to persons with disabilities the enjoyment or exercise on an equal basis with others of all human rights and fundamental freedoms;

'Universal design' means the design of products, environments, programmes and services to be usable by all people, to the greatest extent possible, without the need for adaptation or specialized design. 'Universal design' shall not exclude assistive devices for particular groups of persons with disabilities where this is needed.

Article 3   General principles
The principles of the present Convention shall be:
- (a) Respect for inherent dignity, individual autonomy including the freedom to make one's own choices, and independence of persons;
- (b) Non-discrimination;
- (c) Full and effective participation and inclusion in society;
- (d) Respect for difference and acceptance of persons with disabilities as part of human diversity and humanity;
- (e) Equality of opportunity;
- (f) Accessibility;
- (g) Equality between men and women;
- (h) Respect for the evolving capacities of children with disabilities and respect for the right of children with disabilities to preserve their identities.

Article 4   General obligations
1. States Parties undertake to ensure and promote the full realization of all human rights and fundamental freedoms for all persons with disabilities without discrimination of any kind on the basis of disability. To this end, States Parties undertake:
- (a) To adopt all appropriate legislative, administrative and other measures for the implementation of the rights recognized in the present Convention;
- (b) To take all appropriate measures, including legislation, to modify or abolish existing laws, regulations, customs and practices that constitute discrimination against persons with disabilities;
- (c) To take into account the protection and promotion of the human rights of persons with disabilities in all policies and programmes;
- (d) To refrain from engaging in any act or practice that is inconsistent with the present Convention and to ensure that public authorities and institutions act in conformity with the present Convention;
- (e) To take all appropriate measures to eliminate discrimination on the basis of disability by any person, organization or private enterprise;
- (f) To undertake or promote research and development of universally designed goods, services, equipment and facilities, as defined in article 2 of the present Convention, which should require the minimum possible adaptation and the least cost to meet the specific needs of a person with disabilities, to promote their availability and use, and to promote universal design in the development of standards and guidelines;
- (g) To undertake or promote research and development of, and to promote the availability and use of new technologies, including information and communications technologies, mobility aids, devices and assistive technologies, suitable for persons with disabilities, giving priority to technologies at an affordable cost;
- (h) To provide accessible information to persons with disabilities about mobility aids, devices and assistive technologies, including new technologies, as well as other forms of assistance, support services and facilities;
- (i) To promote the training of professionals and staff working with persons with disabilities in the rights recognized in the present Convention so as to better provide the assistance and services guaranteed by those rights.

2. With regard to economic, social and cultural rights, each State Party undertakes to take measures to the maximum of its available resources and, where needed, within the framework of international cooperation, with a view to achieving progressively the full realization of these rights, without prejudice to those obligations contained in the present Convention that are immediately applicable according to international law.

3. In the development and implementation of legislation and policies to implement the present Convention, and in other decision-making processes concerning issues relating to persons with disabilities, States Parties shall closely consult with and actively involve persons with disabilities, including children with disabilities, through their representative organizations.

4. Nothing in the present Convention shall affect any provisions which are more conducive to the realization of the rights of persons with disabilities and which may be contained in the law of a State Party or international law in force for that State. There shall be no restriction upon or derogation from any of the human rights and fundamental freedoms recognized or existing in any State Party to the present Convention pursuant to law, conventions, regulation or custom on the pretext that the present Convention does not recognize such rights or freedoms or that it recognizes them to a lesser extent.

5. The provisions of the present Convention shall extend to all parts of federal States without any limitations or exceptions.

Article 5 Equality and non-discrimination

1. States Parties recognize that all persons are equal before and under the law and are entitled without any discrimination to the equal protection and equal benefit of the law.

2. States Parties shall prohibit all discrimination on the basis of disability and guarantee to persons with disabilities equal and effective legal protection against discrimination on all grounds.

3. In order to promote equality and eliminate discrimination, States Parties shall take all appropriate steps to ensure that reasonable accommodation is provided.

4. Specific measures which are necessary to accelerate or achieve de facto equality of persons with disabilities shall not be considered discrimination under the terms of the present Convention.

Article 6 Women with disabilities

1. States Parties recognize that women and girls with disabilities are subject to multiple discrimination, and in this regard shall take measures to ensure the full and equal enjoyment by them of all human rights and fundamental freedoms.

2. States Parties shall take all appropriate measures to ensure the full development, advancement and empowerment of women, for the purpose of guaranteeing them the exercise and enjoyment of the human rights and fundamental freedoms set out in the present Convention.

Article 7 Children with disabilities

1. States Parties shall take all necessary measures to ensure the full enjoyment by children with disabilities of all human rights and fundamental freedoms on an equal basis with other children.

2. In all actions concerning children with disabilities, the best interests of the child shall be a primary consideration.

3. States Parties shall ensure that children with disabilities have the right to express their views freely on all matters affecting them, their views being given due weight in accordance with their age and maturity, on an equal basis with other children, and to be provided with disability and age-appropriate assistance to realize that right.

Article 8 Awareness-raising

1. States Parties undertake to adopt immediate, effective and appropriate measures:
   (a) To raise awareness throughout society, including at the family level, regarding persons with disabilities, and to foster respect for the rights and dignity of persons with disabilities;
   (b) To combat stereotypes, prejudices and harmful practices relating to persons with disabilities, including those based on sex and age, in all areas of life;
   (c) To promote awareness of the capabilities and contributions of persons with disabilities.
2. Measures to this end include:
   (a) Initiating and maintaining effective public awareness campaigns designed:
      (i) To nurture receptiveness to the rights of persons with disabilities;
      (ii) To promote positive perceptions and greater social awareness towards persons with disabilities;

      (iii) To promote recognition of the skills, merits and abilities of persons with disabilities, and of their contributions to the workplace and the labour market;

  (b) Fostering at all levels of the education system, including in all children from an early age, an attitude of respect for the rights of persons with disabilities;

  (c) Encouraging all organs of the media to portray persons with disabilities in a manner consistent with the purpose of the present Convention;

  (d) Promoting awareness-training programmes regarding persons with disabilities and the rights of persons with disabilities.

Article 9   Accessibility

1. To enable persons with disabilities to live independently and participate fully in all aspects of life, States Parties shall take appropriate measures to ensure to persons with disabilities access, on an equal basis with others, to the physical environment, to transportation, to information and communications, including information and communications technologies and systems, and to other facilities and services open or provided to the public, both in urban and in rural areas. These measures, which shall include the identification and elimination of obstacles and barriers to accessibility, shall apply to, inter alia:

  (a) Buildings, roads, transportation and other indoor and outdoor facilities, including schools, housing, medical facilities and workplaces;

  (b) Information, communications and other services, including electronic services and emergency services.

2. States Parties shall also take appropriate measures:

  (a) To develop, promulgate and monitor the implementation of minimum standards and guidelines for the accessibility of facilities and services open or provided to the public;

  (b) To ensure that private entities that offer facilities and services which are open or provided to the public take into account all aspects of accessibility for persons with disabilities;

  (c) To provide training for stakeholders on accessibility issues facing persons with disabilities;

  (d) To provide in buildings and other facilities open to the public signage in Braille and in easy to read and understand forms;

  (e) To provide forms of live assistance and intermediaries, including guides, readers and professional sign language interpreters, to facilitate accessibility to buildings and other facilities open to the public;

  (f) To promote other appropriate forms of assistance and support to persons with disabilities to ensure their access to information;

  (g) To promote access for persons with disabilities to new information and communications technologies and systems, including the Internet;

  (h) To promote the design, development, production and distribution of accessible information and communications technologies and systems at an early stage, so that these technologies and systems become accessible at minimum cost.

Article 10   Right to life

States Parties reaffirm that every human being has the inherent right to life and shall take all necessary measures to ensure its effective enjoyment by persons with disabilities on an equal basis with others.

Article 11   Situations of risk and humanitarian emergencies

States Parties shall take, in accordance with their obligations under international law, including international humanitarian law and international human rights law, all necessary measures to ensure the protection and safety of persons with disabilities in situations of risk, including situations of armed conflict, humanitarian emergencies and the occurrence of natural disasters.

Article 12   Equal recognition before the law

1. States Parties reaffirm that persons with disabilities have the right to recognition everywhere as persons before the law.

2. States Parties shall recognize that persons with disabilities enjoy legal capacity on an equal basis with others in all aspects of life.

3. States Parties shall take appropriate measures to provide access by persons with disabilities to the support they may require in exercising their legal capacity.

4. States Parties shall ensure that all measures that relate to the exercise of legal capacity provide for appropriate and effective safeguards to prevent abuse in accordance with international human rights law. Such safeguards shall ensure that measures relating to the exercise of legal capacity respect the rights, will and preferences of the person, are free of conflict of interest and undue influence, are proportional and tailored to the person's circumstances, apply for the shortest time possible and are subject to regular review by a competent, independent and impartial authority or judicial body. The safeguards shall be proportional to the degree to which such measures affect the person's rights and interests.

5. Subject to the provisions of this article, States Parties shall take all appropriate and effective measures to ensure the equal right of persons with disabilities to own or inherit property, to control their own financial affairs and to have equal access to bank loans, mortgages and other forms of financial credit, and shall ensure that persons with disabilities are not arbitrarily deprived of their property.

Article 13   Access to justice

1. States Parties shall ensure effective access to justice for persons with disabilities on an equal basis with others, including through the provision of procedural and age-appropriate accommodations, in order to facilitate their effective role as direct and indirect participants, including as witnesses, in all legal proceedings, including at investigative and other preliminary stages.

2. In order to help to ensure effective access to justice for persons with disabilities, States Parties shall promote appropriate training for those working in the field of administration of justice, including police and prison staff.

Article 14   Liberty and security of person

1. States Parties shall ensure that persons with disabilities, on an equal basis with others:
   (a) Enjoy the right to liberty and security of person;
   (b) Are not deprived of their liberty unlawfully or arbitrarily, and that any deprivation of liberty is in conformity with the law, and that the existence of a disability shall in no case justify a deprivation of liberty.

2. States Parties shall ensure that if persons with disabilities are deprived of their liberty through any process, they are, on an equal basis with others, entitled to guarantees in accordance with international human rights law and shall be treated in compliance with the objectives and principles of the present Convention, including by provision of reasonable accommodation.

Article 15   Freedom from torture or cruel, inhuman or degrading treatment or punishment

1 No one shall be subjected to torture or to cruel, inhuman or degrading treatment or punishment. In particular, no one shall be subjected without his or her free consent to medical or scientific experimentation.

2. States Parties shall take all effective legislative, administrative, judicial or other measures to prevent persons with disabilities, on an equal basis with others, from being subjected to torture or cruel, inhuman or degrading treatment or punishment.

Article 16   Freedom from exploitation, violence and abuse

1. States Parties shall take all appropriate legislative, administrative, social, educational and other measures to protect persons with disabilities, both within and outside the home, from all forms of exploitation, violence and abuse, including their gender-based aspects.

2. States Parties shall also take all appropriate measures to prevent all forms of exploitation, violence and abuse by ensuring, inter alia, appropriate forms of gender- and age-sensitive assistance and support for persons with disabilities and their families and caregivers, including through the provision of information and education on how to avoid, recognize and report instances of

exploitation, violence and abuse. States Parties shall ensure that protection services are age-, gender- and disability-sensitive.

3. In order to prevent the occurrence of all forms of exploitation, violence and abuse, States Parties shall ensure that all facilities and programmes designed to serve persons with disabilities are effectively monitored by independent authorities.

4. States Parties shall take all appropriate measures to promote the physical, cognitive and psychological recovery, rehabilitation and social reintegration of persons with disabilities who become victims of any form of exploitation, violence or abuse, including through the provision of protection services. Such recovery and reintegration shall take place in an environment that fosters the health, welfare, self-respect, dignity and autonomy of the person and takes into account gender- and age-specific needs.

5. States Parties shall put in place effective legislation and policies, including women- and child-focused legislation and policies, to ensure that instances of exploitation, violence and abuse against persons with disabilities are identified, investigated and, where appropriate, prosecuted.

Article 17   Protecting the integrity of the person

Every person with disabilities has a right to respect for his or her physical and mental integrity on an equal basis with others.

Article 18   Liberty of movement and nationality

1. States Parties shall recognize the rights of persons with disabilities to liberty of movement, to freedom to choose their residence and to a nationality, on an equal basis with others, including by ensuring that persons with disabilities:

    (a) Have the right to acquire and change a nationality and are not deprived of their nationality arbitrarily or on the basis of disability;

    (b) Are not deprived, on the basis of disability, of their ability to obtain, possess and utilize documentation of their nationality or other documentation of identification, or to utilize relevant processes such as immigration proceedings, that may be needed to facilitate exercise of the right to liberty of movement;

    (c) Are free to leave any country, including their own;

    (d) Are not deprived, arbitrarily or on the basis of disability, of the right to enter their own country.

2. Children with disabilities shall be registered immediately after birth and shall have the right from birth to a name, the right to acquire a nationality and, as far as possible, the right to know and be cared for by their parents.

Article 19   Living independently and being included in the community

States Parties to the present Convention recognize the equal right of all persons with disabilities to live in the community, with choices equal to others, and shall take effective and appropriate measures to facilitate full enjoyment by persons with disabilities of this right and their full inclusion and participation in the community, including by ensuring that:

    (a) Persons with disabilities have the opportunity to choose their place of residence and where and with whom they live on an equal basis with others and are not obliged to live in a particular living arrangement;

    (b) Persons with disabilities have access to a range of in-home, residential and other community support services, including personal assistance necessary to support living and inclusion in the community, and to prevent isolation or segregation from the community;

    (c) Community services and facilities for the general population are available on an equal basis to persons with disabilities and are responsive to their needs.

Article 20 Personal mobility

States Parties shall take effective measures to ensure personal mobility with the greatest possible independence for persons with disabilities, including by:

(a) Facilitating the personal mobility of persons with disabilities in the manner and at the time of their choice, and at affordable cost;

(b) Facilitating access by persons with disabilities to quality mobility aids, devices, assistive technologies and forms of live assistance and intermediaries, including by making them available at affordable cost;

(c) Providing training in mobility skills to persons with disabilities and to specialist staff working with persons with disabilities;

(d) Encouraging entities that produce mobility aids, devices and assistive technologies to take into account all aspects of mobility for persons with disabilities.

Article 21 Freedom of expression and opinion, and access to information

States Parties shall take all appropriate measures to ensure that persons with disabilities can exercise the right to freedom of expression and opinion, including the freedom to seek, receive and impart information and ideas on an equal basis with others and through all forms of communication of their choice, as defined in article 2 of the present Convention, including by:

(a) Providing information intended for the general public to persons with disabilities in accessible formats and technologies appropriate to different kinds of disabilities in a timely manner and without additional cost;

(b) Accepting and facilitating the use of sign languages, Braille, augmentative and alternative communication, and all other accessible means, modes and formats of communication of their choice by persons with disabilities in official interactions;

(c) Urging private entities that provide services to the general public, including through the Internet, to provide information and services in accessible and usable formats for persons with disabilities;

(d) Encouraging the mass media, including providers of information through the Internet, to make their services accessible to persons with disabilities;

(e) Recognizing and promoting the use of sign languages.

Article 22 Respect for privacy

1. No person with disabilities, regardless of place of residence or living arrangements, shall be subjected to arbitrary or unlawful interference with his or her privacy, family, home or correspondence or other types of communication or to unlawful attacks on his or her honour and reputation. Persons with disabilities have the right to the protection of the law against such interference or attacks.

2. States Parties shall protect the privacy of personal, health and rehabilitation information of persons with disabilities on an equal basis with others.

Article 23 Respect for home and the family

1. States Parties shall take effective and appropriate measures to eliminate discrimination against persons with disabilities in all matters relating to marriage, family, parenthood and relationships, on an equal basis with others, so as to ensure that:

(a) The right of all persons with disabilities who are of marriageable age to marry and to found a family on the basis of free and full consent of the intending spouses is recognized;

(b) The rights of persons with disabilities to decide freely and responsibly on the number and spacing of their children and to have access to age-appropriate information, reproductive and family planning education are recognized, and the means necessary to enable them to exercise these rights are provided;

(c) Persons with disabilities, including children, retain their fertility on an equal basis with others.

2. States Parties shall ensure the rights and responsibilities of persons with disabilities, with regard to guardianship, wardship, trusteeship, adoption of children or similar institutions, where these

concepts exist in national legislation; in all cases the best interests of the child shall be paramount. States Parties shall render appropriate assistance to persons with disabilities in the performance of their child-rearing responsibilities.

3. States Parties shall ensure that children with disabilities have equal rights with respect to family life. With a view to realizing these rights, and to prevent concealment, abandonment, neglect and segregation of children with disabilities, States Parties shall undertake to provide early and comprehensive information, services and support to children with disabilities and their families.

4. States Parties shall ensure that a child shall not be separated from his or her parents against their will, except when competent authorities subject to judicial review determine, in accordance with applicable law and procedures, that such separation is necessary for the best interests of the child. In no case shall a child be separated from parents on the basis of a disability of either the child or one or both of the parents.

5. States Parties shall, where the immediate family is unable to care for a child with disabilities, undertake every effort to provide alternative care within the wider family, and failing that, within the community in a family setting.

Article 24   Education

1. States Parties recognize the right of persons with disabilities to education. With a view to realizing this right without discrimination and on the basis of equal opportunity, States Parties shall ensure an inclusive education system at all levels and lifelong learning directed to:
   (a) The full development of human potential and sense of dignity and self-worth, and the strengthening of respect for human rights, fundamental freedoms and human diversity;
   (b) The development by persons with disabilities of their personality, talents and creativity, as well as their mental and physical abilities, to their fullest potential;
   (c) Enabling persons with disabilities to participate effectively in a free society.

2. In realizing this right, States Parties shall ensure that:
   (a) Persons with disabilities are not excluded from the general education system on the basis of disability, and that children with disabilities are not excluded from free and compulsory primary education, or from secondary education, on the basis of disability;
   (b) Persons with disabilities can access an inclusive, quality and free primary education and secondary education on an equal basis with others in the communities in which they live;
   (c) Reasonable accommodation of the individual's requirements is provided;
   (d) Persons with disabilities receive the support required, within the general education system, to facilitate their effective education;
   (e) Effective individualized support measures are provided in environments that maximize academic and social development, consistent with the goal of full inclusion.

3. States Parties shall enable persons with disabilities to learn life and social development skills to facilitate their full and equal participation in education and as members of the community. To this end, States Parties shall take appropriate measures, including:
   (a) Facilitating the learning of Braille, alternative script, augmentative and alternative modes, means and formats of communication and orientation and mobility skills, and facilitating peer support and mentoring;
   (b) Facilitating the learning of sign language and the promotion of the linguistic identity of the deaf community;
   (c) Ensuring that the education of persons, and in particular children, who are blind, deaf or deaf blind, is delivered in the most appropriate languages and modes and means of communication for the individual, and in environments which maximize academic and social development.

4. In order to help ensure the realization of this right, States Parties shall take appropriate measures to employ teachers, including teachers with disabilities, who are qualified in sign language and/or Braille, and to train professionals and staff who work at all levels of education. Such training shall

incorporate disability awareness and the use of appropriate augmentative and alternative modes, means and formats of communication, educational techniques and materials to support persons with disabilities.

5. States Parties shall ensure that persons with disabilities are able to access general tertiary education, vocational training, adult education and lifelong learning without discrimination and on an equal basis with others. To this end, States Parties shall ensure that reasonable accommodation is provided to persons with disabilities.

Article 25   Health

States Parties recognize that persons with disabilities have the right to the enjoyment of the highest attainable standard of health without discrimination on the basis of disability. States Parties shall take all appropriate measures to ensure access for persons with disabilities to health services that are gender-sensitive, including health-related rehabilitation. In particular, States Parties shall:

(a) Provide persons with disabilities with the same range, quality and standard of free or affordable health care and programmes as provided to other persons, including in the area of sexual and reproductive health and population-based public health programmes;

(b) Provide those health services needed by persons with disabilities specifically because of their disabilities, including early identification and intervention as appropriate, and services designed to minimize and prevent further disabilities, including among children and older persons;

(c) Provide these health services as close as possible to people's own communities, including in rural areas;

(d) Require health professionals to provide care of the same quality to persons with disabilities as to others, including on the basis of free and informed consent by, *inter alia*, raising awareness of the human rights, dignity, autonomy and needs of persons with disabilities through training and the promulgation of ethical standards for public and private health care;

(e) Prohibit discrimination against persons with disabilities in the provision of health insurance, and life insurance where such insurance is permitted by national law, which shall be provided in a fair and reasonable manner;

(f) Prevent discriminatory denial of health care or health services or food and fluids on the basis of disability.

Article 26   Habilitation and rehabilitation

1. States Parties shall take effective and appropriate measures, including through peer support, to enable persons with disabilities to attain and maintain maximum independence, full physical, mental, social and vocational ability, and full inclusion and participation in all aspects of life. To that end, States Parties shall organize, strengthen and extend comprehensive habilitation and rehabilitation services and programmes, particularly in the areas of health, employment, education and social services, in such a way that these services and programmes:

(a) Begin at the earliest possible stage, and are based on the multidisciplinary assessment of individual needs and strengths;

(b) Support participation and inclusion in the community and all aspects of society, are voluntary, and are available to persons with disabilities as close as possible to their own communities, including in rural areas.

2. States Parties shall promote the development of initial and continuing training for professionals and staff working in habilitation and rehabilitation services.

3. States Parties shall promote the availability, knowledge and use of assistive devices and technologies, designed for persons with disabilities, as they relate to habilitation and rehabilitation.

Article 27   Work and employment

1. States Parties recognize the right of persons with disabilities to work, on an equal basis with others; this includes the right to the opportunity to gain a living by work freely chosen or accepted in a labour market and work environment that is open, inclusive and accessible to persons with

disabilities. States Parties shall safeguard and promote the realization of the right to work, including for those who acquire a disability during the course of employment, by taking appropriate steps, including through legislation, to, inter alia:

(a) Prohibit discrimination on the basis of disability with regard to all matters concerning all forms of employment, including conditions of recruitment, hiring and employment, continuance of employment, career advancement and safe and healthy working conditions;

(b) Protect the rights of persons with disabilities, on an equal basis with others, to just and favourable conditions of work, including equal opportunities and equal remuneration for work of equal value, safe and healthy working conditions, including protection from harassment, and the redress of grievances;

(c) Ensure that persons with disabilities are able to exercise their labour and trade union rights on an equal basis with others;

(d) Enable persons with disabilities to have effective access to general technical and vocational guidance programmes, placement services and vocational and continuing training;

(e) Promote employment opportunities and career advancement for persons with disabilities in the labour market, as well as assistance in finding, obtaining, maintaining and returning to employment;

(f) Promote opportunities for self-employment, entrepreneurship, the development of cooperatives and starting one's own business;

(g) Employ persons with disabilities in the public sector;

(h) Promote the employment of persons with disabilities in the private sector through appropriate policies and measures, which may include affirmative action programmes, incentives and other measures;

(i) Ensure that reasonable accommodation is provided to persons with disabilities in the workplace;

(j) Promote the acquisition by persons with disabilities of work experience in the open labour market;

(k) Promote vocational and professional rehabilitation, job retention and return-to-work programmes for persons with disabilities.

2. States Parties shall ensure that persons with disabilities are not held in slavery or in servitude, and are protected, on an equal basis with others, from forced or compulsory labour.

Article 28   Adequate standard of living and social protection

1. States Parties recognize the right of persons with disabilities to an adequate standard of living for themselves and their families, including adequate food, clothing and housing, and to the continuous improvement of living conditions, and shall take appropriate steps to safeguard and promote the realization of this right without discrimination on the basis of disability.

2. States Parties recognize the right of persons with disabilities to social protection and to the enjoyment of that right without discrimination on the basis of disability, and shall take appropriate steps to safeguard and promote the realization of this right, including measures:

(a) To ensure equal access by persons with disabilities to clean water services, and to ensure access to appropriate and affordable services, devices and other assistance for disability-related needs;

(b) To ensure access by persons with disabilities, in particular women and girls with disabilities and older persons with disabilities, to social protection programmes and poverty reduction programmes;

(c) To ensure access by persons with disabilities and their families living in situations of poverty to assistance from the State with disability-related expenses, including adequate training, counselling, financial assistance and respite care;

(d) To ensure access by persons with disabilities to public housing programmes;

(e) To ensure equal access by persons with disabilities to retirement benefits and programmes.

Article 29 Participation in political and public life

States Parties shall guarantee to persons with disabilities political rights and the opportunity to enjoy them on an equal basis with others, and shall undertake:

(a) To ensure that persons with disabilities can effectively and fully participate in political and public life on an equal basis with others, directly or through freely chosen representatives, including the right and opportunity for persons with disabilities to vote and be elected, *inter alia*, by:

   (i) Ensuring that voting procedures, facilities and materials are appropriate, accessible and easy to understand and use;

   (ii) Protecting the right of persons with disabilities to vote by secret ballot in elections and public referendums without intimidation, and to stand for elections, to effectively hold office and perform all public functions at all levels of government, facilitating the use of assistive and new technologies where appropriate;

   (iii) Guaranteeing the free expression of the will of persons with disabilities as electors and to this end, where necessary, at their request, allowing assistance in voting by a person of their own choice;

(b) To promote actively an environment in which persons with disabilities can effectively and fully participate in the conduct of public affairs, without discrimination and on an equal basis with others, and encourage their participation in public affairs, including:

   (i) Participation in non-governmental organizations and associations concerned with the public and political life of the country, and in the activities and administration of political parties;

   (ii) Forming and joining organizations of persons with disabilities to represent persons with disabilities at international, national, regional and local levels.

Article 30 Participation in cultural life, recreation, leisure and sport

1. States Parties recognize the right of persons with disabilities to take part on an equal basis with others in cultural life, and shall take all appropriate measures to ensure that persons with disabilities:

(a) Enjoy access to cultural materials in accessible formats;

(b) Enjoy access to television programmes, films, theatre and other cultural activities, in accessible formats;

(c) Enjoy access to places for cultural performances or services, such as theatres, museums, cinemas, libraries and tourism services, and, as far as possible, enjoy access to monuments and sites of national cultural importance.

2. States Parties shall take appropriate measures to enable persons with disabilities to have the opportunity to develop and utilize their creative, artistic and intellectual potential, not only for their own benefit, but also for the enrichment of society.

3. States Parties shall take all appropriate steps, in accordance with international law, to ensure that laws protecting intellectual property rights do not constitute an unreasonable or discriminatory barrier to access by persons with disabilities to cultural materials.

4. Persons with disabilities shall be entitled, on an equal basis with others, to recognition and support of their specific cultural and linguistic identity, including sign languages and deaf culture.

5. With a view to enabling persons with disabilities to participate on an equal basis with others in recreational, leisure and sporting activities, States Parties shall take appropriate measures:

(a) To encourage and promote the participation, to the fullest extent possible, of persons with disabilities in mainstream sporting activities at all levels;

(b) To ensure that persons with disabilities have an opportunity to organize, develop and participate in disability-specific sporting and recreational activities and, to this end, encourage the provision, on an equal basis with others, of appropriate instruction, training and resources;

(c) To ensure that persons with disabilities have access to sporting, recreational and tourism venues;

(d) To ensure that children with disabilities have equal access with other children to participation in play, recreation and leisure and sporting activities, including those activities in
the school system;

(e) To ensure that persons with disabilities have access to services from those involved in the
organization of recreational, tourism, leisure and sporting activities.

Article 31   Statistics and data collection

1. States Parties undertake to collect appropriate information, including statistical and research
data, to enable them to formulate and implement policies to give effect to the present Convention. The
process of collecting and maintaining this information shall:

(a) Comply with legally established safeguards, including legislation on data protection, to
ensure confidentiality and respect for the privacy of persons with disabilities;

(b) Comply with internationally accepted norms to protect human rights and fundamental
freedoms and ethical principles in the collection and use of statistics.

2. The information collected in accordance with this article shall be disaggregated, as appropriate, and used to help assess the implementation of States Parties' obligations under the present
Convention and to identify and address the barriers faced by persons with disabilities in exercising
their rights.

3. States Parties shall assume responsibility for the dissemination of these statistics and ensure
their accessibility to persons with disabilities and others.

Article 32   International cooperation

1. States Parties recognize the importance of international cooperation and its promotion,
in support of national efforts for the realization of the purpose and objectives of the present
Convention, and will undertake appropriate and effective measures in this regard, between and
among States and, as appropriate, in partnership with relevant international and regional organizations and civil society, in particular organizations of persons with disabilities. Such measures
could include, inter alia:

(a) Ensuring that international cooperation, including international development programmes, is inclusive of and accessible to persons with disabilities;

(b) Facilitating and supporting capacity-building, including through the exchange and sharing of information, experiences, training programmes and best practices;

(c) Facilitating cooperation in research and access to scientific and technical knowledge;

(d) Providing, as appropriate, technical and economic assistance, including by facilitating
access to and sharing of accessible and assistive technologies, and through the transfer of
technologies.

2. The provisions of this article are without prejudice to the obligations of each State Party to
fulfil its obligations under the present Convention.

Article 33   National implementation and monitoring

1. States Parties, in accordance with their system of organization, shall designate one or more
focal points within government for matters relating to the implementation of the present Convention,
and shall give due consideration to the establishment or designation of a coordination mechanism
within government to facilitate related action in different sectors and at different levels.

2. States Parties shall, in accordance with their legal and administrative systems, maintain,
strengthen, designate or establish within the State Party, a framework, including one or more independent mechanisms, as appropriate, to promote, protect and monitor implementation of the present Convention. When designating or establishing such a mechanism, States Parties shall take into
account the principles relating to the status and functioning of national institutions for protection and
promotion of human rights.

3. Civil society, in particular persons with disabilities and their representative organizations,
shall be involved and participate fully in the monitoring process.

Article 34   Committee on the Rights of Persons with Disabilities

1. There shall be established a Committee on the Rights of Persons with Disabilities (hereafter referred to as 'the Committee'), which shall carry out the functions hereinafter provided.

2. The Committee shall consist, at the time of entry into force of the present Convention, of twelve experts. After an additional sixty ratifications or accessions to the Convention, the membership of the Committee shall increase by six members, attaining a maximum number of eighteen members.

3. The members of the Committee shall serve in their personal capacity and shall be of high moral standing and recognized competence and experience in the field covered by the present Convention. When nominating their candidates, States Parties are invited to give due consideration to the provision set out in article 4, paragraph 3, of the present Convention.

4. The members of the Committee shall be elected by States Parties, consideration being given to equitable geographical distribution, representation of the different forms of civilization and of the principal legal systems, balanced gender representation and participation of experts with disabilities.

5. The members of the Committee shall be elected by secret ballot from a list of persons nominated by the States Parties from among their nationals at meetings of the Conference of States Parties. At those meetings, for which two thirds of States Parties shall constitute a quorum, the persons elected to the Committee shall be those who obtain the largest number of votes and an absolute majority of the votes of the representatives of States Parties present and voting.

6. The initial election shall be held no later than six months after the date of entry into force of the present Convention. At least four months before the date of each election, the Secretary-General of the United Nations shall address a letter to the States Parties inviting them to submit the nominations within two months. The Secretary-General shall subsequently prepare a list in alphabetical order of all persons thus nominated, indicating the State Parties which have nominated them, and shall submit it to the States Parties to the present Convention.

7. The members of the Committee shall be elected for a term of four years. They shall be eligible for re-election once. However, the term of six of the members elected at the first election shall expire at the end of two years; immediately after the first election, the names of these six members shall be chosen by lot by the chairperson of the meeting referred to in paragraph 5 of this article.

8. The election of the six additional members of the Committee shall be held on the occasion of regular elections, in accordance with the relevant provisions of this article.

9. If a member of the Committee dies or resigns or declares that for any other cause she or he can no longer perform her or his duties, the State Party which nominated the member shall appoint another expert possessing the qualifications and meeting the requirements set out in the relevant provisions of this article, to serve for the remainder of the term.

10. The Committee shall establish its own rules of procedure.

11. The Secretary-General of the United Nations shall provide the necessary staff and facilities for the effective performance of the functions of the Committee under the present Convention, and shall convene its initial meeting.

12. With the approval of the General Assembly of the United Nations, the members of the Committee established under the present Convention shall receive emoluments from United Nations resources on such terms and conditions as the Assembly may decide, having regard to the importance of the Committee's responsibilities.

13. The members of the Committee shall be entitled to the facilities, privileges and immunities of experts on mission for the United Nations as laid down in the relevant sections of the Convention on the Privileges and Immunities of the United Nations.

Article 35   Reports by States Parties

1. Each State Party shall submit to the Committee, through the Secretary-General of the United Nations, a comprehensive report on measures taken to give effect to its obligations under the present Convention and on the progress made in that regard, within two years after the entry into force of the present Convention for the State Party concerned.

2. Thereafter, States Parties shall submit subsequent reports at least every four years and further whenever the Committee so requests.

3. The Committee shall decide any guidelines applicable to the content of the reports.

4. A State Party which has submitted a comprehensive initial report to the Committee need not, in its subsequent reports, repeat information previously provided. When preparing reports to the Committee, States Parties are invited to consider doing so in an open and transparent process and to give due consideration to the provision set out in article 4, paragraph 3, of the present Convention.

5. Reports may indicate factors and difficulties affecting the degree of fulfilment of obligations under the present Convention.

Article 36   Consideration of reports

1. Each report shall be considered by the Committee, which shall make such suggestions and general recommendations on the report as it may consider appropriate and shall forward these to the State Party concerned. The State Party may respond with any information it chooses to the Committee. The Committee may request further information from States Parties relevant to the implementation of the present Convention.

2. If a State Party is significantly overdue in the submission of a report, the Committee may notify the State Party concerned of the need to examine the implementation of the present Convention in that State Party, on the basis of reliable information available to the Committee, if the relevant report is not submitted within three months following the notification. The Committee shall invite the State Party concerned to participate in such examination. Should the State Party respond by submitting the relevant report, the provisions of paragraph 1 of this article will apply.

3. The Secretary-General of the United Nations shall make available the reports to all States Parties.

4. States Parties shall make their reports widely available to the public in their own countries and facilitate access to the suggestions and general recommendations relating to these reports.

5. The Committee shall transmit, as it may consider appropriate, to the specialized agencies, funds and programmes of the United Nations, and other competent bodies, reports from States Parties in order to address a request or indication of a need for technical advice or assistance contained therein, along with the Committee's observations and recommendations, if any, on these requests or indications.

Article 37   Cooperation between States Parties and the Committee

1. Each State Party shall cooperate with the Committee and assist its members in the fulfilment of their mandate.

2. In its relationship with States Parties, the Committee shall give due consideration to ways and means of enhancing national capacities for the implementation of the present Convention, including through international cooperation.

Article 38   Relationship of the Committee with other bodies

In order to foster the effective implementation of the present Convention and to encourage international cooperation in the field covered by the present Convention:

   (a) The specialized agencies and other United Nations organs shall be entitled to be represented at the consideration of the implementation of such provisions of the present Convention as fall within the scope of their mandate. The Committee may invite the specialized agencies and other competent bodies as it may consider appropriate to provide expert advice on the implementation of the Convention in areas falling within the scope of their respective mandates. The Committee may invite specialized agencies and other United Nations organs to submit reports on the implementation of the Convention in areas falling within the scope of their activities;

   (b) The Committee, as it discharges its mandate, shall consult, as appropriate, other relevant bodies instituted by international human rights treaties, with a view to ensuring the consistency of their respective reporting guidelines, suggestions and general recommendations, and avoiding duplication and overlap in the performance of their functions.

Article 39   Report of the Committee

The Committee shall report every two years to the General Assembly and to the Economic and Social Council on its activities, and may make suggestions and general recommendations based on the examination of reports and information received from the States Parties. Such suggestions and general recommendations shall be included in the report of the Committee together with comments, if any, from States Parties.

Article 40   Conference of States Parties

1. The States Parties shall meet regularly in a Conference of States Parties in order to consider any matter with regard to the implementation of the present Convention.

2. No later than six months after the entry into force of the present Convention, the Conference of States Parties shall be convened by the Secretary-General of the United Nations. The subsequent meetings shall be convened by the Secretary-General biennially or upon the decision of the Conference of States Parties.

Article 41   Depositary

The Secretary-General of the United Nations shall be the depositary of the present Convention.

Article 42   Signature

The present Convention shall be open for signature by all States and by regional integration organizations at United Nations Headquarters in New York as of 30 March 2007.

Article 43   Consent to be bound

The present Convention shall be subject to ratification by signatory States and to formal confirmation by signatory regional integration organizations. It shall be open for accession by any State or regional integration organization which has not signed the Convention.

Article 44   Regional integration organizations

1. 'Regional integration organization' shall mean an organization constituted by sovereign States of a given region, to which its member States have transferred competence in respect of matters governed by the present Convention. Such organizations shall declare, in their instruments of formal confirmation or accession, the extent of their competence with respect to matters governed by the present Convention. Subsequently, they shall inform the depositary of any substantial modification in the extent of their competence.

2. References to 'States Parties' in the present Convention shall apply to such organizations within the limits of their competence.

3. For the purposes of article 45, paragraph 1, and article 47, paragraphs 2 and 3, of the present Convention, any instrument deposited by a regional integration organization shall not be counted.

4. Regional integration organizations, in matters within their competence, may exercise their right to vote in the Conference of States Parties, with a number of votes equal to the number of their member States that are Parties to the present Convention. Such an organization shall not exercise its right to vote if any of its member States exercises its right, and vice versa.

Article 45   Entry into force

1. The present Convention shall enter into force on the thirtieth day after the deposit of the twentieth instrument of ratification or accession.

2. For each State or regional integration organization ratifying, formally confirming or acceding to the present Convention after the deposit of the twentieth such instrument, the Convention shall enter into force on the thirtieth day after the deposit of its own such instrument.

Article 46   Reservations

1. Reservations incompatible with the object and purpose of the present Convention shall not be permitted.

2. Reservations may be withdrawn at any time.

Article 47   Amendments

1. Any State Party may propose an amendment to the present Convention and submit it to the Secretary-General of the United Nations. The Secretary-General shall communicate any proposed amendments to States Parties, with a request to be notified whether they favour a conference of States Parties for the purpose of considering and deciding upon the proposals. In the event that, within four months from the date of such communication, at least one third of the States Parties favour such a conference, the Secretary-General shall convene the conference under the auspices of the United Nations. Any amendment adopted by a majority of two thirds of the States Parties present and voting shall be submitted by the Secretary-General to the General Assembly of the United Nations for approval and thereafter to all States Parties for acceptance.

2. An amendment adopted and approved in accordance with paragraph 1 of this article shall enter into force on the thirtieth day after the number of instruments of acceptance deposited reaches two thirds of the number of States Parties at the date of adoption of the amendment. Thereafter, the amendment shall enter into force for any State Party on the thirtieth day following the deposit of its own instrument of acceptance. An amendment shall be binding only on those States Parties which have accepted it.

3. If so decided by the Conference of States Parties by consensus, an amendment adopted and approved in accordance with paragraph 1 of this article which relates exclusively to articles 34, 38, 39 and 40 shall enter into force for all States Parties on the thirtieth day after the number of instruments of acceptance deposited reaches two thirds of the number of States Parties at the date of adoption of the amendment.

Article 48   Denunciation

A State Party may denounce the present Convention by written notification to the Secretary-General of the United Nations. The denunciation shall become effective one year after the date of receipt of the notification by the Secretary-General.

Article 49   Accessible format

The text of the present Convention shall be made available in accessible formats.

Article 50   Authentic texts

The Arabic, Chinese, English, French, Russian and Spanish texts of the present Convention shall be equally authentic.

Optional Protocol to the Convention on the Rights of Persons with Disabilities (2006)*

The States Parties to the present Protocol have agreed as follows:

Article 1

1. A State Party to the present Protocol ('State Party') recognizes the competence of the Committee on the Rights of Persons with Disabilities ('the Committee') to receive and consider communications from or on behalf of individuals or groups of individuals subject to its jurisdiction who claim to be victims of a violation by that State Party of the provisions of the Convention.

2. No communication shall be received by the Committee if it concerns a State Party to the Convention that is not a party to the present Protocol.

Article 2

The Committee shall consider a communication inadmissible when:
    (a) The communication is anonymous;
    (b) The communication constitutes an abuse of the right of submission of such communications or is incompatible with the provisions of the Convention;

(c) The same matter has already been examined by the Committee or has been or is being examined under another procedure of international investigation or settlement;

(d) All available domestic remedies have not been exhausted. This shall not be the rule where the application of the remedies is unreasonably prolonged or unlikely to bring effective relief;

(e) It is manifestly ill-founded or not sufficiently substantiated; or when

(f) The facts that are the subject of the communication occurred prior to the entry into force of the present Protocol for the State Party concerned unless those facts continued after that date.

Article 3

Subject to the provisions of article 2 of the present Protocol, the Committee shall bring any communications submitted to it confidentially to the attention of the State Party. Within six months, the receiving State shall submit to the Committee written explanations or statements clarifying the matter and the remedy, if any, that may have been taken by that State.

Article 4

1. At any time after the receipt of a communication and before a determination on the merits has been reached, the Committee may transmit to the State Party concerned for its urgent consideration a request that the State Party take such interim measures as may be necessary to avoid possible irreparable damage to the victim or victims of the alleged violation.

2. Where the Committee exercises its discretion under paragraph 1 of this article, this does not imply a determination on admissibility or on the merits of the communication.

Article 5

The Committee shall hold closed meetings when examining communications under the present Protocol. After examining a communication, the Committee shall forward its suggestions and recommendations, if any, to the State Party concerned and to the petitioner.

Article 6

1. If the Committee receives reliable information indicating grave or systematic violations by a State Party of rights set forth in the Convention, the Committee shall invite that State Party to co-operate in the examination of the information and to this end submit observations with regard to the information concerned.

2. Taking into account any observations that may have been submitted by the State Party concerned as well as any other reliable information available to it, the Committee may designate one or more of its members to conduct an inquiry and to report urgently to the Committee. Where warranted and with the consent of the State Party, the inquiry may include a visit to its territory.

3. After examining the findings of such an inquiry, the Committee shall transmit these findings to the State Party concerned together with any comments and recommendations.

4. The State Party concerned shall, within six months of receiving the findings, comments and recommendations transmitted by the Committee, submit its observations to the Committee.

5. Such an inquiry shall be conducted confidentially and the cooperation of the State Party shall be sought at all stages of the proceedings.

Article 7

1. The Committee may invite the State Party concerned to include in its report under article 35 of the Convention details of any measures taken in response to an inquiry conducted under article 6 of the present Protocol.

2. The Committee may, if necessary, after the end of the period of six months referred to in article 6, paragraph 4, invite the State Party concerned to inform it of the measures taken in response to such an inquiry.

Article 8

Each State Party may, at the time of signature or ratification of the present Protocol or accession thereto, declare that it does not recognize the competence of the Committee provided for in articles 6 and 7.

Article 9
The Secretary-General of the United Nations shall be the depositary of the present Protocol.

Article 10
The present Protocol shall be open for signature by signatory States and regional integration organizations of the Convention at United Nations Headquarters in New York as of 30 March 2007.

Article 11
The present Protocol shall be subject to ratification by signatory States of the present Protocol which have ratified or acceded to the Convention. It shall be subject to formal confirmation by signatory regional integration organizations of the present Protocol which have formally confirmed or acceded to the Convention. It shall be open for accession by any State or regional integration organization which has ratified, formally confirmed or acceded to the Convention and which has not signed the Protocol.

Article 12
1. 'Regional integration organization' shall mean an organization constituted by sovereign States of a given region, to which its member States have transferred competence in respect of matters governed by the Convention and the present Protocol. Such organizations shall declare, in their instruments of formal confirmation or accession, the extent of their competence with respect to matters governed by the Convention and the present Protocol. Subsequently, they shall inform the depositary of any substantial modification in the extent of their competence.

2. References to 'States Parties' in the present Protocol shall apply to such organizations within the limits of their competence.

3. For the purposes of article 13, paragraph 1, and article 15, paragraph 2, of the present Protocol, any instrument deposited by a regional integration organization shall not be counted.

4. Regional integration organizations, in matters within their competence, may exercise their right to vote in the meeting of States Parties, with a number of votes equal to the number of their member States that are Parties to the present Protocol. Such an organization shall not exercise its right to vote if any of its member States exercises its right, and vice versa.

Article 13
1. Subject to the entry into force of the Convention, the present Protocol shall enter into force on the thirtieth day after the deposit of the tenth instrument of ratification or accession.

2. For each State or regional integration organization ratifying, formally confirming or acceding to the present Protocol after the deposit of the tenth such instrument, the Protocol shall enter into force on the thirtieth day after the deposit of its own such instrument.

Article 14
1. Reservations incompatible with the object and purpose of the present Protocol shall not be permitted.

2. Reservations may be withdrawn at any time.

Article 15
1. Any State Party may propose an amendment to the present Protocol and submit it to the Secretary-General of the United Nations. The Secretary-General shall communicate any proposed amendments to States Parties, with a request to be notified whether they favour a meeting of States Parties for the purpose of considering and deciding upon the proposals. In the event that, within four months from the date of such communication, at least one third of the States Parties favour such a meeting, the Secretary-General shall convene the meeting under the auspices of the United Nations. Any amendment adopted by a majority of two thirds of the States Parties present and voting shall be submitted by the Secretary-General to the General Assembly of the United Nations for approval and thereafter to all States Parties for acceptance.

2. An amendment adopted and approved in accordance with paragraph 1 of this article shall enter into force on the thirtieth day after the number of instruments of acceptance deposited reaches two thirds of the number of States Parties at the date of adoption of the amendment. Thereafter, the

amendment shall enter into force for any State Party on the thirtieth day following the deposit of its own instrument of acceptance. An amendment shall be binding only on those States Parties which have accepted it.

Article 16

A State Party may denounce the present Protocol by written notification to the Secretary-General of the United Nations. The denunciation shall become effective one year after the date of receipt of the notification by the Secretary-General.

Article 17

The text of the present Protocol shall be made available in accessible formats.

Article 18

The Arabic, Chinese, English, French, Russian and Spanish texts of the present Protocol shall be equally authentic.

International Convention for the Protection of All Persons from Enforced Disappearance (2006)*

PREAMBLE

The States Parties to this Convention,

Considering the obligation of States under the Charter of the United Nations to promote universal respect for, and observance of, human rights and fundamental freedoms,

Having regard to the Universal Declaration of Human Rights,

Recalling the International Covenant on Economic, Social and Cultural Rights, the International Covenant on Civil and Political Rights and the other relevant international instruments in the fields of human rights, humanitarian law and international criminal law,

Also recalling the Declaration on the Protection of All Persons from Enforced Disappearance adopted by the General Assembly of the United Nations in its resolution 47/133 of 18 December 1992,

Aware of the extreme seriousness of enforced disappearance, which constitutes a crime and, in certain circumstances defined in international law, a crime against humanity,

Determined to prevent enforced disappearances and to combat impunity for the crime of enforced disappearance,

Considering the right of any person not to be subjected to enforced disappearance, the right of victims to justice and to reparation,

Affirming the right of any victim to know the truth about the circumstances of an enforced disappearance and the fate of the disappeared person, and the right to freedom to seek, receive and impart information to this end,

Have agreed on the following articles:

PART I

Article 1

1. No one shall be subjected to enforced disappearance.

2. No exceptional circumstances whatsoever, whether a state of war or a threat of war, internal political instability or any other public emergency, may be invoked as a justification for enforced disappearance.

Article 2

For the purposes of this Convention, 'enforced disappearance' is considered to be the arrest, detention, abduction or any other form of deprivation of liberty by agents of the State or by persons or groups of persons acting with the authorization, support or acquiescence of the State, followed by a refusal to acknowledge the deprivation of liberty or by concealment of the fate or whereabouts of the disappeared person, which place such a person outside the protection of the law.

Article 3
Each State Party shall take appropriate measures to investigate acts defined in article 2 committed by persons or groups of persons acting without the authorization, support or acquiescence of the State and to bring those responsible to justice.

Article 4
Each State Party shall take the necessary measures to ensure that enforced disappearance constitutes an offence under its criminal law.

Article 5
The widespread or systematic practice of enforced disappearance constitutes a crime against humanity as defined in applicable international law and shall attract the consequences provided for under such applicable international law.

Article 6
1. Each State Party shall take the necessary measures to hold criminally responsible at least:
    (a) Any person who commits, orders, solicits or induces the commission of, attempts to commit, is an accomplice to or participates in an enforced disappearance;
    (b) A superior who:
        (i) Knew, or consciously disregarded information which clearly indicated, that subordinates under his or her effective authority and control were committing or about to commit a crime of enforced disappearance;
        (ii) Exercised effective responsibility for and control over activities which were concerned with the crime of enforced disappearance; and
        (iii) Failed to take all necessary and reasonable measures within his or her power to prevent or repress the commission of an enforced disappearance or to submit the matter to the competent authorities for investigation and prosecution;
    (c) Subparagraph (b) above is without prejudice to the higher standards of responsibility applicable under relevant international law to a military commander or to a person effectively acting as a military commander.
2. No order or instruction from any public authority, civilian, military or other, may be invoked to justify an offence of enforced disappearance.

Article 7
1. Each State Party shall make the offence of enforced disappearance punishable by appropriate penalties which take into account its extreme seriousness.
2. Each State Party may establish:
    (a) Mitigating circumstances, in particular for persons who, having been implicated in the commission of an enforced disappearance, effectively contribute to bringing the disappeared person forward alive or make it possible to clarify cases of enforced disappearance or to identify the perpetrators of an enforced disappearance;
    (b) Without prejudice to other criminal procedures, aggravating circumstances, in particular in the event of the death of the disappeared person or the commission of an enforced disappearance in respect of pregnant women, minors, persons with disabilities or other particularly vulnerable persons.

Article 8
Without prejudice to article 5,
1. A State Party which applies a statute of limitations in respect of enforced disappearance shall take the necessary measures to ensure that the term of limitation for criminal proceedings:
    (a) Is of long duration and is proportionate to the extreme seriousness of this offence;
    (b) Commences from the moment when the offence of enforced disappearance ceases, taking into account its continuous nature.

2. Each State Party shall guarantee the right of victims of enforced disappearance to an effective remedy during the term of limitation.

Article 9

1. Each State Party shall take the necessary measures to establish its competence to exercise jurisdiction over the offence of enforced disappearance:

    (a) When the offence is committed in any territory under its jurisdiction or on board a ship or aircraft registered in that State;

    (b) When the alleged offender is one of its nationals;

    (c) When the disappeared person is one of its nationals and the State Party considers it appropriate.

2. Each State Party shall likewise take such measures as may be necessary to establish its competence to exercise jurisdiction over the offence of enforced disappearance when the alleged offender is present in any territory under its jurisdiction, unless it extradites or surrenders him or her to another State in accordance with its international obligations or surrenders him or her to an international criminal tribunal whose jurisdiction it has recognized.

3. This Convention does not exclude any additional criminal jurisdiction exercised in accordance with national law.

Article 10

1. Upon being satisfied, after an examination of the information available to it, that the circumstances so warrant, any State Party in whose territory a person suspected of having committed an offence of enforced disappearance is present shall take him or her into custody or take such other legal measures as are necessary to ensure his or her presence. The custody and other legal measures shall be as provided for in the law of that State Party but may be maintained only for such time as is necessary to ensure the person's presence at criminal, surrender or extradition proceedings.

2. A State Party which has taken the measures referred to in paragraph 1 of this article shall immediately carry out a preliminary inquiry or investigations to establish the facts. It shall notify the States Parties referred to in article 9, paragraph 1, of the measures it has taken in pursuance of paragraph 1 of this article, including detention and the circumstances warranting detention, and of the findings of its preliminary inquiry or its investigations, indicating whether it intends to exercise its jurisdiction.

3. Any person in custody pursuant to paragraph 1 of this article may communicate immediately with the nearest appropriate representative of the State of which he or she is a national, or, if he or she is a stateless person, with the representative of the State where he or she usually resides.

Article 11

1. The State Party in the territory under whose jurisdiction a person alleged to have committed an offence of enforced disappearance is found shall, if it does not extradite that person or surrender him or her to another State in accordance with its international obligations or surrender him or her to an international criminal tribunal whose jurisdiction it has recognized, submit the case to its competent authorities for the purpose of prosecution.

2. These authorities shall take their decision in the same manner as in the case of any ordinary offence of a serious nature under the law of that State Party. In the cases referred to in article 9, paragraph 2, the standards of evidence required for prosecution and conviction shall in no way be less stringent than those which apply in the cases referred to in article 9, paragraph 1.

3. Any person against whom proceedings are brought in connection with an offence of enforced disappearance shall be guaranteed fair treatment at all stages of the proceedings. Any person tried for an offence of enforced disappearance shall benefit from a fair trial before a competent, independent and impartial court or tribunal established by law.

Article 12

1. Each State Party shall ensure that any individual who alleges that a person has been subjected to enforced disappearance has the right to report the facts to the competent authorities, which shall

examine the allegation promptly and impartially and, where necessary, undertake without delay a thorough and impartial investigation. Appropriate steps shall be taken, where necessary, to ensure that the complainant, witnesses, relatives of the disappeared person and their defence counsel, as well as persons participating in the investigation, are protected against all ill-treatment or intimidation as a consequence of the complaint or any evidence given.

2. Where there are reasonable grounds for believing that a person has been subjected to enforced disappearance, the authorities referred to in paragraph 1 of this article shall undertake an investigation, even if there has been no formal complaint.

3. Each State Party shall ensure that the authorities referred to in paragraph 1 of this article:

(a) Have the necessary powers and resources to conduct the investigation effectively, including access to the documentation and other information relevant to their investigation;

(b) Have access, if necessary with the prior authorization of a judicial authority, which shall rule promptly on the matter, to any place of detention or any other place where there are reasonable grounds to believe that the disappeared person may be present.

4. Each State Party shall take the necessary measures to prevent and sanction acts that hinder the conduct of an investigation. It shall ensure in particular that persons suspected of having committed an offence of enforced disappearance are not in a position to influence the progress of an investigation by means of pressure or acts of intimidation or reprisal aimed at the complainant, witnesses, relatives of the disappeared person or their defence counsel, or at persons participating in the investigation.

Article 13

1. For the purposes of extradition between States Parties, the offence of enforced disappearance shall not be regarded as a political offence or as an offence connected with a political offence or as an offence inspired by political motives. Accordingly, a request for extradition based on such an offence may not be refused on these grounds alone.

2. The offence of enforced disappearance shall be deemed to be included as an extraditable offence in any extradition treaty existing between States Parties before the entry into force of this Convention.

3. States Parties undertake to include the offence of enforced disappearance as an extraditable offence in any extradition treaty subsequently to be concluded between them.

4. If a State Party which makes extradition conditional on the existence of a treaty receives a request for extradition from another State Party with which it has no extradition treaty, it may consider this Convention as the necessary legal basis for extradition in respect of the offence of enforced disappearance.

5. States Parties which do not make extradition conditional on the existence of a treaty shall recognize the offence of enforced disappearance as an extraditable offence between themselves.

6. Extradition shall, in all cases, be subject to the conditions provided for by the law of the requested State Party or by applicable extradition treaties, including, in particular, conditions relating to the minimum penalty requirement for extradition and the grounds upon which the requested State Party may refuse extradition or make it subject to certain conditions.

7. Nothing in this Convention shall be interpreted as imposing an obligation to extradite if the requested State Party has substantial grounds for believing that the request has been made for the purpose of prosecuting or punishing a person on account of that person's sex, race, religion, nationality, ethnic origin, political opinions or membership of a particular social group, or that compliance with the request would cause harm to that person for any one of these reasons.

Article 14

1. States Parties shall afford one another the greatest measure of mutual legal assistance in connection with criminal proceedings brought in respect of an offence of enforced disappearance, including the supply of all evidence at their disposal that is necessary for the proceedings.

2. Such mutual legal assistance shall be subject to the conditions provided for by the domestic law of the requested State Party or by applicable treaties on mutual legal assistance, including, in

particular, the conditions in relation to the grounds upon which the requested State Party may refuse to grant mutual legal assistance or may make it subject to conditions.

Article 15

States Parties shall cooperate with each other and shall afford one another the greatest measure of mutual assistance with a view to assisting victims of enforced disappearance, and in searching for, locating and releasing disappeared persons and, in the event of death, in exhuming and identifying them and returning their remains.

Article 16

1. No State Party shall expel, return ('refouler'), surrender or extradite a person to another State where there are substantial grounds for believing that he or she would be in danger of being subjected to enforced disappearance.

2. For the purpose of determining whether there are such grounds, the competent authorities shall take into account all relevant considerations, including, where applicable, the existence in the State concerned of a consistent pattern of gross, flagrant or mass violations of human rights or of serious violations of international humanitarian law.

Article 17

1. No one shall be held in secret detention.

2. Without prejudice to other international obligations of the State Party with regard to the deprivation of liberty, each State Party shall, in its legislation:

    (a) Establish the conditions under which orders of deprivation of liberty may be given;

    (b) Indicate those authorities authorized to order the deprivation of liberty;

    (c) Guarantee that any person deprived of liberty shall be held solely in officially recognized and supervised places of deprivation of liberty;

    (d) Guarantee that any person deprived of liberty shall be authorized to communicate with and be visited by his or her family, counsel or any other person of his or her choice, subject only to the conditions established by law, or, if he or she is a foreigner, to communicate with his or her consular authorities, in accordance with applicable international law;

    (e) Guarantee access by the competent and legally authorized authorities and institutions to the places where persons are deprived of liberty, if necessary with prior authorization from a judicial authority;

    (f) Guarantee that any person deprived of liberty or, in the case of a suspected enforced disappearance, since the person deprived of liberty is not able to exercise this right, any persons with a legitimate interest, such as relatives of the person deprived of liberty, their representatives or their counsel, shall, in all circumstances, be entitled to take proceedings before a court, in order that the court may decide without delay on the lawfulness of the deprivation of liberty and order the person's release if such deprivation of liberty is not lawful.

3. Each State Party shall assure the compilation and maintenance of one or more up-to-date official registers and/or records of persons deprived of liberty, which shall be made promptly available, upon request, to any judicial or other competent authority or institution authorized for that purpose by the law of the State Party concerned or any relevant international legal instrument to which the State concerned is a party. The information contained therein shall include, as a minimum:

    (a) The identity of the person deprived of liberty;

    (b) The date, time and place where the person was deprived of liberty and the identity of the authority that deprived the person of liberty;

    (c) The authority that ordered the deprivation of liberty and the grounds for the deprivation of liberty;

    (d) The authority responsible for supervising the deprivation of liberty;

    (e) The place of deprivation of liberty, the date and time of admission to the place of deprivation of liberty and the authority responsible for the place of deprivation of liberty;

    (f) Elements relating to the state of health of the person deprived of liberty;

    (g) In the event of death during the deprivation of liberty, the circumstances and cause of death and the destination of the remains;

    (h) The date and time of release or transfer to another place of detention, the destination and the authority responsible for the transfer.

Article 18

  1. Subject to articles 19 and 20, each State Party shall guarantee to any person with a legitimate interest in this information, such as relatives of the person deprived of liberty, their representatives or their counsel, access to at least the following information:

    (a) The authority that ordered the deprivation of liberty;

    (b) The date, time and place where the person was deprived of liberty and admitted to the place of deprivation of liberty;

    (c) The authority responsible for supervising the deprivation of liberty;

    (d) The whereabouts of the person deprived of liberty, including, in the event of a transfer to another place of deprivation of liberty, the destination and the authority responsible for the transfer;

    (e) The date, time and place of release;

    (f) Elements relating to the state of health of the person deprived of liberty;

    (g) In the event of death during the deprivation of liberty, the circumstances and cause of death and the destination of the remains.

  2. Appropriate measures shall be taken, where necessary, to protect the persons referred to in paragraph 1 of this article, as well as persons participating in the investigation, from any ill-treatment, intimidation or sanction as a result of the search for information concerning a person deprived of liberty.

Article 19

  1. Personal information, including medical and genetic data, which is collected and/or transmitted within the framework of the search for a disappeared person shall not be used or made available for purposes other than the search for the disappeared person. This is without prejudice to the use of such information in criminal proceedings relating to an offence of enforced disappearance or the exercise of the right to obtain reparation.

  2. The collection, processing, use and storage of personal information, including medical and genetic data, shall not infringe or have the effect of infringing the human rights, fundamental freedoms or human dignity of an individual.

Article 20

  1. Only where a person is under the protection of the law and the deprivation of liberty is subject to judicial control may the right to information referred to in article 18 be restricted, on an exceptional basis, where strictly necessary and where provided for by law, and if the transmission of the information would adversely affect the privacy or safety of the person, hinder a criminal investigation, or for other equivalent reasons in accordance with the law, and in conformity with applicable international law and with the objectives of this Convention. In no case shall there be restrictions on the right to information referred to in article 18 that could constitute conduct defined in article 2 or be in violation of article 17, paragraph 1.

  2. Without prejudice to consideration of the lawfulness of the deprivation of a person's liberty, States Parties shall guarantee to the persons referred to in article 18, paragraph 1, the right to a prompt and effective judicial remedy as a means of obtaining without delay the information referred to in article 18, paragraph 1. This right to a remedy may not be suspended or restricted in any circumstances.

Article 21

Each State Party shall take the necessary measures to ensure that persons deprived of liberty are released in a manner permitting reliable verification that they have actually been released. Each State Party shall also take the necessary measures to assure the physical integrity of such persons and their ability to exercise fully their rights at the time of release, without prejudice to any obligations to which such persons may be subject under national law.

Article 22
Without prejudice to article 6, each State Party shall take the necessary measures to prevent and impose sanctions for the following conduct:
  (a) Delaying or obstructing the remedies referred to in article 17, paragraph 2 (f), and article 20, paragraph 2;
  (b) Failure to record the deprivation of liberty of any person, or the recording of any information which the official responsible for the official register knew or should have known to be inaccurate;
  (c) Refusal to provide information on the deprivation of liberty of a person, or the provision of inaccurate information, even though the legal requirements for providing such information have been met.

Article 23
1. Each State Party shall ensure that the training of law enforcement personnel, civil or military, medical personnel, public officials and other persons who may be involved in the custody or treatment of any person deprived of liberty includes the necessary education and information regarding the relevant provisions of this Convention, in order to:
  (a) Prevent the involvement of such officials in enforced disappearances;
  (b) Emphasize the importance of prevention and investigations in relation to enforced disappearances;
  (c) Ensure that the urgent need to resolve cases of enforced disappearance is recognized.
2. Each State Party shall ensure that orders or instructions prescribing, authorizing or encouraging enforced disappearance are prohibited. Each State Party shall guarantee that a person who refuses to obey such an order will not be punished.
3. Each State Party shall take the necessary measures to ensure that the persons referred to in paragraph 1 of this article who have reason to believe that an enforced disappearance has occurred or is planned report the matter to their superiors and, where necessary, to the appropriate authorities or bodies vested with powers of review or remedy.

Article 24
1. For the purposes of this Convention, 'victim' means the disappeared person and any individual who has suffered harm as the direct result of an enforced disappearance.
2. Each victim has the right to know the truth regarding the circumstances of the enforced disappearance, the progress and results of the investigation and the fate of the disappeared person. Each State Party shall take appropriate measures in this regard.
3. Each State Party shall take all appropriate measures to search for, locate and release disappeared persons and, in the event of death, to locate, respect and return their remains.
4. Each State Party shall ensure in its legal system that the victims of enforced disappearance have the right to obtain reparation and prompt, fair and adequate compensation.
5. The right to obtain reparation referred to in paragraph 4 of this article covers material and moral damages and, where appropriate, other forms of reparation such as:
  (a) Restitution;
  (b) Rehabilitation;
  (c) Satisfaction, including restoration of dignity and reputation;
  (d) Guarantees of non-repetition.
6. Without prejudice to the obligation to continue the investigation until the fate of the disappeared person has been clarified, each State Party shall take the appropriate steps with regard to the legal situation of disappeared persons whose fate has not been clarified and that of their relatives, in fields such as social welfare, financial matters, family law and property rights.

7. Each State Party shall guarantee the right to form and participate freely in organizations and associations concerned with attempting to establish the circumstances of enforced disappearances and the fate of disappeared persons, and to assist victims of enforced disappearance.

Article 25

1. Each State Party shall take the necessary measures to prevent and punish under its criminal law:
   (a) The wrongful removal of children who are subjected to enforced disappearance, children whose father, mother or legal guardian is subjected to enforced disappearance or children born during the captivity of a mother subjected to enforced disappearance;
   (b) The falsification, concealment or destruction of documents attesting to the true identity of the children referred to in subparagraph (a) above.

2. Each State Party shall take the necessary measures to search for and identify the children referred to in paragraph 1 (a) of this article and to return them to their families of origin, in accordance with legal procedures and applicable international agreements.

3. States Parties shall assist one another in searching for, identifying and locating the children referred to in paragraph 1 (a) of this article.

4. Given the need to protect the best interests of the children referred to in paragraph 1 (a) of this article and their right to preserve, or to have re-established, their identity, including their nationality, name and family relations as recognized by law, States Parties which recognize a system of adoption or other form of placement of children shall have legal procedures in place to review the adoption or placement procedure, and, where appropriate, to annul any adoption or placement of children that originated in an enforced disappearance.

5. In all cases, and in particular in all matters relating to this article, the best interests of the child shall be a primary consideration, and a child who is capable of forming his or her own views shall have the right to express those views freely, the views of the child being given due weight in accordance with the age and maturity of the child.

PART II

Article 26

1. A Committee on Enforced Disappearances (hereinafter referred to as 'the Committee') shall be established to carry out the functions provided for under this Convention. The Committee shall consist of ten experts of high moral character and recognized competence in the field of human rights, who shall serve in their personal capacity and be independent and impartial. The members of the Committee shall be elected by the States Parties according to equitable geographical distribution. Due account shall be taken of the usefulness of the participation in the work of the Committee of persons having relevant legal experience and of balanced gender representation.

2. The members of the Committee shall be elected by secret ballot from a list of persons nominated by States Parties from among their nationals, at biennial meetings of the States Parties convened by the Secretary-General of the United Nations for this purpose. At those meetings, for which two thirds of the States Parties shall constitute a quorum, the persons elected to the Committee shall be those who obtain the largest number of votes and an absolute majority of the votes of the representatives of States Parties present and voting.

3. The initial election shall be held no later than six months after the date of entry into force of this Convention. Four months before the date of each election, the Secretary-General of the United Nations shall address a letter to the States Parties inviting them to submit nominations within three months. The Secretary-General shall prepare a list in alphabetical order of all persons thus nominated, indicating the State Party which nominated each candidate, and shall submit this list to all States Parties.

4. The members of the Committee shall be elected for a term of four years. They shall be eligible for re-election once. However, the term of five of the members elected at the first election shall expire at the end of two years; immediately after the first election, the names of these five members shall be chosen by lot by the chairman of the meeting referred to in paragraph 2 of this article.

5. If a member of the Committee dies or resigns or for any other reason can no longer perform his or her Committee duties, the State Party which nominated him or her shall, in accordance with the criteria set out in paragraph 1 of this article, appoint another candidate from among its nationals to serve out his or her term, subject to the approval of the majority of the States Parties. Such approval shall be considered to have been obtained unless half or more of the States Parties respond negatively within six weeks of having been informed by the Secretary-General of the United Nations of the proposed appointment.

6. The Committee shall establish its own rules of procedure.

7. The Secretary-General of the United Nations shall provide the Committee with the necessary means, staff and facilities for the effective performance of its functions. The Secretary-General of the United Nations shall convene the initial meeting of the Committee.

8. The members of the Committee shall be entitled to the facilities, privileges and immunities of experts on mission for the United Nations, as laid down in the relevant sections of the Convention on the Privileges and Immunities of the United Nations.

9. Each State Party shall cooperate with the Committee and assist its members in the fulfilment of their mandate, to the extent of the Committee's functions that the State Party has accepted.

Article 27

A Conference of the States Parties will take place at the earliest four years and at the latest six years following the entry into force of this Convention to evaluate the functioning of the Committee and to decide, in accordance with the procedure described in article 44, paragraph 2, whether it is appropriate to transfer to another body—without excluding any possibility—the monitoring of this Convention, in accordance with the functions defined in articles 28 to 36.

Article 28

1. In the framework of the competencies granted by this Convention, the Committee shall cooperate with all relevant organs, offices and specialized agencies and funds of the United Nations, with the treaty bodies instituted by international instruments, with the special procedures of the United Nations and with the relevant regional intergovernmental organizations or bodies, as well as with all relevant State institutions, agencies or offices working towards the protection of all persons against enforced disappearances.

2. As it discharges its mandate, the Committee shall consult other treaty bodies instituted by relevant international human rights instruments, in particular the Human Rights Committee instituted by the International Covenant on Civil and Political Rights, with a view to ensuring the consistency of their respective observations and recommendations.

Article 29

1. Each State Party shall submit to the Committee, through the Secretary-General of the United Nations, a report on the measures taken to give effect to its obligations under this Convention, within two years after the entry into force of this Convention for the State Party concerned.

2. The Secretary-General of the United Nations shall make this report available to all States Parties.

3. Each report shall be considered by the Committee, which shall issue such comments, observations or recommendations as it may deem appropriate. The comments, observations or recommendations shall be communicated to the State Party concerned, which may respond to them, on its own initiative or at the request of the Committee.

4. The Committee may also request States Parties to provide additional information on the implementation of this Convention.

Article 30

1. A request that a disappeared person should be sought and found may be submitted to the Committee, as a matter of urgency, by relatives of the disappeared person or their legal representatives, their counsel or any person authorized by them, as well as by any other person having a legitimate interest.

2. If the Committee considers that a request for urgent action submitted in pursuance of paragraph 1 of this article:

(a) Is not manifestly unfounded;

(b) Does not constitute an abuse of the right of submission of such requests;

(c) Has already been duly presented to the competent bodies of the State Party concerned, such as those authorized to undertake investigations, where such a possibility exists;

(d) Is not incompatible with the provisions of this Convention; and

(e) The same matter is not being examined under another procedure of international investigation or settlement of the same nature;

it shall request the State Party concerned to provide it with information on the situation of the persons sought, within a time limit set by the Committee.

3. In the light of the information provided by the State Party concerned in accordance with paragraph 2 of this article, the Committee may transmit recommendations to the State Party, including a request that the State Party should take all the necessary measures, including interim measures, to locate and protect the person concerned in accordance with this Convention and to inform the Committee, within a specified period of time, of measures taken, taking into account the urgency of the situation. The Committee shall inform the person submitting the urgent action request of its recommendations and of the information provided to it by the State as it becomes available.

4. The Committee shall continue its efforts to work with the State Party concerned for as long as the fate of the person sought remains unresolved. The person presenting the request shall be kept informed.

Article 31

1. A State Party may at the time of ratification of this Convention or at any time afterwards declare that it recognizes the competence of the Committee to receive and consider communications from or on behalf of individuals subject to its jurisdiction claiming to be victims of a violation by this State Party of provisions of this Convention. The Committee shall not admit any communication concerning a State Party which has not made such a declaration.

2. The Committee shall consider a communication inadmissible where:

(a) The communication is anonymous;

(b) The communication constitutes an abuse of the right of submission of such communications or is incompatible with the provisions of this Convention;

(c) The same matter is being examined under another procedure of international investigation or settlement of the same nature; or where

(d) All effective available domestic remedies have not been exhausted. This rule shall not apply where the application of the remedies is unreasonably prolonged.

3. If the Committee considers that the communication meets the requirements set out in paragraph 2 of this article, it shall transmit the communication to the State Party concerned, requesting it to provide observations and comments within a time limit set by the Committee.

4. At any time after the receipt of a communication and before a determination on the merits has been reached, the Committee may transmit to the State Party concerned for its urgent consideration a request that the State Party will take such interim measures as may be necessary to avoid possible irreparable damage to the victims of the alleged violation. Where the Committee exercises its discretion, this does not imply a determination on admissibility or on the merits of the communication.

5. The Committee shall hold closed meetings when examining communications under the present article. It shall inform the author of a communication of the responses provided by the State Party concerned. When the Committee decides to finalize the procedure, it shall communicate its views to the State Party and to the author of the communication.

Article 32

A State Party to this Convention may at any time declare that it recognizes the competence of the Committee to receive and consider communications in which a State Party claims that another State Party is not fulfilling its obligations under this Convention. The Committee shall not receive communications concerning a State Party which has not made such a declaration, nor communications from a State Party which has not made such a declaration.

Article 33

1. If the Committee receives reliable information indicating that a State Party is seriously violating the provisions of this Convention, it may, after consultation with the State Party concerned, request one or more of its members to undertake a visit and report back to it without delay.

2. The Committee shall notify the State Party concerned, in writing, of its intention to organize a visit, indicating the composition of the delegation and the purpose of the visit. The State Party shall answer the Committee within a reasonable time.

3. Upon a substantiated request by the State Party, the Committee may decide to postpone or cancel its visit.

4. If the State Party agrees to the visit, the Committee and the State Party concerned shall work together to define the modalities of the visit and the State Party shall provide the Committee with all the facilities needed for the successful completion of the visit.

5. Following its visit, the Committee shall communicate to the State Party concerned its observations and recommendations.

Article 34

If the Committee receives information which appears to it to contain well-founded indications that enforced disappearance is being practised on a widespread or systematic basis in the territory under the jurisdiction of a State Party, it may, after seeking from the State Party concerned all relevant information on the situation, urgently bring the matter to the attention of the General Assembly of the United Nations, through the Secretary-General of the United Nations.

Article 35

1. The Committee shall have competence solely in respect of enforced disappearances which commenced after the entry into force of this Convention.

2. If a State becomes a party to this Convention after its entry into force, the obligations of that State vis-à-vis the Committee shall relate only to enforced disappearances which commenced after the entry into force of this Convention for the State concerned.

Article 36

1. The Committee shall submit an annual report on its activities under this Convention to the States Parties and to the General Assembly of the United Nations.

2. Before an observation on a State Party is published in the annual report, the State Party concerned shall be informed in advance and shall be given reasonable time to answer. This State Party may request the publication of its comments or observations in the report.

PART III

Article 37

Nothing in this Convention shall affect any provisions which are more conducive to the protection of all persons from enforced disappearance and which may be contained in:

    (a) The law of a State Party;

    (b) International law in force for that State.

Article 38

1. This Convention is open for signature by all Member States of the United Nations.

2. This Convention is subject to ratification by all Member States of the United Nations. Instruments of ratification shall be deposited with the Secretary-General of the United Nations.

3. This Convention is open to accession by all Member States of the United Nations. Accession shall be effected by the deposit of an instrument of accession with the Secretary-General.

Article 39

1. This Convention shall enter into force on the thirtieth day after the date of deposit with the Secretary-General of the United Nations of the twentieth instrument of ratification or accession.

2. For each State ratifying or acceding to this Convention after the deposit of the twentieth instrument of ratification or accession, this Convention shall enter into force on the thirtieth day after the date of the deposit of that State's instrument of ratification or accession.

Article 40

The Secretary-General of the United Nations shall notify all States Members of the United Nations and all States which have signed or acceded to this Convention of the following:

(a) Signatures, ratifications and accessions under article 38;

(b) The date of entry into force of this Convention under article 39.

Article 41

The provisions of this Convention shall apply to all parts of federal States without any limitations or exceptions.

Article 42

1. Any dispute between two or more States Parties concerning the interpretation or application of this Convention which cannot be settled through negotiation or by the procedures expressly provided for in this Convention shall, at the request of one of them, be submitted to arbitration. If within six months from the date of the request for arbitration the Parties are unable to agree on the organization of the arbitration, any one of those Parties may refer the dispute to the International Court of Justice by request in conformity with the Statute of the Court.

2. A State may, at the time of signature or ratification of this Convention or accession thereto, declare that it does not consider itself bound by paragraph 1 of this article. The other States Parties shall not be bound by paragraph 1 of this article with respect to any State Party having made such a declaration.

3. Any State Party having made a declaration in accordance with the provisions of paragraph 2 of this article may at any time withdraw this declaration by notification to the Secretary-General of the United Nations.

Article 43

This Convention is without prejudice to the provisions of international humanitarian law, including the obligations of the High Contracting Parties to the four Geneva Conventions of 12 August 1949 and the two Additional Protocols thereto of 8 June 1977, or to the opportunity available to any State Party to authorize the International Committee of the Red Cross to visit places of detention in situations not covered by international humanitarian law.

Article 44

1. Any State Party to this Convention may propose an amendment and file it with the Secretary-General of the United Nations. The Secretary-General shall thereupon communicate the proposed amendment to the States Parties to this Convention with a request that they indicate whether they favour a conference of States Parties for the purpose of considering and voting upon the proposal. In the event that within four months from the date of such communication at least one third of the States Parties favour such a conference, the Secretary-General shall convene the conference under the auspices of the United Nations.

2. Any amendment adopted by a majority of two thirds of the States Parties present and voting at the conference shall be submitted by the Secretary-General of the United Nations to all the States Parties for acceptance.

3. An amendment adopted in accordance with paragraph 1 of this article shall enter into force when two thirds of the States Parties to this Convention have accepted it in accordance with their respective constitutional processes.

4. When amendments enter into force, they shall be binding on those States Parties which have accepted them, other States Parties still being bound by the provisions of this Convention and any earlier amendment which they have accepted.

Article 45

1. This Convention, of which the Arabic, Chinese, English, French, Russian and Spanish texts are equally authentic, shall be deposited with the Secretary-General of the United Nations.

2. The Secretary-General of the United Nations shall transmit certified copies of this Convention to all States referred to in article 38.

United Nations Declaration on the Rights of Indigenous Peoples (2007)*

The General Assembly,

Taking note of the recommendation of the Human Rights Council contained in its resolution 1/2 of 29 June 2006, by which the Council adopted the text of the United Nations Declaration on the Rights of Indigenous Peoples,

Recalling its resolution 61/178 of 20 December 2006, by which it decided to defer consideration of and action on the Declaration to allow time for further consultations thereon, and also decided to conclude its consideration before the end of the sixty-first session of the General Assembly,

Adopts the United Nations Declaration on the Rights of Indigenous Peoples as contained in the annex to the present resolution.

Annex
United Nations Declaration on the Rights of Indigenous Peoples

The General Assembly,

Guided by the purposes and principles of the Charter of the United Nations, and good faith in the fulfilment of the obligations assumed by States in accordance with the Charter,

Affirming that indigenous peoples are equal to all other peoples, while recognizing the right of all peoples to be different, to consider themselves different, and to be respected as such,

Affirming also that all peoples contribute to the diversity and richness of civilizations and cultures, which constitute the common heritage of humankind,

Affirming further that all doctrines, policies and practices based on or advocating superiority of peoples or individuals on the basis of national origin or racial, religious, ethnic or cultural differences are racist, scientifically false, legally invalid, morally condemnable and socially unjust,

Reaffirming that indigenous peoples, in the exercise of their rights, should be free from discrimination of any kind,

Concerned that indigenous peoples have suffered from historic injustices as a result of, inter alia, their colonization and dispossession of their lands, territories and resources, thus preventing them from exercising, in particular, their right to development in accordance with their own needs and interests,

Recognizing the urgent need to respect and promote the inherent rights of indigenous peoples which derive from their political, economic and social structures and from their cultures, spiritual traditions, histories and philosophies, especially their rights to their lands, territories and resources,

Recognizing also the urgent need to respect and promote the rights of indigenous peoples affirmed in treaties, agreements and other constructive arrangements with States,

Welcoming the fact that indigenous peoples are organizing themselves for political, economic, social and cultural enhancement and in order to bring to an end all forms of discrimination and oppression wherever they occur,

Convinced that control by indigenous peoples over developments affecting them and their lands, territories and resources will enable them to maintain and strengthen their institutions, cultures and traditions, and to promote their development in accordance with their aspirations and needs,

Recognizing that respect for indigenous knowledge, cultures and traditional practices contributes to sustainable and equitable development and proper management of the environment,

Emphasizing the contribution of the demilitarization of the lands and territories of indigenous peoples to peace, economic and social progress and development, understanding and friendly relations among nations and peoples of the world,

Recognizing in particular the right of indigenous families and communities to retain shared responsibility for the upbringing, training, education and well-being of their children, consistent with the rights of the child,

Considering that the rights affirmed in treaties, agreements and other constructive arrangements between States and indigenous peoples are, in some situations, matters of international concern, interest, responsibility and character,

Considering also that treaties, agreements and other constructive arrangements, and the relationship they represent, are the basis for a strengthened partnership between indigenous peoples and States,

Acknowledging that the Charter of the United Nations, the International Covenant on Economic, Social and Cultural Rights and the International Covenant on Civil and Political Rights as well as the Vienna Declaration and Programme of Action, affirm the fundamental importance of the right to self-determination of all peoples, by virtue of which they freely determine their political status and freely pursue their economic, social and cultural development,

Bearing in mind that nothing in this Declaration may be used to deny any peoples their right to self-determination, exercised in conformity with international law,

Convinced that the recognition of the rights of indigenous peoples in this Declaration will enhance harmonious and cooperative relations between the State and indigenous peoples, based on principles of justice, democracy, respect for human rights, non-discrimination and good faith,

Encouraging States to comply with and effectively implement all their obligations as they apply to indigenous peoples under international instruments, in particular those related to human rights, in consultation and cooperation with the peoples concerned,

Emphasizing that the United Nations has an important and continuing role to play in promoting and protecting the rights of indigenous peoples,

Believing that this Declaration is a further important step forward for the recognition, promotion and protection of the rights and freedoms of indigenous peoples and in the development of relevant activities of the United Nations system in this field,

Recognizing and reaffirming that indigenous individuals are entitled without discrimination to all human rights recognized in international law, and that indigenous peoples possess collective rights which are indispensable for their existence, well-being and integral development as peoples,

Recognizing also that the situation of indigenous peoples varies from region to region and from country to country and that the significance of national and regional particularities and various historical and cultural backgrounds should be taken into consideration,

Solemnly proclaims the following United Nations Declaration on the Rights of Indigenous Peoples as a standard of achievement to be pursued in a spirit of partnership and mutual respect:

Article 1

Indigenous peoples have the right to the full enjoyment, as a collective or as individuals, of all human rights and fundamental freedoms as recognized in the Charter of the United Nations, the Universal Declaration of Human Rights and international human rights law.

Article 2

Indigenous peoples and individuals are free and equal to all other peoples and individuals and have the right to be free from any kind of discrimination, in the exercise of their rights, in particular that based on their indigenous origin or identity.

Article 3

Indigenous peoples have the right to self-determination. By virtue of that right they freely determine their political status and freely pursue their economic, social and cultural development.

Article 4

Indigenous peoples, in exercising their right to self-determination, have the right to autonomy or self-government in matters relating to their internal and local affairs, as well as ways and means for financing their autonomous functions.

Article 5

Indigenous peoples have the right to maintain and strengthen their distinct political, legal, economic, social and cultural institutions, while retaining their right to participate fully, if they so choose, in the political, economic, social and cultural life of the State.

Article 6

Every indigenous individual has the right to a nationality.

Article 7

1. Indigenous individuals have the rights to life, physical and mental integrity, liberty and security of person.

2. Indigenous peoples have the collective right to live in freedom, peace and security as distinct peoples and shall not be subjected to any act of genocide or any other act of violence, including forcibly removing children of the group to another group.

Article 8

1. Indigenous peoples and individuals have the right not to be subjected to forced assimilation or destruction of their culture.

2. States shall provide effective mechanisms for prevention of, and redress for:

    (a) Any action which has the aim or effect of depriving them of their integrity as distinct peoples, or of their cultural values or ethnic identities;

    (b) Any action which has the aim or effect of dispossessing them of their lands, territories or resources;

    (c) Any form of forced population transfer which has the aim or effect of violating or undermining any of their rights;

    (d) Any form of forced assimilation or integration;

    (e) Any form of propaganda designed to promote or incite racial or ethnic discrimination directed against them.

Article 9

Indigenous peoples and individuals have the right to belong to an indigenous community or nation, in accordance with the traditions and customs of the community or nation concerned. No discrimination of any kind may arise from the exercise of such a right.

Article 10

Indigenous peoples shall not be forcibly removed from their lands or territories. No relocation shall take place without the free, prior and informed consent of the indigenous peoples concerned and after agreement on just and fair compensation and, where possible, with the option of return.

Article 11

1. Indigenous peoples have the right to practise and revitalize their cultural traditions and customs. This includes the right to maintain, protect and develop the past, present and future manifestations of their cultures, such as archaeological and historical sites, artefacts, designs, technologies and visual and performing arts and literature.

2. States shall provide redress through effective mechanisms, which may include restitution, developed in conjunction with indigenous peoples, with respect to their cultural, intellectual,

religious and spiritual property taken without their free, prior and informed consent or in violation of their laws, traditions and customs.

Article 12

1. Indigenous peoples have the right to manifest, practice, develop and teach their spiritual and religious traditions, customs and ceremonies; the right to maintain, protect, and have access in privacy to their religious and cultural sites; the right to the use and control of their ceremonial objects; and the right to the repatriation of their human remains.

2. States shall seek to enable the access and/or repatriation of ceremonial objects and human remains in their possession through fair, transparent and effective mechanisms developed in conjunction with indigenous peoples concerned.

Article 13

1. Indigenous peoples have the right to revitalize, use, develop and transmit to future generations their histories, languages, oral traditions, philosophies, writing systems and literatures, and to designate and retain their own names for communities, places and persons.

2. States shall take effective measures to ensure that this right is protected and also to ensure that indigenous peoples can understand and be understood in political, legal and administrative proceedings, where necessary through the provision of interpretation or by other appropriate means.

Article 14

1. Indigenous peoples have the right to establish and control their educational systems and institutions providing education in their own languages, in a manner appropriate to their cultural methods of teaching and learning.

2. Indigenous individuals, particularly children, have the right to all levels and forms of education of the State without discrimination.

3. States shall, in conjunction with indigenous peoples, take effective measures, in order for indigenous individuals, particularly children, including those living outside their communities, to have access, when possible, to an education in their own culture and provided in their own language.

Article 15

1. Indigenous peoples have the right to the dignity and diversity of their cultures, traditions, histories and aspirations which shall be appropriately reflected in education and public information.

2. States shall take effective measures, in consultation and cooperation with the indigenous peoples concerned, to combat prejudice and eliminate discrimination and to promote tolerance, understanding and good relations among indigenous peoples and all other segments of society.

Article 16

1. Indigenous peoples have the right to establish their own media in their own languages and to have access to all forms of non-indigenous media without discrimination.

2. States shall take effective measures to ensure that State-owned media duly reflect indigenous cultural diversity. States, without prejudice to ensuring full freedom of expression, should encourage privately owned media to adequately reflect indigenous cultural diversity.

Article 17

1. Indigenous individuals and peoples have the right to enjoy fully all rights established under applicable international and domestic labour law.

2. States shall in consultation and cooperation with indigenous peoples take specific measures to protect indigenous children from economic exploitation and from performing any work that is likely to be hazardous or to interfere with the child's education, or to be harmful to the child's health or physical, mental, spiritual, moral or social development, taking into account their special vulnerability and the importance of education for their empowerment.

3. Indigenous individuals have the right not to be subjected to any discriminatory conditions of labour and, inter alia, employment or salary.

Article 18

Indigenous peoples have the right to participate in decision-making in matters which would affect their rights, through representatives chosen by themselves in accordance with their own procedures, as well as to maintain and develop their own indigenous decision-making institutions.

Article 19

States shall consult and cooperate in good faith with the indigenous peoples concerned through their own representative institutions in order to obtain their free, prior and informed consent before adopting and implementing legislative or administrative measures that may affect them.

Article 20

1. Indigenous peoples have the right to maintain and develop their political, economic and social systems or institutions, to be secure in the enjoyment of their own means of subsistence and development, and to engage freely in all their traditional and other economic activities.

2. Indigenous peoples deprived of their means of subsistence and development are entitled to just and fair redress.

Article 21

1. Indigenous peoples have the right, without discrimination, to the improvement of their economic and social conditions, including, *inter alia*, in the areas of education, employment, vocational training and retraining, housing, sanitation, health and social security.

2. States shall take effective measures and, where appropriate, special measures to ensure continuing improvement of their economic and social conditions. Particular attention shall be paid to the rights and special needs of indigenous elders, women, youth, children and persons with disabilities.

Article 22

1. Particular attention shall be paid to the rights and special needs of indigenous elders, women, youth, children and persons with disabilities in the implementation of this Declaration.

2. States shall take measures, in conjunction with indigenous peoples, to ensure that indigenous women and children enjoy the full protection and guarantees against all forms of violence and discrimination.

Article 23

Indigenous peoples have the right to determine and develop priorities and strategies for exercising their right to development. In particular, indigenous peoples have the right to be actively involved in developing and determining health, housing and other economic and social programmes affecting them and, as far as possible, to administer such programmes through their own institutions.

Article 24

1. Indigenous peoples have the right to their traditional medicines and to maintain their health practices, including the conservation of their vital medicinal plants, animals and minerals. Indigenous individuals also have the right to access, without any discrimination, to all social and health services.

2. Indigenous individuals have an equal right to the enjoyment of the highest attainable standard of physical and mental health. States shall take the necessary steps with a view to achieving progressively the full realization of this right.

Article 25

Indigenous peoples have the right to maintain and strengthen their distinctive spiritual relationship with their traditionally owned or otherwise occupied and used lands, territories, waters and coastal seas and other resources and to uphold their responsibilities to future generations in this regard.

Article 26

1. Indigenous peoples have the right to the lands, territories and resources which they have traditionally owned, occupied or otherwise used or acquired.

2. Indigenous peoples have the right to own, use, develop and control the lands, territories and resources that they possess by reason of traditional ownership or other traditional occupation or use, as well as those which they have otherwise acquired.

3. States shall give legal recognition and protection to these lands, territories and resources. Such recognition shall be conducted with due respect to the customs, traditions and land tenure systems of the indigenous peoples concerned.

Article 27

States shall establish and implement, in conjunction with indigenous peoples concerned, a fair, independent, impartial, open and transparent process, giving due recognition to indigenous peoples' laws, traditions, customs and land tenure systems, to recognize and adjudicate the rights of indigenous peoples pertaining to their lands, territories and resources, including those which were traditionally owned or otherwise occupied or used. Indigenous peoples shall have the right to participate in this process.

Article 28

1. Indigenous peoples have the right to redress, by means that can include restitution or, when this is not possible, just, fair and equitable compensation, for the lands, territories and resources which they have traditionally owned or otherwise occupied or used, and which have been confiscated, taken, occupied, used or damaged without their free, prior and informed consent.

2. Unless otherwise freely agreed upon by the peoples concerned, compensation shall take the form of lands, territories and resources equal in quality, size and legal status or of monetary compensation or other appropriate redress.

Article 29

1. Indigenous peoples have the right to the conservation and protection of the environment and the productive capacity of their lands or territories and resources. States shall establish and implement assistance programmes for indigenous peoples for such conservation and protection, without discrimination.

2. States shall take effective measures to ensure that no storage or disposal of hazardous materials shall take place in the lands or territories of indigenous peoples without their free, prior and informed consent.

3. States shall also take effective measures to ensure, as needed, that programmes for monitoring, maintaining and restoring the health of indigenous peoples, as developed and implemented by the peoples affected by such materials, are duly implemented.

Article 30

1. Military activities shall not take place in the lands or territories of indigenous peoples, unless justified by a significant threat to relevant public interest or otherwise freely agreed with or requested by the indigenous peoples concerned.

2. States shall undertake effective consultations with the indigenous peoples concerned, through appropriate procedures and in particular through their representative institutions, prior to using their lands or territories for military activities.

Article 31

1. Indigenous peoples have the right to maintain, control, protect and develop their cultural heritage, traditional knowledge and traditional cultural expressions, as well as the manifestations of their sciences, technologies and cultures, including human and genetic resources, seeds, medicines, knowledge of the properties of fauna and flora, oral traditions, literatures, designs, sports and traditional games and visual and performing arts. They also have the right to maintain, control, protect and develop their intellectual property over such cultural heritage, traditional knowledge, and traditional cultural expressions.

2. In conjunction with indigenous peoples, States shall take effective measures to recognize and protect the exercise of these rights.

Article 32

1. Indigenous peoples have the right to determine and develop priorities and strategies for the development or use of their lands or territories and other resources.

2. States shall consult and cooperate in good faith with the indigenous peoples concerned through their own representative institutions in order to obtain their free and informed consent prior to the approval of any project affecting their lands or territories and other resources, particularly in connection with the development, utilization or exploitation of mineral, water or other resources.

3. States shall provide effective mechanisms for just and fair redress for any such activities, and appropriate measures shall be taken to mitigate adverse environmental, economic, social, cultural or spiritual impact.

Article 33

1. Indigenous peoples have the right to determine their own identity or membership in accordance with their customs and traditions. This does not impair the right of indigenous individuals to obtain citizenship of the States in which they live.

2. Indigenous peoples have the right to determine the structures and to select the membership of their institutions in accordance with their own procedures.

Article 34

Indigenous peoples have the right to promote, develop and maintain their institutional structures and their distinctive customs, spirituality, traditions, procedures, practices and, in the cases where they exist, juridical systems or customs, in accordance with international human rights standards.

Article 35

Indigenous peoples have the right to determine the responsibilities of individuals to their communities.

Article 36

1. Indigenous peoples, in particular those divided by international borders, have the right to maintain and develop contacts, relations and cooperation, including activities for spiritual, cultural, political, economic and social purposes, with their own members as well as other peoples across borders.

2. States, in consultation and cooperation with indigenous peoples, shall take effective measures to facilitate the exercise and ensure the implementation of this right.

Article 37

1. Indigenous peoples have the right to the recognition, observance and enforcement of treaties, agreements and other constructive arrangements concluded with States or their successors and to have States honour and respect such treaties, agreements and other constructive arrangements.

2. Nothing in this Declaration may be interpreted as diminishing or eliminating the rights of indigenous peoples contained in treaties, agreements and other constructive arrangements.

Article 38

States in consultation and cooperation with indigenous peoples, shall take the appropriate measures, including legislative measures, to achieve the ends of this Declaration.

Article 39

Indigenous peoples have the right to have access to financial and technical assistance from States and through international cooperation, for the enjoyment of the rights contained in this Declaration.

Article 40

Indigenous peoples have the right to access to and prompt decision through just and fair procedures for the resolution of conflicts and disputes with States or other parties, as well as to effective remedies for all infringements of their individual and collective rights. Such a decision shall give due consideration to the customs, traditions, rules and legal systems of the indigenous peoples concerned and international human rights.

Article 41

The organs and specialized agencies of the United Nations system and other intergovernmental organizations shall contribute to the full realization of the provisions of this Declaration through the mobilization, *inter alia*, of financial cooperation and technical assistance. Ways and means of ensuring participation of indigenous peoples on issues affecting them shall be established.

Article 42

The United Nations, its bodies, including the Permanent Forum on Indigenous Issues, and specialized agencies, including at the country level, and States shall promote respect for and full application of the provisions of this Declaration and follow up the effectiveness of this Declaration.

Article 43

The rights recognized herein constitute the minimum standards for the survival, dignity and well-being of the indigenous peoples of the world.

Article 44

All the rights and freedoms recognized herein are equally guaranteed to male and female indigenous individuals.

Article 45

Nothing in this Declaration may be construed as diminishing or extinguishing the rights indigenous peoples have now or may acquire in the future.

Article 46

1. Nothing in this Declaration may be interpreted as implying for any State, people, group or person any right to engage in any activity or to perform any act contrary to the Charter of the United Nations or construed as authorizing or encouraging any action which would dismember or impair, totally or in part, the territorial integrity or political unity of sovereign and independent States.

2. In the exercise of the rights enunciated in the present Declaration, human rights and fundamental freedoms of all shall be respected. The exercise of the rights set forth in this Declaration shall be subject only to such limitations as are determined by law, and in accordance with international human rights obligations. Any such limitations shall be non-discriminatory and strictly necessary solely for the purpose of securing due recognition and respect for the rights and freedoms of others and for meeting the just and most compelling requirements of a democratic society.

3. The provisions set forth in this Declaration shall be interpreted in accordance with the principles of justice, democracy, respect for human rights, equality, non-discrimination, good governance and good faith.

United Nations Guiding Principles on Business and Human Rights (2011)*

I. THE STATE DUTY TO PROTECT HUMAN RIGHTS

A. FOUNDATIONAL PRINCIPLES

Principle 1

States must protect against human rights abuse within their territory and/or jurisdiction by third parties, including business enterprises. This requires taking appropriate steps to prevent, investigate, punish and redress such abuse through effective policies, legislation, regulations and adjudication.

Principle 2

States should set out clearly the expectation that all business enterprises domiciled in their territory and/or jurisdiction respect human rights throughout their operations.

B. OPERATIONAL PRINCIPLES

GENERAL STATE REGULATORY AND POLICY FUNCTIONS

Principle 3

In meeting their duty to protect, States should:

(a) Enforce laws that are aimed at, or have the effect of, requiring business enterprises to respect human rights, and periodically to assess the adequacy of such laws and address any gaps;

(b) Ensure that other laws and policies governing the creation and ongoing operation of business enterprises, such as corporate law, do not constrain but enable business respect for human rights;

(c) Provide effective guidance to business enterprises on how to respect human rights throughout their operations;

(d) Encourage, and where appropriate require, business enterprises to communicate how they address their human rights impacts.

THE STATE-BUSINESS NEXUS

Principle 4

States should take additional steps to protect against human rights abuses by business enterprises that are owned or controlled by the State, or that receive substantial support and services from State agencies such as export credit agencies and official investment insurance or guarantee agencies, including, where appropriate, by requiring human rights due diligence.

Principle 5

States should exercise adequate oversight in order to meet their international human rights obligations when they contract with, or legislate for, business enterprises to provide services that may impact upon the enjoyment of human rights.

Principle 6

States should promote respect for human rights by business enterprises with which they conduct commercial transactions.

SUPPORTING BUSINESS RESPECT FOR HUMAN RIGHTS IN CONFLICT-AFFECTED AREAS

Principle 7

Because the risk of gross human rights abuses is heightened in conflict-affected areas, States should help ensure that business enterprises operating in those contexts are not involved with such abuses, including by:

(a) Engaging at the earliest stage possible with business enterprises to help them identify, prevent and mitigate the human rights-related risks of their activities and business relationships;

(b) Providing adequate assistance to business enterprises to assess and address the heightened risks of abuses, paying special attention to both gender-based and sexual violence;

(c) Denying access to public support and services for a business enterprise that is involved with gross human rights abuses and refuses to cooperate in addressing the situation;

(d) Ensuring that their current policies, legislation, regulations and enforcement measures are effective in addressing the risk of business involvement in gross human rights abuses.

ENSURING POLICY COHERENCE

Principle 8

States should ensure that governmental departments, agencies and other State-based institutions that shape business practices are aware of and observe the State's human rights obligations when fulfilling their respective mandates, including by providing them with relevant information, training and support.

Principle 9

States should maintain adequate domestic policy space to meet their human rights obligations when pursuing business-related policy objectives with other States or business enterprises, for instance through investment treaties or contracts.

Principle 10

States, when acting as members of multilateral institutions that deal with business-related issues, should:

(a) Seek to ensure that those institutions neither restrain the ability of their member States to meet their duty to protect nor hinder business enterprises from respecting human rights;

(b) Encourage those institutions, within their respective mandates and capacities, to promote business respect for human rights and, where requested, to help States meet their duty to protect against human rights abuse by business enterprises, including through technical assistance, capacity-building and awareness-raising;

(c) Draw on these Guiding Principles to promote shared understanding and advance international cooperation in the management of business and human rights challenges.

II. THE CORPORATE RESPONSIBILITY TO RESPECT HUMAN RIGHTS

A. FOUNDATIONAL PRINCIPLES

Principle 11

Business enterprises should respect human rights. This means that they should avoid infringing on the human rights of others and should address adverse human rights impacts with which they are involved.

Principle 12

The responsibility of business enterprises to respect human rights refers to internationally recognized human rights—understood, at a minimum, as those expressed in the International Bill of Human Rights and the principles concerning fundamental rights set out in the International Labour Organization's Declaration on Fundamental Principles and Rights at Work.

Principle 13

The responsibility to respect human rights requires that business enterprises:

(a) Avoid causing or contributing to adverse human rights impacts through their own activities, and address such impacts when they occur;

(b) Seek to prevent or mitigate adverse human rights impacts that are directly linked to their operations, products or services by their business relationships, even if they have not contributed to those impacts.

Principle 14

The responsibility of business enterprises to respect human rights applies to all enterprises regardless of their size, sector, operational context, ownership and structure. Nevertheless, the scale and complexity of the means through which enterprises meet that responsibility may vary according to these factors and with the severity of the enterprise's adverse human rights impacts.

Principle 15

In order to meet their responsibility to respect human rights, business enterprises should have in place policies and processes appropriate to their size and circumstances, including:

    (a) A policy commitment to meet their responsibility to respect human rights;

    (b) A human rights due diligence process to identify, prevent, mitigate and account for how they address their impacts on human rights;

    (c) Processes to enable the remediation of any adverse human rights impacts they cause or to which they contribute.

B. OPERATIONAL PRINCIPLES

POLICY COMMITMENT

Principle 16

As the basis for embedding their responsibility to respect human rights, business enterprises should express their commitment to meet this responsibility through a statement of policy that:

    (a) Is approved at the most senior level of the business enterprise;

    (b) Is informed by relevant internal and/or external expertise;

    (c) Stipulates the enterprise's human rights expectations of personnel, business partners and other parties directly linked to its operations, products or services;

    (d) Is publicly available and communicated internally and externally to all personnel, business partners and other relevant parties;

    (e) Is reflected in operational policies and procedures necessary to embed it throughout the business enterprise.

HUMAN RIGHTS DUE DILIGENCE

Principle 17

In order to identify, prevent, mitigate and account for how they address their adverse human rights impacts, business enterprises should carry out human rights due diligence. The process should include assessing actual and potential human rights impacts, integrating and acting upon the findings, tracking responses, and communicating how impacts are addressed. Human rights due diligence:

    (a) Should cover adverse human rights impacts that the business enterprise may cause or contribute to through its own activities, or which may be directly linked to its operations, products or services by its business relationships;

    (b) Will vary in complexity with the size of the business enterprise, the risk of severe human rights impacts, and the nature and context of its operations;

    (c) Should be ongoing, recognizing that the human rights risks may change over time as the business enterprise's operations and operating context evolve.

Principle 18

In order to gauge human rights risks, business enterprises should identify and assess any actual or potential adverse human rights impacts with which they may be involved either through their own activities or as a result of their business relationships. This process should:

    (a) Draw on internal and/or independent external human rights expertise;

    (b) Involve meaningful consultation with potentially affected groups and other relevant stakeholders, as appropriate to the size of the business enterprise and the nature and context of the operation.

Principle 19

In order to prevent and mitigate adverse human rights impacts, business enterprises should integrate the findings from their impact assessments across relevant internal functions and processes, and take appropriate action.

(a) Effective integration requires that:
  (i) Responsibility for addressing such impacts is assigned to the appropriate level and function within the business enterprise;
  (ii) Internal decision-making, budget allocations and oversight processes enable effective responses to such impacts.
(b) Appropriate action will vary according to:
  (i) Whether the business enterprise causes or contributes to an adverse impact, or whether it is involved solely because the impact is directly linked to its operations, products or services by a business relationship;
  (ii) The extent of its leverage in addressing the adverse impact.

Principle 20

In order to verify whether adverse human rights impacts are being addressed, business enterprises should track the effectiveness of their response. Tracking should:
(a) Be based on appropriate qualitative and quantitative indicators;
(b) Draw on feedback from both internal and external sources, including affected stakeholders.

Principle 21

In order to account for how they address their human rights impacts, business enterprises should be prepared to communicate this externally, particularly when concerns are raised by or on behalf of affected stakeholders. Business enterprises whose operations or operating contexts pose risks of severe human rights impacts should report formally on how they address them. In all instances, communications should:
(a) Be of a form and frequency that reflect an enterprise's human rights impacts and that are accessible to its intended audiences;
(b) Provide information that is sufficient to evaluate the adequacy of an enterprise's response to the particular human rights impact involved;
(c) In turn not pose risks to affected stakeholders, personnel or to legitimate requirements of commercial confidentiality.

REMEDIATION

Principle 22

Where business enterprises identify that they have caused or contributed to adverse impacts, they should provide for or cooperate in their remediation through legitimate processes.

ISSUES OF CONTEXT

Principle 23

In all contexts, business enterprises should:
(a) Comply with all applicable laws and respect internationally recognized human rights, wherever they operate;
(b) Seek ways to honour the principles of internationally recognized human rights when faced with conflicting requirements;
(c) Treat the risk of causing or contributing to gross human rights abuses as a legal compliance issue wherever they operate.

Principle 24

Where it is necessary to prioritize actions to address actual and potential adverse human rights impacts, business enterprises should first seek to prevent and mitigate those that are most severe or where delayed response would make them irremediable.

III. ACCESS TO A REMEDY

A. FOUNDATIONAL PRINCIPLE

Principle 25

As part of their duty to protect against business-related human rights abuse, States must take appropriate steps to ensure, through judicial, administrative, legislative or other appropriate means, that when such abuses occur within their territory and/or jurisdiction those affected have access to effective remedy.

B. OPERATIONAL PRINCIPLES

STATE-BASED JUDICIAL MECHANISMS

Principle 26

States should take appropriate steps to ensure the effectiveness of domestic judicial mechanisms when addressing business-related human rights abuses, including considering ways to reduce legal, practical and other relevant barriers that could lead to a denial of access to remedy.

STATE-BASED NON-JUDICIAL GRIEVANCE MECHANISMS

Principle 27

States should provide effective and appropriate non-judicial grievance mechanisms, alongside judicial mechanisms, as part of a comprehensive State-based system for the remedy of business-related human rights abuse.

NON-STATE-BASED GRIEVANCE MECHANISMS

Principle 28

States should consider ways to facilitate access to effective non-State-based grievance mechanisms dealing with business-related human rights harms.

Principle 29

To make it possible for grievances to be addressed early and remediated directly, business enterprises should establish or participate in effective operational-level grievance mechanisms for individuals and communities who may be adversely impacted.

Principle 30

Industry, multi-stakeholder and other collaborative initiatives that are based on respect for human rights-related standards should ensure that effective grievance mechanisms are available.

EFFECTIVENESS CRITERIA FOR NON-JUDICIAL GRIEVANCE MECHANISMS

Principle 31

In order to ensure their effectiveness, non-judicial grievance mechanisms, both State-based and non-State-based, should be:

    (a) Legitimate: enabling trust from the stakeholder groups for whose use they are intended, and being accountable for the fair conduct of grievance processes;

    (b) Accessible: being known to all stakeholder groups for whose use they are intended, and providing adequate assistance for those who may face particular barriers to access;

    (c) Predictable: providing a clear and known procedure with an indicative time frame for each stage, and clarity on the types of process and outcome available and means of monitoring implementation;

(d) Equitable: seeking to ensure that aggrieved parties have reasonable access to sources of information, advice and expertise necessary to engage in a grievance process on fair, informed and respectful terms;

(e) Transparent: keeping parties to a grievance informed about its progress, and providing sufficient information about the mechanism's performance to build confidence in its effectiveness and meet any public interest at stake;

(f) Rights-compatible: ensuring that outcomes and remedies accord with internationally recognized human rights;

(g) A source of continuous learning: drawing on relevant measures to identify lessons for improving the mechanism and preventing future grievances and harms;

Operational-level mechanisms should also be:

(h) Based on engagement and dialogue: consulting the stakeholder groups for whose use they are intended on their design and performance, and focusing on dialogue as the means to address and resolve grievances.

United Nations Declaration on the Rights of Peasants and Other People Working in Rural Areas (2018)*

The General Assembly,

Welcoming the adoption by the Human Rights Council, in its resolution 39/12 of 28 September 2018,[1] of the United Nations Declaration on the Rights of Peasants and Other People Working in Rural Areas,

1. *Adopts* the United Nations Declaration on the Rights of Peasants and Other People Working in Rural Areas, as contained in the annex to the present resolution;

2. *Invites* Governments, agencies and organizations of the United Nations system and intergovernmental and non-governmental organizations to disseminate the Declaration and to promote universal respect and understanding thereof;

3. *Requests* the Secretary-General to include the text of the Declaration in the next edition of *Human Rights: A Compilation of International Instruments*

Annex

United Nations Declaration on the Rights of Peasants and Other People Working in Rural Areas

The General Assembly,

Recalling the principles proclaimed in the Charter of the United Nations, which recognize the inherent dignity and worth and the equal and inalienable rights of all members of the human family as the foundation of freedom, justice and peace in the world,

Taking into account the principles proclaimed in the Universal Declaration of Human Rights,[2] the International Convention on the Elimination of All Forms of Racial Discrimination,[3] the International Covenant on Economic, Social and Cultural Rights,[4] the International Covenant on Civil and Political Rights,[4] the Convention on the Elimination of All Forms of Discrimination against Women,[5] the Convention on the Rights of the Child,[6] the International Convention on the Protection of the Rights of All Migrant Workers and Members of Their Families,[7] relevant conventions of the International Labour Organization and other relevant international instruments that have been adopted at the universal or regional level,

---

* From United Nations Declaration on the Rights of Peasants and Other People Working in Rural Areas, © 2018 United Nations. Reprinted with the permission of the United Nations.

[1] See *Official Records of the General Assembly, Seventy-third Session, Supplement No. 53A* (A/73/53/Add.1), chap. II.

[2] Resolution 217 A (III).

[3] United Nations, *Treaty Series*, vol. 660, No. 9464.

[4] See resolution 2200 A (XXI), annex.

[5] United Nations, *Treaty Series*, vol. 1249, No. 20378.

[6] Ibid., vol. 1577, No. 27531.

[7] Ibid., vol. 2220, No. 39481.

Reaffirming the Declaration on the Right to Development,[8] and that the right to development is an inalienable human right by virtue of which every human person and all peoples are entitled to participate in, contribute to and enjoy economic, social, cultural and political development, in which all human rights and fundamental freedoms can be fully realized,

Reaffirming also the United Nations Declaration on the Rights of Indigenous Peoples,[9]

Reaffirming further that all human rights are universal, indivisible, interrelated, interdependent and mutually reinforcing and must be treated in a fair and equal manner, on the same footing and with the same emphasis, and recalling that the promotion and protection of one category of rights should never exempt States from the promotion and protection of the other rights,

Recognizing the special relationship and interaction between peasants and other people working in rural areas and the land, water and nature to which they are attached and on which they depend for their livelihood,

Recognizing also the past, present and future contributions of peasants and other people working in rural areas in all regions of the world to development and to conserving and improving biodiversity, which constitute the basis of food and agricultural production throughout the world, and their contribution in ensuring the right to adequate food and food security, which are fundamental to attaining the internationally agreed development goals, including the 2030 Agenda for Sustainable Development,[10]

Concerned that peasants and other people working in rural areas suffer disproportionately from poverty, hunger and malnutrition,

Concerned also that peasants and other people working in rural areas suffer from the burdens caused by environmental degradation and climate change,

Concerned further about peasants ageing around the world and youth increasingly migrating to urban areas and turning their backs on agriculture owing to the lack of incentives and the drudgery of rural life, and recognizing the need to improve the economic diversification of rural areas and the creation of non-farm opportunities, especially for rural youth,

Alarmed by the increasing number of peasants and other people working in rural areas forcibly evicted or displaced every year,

Alarmed also by the high incidence of suicide of peasants in several countries,

Stressing that peasant women and other rural women play a significant role in the economic survival of their families and in contributing to the rural and national economy, including through their work in the non-monetized sectors of the economy, but are often denied tenure and ownership of land, equal access to land, productive resources, financial services, information, employment or social protection, and are often victims of violence and discrimination in a variety of forms and manifestations,

Stressing also the importance of promoting and protecting the rights of the child in rural areas, including through the eradication of poverty, hunger and malnutrition, the promotion of quality education and health, protection from exposure to chemicals and wastes, and the elimination of child labour, in accordance with relevant human rights obligations,

Stressing further that several factors make it difficult for peasants and other people working in rural areas, including small-scale fishers and fish workers, pastoralists, foresters and other local communities, to make their voices heard, to defend their human rights and tenure rights, and to secure the sustainable use of the natural resources on which they depend,

Recognizing that access to land, water, seeds and other natural resources is an increasing challenge for rural people, and stressing the importance of improving access to productive resources and investment in appropriate rural development,

Convinced that peasants and other people working in rural areas should be supported in their efforts to promote and undertake sustainable practices of agricultural production that support and are in harmony with nature, also referred to as Mother Earth in a number of countries and regions, including by respecting the biological and natural ability of ecosystems to adapt and regenerate through natural processes and cycles,

Considering the hazardous and exploitative conditions that exist in many parts of the world under which many peasants and other people working in rural areas have to work, often denied

---

[8] Resolution 41/128, annex.
[9] Resolution 61/295, annex.
[10] Resolution 70/1.

the opportunity to exercise their fundamental rights at work and lacking living wages and social protection,

Concerned that individuals, groups and institutions that promote and protect the human rights of those working on land and natural resources issues face a high risk of being subjected to different forms of intimidation and of violations of their physical integrity,

Noting that peasants and other people working in rural areas often face difficulties in gaining access to courts, police officers, prosecutors and lawyers to the extent that they are unable to seek immediate redress or protection from violence, abuse and exploitation,

Concerned about speculation on food products, the increasing concentration and unbalanced distribution of food systems and the uneven power relations along the value chains, which impair the enjoyment of human rights,

Reaffirming that the right to development is an inalienable human right by virtue of which every human person and all peoples are entitled to participate in, contribute to and enjoy economic, social, cultural and political development, in which all human rights and fundamental freedoms can be fully realized,

Recalling the right of peoples to exercise, subject to the relevant provisions of both International Covenants on Human Rights, full and complete sovereignty over all their natural wealth and resources,

Recognizing that the concept of food sovereignty has been used in many States and regions to designate the right to define their food and agriculture systems and the right to healthy and culturally appropriate food produced through ecologically sound and sustainable methods that respect human rights,

Realizing that the individual, having duties to other individuals and to the community to which he or she belongs, is under a responsibility to strive for the promotion and observance of the rights recognized in the present Declaration and in national law,

Reaffirming the importance of respecting the diversity of cultures and of promoting tolerance, dialogue and cooperation,

Recalling the extensive body of conventions and recommendations of the International Labour Organization on labour protection and decent work,

Recalling also the Convention on Biological Diversity[11] and the Nagoya Protocol on Access to Genetic Resources and the Fair and Equitable Sharing of Benefits Arising from Their Utilization to the Convention on Biological Diversity,[12]

Recalling further the extensive work of the Food and Agriculture Organization of the United Nations and the Committee on World Food Security on the right to food, tenure rights, access to natural resources and other rights of peasants, in particular the International Treaty on Plant Genetic Resources for Food and Agriculture,[13] and the Organization's Voluntary Guidelines on the Responsible Governance of Tenure of Land, Fisheries and Forests in the Context of National Food Security,[14] the Voluntary Guidelines for Securing Sustainable Small-Scale Fisheries in the Context of Food Security and Poverty Eradication and the Voluntary Guidelines to Support the Progressive Realization of the Right to Adequate Food in the Context of National Food Security,[15]

Recalling the outcome of the World Conference on Agrarian Reform and Rural Development, and the Peasants' Charter adopted thereat, in which the need for the formulation of appropriate national strategies for agrarian reform and rural development, and their integration with overall national development strategies, was emphasized,

Reaffirming that the present Declaration and relevant international agreements shall be mutually supportive with a view to enhancing the protection of human rights,

Determined to take new steps forward in the commitment of the international community with a view to achieving substantial progress in human rights endeavours by an increased and sustained effort of international cooperation and solidarity,

Convinced of the need for greater protection of the human rights of peasants and other people working in rural areas, and for a coherent interpretation and application of existing international human rights norms and standards in this matter,

Declares the following:

---

[11] United Nations, *Treaty Series*, vol. 1760, No. 30619.
[12] United Nations Environment Programme, document UNEP/CBD/COP/10/27, annex, decision X/1.
[13] United Nations, *Treaty Series*, vol. 2400, No. 43345.
[14] Food and Agriculture Organization of the United Nations, document CL 144/9 (C 2013/20), appendix D.
[15] E/CN.4/2005/131, annex.

Article 1

1. For the purposes of the present Declaration, a peasant is any person who engages or who seeks to engage, alone, or in association with others or as a community, in small-scale agricultural production for subsistence and/or for the market, and who relies significantly, though not necessarily exclusively, on family or household labour and other non-monetized ways of organizing labour, and who has a special dependency on and attachment to the land.

2. The present Declaration applies to any person engaged in artisanal or small-scale agriculture, crop planting, livestock raising, pastoralism, fishing, forestry, hunting or gathering, and handicrafts related to agriculture or a related occupation in a rural area. It also applies to dependent family members of peasants.

3. The present Declaration also applies to indigenous peoples and local communities working on the land, transhumant, nomadic and semi-nomadic communities, and the landless engaged in the above-mentioned activities.

4. The present Declaration further applies to hired workers, including all migrant workers regardless of their migration status, and seasonal workers, on plantations, agricultural farms, forests and farms in aquaculture and in agro-industrial enterprises.

Article 2

1. States shall respect, protect and fulfil the rights of peasants and other people working in rural areas. They shall promptly take legislative, administrative and other appropriate steps to achieve progressively the full realization of the rights set forth in the present Declaration that cannot be immediately guaranteed.

2. Particular attention shall be paid in the implementation of the present Declaration to the rights and special needs of peasants and other people working in rural areas, including older persons, women, youth, children and persons with disabilities, taking into account the need to address multiple forms of discrimination.

3. Without disregarding specific legislation on indigenous peoples, before adopting and implementing legislation and policies, international agreements and other decision-making processes that may affect the rights of peasants and other people working in rural areas, States shall consult and cooperate in good faith with peasants and other people working in rural areas through their own representative institutions, engaging with and seeking the support of peasants and other people working in rural areas who could be affected by decisions before those decisions are made, and responding to their contributions, taking into consideration existing power imbalances between different parties and ensuring active, free, effective, meaningful and informed participation of individuals and groups in associated decision-making processes.

4. States shall elaborate, interpret and apply relevant international agreements and standards to which they are a party in a manner consistent with their human rights obligations as applicable to peasants and other people working in rural areas.

5. States shall take all necessary measures to ensure that non-State actors that they are in a position to regulate, such as private individuals and organizations, and transnational corporations and other business enterprises, respect and strengthen the rights of peasants and other people working in rural areas.

6. States, recognizing the importance of international cooperation in support of national efforts for the realization of the purposes and objectives of the present Declaration, shall take appropriate and effective measures in this regard, between and among States and, as appropriate, in partnership with relevant international and regional organizations and civil society, in particular organizations of peasants and other people working in rural areas, among others. Such measures could include:

   (a) Ensuring that relevant international cooperation, including international development programmes, is inclusive, accessible and pertinent to peasants and other people working in rural areas;

   (b) Facilitating and supporting capacity-building, including through the exchange and sharing of information, experiences, training programmes and best practices;

   (c) Facilitating cooperation in research and in access to scientific and technical knowledge;

   (d) Providing, as appropriate, technical and economic assistance, facilitating access to and sharing of accessible technologies, and through the transfer of technologies, particularly to developing countries, on mutually agreed terms;

(e) Improving the functioning of markets at the global level and facilitating timely access to market information, including on food reserves, in order to help to limit extreme food price volatility and the attractiveness of speculation.

Article 3

1. Peasants and other people working in rural areas have the right to the full enjoyment of all human rights and fundamental freedoms recognized in the Charter of the United Nations, the Universal Declaration of Human Rights and all other international human rights instruments, free from any kind of discrimination in the exercise of their rights based on any grounds such as origin, nationality, race, colour, descent, sex, language, culture, marital status, property, disability, age, political or other opinion, religion, birth or economic, social or other status.

2. Peasants and other people working in rural areas have the right to determine and develop priorities and strategies to exercise their right to development.

3. States shall take appropriate measures to eliminate conditions that cause or help to perpetuate discrimination, including multiple and intersecting forms of discrimination, against peasants and other people working in rural areas.

Article 4

1. States shall take all appropriate measures to eliminate all forms of discrimination against peasant women and other women working in rural areas and to promote their empowerment in order to ensure, on the basis of equality between men and women, that they fully and equally enjoy all human rights and fundamental freedoms and that they are able to freely pursue, participate in and benefit from rural economic, social, political and cultural development.

2. States shall ensure that peasant women and other women working in rural areas enjoy without discrimination all the human rights and fundamental freedoms set out in the present Declaration and in other international human rights instruments, including the rights:
   (a) To participate equally and effectively in the formulation and implementation of development planning at all levels;
   (b) To have equal access to the highest attainable standard of physical and mental health, including adequate health-care facilities, information, counselling and services in family planning;
   (c) To benefit directly from social security programmes;
   (d) To receive all types of training and education, whether formal or non-formal, including training and education relating to functional literacy, and to benefit from all community and extension services in order to increase their technical proficiency;
   (e) To organize self-help groups, associations and cooperatives in order to obtain equal access to economic opportunities through employment or self-employment;
   (f) To participate in all community activities;
   (g) To have equal access to financial services, agricultural credit and loans, marketing facilities and appropriate technology;
   (h) To equal access to, use of and management of land and natural resources, and to equal or priority treatment in land and agrarian reform and in land resettlement schemes;
   (i) To decent employment, equal remuneration and social protection benefits, and to have access to income-generating activities;
   (j) To be free from all forms of violence.

Article 5

1. Peasants and other people working in rural areas have the right to have access to and to use in a sustainable manner the natural resources present in their communities that are required to enjoy adequate living conditions, in accordance with article 28 of the present Declaration. They also have the right to participate in the management of these resources.

2. States shall take measures to ensure that any exploitation affecting the natural resources that peasants and other people working in rural areas traditionally hold or use is permitted based on, but not limited to:
   (a) A duly conducted social and environmental impact assessment;
   (b) Consultations in good faith, in accordance with article 2 (3) of the present Declaration;

(c) Modalities for the fair and equitable sharing of the benefits of such exploitation that have been established on mutually agreed terms between those exploiting the natural resources and the peasants and other people working in rural areas.

Article 6

1. Peasants and other people working in rural areas have the right to life, physical and mental integrity, liberty and security of person.

2. Peasants and other people working in rural areas shall not be subjected to arbitrary arrest or detention, torture or other cruel, inhuman or degrading treatment or punishment, and shall not be held in slavery or servitude.

Article 7

1. Peasants and other people working in rural areas have the right to recognition everywhere as persons before the law.

2. States shall take appropriate measures to facilitate the freedom of movement of peasants and other people working in rural areas.

3. States shall, where required, take appropriate measures to cooperate with a view to addressing transboundary tenure issues affecting peasants and other people working in rural areas that cross international boundaries, in accordance with article 28 of the present Declaration.

Article 8

1. Peasants and other people working in rural areas have the right to freedom of thought, belief, conscience, religion, opinion, expression and peaceful assembly. They have the right to express their opinion, either orally, in writing or in print, in the form of art, or through any other media of their choice, at the local, regional, national and international levels.

2. Peasants and other people working in rural areas have the right, individually and/or collectively, in association with others or as a community, to participate in peaceful activities against violations of human rights and fundamental freedoms.

3. The exercise of the rights provided for in the present article carries with it special duties and responsibilities. It may therefore be subject to certain restrictions, but these shall only be such as are provided for by law and are necessary:

(a) For respect of the rights or reputations of others;

(b) For the protection of national security or of public order (*ordre public*), or of public health or morals.

4. States shall take all necessary measures to ensure protection by the competent authorities of everyone, individually and in association with others, against any violence, threat, retaliation, de jure or de facto discrimination, pressure or any other arbitrary action as a consequence of his or her legitimate exercise and defence of the rights described in the present Declaration.

Article 9

1. Peasants and other people working in rural areas have the right to form and join organizations, trade unions, cooperatives or any other organization or association of their own choosing for the protection of their interests, and to bargain collectively. Such organizations shall be independent and voluntary in character, and remain free from all interference, coercion or repression.

2. No restrictions may be placed on the exercise of this right other than those which are prescribed by law and are necessary in a democratic society in the interests of national security or public safety, public order (*ordre public*), the protection of public health or morals or the protection of the rights and freedoms of others.

3. States shall take appropriate measures to encourage the establishment of organizations of peasants and other people working in rural areas, including unions, cooperatives or other organizations, particularly with a view to eliminating obstacles to their establishment, growth and pursuit of lawful activities, including any legislative or administrative discrimination against such organizations and their members, and provide them with support to strengthen their position when negotiating contractual arrangements in order to ensure that conditions and prices are fair and stable and do not violate their rights to dignity and to a decent life.

Article 10

1. Peasants and other people working in rural areas have the right to active and free participation, directly and/or through their representative organizations, in the preparation and implementation of policies, programmes and projects that may affect their lives, land and livelihoods.

2. States shall promote the participation, directly and/or through their representative organizations, of peasants and other people working in rural areas in decision-making processes that may affect their lives, land and livelihoods; this includes respecting the establishment and growth of strong and independent organizations of peasants and other people working in rural areas and promoting their participation in the preparation and implementation of food safety, labour and environmental standards that may affect them.

Article 11

1. Peasants and other people working in rural areas have the right to seek, receive, develop and impart information, including information about factors that may affect the production, processing, marketing and distribution of their products.

2. States shall take appropriate measures to ensure that peasants and other people working in rural areas have access to relevant, transparent, timely and adequate information in a language and form and through means adequate to their cultural methods so as to promote their empowerment and to ensure their effective participation in decision-making in matters that may affect their lives, land and livelihoods.

3. States shall take appropriate measures to promote the access of peasants and other people working in rural areas to a fair, impartial and appropriate system of evaluation and certification of the quality of their products at the local, national and international levels, and to promote their participation in its formulation.

Article 12

1. Peasants and other people working in rural areas have the right to effective and non-discriminatory access to justice, including access to fair procedures for the resolution of disputes and to effective remedies for all infringements of their human rights. Such decisions shall give due consideration to their customs, traditions, rules and legal systems in conformity with relevant obligations under international human rights law.

2. States shall provide for non-discriminatory access, through impartial and competent judicial and administrative bodies, to timely, affordable and effective means of resolving disputes in the language of the persons concerned, and shall provide effective and prompt remedies, which may include a right of appeal, restitution, indemnity, compensation and reparation.

3. Peasants and other people working in rural areas have the right to legal assistance. States shall consider additional measures, including legal aid, to support peasants and other people working in rural areas who would otherwise not have access to administrative and judicial services.

4. States shall consider measures to strengthen relevant national institutions for the promotion and protection of all human rights, including the rights described in the present Declaration.

5. States shall provide peasants and other people working in rural areas with effective mechanisms for the prevention of and redress for any action that has the aim or effect of violating their human rights, arbitrarily dispossessing them of their land and natural resources or of depriving them of their means of subsistence and integrity, and for any form of forced sedentarization or population displacement.

Article 13

1. Peasants and other people working in rural areas have the right to work, which includes the right to choose freely the way they earn their living.

2. Children of peasants and other people working in rural areas have the right to be protected from any work that is likely to be hazardous or to interfere with the child's education, or to be harmful to a child's health or physical, mental, spiritual, moral or social development.

3. States shall create an enabling environment with opportunities for work for peasants and other people working in rural areas and their families that provide remuneration allowing for an adequate standard of living.

4. In States facing high levels of rural poverty and in the absence of employment opportunities in other sectors, States shall take appropriate measures to establish and promote sustainable food systems that are sufficiently labour-intensive to contribute to the creation of decent employment.

5. States, taking into account the specific characteristics of peasant agriculture and small-scale fisheries, shall monitor compliance with labour legislation by allocating, where required, appropriate resources to ensure the effective operation of labour inspectorates in rural areas.

6. No one shall be required to perform forced, bonded or compulsory labour, be subjected to the risk of becoming a victim of human trafficking or be held in any other form of contemporary slavery. States shall, in consultation and cooperation with peasants and other people working in rural areas and their representative organizations, take appropriate measures to protect them from economic exploitation, child labour and all forms of contemporary slavery, such as debt bondage of women, men and children, and forced labour, including of fishers and fish workers, forest workers, or seasonal or migrant workers.

Article 14

1. Peasants and other people working in rural areas, irrespective of whether they are temporary, seasonal or migrant workers, have the rights to work in safe and healthy working conditions, to participate in the application and review of safety and health measures, to select safety and health representatives and representatives in safety and health committees, to the implementation of measures to prevent, reduce and control hazards and risks, to have access to adequate and appropriate protective clothing and equipment and to adequate information and training on occupational safety, to work free from violence and harassment, including sexual harassment, to report unsafe and unhealthy working conditions and to remove themselves from danger resulting from their work activity when they reasonably believe that there is an imminent and serious risk to their safety or health, without being subjected to any work-related retaliation for exercising such rights.

2. Peasants and other people working in rural areas have the right not to use or to be exposed to hazardous substances or toxic chemicals, including agrochemicals or agricultural or industrial pollutants.

3. States shall take appropriate measures to ensure favourable safe and healthy working conditions for peasants and other people working in rural areas, and shall in particular designate appropriate competent authorities responsible and establish mechanisms for intersectoral coordination for the implementation of policies and enforcement of national laws and regulations on occupational safety and health in agriculture, the agro-industry and fisheries, provide for corrective measures and appropriate penalties, and establish and support adequate and appropriate systems of inspection for rural workplaces.

4. States shall take all measures necessary to ensure:
   (a) The prevention of risks to health and safety derived from technologies, chemicals and agricultural practices, including through their prohibition and restriction;
   (b) An appropriate national system or any other system approved by the competent authority establishing specific criteria for the importation, classification, packaging, distribution, labelling and use of chemicals used in agriculture, and for their prohibition or restriction;
   (c) That those who produce, import, provide, sell, transfer, store or dispose of chemicals used in agriculture comply with national or other recognized safety and health standards, and provide adequate and appropriate information to users in the appropriate official language or languages of the country and, on request, to the competent authority;
   (d) That there is a suitable system for the safe collection, recycling and disposal of chemical waste, obsolete chemicals and empty containers of chemicals so as to avoid their use for other purposes and to eliminate or minimize the risks to safety and health and to the environment;
   (e) The development and implementation of educational and public awareness programmes on the health and environmental effects of chemicals commonly used in rural areas, and on alternatives to them.

Article 15

1. Peasants and other people working in rural areas have the right to adequate food and the fundamental right to be free from hunger. This includes the right to produce food and the right to adequate nutrition, which guarantee the possibility of enjoying the highest degree of physical, emotional and intellectual development.

2. States shall ensure that peasants and other people working in rural areas enjoy physical and economic access at all times to sufficient and adequate food that is produced and consumed sustainably and equitably, respecting their cultures, preserving access to food for future generations, and that ensures a physically and mentally fulfilling and dignified life for them, individually and/or collectively, responding to their needs.

3. States shall take appropriate measures to combat malnutrition in rural children, including within the framework of primary health care through, inter alia, the application of readily available technology and the provision of adequate nutritious food and by ensuring that women have adequate nutrition during pregnancy and lactation. States shall also ensure that all segments of society, in particular parents and children, are informed, have access to nutritional education and are supported in the use of basic knowledge on child nutrition and the advantages of breastfeeding.

4. Peasants and other people working in rural areas have the right to determine their own food and agriculture systems, recognized by many States and regions as the right to food sovereignty. This includes the right to participate in decision-making processes on food and agriculture policy and the right to healthy and adequate food produced through ecologically sound and sustainable methods that respect their cultures.

5. States shall formulate, in partnership with peasants and other people working in rural areas, public policies at the local, national, regional and international levels to advance and protect the right to adequate food, food security and food sovereignty and sustainable and equitable food systems that promote and protect the rights contained in the present Declaration. States shall establish mechanisms to ensure the coherence of their agricultural, economic, social, cultural and development policies with the realization of the rights contained in the present Declaration.

Article 16

1. Peasants and other people working in rural areas have the right to an adequate standard of living for themselves and their families and to facilitated access to the means of production necessary to achieve them, including production tools, technical assistance, credit, insurance and other financial services. They also have the right to engage freely, individually and/or collectively, in association with others or as a community, in traditional ways of farming, fishing, livestock rearing and forestry and to develop community-based commercialization systems.

2. States shall take appropriate measures to favour the access of peasants and other people working in rural areas to the means of transportation and the processing, drying and storage facilities necessary for selling their products on local, national and regional markets at prices that guarantee them a decent income and livelihood.

3. States shall take appropriate measures to strengthen and support local, national and regional markets in ways that facilitate and ensure that peasants and other people working in rural areas have full and equitable access and participation in these markets to sell their products at prices that allow them and their families to attain an adequate standard of living.

4. States shall take all appropriate measures to ensure that their rural development, agricultural, environmental, trade and investment policies and programmes contribute effectively to protecting and strengthening local livelihood options and to the transition to sustainable modes of agricultural production. States shall stimulate sustainable production, including agroecological and organic production, whenever possible, and facilitate direct farmer-to-consumer sales.

5. States shall take appropriate measures to strengthen the resilience of peasants and other people working in rural areas against natural disasters and other severe disruptions, such as market failures.

6. States shall take appropriate measures to ensure fair wages and equal remuneration for work of equal value, without distinction of any kind.

Article 17

1. Peasants and other people living in rural areas have the right to land, individually and/or collectively, in accordance with article 28 of the present Declaration, including the right to have access to, sustainably use and manage land and the water bodies, coastal seas, fisheries, pastures and forests therein, to achieve an adequate standard of living, to have a place to live in security, peace and dignity and to develop their cultures.

2. States shall take appropriate measures to remove and prohibit all forms of discrimination relating to the right to land, including those resulting from change of marital status, lack of legal capacity or lack of access to economic resources.

3. States shall take appropriate measures to provide legal recognition for land tenure rights, including customary land tenure rights not currently protected by law, recognizing the existence of different models and systems. States shall protect legitimate tenure and ensure that peasants and other people working in rural areas are not arbitrarily or unlawfully evicted and that their rights are not otherwise extinguished or infringed. States shall recognize and protect the natural commons and their related systems of collective use and management.

4. Peasants and other people working in rural areas have the right to be protected against arbitrary and unlawful displacement from their land or place of habitual residence, or from other natural resources used in their activities and necessary for the enjoyment of adequate living conditions. States shall incorporate protections against displacement into domestic legislation that are consistent with international human rights and humanitarian law. States shall prohibit arbitrary and unlawful forced eviction, the destruction of agricultural areas and the confiscation or expropriation of land and other natural resources, including as a punitive measure or as a means or method of war.

5. Peasants and other people working in rural areas who have been arbitrarily or unlawfully deprived of their lands have the right, individually and/or collectively, in association with others or as a community, to return to their land of which they were arbitrarily or unlawfully deprived, including in cases of natural disasters and/or armed conflict, and to have restored their access to the natural resources used in their activities and necessary for the enjoyment of adequate living conditions, whenever possible, or to receive just, fair and lawful compensation when their return is not possible.

6. Where appropriate, States shall take appropriate measures to carry out agrarian reforms in order to facilitate the broad and equitable access to land and other natural resources necessary to ensure that peasants and other people working in rural areas enjoy adequate living conditions, and to limit excessive concentration and control of land, taking into account its social function. Landless peasants, young people, small-scale fishers and other rural workers should be given priority in the allocation of public lands, fisheries and forests.

7. States shall take measures aimed at the conservation and sustainable use of land and other natural resources used in their production, including through agroecology, and ensure the conditions for the regeneration of biological and other natural capacities and cycles.

Article 18

1. Peasants and other people working in rural areas have the right to the conservation and protection of the environment and the productive capacity of their lands, and of the resources that they use and manage.

2. States shall take appropriate measures to ensure that peasants and other people working in rural areas enjoy, without discrimination, a safe, clean and healthy environment.

3. States shall comply with their respective international obligations to combat climate change. Peasants and other people working in rural areas have the right to contribute to the design and implementation of national and local climate change adaptation and mitigation policies, including through the use of practices and traditional knowledge.

4. States shall take effective measures to ensure that no hazardous material, substance or waste is stored or disposed of on the land of peasants and other people working in rural areas, and shall cooperate to address the threats to the enjoyment of their rights that result from transboundary environmental harm.

5. States shall protect peasants and other people working in rural areas against abuses by non-State actors, including by enforcing environmental laws that contribute, directly or indirectly, to the protection of the rights of peasants or other people working in rural areas.

Article 19

1. Peasants and other people working in rural areas have the right to seeds, in accordance with article 28 of the present Declaration, including:

    (a) The right to the protection of traditional knowledge relevant to plant genetic resources for food and agriculture;

    (b) The right to equitably participate in sharing the benefits arising from the utilization of plant genetic resources for food and agriculture;

    (c) The right to participate in the making of decisions on matters relating to the conservation and sustainable use of plant genetic resources for food and agriculture;

    (d) The right to save, use, exchange and sell their farm-saved seed or propagating material.

    2. Peasants and other people working in rural areas have the right to maintain, control, protect and develop their own seeds and traditional knowledge.

    3. States shall take measures to respect, protect and fulfil the right to seeds of peasants and other people working in rural areas.

    4. States shall ensure that seeds of sufficient quality and quantity are available to peasants at the most suitable time for planting and at an affordable price.

    5. States shall recognize the rights of peasants to rely either on their own seeds or on other locally available seeds of their choice and to decide on the crops and species that they wish to grow.

    6. States shall take appropriate measures to support peasant seed systems and promote the use of peasant seeds and agrobiodiversity.

    7. States shall take appropriate measures to ensure that agricultural research and development integrates the needs of peasants and other people working in rural areas and to ensure their active participation in the definition of priorities and the undertaking of research and development, taking into account their experience, and increase investment in research and the development of orphan crops and seeds that respond to the needs of peasants and other people working in rural areas.

    8. States shall ensure that seed policies, plant variety protection and other intellectual property laws, certification schemes and seed marketing laws respect and take into account the rights, needs and realities of peasants and other people working in rural areas.

Article 20

    1. States shall take appropriate measures, in accordance with their relevant international obligations, to prevent the depletion and ensure the conservation and sustainable use of biodiversity in order to promote and protect the full enjoyment of the rights of peasants and other people working in rural areas.

    2. States shall take appropriate measures to promote and protect the traditional knowledge, innovation and practices of peasants and other people working in rural areas, including traditional agrarian, pastoral, forestry, fisheries, livestock and agroecological systems relevant to the conservation and sustainable use of biological diversity.

    3. States shall prevent risks of violation of the rights of peasants and other people working in rural areas arising from the development, handling, transport, use, transfer or release of any living modified organisms.

Article 21

    1. Peasants and other people working in rural areas have the human rights to safe and clean drinking water and to sanitation, which are essential for the full enjoyment of life and all human rights and human dignity. These rights include water supply systems and sanitation facilities that are of good quality, affordable and physically accessible, and non-discriminatory and acceptable in cultural and gender terms.

    2. Peasants and other people working in rural areas have the right to water for personal and domestic use, farming, fishing and livestock keeping and for securing other water-related livelihoods, ensuring the conservation, restoration and sustainable use of water. They have the right to equitable access to water and water management systems, and to be free from arbitrary disconnections or the contamination of water supplies.

    3. States shall respect, protect and ensure access to water, including in customary and community-based water management systems, on a non-discriminatory basis, and shall take measures to guarantee affordable water for personal, domestic and productive uses, and improved sanitation, in particular for rural women and girls and persons belonging to disadvantaged or marginalized groups, such as nomadic pastoralists, workers on plantations, all migrants regardless of their migration status and persons living in irregular or informal settlements. States shall promote appropriate and affordable technologies, including irrigation technology, and technologies for the reuse of treated wastewater and for water collection and storage.

4. States shall protect and restore water-related ecosystems, including mountains, forests, wetlands, rivers, aquifers and lakes, from overuse and contamination by harmful substances, in particular by industrial effluent and concentrated minerals and chemicals that result in slow and fast poisoning.

5. States shall prevent third parties from impairing the enjoyment of the right to water of peasants and other people working in rural areas. States shall prioritize water for human needs before other uses, promoting its conservation, restoration and sustainable use.

Article 22

1. Peasants and other people working in rural areas have the right to social security, including social insurance.

2. States shall, according to their national circumstances, take appropriate steps to promote the enjoyment of the right to social security of all migrant workers in rural areas.

3. States shall recognize the rights of peasants and other people working in rural areas to social security, including social insurance, and, in accordance with national circumstances, should establish or maintain their social protection floors comprising basic social security guarantees. The guarantees should ensure at a minimum that, over the life cycle, all in need have access to essential health care and to basic income security, which together secure effective access to goods and services defined as necessary at the national level.

4. Basic social security guarantees should be established by law. Impartial, transparent, effective, accessible and affordable grievance and appeal procedures should also be specified. Systems should be in place to enhance compliance with national legal frameworks.

Article 23

1. Peasants and other people working in rural areas have the right to the enjoyment of the highest attainable standard of physical and mental health. They also have the right to have access, without any discrimination, to all social and health services.

2. Peasants and other people working in rural areas have the right to use and protect their traditional medicines and to maintain their health practices, including access to and conservation of their plants, animals and minerals for medicinal use.

3. States shall guarantee access to health facilities, goods and services in rural areas on a non-discriminatory basis, especially for groups in vulnerable situations, access to essential medicines, immunization against major infectious diseases, reproductive health, information concerning the main health problems affecting the community, including methods of preventing and controlling them, maternal and child health care, as well as training for health personnel, including education on health and human rights.

Article 24

1. Peasants and other people working in rural areas have the right to adequate housing. They have the right to sustain a secure home and community in which to live in peace and dignity, and the right to non-discrimination in this context.

2. Peasants and other people working in rural areas have the right to be protected against forced eviction from their home, harassment and other threats.

3. States shall not, arbitrarily or unlawfully, either temporarily or permanently, remove peasants or other people working in rural areas against their will from the homes or land that they occupy without providing or affording access to appropriate forms of legal or other protection. When eviction is unavoidable, the State must provide or ensure fair and just compensation for any material or other losses.

Article 25

1. Peasants and other people working in rural areas have the right to adequate training suited to the specific agroecological, sociocultural and economic environments in which they find themselves. Issues covered by training programmes should include, but not be limited to, improving productivity, marketing and the ability to cope with pests, pathogens, system shocks, the effects of chemicals, climate change and weather-related events.

2. All children of peasants and other people working in rural areas have the right to education in accordance with their culture and with all the rights contained in human rights instruments.

3. States shall encourage equitable and participatory farmer-scientist partnerships, such as farmer field schools, participatory plant breeding and plant and animal health clinics, to respond more appropriately to the immediate and emerging challenges that peasants and other people working in rural areas face.

4. States shall invest in providing training, market information and advisory services at the farm level.

Article 26

1. Peasants and other people working in rural areas have the right to enjoy their own culture and to pursue freely their cultural development, without interference or any form of discrimination. They also have the right to maintain, express, control, protect and develop their traditional and local knowledge, such as ways of life, methods of production or technology, or customs and tradition. No one may invoke cultural rights to infringe upon the human rights guaranteed by international law or to limit their scope.

2. Peasants and other people working in rural areas have the right, individually and/or collectively, in association with others or as a community, to express their local customs, languages, culture, religions, literature and art, in conformity with international human rights standards.

3. States shall respect, and take measures to recognize and protect, the rights of peasants and other people working in rural areas relating to their traditional knowledge and eliminate discrimination against the traditional knowledge, practices and technologies of peasants and other people working in rural areas.

Article 27

1. The specialized agencies, funds and programmes of the United Nations system and other intergovernmental organizations, including international and regional financial organizations, shall contribute to the full realization of the present Declaration, including through the mobilization of, inter alia, development assistance and cooperation. Ways and means of ensuring the participation of peasants and other people working in rural areas on issues affecting them shall be considered.

2. The United Nations and its specialized agencies, funds and programmes, and other intergovernmental organizations, including international and regional financial organizations, shall promote respect for and the full application of the present Declaration and follow up on its effectiveness.

Article 28

1. Nothing in the present Declaration may be construed as diminishing, impairing or nullifying the rights that peasants and other people working in rural areas and indigenous peoples currently have or may acquire in the future.

2. The human rights and fundamental freedoms of all, without discrimination of any kind, shall be respected in the exercise of the rights enunciated in the present Declaration. The exercise of the rights set forth in the present Declaration shall be subject only to such limitations as are determined by law and that are compliant with international human rights obligations. Any such limitations shall be non-discriminatory and necessary solely for the purpose of securing due recognition and respect for the rights and freedoms of others and for meeting the just and most compelling requirements of a democratic society.

ILC Draft Articles on Prevention and Punishment of Crimes Against Humanity (2019)*

Mindful that throughout history millions of children, women and men have been victims of crimes that deeply shock the conscience of humanity,

Recognizing that crimes against humanity threaten the peace, security and well-being of the world,

Recalling the principles of international law embodied in the Charter of the United Nations,

Recalling also that the prohibition of crimes against humanity is a peremptory norm of general international law (*jus cogens*),

Affirming that crimes against humanity, which are among the most serious crimes of concern to the international community as a whole, must be prevented in conformity with international law,

Determined to put an end to impunity for the perpetrators of these crimes and thus to contribute to the prevention of such crimes,

Considering the definition of crimes against humanity set forth in article 7 of the Rome Statute of the International Criminal Court,

Recalling that it is the duty of every State to exercise its criminal jurisdiction with respect to crimes against humanity,

Considering the rights of victims, witnesses and others in relation to crimes against humanity, as well as the right of alleged offenders to fair treatment,

Considering also that, because crimes against humanity must not go unpunished, the effective prosecution of such crimes must be ensured by taking measures at the national level and by enhancing international cooperation, including with respect to extradition and mutual legal assistance,

Article 1   Scope
The present draft articles apply to the prevention and punishment of crimes against humanity.

Article 2   Definition of crimes against humanity
1. For the purpose of the present draft articles, 'crime against humanity' means any of the following acts when committed as part of a widespread or systematic attack directed against any civilian population, with knowledge of the attack:
    (a) murder;
    (b) extermination;
    (c) enslavement;
    (d) deportation or forcible transfer of population;
    (e) imprisonment or other severe deprivation of physical liberty in violation of fundamental rules of international law;
    (f) torture;
    (g) rape, sexual slavery, enforced prostitution, forced pregnancy, enforced sterilization, or any other form of sexual violence of comparable gravity;
    (h) persecution against any identifiable group or collectivity on political, racial, national, ethnic, cultural, religious, gender, or other grounds that are universally recognized as impermissible under international law, in connection with any act referred to in this paragraph;
    (i) enforced disappearance of persons;
    (j) the crime of apartheid;
    (k) other inhumane acts of a similar character intentionally causing great suffering, or serious injury to body or to mental or physical health.
2. For the purpose of paragraph 1:
    (a) 'attack directed against any civilian population' means a course of conduct involving the multiple commission of acts referred to in paragraph 1 against any civilian population, pursuant to or in furtherance of a State or organizational policy to commit such attack;
    (b) 'extermination' includes the intentional infliction of conditions of life, *inter alia* the deprivation of access to food and medicine, calculated to bring about the destruction of part of a population;
    (c) 'enslavement' means the exercise of any or all of the powers attaching to the right of ownership over a person and includes the exercise of such power in the course of trafficking in persons, in particular women and children;
    (d) 'deportation or forcible transfer of population' means forced displacement of the persons concerned by expulsion or other coercive acts from the area in which they are lawfully present, without grounds permitted under international law;
    (e) 'torture' means the intentional infliction of severe pain or suffering, whether physical or mental, upon a person in the custody or under the control of the accused; except that torture shall not include pain or suffering arising only from, inherent in or incidental to, lawful sanctions;
    (f) 'forced pregnancy' means the unlawful confinement of a woman forcibly made pregnant, with the intent of affecting the ethnic composition of any population or carrying out other grave violations of international law. This definition shall not in any way be interpreted as affecting national laws relating to pregnancy;

(g) 'persecution' means the intentional and severe deprivation of fundamental rights contrary to international law by reason of the identity of the group or collectivity;

(h) 'the crime of apartheid' means inhumane acts of a character similar to those referred to in paragraph 1, committed in the context of an institutionalized regime of systematic oppression and domination by one racial group over any other racial group or groups and committed with the intention of maintaining that regime;

(i) 'enforced disappearance of persons' means the arrest, detention or abduction of persons by, or with the authorization, support or acquiescence of, a State or a political organization, followed by a refusal to acknowledge that deprivation of freedom or to give information on the fate or whereabouts of those persons, with the intention of removing them from the protection of the law for a prolonged period of time.

3. This draft article is without prejudice to any broader definition provided for in any international instrument, in customary international law or in national law.

Article 3   General obligations

1. Each State has the obligation not to engage in acts that constitute crimes against humanity.

2. Each State undertakes to prevent and to punish crimes against humanity, which are crimes under international law, whether or not committed in time of armed conflict.

3. No exceptional circumstances whatsoever, such as armed conflict, internal political instability or other public emergency, may be invoked as a justification of crimes against humanity.

Article 4   Obligation of prevention

Each State undertakes to prevent crimes against humanity, in conformity with international law, through:

(a) effective legislative, administrative, judicial or other appropriate preventive measures in any territory under its jurisdiction; and

(b) cooperation with other States, relevant intergovernmental organizations, and, as appropriate, other organizations.

Article 5   *Non-refoulement*

1. No State shall expel, return (*refouler*), surrender or extradite a person to another State where there are substantial grounds for believing that he or she would be in danger of being subjected to a crime against humanity.

2. For the purpose of determining whether there are such grounds, the competent authorities shall take into account all relevant considerations, including, where applicable, the existence in the State concerned of a consistent pattern of gross, flagrant or mass violations of human rights or of serious violations of international humanitarian law.

Article 6   Criminalization under national law

1. Each State shall take the necessary measures to ensure that crimes against humanity constitute offences under its criminal law.

2. Each State shall take the necessary measures to ensure that the following acts are offences under its criminal law:

(a) committing a crime against humanity;

(b) attempting to commit such a crime; and

(c) ordering, soliciting, inducing, aiding, abetting or otherwise assisting in or contributing to the commission or attempted commission of such a crime.

3. Each State shall also take the necessary measures to ensure that commanders and other superiors are criminally responsible for crimes against humanity committed by their subordinates if they knew, or had reason to know, that the subordinates were about to commit or were committing such crimes and did not take all necessary and reasonable measures in their power to prevent their commission, or if such crimes had been committed, to punish the persons responsible.

4. Each State shall take the necessary measures to ensure that, under its criminal law, the fact that an offence referred to in this draft article was committed pursuant to an order of a Government or of a superior, whether military or civilian, is not a ground for excluding criminal responsibility of a subordinate.

5. Each State shall take the necessary measures to ensure that, under its criminal law, the fact that an offence referred to in this draft article was committed by a person holding an official position is not a ground for excluding criminal responsibility.

6. Each State shall take the necessary measures to ensure that, under its criminal law, the offences referred to in this draft article shall not be subject to any statute of limitations.

7. Each State shall take the necessary measures to ensure that, under its criminal law, the offences referred to in this draft article shall be punishable by appropriate penalties that take into account their grave nature.

8. Subject to the provisions of its national law, each State shall take measures, where appropriate, to establish the liability of legal persons for the offences referred to in this draft article. Subject to the legal principles of the State, such liability of legal persons may be criminal, civil or administrative.

Article 7   Establishment of national jurisdiction

1. Each State shall take the necessary measures to establish its jurisdiction over the offences covered by the present draft articles in the following cases:

   (a) when the offence is committed in any territory under its jurisdiction or on board a ship or aircraft registered in that State;

   (b) when the alleged offender is a national of that State or, if that State considers it appropriate, a stateless person who is habitually resident in that State's territory;

   (c) when the victim is a national of that State if that State considers it appropriate.

2. Each State shall also take the necessary measures to establish its jurisdiction over the offences covered by the present draft articles in cases where the alleged offender is present in any territory under its jurisdiction and it does not extradite or surrender the person in accordance with the present draft articles.

3. The present draft articles do not exclude the exercise of any criminal jurisdiction established by a State in accordance with its national law.

Article 8   Investigation

Each State shall ensure that its competent authorities proceed to a prompt, thorough and impartial investigation whenever there is reasonable ground to believe that acts constituting crimes against humanity have been or are being committed in any territory under its jurisdiction.

Article 9   Preliminary measures when an alleged offender is present

1. Upon being satisfied, after an examination of information available to it, that the circumstances so warrant, any State in the territory under whose jurisdiction a person alleged to have committed any offence covered by the present draft articles is present shall take the person into custody or take other legal measures to ensure his or her presence. The custody and other legal measures shall be as provided in the law of that State, but may be continued only for such time as is necessary to enable any criminal, extradition or surrender proceedings to be instituted.

2. Such State shall immediately make a preliminary inquiry into the facts.

3. When a State, pursuant to this draft article, has taken a person into custody, it shall immediately notify the States referred to in draft article 7, paragraph 1, of the fact that such person is in custody and of the circumstances which warrant his or her detention. The State which makes the preliminary inquiry contemplated in paragraph 2 of this draft article shall, as appropriate, promptly report its findings to the said States and shall indicate whether it intends to exercise jurisdiction.

Article 10   *Aut dedere aut judicare*

The State in the territory under whose jurisdiction the alleged offender is present shall, if it does not extradite or surrender the person to another State or competent international criminal court or tribunal, submit the case to its competent authorities for the purpose of prosecution. Those authorities shall take their decision in the same manner as in the case of any other offence of a grave nature under the law of that State.

Article 11   Fair treatment of the alleged offender

1. Any person against whom measures are being taken in connection with an offence covered by the present draft articles shall be guaranteed at all stages of the proceedings fair treatment, including a fair trial, and full protection of his or her rights under applicable national and international law, including human rights law and international humanitarian law.

2. Any such person who is in prison, custody or detention in a State that is not of his or her nationality shall be entitled:

    (a) to communicate without delay with the nearest appropriate representative of the State or States of which such person is a national or which is otherwise entitled to protect that person's rights or, if such person is a stateless person, of the State which, at that person's request, is willing to protect that person's rights;

    (b) to be visited by a representative of that State or those States; and

    (c) to be informed without delay of his or her rights under this paragraph.

3. The rights referred to in paragraph 2 shall be exercised in conformity with the laws and regulations of the State in the territory under whose jurisdiction the person is present, subject to the proviso that the said laws and regulations must enable full effect to be given to the purpose for which the rights accorded under paragraph 2 are intended.

Article 12   Victims, witnesses and others

1. Each State shall take the necessary measures to ensure that:

    (a) any person who alleges that acts constituting crimes against humanity have been or are being committed has the right to complain to the competent authorities; and

    (b) complainants, victims, witnesses, and their relatives and representatives, as well as other persons participating in any investigation, prosecution, extradition or other proceeding within the scope of the present draft articles, shall be protected against ill-treatment or intimidation as a consequence of any complaint, information, testimony or other evidence given. Protective measures shall be without prejudice to the rights of the alleged offender referred to in draft article 11.

2. Each State shall, in accordance with its national law, enable the views and concerns of victims of a crime against humanity to be presented and considered at appropriate stages of criminal proceedings against alleged offenders in a manner not prejudicial to the rights referred to in draft article 11.

3. Each State shall take the necessary measures to ensure in its legal system that the victims of a crime against humanity, committed through acts attributable to the State under international law or committed in any territory under its jurisdiction, have the right to obtain reparation for material and moral damages, on an individual or collective basis, consisting, as appropriate, of one or more of the following or other forms: restitution; compensation; satisfaction; rehabilitation; cessation and guarantees of non-repetition.

Article 13   Extradition

1. This draft article shall apply to the offences covered by the present draft articles when a requesting State seeks the extradition of a person who is present in territory under the jurisdiction of a requested State.

2. Each of the offences covered by the present draft articles shall be deemed to be included as an extraditable offence in any extradition treaty existing between States. States undertake to include such offences as extraditable offences in every extradition treaty to be concluded between them.

3. For the purposes of extradition between States, an offence covered by the present draft articles shall not be regarded as a political offence or as an offence connected with a political offence or as an offence inspired by political motives. Accordingly, a request for extradition based on such an offence may not be refused on these grounds alone.

4. If a State that makes extradition conditional on the existence of a treaty receives a request for extradition from another State with which it has no extradition treaty, it may consider the present draft articles as the legal basis for extradition in respect of any offence covered by the present draft articles.

5. A State that makes extradition conditional on the existence of a treaty shall, for any offence covered by the present draft articles:

    (a) inform the Secretary-General of the United Nations whether it will use the present draft articles as the legal basis for cooperation on extradition with other States; and

    (b) if it does not use the present draft articles as the legal basis for cooperation on extradition, seek, where appropriate, to conclude treaties on extradition with other States in order to implement this draft article.

6. States that do not make extradition conditional on the existence of a treaty shall recognize the offences covered by the present draft articles as extraditable offences between themselves.

7. Extradition shall be subject to the conditions provided for by the national law of the requested State or by applicable extradition treaties, including the grounds upon which the requested State may refuse extradition.

8. The requesting and requested States shall, subject to their national law, endeavour to expedite extradition procedures and to simplify evidentiary requirements relating thereto.

9. If necessary, the offences covered by the present draft articles shall be treated, for the purposes of extradition between States, as if they had been committed not only in the place in which they occurred but also in the territory of the States that have established jurisdiction in accordance with draft article 7, paragraph 1.

10. If extradition, sought for purposes of enforcing a sentence, is refused because the person sought is a national of the requested State, the requested State shall, if its national law so permits and in conformity with the requirements of such law, upon application of the requesting State, consider the enforcement of the sentence imposed under the national law of the requesting State or the remainder thereof.

11. Nothing in the present draft articles shall be interpreted as imposing an obligation to extradite if the requested State has substantial grounds for believing that the request has been made for the purpose of prosecuting or punishing a person on account of that person's gender, race, religion, nationality, ethnic origin, culture, membership of a particular social group, political opinions or other grounds that are universally recognized as impermissible under international law, or that compliance with the request would cause prejudice to that person's position for any of these reasons.

12. A requested State shall give due consideration to the request of the State in the territory under whose jurisdiction the alleged offence has occurred.

13. Before refusing extradition, the requested State shall consult, as appropriate, with the requesting State to provide it with ample opportunity to present its opinions and to provide information relevant to its allegation.

Article 14   Mutual legal assistance

1. States shall afford one another the widest measure of mutual legal assistance in investigations, prosecutions and judicial proceedings in relation to the offences covered by the present draft articles in accordance with this draft article.

2. In relation to the offences for which a legal person may be held liable in accordance with draft article 6, paragraph 8, in the requesting State, mutual legal assistance shall be afforded to the fullest extent possible under relevant laws, treaties, agreements and arrangements of the requested State with respect to investigations, prosecutions, judicial and other proceedings.

3. Mutual legal assistance to be afforded in accordance with this draft article may be requested for any of the following purposes:

(a) identifying and locating alleged offenders and, as appropriate, victims, witnesses or others;

(b) taking evidence or statements from persons, including by video conference;

(c) effecting service of judicial documents;

(d) executing searches and seizures;

(e) examining objects and sites, including obtaining forensic evidence;

(f) providing information, evidentiary items and expert evaluations;

(g) providing originals or certified copies of relevant documents and records;

(h) identifying, tracing or freezing proceeds of crime, property, instrumentalities or other things for evidentiary or other purposes;

(i) facilitating the voluntary appearance of persons in the requesting State; or

(j) any other type of assistance that is not contrary to the national law of the requested State.

4. States shall not decline to render mutual legal assistance pursuant to this draft article on the ground of bank secrecy.

5. States shall consider, as may be necessary, the possibility of concluding bilateral or multilateral agreements or arrangements that would serve the purposes of, give practical effect to, or enhance the provisions of this draft article.

6. Without prejudice to its national law, the competent authorities of a State may, without prior request, transmit information relating to crimes against humanity to a competent authority in another State where they believe that such information could assist the authority in undertaking or

successfully concluding investigations, prosecutions and judicial proceedings or could result in a request formulated by the latter State pursuant to the present draft articles.

7. The provisions of this draft article shall not affect the obligations under any other treaty, bilateral or multilateral, that governs or will govern, in whole or in part, mutual legal assistance between the States in question.

8. The draft annex to the present draft articles shall apply to requests made pursuant to this draft article if the States in question are not bound by a treaty of mutual legal assistance. If those States are bound by such a treaty, the corresponding provisions of that treaty shall apply, unless the States agree to apply the provisions of the draft annex in lieu thereof. States are encouraged to apply the draft annex if it facilitates cooperation.

9. States shall consider, as appropriate, entering into agreements or arrangements with international mechanisms that are established by the United Nations or by other international organizations and that have a mandate to collect evidence with respect to crimes against humanity.

Article 15   Settlement of disputes

1. States shall endeavour to settle disputes concerning the interpretation or application of the present draft articles through negotiations.

2. Any dispute between two or more States concerning the interpretation or application of the present draft articles that is not settled through negotiation shall, at the request of one of those States, be submitted to the International Court of Justice, unless those States agree to submit the dispute to arbitration.

3. Each State may declare that it does not consider itself bound by paragraph 2 of this draft article. The other States shall not be bound by paragraph 2 of this draft article with respect to any State that has made such a declaration.

4. Any State that has made a declaration in accordance with paragraph 3 of this draft article may at any time withdraw that declaration.

Annex

1. This draft annex applies in accordance with draft article 14, paragraph 8.

Designation of a central authority

2. Each State shall designate a central authority that shall have the responsibility and power to receive requests for mutual legal assistance and either to execute them or to transmit them to the competent authorities for execution. Where a State has a special region or territory with a separate system of mutual legal assistance, it may designate a distinct central authority that shall have the same function for that region or territory. Central authorities shall ensure the speedy and proper execution or transmission of the requests received. Where the central authority transmits the request to a competent authority for execution, it shall encourage the speedy and proper execution of the request by the competent authority. The Secretary-General of the United Nations shall be notified by each State of the central authority designated for this purpose. Requests for mutual legal assistance and any communication related thereto shall be transmitted to the central authorities designated by the States. This requirement shall be without prejudice to the right of a State to require that such requests and communications be addressed to it through diplomatic channels and, in urgent circumstances, where the States agree, through the International Criminal Police Organization, if possible.

Procedures for making a request

3. Requests shall be made in writing or, where possible, by any means capable of producing a written record, in a language acceptable to the requested State, under conditions allowing that State to establish authenticity. The Secretary-General of the United Nations shall be notified by each State of the language or languages acceptable to that State. In urgent circumstances and where agreed by the States, requests may be made orally, but shall be confirmed in writing forthwith.

4. A request for mutual legal assistance shall contain:
    (a) the identity of the authority making the request;
    (b) the subject matter and nature of the investigation, prosecution or judicial proceeding to which the request relates and the name and functions of the authority conducting the investigation, prosecution or judicial proceeding;

(c) a summary of the relevant facts, except in relation to requests for the purpose of service of judicial documents;

(d) a description of the assistance sought and details of any particular procedure that the requesting State wishes to be followed;

(e) where possible, the identity, location and nationality of any person concerned; and

(f) the purpose for which the evidence, information or action is sought.

5. The requested State may request additional information when it appears necessary for the execution of the request in accordance with its national law or when it can facilitate such execution.

Response to the request by the requested State

6. A request shall be executed in accordance with the national law of the requested State and, to the extent not contrary to the national law of the requested State and where possible, in accordance with the procedures specified in the request.

7. The requested State shall execute the request for mutual legal assistance as soon as possible and shall take as full account as possible of any deadlines suggested by the requesting State and for which reasons are given, preferably in the request. The requested State shall respond to reasonable requests by the requesting State on progress of its handling of the request. The requesting State shall promptly inform the requested State when the assistance sought is no longer required.

8. Mutual legal assistance may be refused:

(a) if the request is not made in conformity with the provisions of this draft annex;

(b) if the requested State considers that execution of the request is likely to prejudice its sovereignty, security, *ordre public* or other essential interests;

(c) if the authorities of the requested State would be prohibited by its national law from carrying out the action requested with regard to any similar offence, had it been subject to investigation, prosecution or judicial proceedings under their own jurisdiction;

(d) if it would be contrary to the legal system of the requested State relating to mutual legal assistance for the request to be granted.

9. Reasons shall be given for any refusal of mutual legal assistance.

10. Mutual legal assistance may be postponed by the requested State on the ground that it interferes with an ongoing investigation, prosecution or judicial proceeding.

11. Before refusing a request pursuant to paragraph 8 of this draft annex or postponing its execution pursuant to paragraph 10 of this draft annex, the requested State shall consult with the requesting State to consider whether assistance may be granted subject to such terms and conditions as it deems necessary. If the requesting State accepts assistance subject to those conditions, it shall comply with the conditions.

12. The requested State:

(a) shall provide to the requesting State copies of government records, documents or information in its possession that under its national law are available to the general public; and

(b) may, at its discretion, provide to the requesting State in whole, in part or subject to such conditions as it deems appropriate, copies of any government records, documents or information in its possession that under its national law are not available to the general public.

Use of information by the requesting State

13. The requesting State shall not transmit or use information or evidence furnished by the requested State for investigations, prosecutions or judicial proceedings other than those stated in the request without the prior consent of the requested State. Nothing in this paragraph shall prevent the requesting State from disclosing in its proceedings information or evidence that is exculpatory to an accused person. In the latter case, the requesting State shall notify the requested State prior to the disclosure and, if so requested, consult with the requested State. If, in an exceptional case, advance notice is not possible, the requesting State shall inform the requested State of the disclosure without delay.

14. The requesting State may require that the requested State keep confidential the fact and substance of the request, except to the extent necessary to execute the request. If the requested State cannot comply with the requirement of confidentiality, it shall promptly inform the requesting State.

Testimony of person from the requested State

15. Without prejudice to the application of paragraph 19 of this draft annex, a witness, expert or other person who, at the request of the requesting State, consents to give evidence in a proceeding or to assist in an investigation, prosecution or judicial proceeding in territory under the jurisdiction of the requesting State shall not be prosecuted, detained, punished or subjected to any other restriction of his or her personal liberty in that territory in respect of acts, omissions or convictions prior to his or her departure from territory under the jurisdiction of the requested State. Such safe conduct shall cease when the witness, expert or other person having had, for a period of fifteen consecutive days or for any period agreed upon by the States from the date on which he or she has been officially informed that his or her presence is no longer required by the judicial authorities, an opportunity of leaving, has nevertheless remained voluntarily in territory under the jurisdiction of the requesting State or, having left it, has returned of his or her own free will.

16. Wherever possible and consistent with fundamental principles of national law, when an individual is in territory under the jurisdiction of a State and has to be heard as a witness or expert by the judicial authorities of another State, the first State may, at the request of the other, permit the hearing to take place by video conference if it is not possible or desirable for the individual in question to appear in person in territory under the jurisdiction of the requesting State. States may agree that the hearing shall be conducted by a judicial authority of the requesting State and attended by a judicial authority of the requested State.

Transfer for testimony of person detained in the requested State

17. A person who is being detained or is serving a sentence in the territory under the jurisdiction of one State whose presence in another State is requested for purposes of identification, testimony or otherwise providing assistance in obtaining evidence for investigations, prosecutions or judicial proceedings in relation to offences covered by the present draft articles, may be transferred if the following conditions are met:

    (a) the person freely gives his or her informed consent; and

    (b) the competent authorities of both States agree, subject to such conditions as those States may deem appropriate.

18. For the purposes of paragraph 17 of this draft annex:

    (a) the State to which the person is transferred shall have the authority and obligation to keep the person transferred in custody, unless otherwise requested or authorized by the State from which the person was transferred;

    (b) the State to which the person is transferred shall without delay implement its obligation to return the person to the custody of the State from which the person was transferred as agreed beforehand, or as otherwise agreed, by the competent authorities of both States;

    (c) the State to which the person is transferred shall not require the State from which the person was transferred to initiate extradition proceedings for the return of the person; and

    (d) the person transferred shall receive credit for service of the sentence being served from the State from which he or she was transferred for time spent in the custody of the State to which he or she was transferred.

19. Unless the State from which a person is to be transferred in accordance with paragraphs 17 and 18 of this draft annex so agrees, that person, whatever his or her nationality, shall not be prosecuted, detained, punished or subjected to any other restriction of his or her personal liberty in territory under the jurisdiction of the State to which that person is transferred in respect of acts, omissions or convictions prior to his or her departure from territory under the jurisdiction of the State from which he or she was transferred.

Costs

20. The ordinary costs of executing a request shall be borne by the requested State, unless otherwise agreed by the States concerned. If expenses of a substantial or extraordinary nature are or will be required to fulfil the request, the States shall consult to determine the terms and conditions under which the request will be executed, as well as the manner in which the costs shall be borne.

Part II

UN Human Rights Council

Resolution adopted by the General Assembly 60/251: Human Rights Council (2006)*

The General Assembly,

Reaffirming the purposes and principles contained in the Charter of the United Nations, including developing friendly relations among nations based on respect for the principle of equal rights and self-determination of peoples, and achieving international cooperation in solving international problems of an economic, social, cultural or humanitarian character and in promoting and encouraging respect for human rights and fundamental freedoms for all,

Reaffirming also the Universal Declaration of Human Rights[a] and the Vienna Declaration and Programme of Action,[b] and recalling the International Covenant on Civil and Political Rights,[c] the International Covenant on Economic, Social and Cultural Rights and other human rights instruments,

Reaffirming further that all human rights are universal, indivisible, interrelated, interdependent and mutually reinforcing, and that all human rights must be treated in a fair and equal manner, on the same footing and with the same emphasis,

Reaffirming that, while the significance of national and regional particularities and various historical, cultural and religious backgrounds must be borne in mind, all States, regardless of their political, economic and cultural systems, have the duty to promote and protect all human rights and fundamental freedoms,

Emphasizing the responsibilities of all States, in conformity with the Charter, to respect human rights and fundamental freedoms for all, without distinction of any kind as to race, colour, sex, language or religion, political or other opinion, national or social origin, property, birth or other status,

Acknowledging that peace and security, development and human rights are the pillars of the United Nations system and the foundations for collective security and well-being, and recognizing that development, peace and security and human rights are interlinked and mutually reinforcing,

Affirming the need for all States to continue international efforts to enhance dialogue and broaden understanding among civilizations, cultures and religions, and emphasizing that States, regional organizations, non-governmental organizations, religious bodies and the media have an important role to play in promoting tolerance, respect for and freedom of religion and belief,

Recognizing the work undertaken by the Commission on Human Rights and the need to preserve and build on its achievements and to redress its shortcomings,

Recognizing also the importance of ensuring universality, objectivity and non-selectivity in the consideration of human rights issues, and the elimination of double standards and politicization,

---

* From General Assembly Resolution 60/251: Human Rights Council, © 2006 United Nations. Reprinted with the permission of the United Nations.
 [a] Resolution 217 A (III).
 [b] A/CONF.157/24 (Part I), chap. III.
 [c] See resolution 2200 A (XXI), annex.

Recognizing further that the promotion and protection of human rights should be based on the principles of cooperation and genuine dialogue and aimed at strengthening the capacity of Member States to comply with their human rights obligations for the benefit of all human beings,

Acknowledging that non-governmental organizations play an important role at the national, regional and international levels, in the promotion and protection of human rights,

Reaffirming the commitment to strengthen the United Nations human rights machinery, with the aim of ensuring effective enjoyment by all of all human rights, civil, political, economic, social and cultural rights, including the right to development, and to that end, the resolve to create a Human Rights Council,

1. *Decides* to establish the Human Rights Council, based in Geneva, in replacement of the Commission on Human Rights, as a subsidiary organ of the General Assembly; the Assembly shall review the status of the Council within five years;

2. *Decides* that the Council shall be responsible for promoting universal respect for the protection of all human rights and fundamental freedoms for all, without distinction of any kind and in a fair and equal manner;

3. *Decides also* that the Council should address situations of violations of human rights, including gross and systematic violations, and make recommendations thereon. It should also promote the effective coordination and the mainstreaming of human rights within the United Nations system;

4. *Decides further* that the work of the Council shall be guided by the principles of universality, impartiality, objectivity and non-selectivity, constructive international dialogue and cooperation, with a view to enhancing the promotion and protection of all human rights, civil, political, economic, social and cultural rights, including the right to development;

5. *Decides* that the Council shall, *inter alia*:

   (a) Promote human rights education and learning as well as advisory services, technical assistance and capacity-building, to be provided in consultation with and with the consent of Member States concerned;

   (b) Serve as a forum for dialogue on thematic issues on all human rights;

   (c) Make recommendations to the General Assembly for the further development of international law in the field of human rights;

   (d) Promote the full implementation of human rights obligations undertaken by States and follow-up to the goals and commitments related to the promotion and protection of human rights emanating from United Nations conferences and summits;

   (e) Undertake a universal periodic review, based on objective and reliable information, of the fulfilment by each State of its human rights obligations and commitments in a manner which ensures universality of coverage and equal treatment with respect to all States; the review shall be a cooperative mechanism, based on an interactive dialogue, with the full involvement of the country concerned and with consideration given to its capacity-building needs; such a mechanism shall complement and not duplicate the work of treaty bodies; the Council shall develop the modalities and necessary time allocation for the universal periodic review mechanism within one year after the holding of its first session;

   (f) Contribute, through dialogue and cooperation, towards the prevention of human rights violations and respond promptly to human rights emergencies;

   (g) Assume the role and responsibilities of the Commission on Human Rights relating to the work of the Office of the United Nations High Commissioner for Human Rights, as decided by the General Assembly in its resolution 48/141 of 20 December 1993;

   (h) Work in close cooperation in the field of human rights with Governments, regional organizations, national human rights institutions and civil society;

   (i) Make recommendations with regard to the promotion and protection of human rights;

   (j) Submit an annual report to the General Assembly;

6. *Decides also* that the Council shall assume, review and, where necessary, improve and rationalize all mandates, mechanisms, functions and responsibilities of the Commission on Human Rights in order to maintain a system of special procedures, expert advice and a complaint procedure; the Council shall complete this review within one year after the holding of its first session;

7. *Decides further* that the Council shall consist of forty-seven Member States, which shall be elected directly and individually by secret ballot by the majority of the members of the General Assembly; the membership shall be based on equitable geographical distribution, and seats shall be distributed as follows among regional groups: Group of African States, thirteen; Group of Asian States, thirteen; Group of Eastern European States, six; Group of Latin American and Caribbean States, eight; and Group of Western European and other States, seven; the members of the Council shall serve for a period of three years and shall not be eligible for immediate re-election after two consecutive terms;

8. *Decides* that the membership in the Council shall be open to all States Members of the United Nations; when electing members of the Council, Member States shall take into account the contribution of candidates to the promotion and protection of human rights and their voluntary pledges and commitments made thereto; the General Assembly, by a two-thirds majority of the members present and voting, may suspend the rights of membership in the Council of a member of the Council that commits gross and systematic violations of human rights;

9. *Decides also* that members elected to the Council shall uphold the highest standards in the promotion and protection of human rights, shall fully cooperate with the Council and be reviewed under the universal periodic review mechanism during their term of membership;

10. *Decides further* that the Council shall meet regularly throughout the year and schedule no fewer than three sessions per year, including a main session, for a total duration of no less than ten weeks, and shall be able to hold special sessions, when needed, at the request of a member of the Council with the support of one third of the membership of the Council;

11. *Decides* that the Council shall apply the rules of procedure established for committees of the General Assembly, as applicable, unless subsequently otherwise decided by the Assembly or the Council, and also decides that the participation of and consultation with observers, including States that are not members of the Council, the specialized agencies, other intergovernmental organizations and national human rights institutions, as well as non-governmental organizations, shall be based on arrangements, including Economic and Social Council resolution 1996/31 of 25 July 1996 and practices observed by the Commission on Human Rights, while ensuring the most effective contribution of these entities;

12. *Decides also* that the methods of work of the Council shall be transparent, fair and impartial and shall enable genuine dialogue, be results-oriented, allow for subsequent follow-up discussions to recommendations and their implementation and also allow for substantive interaction with special procedures and mechanisms;

13. *Recommends* that the Economic and Social Council request the Commission on Human Rights to conclude its work at its sixty-second session, and that it abolish the Commission on 16 June 2006;

14. *Decides* to elect the new members of the Council; the terms of membership shall be staggered, and such decision shall be taken for the first election by the drawing of lots, taking into consideration equitable geographical distribution;

15. *Decides also* that elections of the first members of the Council shall take place on 9 May 2006, and that the first meeting of the Council shall be convened on 19 June 2006;

16. *Decides further* that the Council shall review its work and functioning five years after its establishment and report to the General Assembly.

72nd plenary meeting
15 March 2006

Resolution adopted by the Human Rights Council 5/1: Institution-building of the United Nations Human Rights Council (2007)*¹

The Human Rights Council,

Acting in compliance with the mandate entrusted to it by the United Nations General Assembly in resolution 60/251 of 15 March 2006,

Having considered the draft text on institution-building submitted by the President of the Council,

1. *Adopts* the draft text entitled 'United Nations Human Rights Council: Institution-Building', as contained in the annex to the present resolution, including its appendix(ces);

2. *Decides* to submit the following draft resolution to the General Assembly for its adoption as a matter of priority in order to facilitate the timely implementation of the text contained thereafter:

'The General Assembly,

'*Taking note* of Human Rights Council Resolution 5/1 of 18 June 2007,

'1. *Welcomes* the text entitled 'United Nations Human Rights Council: Institution-Building', as contained in the annex to the present resolution, including its appendix(ces).'

9th meeting
18 June 2007

Annex

United Nations Human Rights Council: Institution-Building

I Universal Periodic Review Mechanism

A Basis of the review

1. The basis of the review is:
   (a) The Charter of the United Nations;
   (b) The Universal Declaration of Human Rights;
   (c) Human rights instruments to which a State is party;
   (d) Voluntary pledges and commitments made by States, including those undertaken when presenting their candidatures for election to the Human Rights Council (hereinafter 'the Council').

2. In addition to the above and given the complementary and mutually interrelated nature of international human rights law and international humanitarian law, the review shall take into account applicable international humanitarian law.

B Principles and objectives

1 Principles

3. The universal periodic review should:
   (a) Promote the universality, interdependence, indivisibility and interrelatedness of all human rights;
   (b) Be a cooperative mechanism based on objective and reliable information and on inter-active dialogue;
   (c) Ensure universal coverage and equal treatment of all States;

(d) Be an intergovernmental process, United Nations Member-driven and action-oriented;

(e) Fully involve the country under review;

(f) Complement and not duplicate other human rights mechanisms, thus representing an added value;

(g) Be conducted in an objective, transparent, non-selective, constructive, non-confrontational and non-politicized manner;

(h) Not be overly burdensome to the concerned State or to the agenda of the Council;

(i) Not be overly long; it should be realistic and not absorb a disproportionate amount of time, human and financial resources;

(j) Not diminish the Council's capacity to respond to urgent human rights situations;

(k) Fully integrate a gender perspective;

(l) Without prejudice to the obligations contained in the elements provided for in the basis of review, take into account the level of development and specificities of countries;

(m) Ensure the participation of all relevant stakeholders, including non-governmental organizations and national human rights institutions, in accordance with General Assembly resolution 60/251 of 15 March 2006 and Economic and Social Council resolution 1996/31 of 25 July 1996, as well as any decisions that the Council may take in this regard.

2 Objectives

4. The objectives of the review are:

(a) The improvement of the human rights situation on the ground;

(b) The fulfilment of the State's human rights obligations and commitments and assessment of positive developments and challenges faced by the State;

(c) The enhancement of the State's capacity and of technical assistance, in consultation with, and with the consent of, the State concerned;

(d) The sharing of best practice among States and other stakeholders;

(e) Support for cooperation in the promotion and protection of human rights;

(f) The encouragement of full cooperation and engagement with the Council, other human rights bodies and the Office of the United Nations High Commissioner for Human Rights.

C Periodicity and order of the review

5. The review begins after the adoption of the universal periodic review mechanism by the Council.

6. The order of review should reflect the principles of universality and equal treatment.

7. The order of the review should be established as soon as possible in order to allow States to prepare adequately.

8. All member States of the Council shall be reviewed during their term of membership.

9. The initial members of the Council, especially those elected for one or two-year terms, should be reviewed first.

10. A mix of member and observer States of the Council should be reviewed.

11. Equitable geographic distribution should be respected in the selection of countries for review.

12. The first member and observer States to be reviewed will be chosen by the drawing of lots from each Regional Group in such a way as to ensure full respect for equitable geographic distribution. Alphabetical order will then be applied beginning with those countries thus selected, unless other countries volunteer to be reviewed.

13. The period between review cycles should be reasonable so as to take into account the capacity of States to prepare for, and the capacity of other stakeholders to respond to, the requests arising from the review.

14. The periodicity of the review for the first cycle will be of four years. This will imply the consideration of 48 States per year during three sessions of the working group of two weeks each.[a]

---

[a] The universal periodic review is an evolving process; the Council, after the conclusion of the first review cycle, may review the modalities and the periodicity of this mechanism, based on best practices and lessons learned.

D Process and modalities of the review

1 Documentation

15. The documents on which the review would be based are:

(a) Information prepared by the State concerned, which can take the form of a national report, on the basis of general guidelines to be adopted by the Council at its sixth session (first session of the second cycle), and any other information considered relevant by the State concerned, which could be presented either orally or in writing, provided that the written presentation summarizing the information will not exceed 20 pages, to guarantee equal treatment to all States and not to overburden the mechanism. States are encouraged to prepare the information through a broad consultation process at the national level with all relevant stakeholders;

(b) Additionally a compilation prepared by the Office of the High Commissioner for Human Rights of the information contained in the reports of treaty bodies, special procedures, including observations and comments by the State concerned, and other relevant official United Nations documents, which shall not exceed 10 pages;

(c) Additional, credible and reliable information provided by other relevant stakeholders to the universal periodic review which should also be taken into consideration by the Council in the review. The Office of the High Commissioner for Human Rights will prepare a summary of such information which shall not exceed 10 pages.

16. The documents prepared by the Office of the High Commissioner for Human Rights should be elaborated following the structure of the general guidelines adopted by the Council regarding the information prepared by the State concerned.

17. Both the State's written presentation and the summaries prepared by the Office of the High Commissioner for Human Rights shall be ready six weeks prior to the review by the working group to ensure the distribution of documents simultaneously in the six official languages of the United Nations, in accordance with General Assembly resolution 53/208 of 14 January 1999.

2 Modalities

18. The modalities of the review shall be as follows:

(a) The review will be conducted in one working group, chaired by the President of the Council and composed of the 47 member States of the Council. Each member State will decide on the composition of its delegation;[b]

(b) Observer States may participate in the review, including in the interactive dialogue;

(c) Other relevant stakeholders may attend the review in the Working Group;

(d) A group of three rapporteurs, selected by the drawing of lots among the members of the Council and from different Regional Groups (*troika*) will be formed to facilitate each review, including the preparation of the report of the working group. The Office of the High Commissioner for Human Rights will provide the necessary assistance and expertise to the rapporteurs.

19. The country concerned may request that one of the rapporteurs be from its own Regional Group and may also request the substitution of a rapporteur on only one occasion.

20. A rapporteur may request to be excused from participation in a specific review process.

21. Interactive dialogue between the country under review and the Council will take place in the working group. The rapporteurs may collate issues or questions to be transmitted to the State under review to facilitate its preparation and focus the interactive dialogue, while guaranteeing fairness and transparency.

---

[b] A Universal Periodic Review Voluntary Trust Fund should be established to facilitate the participation of developing countries, particularly the Least Developed Countries, in the universal periodic review mechanism.

22. The duration of the review will be three hours for each country in the working group. Additional time of up to one hour will be allocated for the consideration of the outcome by the plenary of the Council.

23. Half an hour will be allocated for the adoption of the report of each country under review in the working group.

24. A reasonable time frame should be allocated between the review and the adoption of the report of each State in the working group.

25. The final outcome will be adopted by the plenary of the Council.

E Outcome of the review

1 Format of the outcome

26. The format of the outcome of the review will be a report consisting of a summary of the proceedings of the review process; conclusions and/or recommendations, and the voluntary commitments of the State concerned.

2 Content of the outcome

27. The universal periodic review is a cooperative mechanism. Its outcome may include, *inter alia*:

(a) An assessment undertaken in an objective and transparent manner of the human rights situation in the country under review, including positive developments and the challenges faced by the country;

(b) Sharing of best practices;

(c) An emphasis on enhancing cooperation for the promotion and protection of human rights;

(d) The provision of technical assistance and capacity-building in consultation with, and with the consent of, the country concerned;[c]

(e) Voluntary commitments and pledges made by the country under review.

3 Adoption of the outcome

28. The country under review should be fully involved in the outcome.

29. Before the adoption of the outcome by the plenary of the Council, the State concerned should be offered the opportunity to present replies to questions or issues that were not sufficiently addressed during the interactive dialogue.

30. The State concerned and the member States of the Council, as well as observer States, will be given the opportunity to express their views on the outcome of the review before the plenary takes action on it.

31. Other relevant stakeholders will have the opportunity to make general comments before the adoption of the outcome by the plenary.

32. Recommendations that enjoy the support of the State concerned will be identified as such. Other recommendations, together with the comments of the State concerned thereon, will be noted. Both will be included in the outcome report to be adopted by the Council.

F Follow-up to the review

33. The outcome of the universal periodic review, as a cooperative mechanism, should be implemented primarily by the State concerned and, as appropriate, by other relevant stakeholders.

34. The subsequent review should focus, *inter alia*, on the implementation of the preceding outcome.

35. The Council should have a standing item on its agenda devoted to the universal periodic review.

36. The international community will assist in implementing the recommendations and conclusions regarding capacity-building and technical assistance, in consultation with, and with the consent of, the country concerned.

---

[c] A decision should be taken by the Council on whether to resort to existing financing mechanisms or to create a new mechanism.

37. In considering the outcome of the universal periodic review, the Council will decide if and when any specific follow-up is necessary.

38. After exhausting all efforts to encourage a State to cooperate with the universal periodic review mechanism, the Council will address, as appropriate, cases of persistent non-cooperation with the mechanism.

II Special Procedures

A Selection and appointment of mandate-holders

39. The following general criteria will be of paramount importance while nominating, selecting and appointing mandate-holders: (a) expertise; (b) experience in the field of the mandate; (c) independence; (d) impartiality; (e) personal integrity; and (f) objectivity.

40. Due consideration should be given to gender balance and equitable geographic representation, as well as to an appropriate representation of different legal systems.

41. Technical and objective requirements for eligible candidates for mandate-holders will be approved by the Council at its sixth session (first session of the second cycle), in order to ensure that eligible candidates are highly qualified individuals who possess established competence, relevant expertise and extensive professional experience in the field of human rights.

42. The following entities may nominate candidates as special procedures mandate-holders: (a) Governments; (b) Regional Groups operating within the United Nations human rights system; (c) international organizations or their offices (e.g. the Office of the High Commissioner for Human Rights); (d) non-governmental organizations; (e) other human rights bodies; (f) individual nominations.

43. The Office of the High Commissioner for Human Rights shall immediately prepare, maintain and periodically update a public list of eligible candidates in a standardized format, which shall include personal data, areas of expertise and professional experience. Upcoming vacancies of mandates shall be publicized.

44. The principle of non-accumulation of human rights functions at a time shall be respected.

45. A mandate-holder's tenure in a given function, whether a thematic or country mandate, will be no longer than six years (two terms of three years for thematic mandate-holders).

46. Individuals holding decision-making positions in Government or in any other organization or entity which may give rise to a conflict of interest with the responsibilities inherent to the mandate shall be excluded. Mandate-holders will act in their personal capacity.

47. A consultative group would be established to propose to the President, at least one month before the beginning of the session in which the Council would consider the selection of mandate-holders, a list of candidates who possess the highest qualifications for the mandates in question and meet the general criteria and particular requirements.

48. The consultative group shall also give due consideration to the exclusion of nominated candidates from the public list of eligible candidates brought to its attention.

49. At the beginning of the annual cycle of the Council, Regional Groups would be invited to appoint a member of the consultative group, who would serve in his/her personal capacity. The Group will be assisted by the Office of the High Commissioner for Human Rights.

50. The consultative group will consider candidates included in the public list; however, under exceptional circumstances and if a particular post justifies it, the Group may consider additional nominations with equal or more suitable qualifications for the post. Recommendations to the President shall be public and substantiated.

51. The consultative group should take into account, as appropriate, the views of stakeholders, including the current or outgoing mandate-holders, in determining the necessary expertise, experience, skills, and other relevant requirements for each mandate.

52. On the basis of the recommendations of the consultative group and following broad consultations, in particular through the regional coordinators, the President of the Council will identify an appropriate candidate for each vacancy. The President will present to member States and observers a list of candidates to be proposed at least two weeks prior to the beginning of the session in which the Council will consider the appointments.

53. If necessary, the President will conduct further consultations to ensure the endorsement of the proposed candidates. The appointment of the special procedures mandate-holders will be completed upon the subsequent approval of the Council. Mandate-holders shall be appointed before the end of the session.

B Review, rationalization and improvement of mandates

54. The review, rationalization and improvement of mandates, as well as the creation of new ones, must be guided by the principles of universality, impartiality, objectivity and non-selectivity, constructive international dialogue and cooperation, with a view to enhancing the promotion and protection of all human rights, civil, political, economic, social and cultural rights, including the right to development.

55. The review, rationalization and improvement of each mandate would take place in the context of the negotiations of the relevant resolutions. An assessment of the mandate may take place in a separate segment of the interactive dialogue between the Council and special procedures mandate-holders.

56. The review, rationalization and improvement of mandates would focus on the relevance, scope and contents of the mandates, having as a framework the internationally recognized human rights standards, the system of special procedures and General Assembly resolution 60/251.

57. Any decision to streamline, merge or possibly discontinue mandates should always be guided by the need for improvement of the enjoyment and protection of human rights.

58. The Council should always strive for improvements:

    (a) Mandates should always offer a clear prospect of an increased level of human rights protection and promotion as well as being coherent within the system of human rights;

    (b) Equal attention should be paid to all human rights. The balance of thematic mandates should broadly reflect the accepted equal importance of civil, political, economic, social and cultural rights, including the right to development;

    (c) Every effort should be made to avoid unnecessary duplication;

    (d) Areas which constitute thematic gaps will be identified and addressed, including by means other than the creation of special procedures mandates, such as by expanding an existing mandate, bringing a cross-cutting issue to the attention of mandate-holders or by requesting a joint action to the relevant mandate-holders;

    (e) Any consideration of merging mandates should have regard to the content and predominant functions of each mandate, as well as to the workload of individual mandate-holders;

    (f) In creating or reviewing mandates, efforts should be made to identify whether the structure of the mechanism (expert, rapporteur or working group) is the most effective in terms of increasing human rights protection;

    (g) New mandates should be as clear and specific as possible, so as to avoid ambiguity.

59. It should be considered desirable to have a uniform nomenclature of mandate-holders, titles of mandates as well as a selection and appointment process, to make the whole system more understandable.

60. Thematic mandate periods will be of three years. Country mandate periods will be of one year.

61. Mandates included in Appendix I, where applicable, will be renewed until the date on which they are considered by the Council according to the programme of work.[d]

---

[d] Country mandates meet the following criteria:
- There is a pending mandate of the Council to be accomplished; or
- There is a pending mandate of the General Assembly to be accomplished; or
- The nature of the mandate is for advisory services and technical assistance.

62. Current mandate-holders may continue serving, provided they have not exceeded the six-year term limit (Appendix II). On an exceptional basis, the term of those mandate-holders who have served more than six years may be extended until the relevant mandate is considered by the Council and the selection and appointment process has concluded.

63. Decisions to create, review or discontinue country mandates should also take into account the principles of cooperation and genuine dialogue aimed at strengthening the capacity of Member States to comply with their human rights obligations.

64. In case of situations of violations of human rights or a lack of cooperation that require the Council's attention, the principles of objectivity, non-selectivity, and the elimination of double standards and politicization should apply.

III Human Rights Council Advisory Committee

65. The Human Rights Council Advisory Committee (hereinafter 'the Advisory Committee'), composed of 18 experts serving in their personal capacity, will function as a think-tank for the Council and work at its direction. The establishment of this subsidiary body and its functioning will be executed according to the guidelines stipulated below.

A Nomination

66. All Member States of the United Nations may propose or endorse candidates from their own region. When selecting their candidates, States should consult their national human rights institutions and civil society organizations and, in this regard, include the names of those supporting their candidates.

67. The aim is to ensure that the best possible expertise is made available to the Council. For this purpose, technical and objective requirements for the submission of candidatures will be established and approved by the Council at its sixth session (first session of the second cycle). These should include:

    (a) Recognized competence and experience in the field of human rights;

    (b) High moral standing;

    (c) Independence and impartiality.

68. Individuals holding decision-making positions in Government or in any other organization or entity which might give rise to a conflict of interest with the responsibilities inherent in the mandate shall be excluded. Elected members of the Committee will act in their personal capacity.

69. The principle of non-accumulation of human rights functions at the same time shall be respected.

B Election

70. The Council shall elect the members of the Advisory Committee, in secret ballot, from the list of candidates whose names have been presented in accordance with the agreed requirements.

71. The list of candidates shall be closed two months prior to the election date. The Secretariat will make available the list of candidates and relevant information to member States and to the public at least one month prior to their election.

72. Due consideration should be given to gender balance and appropriate representation of different civilizations and legal systems.

73. The geographic distribution will be as follows:

    African States: 5

    Asian States: 5

    Eastern European States: 2

    Latin American and Caribbean States: 3

    Western European and other States: 3

74. The members of the Advisory Committee shall serve for a period of three years. They shall be eligible for re-election once. In the first term, one third of the experts will serve for one year and another third for two years. The staggering of terms of membership will be defined by the drawing of lots.

C Functions

75. The function of the Advisory Committee is to provide expertise to the Council in the manner and form requested by the Council, focusing mainly on studies and research-based advice. Further, such expertise shall be rendered only upon the latter's request, in compliance with its resolutions and under its guidance.

76. The Advisory Committee should be implementation-oriented and the scope of its advice should be limited to thematic issues pertaining to the mandate of the Council; namely promotion and protection of all human rights.

77. The Advisory Committee shall not adopt resolutions or decisions. The Advisory Committee may propose within the scope of the work set out by the Council, for the latter's consideration and approval, suggestions for further enhancing its procedural efficiency, as well as further research proposals within the scope of the work set out by the Council.

78. The Council shall issue specific guidelines for the Advisory Committee when it requests a substantive contribution from the latter and shall review all or any portion of those guidelines if it deems necessary in the future.

D Methods of work

79. The Advisory Committee shall convene up to two sessions for a maximum of 10 working days per year. Additional sessions may be scheduled on an ad hoc basis with prior approval of the Council.

80. The Council may request the Advisory Committee to undertake certain tasks that could be performed collectively, through a smaller team or individually. The Advisory Committee will report on such efforts to the Council.

81. Members of the Advisory Committee are encouraged to communicate between sessions, individually or in teams. However, the Advisory Committee shall not establish subsidiary bodies unless the Council authorizes it to do so.

82. In the performance of its mandate, the Advisory Committee is urged to establish interaction with States, national human rights institutions, non-governmental organizations and other civil society entities in accordance with the modalities of the Council.

83. Member States and observers, including States that are not members of the Council, the specialized agencies, other intergovernmental organizations and national human rights institutions, as well as non-governmental organizations shall be entitled to participate in the work of the Advisory Committee based on arrangements, including Economic and Social Council resolution 1996/31 and practices observed by the Commission on Human Rights and the Council, while ensuring the most effective contribution of these entities.

84. The Council will decide at its sixth session (first session of its second cycle) on the most appropriate mechanisms to continue the work of the Working Groups on Indigenous Populations; Contemporary Forms of Slavery; Minorities; and the Social Forum.

IV Complaint Procedure

A Objective and scope

85. A complaint procedure is being established to address consistent patterns of gross and reliably attested violations of all human rights and all fundamental freedoms occurring in any part of the world and under any circumstances.

86. Economic and Social Council resolution 1503 (XLVIII) of 27 May 1970 as revised by resolution 2000/3 of 19 June 2000 served as a working basis and was improved where necessary, so as to

ensure that the complaint procedure is impartial, objective, efficient, victims-oriented and conducted in a timely manner. The procedure will retain its confidential nature, with a view to enhancing cooperation with the State concerned.

B Admissibility criteria for communications

87. A communication related to a violation of human rights and fundamental freedoms, for the purpose of this procedure, shall be admissible, provided that:

(a) It is not manifestly politically motivated and its object is consistent with the Charter of the United Nations, the Universal Declaration of Human Rights and other applicable instruments in the field of human rights law;

(b) It gives a factual description of the alleged violations, including the rights which are alleged to be violated;

(c) Its language is not abusive. However, such a communication may be considered if it meets the other criteria for admissibility after deletion of the abusive language;

(d) It is submitted by a person or a group of persons claiming to be the victims of violations of human rights and fundamental freedoms, or by any person or group of persons, including non-governmental organizations, acting in good faith in accordance with the principles of human rights, not resorting to politically motivated stands contrary to the provisions of the Charter of the United Nations and claiming to have direct and reliable knowledge of the violations concerned. Nonetheless, reliably attested communications shall not be inadmissible solely because the knowledge of the individual authors is second-hand, provided that they are accompanied by clear evidence;

(e) It is not exclusively based on reports disseminated by mass media;

(f) It does not refer to a case that appears to reveal a consistent pattern of gross and reliably attested violations of human rights already being dealt with by a special procedure, a treaty body or other United Nations or similar regional complaints procedure in the field of human rights;

(g) Domestic remedies have been exhausted, unless it appears that such remedies would be ineffective or unreasonably prolonged.

88. National human rights institutions, established and operating under the Principles Relating to the Status of National Institutions (the Paris Principles), in particular in regard to quasi-judicial competence, may serve as effective means of addressing individual human rights violations.

C Working groups

89. Two distinct working groups shall be established with the mandate to examine the communications and to bring to the attention of the Council consistent patterns of gross and reliably attested violations of human rights and fundamental freedoms.

90. Both working groups shall, to the greatest possible extent, work on the basis of consensus. In the absence of consensus, decisions shall be taken by simple majority of the votes. They may establish their own rules of procedure.

1 Working Group on Communications: composition, mandate and powers

91. The Human Rights Council Advisory Committee shall appoint five of its members, one from each Regional Group, with due consideration to gender balance, to constitute the Working Group on Communications.

92. In case of a vacancy, the Advisory Committee shall appoint an independent and highly qualified expert of the same Regional Group from the Advisory Committee.

93. Since there is a need for independent expertise and continuity with regard to the examination and assessment of communications received, the independent and highly qualified experts of the Working Group on Communications shall be appointed for three years. Their mandate is renewable only once.

94. The Chairperson of the Working Group on Communications is requested, together with the secretariat, to undertake an initial screening of communications received, based on the admissibility

criteria, before transmitting them to the States concerned. Manifestly ill-founded or anonymous communications shall be screened out by the Chairperson and shall therefore not be transmitted to the State concerned. In a perspective of accountability and transparency, the Chairperson of the Working Group on Communications shall provide all its members with a list of all communications rejected after initial screening. This list should indicate the grounds of all decisions resulting in the rejection of a communication. All other communications, which have not been screened out, shall be transmitted to the State concerned, so as to obtain the views of the latter on the allegations of violations.

95. The members of the Working Group on Communications shall decide on the admissibility of a communication and assess the merits of the allegations of violations, including whether the communication alone or in combination with other communications appear to reveal a consistent pattern of gross and reliably attested violations of human rights and fundamental freedoms. The Working Group on Communications shall provide the Working Group on Situations with a file containing all admissible communications as well as recommendations thereon. When the Working Group on Communications requires further consideration or additional information, it may keep a case under review until its next session and request such information from the State concerned. The Working Group on Communications may decide to dismiss a case. All decisions of the Working Group on Communications shall be based on a rigorous application of the admissibility criteria and duly justified.

2 Working Group on Situations: composition, mandate and powers

96. Each Regional Group shall appoint a representative of a member State of the Council, with due consideration to gender balance, to serve on the Working Group on Situations. Members shall be appointed for one year. Their mandate may be renewed once, if the State concerned is a member of the Council.

97. Members of the Working Group on Situations shall serve in their personal capacity. In order to fill a vacancy, the respective Regional Group to which the vacancy belongs, shall appoint a representative from member States of the same Regional Group.

98. The Working Group on Situations is requested, on the basis of the information and recommendations provided by the Working Group on Communications, to present the Council with a report on consistent patterns of gross and reliably attested violations of human rights and fundamental freedoms and to make recommendations to the Council on the course of action to take, normally in the form of a draft resolution or decision with respect to the situations referred to it. When the Working Group on Situations requires further consideration or additional information, its members may keep a case under review until its next session. The Working Group on Situations may also decide to dismiss a case.

99. All decisions of the Working Group on Situations shall be duly justified and indicate why the consideration of a situation has been discontinued or action recommended thereon. Decisions to discontinue should be taken by consensus; if that is not possible, by simple majority of the votes.

D Working modalities and confidentiality

100. Since the complaint procedure is to be, *inter alia*, victims-oriented and conducted in a confidential and timely manner, both Working Groups shall meet at least twice a year for five working days each session, in order to promptly examine the communications received, including replies of States thereon, and the situations of which the Council is already seized under the complaint procedure.

101. The State concerned shall cooperate with the complaint procedure and make every effort to provide substantive replies in one of the United Nations official languages to any of the requests of the Working Groups or the Council. The State concerned shall also make every effort to provide a reply not later than three months after the request has been made. If necessary, this deadline may however be extended at the request of the State concerned.

102. The Secretariat is requested to make the confidential files available to all members of the Council, at least two weeks in advance, so as to allow sufficient time for the consideration of the files.

103. The Council shall consider consistent patterns of gross and reliably attested violations of human rights and fundamental freedoms brought to its attention by the Working Group on Situations as frequently as needed, but at least once a year.

104. The reports of the Working Group on Situations referred to the Council shall be examined in a confidential manner, unless the Council decides otherwise. When the Working Group on Situations recommends to the Council that it consider a situation in a public meeting, in particular in the case of manifest and unequivocal lack of cooperation, the Council shall consider such recommendation on a priority basis at its next session.

105. So as to ensure that the complaint procedure is victims-oriented, efficient and conducted in a timely manner, the period of time between the transmission of the complaint to the State concerned and consideration by the Council shall not, in principle, exceed 24 months.

E Involvement of the complainant and of the State concerned

106. The complaint procedure shall ensure that both the author of a communication and the State concerned are informed of the proceedings at the following key stages:

 (a) When a communication is deemed inadmissible by the Working Group on Communications or when it is taken up for consideration by the Working Group on Situations; or when a communication is kept pending by one of the Working Groups or by the Council;
 (b) At the final outcome.

107. In addition, the complainant shall be informed when his/her communication is registered by the complaint procedure.

108. Should the complainant request that his/her identity be kept confidential, it will not be transmitted to the State concerned.

F Measures

109. In accordance with established practice the action taken in respect of a particular situation should be one of the following options:

 (a) To discontinue considering the situation when further consideration or action is not warranted;
 (b) To keep the situation under review and request the State concerned to provide further information within a reasonable period of time;
 (c) To keep the situation under review and appoint an independent and highly qualified expert to monitor the situation and report back to the Council;
 (d) To discontinue reviewing the matter under the confidential complaint procedure in order to take up public consideration of the same;
 (e) To recommend to OHCHR to provide technical cooperation, capacity-building assistance or advisory services to the State concerned.

V Agenda and Framework for the Programme of Work

A Principles

Universality
Impartiality
Objectivity
Non-selectiveness
Constructive dialogue and cooperation
Predictability
Flexibility
Transparency
Accountability
Balance

Inclusive/comprehensive

Gender perspective

Implementation and follow-up of decisions

B Agenda

Item 1.   Organizational and procedural matters

Item 2.   Annual report of the United Nations High Commissioner for Human Rights and reports of the Office of the High Commissioner and the Secretary-General

Item 3.   Promotion and protection of all human rights, civil, political, economic, social and cultural rights, including the right to development

Item 4.   Human rights situations that require the Council's attention

Item 5.   Human rights bodies and mechanisms

Item 6.   Universal Periodic Review

Item 7.   Human rights situation in Palestine and other occupied Arab territories

Item 8.   Follow-up and implementation of the Vienna Declaration and Programme of Action

Item 9.   Racism, racial discrimination, xenophobia and related forms of intolerance, follow-up and implementation of the Durban Declaration and Programme of Action

Item 10. Technical assistance and capacity-building

C Framework for the programme of work

Item 1.   Organizational and procedural matters

Election of the Bureau

Adoption of the annual programme of work

Adoption of the programme of work of the session, including other business

Selection and appointment of mandate-holders

Election of members of the Human Rights Council Advisory Committee

Adoption of the report of the session

Adoption of the annual report

Item 2.   Annual report of the United Nations High Commissioner for Human Rights and reports of the Office of the High Commissioner and the Secretary-General

Presentation of the annual report and updates

Item 3.   Promotion and protection of all human rights, civil, political, economic, social and cultural rights, including the right to development

Economic, social and cultural rights

Civil and political rights

Rights of peoples, and specific groups and individuals

Right to development

Interrelation of human rights and human rights thematic issues

Item 4.   Human rights situations that require the Council's attention

Item 5.   Human rights bodies and mechanisms

Report of the Human Rights Council Advisory Committee

Report of the complaint procedure

Item 6.   Universal Periodic Review

Item 7.   Human rights situation in Palestine and other occupied Arab territories

Human rights violations and implications of the Israeli occupation of Palestine and other occupied Arab territories

Right to self-determination of the Palestinian people

Item 8.   Follow-up and implementation of the Vienna Declaration and Programme of Action

Item 9.   Racism, racial discrimination, xenophobia and related forms of intolerance, follow-up and implementation of the Durban Declaration and Programme of Action

Item 10. Technical assistance and capacity-building

VI Methods of Work

110. The methods of work, pursuant to General Assembly resolution 60/251 should be transparent, impartial, equitable, fair, pragmatic; lead to clarity, predictability, and inclusiveness. They may also be updated and adjusted over time.

A Institutional arrangements

1 Briefings on prospective resolutions or decisions

111. The briefings on prospective resolutions or decisions would be informative only, whereby delegations would be apprised of resolutions and/or decisions tabled or intended to be tabled. These briefings will be organized by interested delegations.

2 President's open-ended information meetings on resolutions, decisions and other related business

112. The President's open-ended information meetings on resolutions, decisions and other related business shall provide information on the status of negotiations on draft resolutions and/or decisions so that delegations may gain a bird's eye view of the status of such drafts. The consultations shall have a purely informational function, combined with information on the extranet, and be held in a transparent and inclusive manner. They shall not serve as a negotiating forum.

3 Informal consultations on proposals convened by main sponsors

113. Informal consultations shall be the primary means for the negotiation of draft resolutions and/or decisions, and their convening shall be the responsibility of the sponsor(s). At least one informal open-ended consultation should be held on each draft resolution and/or decision before it is considered for action by the Council. Consultations should, as much as possible, be scheduled in a timely, transparent and inclusive manner that takes into account the constraints faced by delegations, particularly smaller ones.

4 Role of the Bureau

114. The Bureau shall deal with procedural and organizational matters. The Bureau shall regularly communicate the contents of its meetings through a timely summary report.

5 Other work formats may include panel debates, seminars and round tables

115. Utilization of these other work formats, including topics and modalities, would be decided by the Council on a case-by-case basis. They may serve as tools of the Council for enhancing dialogue and mutual understanding on certain issues. They should be utilized in the context of the Council's agenda and annual programme of work, and reinforce and/or complement its intergovernmental nature. They shall not be used to substitute or replace existing human rights mechanisms and established methods of work.

6 High-Level Segment

116. The High-Level Segment shall be held once a year during the main session of the Council. It shall be followed by a general segment wherein delegations that did not participate in the High-Level Segment may deliver general statements.

B Working culture

117. There is a need for:
  (a) Early notification of proposals;
  (b) Early submission of draft resolutions and decisions, preferably by the end of the penultimate week of a session;
  (c) Early distribution of all reports, particularly those of special procedures, to be transmitted to delegations in a timely fashion, at least 15 days in advance of their consideration by the Council, and in all official United Nations languages;

(d) Proposers of a country resolution to have the responsibility to secure the broadest possible support for their initiatives (preferably 15 members), before action is taken;

(e) Restraint in resorting to resolutions, in order to avoid proliferation of resolutions without prejudice to the right of States to decide on the periodicity of presenting their draft proposals by:

(i) Minimizing unnecessary duplication of initiatives with the General Assembly/Third Committee;

(ii) Clustering of agenda items;

(iii) Staggering the tabling of decisions and/or resolutions and consideration of action on agenda items/issues.

C Outcomes other than resolutions and decisions

118. These may include recommendations, conclusions, summaries of discussions and President's Statement. As such outcomes would have different legal implications, they should supplement and not replace resolutions and decisions.

D Special sessions of the Council

119. The following provisions shall complement the general framework provided by General Assembly resolution 60/251 and the rules of procedure of the Human Rights Council.

120. The rules of procedure of special sessions shall be in accordance with the rules of procedure applicable for regular sessions of the Council.

121. The request for the holding of a special session, in accordance with the requirement established in paragraph 10 of General Assembly resolution 60/251, shall be submitted to the President and to the secretariat of the Council. The request shall specify the item proposed for consideration and include any other relevant information the sponsors may wish to provide.

122. The special session shall be convened as soon as possible after the formal request is communicated, but, in principle, not earlier than two working days, and not later than five working days after the formal receipt of the request. The duration of the special session shall not exceed three days (six working sessions), unless the Council decides otherwise.

123. The secretariat of the Council shall immediately communicate the request for the holding of a special session and any additional information provided by the sponsors in the request, as well as the date for the convening of the special session, to all United Nations Member States and make the information available to the specialized agencies, other intergovernmental organizations and national human rights institutions, as well as to non-governmental organizations in consultative status by the most expedient and expeditious means of communication. Special session documentation, in particular draft resolutions and decisions, should be made available in all official United Nations languages to all States in an equitable, timely and transparent manner.

124. The President of the Council should hold open-ended informative consultations before the special session on its conduct and organization. In this regard, the secretariat may also be requested to provide additional information, including, on the methods of work of previous special sessions.

125. Members of the Council, concerned States, observer States, specialized agencies, other intergovernmental organizations and national human rights institutions, as well as non-governmental organizations in consultative status may contribute to the special session in accordance with the rules of procedure of the Council.

126. If the requesting or other States intend to present draft resolutions or decisions at the special session, texts should be made available in accordance with the Council's relevant rules of procedure. Nevertheless, sponsors are urged to present such texts as early as possible.

127. The sponsors of a draft resolution or decision should hold open-ended consultations on the text of their draft resolution(s) or decision(s) with a view to achieving the widest participation in their consideration and, if possible, achieving consensus on them.

128. A special session should allow participatory debate, be results-oriented and geared to achieving practical outcomes, the implementation of which can be monitored and reported on at the following regular session of the Council for possible follow-up decision.

VII Rules of procedure[e]

SESSIONS

Rules of procedure

Rule 1

The Human Rights Council shall apply the rules of procedure established for the Main Committees of the General Assembly, as applicable, unless subsequently otherwise decided by the Assembly or the Council.

REGULAR SESSIONS

Number of sessions

Rule 2

The Human Rights Council shall meet regularly throughout the year and schedule no fewer than three sessions per Council year, including a main session, for a total duration of no less than 10 weeks.

Assumption of membership

Rule 3

Newly-elected member States of the Human Rights Council shall assume their membership on the first day of the Council year, replacing member States that have concluded their respective membership terms.

Place of meeting

Rule 4

The Human Rights Council shall be based in Geneva.

SPECIAL SESSIONS

Convening of special sessions

Rule 5

The rules of procedure of special sessions of the Human Rights Council will be the same as the rules of procedure applicable for regular sessions of the Human Rights Council.

Rule 6

The Human Rights Council shall hold special sessions, when needed, at the request of a member of the Council with the support of one third of the membership of the Council.

PARTICIPATION OF AND CONSULTATION WITH OBSERVERS OF THE COUNCIL

Rule 7

    (a) The Council shall apply the rules of procedure established for committees of the General Assembly, as applicable, unless subsequently otherwise decided by the Assembly or the Council, and the participation of and consultation with observers, including States that

---

[e] Figures indicated in square brackets refer to identical or corresponding rules of the General Assembly or its Main Committees (A/520/Rev.16).

are not members of the Council, the specialized agencies, other intergovernmental organizations and national human rights institutions, as well as non-governmental organizations, shall be based on arrangements, including Economic and Social Council resolution 1996/31 of 25 July 1996, and practices observed by the Commission on Human Rights, while ensuring the most effective contribution of these entities.

(b) Participation of national human rights institutions shall be based on arrangements and practices agreed upon by the Commission on Human Rights, including resolution 2005/74 of 20 April 2005, while ensuring the most effective contribution of these entities.

ORGANIZATION OF WORK AND AGENDA FOR REGULAR SESSIONS

Organizational meetings

Rule 8

(a) At the beginning of each Council year, the Council shall hold an organizational meeting to elect its Bureau and to consider and adopt the agenda, programme of work, and calendar of regular sessions for the Council year indicating, if possible, a target date for the conclusion of its work, the approximate dates of consideration of items and the number of meetings to be allocated to each item.

(b) The President of the Council shall also convene organizational meetings two weeks before the beginning of each session and, if necessary, during the Council sessions to discuss organizational and procedural issues pertinent to that session.

PRESIDENT AND VICE-PRESIDENTS

Elections

Rule 9

(a) At the beginning of each Council year, at its organizational meeting, the Council shall elect, from among the representatives of its members, a President and four Vice-Presidents. The President and the Vice-Presidents shall constitute the Bureau. One of the Vice-Presidents shall serve as Rapporteur.

(b) In the election of the President of the Council, regard shall be had for the equitable geographical rotation of this office among the following Regional Groups: African States, Asian States, Eastern European States, Latin American and Caribbean States, and Western European and other States. The four Vice-Presidents of the Council shall be elected on the basis of equitable geographical distribution from the Regional Groups other than the one to which the President belongs. The selection of the Rapporteur shall be based on geographic rotation.

Bureau

Rule 10

The Bureau shall deal with procedural and organizational matters.

Term of office

Rule 11

The President and the Vice-Presidents shall, subject to rule 13, hold office for a period of one year. They shall not be eligible for immediate re-election to the same post.

Absence of officers

Rule 12 [105]

If the President finds it necessary to be absent during a meeting or any part thereof, he/she shall designate one of the Vice-Presidents to take his/her place. A Vice-President acting as President shall have the same powers and duties as the President. If the President ceases to hold office pursuant to rule 13, the remaining members of the Bureau shall designate one of the Vice-Presidents to take his/her place until the election of a new President.

Replacement of the President or a Vice-President

Rule 13

If the President or any Vice-President ceases to be able to carry out his/her functions or ceases to be a representative of a member of the Council, or if the Member of the United Nations of which he/she is a representative ceases to be a member of the Council, he/she shall cease to hold such office and a new President or Vice-President shall be elected for the unexpired term.

SECRETARIAT

Duties of the secretariat

Rule 14 [47]

The Office of the United Nations High Commissioner for Human Rights shall act as secretariat for the Council. In this regard, it shall receive, translate, print and circulate in all official United Nations languages, documents, reports and resolutions of the Council, its committees and its organs; interpret speeches made at the meetings; prepare, print and circulate the records of the session; have the custody and proper preservation of the documents in the archives of the Council; distribute all documents of the Council to the members of the Council and observers and, generally, perform all other support functions which the Council may require.

RECORDS AND REPORT

Report to the General Assembly

Rule 15

The Council shall submit an annual report to the General Assembly.

PUBLIC AND PRIVATE MEETINGS OF THE HUMAN RIGHTS COUNCIL

General principles

Rule 16 [60]

The meetings of the Council shall be held in public unless the Council decides that exceptional circumstances require the meeting be held in private.

Private meetings

Rule 17 [61]

All decisions of the Council taken at a private meeting shall be announced at an early public meeting of the Council.

CONDUCT OF BUSINESS

Working groups and other arrangements

Rule 18

The Council may set up working groups and other arrangements. Participation in these bodies shall be decided upon by the members, based on rule 7. The rules of procedure of these bodies shall follow those of the Council, as applicable, unless decided otherwise by the Council.

Quorum

Rule 19 [67]

The President may declare a meeting open and permit the debate to proceed when at least one third of the members of the Council are present. The presence of a majority of the members shall be required for any decision to be taken.

Majority required

Rule 20 [125]

Decisions of the Council shall be made by a simple majority of the members present and voting, subject to rule 19.

Part III

Regional Instruments

A. EUROPE

Convention for the Protection of Human Rights and Fundamental Freedoms (1950), as amended by Protocols No. 11, 14 and 15*[1]

The governments signatory hereto, being members of the Council of Europe,

Considering the Universal Declaration of Human Rights proclaimed by the General Assembly of the United Nations on 10th December 1948;

Considering that this Declaration aims at securing the universal and effective recognition and observance of the Rights therein declared;

Considering that the aim of the Council of Europe is the achievement of greater unity between its members and that one of the methods by which that aim is to be pursued is the maintenance and further realisation of human rights and fundamental freedoms;

Reaffirming their profound belief in those fundamental freedoms which are the foundation of justice and peace in the world and are best maintained on the one hand by an effective political democracy and on the other by a common understanding and observance of the human rights upon which they depend;

Being resolved, as the governments of European countries which are like-minded and have a common heritage of political traditions, ideals, freedom and the rule of law, to take the first steps for the collective enforcement of certain of the rights stated in the Universal Declaration,

Affirming that the High Contracting Parties, in accordance with the principle of subsidiarity, have the primary responsibility to secure the rights and freedoms defined in this Convention and the Protocols thereto, and that in doing so they enjoy a margin of appreciation, subject to the supervisory jurisdiction of the European Court of Human Rights established by this Convention,

Have agreed as follows:

Article 1   Obligation to respect human rights

The High Contracting Parties shall secure to everyone within their jurisdiction the rights and freedoms defined in Section I of this Convention.

---

[1] Text amended by the provisions of Protocol No. 15 (CETS No. 213) as from the date of its entry into force on 1 August 2021 and of Protocol No. 14 (CETS No. 194) as from the date of its entry into force on 1 June 2010. The text of the Convention had been previously amended according to the provisions of Protocol No. 3 (ETS No. 45), which entered into force on 21 September 1970, of Protocol No. 5 (ETS No. 55), which entered into force on 20 December 1971 and of Protocol No. 8 (ETS No. 118), which entered into force on 1 January 1990, and comprised also the text of Protocol No. 2 (ETS No. 44) which, in accordance with Article 5, paragraph 3 thereof, had been an integral part of the Convention since its entry into force on 21 September 1970. All provisions which had been amended or added by these Protocols were replaced by Protocol No. 11 (ETS No. 155), as from the date of its entry into force on 1 November 1998. As from that date, Protocol No. 9 (ETS No. 140), which entered into force on 1 October 1994, was repealed and Protocol No. 10 (ETS No. 146) had lost its purpose.

Section I   Rights and freedoms

Article 2   Right to life

1. Everyone's right to life shall be protected by law. No one shall be deprived of his life intentionally save in the execution of a sentence of a court following his conviction of a crime for which this penalty is provided by law.

2. Deprivation of life shall not be regarded as inflicted in contravention of this article when it results from the use of force which is no more than absolutely necessary:

    (a) in defence of any person from unlawful violence;

    (b) in order to effect a lawful arrest or to prevent the escape of a person lawfully detained;

    (c) in action lawfully taken for the purpose of quelling a riot or insurrection.

Article 3   Prohibition of torture

No one shall be subjected to torture or to inhuman or degrading treatment or punishment.

Article 4   Prohibition of slavery and forced labour

1. No one shall be held in slavery or servitude.

2. No one shall be required to perform forced or compulsory labour.

3. For the purpose of this article the term 'forced or compulsory labour' shall not include:

    (a) any work required to be done in the ordinary course of detention imposed according to the provisions of Article 5 of this Convention or during conditional release from such detention;

    (b) any service of a military character or, in case of conscientious objectors in countries where they are recognised, service exacted instead of compulsory military service;

    (c) any service exacted in case of an emergency or calamity threatening the life or well-being of the community;

    (d) any work or service which forms part of normal civic obligations.

Article 5   Right to liberty and security

1. Everyone has the right to liberty and security of person. No one shall be deprived of his liberty save in the following cases and in accordance with a procedure prescribed by law:

    (a) the lawful detention of a person after conviction by a competent court;

    (b) the lawful arrest or detention of a person for non-compliance with the lawful order of a court or in order to secure the fulfilment of any obligation prescribed by law;

    (c) the lawful arrest or detention of a person effected for the purpose of bringing him before the competent legal authority on reasonable suspicion of having committed an offence or when it is reasonably considered necessary to prevent his committing an offence or fleeing after having done so;

    (d) the detention of a minor by lawful order for the purpose of educational supervision or his lawful detention for the purpose of bringing him before the competent legal authority;

    (e) the lawful detention of persons for the prevention of the spreading of infectious diseases, of persons of unsound mind, alcoholics or drug addicts or vagrants;

    (f) the lawful arrest or detention of a person to prevent his effecting an unauthorised entry into the country or of a person against whom action is being taken with a view to deportation or extradition.

2. Everyone who is arrested shall be informed promptly, in a language which he understands, of the reasons for his arrest and of any charge against him.

3. Everyone arrested or detained in accordance with the provisions of paragraph 1.c of this article shall be brought promptly before a judge or other officer authorised by law to exercise judicial power and shall be entitled to trial within a reasonable time or to release pending trial. Release may be conditioned by guarantees to appear for trial.

4. Everyone who is deprived of his liberty by arrest or detention shall be entitled to take proceedings by which the lawfulness of his detention shall be decided speedily by a court and his release ordered if the detention is not lawful.

5. Everyone who has been the victim of arrest or detention in contravention of the provisions of this article shall have an enforceable right to compensation.

Article 6   Right to a fair trial

1. In the determination of his civil rights and obligations or of any criminal charge against him, everyone is entitled to a fair and public hearing within a reasonable time by an independent and impartial tribunal established by law. Judgment shall be pronounced publicly but the press and public may be excluded from all or part of the trial in the interests of morals, public order or national security in a democratic society, where the interests of juveniles or the protection of the private life of the parties so require, or to the extent strictly necessary in the opinion of the court in special circumstances where publicity would prejudice the interests of justice.

2. Everyone charged with a criminal offence shall be presumed innocent until proved guilty according to law.

3. Everyone charged with a criminal offence has the following minimum rights:

    (a) to be informed promptly, in a language which he understands and in detail, of the nature and cause of the accusation against him;

    (b) to have adequate time and facilities for the preparation of his defence;

    (c) to defend himself in person or through legal assistance of his own choosing or, if he has not sufficient means to pay for legal assistance, to be given it free when the interests of justice so require;

    (d) to examine or have examined witnesses against him and to obtain the attendance and examination of witnesses on his behalf under the same conditions as witnesses against him;

    (e) to have the free assistance of an interpreter if he cannot understand or speak the language used in court.

Article 7   No punishment without law

1. No one shall be held guilty of any criminal offence on account of any act or omission which did not constitute a criminal offence under national or international law at the time when it was committed. Nor shall a heavier penalty be imposed than the one that was applicable at the time the criminal offence was committed.

2. This article shall not prejudice the trial and punishment of any person for any act or omission which, at the time when it was committed, was criminal according to the general principles of law recognised by civilised nations.

Article 8   Right to respect for private and family life

1. Everyone has the right to respect for his private and family life, his home and his correspondence.

2. There shall be no interference by a public authority with the exercise of this right except such as is in accordance with the law and is necessary in a democratic society in the interests of national security, public safety or the economic well-being of the country, for the prevention of disorder or crime, for the protection of health or morals, or for the protection of the rights and freedoms of others.

Article 9   Freedom of thought, conscience and religion

1. Everyone has the right to freedom of thought, conscience and religion; this right includes freedom to change his religion or belief and freedom, either alone or in community with others and in public or private, to manifest his religion or belief, in worship, teaching, practice and observance.

2. Freedom to manifest one's religion or beliefs shall be subject only to such limitations as are prescribed by law and are necessary in a democratic society in the interests of public safety, for the protection of public order, health or morals, or for the protection of the rights and freedoms of others.

Article 10   Freedom of expression

1. Everyone has the right to freedom of expression. This right shall include freedom to hold opinions and to receive and impart information and ideas without interference by public authority and regardless of frontiers. This article shall not prevent States from requiring the licensing of broadcasting, television or cinema enterprises.

2. The exercise of these freedoms, since it carries with it duties and responsibilities, may be subject to such formalities, conditions, restrictions or penalties as are prescribed by law and are necessary in a democratic society, in the interests of national security, territorial integrity or public safety, for the prevention of disorder or crime, for the protection of health or morals, for the protection of the

reputation or rights of others, for preventing the disclosure of information received in confidence, or for maintaining the authority and impartiality of the judiciary.

Article 11   Freedom of assembly and association

1. Everyone has the right to freedom of peaceful assembly and to freedom of association with others, including the right to form and to join trade unions for the protection of his interests.

2. No restrictions shall be placed on the exercise of these rights other than such as are prescribed by law and are necessary in a democratic society in the interests of national security or public safety, for the prevention of disorder or crime, for the protection of health or morals or for the protection of the rights and freedoms of others. This article shall not prevent the imposition of lawful restrictions on the exercise of these rights by members of the armed forces, of the police or of the administration of the State.

Article 12   Right to marry

Men and women of marriageable age have the right to marry and to found a family, according to the national laws governing the exercise of this right.

Article 13   Right to an effective remedy

Everyone whose rights and freedoms as set forth in this Convention are violated shall have an effective remedy before a national authority notwithstanding that the violation has been committed by persons acting in an official capacity.

Article 14   Prohibition of discrimination

The enjoyment of the rights and freedoms set forth in this Convention shall be secured without discrimination on any ground such as sex, race, colour, language, religion, political or other opinion, national or social origin, association with a national minority, property, birth or other status.

Article 15   Derogation in time of emergency

1. In time of war or other public emergency threatening the life of the nation any High Contracting Party may take measures derogating from its obligations under this Convention to the extent strictly required by the exigencies of the situation, provided that such measures are not inconsistent with its other obligations under international law.

2. No derogation from Article 2, except in respect of deaths resulting from lawful acts of war, or from Articles 3, 4 (paragraph 1) and 7 shall be made under this provision.

3. Any High Contracting Party availing itself of this right of derogation shall keep the Secretary General of the Council of Europe fully informed of the measures which it has taken and the reasons therefor. It shall also inform the Secretary General of the Council of Europe when such measures have ceased to operate and the provisions of the Convention are again being fully executed.

Article 16   Restrictions on political activity of aliens

Nothing in Articles 10, 11 and 14 shall be regarded as preventing the High Contracting Parties from imposing restrictions on the political activity of aliens.

Article 17   Prohibition of abuse of rights

Nothing in this Convention may be interpreted as implying for any State, group or person any right to engage in any activity or perform any act aimed at the destruction of any of the rights and freedoms set forth herein or at their limitation to a greater extent than is provided for in the Convention.

Article 18   Limitation on use of restrictions on rights

The restrictions permitted under this Convention to the said rights and freedoms shall not be applied for any purpose other than those for which they have been prescribed.

Section II   European Court of Human Rights

Article 19   Establishment of the Court

To ensure the observance of the engagements undertaken by the High Contracting Parties in the Convention and the Protocols thereto, there shall be set up a European Court of Human Rights, hereinafter referred to as 'the Court'. It shall function on a permanent basis.

Article 20 Number of judges

The Court shall consist of a number of judges equal to that of the High Contracting Parties.

Article 21 Criteria for office*

1. The judges shall be of high moral character and must either possess the qualifications required for appointment to high judicial office or be jurisconsults of recognised competence.

2. Candidates shall be less than 65 years of age at the date by which the list of three candidates has been requested by the Parliamentary Assembly, further to Article 22.

3. The judges shall sit on the Court in their individual capacity.

4. During their term of office the judges shall not engage in any activity which is incompatible with their independence, impartiality or with the demands of a full-time office; all questions arising from the application of this paragraph shall be decided by the Court.

Article 22 Election of judges**

The judges shall be elected by the Parliamentary Assembly with respect to each High Contracting Party by a majority of votes cast from a list of three candidates nominated by the High Contracting Party.

Article 23 Terms of office and dismissal***

1. The judges shall be elected for a period of nine years. They may not be re-elected.

2. The judges shall hold office until replaced. They shall, however, continue to deal with such cases as they already have under consideration.

3. No judge may be dismissed from office unless the other judges decide by a majority of two-thirds that that judge has ceased to fulfil the required conditions.

Article 24 Registry and rapporteurs****

1. The Court shall have a registry, the functions and organisation of which shall be laid down in the rules of the Court.

2. When sitting in a single-judge formation, the Court shall be assisted by rapporteurs who shall function under the authority of the President of the Court. They shall form part of the Court's registry.

Article 25 Plenary Court*****

The plenary Court shall

(a) elect its President and one or two Vice-Presidents for a period of three years; they may be re-elected;

(b) set up Chambers, constituted for a fixed period of time;

(c) elect the Presidents of the Chambers of the Court; they may be re-elected;

(d) adopt the rules of the Court;

(e) elect the Registrar and one or more Deputy Registrars;

(f) make any request under Article 26, paragraph 2.

Article 26 Single-judge formation, committees, Chambers and Grand Chamber******

1. To consider cases brought before it, the Court shall sit in a single-judge formation, in committees of three judges, in Chambers of seven judges and in a Grand Chamber of seventeen judges. The Court's Chambers shall set up committees for a fixed period of time.

2. At the request of the plenary Court, the Committee of Ministers may, by a unanimous decision and for a fixed period, reduce to five the number of judges of the Chambers.

3. When sitting as a single judge, a judge shall not examine any application against the High Contracting Party in respect of which that judge has been elected.

---

* **Editor's Note:** Text amended according to the provisions of Protocol No. 15 (CETS No. 213).

** **Editor's Note:** Text amended according to the provisions of Protocol No. 14 (CETS No. 194).

*** **Editor's Note:** Article renumbered, heading and text amended according to the provisions of Protocol No. 14 (CETS No. 194) and Protocol No. 15 (CETS No. 213).

**** **Editor's Note:** Text amended according to the provisions of Protocol No. 14 (CETS No. 194).

***** **Editor's Note:** Article renumbered, heading and text amended according to the provisions of Protocol No. 14 (CETS No. 194).

****** **Editor's Note:** Article renumbered, heading and text amended according to the provisions of Protocol No. 14 (CETS No. 194).

4. There shall sit as an *ex officio* member of the Chamber and the Grand Chamber the judge elected in respect of the High Contracting Party concerned. If there is none or if that judge is unable to sit, a person chosen by the President of the Court from a list submitted in advance by that Party shall sit in the capacity of judge.

5. The Grand Chamber shall also include the President of the Court, the Vice-Presidents, the Presidents of the Chambers and other judges chosen in accordance with the rules of the Court. When a case is referred to the Grand Chamber under Article 43, no judge from the Chamber which rendered the judgment shall sit in the Grand Chamber, with the exception of the President of the Chamber and the judge who sat in respect of the High Contracting Party concerned.

Article 27   Competence of single judges*

1. A single judge may declare inadmissible or strike out of the Court's list of cases an application submitted under Article 34, where such a decision can be taken without further examination.

2. The decision shall be final.

3. If the single judge does not declare an application inadmissible or strike it out, that judge shall forward it to a committee or to a Chamber for further examination.

Article 28   Competence of committees**

1. In respect of an application submitted under Article 34, a committee may, by a unanimous vote,

    (a) declare it inadmissible or strike it out of its list of cases, where such decision can be taken without further examination; or

    (b) declare it admissible and render at the same time a judgment on the merits, if the underlying question in the case, concerning the interpretation or the application of the Convention or the Protocols thereto, is already the subject of well-established case-law of the Court.

2. Decisions and judgments under paragraph 1 shall be final.

3. If the judge elected in respect of the High Contracting Party concerned is not a member of the committee, the committee may at any stage of the proceedings invite that judge to take the place of one of the members of the committee, having regard to all relevant factors, including whether that Party has contested the application of the procedure under paragraph 1.b.

Article 29   Decisions by Chambers on admissibility and merits***

1. If no decision is taken under Article 27 or 28, or no judgment rendered under Article 28, a Chamber shall decide on the admissibility and merits of individual applications submitted under Article 34. The decision on admissibility may be taken separately.

2. A Chamber shall decide on the admissibility and merits of inter-State applications submitted under Article 33. The decision on admissibility shall be taken separately unless the Court, in exceptional cases, decides otherwise.

Article 30   Relinquishment of jurisdiction to the Grand Chamber****

Where a case pending before a Chamber raises a serious question affecting the interpretation of the Convention or the protocols thereto, or where the resolution of a question before the Chamber might have a result inconsistent with a judgment previously delivered by the Court, the Chamber may, at any time before it has rendered its judgment, relinquish jurisdiction in favour of the Grand Chamber.

Article 31   Powers of the Grand Chamber*****

The Grand Chamber shall

---

* **Editor's Note:** New article according to the provisions of Protocol No. 14 (CETS No. 194).

** **Editor's Note:** Heading and text amended according to the provisions of Protocol No. 14 (CETS No. 194).

*** **Editor's Note:** Text amended according to the provisions of Protocol No. 14 (CETS No. 194).

**** **Editor's Note:** Text amended according to the provisions of Protocol No. 15 (CETS No. 213).

***** **Editor's Note:** Text amended according to the provisions of Protocol No. 14 (CETS No. 194).

(a) determine applications submitted either under Article 33 or Article 34 when a Chamber has relinquished jurisdiction under Article 30 or when the case has been referred to it under Article 43;

(b) decide on issues referred to the Court by the Committee of Ministers in accordance with Article 46, paragraph 4; and

(c) consider requests for advisory opinions submitted under Article 47.

Article 32   Jurisdiction of the Court*

1. The jurisdiction of the Court shall extend to all matters concerning the interpretation and application of the Convention and the protocols thereto which are referred to it as provided in Articles 33, 34, 46 and 47.

2. In the event of dispute as to whether the Court has jurisdiction, the Court shall decide.

Article 33   Inter-State cases

Any High Contracting Party may refer to the Court any alleged breach of the provisions of the Convention and the protocols thereto by another High Contracting Party.

Article 34   Individual applications

The Court may receive applications from any person, non-governmental organisation or group of individuals claiming to be the victim of a violation by one of the High Contracting Parties of the rights set forth in the Convention or the protocols thereto. The High Contracting Parties undertake not to hinder in any way the effective exercise of this right.

Article 35   Admissibility criteria**

1. The Court may only deal with the matter after all domestic remedies have been exhausted, according to the generally recognised rules of international law, and within a period of four months from the date on which the final decision was taken.

2. The Court shall not deal with any application submitted under Article 34 that

(a) is anonymous; or

(b) is substantially the same as a matter that has already been examined by the Court or has already been submitted to another procedure of international investigation or settlement and contains no relevant new information.

3. The Court shall declare inadmissible any individual application submitted under Article 34 if it considers that:

(a) the application is incompatible with the provisions of the Convention or the Protocols thereto, manifestly ill-founded, or an abuse of the right of individual application; or

(b) the applicant has not suffered a significant disadvantage, unless respect for human rights as defined in the Convention and the Protocols thereto requires an examination of the application on the merits and provided that no case may be rejected on this ground which has not been duly considered by a domestic tribunal.

4. The Court shall reject any application which it considers inadmissible under this Article. It may do so at any stage of the proceedings.

Article 36   Third party intervention***

1. In all cases before a Chamber or the Grand Chamber, a High Contracting Party one of whose nationals is an applicant shall have the right to submit written comments and to take part in hearings.

2. The President of the Court may, in the interest of the proper administration of justice, invite any High Contracting Party which is not a party to the proceedings or any person concerned who is not the applicant to submit written comments or take part in hearings.

* **Editor's Note:** Text amended according to the provisions of Protocol No. 14 (CETS No. 194).
** **Editor's Note:** Text amended according to the provisions of Protocol No. 14 (CETS No. 194) and Protocol No. 15 (CETS No. 213).
*** **Editor's Note:** Text amended according to the provisions of Protocol No. 14 (CETS No. 194).

3. In all cases before a Chamber or the Grand Chamber, the Council of Europe Commissioner for Human Rights may submit written comments and take part in hearings.

Article 37   Striking out applications

1. The Court may at any stage of the proceedings decide to strike an application out of its list of cases where the circumstances lead to the conclusion that
   (a) the applicant does not intend to pursue his application; or
   (b) the matter has been resolved; or
   (c) for any other reason established by the Court, it is no longer justified to continue the examination of the application.

However, the Court shall continue the examination of the application if respect for human rights as defined in the Convention and the protocols thereto so requires.

2. The Court may decide to restore an application to its list of cases if it considers that the circumstances justify such a course.

Article 38   Examination of the case*

The Court shall examine the case together with the representatives of the parties and, if need be, undertake an investigation, for the effective conduct of which the High Contracting Parties concerned shall furnish all necessary facilities.

Article 39   Friendly settlements**

1. At any stage of the proceedings, the Court may place itself at the disposal of the parties concerned with a view to securing a friendly settlement of the matter on the basis of respect for human rights as defined in the Convention and the Protocols thereto.

2. Proceedings conducted under paragraph 1 shall be confidential.

3. If a friendly settlement is effected, the Court shall strike the case out of its list by means of a decision which shall be confined to a brief statement of the facts and of the solution reached.

4. This decision shall be transmitted to the Committee of Ministers, which shall supervise the execution of the terms of the friendly settlement as set out in the decision.

Article 40   Public hearings and access to documents

1. Hearings shall be in public unless the Court in exceptional circumstances decides otherwise.

2. Documents deposited with the Registrar shall be accessible to the public unless the President of the Court decides otherwise.

Article 41   Just satisfaction

If the Court finds that there has been a violation of the Convention or the protocols thereto, and if the internal law of the High Contracting Party concerned allows only partial reparation to be made, the Court shall, if necessary, afford just satisfaction to the injured party.

Article 42   Judgments of Chambers

Judgments of Chambers shall become final in accordance with the provisions of Article 44, paragraph 2.

Article 43   Referral to the Grand Chamber

1. Within a period of three months from the date of the judgment of the Chamber, any party to the case may, in exceptional cases, request that the case be referred to the Grand Chamber.

2. A panel of five judges of the Grand Chamber shall accept the request if the case raises a serious question affecting the interpretation or application of the Convention or the protocols thereto, or a serious issue of general importance.

3. If the panel accepts the request, the Grand Chamber shall decide the case by means of a judgment.

---

* **Editor's Note:** Heading and text amended according to the provisions of Protocol No. 14 (CETS No. 194).
** **Editor's Note:** Heading and text amended according to the provisions of Protocol No. 14 (CETS No. 194).

Article 44   Final judgments

1. The judgment of the Grand Chamber shall be final.
2. The judgment of a Chamber shall become final
   (a) when the parties declare that they will not request that the case be referred to the Grand Chamber; or
   (b) three months after the date of the judgment, if reference of the case to the Grand Chamber has not been requested; or
   (c) when the panel of the Grand Chamber rejects the request to refer under Article 43.
3. The final judgment shall be published.

Article 45   Reasons for judgments and decisions

1. Reasons shall be given for judgments as well as for decisions declaring applications admissible or inadmissible.
2. If a judgment does not represent, in whole or in part, the unanimous opinion of the judges, any judge shall be entitled to deliver a separate opinion.

Article 46   Binding force and execution of judgments*

1. The High Contracting Parties undertake to abide by the final judgment of the Court in any case to which they are parties.
2. The final judgment of the Court shall be transmitted to the Committee of Ministers, which shall supervise its execution.
3. If the Committee of Ministers considers that the supervision of the execution of a final judgment is hindered by a problem of interpretation of the judgment, it may refer the matter to the Court for a ruling on the question of interpretation. A referral decision shall require a majority vote of two thirds of the representatives entitled to sit on the Committee.
4. If the Committee of Ministers considers that a High Contracting Party refuses to abide by a final judgment in a case to which it is a party, it may, after serving formal notice on that Party and by decision adopted by a majority vote of two thirds of the representatives entitled to sit on the Committee, refer to the Court the question whether that Party has failed to fulfil its obligation under paragraph 1.
5. If the Court finds a violation of paragraph 1, it shall refer the case to the Committee of Ministers for consideration of the measures to be taken. If the Court finds no violation of paragraph 1, it shall refer the case to the Committee of Ministers, which shall close its examination of the case.

Article 47   Advisory opinions

1. The Court may, at the request of the Committee of Ministers, give advisory opinions on legal questions concerning the interpretation of the Convention and the protocols thereto.
2. Such opinions shall not deal with any question relating to the content or scope of the rights or freedoms defined in Section I of the Convention and the protocols thereto, or with any other question which the Court or the Committee of Ministers might have to consider in consequence of any such proceedings as could be instituted in accordance with the Convention.
3. Decisions of the Committee of Ministers to request an advisory opinion of the Court shall require a majority vote of the representatives entitled to sit on the Committee.

Article 48   Advisory jurisdiction of the Court

The Court shall decide whether a request for an advisory opinion submitted by the Committee of Ministers is within its competence as defined in Article 47.

Article 49   Reasons for advisory opinions

1. Reasons shall be given for advisory opinions of the Court.
2. If the advisory opinion does not represent, in whole or in part, the unanimous opinion of the judges, any judge shall be entitled to deliver a separate opinion.
3. Advisory opinions of the Court shall be communicated to the Committee of Ministers.

---

* **Editor's Note:** Text amended according to the provisions of Protocol No. 14 (CETS No. 194).

Article 50   Expenditure on the Court

The expenditure on the Court shall be borne by the Council of Europe.

Article 51   Privileges and immunities of judges

The judges shall be entitled, during the exercise of their functions, to the privileges and immunities provided for in Article 40 of the Statute of the Council of Europe and in the agreements made thereunder.

Section III   Miscellaneous provisions

Article 52   Inquiries by the Secretary General

On receipt of a request from the Secretary General of the Council of Europe any High Contracting Party shall furnish an explanation of the manner in which its internal law ensures the effective implementation of any of the provisions of the Convention.

Article 53   Safeguard for existing human rights

Nothing in this Convention shall be construed as limiting or derogating from any of the human rights and fundamental freedoms which may be ensured under the laws of any High Contracting Party or under any other agreement to which it is a Party.

Article 54   Powers of the Committee of Ministers

Nothing in this Convention shall prejudice the powers conferred on the Committee of Ministers by the Statute of the Council of Europe.

Article 55   Exclusion of other means of dispute settlement

The High Contracting Parties agree that, except by special agreement, they will not avail themselves of treaties, conventions or declarations in force between them for the purpose of submitting, by way of petition, a dispute arising out of the interpretation or application of this Convention to a means of settlement other than those provided for in this Convention.

Article 56   Territorial application

1. Any State may at the time of its ratification or at any time thereafter declare by notification addressed to the Secretary General of the Council of Europe that the present Convention shall, subject to paragraph 4 of this Article, extend to all or any of the territories for whose international relations it is responsible.

2. The Convention shall extend to the territory or territories named in the notification as from the thirtieth day after the receipt of this notification by the Secretary General of the Council of Europe.

3. The provisions of this Convention shall be applied in such territories with due regard, however, to local requirements.

4. Any State which has made a declaration in accordance with paragraph 1 of this article may at any time thereafter declare on behalf of one or more of the territories to which the declaration relates that it accepts the competence of the Court to receive applications from individuals, non-governmental organisations or groups of individuals as provided by Article 34 of the Convention.

Article 57   Reservations

1. Any State may, when signing this Convention or when depositing its instrument of ratification, make a reservation in respect of any particular provision of the Convention to the extent that any law then in force in its territory is not in conformity with the provision. Reservations of a general character shall not be permitted under this article.

2. Any reservation made under this article shall contain a brief statement of the law concerned.

Article 58   Denunciation

1. A High Contracting Party may denounce the present Convention only after the expiry of five years from the date on which it became a party to it and after six months' notice contained in a notification addressed to the Secretary General of the Council of Europe, who shall inform the other High Contracting Parties.

2. Such a denunciation shall not have the effect of releasing the High Contracting Party concerned from its obligations under this Convention in respect of any act which, being capable of constituting a violation of such obligations, may have been performed by it before the date at which the denunciation became effective.

3. Any High Contracting Party which shall cease to be a member of the Council of Europe shall cease to be a Party to this Convention under the same conditions.

4. The Convention may be denounced in accordance with the provisions of the preceding paragraphs in respect of any territory to which it has been declared to extend under the terms of Article 56.

Article 59   Signature and ratification

1. This Convention shall be open to the signature of the members of the Council of Europe. It shall be ratified. Ratifications shall be deposited with the Secretary General of the Council of Europe.

2. The European Union may accede to this Convention.

3. The present Convention shall come into force after the deposit of ten instruments of ratification.

4. As regards any signatory ratifying subsequently, the Convention shall come into force at the date of the deposit of its instrument of ratification.

5. The Secretary General of the Council of Europe shall notify all the members of the Council of Europe of the entry into force of the Convention, the names of the High Contracting Parties who have ratified it, and the deposit of all instruments of ratification which may be effected subsequently.

Done at Rome this 4th day of November 1950, in English and French, both texts being equally authentic, in a single copy which shall remain deposited in the archives of the Council of Europe. The Secretary General shall transmit certified copies to each of the signatories.

First Protocol (1952)*

The Governments signatory hereto, being members of the Council of Europe,

Being resolved to take steps to ensure the collective enforcement of certain rights and freedoms other than those already included in Section I of the Convention for the Protection of Human Rights and Fundamental Freedoms signed at Rome on 4th November, 1950 (hereinafter referred to as 'the Convention'),

Have agreed as follows:

Article 1   Protection of property

Every natural or legal person is entitled to the peaceful enjoyment of his possessions. No one shall be deprived of his possessions except in the public interest and subject to the conditions provided for by law and by the general principles of international law.

The preceding provisions shall not, however, in any way impair the right of a State to enforce such laws as it deems necessary to control the use of property in accordance with the general interest or to secure the payment of taxes or other contributions or penalties.

Article 2   Right to education

No person shall be denied the right to education. In the exercise of any functions which it assumes in relation to education and to teaching, the State shall respect the right of parents to ensure such education and teaching in conformity with their own religious and philosophical convictions.

---

* **Editor's Note:** Text amended according to the provisions of Protocol No. 14 (CETS No. 194).

Article 3   Right to free elections

The High Contracting Parties undertake to hold free elections at reasonable intervals by secret ballot, under conditions which will ensure the free expression of the opinion of the people in the choice of the legislature.

Article 4   Territorial application

Any High Contracting Party may at the time of signature or ratification or at any time thereafter communicate to the Secretary-General of the Council of Europe a declaration stating the extent to which it undertakes that the provisions of the present Protocol shall apply to such of the territories for the international relations of which it is responsible as are named therein.

   Any High Contracting Party which has communicated a declaration in virtue of the preceding paragraph may from time to time communicate a further declaration modifying the terms of any former declaration or terminating the application of the provisions of this Protocol in respect of any territory.

   A declaration made in accordance with this Article shall be deemed to have been made in accordance with paragraph (1) of Article 56 of the Convention.

Article 5   Relationship to the Convention

As between the High Contracting Parties the provisions of Articles 1, 2, 3 and 4 of this Protocol shall be regarded as additional Articles to the Convention and all the provisions of the Convention shall apply accordingly.

Article 6   Signature and ratification

This Protocol shall be open for signature by the Members of the Council of Europe, who are the signatories of the Convention: it shall be ratified at the same time as or after the ratification of the Convention. It shall enter into force after the deposit of ten instruments of ratification. As regards any signatory ratifying subsequently, the Protocol shall enter into force at the date of the deposit of its instrument of ratification.

   The instruments of ratification shall be deposited with the Secretary-General of the Council of Europe, who will notify all Members of the names of those who have ratified.

Done at Paris on the 20th day of March 1952, in English and French, both texts being equally authentic, in a single copy which shall remain deposited in the archives of the Council of Europe. The Secretary-General shall transmit certified copies to each of the signatory Governments.

Fourth Protocol (1963)*

[Securing certain rights and freedoms other than those already included in the Convention and in the first Protocol thereto]

The Governments signatory hereto, being members of the Council of Europe

   Being resolved to take steps to ensure the collective enforcement of certain rights and freedoms other than those already included in Section I of the Convention for the Protection of Human Rights and Fundamental Freedoms signed at Rome on 4th November 1950 (hereinafter referred to as 'the Convention') and in Articles 1 to 3 of the First Protocol to the Convention, signed at Paris on 20th March 1952,

   Have agreed as follows:

Article 1   Prohibition of imprisonment for debt

No one shall be deprived of his liberty merely on the ground of inability to fulfil a contractual obligation.

Article 2   Freedom of movement

   1. Everyone lawfully within the territory of a State shall, within that territory, have the right to liberty of movement and freedom to choose his residence.

2. Everyone shall be free to leave any country, including his own.

3. No restrictions shall be placed on the exercise of these rights other than such as are in accordance with law and are necessary in a democratic society in the interests of national security or public safety, for the maintenance of *ordre public*, for the prevention of crime, for the protection of health or morals, or for the protection of the rights and freedoms of others.

4. The rights set forth in paragraph 1 may also be subject, in particular areas, to restrictions imposed in accordance with law and justified by the public interest in a democratic society.

Article 3   Prohibition of expulsion of nationals

1. No one shall be expelled, by means either of an individual or of a collective measure, from the territory of the State of which he is a national.

2. No one shall be deprived of the right to enter the territory of the State of which he is a national.

Article 4   Prohibition of collective expulsion of aliens

Collective expulsion of aliens is prohibited.

Article 5   Territorial application

1. Any High Contracting Party may, at the time of signature or ratification of this Protocol, or at any time thereafter, communicate to the Secretary-General of the Council of Europe a declaration stating the extent to which it undertakes that the provisions of this Protocol shall apply to such of the territories for the international relations of which it is responsible as are named therein.

2. Any High Contracting Party which has communicated a declaration in virtue of the preceding paragraph may, from time to time, communicate a further declaration modifying the terms of any former declaration or terminating the application of the provisions of this Protocol in respect of any territory.

3. A declaration made in accordance with this Article shall be deemed to have been made in accordance with paragraph 1 of Article 56 of the Convention.

4. The territory of any State to which this Protocol applies by virtue of ratification or acceptance by that State, and each territory to which this Protocol is applied by virtue of a declaration by that State under this Article, shall be treated as separate territories for the purpose of the references in Articles 2 and 3 to the territory of a State.

5. Any State which has made a declaration in accordance with paragraph 1 or 2 of this Article may at any time thereafter declare on behalf of one or more of the territories to which the declaration relates that it accepts the competence of the Court to receive applications from individuals, non-governmental organizations or groups of individuals as provided in Article 34 of the Convention in respect of all or any of Articles 1 to 4 of this Protocol.

Article 6   Relationship to the Convention

As between the High Contracting Parties the provisions of Articles 1 to 5 of this Protocol shall be regarded as additional Articles to the Convention, and all the provisions of the Convention shall apply accordingly.

Article 7   Signature and ratification

1. This Protocol shall be open for signature by the members of the Council of Europe who are the signatories of the Convention; it shall be ratified at the same time as or after the ratification of the Convention. It shall enter into force after the deposit of five instruments of ratification. As regards any signatory ratifying subsequently, the Protocol shall enter into force at the date of the deposit of its instrument of ratification.

2. The instruments of ratification shall be deposited with the Secretary-General of the Council of Europe, who will notify all members of the names of those who have ratified.

In witness whereof, the under signed, being duly authorised thereto, have signed this Protocol.

Done at Strasbourg, this 16th day of September 1963, in English and in French, both texts being equally authoritative, in a single copy which shall remain deposited in the archives of the Council of Europe. The Secretary-General shall transmit certified copies to each of the signatory States.

Sixth Protocol (1983)*

[Concerning the abolition of the death penalty]
The member States of the Council of Europe, signatory to this Protocol to the Convention for the Protection of Human Rights and Fundamental Freedoms, signed at Rome on 4 November 1950 (hereinafter referred to as 'the Convention'),

Considering that the evolution that has occurred in several member States of the Council of Europe expresses a general tendency in favour of abolition of the death penalty,

Have agreed as follows:

Article 1   Abolition of the death penalty
The death penalty shall be abolished. No one shall be condemned to such penalty or executed.

Article 2   Death penalty in time of war
A State may make provision in its law for the death penalty in respect of acts committed in time of war or of imminent threat of war; such penalty shall be applied only in the instances laid down in the law and in accordance with its provisions. The State shall communicate to the Secretary of the Council of Europe the relevant provisions of that law.

Article 3   Prohibition of derogations
No derogation from the provisions of this Protocol shall be made under Article 15 of the Convention.

Article 4   Prohibition of reservations
No reservation may be made under Article 57 of the Convention in respect of the provisions of this Protocol.

Article 5   Territorial application
1. Any State may at the time of signature or when depositing its instrument of ratification, acceptance or approval, specify the territory or territories to which this Protocol shall apply.

2. Any State may at any later date, by a declaration addressed to the Secretary-General of the Council of Europe, extend the application of this Protocol to any other territory specified in the declaration. In respect of such territory the Protocol shall enter into force on the first day of the month following the date of receipt of such a declaration by the Secretary-General.

3. Any declaration made under the two preceding paragraphs may, in respect of any territory specified in such declaration, be withdrawn by a notification addressed to the Secretary-General. The withdrawal shall become effective on the first day of the month following the date of receipt of such notification by the Secretary-General.

Article 6   Relationship to the Convention
As between the States Parties the provisions of Articles 1 to 5 of this Protocol shall be regarded as additional articles to the Convention and all the provisions of the Convention shall apply accordingly.

Article 7   Signature and ratification
This Protocol shall be open for signature by the member States of the Council of Europe, signatories to the Convention. It shall be subject to ratification, acceptance or approval. A member State of the Council of Europe may not ratify, accept or approve this Protocol unless it has, simultaneously or previously, ratified the Convention. Instruments of ratification, acceptance or approval shall be deposited with the Secretary-General of the Council of Europe.

Article 8   Entry into force
1. This Protocol shall enter into force on the first day of the month following the date on which five member States of the Council of Europe have expressed their consent to be bound by the Protocol in accordance with the provisions of Article 7.

2. In respect of any member State which subsequently expresses its consent to be bound by it, the Protocol shall enter into force on the first day of the month following the date of the deposit of the instrument of ratification, acceptance or approval.

---

* © Council of Europe

Article 9   Depositary functions

The Secretary-General of the Council of Europe shall notify the member States of the Council of:

    (a) any signature;

    (b) the deposit of any instrument of ratification, acceptance or approval;

    (c) any date of entry into force of this Protocol in accordance with Articles 5 and 8;

    (d) any other act, notification or communication relating to this Protocol.

In witness whereof the undersigned, being duly authorised thereto, have signed this Protocol.

Done at Strasbourg, this 28th day of April 1983, in English and French, both texts being equally authentic, in a single copy which shall be deposited in the archives of the Council of Europe. The Secretary-General of the Council of Europe shall transmit certified copies to each member State of the Council of Europe.

Seventh Protocol (1984)*

The member States of the Council of Europe signatory hereto

    Being resolved to take further steps to ensure the collective enforcement of certain rights and freedoms by means of the Convention for the Protection of Human Rights and Fundamental Freedoms signed at Rome on 4 November 1950 (hereinafter referred to as 'the Convention'),

    Have agreed as follows:

Article 1   Procedural safeguards relating to expulsion of aliens

    1. An alien lawfully resident in the territory of a State shall not be expelled therefrom except in pursuance of a decision reached in accordance with law and shall be allowed:

    (a) to submit reasons against his expulsion;

    (b) to have his case reviewed; and

    (c) to be represented for these purposes before the competent authority or a person or persons designated by that authority.

    2. An alien may be expelled before the exercise of his rights under paragraph 1(a), (b) and (c) of this Article, when such expulsion is necessary in the interests of public order or is grounded on reasons of national security.

Article 2   Right of appeal in criminal matters

    1. Everyone convicted of a criminal offence by a tribunal shall have the right to have conviction or sentence reviewed by a higher tribunal. The exercise of this right, including the grounds on which it may be exercised, shall be governed by law.

    2. This right may be subject to exceptions in regard to offences of a minor character, as prescribed by law, or in cases in which the person concerned was tried in the first instance by the highest tribunal or was convicted following an appeal against acquittal.

Article 3   Compensation for wrongful conviction

When a person has by a final decision been convicted of a criminal offence and when subsequently his conviction has been reversed, or he has been pardoned, on the ground that a new or newly discovered fact shows conclusively that there has been a miscarriage of justice, the person who has suffered punishment as a result of such conviction shall be compensated according to the law or the practice of the State concerned, unless it is proved that the non-disclosure of the unknown fact in time is wholly or partly attributable to him.

Article 4   Right not to be tried or punished twice

    1. No one shall be liable to be tried or punished again in criminal proceedings under the jurisdiction of the same State for an offence for which he has already been finally acquitted or convicted in accordance with the law and penal procedure of that State.

    2. The provisions of the preceding paragraph shall not prevent the re-opening of the case in accordance with the law and penal procedure of the State concerned, if there is evidence of new or

newly discovered facts, or if there has been a fundamental defect in the previous proceedings, which could affect the outcome of the case.

3. No derogation from this Article shall be made under Article 15 of the Convention.

Article 5   Equality between spouses

1. Spouses shall enjoy equality of rights and responsibilities of a private law character between them, and in their relations with their children, as to marriage, during marriage and in the event of its dissolution. This Article shall not prevent States from taking such measures as are necessary in the interests of the children.

Article 6   Territorial application

1. Any State may at the time of signature or when depositing its instrument of ratification, acceptance or approval, specify the territory or territories to which this Protocol shall apply and state the extent to which it undertakes that the provisions of this Protocol shall apply to this or these territories.

2. Any State may at any later date, by a declaration addressed to the Secretary-General of the Council of Europe, extend the application of this Protocol to any other territory specified in the declaration. In respect of such territory the Protocol shall enter into force on the first day of the month following the expiration of a period of two months after the date of receipt by the Secretary-General of such declaration.

3. Any declaration made under the two preceding paragraphs may, in respect of any territory specified in such declaration, be withdrawn or modified by a notification addressed to the Secretary-General. The withdrawal or modification shall become effective on the first day of the month following the expiration of a period of two months after the date of receipt of such notification by the Secretary-General.

4. A declaration made in accordance with this Article shall be deemed to have been made in accordance with paragraph 1 of Article 56 of the Convention.

5. The territory of any State to which this Protocol applies by virtue of ratification, acceptance or approval by that State, and each territory to which this Protocol is applied by virtue of a declaration by that State under this Article, may be treated as separate territories for the purpose of the reference in Article 1 to the territory of a State.

6. Any State which has made a declaration in accordance with paragraph 1 or 2 of this Article may at any time thereafter declare on behalf of one or more of the territories to which the declaration relates that it accepts the competence of the Court to receive applications from individuals, non-governmental organizations or groups of individuals as provided in Article 34 of the Convention in respect of Articles 1 to 5 of this Protocol.

Article 7   Relationship to the Convention

As between the States Parties, the provisions of Articles 1 to 6 of this Protocol shall be regarded as additional Articles to the Convention, and all the provisions of the Convention shall apply accordingly.

Article 8   Signature and ratification

This Protocol shall be open for signature by member States of the Council of Europe which have signed the Convention. It is subject to ratification, acceptance or approval. A member State of the Council of Europe may not ratify, accept or approve this Protocol without previously or simultaneously ratifying the Convention. Instruments of ratification, acceptance or approval shall be deposited with the Secretary-General of the Council of Europe.

Article 9   Entry into force

1. This Protocol shall enter into force on the first day of the month following the expiration of a period of two months after the date on which seven member States of the Council of Europe have expressed their consent to be bound by the Protocol in accordance with the provisions of Article 8.

2. In respect of any member State which subsequently expresses its consent to be bound by it, the Protocol shall enter into force on the first day of the month following the expiration of a period of two months after the date of the deposit of the instrument of ratification, acceptance or approval.

Article 10   Depository functions

The Secretary-General of the Council of Europe shall notify all the member States of the Council of:

(a) any signature;

(b) the deposit of any instrument of ratification, acceptance or approval;

(c) any date of entry into force of this Protocol in accordance with Articles 6 and 9;

(d) any other act, notification or declaration relating to this Protocol.

In witness whereof the undersigned, being duly authorised thereto, have signed this Protocol.

Done at Strasbourg, this 22nd day of November 1984, in English and French, both texts being equally authentic, in a single copy which shall be deposited in the archives of the Council of Europe. The Secretary-General of the Council of Europe shall transmit certified copies to each member State of the Council.

Twelfth Protocol (2000)*

The member States of the Council of Europe signatory hereto,

Having regard to the fundamental principle according to which all persons are equal before the law and are entitled to the equal protection of the law;

Being resolved to take further steps to promote the equality of all persons through the collective enforcement of a general prohibition of discrimination by means of the Convention for the Protection of Human Rights and Fundamental Freedoms signed at Rome on 4 November 1950 (hereinafter referred to as 'the Convention');

Reaffirming that the principle of non-discrimination does not prevent States Parties from taking measures in order to promote full and effective equality, provided that there is an objective and reasonable justification for those measures,

Have agreed as follows:

Article 1   General prohibition of discrimination

1. The enjoyment of any right set forth by law shall be secured without discrimination on any ground such as sex, race, colour, language, religion, political or other opinion, national or social origin, association with a national minority, property, birth or other status.

2. No one shall be discriminated against by any public authority on any ground such as those mentioned in paragraph 1.

Article 2   Territorial application

1. Any State may, at the time of signature or when depositing its instrument of ratification, acceptance or approval, specify the territory or territories to which this Protocol shall apply.

2. Any State may at any later date, by a declaration addressed to the Secretary General of the Council of Europe, extend the application of this Protocol to any other territory specified in the declaration. In respect of such territory the Protocol shall enter into force on the first day of the month following the expiration of a period of three months after the date of receipt by the Secretary General of such declaration.

3. Any declaration made under the two preceding paragraphs may, in respect of any territory specified in such declaration, be withdrawn or modified by a notification addressed to the Secretary General of the Council of Europe. The withdrawal or modification shall become effective on the first day of the month following the expiration of a period of three months after the date of receipt of such notification by the Secretary General.

4. A declaration made in accordance with this article shall be deemed to have been made in accordance with paragraph 1 of Article 56 of the Convention.

5. Any State which has made a declaration in accordance with paragraph 1 or 2 of this article may at any time thereafter declare on behalf of one or more of the territories to which the declaration relates that it accepts the competence of the Court to receive applications from individuals,

non-governmental organisations or groups of individuals as provided by Article 34 of the Convention in respect of Article 1 of this Protocol.

Article 3   Relationship to the Convention

As between the States Parties, the provisions of Articles 1 and 2 of this Protocol shall be regarded as additional articles to the Convention, and all the provisions of the Convention shall apply accordingly.

Article 4   Signature and ratification

This Protocol shall be open for signature by member States of the Council of Europe which have signed the Convention. It is subject to ratification, acceptance or approval. A member State of the Council of Europe may not ratify, accept or approve this Protocol without previously or simultaneously ratifying the Convention. Instruments of ratification, acceptance or approval shall be deposited with the Secretary General of the Council of Europe.

Article 5   Entry into force

1. This Protocol shall enter into force on the first day of the month following the expiration of a period of three months after the date on which ten member States of the Council of Europe have expressed their consent to be bound by the Protocol in accordance with the provisions of Article 4.

2. In respect of any member State which subsequently expresses its consent to be bound by it, the Protocol shall enter into force on the first day of the month following the expiration of a period of three months after the date of the deposit of the instrument of ratification, acceptance or approval.

Article 6   Depositary functions

The Secretary General of the Council of Europe shall notify all the member States of the Council of Europe of:

(a) any signature;
(b) the deposit of any instrument of ratification, acceptance or approval;
(c) any date of entry into force of this Protocol in accordance with Articles 2 and 5;
(d) any other act, notification or communication relating to this Protocol.

In witness whereof the undersigned, being duly authorised thereto, have signed this Protocol.

Done at Rome, this 4th day of November 2000, in English and in French, both texts being equally authentic, in a single copy which shall be deposited in the archives of the Council of Europe. The Secretary General of the Council of Europe shall transmit certified copies to each member State of the Council of Europe.

Thirteenth Protocol (2002)*

The member States of the Council of Europe signatory hereto,

Convinced that everyone's right to life is a basic value in a democratic society and that the abolition of the death penalty is essential for the protection of this right and for the full recognition of the inherent dignity of all human beings;

Wishing to strengthen the protection of the right to life guaranteed by the Convention for the Protection of Human Rights and Fundamental Freedoms signed at Rome on 4 November 1950 (hereinafter referred to as 'the Convention');

Noting that Protocol No. 6 to the Convention, concerning the Abolition of the Death Penalty, signed at Strasbourg on 28 April 1983, does not exclude the death penalty in respect of acts committed in time of war or of imminent threat of war;

Being resolved to take the final step in order to abolish the death penalty in all circumstances,

Have agreed as follows:

Article 1   Abolition of the death penalty

The death penalty shall be abolished. No one shall be condemned to such penalty or executed.

Article 2   Prohibition of derogations

No derogation from the provisions of this Protocol shall be made under Article 15 of the Convention.

Article 3   Prohibition of reservations

No reservation may be made under Article 57 of the Convention in respect of the provisions of this Protocol.

Article 4   Territorial application

1. Any State may, at the time of signature or when depositing its instrument of ratification, acceptance or approval, specify the territory or territories to which this Protocol shall apply.

2. Any State may at any later date, by a declaration addressed to the Secretary General of the Council of Europe, extend the application of this Protocol to any other territory specified in the declaration. In respect of such territory the Protocol shall enter into force on the first day of the month following the expiration of a period of three months after the date of receipt of such declaration by the Secretary General.

3. Any declaration made under the two preceding paragraphs may, in respect of any territory specified in such declaration, be withdrawn or modified by a notification addressed to the Secretary General. The withdrawal or modification shall become effective on the first day of the month following the expiration of a period of three months after the date of receipt of such notification by the Secretary General.

Article 5   Relationship to the Convention

As between the States Parties the provisions of Articles 1 to 4 of this Protocol shall be regarded as additional articles to the Convention, and all the provisions of the Convention shall apply accordingly.

Article 6   Signature and ratification

This Protocol shall be open for signature by member States of the Council of Europe which have signed the Convention. It is subject to ratification, acceptance or approval. A member State of the Council of Europe may not ratify, accept or approve this Protocol without previously or simultaneously ratifying the Convention. Instruments of ratification, acceptance or approval shall be deposited with the Secretary General of the Council of Europe.

Article 7   Entry into force

1. This Protocol shall enter into force on the first day of the month following the expiration of a period of three months after the date on which ten member States of the Council of Europe have expressed their consent to be bound by the Protocol in accordance with the provisions of Article 6.

2. In respect of any member State which subsequently expresses its consent to be bound by it, the Protocol shall enter into force on the first day of the month following the expiration of a period of three months after the date of the deposit of the instrument of ratification, acceptance or approval.

Article 8   Depositary functions

The Secretary General of the Council of Europe shall notify all the member States of the Council of Europe of:

    (a) any signature;
    (b) the deposit of any instrument of ratification, acceptance or approval;
    (c) any date of entry into force of this Protocol in accordance with Articles 4 and 7;
    (d) any other act, notification or communication relating to this Protocol.

In witness whereof the undersigned, being duly authorised thereto, have signed this Protocol.

Done at Vilnius, this 3rd day of May 2002, in English and in French, both texts being equally authentic, in a single copy which shall be deposited in the archives of the Council of Europe. The Secretary General of the Council of Europe shall transmit certified copies to each member State of the Council of Europe.

Sixteenth Protocol (2013)*

PREAMBLE

The member States of the Council of Europe and other High Contracting Parties to the Convention for the Protection of Human Rights and Fundamental Freedoms, signed at Rome on 4 November 1950 (hereinafter referred to as 'the Convention'), signatories hereto,

Having regard to the provisions of the Convention and, in particular, Article 19 establishing the European Court of Human Rights (hereinafter referred to as 'the Court');

Considering that the extension of the Court's competence to give advisory opinions will further enhance the interaction between the Court and national authorities and thereby reinforce implementation of the Convention, in accordance with the principle of subsidiarity;

Having regard to Opinion No. 285 (2013) adopted by the Parliamentary Assembly of the Council of Europe on 28 June 2013,

Have agreed as follows:

Article 1

1. Highest courts and tribunals of a High Contracting Party, as specified in accordance with Article 10, may request the Court to give advisory opinions on questions of principle relating to the interpretation or application of the rights and freedoms defined in the Convention or the protocols thereto.

2. The requesting court or tribunal may seek an advisory opinion only in the context of a case pending before it.

3. The requesting court or tribunal shall give reasons for its request and shall provide the relevant legal and factual background of the pending case.

Article 2

1. A panel of five judges of the Grand Chamber shall decide whether to accept the request for an advisory opinion, having regard to Article 1. The panel shall give reasons for any refusal to accept the request.

2. If the panel accepts the request, the Grand Chamber shall deliver the advisory opinion.

3. The panel and the Grand Chamber, as referred to in the preceding paragraphs, shall include *ex officio* the judge elected in respect of the High Contracting Party to which the requesting court or tribunal pertains. If there is none or if that judge is unable to sit, a person chosen by the President of the Court from a list submitted in advance by that Party shall sit in the capacity of judge.

Article 3

The Council of Europe Commissioner for Human Rights and the High Contracting Party to which the requesting court or tribunal pertains shall have the right to submit written comments and take part in any hearing. The President of the Court may, in the interest of the proper administration of justice, invite any other High Contracting Party or person also to submit written comments or take part in any hearing.

Article 4

1. Reasons shall be given for advisory opinions.

2. If the advisory opinion does not represent, in whole or in part, the unanimous opinion of the judges, any judge shall be entitled to deliver a separate opinion.

3. Advisory opinions shall be communicated to the requesting court or tribunal and to the High Contracting Party to which that court or tribunal pertains.

4. Advisory opinions shall be published.

* © Council of Europe

Article 5
Advisory opinions shall not be binding.

Article 6
As between the High Contracting Parties the provisions of Articles 1 to 5 of this Protocol shall be regarded as additional articles to the Convention, and all the provisions of the Convention shall apply accordingly.

Article 7
1. This Protocol shall be open for signature by the High Contracting Parties to the Convention, which may express their consent to be bound by:
   (a) signature without reservation as to ratification, acceptance or approval; or
   (b) signature subject to ratification, acceptance or approval, followed by ratification, acceptance or approval.
2. The instruments of ratification, acceptance or approval shall be deposited with the Secretary General of the Council of Europe.

Article 8
1. This Protocol shall enter into force on the first day of the month following the expiration of a period of three months after the date on which ten High Contracting Parties to the Convention have expressed their consent to be bound by the Protocol in accordance with the provisions of Article 7.
2. In respect of any High Contracting Party to the Convention which subsequently expresses its consent to be bound by it, the Protocol shall enter into force on the first day of the month following the expiration of a period of three months after the date of the expression of its consent to be bound by the Protocol in accordance with the provisions of Article 7.

Article 9
No reservation may be made under Article 57 of the Convention in respect of the provisions of this Protocol.

Article 10
Each High Contracting Party to the Convention shall, at the time of signature or when depositing its instrument of ratification, acceptance or approval, by means of a declaration addressed to the Secretary General of the Council of Europe, indicate the courts or tribunals that it designates for the purposes of Article 1, paragraph 1, of this Protocol. This declaration may be modified at any later date and in the same manner.

Article 11
The Secretary General of the Council of Europe shall notify the member States of the Council of Europe and the other High Contracting Parties to the Convention of:
   (a) any signature;
   (b) the deposit of any instrument of ratification, acceptance or approval;
   (c) any date of entry into force of this Protocol in accordance with Article 8;
   (d) any declaration made in accordance with Article 10; and
   (e) any other act, notification or communication relating to this Protocol.

In witness whereof the undersigned, being duly authorised thereto, have signed this Protocol.

Done at Strasbourg, this 2nd day of October 2013, in English and French, both texts being equally authentic, in a single copy which shall be deposited in the archives of the Council of Europe. The Secretary General of the Council of Europe shall transmit certified copies to each member State of the Council of Europe and to the other High Contracting Parties to the Convention.

European Social Charter (1961)*

The governments signatory hereto, being members of the Council of Europe,

Considering that the aim of the Council of Europe is the achievement of greater unity between its members for the purpose of safeguarding and realising the ideals and principles which are their common heritage and of facilitating their economic and social progress, in particular by the maintenance and further realisation of human rights and fundamental freedoms;

Considering that in the European Convention for the Protection of Human Rights and Fundamental Freedoms signed at Rome on 4 November 1950, and the Protocol thereto signed at Paris on 20 March 1952, the member States of the Council of Europe agreed to secure to their populations the civil and political rights and freedoms therein specified;

Considering that the enjoyment of social rights should be secured without discrimination on grounds of race, colour, sex, religion, political opinion, national extraction or social origin;

Being resolved to make every effort in common to improve the standard of living and to promote the social well-being of both their urban and rural populations by means of appropriate institutions and action,

Have agreed as follows:

PART I

The Contracting Parties accept as the aim of their policy, to be pursued by all appropriate means, both national and international in character, the attainment of conditions in which the following rights and principles may be effectively realised:

1. Everyone shall have the opportunity to earn his living in an occupation freely entered upon.
2. All workers have the right to just conditions of work.
3. All workers have the right to safe and healthy working conditions.
4. All workers have the right to a fair remuneration sufficient for a decent standard of living for themselves and their families.
5. All workers and employers have the right to freedom of association in national or international organisations for the protection of their economic and social interests.
6. All workers and employers have the right to bargain collectively.
7. Children and young persons have the right to a special protection against the physical and moral hazards to which they are exposed.
8. Employed women, in case of maternity, and other employed women as appropriate, have the right to a special protection in their work.
9. Everyone has the right to appropriate facilities for vocational guidance with a view to helping him choose an occupation suited to his personal aptitude and interests.
10. Everyone has the right to appropriate facilities for vocational training.
11. Everyone has the right to benefit from any measures enabling him to enjoy the highest possible standard of health attainable.
12. All workers and their dependants have the right to social security.
13. Anyone without adequate resources has the right to social and medical assistance.
14. Everyone has the right to benefit from social welfare services.
15. Disabled persons have the right to vocational training, rehabilitation and resettlement, whatever the origin and nature of their disability.
16. The family as a fundamental unit of society has the right to appropriate social, legal and economic protection to ensure its full development.
17. Mothers and children, irrespective of marital status and family relations, have the right to appropriate social and economic protection.
18. The nationals of any one of the Contracting Parties have the right to engage in any gainful occupation in the territory of any one of the others on a footing of equality with the nationals of the latter, subject to restrictions based on cogent economic or social reasons.

19. Migrant workers who are nationals of a Contracting Party and their families have the right to protection and assistance in the territory of any other Contracting Party.

PART II

The Contracting Parties undertake, as provided for in Part III, to consider themselves bound by the obligations laid down in the following articles and paragraphs.

Article 1   The right to work
With a view to ensuring the effective exercise of the right to work, the Contracting Parties undertake:

1. to accept as one of their primary aims and responsibilities the achievement and maintenance of as high and stable a level of employment as possible, with view to the attainment of full employment;

2. to protect effectively the right of the worker to earn his living in an occupation freely entered upon;

3. to establish or maintain free employment services for all workers;

4. to provide or promote appropriate vocational guidance, training and rehabilitation.

Article 2   The right to just conditions of work
With a view to ensuring the effective exercise of the right to just conditions of work, the Contracting Parties undertake:

1. to provide for reasonable daily and weekly working hours, the working week to be progressively reduced to the extent that the increase of productivity and other relevant factors permit;

2. to provide for public holidays with pay;

3. to provide for a minimum of two weeks' annual holiday with pay;

4. to provide for additional paid holidays or reduced working hours for workers engaged in dangerous or unhealthy occupations as prescribed;

5. to ensure a weekly rest period which shall, as far as possible, coincide with the day recognised by tradition or custom in the country or region concerned as a day of rest.

Article 3   The right to safe and healthy working conditions
With a view to ensuring the effective exercise of the right to safe and healthy working conditions, the Contracting Parties undertake:

1. to issue safety and health regulations;

2. to provide for the enforcement of such regulations by measures of supervision;

3. to consult, as appropriate, employers' and workers' organisations on measures intended to improve industrial safety and health.

Article 4   The right to a fair remuneration
With a view to ensuring the effective exercise of the right to a fair remuneration, the Contracting Parties undertake:

1. to recognise the right of workers to a remuneration such as will give them and their families a decent standard of living;

2. to recognise the right of workers to an increased rate of remuneration for overtime work, subject to exceptions in particular cases;

3. to recognise the right of men and women workers to equal pay for work of equal value;

4. to recognise the right of all workers to a reasonable period of notice for termination of employment;

5. to permit deductions from wages only under conditions and to the extent prescribed by national laws or regulations or fixed by collective agreements or arbitration awards.

The exercise of these rights shall be achieved by freely concluded collective agreements, by statutory wage-fixing machinery, or by other means appropriate to national conditions.

Article 5   The right to organise

With a view to ensuring or promoting the freedom of workers and employers to form local, national or international organisations for the protection of their economic and social interests and to join those organisations the Contracting Parties undertake that national law shall not be such as to impair, nor shall it be so applied as to impair, this freedom. The extent to which the guarantees provided for in this article shall apply to the police shall be determined by national laws or regulations. The principle governing the application to the members of the armed forces of these guarantees and the extent to which they shall apply to persons in this category shall equally be determined by national laws or regulations.

Article 6   The right to bargain collectively

With a view to ensuring the effective exercise of the right to bargain collectively, the Contracting Parties undertake:

1. to promote joint consultation between workers and employers;
2. to promote, where necessary and appropriate, machinery for voluntary negotiations between employers or employers' organisations and workers' organisations, with a view to the regulation of terms and conditions of employment by means of collective agreements;
3. to promote the establishment and use of appropriate machinery for conciliation and voluntary arbitration for the settlement of labour disputes;

and recognise:

4. the right of workers and employers to collective action in cases of conflicts of interest, including the right to strike, subject to obligations that might arise out of collective agreements previously entered into.

Article 7   The right of children and young persons to protection

With a view to ensuring the effective exercise of the right of children and young persons to protection, the Contracting Parties undertake:

1. to provide that the minimum age of admission to employment shall be 15 years, subject to exceptions for children employed in prescribed light work without harm to their health, morals or education;
2. to provide that a higher minimum age of admission to employment shall be fixed with respect to prescribed occupations regarded as dangerous or unhealthy;
3. to provide that persons who are still subject to compulsory education shall not be employed in such work as would deprive them of the full benefit of their education;
4. to provide that the working hours of persons under 16 years of age shall be limited in accordance with the needs of their development, and particularly with their need for vocational training;
5. to recognise the right of young workers and apprentices to a fair wage or other appropriate allowances;
6. to provide that the time spent by young persons in vocational training during the normal working hours with the consent of the employer shall be treated as forming part of the working day;
7. to provide that employed persons of under 18 years of age shall be entitled to not less than three weeks' annual holiday with pay;
8. to provide that persons under 18 years of age shall not be employed in night work with the exception of certain occupations provided for by national laws or regulations;
9. to provide that persons under 18 years of age employed in occupations prescribed by national laws or regulations shall be subject to regular medical control;
10. to ensure special protection against physical and moral dangers to which children and young persons are exposed, and particularly against those resulting directly or indirectly from their work.

Article 8   The right of employed women to protection

With a view to ensuring the effective exercise of the right of employed women to protection the Contracting Parties undertake:

1. to provide either by paid leave, by adequate social security benefits or by benefits from public funds for women to take leave before and after childbirth up to a total of at least 12 weeks;

2. to consider it as unlawful for an employer to give a woman notice of dismissal during her absence on maternity leave or to give her notice of dismissal at such a time that the notice would expire during such absence;

3. to provide that mothers who are nursing their infants shall be entitled to sufficient time off for this purpose;

4. (a) to regulate the employment of women workers on night work in industrial employment;

(b) to prohibit the employment of women workers in underground mining, and, as appropriate, on all other work which is unsuitable for them by reason of its dangerous, unhealthy, or arduous nature.

Article 9   The right to vocational guidance

With a view to ensuring the effective exercise of the right to vocational guidance, the Contracting Parties undertake to provide or promote, as necessary, a service which will assist all persons, including the handicapped, to solve problems related to occupational choice and progress, with due regard to the individual's characteristics and their relation to occupational opportunity; this assistance should be available free of charge, both to young persons, including school children, and to adults.

Article 10   The right to vocational training

With a view to ensuring the effective exercise of the right to vocational training, the Contracting Parties undertake:

1. to provide or promote, as necessary, the technical and vocational training of all persons, including the handicapped, in consultation with employers' and workers' organisations and to grant facilities for access to higher technical and university education, based solely on individual aptitude;

2. to provide or promote a system of apprenticeship and other systematic arrangements for training young boys and girls in their various employments;

3. to provide or promote, as necessary:
    (a) adequate and readily available training facilities for adult workers;
    (b) special facilities for the re-training of adult workers needed as a result of technological development or new trends in employment;

4. to encourage the full utilisation of the facilities provided by appropriate measures such as:
    (a) reducing or abolishing any fees or charges;
    (b) granting financial assistance in appropriate cases;
    (c) including in the normal working hours time spent on supplementary training taken by the worker, at the request of his employer, during employment;
    (d) ensuring, through adequate supervision in consultation with the employers' and workers' organisations the efficiency of apprenticeship and other training arrangements for young workers, and the adequate protection of young workers generally.

Article 11   The right to protection of health

With a view to ensuring the effective exercise of the right to protection of health, the Contracting Parties undertake, either directly or in cooperation with public or private organisations to take appropriate measures designed *inter alia*:

1. to remove as far as possible the causes of ill-health;

2. to provide advisory and educational facilities for the promotion of health and the encouragement of individual responsibility in matters of health;

3. to prevent as far as possible epidemic, endemic and other diseases.

Article 12   The right to social security

With a view to ensuring the effective exercise of the right to social security, the Contracting Parties undertake:

1. to establish or maintain a system of social security;

2. to maintain the social security system at a satisfactory level at least equal to that required for ratification of International Labour Convention (No. 102) Concerning Minimum Standards of Social Security;

3. to endeavour to raise progressively the system of social security to a higher level;

4. to take steps, by the conclusion of appropriate bilateral and multilateral agreements, or by other means, and subject to the conditions laid down in such agreements, in order to ensure:

(a) equal treatment with their own nationals of the nationals of other Contracting Parties in respect of social security rights, including the retention of benefits arising out of social security legislation, whatever movements the persons protected may undertake between the territories of the Contracting Parties;

(b) the granting, maintenance and resumption of social security rights by such means as the accumulation of insurance or employment periods completed under the legislation of each of the Contracting Parties.

Article 13   The right to social and medical assistance

With a view to ensuring the effective exercise of the right to social and medical assistance, the Contracting Parties undertake:

1. to ensure that any person who is without adequate resources and who is unable to secure such resources either by his own efforts or from other sources, in particular by benefits under a social security scheme, be granted adequate assistance, and, in case of sickness, the care necessitated by this condition;

2. to ensure that persons receiving such assistance shall not, for that reason, suffer from a diminution of their political or social rights;

3. to provide that everyone may receive by appropriate public or private services such advice and personal help as may be required to prevent, to remove, or to alleviate personal or family want;

4. to apply the provisions referred to in paragraphs 1, 2 and 3 of this article on an equal footing with their nationals to nationals of other Contracting Parties lawfully within their territories, in accordance with their obligations under the European Convention on Social and Medical Assistance, signed at Paris on 11 December 1953.

Article 14   The right to benefit from social welfare services

With a view to ensuring the effective exercise of the right to benefit from social welfare services, the Contracting Parties undertake:

1. to promote or provide services which, by using methods of social work, would contribute to the welfare and development of both individuals and groups in the community, and to their adjustment to the social environment;

2. to encourage the participation of individuals and voluntary or other organisations in the establishment and maintenance of such services.

Article 15   The right of physically or mentally disabled persons to vocational training, rehabilitation and social resettlement

With a view to ensuring the effective exercise of the right of the physically or mentally disabled to vocational training, rehabilitation and resettlement, the Contracting Parties undertake:

1. to take adequate measures for the provision of training facilities, including, where necessary, specialised institutions, public or private;

2. to take adequate measures for the placing of disabled persons in employment, such as specialised placing services, facilities for sheltered employment and measures to encourage employers to admit disabled persons to employment.

Article 16   The right of the family to social, legal and economic protection

With a view to ensuring the necessary conditions for the full development of the family, which is a fundamental unit of society, the Contracting Parties undertake to promote the economic, legal and social protection of family life by such means as social and family benefits, fiscal arrangements, provision of family housing, benefits for the newly married, and other appropriate means.

Article 17   The right of mothers and children to social and economic protection

With a view to ensuring the effective exercise of the right of mothers and children to social and economic protection, the Contracting Parties will take all appropriate and necessary measures to that end, including the establishment or maintenance of appropriate institutions or services.

Article 18   The right to engage in a gainful occupation in the territory of other Contracting Parties

With a view to ensuring the effective exercise of the right to engage in a gainful occupation in the territory of any other Contracting Party, the Contracting Parties undertake:

1. to apply existing regulations in a spirit of liberality;
2. to simplify existing formalities and to reduce or abolish chancery dues and other charges payable by foreign workers or their employers;
3. to liberalise, individually or collectively, regulations governing the employment of foreign workers; and recognise:
4. the right of their nationals to leave the country to engage in a gainful occupation in the territories of the other Contracting Parties.

Article 19   The right of migrant workers and their families to protection and assistance

With a view to ensuring the effective exercise of the right of migrant workers and their families to protection and assistance in the territory of any other Contracting Party, the Contracting Parties undertake:

1. to maintain or to satisfy themselves that there are maintained adequate and free services to assist such workers, particularly in obtaining accurate information, and to take all appropriate steps, so far as national laws and regulations permit, against misleading propaganda relating to emigration and immigration;
2. to adopt appropriate measures within their own jurisdiction to facilitate the departure, journey and reception of such workers and their families, and to provide, within their own jurisdiction, appropriate services for health, medical attention and good hygienic conditions during the journey;
3. to promote co-operation, as appropriate, between social services, public and private, in emigration and immigration countries;
4. to secure for such workers lawfully within their territories, in so far as such matters are regulated by law or regulations or are subject to the control of administrative authorities, treatment not less favourable than that of their own nationals in respect of the following matters:
    (a) remuneration and other employment and working conditions;
    (b) membership of trade unions and enjoyment of the benefits of collective bargaining;
    (c) accommodation;
5. to secure for such workers lawfully within their territories, treatment not less favourable than that of their own nationals with regard to employment taxes, dues or contributions payable in respect of employed persons;
6. to facilitate as far as possible the reunion of the family of a foreign worker permitted to establish himself in the territory;
7. to secure for such workers lawfully within their territories treatment not less favourable than that of their own nationals in respect of legal proceedings relating to matters referred to in this article;
8. to secure that such workers lawfully residing within their territories are not expelled unless they endanger national security or offend against public interest or morality;
9. to permit, within legal limits, the transfer of such parts of the earnings and savings of such workers as they may desire;
10. to extend the protection and assistance provided for in this article to self employed migrants in so far as such measures apply.

PART III

Article 20   Undertakings
1. Each of the Contracting Parties undertakes:
    (a) to consider Part I of this Charter as a declaration of the aims which it will pursue by all appropriate means, as stated in the introductory paragraph of that part;
    (b) to consider itself bound by at least five of the following articles of Part II of this Charter: Articles, 1, 5, 6, 12, 13, 16 and 19;
    (c) in addition to the articles selected by it in accordance with the preceding sub- paragraph, to consider itself bound by such a number of articles or numbered paragraphs of Part 11 of the Charter as it may select, provided that the total number of articles or numbered paragraphs by which it is bound is not less than 10 articles or 45 numbered paragraphs.

2. The articles or paragraphs selected in accordance with sub-paragraphs b and c of paragraph 1 of this article shall be notified to the Secretary General of the Council of Europe at the time when the instrument of ratification or approval of the Contracting Party concerned is deposited.

3. Any Contracting Party may, at a later date, declare by notification to the Secretary General that it considers itself bound by any articles or any numbered paragraphs of Part II of the Charter which it has not already accepted under the terms of paragraph 1 of this article. Such undertakings subsequently given shall be deemed to be an integral part of the ratification or approval, and shall have the same effect as from the thirtieth day after the date of the notification.

4. The Secretary General shall communicate to all the signatory governments and to the Director General of the International Labour Office any notification which he shall have received pursuant to this part of the Charter.

5. Each Contracting Party shall maintain a system of labour inspection appropriate to national conditions.

PART IV

Article 21   Reports concerning accepted provisions
The Contracting Parties shall send to the Secretary General of the Council of Europe a report at two-yearly intervals, in a form to be determined by the Committee of Ministers, concerning the application of such provisions of Part II of the Charter as they have accepted.

Article 22   Reports concerning provisions which are not accepted
The Contracting Parties shall send to the Secretary General, at appropriate intervals as requested by the Committee of Ministers, reports relating to the provisions of Part II of the Charter which they did not accept at the time of their ratification or approval or in a subsequent notification. The Committee of Ministers shall determine from time to time in respect of which provisions such reports shall be requested and the form of the reports to be provided.

Article 23   Communication of copies
1. Each Contracting Party shall communicate copies of its reports referred to in Articles 21 and 22 to such of its national organisations as are members of the international organisations of employers and trade unions to be invited under Article 27, paragraph 2, to be represented at meetings of the Sub-committee of the Governmental Social Committee.

2. The Contracting Parties shall forward to the Secretary General any comments on the said reports received from these national organisations if so requested by them.

Article 24   Examination of the reports
The reports sent to the Secretary General in accordance with Articles 21 and 22 shall be examined by a committee of experts who shall have also before them any comments forwarded to the Secretary General in accordance with paragraph 2 of Article 23.

Article 25   Committee of Experts

1. The Committee of Experts shall consist of not more than seven members appointed by the Committee of Ministers from a list of independent experts of the highest integrity and of recognised competence in international social questions, nominated by the Contracting Parties.

2. The members of the committee shall be appointed for a period of six years. They may be reappointed. However, of the members first appointed, the terms of office of two members shall expire at the end of four years.

3. The members whose terms of office are to expire at the end of the initial period of four years shall be chosen by lot by the Committee of Ministers immediately after the first appointment has been made.

4. A member of the Committee of Experts appointed to replace a member whose term of office has not expired shall hold office for the remainder of his predecessor's term.

Article 26   Participation of the International Labour Organisation

The International Labour Organisation shall be invited to nominate a representative to participate in a consultative capacity in the deliberations of the Committee of Experts.

Article 27   Sub-committee of the Governmental Social Committee

1. The reports of the Contracting Parties and the conclusions of the Committee of Experts shall be submitted for examination to a sub-committee of the Governmental Social Committee of the Council of Europe.

2. The sub-committee shall be composed of one representative of each of the Contracting Parties. It shall invite no more than two international organisations of employers and no more than two international trade union organisations as it may designate to be represented as observers in a consultative capacity at its meetings. Moreover, it may consult no more than two representatives of international non-governmental organisations having consultative status with the Council of Europe, in respect of questions with which the organisations are particularly qualified to deal, such as social welfare, and the economic and social protection of the family.

3. The sub-committee shall present to the Committee of Ministers a report containing its conclusions and append the report of the Committee of Experts.

Article 28   Consultative Assembly

The Secretary General of the Council of Europe shall transmit to the Consultative Assembly the conclusions of the Committee of Experts.

The Consultative Assembly shall communicate its views on these conclusions to the Committee of Ministers.

Article 29   Committee of Ministers

By a majority of two-thirds of the members entitled to sit on the Committee, the Committee of Ministers may, on the basis of the report of the sub-committee, and after consultation with the Consultative Assembly, make to each Contracting Party any necessary recommendations.

PART V

Article 30   Derogations in time of war or public emergency

1. In time of war or other public emergency threatening the life of the nation any Contracting Party may take measures derogating from its obligations under this Charter to the extent strictly required by the exigencies of the situation, provided that such measures are not inconsistent with its other obligations under international law.

2. Any Contracting Party which has availed itself of this right of derogation shall, within a reasonable lapse of time, keep the Secretary General of the Council of Europe fully informed of the measures taken and of the reasons therefor. It shall likewise inform the Secretary General when such measures

have ceased to operate and the provisions of the Charter which it has accepted are again being fully executed.

3. The Secretary General shall in turn inform other Contracting Parties and the Director General of the International Labour Office of all communications received in accordance with paragraph 2 of this article.

Article 31 Restrictions

1. The rights and principles set forth in Part I when effectively realised, and their effective exercise as provided for in Part II, shall not be subject to any restrictions or limitations not specified in those parts, except such as are prescribed bylaw and are necessary in a democratic society for the protection of the rights and freedoms of others or for the protection of public interest, national security, public health, or morals.

2. The restrictions permitted under this Charter to the rights and obligations set forth herein shall not be applied for any purpose other than that for which they have been prescribed.

Article 32 Relations between the Charter and domestic law or international agreements

The provisions of this Charter shall not prejudice the provisions of domestic law or of any bilateral or multilateral treaties, conventions or agreements which are already in force, or may come into force, under which more favourable treatment would be accorded to the persons protected.

Article 33 Implementation by collective agreements

1. In member States where the provisions of paragraphs 1, 2, 3, 4 and 5 of Article 2, paragraphs 4, 6 and 7 of Article 7 and paragraphs 1, 2, 3 and 4 of Article 10 of Part II of this Charter are matters normally left to agreements between employers or employers' organisations and workers' organisations, or are normally carried out otherwise than by law, the undertakings of those paragraphs may be given and compliance with them shall be treated as effective if their provisions are applied through such agreements or other means to the great majority of the workers concerned.

2. In member States where these provisions are normally the subject of legislation, the undertakings concerned may likewise be given, and compliance with them shall be regarded as effective if the provisions are applied by law to the great majority of the workers concerned.

Article 34 Territorial application

1. This Charter shall apply to the metropolitan territory of each Contracting Party. Each signatory government may, at the time of signature or of the deposit of its instrument of ratification or approval, specify, by declaration addressed to the Secretary General of the Council of Europe, the territory which shall be considered to be its metropolitan territory for this purpose.

2. Any Contracting Party may, at the time of ratification or approval of this Charter or at any time thereafter, declare by notification addressed to the Secretary General of the Council of Europe, that the Charter shall extend in whole or in part to a non-metropolitan territory or territories specified in the said declaration for whose international relations it is responsible or for which it assumes international responsibility, It shall specify in the declaration the articles or paragraphs of Part II of the Charter which it accepts as binding in respect of the territories named in the declaration.

3. The Charter shall extend to the territory or territories named in the aforesaid declarations as from the thirtieth day after the date on which the Secretary General shall have received notification of such declaration.

4. Any Contracting Party may declare at a later date by notification addressed to the Secretary General of the Council of Europe, that, in respect of one or more of the territories to which the Charter has been extended in accordance with paragraph 2 of this article, it accepts as binding any articles or any numbered paragraphs which it has not already accepted in respect of that territory or territories. Such undertakings subsequently given shall be deemed to be an integral part of the original declaration in respect of the territory concerned, and shall have the same effect as from the thirtieth day after the date of the notification.

5. The Secretary General shall communicate to the other signatory governments and to the Director General of the International Labour Office any notification transmitted to him in accordance with this article.

Article 35   Signature, ratification and entry into force

1. This Charter shall be open for signature by the members of the Council of Europe. It shall be ratified or approved. Instruments of ratification or approval shall be deposited with the Secretary General of the Council of Europe.

2. This Charter shall come into force as from the thirtieth day after the date of deposit of the fifth instrument of ratification or approval.

3. In respect of any signatory government ratifying subsequently, the Charter shall come into force as from the thirtieth day after the date of deposit of its instrument of ratification or approval.

4. The Secretary General shall notify all the members of the Council of Europe and the Director General of the International Labour Office of the entry into force of the Charter, the names of the Contracting Parties which have ratified or approved it and the subsequent deposit of any instruments of ratification or approval.

Article 36   Amendments

Any member of the Council of Europe may propose amendments to this Charter in a communication addressed to the Secretary General of the Council of Europe. The Secretary General shall transmit to the other members of the Council of Europe any amendments so proposed, which shall then be considered by the Committee of Ministers and submitted to the Consultative Assembly for opinion. Any amendments approved by the Committee of Ministers shall enter into force as from the thirtieth day after all the Contracting Parties have informed the Secretary General of their acceptance. The Secretary General shall notify all the members of the Council of Europe and the Director General of the International Labour Office of the entry into force of such amendments.

Article 37   Denunciation

1. Any Contracting Party may denounce this Charter only at the end of a period of five years from the date on which the Charter entered into force for it, or at the end of any successive period of two years, and, in each case, after giving six months' notice to the Secretary General of the Council of Europe, who shall inform the other Parties and the Director General of the International Labour Office accordingly. Such denunciation shall not affect the validity of the Charter in respect of the other Contracting. Parties provided that at all times there are not less than five such Contracting Parties.

2. Any Contracting Party may, in accordance with the provisions set out in the preceding paragraph, denounce any article or paragraph of Part II of the Charter accepted by it provided that the number of articles or paragraphs by which this Contracting Party is bound shall never be less than 10 in the former case and 45 in the latter and that this number of articles or paragraphs shall continue to include the articles selected by the Contracting Party among those to which special reference is made in Article 20, paragraph 1, sub-paragraph b.

3. Any Contracting Party may denounce the present Charter or any of the articles or paragraphs of Part II of the Charter, under the conditions specified in paragraph 1 of this article in respect of any territory to which the said Charter is applicable by virtue of a declaration made in accordance with paragraph 2 of Article 34.

Article 38   Appendix

The appendix to this Charter shall form an integral part of it.

In witness whereof, the undersigned, being duly authorised thereto, have signed this Charter.

Done at Turin, this 18th day of October 1961, in English and French, both texts being equally authoritative, in a single copy which shall be deposited within the archives of the Council of Europe. The Secretary General shall transmit certified copies to each of the signatories.

Appendix to the Social Charter

Scope of the Social Charter in terms of persons protected

1. Without prejudice to Article 12, paragraph 4, and Article 13, paragraph 4, the persons covered by Articles 1 to 17 include foreigners only in so far as they are nationals of other Contracting Parties lawfully resident or working regularly within the territory of the Contracting Party concerned, subject to the understanding that these articles are to be interpreted in the light of the provisions of Articles 18 and 19.

This interpretation would not prejudice the extension of similar facilities to other persons by any of the Contracting Parties.

2. Each Contracting Party will grant to refugees as defined in the Convention relating to the Status of Refugees, signed at Geneva on 28 July 1951, and lawfully staying in its territory, treatment as favourable as possible, and in any case not less favourable than under the obligations accepted by the Contracting Party under the said Convention and under any other existing international instruments applicable to those refugees.

PART I PARAGRAPH 18 AND PART II, ARTICLE 18, PARAGRAPH 1

It is understood that these provisions are not concerned with the question of entry into the territories of the Contracting Parties and do not prejudice the provisions of the European Convention on Establishment, signed at Paris on 13 December 1955.

PART II

Article 1, paragraph 2
This provision shall not be interpreted as prohibiting or authorising any union security clause or practice.

Article 4, paragraph 4
This provision shall be so understood as not to prohibit immediate dismissal for any serious offence.

Article 4, paragraph 5
It is understood that a Contracting Party may give the undertaking required in this paragraph if the great majority of workers are not permitted to suffer deductions from wages either by law or through collective agreements or arbitration awards, the exception being those persons not so covered.

Article 6, paragraph 4
It is understood that each Contracting Party may, in so far as it is concerned, regulate the exercise of the right to strike by law, provided that any further restriction that this might place on the right can be justified under the terms of Article 31.

Article 7, paragraph 8
It is understood that a Contracting Party may give the undertaking required in this paragraph if it fulfils the spirit of the undertaking by providing by law that the great majority of persons under 18 years of age shall not be employed in night work.

Article 12, paragraph 4
The words 'and subject to the conditions laid down in such agreements' in the introduction to this paragraph are taken to imply *inter alia* that with regard to benefits which are available independently

of any insurance contribution a Contracting Party may require the completion of a prescribed period of residence before granting such benefits to nationals of other Contracting Parties.

Article 13, paragraph 4

Governments not Parties to the European Convention on Social and Medical Assistance may ratify the Social Charter in respect of this paragraph provided that they grant to nationals of other Contracting Parties a treatment which is in conformity with the provisions of the said convention.

Article 19, paragraph 6

For the purpose of this provision, the term 'family of a foreign worker' is understood to mean at least his wife and dependent children under the age of 21 years.

PART III

It is understood that the Charter contains legal obligations of an international character, the application of which is submitted solely to the supervision provided for in Part IV thereof.

Article 20, paragraph 1

It is understood that the 'numbered paragraphs' may include articles consisting of only one paragraph.

PART V

Article 30

The term 'in time of war or other public emergency' shall be so understood as to cover also the *threat* of war.

Additional Protocol to the European Social Charter (1988)*

PREAMBLE

The member States of the Council of Europe signatory hereto,

Resolved to take new measures to extend the protection of the social and economic rights guaranteed by the European Social Charter, opened for signature in Turin on 18 October 1961 (hereinafter referred to as 'the Charter'),

Have agreed as follows:

PART I

The Parties accept as the aim of their policy to be pursued by all appropriate means, both national and international in character, the attainment of conditions in which the following rights and principles may be effectively realised:

1. All workers have the right to equal opportunities and equal treatment in matters of employment and occupation without discrimination on the grounds of sex.

2. Workers have the right to be informed and to be consulted within the undertaking.

3. Workers have the right to take part in the determination and improvement of the working conditions and working environment in the undertaking.

4. Every elderly person has the right to social protection.

* © Council of Europe

PART II

The Parties undertake, as provided for in Part III, to consider themselves bound by the obligations laid down in the following articles:

Article 1 Right to equal opportunities and equal treatment in matters of employment and occupation without discrimination on the grounds of sex

1. With a view to ensuring the effective exercise of the right to equal opportunities and equal treatment in matters of employment and occupation without discrimination on the grounds of sex, the Parties undertake to recognise that right and to take appropriate measures to ensure or promote its application in the following fields:

— access to employment, protection against dismissal and occupational resettlement;
— vocational guidance, training, retraining and rehabilitation;
— terms of employment and working conditions including remuneration;
— career development including promotion.

2. Provisions concerning the protection of women, particularly as regards pregnancy, confinement and the post-natal period, shall not be deemed to be discrimination as referred to in paragraph 1 of this article.

3. Paragraph 1 of this article shall not prevent the adoption of specific measures aimed at removing de facto inequalities.

4. Occupational activities which, by reason of their nature or the context in which they are carried out, can be entrusted only to persons of a particular sex may be excluded from the scope of this article or some of its provisions.

Article 2 Right to information and consultation

1. With a view to ensuring the effective exercise of the right of workers to be informed and consulted within the undertaking, the Parties undertake to adopt or encourage measures enabling workers or their representatives, in accordance with national legislation and practice:

(a) to be informed regularly or at the appropriate time and in a comprehensible way about the economic and financial situation of the undertaking employing them, on the understanding that the disclosure of certain information which could be prejudicial to the undertaking may be refused or subject to confidentiality; and

(b) to be consulted in good time on proposed decisions which could substantially affect the interests of workers, particularly on those decisions which could have an important impact on the employment situation in the undertaking.

2. The Parties may exclude from the field of application of paragraph 1 of this article those undertakings employing less than a certain number of workers to be determined by national legislation or practice.

Article 3 Right to take part in the determination and improvement of the working conditions and working environment

1. With a view to ensuring the effective exercise of the right of workers to take part in the determination and improvement of the working conditions and working environment in the undertaking, the Parties undertake to adopt or encourage measures enabling workers or their representatives in accordance with national legislation and practice, to contribute:

(a) to the determination and the improvement of the working conditions, work organisation and working environment;

(b) to the protection of health and safety within the undertaking;

(c) to the organisation of social and socio-cultural services and facilities within the undertaking;

(d) to the supervision of the observance of regulations on these matters.

2. The Parties may exclude from the field of application of paragraph 1 of this article, those undertakings employing less than a certain number of workers to be determined by national legislation or practice.

Article 4 Right of elderly persons to social protection

With a view to ensuring the effective exercise of the right of elderly persons to social protection, the Parties undertake to adopt or encourage, either directly or in cooperation with public or private organisations, appropriate measures designed in particular:

1. to enable elderly persons to remain full members of society for as long as possible, by means of:
   - (a) adequate resources enabling them to lead a decent life and play an active part in public, social and cultural life;
   - (b) provision of information about services and facilities available for elderly persons and their opportunities to make use of them;
2. to enable elderly persons to choose their life-style freely and to lead independent lives in their familiar surroundings for as long as they wish and are able, by means of:
   - (a) provision of housing suited to their needs and their state of health or of adequate support for adapting their housing;
   - (b) the health care and the services necessitated by their state;
3. to guarantee elderly persons living in institutions appropriate support, while respecting their privacy, and participation in decisions concerning living conditions in the institution.

PART III

Article 5 Undertakings

1. Each of the Parties undertakes:
   - (a) to consider Part I of this Protocol as a declaration of the aims which it will pursue by all appropriate means, as stated in the introductory paragraph of that part;
   - (b) to consider itself bound by one or more articles of Part II of this Protocol.
2. The article or articles selected in accordance with sub-paragraph b of paragraph 1 of this article shall be notified to the Secretary General of the Council of Europe at the time when the instrument of ratification, acceptance or approval of the Contracting State concerned is deposited.
3. Any Party may, at a later date, declare by notification to the Secretary General that it considers itself bound by any articles of Part II of this Protocol which it has not already accepted under the terms of paragraph 1 of this article. Such undertakings subsequently given shall be deemed to be an integral part of the ratification, acceptance or approval, and shall have the same effect as from the thirtieth day after the date of the notification.

PART IV

Article 6 Supervision of compliance with the undertakings given

The Parties shall submit reports on the application of those provisions of Part II of this Protocol which they have accepted in the reports submitted by virtue of Article 21 of the Charter.

PART V

Article 7 Implementation of the undertakings given

1. The relevant provisions of Articles 1 to 4 of Part II of this Protocol may be implemented by:
   - (a) laws and regulations;
   - (b) agreements between employers or employers' organisations and workers' organisations;

(c) a combination of those two methods; or

(d) other appropriate means.

2. Compliance with the undertakings deriving from Articles 2 and 3 of Part II of this Protocol shall be regarded as effective if the provisions are applied, in accordance with paragraph 1 of this article, to the great majority of the workers concerned.

Article 8   Relations between the Charter and this Protocol

1. The provisions of this Protocol shall not prejudice the provisions of the Charter.

2. Articles 22 to 32 and Article 36 of the Charter shall apply, mutatis mutandis, to this Protocol.

Article 9   Territorial application

1. This Protocol shall apply to the metropolitan territory of each Party. Any State may, at the time of signature or when depositing its instrument of ratification, acceptance or approval, specify, by declaration addressed to the Secretary General of the Council of Europe, the territory which shall be considered to be its metropolitan territory for this purpose.

2. Any Contracting State may, at the time of ratification, acceptance or approval of this Protocol or at any time thereafter, declare by notification addressed to the Secretary General of the Council of Europe that the Protocol shall extend in whole or in part to a non-metropolitan territory or territories specified in the said declaration for whose international relations it is responsible or for which it assumes international responsibility. It shall specify in the declaration the article or articles of Part II of the Protocol which it accepts as binding in respect of the territories named in the declaration.

3. The Protocol shall extend to the territory or territories named in the aforesaid declaration as from the thirtieth day after the date on which the Secretary General shall have notification of such declaration.

4. Any Party may declare at a later date, by notification addressed to the Secretary General of the Council of Europe, that, in respect of one or more of the territories to which this Protocol has been extended in accordance with paragraph 2 of this article, it accepts as binding any articles which it has not already accepted in respect of that territory or territories. Such undertakings subsequently given shall be deemed to be an integral part of the original declaration in respect of the territory concerned, and shall have the same effect as from the thirtieth day after the date on which the Secretary General shall have notification of such declaration.

Article 10   Signature, ratification, acceptance, approval and entry into force

1. This Protocol shall be open for signature by member States of the Council of Europe who are signatories to the Charter. It is subject to ratification, acceptance or approval. No member State of the Council of Europe shall ratify, accept or approve this Protocol except at the same time as or after ratification of the Charter. Instruments of ratification, acceptance or approval shall be deposited with the Secretary General of the Council of Europe.

2. The Protocol shall enter into force on the thirtieth day after the date of deposit of the third instrument of ratification, acceptance or approval.

3. In respect of any signatory State ratifying subsequently, the Protocol shall come into force as from the thirtieth day after the date of deposit of its instrument of ratification, acceptance or approval.

Article 11   Denunciation

1. Any Party may denounce this Protocol only at the end of a period of five years from the date on which the Protocol entered into force for it, or at the end of any successive period of two years and, in each case, after giving six months' notice to the Secretary General of the Council of Europe. Such denunciation shall not affect the validity of the Protocol in respect of the other Parties provided that at all times there are not less than three such Parties.

2. Any Party may, in accordance with the provisions set out in the preceding paragraph, denounce any article of Part II of this Protocol accepted by it, provided that the number of articles by which this Party is bound shall never be less than one.

3. Any Party may denounce this Protocol or any of the articles of Part II of the Protocol, under the conditions specified in paragraph 1 of this article, in respect of any territory to which the Protocol is applicable by virtue of a declaration made in accordance with paragraphs 2 and 4 of Article 9.

4. Any Party bound by the Charter and this Protocol, which denounces the Charter in accordance with the provisions of paragraph 1 of Article 37 thereof, will be considered to have denounced the Protocol likewise.

Article 12   Notifications
The Secretary General of the Council of Europe shall notify the member States of the Council and the Director General of the International Labour Office of:
    (a) any signature;
    (b) the deposit of any instrument of ratification, acceptance or approval;
    (c) any date of entry into force of this Protocol in accordance with Articles 9 and 10;
    (d) any other act, notification or communication relating to this Protocol.

Article 13   Appendix
The appendix to this Protocol shall form an integral part of it.

In witness whereof the undersigned, being duly authorised thereto, have signed this Protocol.

Done at Strasbourg, this 5th day of May 1988, in English and French, both texts being equally authentic, in a single copy which shall be deposited in the archives of the Council of Europe. The Secretary General of the Council of Europe shall transmit certified copies to each member State of the Council of Europe.

Appendix to the Protocol

Scope of the Protocol in terms of persons protected
1. The persons covered by Articles 1 to 4 include foreigners only in so far as they are nationals of other Parties lawfully resident or working regularly within the territory of the Party concerned subject to the understanding that these articles are to be interpreted in the light of the provisions of Articles 18 and 19 of the Charter.

This interpretation would not prejudice the extension of similar facilities to other persons by any of the Parties.

2. Each Party will grant to refugees as defined in the Convention relating to the Status of Refugees, signed at Geneva on 28 July 1951 and in the Protocol of 31 January 1967, and lawfully staying in its territory, treatment as favourable as possible and in any case not less favourable than under the obligations accepted by the Party under the said instruments and under any other existing international instruments applicable to those refugees.

3. Each Party will grant to stateless persons as defined in the Convention on the Status of Stateless Persons done at New York on 28 September 1954 and lawfully staying in its territory, treatment as favourable as possible and in any case not less favourable than under the obligations accepted by the Party under the said instrument and under any other existing international instruments applicable to those stateless persons.

Article 1
It is understood that social security matters, as well as other provisions relating to unemployment benefit, old age benefit and survivor's benefit, may be excluded from the scope of this article.

Article 1, paragraph 4
This provision is not to be interpreted as requiring the Parties to embody in laws or regulations a list of occupations which, by reason of their nature or the context in which they are carried out, may be reserved to persons of a particular sex.

Articles 2 and 3

1. For the purpose of the application of these articles, the term 'workers' representatives' means persons who are recognised as such under national legislation or practice.

2. The term 'national legislation and practice' embraces as the case may be, in addition to laws and regulations, collective agreements, other agreements between employers and workers' representatives, customs, as well as relevant case-law.

3. For the purposes of the application of these articles, the term 'undertaking' is understood as referring to a set of tangible and intangible components, with or without legal personality, formed to produce goods or provide services for financial gain and with power to determine its own market policy.

4. It is understood that religious communities and their institutions may be excluded from the application of these articles, even if these institutions are 'undertakings' within the meaning of paragraph 3. Establishments pursuing activities which are inspired by certain ideals or guided by certain moral concepts, ideals and concepts which are protected by national legislation, may be excluded from the application of these articles to such an extent as is necessary to protect the orientation of the undertaking.

5. It is understood that, where in a State the rights set under Articles 2 and 3 are exercised in the various establishments of the undertaking, the Party concerned is to be considered as fulfilling the obligations deriving from these provisions.

Article 3

This provision affects neither the powers and obligations of States as regards the adoption of health and safety regulations for work-places, nor the powers and responsibilities of the bodies in charge of monitoring their application.

The terms 'social and socio-cultural services and facilities' are understood as referring to the social and/or cultural facilities for workers provided by some undertakings such as welfare assistance, sports fields, rooms for nursing mothers, libraries, children's holiday camps, etc.

Article 4, paragraph 1

For the purpose of the application of this paragraph, the term 'for as long as possible' refers to the elderly person's physical, psychological and intellectual capacities.

Article 7

It is understood that workers excluded in accordance with paragraph 2 of Article 2 and paragraph 2 of Article 3 are not taken into account in establishing the number of workers concerned.

Protocol Amending the European Social Charter (1991)*

The member States of the Council of Europe, signatory to this Protocol to the European Social Charter, opened for signature in Turin on 18 October 1961 (hereinafter referred to as 'the Charter'),

Being resolved to take some measures to improve the effectiveness of the Charter, and particularly the functioning of its supervisory machinery;

Considering therefore that it is desirable to amend certain provisions of the Charter,

Have agreed as follows:

Article 1

Article 23 of the Charter shall read as follows:

'Article 23   Communication of copies of reports and comments

1. When sending to the Secretary General a report pursuant to Articles 21 and 22, each Contracting Party shall forward a copy of that report to such of its national organisations as are members of the international organisations of employers and trade unions invited, under Article 27, paragraph 2, to be represented at meetings of the Governmental Committee. Those organisations shall

send to the Secretary General any comments on the reports of the Contracting Parties. The Secretary General shall send a copy of those comments to the Contracting Parties concerned, who might wish to respond.

2. The Secretary General shall forward a copy of the reports of the Contracting Parties to the international non-governmental organisations which have consultative status with the Council of Europe and have particular competence in the matters governed by the present Charter.

3. The reports and comments referred to in Articles 21 and 22 and in the present article shall be made available to the public on request.'

Article 2
Article 24 of the Charter shall read as follows:

'Article 24   Examination of the reports
1. The reports sent to the Secretary General in accordance with Articles 21 and 22 shall be examined by a Committee of Independent Experts constituted pursuant to Article 25. The committee shall also have before it any comments forwarded to the Secretary General in accordance with paragraph 1 of Article 23. On completion of its examination, the Committee of Independent Experts shall draw up a report containing its conclusions.

2. With regard to the reports referred to in Article 21, the Committee of Independent Experts shall assess from a legal standpoint the compliance of national law and practice with the obligations arising from the Charter for the Contracting Parties concerned.

3. The Committee of Independent Experts may address requests for additional information and clarification directly to Contracting Parties. In this connection the Committee of Independent Experts may also hold, if necessary, a meeting with the representatives of a Contracting Party, either on its own initiative or at the request of the Contracting Party concerned. The organisations referred to in paragraph 1 of Article 23 shall be kept informed.

4. The conclusions of the Committee of Independent Experts shall be made public and communicated by the Secretary General to the Governmental Committee, to the Parliamentary Assembly and to the organisations which are mentioned in paragraph 1 of Article 23 and paragraph 2 of Article 27.'

Article 3
Article 25 of the Charter shall read as follows:

'Article 25 Committee of Independent Experts
1. The Committee of Independent Experts shall consist of at least nine members elected by the Parliamentary Assembly by a majority of votes cast from a list of experts of the highest integrity and of recognised competence in national and international social questions, nominated by the Contracting Parties. The exact number of members shall be determined by the Committee of Ministers.

2. The members of the committee shall be elected for a period of six years. They may stand for re-election once.

3. A member of the Committee of Independent Experts elected to replace a member whose term of office has not expired shall hold office for the remainder of his predecessor's term.

4. The members of the committee shall sit in their individual capacity. Throughout their term of office, they may not perform any function incompatible with the requirements of independence, impartiality and availability inherent in their office.'

Article 4
Article 27 of the Charter shall read as follows:

'Article 27   Governmental Committee
1. The reports of the Contracting Parties, the comments and information communicated in accordance with paragraphs 1 of Article 23 and 3 of Article 24, and the reports of the Committee of Independent Experts shall be submitted to a Governmental Committee.

2. The committee shall be composed of one representative of each of the Contracting Parties. It shall invite no more than two international organisations of employers and no more than two international trade union organisations to send observers in a consultative capacity to its meetings. Moreover, it may consult representatives of international non-governmental organisations which have consultative status with the Council of Europe and have particular competence in the matters governed by the present Charter.

3. The Governmental Committee shall prepare the decisions of the Committee of Ministers. In particular, in the light of the reports of the Committee of Independent Experts and of the Contracting Parties, it shall select, giving reasons for its choice, on the basis of social, economic and other policy considerations the situations which should, in its view, be the subject of recommendations to each Contracting Party concerned, in accordance with Article 28 of the Charter. It shall present to the Committee of Ministers a report which shall be made public.

4. On the basis of its findings on the implementation of the Social Charter in general, the Governmental Committee may submit proposals to the Committee of Ministers aiming at studies to be carried out on social issues and on articles of the Charter which might possibly be updated.'

Article 5
Article 28 of the Charter shall read as follows:

'Article 28   Committee of Ministers
1. The Committee of Ministers shall adopt, by a majority of two-thirds of those voting, with entitlement to voting limited to the Contracting Parties, on the basis of the report of the Governmental Committee, a resolution covering the entire supervision cycle and containing individual recommendations to the Contracting Parties concerned.

2. Having regard to the proposals made by the Governmental Committee pursuant to paragraph 4 of Article 27, the Committee of Ministers shall take such decisions as it deems appropriate.'

Article 6
Article 29 of the Charter shall read as follows:

'Article 29   Parliamentary Assembly
The Secretary General of the Council of Europe shall transmit to the Parliamentary Assembly, with a view to the holding of periodical plenary debates, the reports of the Committee of Independent Experts and of the Governmental Committee, as well as the resolutions of the Committee of Ministers.'

Article 7
1. This Protocol shall be open for signature by member States of the Council of Europe signatories to the Charter, which may express their consent to be bound by:
    (a) signature without reservation as to ratification, acceptance or approval; or
    (b) signature subject to ratification, acceptance or approval, followed by ratification, acceptance or approval.

2. Instruments of ratification, acceptance or approval shall be deposited with the Secretary General of the Council of Europe.

Article 8
This Protocol shall enter into force on the thirtieth day after the date on which all Contracting Parties to the Charter have expressed their consent to be bound by the Protocol in accordance with the provisions of Article 7.

Article 9
The Secretary General of the Council of Europe shall notify the member States of the Council of:
    (a) any signature;
    (b) the deposit of any instrument of ratification, acceptance or approval;

    (c) the date of entry into force of this Protocol in accordance with Article 8;

    (d) any other act, notification or communication relating to this Protocol.

In witness whereof the undersigned, being duly authorised thereto, have signed this Protocol.

Done at Turin, this 21st day of October 1991, in English and French, both texts being equally authentic, in a single copy which shall be deposited in the archives of the Council of Europe. The Secretary General of the Council of Europe shall transmit certified copies to each member State of the Council of Europe.

Additional Protocol to the European Social Charter Providing for a System of Collective Complaints (1995)*

PREAMBLE

The member States of the Council of Europe, signatories to this Protocol to the *European Social Charter*, opened for signature in Turin on 18 October 1961 (hereinafter referred to as 'the Charter');

    Resolved to take new measures to improve the effective enforcement of the social rights guaranteed by The Charter;

    Considering that this aim could be achieved in particular by the establishment of a collective complaints procedure, which, *inter alia*, would strengthen the participation of management and labour and of non-governmental organisations,

    Have agreed as follows:

Article 1

The Contracting Parties to this Protocol recognise the right of the following organisations to submit complaints alleging unsatisfactory application of the Charter:

    (a) International organisations of employers and trade unions referred to in paragraph 2 of Article 27 of the Charter;

    (b) other international non-governmental organisations which have consultative status with the Council of Europe and have been put on a list established for this purpose by the Governmental Committee;

    (c) representative national organisations of employers and trade unions within the jurisdiction of the Contracting Party against which they have lodged a complaint.

Article 2

    1. Any Contracting State may also, when it expresses its consent to be bound by this Protocol, in accordance with the provisions of Article 13, or at any moment thereafter, declare that it recognises the right of any other representative national non-governmental organisation within its jurisdiction which has particular competence in the matters governed by the Charter, to lodge complaints against it.

    2. Such declarations may be made for a specific period.

    3. The declarations shall be deposited with the Secretary General of the Council of Europe who shall transmit copies thereof to the Contracting Parties and publish them.

Article 3

The international non-governmental organisations and the national non-governmental organisations referred to in Article 1.b and Article 2 respectively may submit complaints in accordance with the procedure prescribed by the aforesaid provisions only in respect of those matters regarding which they have been recognised as having particular competence.

---

* © Council of Europe

Article 4

The complaint shall be lodged in writing, relate to a provision of the Charter accepted by the Contracting Party concerned and indicate in what respect the latter has not ensured the satisfactory application of this provision.

Article 5

Any complaint shall be addressed to the Secretary General who shall acknowledge receipt of it, notify it to the Contracting Party concerned and immediately transmit it to the Committee of Independent Experts.

Article 6

The Committee of Independent Experts may request the Contracting Party concerned and the organisation which lodged the complaint to submit written information and observations on the admissibility of the complaint within such time-limit as it shall prescribe.

Article 7

1. If it decides that a complaint is admissible, the Committee of Independent Experts shall notify the Contracting Parties to the Charter through the Secretary General. It shall request the Contracting Party concerned and the organisation which lodged the complaint to submit, within such time-limit as it shall prescribe, all relevant written explanations or information, and the other Contracting Parties to this Protocol, the comments they wish to submit, within the same time-limit.

2. If the complaint has been lodged by a national organisation of employers or a national trade union or by another national or international non-governmental organisation, the Committee of Independent Experts shall notify the international organisations of employers or trade unions referred to in paragraph 2 of Article 27 of the Charter, through the Secretary General, and invite them to submit observations within such time-limit as it shall prescribe.

3. On the basis of the explanations, information or observations submitted under paragraphs 1 and 2 above, the Contracting Party concerned and the organisation which lodged the complaint may submit any additional written information or observations within such time-limit as the Committee of Independent Experts shall prescribe.

4. In the course of the examination of the complaint, the Committee of Independent Experts may organise a hearing with the representatives of the parties.

Article 8

1. The Committee of Independent Experts shall draw up a report in which it shall describe the steps taken by it to examine the complaint and present its conclusions as to whether or not the Contracting Party concerned has ensured the satisfactory application of the provision of the Charter referred to in the complaint.

2. The report shall be transmitted to the Committee of Ministers. It shall also be transmitted to the organisation that lodged the complaint and to the Contracting Parties to the Charter, which shall not be at liberty to publish it.

It shall be transmitted to the Parliamentary Assembly and made public at the same time as the resolution referred to in Article 9 or no later than four months after it has been transmitted to the Committee of Ministers.

Article 9

1. On the basis of the report of the Committee of Independent Experts, the Committee of Ministers shall adopt a resolution by a majority of those voting. If the Committee of Independent Experts finds that the Charter has not been applied in a satisfactory manner, the Committee of Ministers shall adopt, by a majority of two-thirds of those voting, a recommendation addressed to the Contracting Party concerned. In both cases, entitlement to voting shall be limited to the Contracting Parties to the Charter.

2. At the request of the Contracting Party concerned, the Committee of Ministers may decide, where the report of the Committee of Independent Experts raises new issues, by a two-thirds majority of the Contracting Parties to the Charter, to consult the Governmental Committee.

Article 10
The Contracting Party concerned shall provide information on the measures it has taken to give effect to the Committee of Ministers' recommendation, in the next report which it submits to the Secretary General under Article 21 of the Charter.

Article 11
Articles 1 to 10 of this Protocol shall apply also to the articles of Part II of the first Additional Protocol to the Charter in respect of the States Parties to that Protocol, to the extent that these articles have been accepted.

Article 12
The States Parties to this Protocol consider that the first paragraph of the appendix to the Charter, relating to Part III, reads as follows:

'It is understood that the Charter contains legal obligations of an international character, the application of which is submitted solely to the supervision provided for in Part IV thereof and in the provisions of this Protocol.'

Article 13
1. This Protocol shall be open for signature by member States of the Council of Europe signatories to the Charter, which may express their consent to be bound by:
   (a) signature without reservation as to ratification, acceptance or approval; or
   (b) signature subject to ratification, acceptance or approval, followed by ratification, acceptance or approval.

2. A member State of the Council of Europe may not express its consent to be bound by this Protocol without previously or simultaneously ratifying the Charter.

3. Instruments of ratification, acceptance or approval shall be deposited with the Secretary General of the Council of Europe.

Article 14
1. This Protocol shall enter into force on the first day of the month following the expiration of a period of one month after the date on which five member States of the Council of Europe have expressed their consent to be bound by the Protocol in accordance with the provisions of Article 13.

2. In respect of any member State which subsequently expresses its consent to be bound by it, the Protocol shall enter into force on the first day of the month following the expiration of a period of one month after the date of the deposit of the instrument of ratification, acceptance or approval.

Article 15
1. Any Party may at any time denounce this Protocol by means of a notification addressed to the Secretary General of the Council of Europe.

2. Such denunciation shall become effective on the first day of the month following the expiration of a period of twelve months after the date of receipt of such notification by the Secretary General.

Article 16
The Secretary General of the Council of Europe shall notify all the member States of the Council of:
   (a) any signature;
   (b) the deposit of any instrument of ratification, acceptance or approval;
   (c) the date of entry into force of this Protocol in accordance with Article 14;
   (d) any other act, notification or declaration relating to this Protocol.

In witness whereof the undersigned, being duly authorised thereto, have signed this Protocol.

Done at Strasbourg, this 9th day of November 1995, in English and French, both texts being equally authentic, in a single copy which shall be deposited in the archives of the Council of Europe. The Secretary General of the Council of Europe shall transmit certified copies to each member State of the Council of Europe.

European Social Charter (Revised) (1996)*

PREAMBLE

The governments signatory hereto, being members of the Council of Europe,

Considering that the aim of the Council of Europe is the achievement of greater unity between its members for the purpose of safeguarding and realising the ideals and principles which are their common heritage and of facilitating their economic and social progress, in particular by the maintenance and further realisation of human rights and fundamental freedoms;

Considering that in the *European Convention for the Protection of Human Rights and Fundamental Freedoms* signed at Rome on 4 November 1950, and the Protocols thereto, the member States of the Council of Europe agreed to secure to their populations the civil and political rights and freedoms therein specified;

Considering that in the *European Social Charter* opened for signature in Turin on 18 October 1961 and the *Protocols* thereto, the member States of the Council of Europe agreed to secure to their populations the social rights specified therein in order to improve their standard of living and their social well-being;

Recalling that the Ministerial Conference on Human Rights held in Rome on 5 November 1990 stressed the need, on the one hand, to preserve the indivisible nature of all human rights, be they civil, political, economic, social or cultural and, on the other hand, to give the European Social Charter fresh impetus;

Resolved, as was decided during the Ministerial Conference held in Turin on 21 and 22 October 1991, to update and adapt the substantive contents of the Charter in order to take account in particular of the fundamental social changes which have occurred since the text was adopted;

Recognising the advantage of embodying in a Revised Charter, designed progressively to take the place of the European Social Charter, the rights guaranteed by the Charter as amended, the rights guaranteed by the *Additional Protocol* of 1988 and to add new rights,

Have agreed as follows:

PART I

The Parties accept as the aim of their policy, to be pursued by all appropriate means both national and international in character, the attainment of conditions in which the following rights and principles may be effectively realised:

1. Everyone shall have the opportunity to earn his living in an occupation freely entered upon.
2. All workers have the right to just conditions of work.
3. All workers have the right to safe and healthy working conditions.
4. All workers have the right to a fair remuneration sufficient for a decent standard of living for themselves and their families.
5. All workers and employers have the right to freedom of association in national or international organisations for the protection of their economic and social interests.
6. All workers and employers have the right to bargain collectively.
7. Children and young persons have the right to a special protection against the physical and moral hazards to which they are exposed.
8. Employed women, in case of maternity, have the right to a special protection.

---

* © Council of Europe

9. Everyone has the right to appropriate facilities for vocational guidance with a view to helping him choose an occupation suited to his personal aptitude and interests.

10. Everyone has the right to appropriate facilities for vocational training.

11. Everyone has the right to benefit from any measures enabling him to enjoy the highest possible standard of health attainable.

12. All workers and their dependants have the right to social security.

13. Anyone without adequate resources has the right to social and medical assistance.

14. Everyone has the right to benefit from social welfare services.

15. Disabled persons have the right to independence, social integration and participation in the life of the community.

16. The family as a fundamental unit of society has the right to appropriate social, legal and economic protection to ensure its full development.

17. Children and young persons have the right to appropriate social, legal and economic protection.

18. The nationals of anyone of the Parties have the right to engage in any gainful occupation in the territory of any one of the others on a footing of equality with the nationals of the latter, subject to restrictions based on cogent economic or social reasons.

19. Migrant workers who are nationals of a Party and their families have the right to protection and assistance in the territory of any other Party.

20. All workers have the right to equal opportunities and equal treatment in matters of employment and occupation without discrimination on the grounds of sex.

21. Workers have the right to be informed and to be consulted within the undertaking.

22. Workers have the right to take part in the determination and improvement of the working conditions and working environment in the undertaking.

23. Every elderly person has the right to social protection.

24. All workers have the right to protection in cases of termination of employment.

25. All workers have the right to protection of their claims in the event of the insolvency of their employer.

26. All workers have the right to dignity at work.

27. All persons with family responsibilities and who are engaged or wish to engage in employment have a right to do so without being subject to discrimination and as far as possible without conflict between their employment and family responsibilities.

28. Workers' representatives in undertakings have the right to protection against acts prejudicial to them and should be afforded appropriate facilities to carry out their functions.

29. All workers have the right to be informed and consulted in collective redundancy procedures.

30. Everyone has the right to protection against poverty and social exclusion.

31. Everyone has the right to housing.

PART II

The Parties undertake, as provided for in Part III, to consider themselves bound by the obligations laid down in the following articles and paragraphs.

Article 1   The right to work

With a view to ensuring the effective exercise of the right to work, the Contracting Parties undertake:

1. to accept as one of their primary aims and responsibilities the achievement and maintenance of as high and stable a level of employment as possible, with view to the attainment of full employment;

2. to protect effectively the right of the worker to earn his living in an occupation freely entered upon;

3. to establish or maintain free employment services for all workers;

4. to provide or promote appropriate vocational guidance, training and rehabilitation.

Article 2   The right to just conditions of work

With a view to ensuring the effective exercise of the right to just conditions of work, the Contracting Parties undertake:

1. to provide for reasonable daily and weekly working hours, the working week to be progressively reduced to the extent that the increase of productivity and other relevant factors permit;
2. to provide for public holidays with pay;
3. to provide for a minimum of two weeks' annual holiday with pay;
4. to eliminate risks in inherently dangerous or unhealthy occupations, and where it has not yet been possible to eliminate or reduce sufficiently these risks, to provide for either a reduction of working hours or additional paid holidays for workers engaged in such occupations;
5. to ensure a weekly rest period which shall, as far as possible, coincide with the day recognised by tradition or custom in the country or region concerned as a day of rest;
6. to ensure that workers are informed in written form, as soon as possible, and in any event not later than two months after the date of commencing their employment, of the essential aspects of the contract or employment relationship;
7. to ensure that workers performing night work benefit from measures which take account of the special nature of the work.

Article 3   The right to safe and healthy working conditions

With a view to ensuring the effective exercise of the right to safe and healthy working conditions, the Parties undertake, in consultation with employers' and workers' organisations:

1. to formulate, implement and periodically review a coherent national policy on occupational safety, occupational health and the working environment. The primary aim of this policy shall be to improve occupational safety and health and to prevent accidents and injury to health arising out of, linked with or occurring in the course of work, particularly by minimising the causes of hazards inherent in the working environment;
2. to issue safety and health regulations;
3. to provide for the enforcement of such regulations by measures of supervision;
4. to promote the progressive development of occupational health services for all workers with essentially preventive and advisory functions.

Article 4   The right to a fair remuneration

With a view to ensuring the effective exercise of the right to a fair remuneration, the Parties undertake:

1. to recognise the right of workers to a remuneration such as will give them and their families a decent standard of living;
2. to recognise the right of workers to an increased rate of remuneration for overtime work, subject to exceptions in particular cases;
3. to recognise the right of men and women workers to equal pay for work of equal value;
4. to recognise the right of all workers to a reasonable period of notice for termination of employment;
5. to permit deductions from wages only under conditions and to the extent prescribed by national laws or regulations or fixed by collective agreements or arbitration awards.

The exercise of these rights shall be achieved by freely concluded collective agreements, by statutory wage-fixing machinery, or by other means appropriate to national conditions.

Article 5   The right to organise

With a view to ensuring or promoting the freedom of workers and employers to form local, national or international organisations for the protection of their economic and social interests and to join those organisations, the Parties undertake that national law shall not be such as to impair, nor shall it be so applied as to impair, this freedom. The extent to which the guarantees provided for in this article shall apply to the police shall be determined by national laws or regulations. The principle governing the application to the members of the armed forces of these guarantees and the extent to which they shall apply to persons in this category shall equally be determined by national laws or regulations.

Article 6   The right to bargain collectively

With a view to ensuring the effective exercise of the right to bargain collectively, the Parties undertake:

1. to promote joint consultation between workers and employers;

2. to promote, where necessary and appropriate, machinery for voluntary negotiations between employers or employers' organisations and workers' organisations, with a view to the regulation of terms and conditions of employment by means of collective agreements;

3. to promote the establishment and use of appropriate machinery for conciliation and voluntary arbitration for the settlement of labour disputes;

and recognise:

4. the right of workers and employers to collective action in cases of conflicts of interest, including the right to strike, subject to obligations that might arise out of collective agreements previously entered into.

Article 7   The right of children and young persons to protection

With a view to ensuring the effective exercise of the right of children and young persons to protection, the Parties undertake:

1. to provide that the minimum age of admission to employment shall be 15 years, subject to exceptions for children employed in prescribed light work without harm to their health, morals or education;

2. to provide that the minimum age of admission to employment shall be fixed with respect to prescribed occupations regarded as dangerous or unhealthy;

3. to provide that persons who are still subject to compulsory education shall not be employed in such work as would deprive them of the full benefit of their education;

4. to provide that the working hours of persons under 18 years of age shall be limited in accordance with the needs of their development, and particularly with their need for vocational training;

5. to recognise the right of young workers and apprentices to a fair wage or other appropriate allowances;

6. to provide that the time spent by young persons in vocational training during the normal working hours with the consent of the employer shall be treated as forming part of the working day;

7. to provide that employed persons of under 18 years of age shall be entitled to a minimum of four weeks' annual holiday with pay;

8. to provide that persons under 18 years of age shall not be employed in night work with the exception of certain occupations provided for by national laws or regulations;

9. to provide that persons under 18 years of age employed in occupations prescribed by national laws or regulations shall be subject to regular medical control;

10. to ensure special protection against physical and moral dangers to which children and young persons are exposed, and particularly against those resulting directly or indirectly from their work.

Article 8   The right of employed women to protection

With a view to ensuring the effective exercise of the right of employed women to protection the Parties undertake:

1. to provide either by paid leave, by adequate social security benefits or by benefits from public funds for women to take leave before and after childbirth up to a total of at least fourteen weeks;

2. to consider it as unlawful for an employer to give a woman notice of dismissal during the period from the time she notifies her employer that she is pregnant until the end of her maternity leave or to give her notice of dismissal at such a time that the notice would expire during such a period;

3. to provide that mothers who are nursing their infants shall be entitled to sufficient time off for this purpose;

4. to regulate the employment in night work of pregnant women, women who have recently given birth and women nursing their infants;

5. to prohibit the employment of pregnant women, women who have recently given birth or who are nursing their infants in underground mining and all other work which is unsuitable by reason of its dangerous, unhealthy or arduous nature and to take appropriate measures to protect the employment rights of these women.

Article 9   The right to vocational guidance

With a view to ensuring the effective exercise of the right to vocational guidance, the Parties undertake to provide or promote, as necessary, a service which will assist all persons, including the handicapped, to solve problems related to occupational choice and progress, with due regard to the individual's characteristics and their relation to occupational opportunity; this assistance should be available free of charge, both to young persons, including school children, and to adults.

Article 10   The right to vocational training

With a view to ensuring the effective exercise of the right to vocational training, the Parties undertake:

1. to provide or promote, as necessary, the technical and vocational training of all persons, including the handicapped, in consultation with employers' and workers' organisations, and to grant facilities for access to higher technical and university education, based solely on individual aptitude;

2. to provide or promote a system of apprenticeship and other systematic arrangements for training young boys and girls in their various employments;

3. to provide or promote, as necessary:
   (a) adequate and readily available training facilities for adult workers;
   (b) special facilities for the retraining of adult workers needed as a result of technological development or new trends in employment;

4. to provide or promote, as necessary, special measures for the retraining and reintegration of the long-term unemployed;

5. to encourage the full utilisation of the facilities provided by appropriate measures such as:
   (a) reducing or abolishing any fees or charges;
   (b) granting financial assistance in appropriate cases;
   (c) including in the normal working hours time spent on supplementary training taken by the worker, at the request of his employer, during employment;
   (d) ensuring, through adequate supervision, in consultation with the employers' and workers' organisations, the efficiency of apprenticeship and other training arrangements for young workers, and the adequate protection of young workers generally.

Article 11   The right to protection of health

With a view to ensuring the effective exercise of the right to protection of health, the Parties undertake, either directly or in co-operation with public or private organisations to take appropriate measures designed *inter alia*:

1. to remove as far as possible the causes of ill-health;

2. to provide advisory and educational facilities for the promotion of health and the encouragement of individual responsibility in matters of health;

3. to prevent as far as possible epidemic, endemic and other diseases as well as accidents.

Article 12   The right to social security

With a view to ensuring the effective exercise of the right to social security, the Contracting Parties undertake:

1. to establish or maintain a system of social security;

2. to maintain the social security system at a satisfactory level at least equal to that necessary for the ratification of the European Code of Social Security;

3. to endeavour to raise progressively the system of social security to a higher level;

4. to take steps, by the conclusion of appropriate bilateral and multilateral agreements or by other means, and subject to the conditions laid down in such agreements, in order to ensure:

    (a) equal treatment with their own nationals of the nationals of other Parties in respect of social security rights, including the retention of benefits arising out of social security legislation, whatever movements the persons protected may undertake between the territories of the Parties;

    (b) the granting, maintenance and resumption of social security rights by such means as the accumulation of insurance or employment periods completed under the legislation of each of the Parties.

Article 13   The right to social and medical assistance

With a view to ensuring the effective exercise of the right to social and medical assistance, the Parties undertake:

1. to ensure that any person who is without adequate resources and who is unable to secure such resources either by his own efforts or from other sources, in particular by benefits under a social security scheme, be granted adequate assistance, and, in case of sickness, the care necessitated by his condition;

2. to ensure that persons receiving such assistance shall not, for that reason, suffer from a diminution of their political or social rights;

3. to provide that everyone may receive by appropriate public or private services such advice and personal help as may be required to prevent, to remove, or to alleviate personal or family want;

4. to apply the provisions referred to in paragraphs 1, 2 and 3 of this article on an equal footing with their nationals to nationals of other Parties lawfully within their territories, in accordance with their obligations under the *European Convention on Social and Medical Assistance*, signed at Paris on 11 December 1953.

Article 14   The right to benefit from social welfare services

With a view to ensuring the effective exercise of the right to benefit from social welfare services, the Parties undertake:

1. to promote or provide services which, by using methods of social work, would contribute to the welfare and development of both individuals and groups in the community, and to their adjustment to the social environment;

2. to encourage the participation of individuals and voluntary or other organisations in the establishment and maintenance of such services.

Article 15   The right of persons with disabilities to independence, social integration and participation in the life of the community

With a view to ensuring to persons with disabilities, irrespective of age and the nature and origin of their disabilities, the effective exercise of the right to independence, social integration and participation in the life of the community, the Parties undertake, in particular:

1. to take the necessary measures to provide persons with disabilities with guidance, education and vocational training in the framework of general schemes wherever possible or, where this is not possible, through specialised bodies, public or private;

2. to promote their access to employment through all measures tending to encourage employers to hire and keep in employment persons with disabilities in the ordinary working environment and to adjust the working conditions to the needs of the disabled or, where this is not possible by reason of the disability, by arranging for or creating sheltered employment according to the level of disability. In certain cases, such measures may require recourse to specialised placement and support services;

3. to promote their full social integration and participation in the life of the community in particular through measures, including technical aids, aiming to overcome barriers to communication and mobility and enabling access to transport, housing, cultural activities and leisure.

Article 16   The right of the family to social, legal and economic protection

With a view to ensuring the necessary conditions for the full development of the family, which is a fundamental unit of society, the Parties undertake to promote the economic, legal and social protection of family life by such means as social and family benefits, fiscal arrangements, provision of family housing, benefits for the newly married and other appropriate means.

Article 17   The right of children and young persons to social, legal and economic protection

With a view to ensuring the effective exercise of the right of children and young persons to grow up to an environment which encourages the full development of their personality and of their physical and mental capacities, the Parties undertake, either directly or in co-operation with public and private organisations, to take all appropriate and necessary measures designed:

1. (a) to ensure that children and young persons, taking account of the rights and duties of their parents, have the care, the assistance, the education and the training they need, in particular by providing for the establishment or maintenance of institutions and services sufficient and adequate for this purpose;
   (b) to protect children and young persons against negligence, violence or exploitation;
   (c) to provide protection and special aid from the state for children and young persons temporarily or definitively deprived of their family's support;
2. to provide to children and young persons a free primary and secondary education as well as to encourage regular attendance at schools.

Article 18   The right to engage in a gainful occupation in the territory of other Parties

With a view to ensuring the effective exercise of the right to engage in a gainful occupation in the territory of any other Party, the Parties undertake:

1. to apply existing regulations in a spirit of liberality;
2. to simplify existing formalities and to reduce or abolish chancery dues and other charges payable by foreign workers or their employers;
3. to liberalise, individually or collectively, regulations governing the employment of foreign workers; and recognise:
4. the right of their nationals to leave the country to engage in a gainful occupation in the territories of the other Parties.

Article 19   The right of migrant workers and their families to protection and assistance

With a view to ensuring the effective exercise of the right of migrant workers and their families to protection and assistance in the territory of any other Party, the Parties undertake:

1. to maintain or to satisfy themselves that there are maintained adequate and free services to assist such workers, particularly in obtaining accurate information, and to take all appropriate steps, so far as national laws and regulations permit, against misleading propaganda relating to emigration and immigration;
2. to adopt appropriate measures within their own jurisdiction to facilitate the departure, journey and reception of such workers and their families, and to provide, within their own jurisdiction, appropriate services for health, medical attention and good hygienic conditions during the journey;
3. to promote co-operation, as appropriate, between social services, public and private, in emigration and immigration countries;
4. to secure for such workers lawfully within their territories, in so far as such matters are regulated by law or regulations or are subject to the control of administrative authorities, treatment not less favourable than that of their own nationals in respect of the following matters:
   (a) remuneration and other employment and working conditions;
   (b) membership of trade unions and enjoyment of the benefits of collective bargaining;
   (c) accommodation;

5. to secure for such workers lawfully within their territories treatment not less favourable than that of their own nationals with regard to employment taxes, dues or contributions payable in respect of employed persons;

6. to facilitate as far as possible the reunion of the family of a foreign worker permitted to establish himself in the territory;

7. to secure for such workers lawfully within their territories treatment not less favourable than that of their own nationals in respect of legal proceedings relating to matters referred to in this article;

8. to secure that such workers lawfully residing within their territories are not expelled unless they endanger national security or offend against public interest or morality;

9. to permit, within legal limits, the transfer of such parts of the earnings and savings of such workers as they may desire;

10. to extend the protection and assistance provided for in this article to self employed migrants in so far as such measures apply;

11. to promote and facilitate the teaching of the national language of the receiving state or, if there are several, one of these languages, to migrant workers and members of their families;

12. to promote and facilitate, as far as practicable, the teaching of the migrant worker's mother tongue to the children of the migrant worker.

Article 20   The right to equal opportunities and equal treatment in matters of employment and occupation without discrimination on the grounds of sex

With a view to ensuring the effective exercise of the right to equal opportunities and equal treatment in matters of employment and occupation without discrimination on the grounds of sex, the Parties undertake to recognise that right and to take appropriate measures to ensure or promote its application in the following fields:

(a) access to employment, protection against dismissal and occupational reintegration;

(b) vocational guidance, training, retraining and rehabilitation;

(c) terms of employment and working conditions, including remuneration;

(d) career development, including promotion.

Article 21   The right to information and consultation

With a view to ensuring the effective exercise of the right of workers to the informed and consulted within the undertaking, the Parties undertake to adopt or encourage measures enabling workers or their representatives, in accordance with national legislation and practice:

(a) to be informed regularly or at the appropriate time and in a comprehensible way about the economic and financial situation of the undertaking employing them, on the understanding that the disclosure of certain information which could be prejudicial to the undertaking may be refused or subject to confidentiality; and

(b) to be consulted in good time on proposed decisions which could substantially affect the interests of workers, particularly on those decisions which could have an important impact on the employment situation in the undertaking.

Article 22   The right to take part in the determination and improvement of the working conditions and working environment

With a view to ensuring the effective exercise of the right of workers to take part in the determination and improvement of the working conditions and working environment in the undertaking, the Parties undertake to adopt or encourage measures enabling workers or their representatives, in accordance with national legislation and practice, to contribute:

(a) to the determination and the improvement of the working conditions, work organisation and working environment;

(b) to the protection of health and safety within the undertaking;

(c) to the organisation of social and socio-cultural services and facilities within the undertaking;

(d) to the supervision of the observance of regulations on these matters.

Article 23   The right of elderly persons to social protection

With a view to ensuring the effective exercise of the right of elderly persons to social protection, the Parties undertake to adopt or encourage, either directly or in co-operation with public or private organisations, appropriate measures designed in particular:

- to enable elderly persons to remain full members of society for as long as possible, by means of:
  - (a) adequate resources enabling them to lead a decent life and play an active part in public, social and cultural life;
  - (b) provision of information about services and facilities available for elderly persons and their opportunities to make use of them;
- to enable elderly persons to choose their life-style freely and to lead independent lives in their familiar surroundings for as long as they wish and are able, by means of:
  - (a) provision of housing suited to their needs and their state of health or of adequate support for adapting their housing;
  - (b) the health care and the services necessitated by their state;
- to guarantee elderly persons living in institutions appropriate support, while respecting their privacy, and participation in decisions concerning living conditions in the institution.

Article 24   The right to protection in cases of termination of employment

With a view to ensuring the effective exercise of the right of workers to protection in cases of termination of employment, the Parties undertake to recognise:

- (a) the right of all workers not to have their employment terminated without valid reasons for such termination connected with their capacity or conduct or based on the operational requirements of the undertaking, establishment or service;
- (b) the right of workers whose employment is terminated without a valid reason to adequate compensation or other appropriate relief.

To this end the Parties undertake to ensure that a worker who considers that his employment has been terminated without a valid reason shall have the right to appeal to an impartial body.

Article 25   The right of workers to the protection of their claims in the event of the insolvency of their employer

With a view to ensuring the effective exercise of the right of workers to the protection of their claims in the event of the insolvency of their employer, the Parties undertake to provide that workers' claims arising from contracts of employment or employment relationships be guaranteed by a guarantee institution or by any other effective form of protection.

Article 26   The right to dignity at work

With a view to ensuring the effective exercise of the right of all workers to protection of their dignity at work, the Parties undertake, in consultation with employers' and workers' organisations:

1. to promote awareness, information and prevention of sexual harassment in the workplace or in relation to work and to take all appropriate measures to protect workers from such conduct;

2. to promote awareness, information and prevention of recurrent reprehensible or distinctly negative and offensive actions directed against individual workers in the work-place or in relation to work and to take all appropriate measures to protect workers from such conduct.

Article 27   The right of workers with family responsibilities to equal opportunities and equal treatment

With a view to ensuring the exercise of the right to equality of opportunity and treatment for men and women workers with family responsibilities and between such workers and other workers, the Parties undertake:

1. to take appropriate measures:
   - (a) to enable workers with family responsibilities to enter and remain in employment, as well as to re-enter employment after an absence due to those responsibilities, including measures in the field of vocational guidance and training;

(b) to take account of their needs in terms of conditions of employment and social security;

(c) to develop or promote services, public or private, in particular child day care services and other childcare arrangements;

2. to provide a possibility for either parent to obtain, during a period after maternity leave, parental leave to take care of a child, the duration and conditions of which should be determined by national legislation, collective agreements or practice;

3. to ensure that family responsibilities shall not, as such, constitute a valid reason for termination of employment.

Article 28   The right of workers' representatives to protection in the undertaking and facilities to be accorded to them

With a view to ensuring the effective exercise of the right of workers' representatives to carry out their functions, the Parties undertake to ensure that in the undertaking:

(a) they enjoy effective protection against acts prejudicial to them, including dismissal, based on their status or activities as workers' representatives within the undertaking;

(b) they are afforded such facilities as may be appropriate in order to enable them to carry out their functions promptly and efficiently, account being taken of the industrial relations system of the country and the needs, size and capabilities of the undertaking concerned.

Article 29   The right to information and consultation in collective redundancy procedures

With a view to ensuring the effective exercise of the right of workers to be informed and consulted in situations of collective redundancies, the Parties undertake to ensure that employers shall inform and consult workers' representatives, in good time prior to such collective redundancies, on ways and means of avoiding collective redundancies or limiting their occurrence and mitigating their consequences, for example by recourse to accompanying social measures aimed, in particular, at aid for the redeployment or retraining of the workers concerned.

Article 30   The right to protection against poverty and social exclusion

With a view to ensuring the effective exercise of the right to protection against poverty and social exclusion, the Parties undertake:

(a) to take measures within the framework of an overall and co-ordinated approach to promote the effective access of persons who live or risk living in a situation of social exclusion or poverty, as well as their families, to, in particular, employment, housing, training, education, culture and social and medical assistance;

(b) to review these measures with a view to their adaptation if necessary.

Article 31   The right to housing

With a view to ensuring the effective exercise of the right to housing, the Parties undertake to take measures designed:

1. to promote access to housing of an adequate standard;

2. to prevent and reduce homelessness with a view to its gradual elimination;

3. to make the price of housing accessible to those without adequate resources.

PART III

Article A   Undertakings

1. Subject to the provisions of Article B below, each of the Parties undertakes:

(a) to consider Part I of this Charter as a declaration of the aims which it will pursue by all appropriate means, as stated in the introductory paragraph of that part;

(b) to consider itself bound by at least six of the following nine articles of Part II of this Charter: Articles 1, 5, 6, 7, 12, 13, 16, 19 and 20;

    (c) to consider itself bound by an additional number of articles or numbered paragraphs of Part II of the Charter which it may select, provided that the total number of articles or numbered paragraphs by which it is bound is not less than sixteen articles or sixty-three numbered paragraphs.

    2. The articles or paragraphs selected in accordance with sub-paragraphs b and c of paragraph 1 of this article shall be notified to the Secretary General of the Council of Europe at the time when the instrument of ratification, acceptance or approval is deposited.

    3. Any Party may, at a later date, declare by notification addressed to the Secretary General that it considers itself bound by any articles or any numbered paragraphs of Part II of the Charter which it has not already accepted under the terms of paragraph 1 of this article. Such undertakings subsequently given shall be deemed to be an integral part of the ratification, acceptance or approval and shall have the same effect as from the first day of the month following the expiration of a period of one month after the date of the notification.

    4. Each Party shall maintain a system of labour inspection appropriate to national conditions.

Article B   Links with the European Social Charter and the 1988 Additional Protocol

No Contracting Party to the European Social Charter or Party to the Additional Protocol of 5 May 1988 may ratify, accept or approve this Charter without considering itself bound by at least the provisions corresponding to the provisions of the European Social Charter and, where appropriate, of the Additional Protocol, to which it was bound.

    Acceptance of the obligations of any provision of this Charter shall, from the date of entry into force of those obligations for the Party concerned, result in the corresponding provision of the European Social Charter and, where appropriate, of its Additional Protocol of 1988 ceasing to apply to the Party concerned in the event of that Party being bound by the first of those instruments or by both instruments.

PART IV

Article C   Supervision of the implementation of the undertakings contained in this Charter

The implementation of the legal obligations contained in this Charter shall be submitted to the same supervision as the European Social Charter.

Article D   Collective complaints

    1. The provisions of the Additional Protocol to the European Social Charter providing for a system of collective complaints shall apply to the undertakings given in this Charter for the States which have ratified the said Protocol.

    2. Any State which is not bound by the Additional Protocol to the European Social Charter providing for a system of collective complaints may when depositing its instrument of ratification, acceptance or approval of this Charter or at any time thereafter, declare by notification addressed to the Secretary General of the Council of Europe, that it accepts the supervision of its obligations under this Charter following the procedure provided for in the said Protocol.

PART V

Article E   Non-discrimination

The enjoyment of the rights set forth in this Charter shall be secured without discrimination on any ground such as race, colour, sex, language, religion, political or other opinion, national extraction or social origin, health, association with a national minority, birth or other status.

Article F   Derogations in time of war or public emergency

1. In time of war or other public emergency threatening the life of the nation any Party may take measures derogating from its obligations under this Charter to the extent strictly required by the exigencies of the situation, provided that such measures are not inconsistent with its other obligations under international law.

2. Any Party which has availed itself of this right of derogation shall, within a reasonable lapse of time, keep the Secretary General of the Council of Europe fully informed of the measures taken and of the reasons therefor. It shall likewise inform the Secretary General when such measures have ceased to operate and the provisions of the Charter which it has accepted are again being fully executed.

Article G   Restrictions

1. The rights and principles set forth in Part I when effectively realised, and their effective exercise as provided for in Part II, shall not be subject to any restrictions or limitations not specified in those parts, except such as are prescribed by law and are necessary in a democratic society for the protection of the rights and freedoms of others or for the protection of public interest, national security, public health, or morals.

2. The restrictions permitted under this Charter to the rights and obligations set forth herein shall not be applied for any purpose other than that for which they have been prescribed.

Article H   Relations between the Charter and domestic law or international agreements

The provisions of this Charter shall not prejudice the provisions of domestic law or of any bilateral or multilateral treaties, conventions or agreements which are already in force, or may come into force, under which more favourable treatment would be accorded to the persons protected.

Article I   Implementation of the undertakings given

1. Without prejudice to the methods of implementation foreseen in these articles the relevant provisions of Articles 1 to 31 of Part II of this Charter shall be implemented by:
    (a) laws or regulations;
    (b) agreements between employers or employers' organisations and workers' organisations;
    (c) a combination of those two methods;
    (d) other appropriate means.

2. Compliance with the undertakings deriving from the provisions of paragraphs 1, 2, 3, 4, 5 and 7 of Article 2, paragraphs 4, 6 and 7 of Article 7, paragraphs 1, 2, 3 and 5 of Article 10 and Article 21 and 22 of Part II of this Charter shall be regarded as effective if the provisions are applied, in accordance with paragraph 1 of this article, to the great majority of the workers concerned.

Article J   Amendments

1. Any amendment to Parts I and II of this Charter with the purpose of extending the rights guaranteed in this Charter as well as any amendment to Parts III to VI, proposed by a Party or by the Governmental Committee, shall be communicated to the Secretary General of the Council of Europe and forwarded by the Secretary General to the Parties to this Charter.

2. Any amendment proposed in accordance with the provisions of the preceding paragraph shall be examined by the Governmental Committee which shall submit the text adopted to the Committee of Ministers for approval after consultation with the Parliamentary Assembly. After its approval by the Committee of Ministers this text shall be forwarded to the Parties for acceptance.

3. Any amendment to Part I and to Part II of this Charter shall enter into force, in respect of those Parties which have accepted it, on the first day of the month following the expiration of a period of one month after the date on which three Parties have informed the Secretary General that they have accepted it.

In respect of any Party which subsequently accepts it, the amendment shall enter into force on the first day of the month following the expiration of a period of one month after the date on which that Party has informed the Secretary General of its acceptance.

4. Any amendment to Parts III to VI of this Charter shall enter into force on the first day of the month following the expiration of a period of one month after the date on which all Parties have informed the Secretary General that they have accepted it.

PART VI

Article K   Signature, ratification and entry into force

1. This Charter shall be open for signature by the member States of the Council of Europe. It shall be subject to ratification, acceptance or approval. Instruments of ratification, acceptance or approval shall be deposited with the Secretary General of the Council of Europe.

2. This Charter shall enter into force on the first day of the month following the expiration of a period of one month after the date on which three member States of the Council of Europe have expressed their consent to be bound by this Charter in accordance with the preceding paragraph.

3. In respect of any member State which subsequently expresses its consent to be bound by this Charter, it shall enter into force on the first day of the month following the expiration of a period of one month after the date of the deposit of the instrument of ratification, acceptance or approval.

Article L   Territorial application

1. This Charter shall apply to the metropolitan territory of each Party. Each signatory may, at the time of signature or of the deposit of its instrument of ratification, acceptance or approval, specify, by declaration addressed to the Secretary General of the Council of Europe, the territory which shall be considered to be its metropolitan territory for this purpose.

2. Any signatory may, at the time of signature or of the deposit of its instrument of ratification, acceptance or approval, or at any time thereafter, declare by notification addressed to the Secretary General of the Council of Europe, that the Charter shall extend in whole or in part to a non-metropolitan territory or territories specified in the said declaration for whose international relations it is responsible or for which it assumes international responsibility. It shall specify in the declaration the articles or paragraphs of Part II of the Charter which it accepts as binding in respect of the territories named in the declaration.

3. The Charter shall extend its application to the territory or territories named in the aforesaid declaration as from the first day of the month following the expiration of a period of one month after be date of receipt of the notification of such declaration by the Secretary General.

4. Any Party may declare at a later date by notification addressed to the Secretary General of the Council of Europe that, in respect of one or more of the territories to which the Charter has been applied in accordance with paragraph 2 of this article, it accepts as binding any articles or any numbered paragraphs which it has not already accepted in respect of that territory or territories. Such undertakings subsequently given shall be deemed to be an integral part of the original declaration in respect of the territory concerned, and shall have the same effect as from the first day of the month following the expiration of a period of one month after the date of receipt of such notification by the Secretary General.

Article M   Denunciation

1. Any Party may denounce this Charter only at the end of a period of five years from the date on which the Charter entered into force for it, or at the end of any subsequent period of two years, and in either case after giving six months' notice to the Secretary General of the Council of Europe who shall inform the other Parties accordingly.

2. Any Party may, in accordance with the provisions set out in the preceding paragraph, denounce any article or paragraph of Part II of the Charter accepted by it provided that the number of articles or paragraphs by which this Party is bound shall never be less than sixteen in the former case and sixty-three in the latter and that this number of articles or paragraphs shall continue to include

the articles selected by the Party among those to which special reference is made in Article A, paragraph 1, sub-paragraph b.

3. Any Party may denounce the present Charter or any of the articles or paragraphs of Part II of the Charter under the conditions specified in paragraph 1 of this article in respect of any territory to which the said Charter is applicable, by virtue of a declaration made in accordance with paragraph 2 of Article L.

Article N   Appendix

The *appendix* to this Charter shall form an integral part of it.

Article O   Notifications

The Secretary General of the Council of Europe shall notify the member States of the Council and the Director General of the International Labour Office of:

(a) any signature;

(b) the deposit of any instrument of ratification, acceptance or approval;

(c) any date of entry into force of this Charter in accordance with Article K;

(d) any declaration made in application of Articles A, paragraphs 2 and 3, D, paragraphs 1 and 2, F, paragraph 2, L, paragraphs 1, 2, 3 and 4;

(e) any amendment in accordance with Article J;

(f) any denunciation in accordance with Article M;

(g) any other act, notification or communication relating to this Charter.

In witness whereof, the undersigned, being duly authorised thereto, have signed this revised Charter.

Done at Strasbourg, this 3rd day of May 1996, in English and French, both texts being equally authentic, in a single copy which shall be deposited in the archives of the Council of Europe. The Secretary General of the Council of Europe shall transmit certified copies to each member State of the Council of Europe and to the Director General of the International Labour Office.

Appendix to the Revised European Social Charter

Scope of the Revised European Social Charter in terms of persons protected

1. Without prejudice to Article 12, paragraph 4, and Article 13, paragraph 4, the persons covered by Articles 1 to 17 and 20 to 31 include foreigners only in so far as they are nationals of other Parties lawfully resident or working regularly within the territory of the Party concerned, subject to the understanding that these articles are to be interpreted in the light of the provisions of Articles 18 and 19. This interpretation would not prejudice the extension of similar facilities to other persons by any of the Parties.

2. Each Party will grant to refugees as defined in the Convention relating to the Status of Refugees, signed in Geneva on 28 July 1951 and in the Protocol of 31 January 1967, and lawfully staying in its territory, treatment as favourable as possible, and in any case not less favourable than under the obligations accepted by the Party under the said convention and under any other existing international instruments applicable to those refugees.

3. Each Party will grant to stateless persons as defined in the Convention on the Status of Stateless Persons done in New York on 28 September 1954 and lawfully staying in its territory, treatment as favourable as possible and in any case not less favourable than under the obligations accepted by the Party under the said instrument and under any other existing international instruments applicable to those stateless persons.

PART I PARAGRAPH 18, AND PART II, ARTICLE 18, PARAGRAPH 1

It is understood that these provisions are not concerned with the question of entry into the territories of the Parties and do not prejudice the provisions of the European Convention on Establishment, signed in Paris on 13 December 1955.

PART II

Article 1, paragraph 2
This provision shall not be interpreted as prohibiting or authorising any union security clause or practice.

Article 2, paragraph 6
Parties may provide that this provision shall not apply:

    (a) to workers having a contract or employment relationship with a total duration not exceeding one month and/or with a working week not exceeding eight hours;

    (b) where the contract or employment relationship is of a casual and/or specific nature, provided, in these cases, that its non-application is justified by objective considerations.

Article 3, paragraph 4
It is understood that for the purposes of this provision the functions, organisation and conditions of operation of these services shall be determined by national laws or regulations, collective agreements or other means appropriate to national conditions.

Article 4, paragraph 4
This provision shall be so understood as not to prohibit immediate dismissal for any serious offence.

Article 4, paragraph 5
It is understood that a Party may give the undertaking required in this paragraph if the great majority of workers are not permitted to suffer deductions from wages either by law or through collective agreements or arbitration awards, the exceptions being those persons not so covered.

Article 6, paragraph 4
It is understood that each Party may, insofar as it is concerned, regulate the exercise of the right to strike by law, provided that any further restriction that this might place on the right can be justified under the terms of Article G.

Article 7, paragraph 2
This provision does not prevent Parties from providing in their legislation that young persons not having reached the minimum age laid down may perform work in so far as it is absolutely necessary for their vocational training where such work is carried out in accordance with conditions prescribed by the competent authority and measures are taken to protect the health and safety of these young persons.

Article 7, paragraph 8
It is understood that a Party may give the undertaking required in this paragraph if it fulfils the spirit of the undertaking by providing by law that the great majority of persons under eighteen years of age shall not be employed in night work.

Article 8, paragraph 2
This provision shall not be interpreted as laying down an absolute prohibition. Exceptions could be made, for instance, in the following cases:

    (a) if an employed woman has been guilty of misconduct which justifies breaking off the employment relationship;

(b) if the undertaking concerned ceases to operate;

(c) if the period prescribed in the employment contract has expired.

Article 12, paragraph 4

The words 'and subject to the conditions laid down in such agreements' in the introduction to this paragraph are taken to imply *inter alia* that with regard to benefits which are available independently of any insurance contribution, a Party may require the completion of a prescribed period of residence before granting such benefits to nationals of other Parties.

Article 13, paragraph 4

Governments not Parties to the European Convention on Social and Medical Assistance may ratify the Charter in respect of this paragraph provided that they grant to nationals of other Parties a treatment which is in conformity with the provisions of the said convention.

Article 16

It is understood that the protection afforded in this provision covers single-parent families.

Article 17

It is understood that this provision covers all persons below the age of 18 years, unless under the law applicable to the child majority is attained earlier, without prejudice to the other specific provisions provided by the Charter, particularly Article 7.

This does not imply an obligation to provide compulsory education up to the abovementioned age.

Article 19, paragraph 6

For the purpose of applying this provision, the term 'family of a foreign worker' is understood to mean at least the worker's spouse and unmarried children, as long as the latter are considered to be minors by the receiving State and are dependent on the migrant worker.

Article 20

1. It is understood that social security matters, as well as other provisions relating to unemployment benefit, old age benefit and survivor's benefit, may be excluded from the scope of this article.

2. Provisions concerning the protection of women, particularly as regards pregnancy, confinement and the post-natal period, shall not be deemed to be discrimination as referred to in this article.

3. This article shall not prevent the adoption of specific measures aimed at removing *de facto* inequalities.

4. Occupational activities which, by reason of their nature or the context in which they are carried out, can be entrusted only to persons of a particular sex may be excluded from the scope of this article or some of its provisions. This provision is not to be interpreted as requiring the Parties to embody in laws or regulations a list of occupations which, by reason of their nature or the context in which they are carried out, may be reserved to persons of a particular sex.

Articles 21 and 22

1. For the purpose of the application of these articles, the term 'workers' representatives' means persons who are recognised as such under national legislation or practice.

2. The terms 'national legislation and practice' embrace as the case may be, in addition to laws and regulations, collective agreements, other agreements between employers and workers' representatives, customs as well as relevant case law.

3. For the purpose of the application of these articles, the term 'undertaking' is understood as referring to a set of tangible and intangible components, with or without legal personality, formed to produce goods or provide services for financial gain and with power to determine its own market policy.

4. It is understood that religious communities and their institutions may be excluded from the application of these articles, even if these institutions are 'undertakings' within the meaning of paragraph 3. Establishments pursuing activities which are inspired by certain ideals or guided by certain moral concepts, ideals and concepts which are protected by national legislation, may be excluded

from the application of these articles to such an extent as is necessary to protect the orientation of the undertaking.

5. It is understood that where in a state the rights set out in these articles are exercised in the various establishments of the undertaking, the Party concerned is to be considered as fulfilling the obligations deriving from these provisions.

6. The Parties may exclude from the field of application of these articles, those undertakings employing less than a certain number of workers, to be determined by national legislation or practice.

Article 22

1. This provision affects neither the powers and obligations of states as regards the adoption of health and safety regulations for workplaces, nor the powers and responsibilities of the bodies in charge of monitoring their application.

2. The terms 'social and socio-cultural services and facilities' are understood as referring to the social and/or cultural facilities for workers provided by some undertakings such as welfare assistance, sports fields, rooms for nursing mothers, libraries, children's holiday camps, etc.

Article 23, paragraph 1

For the purpose of the application of this paragraph, the term 'for as long as possible' refers to the elderly person's physical, psychological and intellectual capacities.

Article 24

1. It is understood that for the purposes of this article the terms 'termination of employment' and 'terminated' mean termination of employment at the initiative of the employer.

2. It is understood that this article covers all workers but that a Party may exclude from some or all of its protection the following categories of employed persons:
   (a) workers engaged under a contract of employment for a specified period of time or a specified task;
   (b) workers undergoing a period of probation or a qualifying period of employment, provided that this is determined in advance and is of a reasonable duration;
   (c) workers engaged on a casual basis for a short period.

3. For the purpose of this article the following, in particular, shall not constitute valid reasons for termination of employment:
   (a) trade union membership or participation in union activities outside working hours, o r, with the consent of the employer, within working hours;
   (b) seeking office as, acting or having acted in the capacity of a workers' representative;
   (c) the filing of a complaint or the participation in proceedings against an employer involving alleged violation of laws or regulations or recourse to competent administrative authorities;
   (d) race, colour, sex, marital status, family responsibilities, pregnancy, religion, political opinion, national extraction or social origin;
   (e) maternity or parental leave;
   (f) temporary absence from work due to illness or injury.

4. It is understood that compensation or other appropriate relief in case of termination of employment without valid reasons shall be determined by national laws or regulations, collective agreements or other means appropriate to national conditions.

Article 25

1. It is understood that the competent national authority may, by way of exemption and after consulting organisations of employers and workers, exclude certain categories of workers from the protection provided in this provision by reason of the special nature of their employment relationship.

2. It is understood that the definition of the term 'insolvency' must be determined by national law and practice.

3. The workers' claims covered by this provision shall include at least:

    (a) the workers' claims for wages relating to a prescribed period, which shall not be less than three months under a privilege system and eight weeks under a guarantee system, prior to the insolvency or to the termination of employment;

    (b) the workers' claims for holiday pay due as a result of work performed during the year in which the insolvency or the termination of employment occurred;

    (c) the workers' claims for amounts due in respect of other types of paid absence relating to a prescribed period, which shall not be less than three months under a privilege system and eight weeks under a guarantee system, prior to the insolvency or the termination of the employment.

4. National laws or regulations may limit the protection of workers' claims to a prescribed amount, which shall be of a socially acceptable level.

Article 26

It is understood that this article does not require that legislation be enacted by the Parties.

It is understood that paragraph 2 does not cover sexual harassment.

Article 27

It is understood that this article applies to men and women workers with family responsibilities in relation to their dependent children as well as in relation to other members of their immediate family who clearly need their care or support where such responsibilities restrict their possibilities of preparing for, entering, participating in or advancing in economic activity. The terms 'dependent children' and 'other members of their immediate family who clearly need their care and support' mean persons defined as such by the national legislation of the Party concerned.

Articles 28 and 29

For the purpose of the application of this article, the term 'workers' representatives' means persons who are recognised as such under national legislation or practice.

PART III

It is understood that the Charter contains legal obligations of an international character, the application of which is submitted solely to the supervision provided for in *Part IV* thereof.

Article A, paragraph 1

It is understood that the numbered paragraphs may include articles consisting of only one paragraph.

Article B, paragraph 2

For the purpose of paragraph 2 of Article B, the provisions of the revised Charter correspond to the provisions of the Charter with the same article or paragraph number with the exception of:

    (a) Article 3, paragraph 2, of the revised Charter which corresponds to Article 3, paragraphs 1 and 3, of the Charter;

    (b) Article 3, paragraph 3, of the revised Charter which corresponds to Article 3, paragraphs 2 and 3, of the Charter;

    (c) Article 10, paragraph 5, of the revised Charter which corresponds to Article 10, paragraph 4, of the Charter;

    (d) Article 17, paragraph 1, of the revised Charter which corresponds to Article 17 of the Charter.

PART V

Article E

A differential treatment based on an objective and reasonable justification shall not be deemed discriminatory.

Article F

The terms 'in time of war or other public emergency' shall be so understood as to cover also the threat of war.

Article I

It is understood that workers excluded in accordance with the appendix to Articles 21 and 22 are not taken into account in establishing the number of workers concerned.

Article J

The term 'amendment' shall be extended so as to cover also the addition of new articles to the Charter.

European Convention for the Prevention of Torture and Inhuman or Degrading Treatment or Punishment (1987)*

The member States of the Council of Europe, signatory hereto,

Having regard to the provisions of the Convention for the Protection of Human Rights and Fundamental Freedoms,

Recalling that, under Article 3 of the same Convention, 'no one shall be subjected to torture or to inhuman or degrading treatment or punishment';

Noting that the machinery provided for in that Convention operates in relation to persons who allege that they are victims of violations of Article 3;

Convinced that the protection of persons deprived of their liberty against torture and inhuman or degrading treatment or punishment could be strengthened by non-judicial means of a preventive character based on visits,

Have agreed as follows:

Chapter I

Article 1

There shall be established a European Committee for the Prevention of Torture and Inhuman or Degrading Treatment or Punishment (hereinafter referred to as 'the Committee'). The Committee shall, by means of visits, examine the treatment of persons deprived of their liberty with a view to strengthening, if necessary, the protection of such persons from torture and from inhuman or degrading treatment or punishment.

Article 2

Each Party shall permit visits, in accordance with this Convention, to any place within its jurisdiction where persons are deprived of their liberty by a public authority.

Article 3

In the application of this Convention, the Committee and the competent national authorities of the Party concerned shall co-operate with each other.

Chapter II

Article 4

1. The Committee shall consist of a number of members equal to that of the Parties.

2. The members of the Committee shall be chosen from among persons of high moral character, known for their competence in the field of human rights or having professional experience in the areas covered by this Convention.

3. No two members of the Committee may be nationals of the same State.

4. The members shall serve in their individual capacity, shall be independent and impartial, and shall be available to serve the Committee effectively.

Article 5

1. The members of the Committee shall be elected by the Committee of Ministers of the Council of Europe by an absolute majority of votes, from a list of names drawn up by the Bureau of the Consultative Assembly of the Council of Europe; each national delegation of the Parties in the Consultative Assembly shall put forward three candidates, of whom two at least shall be its nationals.

---

* © Council of Europe

2. The same procedure shall be followed in filling casual vacancies.

3. The members of the Committee shall be elected for a period of four years. They may only be re-elected once. However, among the members elected at the first election, the terms of three members shall expire at the end of two years. The members whose terms are to expire at the end of the initial period of two years shall be chosen by lot by the Secretary-General of the Council of Europe immediately after the first election has been completed.

Article 6

1. The Committee shall meet in camera. A quorum shall be equal to the majority of its members. The decisions of the Committee shall be taken by a majority of the members present, subject to the provisions of Article 10, paragraph 2.

2. The Committee shall draw up its own rules of procedure.

3. The Secretariat of the Committee shall be provided by the Secretary-General of the Council of Europe.

Chapter III

Article 7

1. The Committee shall organise visits to places referred to in Article 2. Apart from periodic visits, the Committee may organise such other visits as appear to it to be required in the circumstances.

2. As a general rule, the visits shall be carried out by at least two members of the Committee. The Committee may, if it considers it necessary, be assisted by experts and interpreters.

Article 8

1. The Committee shall notify the Government of the Party concerned of its intention to carry out a visit. After such notification, it may at any time visit any place referred to in Article 2.

2. A Party shall provide the Committee with the following facilities to carry out its task:
   (a) access to its territory and the right to travel without restriction;
   (b) full information on the places where persons deprived of their liberty are being held;
   (c) unlimited access to any place where persons are deprived of their liberty, including the right to move inside such places without restriction;
   (d) other information available to the Party which is necessary for the Committee to carry out its task. In seeking such information, the Committee shall have regard to applicable rules of national law and professional ethics.

3. The Committee may interview in private persons deprived of their liberty.

4. The Committee may communicate freely with any person whom it believes can supply relevant information.

5. If necessary, the Committee may immediately communicate observations to the competent authorities of the Party concerned.

Article 9

1. In exceptional circumstances, the competent authorities of the Party concerned may make representations to the Committee against a visit at the time or to the particular place proposed by the Committee. Such representations may only be made on grounds of national defence, public safety, serious disorder in places where persons are deprived of their liberty, the medical condition of a person or that an urgent interrogation relating to a serious crime is in progress.

2. Following such representations, the Committee and the Party shall immediately enter into consultations in order to clarify the situation and seek agreement on arrangements to enable the Committee to exercise its functions expeditiously. Such arrangements may include the transfer to another place of any person whom the Committee proposed to visit. Until the visit takes place, the Party shall provide information to the Committee about any person concerned.

Article 10

1. After each visit, the Committee shall draw up a report on the facts found during the visit, taking account of any observations which may have been submitted by the Party concerned. It shall transmit to the latter its report containing any recommendations considers necessary. The Committee

may consult with the Party with a view to suggesting, if necessary, improvements in the protection of persons deprived of their liberty.

2. If the Party fails to co-operate or refuses to improve the situation in the light of the Committee's recommendations, the Committee may decide, after the Party has had an opportunity to make known its views, by a majority of two-thirds of its members to make a public statement on the matter.

Article 11

1. The information gathered by the Committee in relation to a visit, its report and its consultations with the Party concerned shall be confidential.

2. The Committee shall publish its report, together with any comments of the Party concerned, whenever requested to do so by that Party.

3. However, no personal data shall be published without the express consent of the person concerned.

Article 12

Subject to the rules of confidentiality in Article 11, the Committee shall every year submit to the Committee of Ministers a general report on its activities which shall be transmitted to the Consultative Assembly and made public.

Article 13

The members of the Committee, experts and other persons assisting the Committee are required, during and after their terms of office, to maintain the confidentiality of the facts or information of which they have become aware during the discharge of their functions.

Article 14

1. The names of persons assisting the Committee shall be specified in the notification under Article 8, paragraph 1.

2. Experts shall act on the instructions and under the authority of the Committee. They shall have particular knowledge and experience in the areas covered by this Convention and shall be bound by the same duties of independence, impartiality and availability as the members of the Committee.

3. A Party may exceptionally declare that an expert or other person assisting the Committee may not be allowed to take part in a visit to a place within its jurisdiction.

Chapter IV

Article 15

Each Party shall inform the Committee of the name and address of the authority competent to receive notifications to its Government, and of any liaison officer it may appoint.

Article 16

The Committee, its members and experts referred to in Article 7, paragraph 2, shall enjoy the privileges and immunities set out in the annex to this Convention.

Article 17

1. This Convention shall not prejudice the provisions of domestic law or any international agreement which provide greater protection for persons deprived of their liberty.

2. Nothing in this Convention shall be construed as limiting or derogating from the competence of the organs of the European Convention on Human Rights or from the obligations assumed by the Parties under that Convention.

3. The Committee shall not visit places which representatives or delegates of protecting powers or the International Committee of the Red Cross effectively visit on a regular basis by virtue of the Geneva Conventions of 12 August 1949 and the Additional Protocols of 8 June 1977 thereto.

Chapter V

Article 18

This Convention shall be open for signature by the member States of the Council of Europe. It is subject to ratification, acceptance or approval. Instruments of ratification, acceptance or approval shall be deposited with the Secretary-General of the Council of Europe.

Article 19

1. This Convention shall enter into force on the first day of the month following the expiration of a period of three months after the date on which seven member States of the Council of Europe have expressed their consent to be bound by the Convention in accordance with the provisions of Article 18.

2. In respect of any member State which subsequently expresses its consent to be bound by it, the Convention shall enter into force on the first day of the month following the expiration of a period of three months after the date of the deposit of the instrument of ratification, acceptance or approval.

Article 20

1. Any State may at the time of signature or when depositing its instrument of ratification, acceptance or approval, specify the territory or territories to which this Convention shall apply.

2. Any State may at any later date, by a declaration addressed to the Secretary-General of the Council of Europe, extend the application of this Convention to any other territory specified in the declaration. In respect of such territory the Convention shall enter into force on the first day of the month following the expiration of a period of three months after the date of receipt of such declaration by the Secretary-General.

3. Any declaration made under the two preceding paragraphs may, in respect of any territory specified in such declaration, be withdrawn by a notification addressed to the Secretary-General. The withdrawal shall become effective on the first day of the month following the expiration of a period of three months after the date of receipt of such notification by the Secretary-General.

Article 21

No reservation may be made in respect of the provisions of this Convention.

Article 22

1. Any Party may, at any time, denounce this Convention by means of a notification addressed to the Secretary-General of the Council of Europe.

2. Such denunciation shall become effective on the first day of the month following the expiration of a period of twelve months after the date of receipt of the notification by the Secretary-General.

Article 23

The Secretary-General of the Council of Europe shall notify the member States of the Council of Europe of:

    (a) any signature;

    (b) the deposit of any instrument of ratification, acceptance or approval;

    (c) any date of entry into force of this Convention in accordance with Articles 19 and 20;

    (d) any other act, notification or communication relating to this Convention, except for action taken in pursuance of Articles 8 and 10.

In witness whereof, the undersigned, being duly authorised thereto, have signed this Convention.

Done at Strasbourg, the 26 November 1987, in English and French, both texts being equally authentic, in a single copy which shall be deposited in the archives of the Council of Europe. The Secretary-General of the Council of Europe shall transmit certified copies to each member State of the Council of Europe.

Annex
Privileges and immunities (Article 16)

1. For the purpose of this annex, references to members of the Committee shall be deemed to include references to experts mentioned in Article 7, paragraph 2.

2. The members of the Committee shall, while exercising their functions and during journeys made in the exercise of their functions, enjoy the following privileges and immunities:

   (a) immunity from personal arrest or detention and from seizure of their personal baggage and, in respect of words spoken or written and all acts done by them in their official capacity, immunity from legal process of every kind;

   (b) exemption from any restrictions on their freedom of movement: on exit from and return to their country of residence, and entry into and exit from the country in which they exercise their functions, and from alien registration in the country which they are visiting or through which they are passing in the exercise of their functions.

3. In the course of journeys undertaken in the exercise of their functions, the members of the Committee shall, in the matter of customs and exchange control, be accorded:

   (a) by their own government, the same facilities as those accorded to senior officials travelling abroad on temporary official duty;

   (b) by the governments of other Parties, the same facilities as those accorded to representatives of foreign governments on temporary official duty.

4. Documents and papers of the Committee, insofar as they relate to the business of the Committee, shall be inviolable.

The official correspondence and other official communications of the Committee may not be held up or subjected to censorship.

5. In order to secure for the members of the Committee complete freedom of speech and complete independence in the discharge of their duties, the immunity from legal process in respect of words spoken or written and all acts done by them in discharging their duties shall continue to be accorded, notwithstanding that the persons concerned are no longer engaged in the discharge of such duties.

6. Privileges and immunities are accorded to the members of the Committee, not for the personal benefit of the individuals themselves but in order to safeguard the independent exercise of their functions. The Committee alone shall be competent to waive the immunity of its members; it has not only the right, but is under a duty, to waive the immunity of one of its members in any case where, in its opinion, the immunity would impede the course of justice, and where it can be waived without prejudice to the purpose for which the immunity is accorded.

First Protocol (1993)*

The member States of the Council of Europe, signatories to this Protocol to the European Convention for the Prevention of Torture and Inhuman or Degrading Treatment or Punishment, signed at Strasbourg on 26 November 1987 (hereinafter referred to as 'the Convention'),

Considering that non-member States of the Council of Europe should be allowed to accede to the Convention at the invitation of the Committee of Ministers,

Have agreed as follows:

Article 1
A sub-paragraph shall be added to Article 5, paragraph 1, of the Convention as follows:

'Where a member is to be elected to the Committee in respect of a non-member State of the Council of Europe, the Bureau of the Consultative Assembly shall invite the Parliament of that State to put

*   © Council of Europe

forward three candidates, of whom two at least shall be its nationals. The election by the Committee of Ministers shall take place after consultation with the Party concerned.'

Article 2
Article 12 of the Convention shall read as follows:

'Subject to the rules of confidentiality in Article 11, the committee shall every year submit to the Committee of Ministers a general report on its activities which shall be transmitted to the consultative Assembly and to any non-member State of the Council of Europe which is a party to the Convention, and made public.'

Article 3
The text of Article 18 of the Convention shall become paragraph 1 of that article and shall be supplemented by the following second paragraph:

'2. The Committee of Ministers of the Council of Europe may invite any non-member State of the Council of Europe to accede to the Convention.'

Article 8
This Protocol shall enter into force on the first day of the month following the expiration of a period of three months after the date on which all Parties to the Convention have expressed their consent to be bound by the Protocol, in accordance with the provisions of Article 7.

Second Protocol (1993)*

The States, signatories to this Protocol to the European Convention for the Prevention of Torture and Inhuman or Degrading Treatment or Punishment, signed at Strasbourg on 26 November 1987 (hereinafter referred to as 'the Convention'),

Convinced of the advisability of enabling members of the European Committee for the Prevention of Torture and Inhuman and Degrading Treatment (hereinafter referred to as 'the Committee') to be re-elected twice;

Also considering the need to guarantee an orderly renewal of the membership of the Committee,

Have agreed as follows:

Article 1
1. In Article 5, paragraph 3, the second sentence shall read as follows:

'They may be re-elected twice.'

2. Article 5 of the Convention shall be supplemented by the following paragraphs 4 and 5:

'4. In order to ensure that, as far as possible, one half of the membership of the Committee shall be renewed every two years, the Committee of Ministers may decide, before proceeding to any subsequent election, that the term or terms of office of one or more members to be elected shall be for a period other than four years but not more than six and not less than two years.

5. In cases where more than one term of office is involved and the Committee of Ministers applies the preceding paragraph, the allocation of the terms of office shall be effected by the drawing of lots by the Secretary-General, immediately after the election.'

Article 3
This Protocol shall enter into force on the first day of the month following the expiration of a period of three months after the date on which all Parties to the Convention have expressed their consent to be bound by the Protocol, in accordance with the provisions of Article 2.

European Charter for Regional or Minority Languages (1992)*

PREAMBLE

The member States of the Council of Europe signatory hereto,

Considering that the aim of the Council of Europe is to achieve a greater unity between its members, particularly for the purpose of safeguarding and realising the ideals and principles which are their common heritage;

Considering that the protection of the historical regional or minority languages of Europe, some of which are in danger of eventual extinction, contributes to the maintenance and development of Europe's cultural wealth and traditions;

Considering that the right to use a regional or minority language in private and public life is an inalienable right conforming to the principles embodied in the United Nations International Covenant on Civil and Political Rights, and according to the spirit of the Council of Europe Convention for the Protection of Human Rights and Fundamental Freedoms;

Having regard to the work carried out within the CSCE and in particular to the Helsinki Final Act of 1975 and the Document of the Copenhagen Meeting of 1990;

Stressing the value of interculturalism and multilingualism and considering that the protection and encouragement of regional or minority languages should not be to the detriment of the official languages and the need to learn them;

Realising that the protection and promotion of regional or minority languages in the different countries and regions of Europe represent an important contribution to the building of a Europe based on the principles of democracy and cultural diversity within the framework of national sovereignty and territorial integrity;

Taking into consideration the specific conditions and historical traditions in the different regions of the European States,

Have agreed as follows:

PART I GENERAL PROVISIONS

Article 1   Definitions

For the purposes of this Charter:

    (a) the term 'regional or minority languages' means languages that are

        (i)   traditionally used within a given territory of a State by nationals of that State who form a group numerically smaller than the rest of the State's population, and

        (ii) different from the official language(s) of that State; it does not include either dialects of the official language(s) of the State or the languages of migrants;

    (b) 'territory in which the regional or minority language is used' means the geographical area in which the said language is the mode of expression of a number of people justifying the adoption of the various protective and promotional measures provided for in this Charter;

    (c) 'non-territorial languages' means languages used by nationals of the State which differ from the language or languages used by the rest of the State's population but which, although traditionally used within the territory of the State, cannot be identified with a particular area thereof.

Article 2   Undertakings

1. Each Party undertakes to apply the provisions of Part II to all the regional or minority languages spoken within its territory and complying with the definition in Article 1.

* © Council of Europe

2. In respect of each language specified at the time of ratification, acceptance or approval, in accordance with Article 3, each Party undertakes to apply a minimum of thirty-five paragraphs or sub-paragraphs chosen from among the provisions of Part III of the Charter, including at least three chosen from each of the Articles 8 and 12 and one from each of the Articles 9, 10, 11 and 13.

Article 3   Practical arrangements

1. Each Contracting State shall specify in its instrument of ratification, acceptance or approval, each regional or minority language, or official language which is less widely used on the whole or part of its territory, to which the paragraphs chosen in accordance with Article 2, paragraph 2, shall apply.

2. Any Party may, at any subsequent time, notify the Secretary General that it accepts the obligations arising out of the provisions of any other paragraph of the Charter not already specified in its instrument of ratification, acceptance or approval, or that it will apply paragraph 1 of the present article to other regional or minority languages, or to other official languages which are less widely used on the whole or part of its territory.

3. The undertakings referred to in the foregoing paragraph shall be deemed to form an integral part of the ratification, acceptance or approval and will have the same effect as from their date of notification.

Article 4   Existing regimes of protection

1. Nothing in this Charter shall be construed as limiting or derogating from any of the rights guaranteed by the European Convention on Human Rights.

2. The provisions of this Charter shall not affect any more favourable provisions concerning the status of regional or minority languages or the legal regime of persons belonging to minorities which may exist in a Party or are provided for by relevant bilateral or multilateral agreements.

Article 5   Existing obligations

Nothing in this Charter may be interpreted as implying any right to engage in any activity or perform any action in contravention of the purposes of the Charter of the United Nations or other obligations under international law, including the principle of the sovereignty and territorial integrity of States.

Article 6   Information

The Parties undertake to see to it that the authorities, organisations and persons concerned are informed of the rights and duties established by this Charter.

PART II OBJECTIVES AND PRINCIPLES PURSUED IN ACCORDANCE WITH ARTICLE 2, PARAGRAPH 1

Article 7 Objectives and principles

1. In respect of regional or minority languages, within the territories in which such languages are used and according to the situation of each language, the Parties shall base their policies, legislation and practice on the following objectives and principles:

   (a) the recognition of the regional or minority languages as an expression of cultural wealth;
   (b) the respect of the geographical area of each regional or minority language in order to ensure that existing or new administrative divisions do not constitute an obstacle to the promotion of the regional or minority language in question;
   (c) the need for resolute action to promote regional or minority languages in order to safeguard them;
   (d) the facilitation and/or encouragement of the use of regional or minority languages, in speech and writing, in public and private life;

(e) the maintenance and development of links, in the fields covered by this Charter, between groups using a regional or minority language and other groups in the State employing a language used in identical or similar form, as well as the establishment of cultural relations with other groups in the State using different languages;

(f) the provision of appropriate forms and means for the teaching and study of regional or minority languages at all appropriate stages;

(g) the provision of facilities enabling non-speakers of a regional or minority language living in the area where it is used to learn it if they so desire;

(h) the promotion of study and research on regional or minority languages at universities or equivalent institutions;

(i) the promotion of appropriate types of transnational exchanges, in the fields covered by this Charter, for regional or minority languages used in identical or similar form in two or more States.

2. The Parties undertake to eliminate, if they have not yet done so, any unjustified distinction, exclusion, restriction or preference relating to the use of a regional or minority language and intended to discourage or endanger the maintenance or development of a regional or minority language. The adoption of special measures in favour of regional or minority languages aimed at promoting equality between the users of these languages and the rest of the population or which take due account of their specific conditions is not considered to be an act of discrimination against the users of more widely-used languages.

3. The Parties undertake to promote, by appropriate measures, mutual understanding between all the linguistic groups of the country and in particular the inclusion of respect, understanding and tolerance in relation to regional or minority languages among the objectives of education and training provided within their countries and encouragement of the mass media to pursue the same objective.

4. In determining their policy with regard to regional or minority languages, the Parties shall take into consideration the needs and wishes expressed by the groups which use such languages. They are encouraged to establish bodies, if necessary, for the purpose of advising the authorities on all matters pertaining to regional or minority languages.

5. The Parties undertake to apply, *mutatis mutandis*, the principles listed in paragraphs 1 to 4 above to non-territorial languages. However, as far as these languages are concerned, the nature and scope of the measures to be taken to give effect to this Charter shall be determined in a flexible manner, bearing in mind the needs and wishes, and respecting the traditions and characteristics, of the groups which use the languages concerned.

PART III MEASURES TO PROMOTE THE USE OF REGIONAL OR MINORITY LANGUAGES IN PUBLIC LIFE IN ACCORDANCE WITH THE UNDERTAKINGS ENTERED INTO UNDER ARTICLE 2, PARAGRAPH 2

Article 8 Education

1. With regard to education, the Parties undertake, within the territory in which such languages are used, according to the situation of each of these languages, and without prejudice to the teaching of the official language(s) of the State, to:

(a) (i) make available pre-school education in the relevant regional or minority languages; or

(ii) make available a substantial part of pre-school education in the relevant regional or minority languages; or

(iii) apply one of the measures provided for under (i) and (ii) above at least to those pupils whose families so request and whose number is considered sufficient; or

(iv) if the public authorities have no direct competence in the field of pre-school education, favour and/or encourage the application of the measures referred to under (i) to (iii) above;

(b) (i)   make available primary education in the relevant regional or minority languages; or

    (ii) make available a substantial part of primary education in the relevant regional or minority languages; or

    (iii) provide, within primary education, for the teaching of the relevant regional or minority languages as an integral part of the curriculum; or

    (iv) apply one of the measures provided for under (i) to (iii) above at least to those pupils whose families so request and whose number is considered sufficient;

(c) (i)   make available secondary education in the relevant regional or minority languages; or

    (ii) make available a substantial part of secondary education in the relevant regional or minority languages; or

    (iii) provide, within secondary education, for the teaching of the relevant regional or minority languages as an integral part of the curriculum; or

    (iv) apply one of the measures provided for under (i) to (iii) above at least to those pupils who, or where appropriate whose families, so wish in a number considered sufficient;

(d) (i)   make available technical and vocational education in the relevant regional or minority languages; or

    (ii) make available a substantial part of technical and vocational education in the relevant regional or minority languages; or

    (iii) provide, within technical and vocational education for the teaching of the relevant regional or minority languages as an integral part of the curriculum; or

    (iv) apply one of the measures provided for under (i) to (iii) above at least to those pupils who, or where appropriate whose families, so wish in a number considered sufficient;

(e) (i)   make available university and other higher education in regional or minority languages; or

    (ii) provide facilities for the study of these languages as university and higher education subjects; or

    (iii) if, by reason of the role of the State in relation to higher education institutions, sub-paragraphs i. and ii. cannot be applied, encourage and/or allow the provision of university and higher education in regional or minority languages or of facilities for the study of these languages as university or higher education subjects;

(f) (i)   arrange for the provision of adult and continuing education courses which are taught mainly or wholly in the regional or minority languages; or

    (ii) offer such languages as subjects of adult and continuing education; or

    (iii) if the public authorities have no direct competence in the field of adult education, favour and/or encourage the offering of such languages as subjects of adult and continuing education;

(g) make arrangements to ensure the teaching of the history and the culture which is reflected by the regional or minority language;

(h) provide the basic and further training of the teachers required to implement those of paragraphs (a) to (g) accepted by the Party;

(i) set up a supervisory body or bodies responsible for monitoring the measures taken and progress achieved in establishing or developing the teaching of regional or minority languages and for drawing up periodic reports of their findings, which will be made public.

2. With regard to education and in respect of territories other than those in which the regional or minority languages are traditionally used, the Parties undertake, if the number of users of a regional or minority language justifies it, to allow, encourage or provide teaching in or of the regional or minority language at all the appropriate stages of education.

Article 9   Judicial authorities

1. The Parties undertake, in respect of those judicial districts in which the number of residents using the regional or minority languages justifies the measures specified below, according to the situation of each of these languages and on condition that the use of the facilities afforded by the present paragraph is not considered by the judge to hamper the proper administration of justice:

    (a) in criminal proceedings:

        (i)   to provide that the courts, at the request of one of the parties, shall conduct the proceedings in the regional or minority languages; and/or

        (ii) to guarantee the accused the right to use his/her regional or minority language; and/or

        (iii) to provide that requests and evidence, whether written or oral, shall not be considered inadmissible solely because they are formulated in a regional or minority language; and/or

        (iv) to produce, on request, documents connected with legal proceedings in the relevant regional or minority language,

        if necessary by the use of interpreters and translations involving no extra expense for the persons concerned;

    (b) in civil proceedings:

        (i)   to provide that the courts, at the request of one of the parties, shall conduct the proceedings in the regional or minority languages; and/or

        (ii) to allow, whenever a litigant has to appear in person before a court, that he or she may use his or her regional or minority language without thereby incurring additional expense; and/or

        (iii) to allow documents and evidence to be produced in the regional or minority languages

        if necessary by the use of interpreters and translations;

    (c) in proceedings before courts concerning administrative matters:

        (i)   to provide that the courts, at the request of one of the parties, shall conduct the proceedings in the regional or minority languages; and/or

        (ii) to allow, whenever a litigant has to appear in person before a court, that he or she may use his or her regional or minority language without thereby incurring additional expense; and/or

        (iii) to allow documents and evidence to be produced in the regional or minority languages

        if necessary by the use of interpreters and translations;

    (d) to take steps to ensure that the application of sub-paragraphs (i) and (iii) of paragraphs (b) and (c) above and any necessary use of interpreters and translations does not involve extra expense for the persons concerned.

2. The Parties undertake:

    (a) not to deny the validity of legal documents drawn up within the State solely because they are drafted in a regional or minority language; or

    (b) not to deny the validity, as between the parties, of legal documents drawn up within the country solely because they are drafted in a regional or minority language, and to provide that they can be invoked against interested third parties who are not users of these languages on condition that the contents of the document are made known to them by the person(s) who invoke(s) it; or

    (c) not to deny the validity, as between the parties, of legal documents drawn up within the country solely because they are drafted in a regional or minority language.

3. The Parties undertake to make available in the regional or minority languages the most important national statutory texts and those relating particularly to users of these languages, unless they are otherwise provided.

Article 10   Administrative authorities and public services

1. Within the administrative districts of the State in which the number of residents who are users of regional or minority languages justifies the measures specified below and according to the situation of each language, the Parties undertake, as far as this is reasonably possible to:

- (a) (i)   ensure that the administrative authorities use the regional or minority languages; or
  - (ii)   ensure that such of their officers as are in contact with the public use the regional or minority languages in their relations with persons applying to them in these languages; or
  - (iii) ensure that users of regional or minority languages may submit oral or written applications and receive a reply in these languages; or
  - (iv) ensure that users of regional or minority languages may submit oral or written applications in these languages; or
  - (v)   ensure that users of regional or minority languages may validly submit a document in these languages;
- (b) make available widely used administrative texts and forms for the population in the regional or minority languages or in bilingual versions;
- (c) allow the administrative authorities to draft documents in a regional or minority language.

2. In respect of the local and regional authorities on whose territory the number of residents who are users of regional or minority languages is such as to justify the measures specified below, the Parties undertake to allow and/or encourage:

- (a) the use of regional or minority languages within the framework of the regional or local authority;
- (b) the possibility for users of regional or minority languages to submit oral or written applications in these languages;
- (c) the publication by regional authorities of their official documents also in the relevant regional or minority languages;
- (d) the publication by local authorities of their official documents also in the relevant regional or minority languages;
- (e) the use by regional authorities of regional or minority languages in debates in their assemblies, without excluding, however, the use of the official language(s) of the State;
- (f) the use by local authorities of regional or minority languages in debates in their assemblies, without excluding, however, the use of the official language(s) of the State;
- (g) the use or adoption, if necessary in conjunction with the name in the official language(s), of traditional and correct forms of place-names in regional or minority languages.

3. With regard to public services provided by the administrative authorities or other persons acting on their behalf, the Parties undertake, within the territory in which regional or minority languages are used, in accordance with the situation of each language and as far as this is reasonably possible, to:

- (a) ensure that the regional or minority languages are used in the provision of the service; or
- (b) allow users of regional or minority languages to submit a request and receive a reply in these languages; or
- (c) allow users of regional or minority languages to submit a request in these languages.

4. With a view to putting into effect those provisions of paragraphs 1, 2 and 3 accepted by them, the Parties undertake to take one or more of the following measures:

- (a) translation or interpretation as may be required;
- (b) recruitment and, where necessary, training of the officials and other public service employees required;
- (c) compliance as far as possible with requests from public service employees having a knowledge of a regional or minority language to be appointed in the territory in which that language is used.

5. The Parties undertake to allow the use or adoption of family names in the regional or minority languages, at the request of those concerned.

Article 11   Media

1. The Parties undertake, for the users of the regional or minority languages within the territories in which those languages are spoken, according to the situation of each language, to the extent that the public authorities, directly or indirectly, are competent, have power or play a role in this field, and respecting the principle of the independence and autonomy of the media:

    (a) to the extent that radio and television carry out a public service mission:

        (i)   to ensure the creation of at least one radio station and one television channel in the regional or minority languages, or

        (ii) to encourage and on facilitate the creation of at least one radio station and one television channel in the regional or minority languages, or

        (iii) to make adequate provision so that broadcasters offer programmes in regional or minority languages;

    (b) (i)   to encourage and/or facilitate the creation of at least one radio station in the regional or minority languages, or

        (ii) to encourage and/or facilitate the broadcasting of radio programmes in the regional or minority languages on a regular basis;

    (c) (i)   to encourage and/or facilitate the creation of at least one television channel in the regional or minority languages, or

        (ii) to encourage and/or facilitate the broadcasting of television programmes in the regional or minority languages on a regular basis;

    (d) to encourage and/or facilitate the production and distribution of audio and audio-visual works in regional or minority languages;

    (e) (i)   to encourage and/or facilitate the creation and/or maintenance of at least one newspaper in the regional or minority languages; or

        (ii) to encourage and/or facilitate the publication of newspaper articles in the regional or minority languages on a regular basis;

    (f) (i)   to cover the additional costs of those media which use regional or minority languages, wherever the law provides for financial assistance in general for the media; or

        (ii) to apply existing measures for financial assistance also to audio-visual productions in regional or minority languages;

    (g) to support the training of journalists and other staff for media using regional or minority languages.

2. The Parties undertake to guarantee freedom of direct reception of radio and television broadcasts from neighbouring countries in a language used in identical or similar form to a regional or minority language, and not to oppose the retransmission of radio and television broadcasts from neighbouring countries in such a language. They further undertake to ensure that no restrictions will be placed on the freedom of expression and free circulation of information in the written press in a language used in identical or similar form to a regional or minority language. The exercise of the above-mentioned freedoms, since it carries with it duties and responsibilities, may be subject to such formalities, conditions, restrictions or penalties as are prescribed by law and are necessary in a democratic society, in the interests of national security, territorial integrity or public safety, for the prevention of disorder or crime, for the protection of health or morals, for the protection of the reputation or rights of others, for preventing disclosure of information received in confidence, or for maintaining the authority and impartiality of the judiciary.

3. The Parties undertake to ensure that the interests of the users of regional or minority languages are represented or taken into account within such bodies as may be established in accordance with the law with responsibility for guaranteeing the freedom and pluralism of the media.

Article 12   Cultural activities and facilities

1. With regard to cultural facilities and activities—especially libraries, video libraries, cultural centres, museums, archives, academies, theatres and cinemas, as well as literary work and film production, vernacular forms of cultural expression, festivals and the culture industries, including *inter*

alia the use of new technologies—the Parties undertake, within the territory in which such languages are used and to the extent that the public authorities are competent, have power or play a role in this field, to:

   (a) encourage types of expression and initiative specific to regional or minority languages and foster the different means of access to works produced in these languages;
   (b) foster the different means of access in other languages to works produced in regional or minority languages by aiding and developing translation, dubbing, post-synchronisation and subtitling activities;
   (c) foster access in regional or minority languages to works produced in other languages by aiding and developing translation, dubbing, post-synchronisation and subtitling activities;
   (d) ensure that the bodies responsible for organising or supporting cultural activities of various kinds make appropriate allowance for incorporating the knowledge and use of regional or minority languages and cultures in the undertakings which they initiate or for which they provide backing;
   (e) promote measures to ensure that the bodies responsible for organising or supporting cultural activities have at their disposal staff who have a full command of the regional or minority language concerned, as well as of the language(s) of the rest of the population;
   (f) encourage direct participation by representatives of the users of a given regional or minority language in providing facilities and planning cultural activities;
   (g) encourage and/or facilitate the creation of a body or bodies responsible for collecting, keeping a copy of and presenting or publishing works produced in the regional or minority languages;
   (h) if necessary create and/or promote and finance translation and terminological research services, particularly with a view to maintaining and developing appropriate administrative, commercial, economic, social, technical or legal terminology in each regional or minority language.

   2. In respect of territories other than those in which the regional or minority languages are traditionally used, the Parties undertake, if the number of users of a regional or minority language justifies it, to allow, encourage and/or provide appropriate cultural activities and facilities in accordance with the preceding paragraph.

   3. The Parties undertake to make appropriate provision, in pursuing their cultural policy abroad, for regional or minority languages and the cultures they reflect.

Article 13   Economic and social life

   1. With regard to economic and social activities, the Parties undertake, within the whole country, to:

   (a) eliminate from their legislation any provision prohibiting or limiting without justifiable reasons the use of regional or minority languages in documents relating to economic or social life, particularly contracts of employment, and in technical documents such as instructions for the use of products or installations;
   (b) prohibit the insertion in internal regulations of companies and private documents of any clauses excluding or restricting the use of regional or minority languages, at least between users of the same language;
   (c) oppose practices designed to discourage the use of regional or minority languages in connection with economic or social activities;
   (d) facilitate and/or encourage the use of regional or minority languages by means other than those specified in the above sub-paragraphs.

   2. With regard to economic and social activities, the Parties undertake, in so far as the public authorities are competent, within the territory in which the regional or minority languages are used, and as far as this is reasonably possible, to:

   (a) include in their financial and banking regulations provisions which allow, by means of procedures compatible with commercial practice, the use of regional or minority languages in drawing up payment orders (cheques, drafts, etc.) or other financial documents, or, where appropriate, ensure the implementation of such provisions;

(b) in the economic and social sectors directly under their control (public sector), organise activities to promote the use of regional or minority languages;

(c) ensure that social care facilities such as hospitals, retirement homes and hostels offer the possibility of receiving and treating in their own language persons using a regional or minority language who are in need of care on grounds of ill-health, old age or for other reasons;

(d) ensure by appropriate means that safety instructions are also accessible in regional or minority languages;

(e) arrange for information provided by the competent public authorities concerning the rights of consumers to be made available in regional or minority languages.

Article 14 Transfrontier exchanges

The Parties undertake:

(a) to apply existing bilateral and multilateral agreements which bind them with the States in which the same language is used in identical or similar form, or if necessary to seek to conclude such agreements, in such a way as to foster contacts between the users of the same language in the States concerned in the fields of culture, education, information, vocational training and permanent education;

(b) for the benefit of regional or minority languages, to facilitate and promote cooperation across borders, in particular between regional or local authorities in whose territory the same language is used in identical or similar form.

PART IV APPLICATION OF THE CHARTER

Article 15 Periodical reports

1. The Parties shall present periodically to the Secretary General of the Council of Europe, in a form to be prescribed by the Committee of Ministers, a report on their policy pursued in accordance with Part II of this Charter and on the measures taken in application of those provisions of Part III which they have accepted. The first report shall be presented within the year following the entry into force of the Charter with respect to the Party concerned, the other reports at three-yearly intervals after the first report.

2. The Parties shall make their reports public.

Article 16 Examination of the reports

1. The reports presented to the Secretary General of the Council of Europe under Article 15 shall be examined by a committee of experts constituted in accordance with Article 17.

2. Bodies or associations legally established in a Party may draw the attention of the committee of experts to matters relating to the undertakings entered into by that Party under Part III of this Charter. After consulting the Party concerned, the committee of experts may take account of this information in the preparation of the report specified in paragraph 3 below. These bodies or associations can furthermore submit statements concerning the policy pursued by a Party in accordance with Part II.

3. On the basis of the reports specified in paragraph 1 and the information mentioned in paragraph 2, the committee of experts shall prepare a report for the Committee of Ministers. This report shall be accompanied by the comments which the Parties have been requested to make and may be made public by the Committee of Ministers.

4. The report specified in paragraph 3 shall contain in particular the proposals of the committee of experts to the Committee of Ministers for the preparation of such recommendations of the latter body to one or more of the Parties as may be required.

5. The Secretary General of the Council of Europe shall make a two-yearly detailed report to the Parliamentary Assembly on the application of the Charter.

Article 17   Committee of experts

1. The committee of experts shall be composed of one member per Party, appointed by the Committee of Ministers from a list of individuals of the highest integrity and recognised competence in the matters dealt with in the Charter who shall be nominated by the Party concerned.

2. Members of the committee shall be appointed for a period of six years and shall be eligible for reappointment. A member who is unable to complete a term of office shall be replaced in accordance with the procedure laid down in paragraph 1, and the replacing member shall complete his predecessor's term of office.

3. The committee of experts shall adopt rules of procedure. Its secretarial services shall be provided by the Secretary General of the Council of Europe.

PART V FINAL PROVISIONS

Article 18

This Charter shall be open for signature by the member States of the Council of Europe. It is subject to ratification, acceptance or approval. Instruments of ratification, acceptance or approval shall be deposited with the Secretary General of the Council of Europe.

Article 19

1. This Charter shall enter into force on the first day of the month following the expiration of a period of three months after the date on which five member States of the Council of Europe have expressed their consent to be bound by the Charter in accordance with the provisions of Article 18.

2. In respect of any member State which subsequently expresses its consent to be bound by it, the Charter shall enter into force on the first day on the month following the expiration of a period of three months after the date of the deposit of the instrument of ratification, acceptance or approval.

Article 20

1. After the entry into force of this Charter, the Committee of Ministers of the Council of Europe may invite any State not a member of the Council of Europe to accede to this Charter.

2. In respect of any acceding State, the Charter shall enter into force on the first day of the month following the expiration of a period of three months after the date of deposit of the instrument of accession with the Secretary General of the Council of Europe.

Article 21

1. Any State may, at the time of signature or when depositing its instrument of ratification, acceptance, approval or accession, make one or more reservations to paragraphs 2 to 5 of Article 7 of this Charter. No other reservation may be made.

2. Any Contracting State which has made a reservation under the preceding paragraph may wholly or partly withdraw it by means of a notification addressed to the Secretary General of the Council of Europe. The withdrawal shall take effect on the date of receipt of such notification by the Secretary General.

Article 22

1. Any Party may at any time denounce this Charter by means of a notification addressed to the Secretary General of the Council of Europe.

2. Such denunciation shall become effective on the first day of the month following the expiration of a period of six months after the date of receipt of the notification by the Secretary General.

Article 23
The Secretary General of the Council of Europe shall notify the member States of the Council and any State which has acceded to this Charter of:

(a) any signature;
(b) the deposit of any instrument of ratification, acceptance, approval or accession;
(c) any date of entry into force of this Charter in accordance with Articles 19 and 20;
(d) any notification received in application of the provisions of Article 3, paragraph 2;
(e) any other act, notification or communication relating to this Charter.

Framework Convention for the Protection of National Minorities (1995)*

The member States of the Council of Europe and the other States, signatories to the present framework Convention,

Considering that the aim of the Council of Europe is to achieve greater unity between its members for the purpose of safeguarding and realising the ideals and principles which are their common heritage;

Considering that one of the methods by which that aim is to be pursued is the maintenance and further realisation of human rights and fundamental freedoms;

Wishing to follow-up the Declaration of the Heads of State and Government of the member States of the Council of Europe adopted in Vienna on 9 October 1993;

Being resolved to protect within their respective territories the existence of national minorities;

Considering that the upheavals of European history have shown that the protection of national minorities is essential to stability, democratic security and peace in this continent;

Considering that a pluralist and genuinely democratic society should not only respect the ethnic, cultural, linguistic and religious identity of each person belonging to a national minority, but also create appropriate conditions enabling them to express, preserve and develop this identity;

Considering that the creation of a climate of tolerance and dialogue is necessary to enable cultural diversity to be a source and a factor, not of division, but of enrichment for each society;

Considering that the realisation of a tolerant and prosperous Europe does not depend solely on co-operation between States but also requires transfrontier co-operation between local and regional authorities without prejudice to the constitution and territorial integrity of each State;

Having regard to the Convention for the Protection of Human Rights and Fundamental Freedoms and the Protocols thereto;

Having regard to the commitments concerning the protection of national minorities in United Nations conventions and declarations and in the documents of the Conference on Security and Co-operation in Europe, particularly the Copenhagen Document of 29 June 1990;

Being resolved to define the principles to be respected and the obligations which flow from them, in order to ensure, in the member States and such other States as may become Parties to the present instrument, the effective protection of national minorities and of the rights and freedoms of persons belonging to those minorities, within the rule of law, respecting the territorial integrity and national sovereignty of states;

Being determined to implement the principles set out in this framework Convention through national legislation and appropriate governmental policies,

Have agreed as follows:

Section I

Article 1
The protection of national minorities and of the rights and freedoms of persons belonging to those minorities forms an integral part of the international protection of human rights, and as such falls within the scope of international co-operation.

* © Council of Europe

Article 2

The provisions of this framework Convention shall be applied in good faith, in a spirit of understanding and tolerance and in conformity with the principles of good neighbourliness, friendly relations and co-operation between States.

Article 3

1. Every person belonging to a national minority shall have the right freely to choose to be treated or not to be treated as such and no disadvantage shall result from this choice or from the exercise of the rights which are connected to that choice.

2. Persons belonging to national minorities may exercise the rights and enjoy the freedoms flowing from the principles enshrined in the present framework Convention individually as well as in community with others.

Section II

Article 4

1. The Parties undertake to guarantee to persons belonging to national minorities the right of equality before the law and of equal protection of the law. In this respect, any discrimination based on belonging to a national minority shall be prohibited.

2. The Parties undertake to adopt, where necessary, adequate measures in order to promote, in all areas of economic, social, political and cultural life, full and effective equality between persons belonging to a national minority and those belonging to the majority. In this respect, they shall take due account of the specific conditions of the persons belonging to national minorities.

3. The measures adopted in accordance with paragraph 2 shall not be considered to be an act of discrimination.

Article 5

1. The Parties undertake to promote the conditions necessary for persons belonging to national minorities to maintain and develop their culture, and to preserve the essential elements of their identity, namely their religion, language, traditions and cultural heritage.

2. Without prejudice to measures taken in pursuance of their general integration policy, the Parties shall refrain from policies or practices aimed at assimilation of persons belonging to national minorities against their will and shall protect these persons from any action aimed at such assimilation.

Article 6

1. The Parties shall encourage a spirit of tolerance and intercultural dialogue and take effective measures to promote mutual respect and understanding and co-operation among all persons living on their territory, irrespective of those persons' ethnic, cultural, linguistic or religious identity, in particular in the fields of education, culture and the media.

2. The Parties undertake to take appropriate measures to protect persons who may be subject to threats or acts of discrimination, hostility or violence as a result of their ethnic, cultural, linguistic or religious identity.

Article 7

The Parties shall ensure respect for the right of every person belonging to a national minority to freedom of peaceful assembly, freedom of association, freedom of expression, and freedom of thought, conscience and religion.

Article 8

The Parties undertake to recognise that every person belonging to a national minority has the right to manifest his or her religion or belief and to establish religious institutions, organisations and associations.

Article 9

1. The Parties undertake to recognise that the right to freedom of expression of every person belonging to a national minority includes freedom to hold opinions and to receive and impart

information and ideas in the minority language, without interference by public authorities and re-gardless of frontiers. The Parties shall ensure, within the framework of their legal systems, that persons belonging to a national minority are not discriminated against in their access to the media.

2. Paragraph 1 shall not prevent Parties from requiring the licensing, without discrimination and based on objective criteria, of sound radio and television broadcasting, or cinema enterprises.

3. The Parties shall not hinder the creation and the use of printed media by persons belonging to national minorities. In the legal framework of sound radio and television broadcasting, they shall ensure, as far as possible, and taking into account the provisions of paragraph 1, that persons belonging to national minorities are granted the possibility of creating and using their own media.

4. In the framework of their legal systems, the Parties shall adopt adequate measures in order to facilitate access to the media for persons belonging to national minorities and in order to promote tolerance and permit cultural pluralism.

Article 10

1. The Parties undertake to recognise that every person belonging to a national minority has the right to use freely and without interference his or her minority language, in private and in public, orally and in writing.

2. In areas inhabited by persons belonging to national minorities traditionally or in substantial numbers, if those persons so request and where such a request corresponds to a real need, the Parties shall endeavour to ensure, as far as possible, the conditions which would make it possible to use the minority language in relations between those persons and the administrative authorities.

3. The Parties undertake to guarantee the right of every person belonging to a national minority to be informed promptly, in a language which he or she understands, of the reasons for his or her arrest, and of the nature and cause of any accusation against him or her, and to defend himself or herself in this language if necessary with the free assistance of an interpreter.

Article 11

1. The Parties undertake to recognise that every person belonging to a national minority has the right to use his or her surname (patronym) and first names in the minority language and the right to official recognition of them, according to modalities provided for in their legal system.

2. The Parties undertake to recognise that every person belonging to a national minority has the right to display in his or her minority language signs, inscriptions and other information of a private nature visible to the public.

3. In areas traditionally inhabited by substantial numbers of persons belonging to a national minority, the Parties shall endeavour, in the framework of their legal system, including, where appropriate, agreements with other States, and taking into account their specific conditions, to display traditional local names, street names and other topographical indications intended for the public also in the minority language when there is a sufficient demand for such indications.

Article 12

1. The Parties shall, where appropriate, take measures in the fields of education and research to foster knowledge of the culture, history, language and religion of their national minorities and of the majority.

2. In this context the Parties shall *inter alia* provide adequate opportunities for teacher training and access to textbooks, and facilitate contacts among students and teachers of different communities.

3. The Parties undertake to promote equal opportunities for access to education at all levels for persons belonging to national minorities.

Article 13

1. Within the framework of their education systems, the Parties shall recognise that persons belonging to a national minority have the right to set up and to manage their own private educational and training establishments.

2. The exercise of this right shall not entail any financial obligation for the Parties.

Article 14

1. The Parties undertake to recognise that every person belonging to a national minority has the right to learn his or her minority language.

2. In areas inhabited by persons belonging to national minorities traditionally or in substantial numbers, if there is sufficient demand, the Parties shall endeavour to ensure, as far as possible and within the framework of their education systems, that persons belonging to those minorities have adequate opportunities for being taught the minority language or for receiving instruction in this language.

3. Paragraph 2 of this article shall be implemented without prejudice to the learning of the official language or the teaching in this language.

Article 15

The Parties shall create the conditions necessary for the effective participation of persons belonging to national minorities in cultural, social and economic life and in public affairs, in particular those affecting them.

Article 16

The Parties shall refrain from measures which alter the proportions of the population in areas inhabited by persons belonging to national minorities and are aimed at restricting the rights and freedoms flowing from the principles enshrined in the present framework Convention.

Article 17

1. The Parties undertake not to interfere with the right of persons belonging to national minorities to establish and maintain free and peaceful contacts across frontiers with persons lawfully staying in other States, in particular those with whom they share an ethnic, cultural, linguistic or religious identity, or a common cultural heritage.

2. The Parties undertake not to interfere with the right of persons belonging to national minorities to participate in the activities of non-governmental organisations, both at the national and international levels.

Article 18

1. The Parties shall endeavour to conclude, where necessary, bilateral and multilateral agreements with other States, in particular neighbouring States, in order to ensure the protection of persons belonging to the national minorities concerned.

2. Where relevant, the Parties shall take measures to encourage transfrontier co-operation.

Article 19

The Parties undertake to respect and implement the principles enshrined in the present framework Convention making, where necessary, only those limitations, restrictions or derogations which are provided for in international legal instruments, in particular the Convention for the Protection of Human Rights and Fundamental Freedoms, in so far as they are relevant to the rights and freedoms flowing from the said principles.

Section III

Article 20

In the exercise of the rights and freedoms flowing from the principles enshrined in the present framework Convention, any person belonging to a national minority shall respect the national legislation and the rights of others, in particular those of persons belonging to the majority or to other national minorities.

Article 21

Nothing in the present framework Convention shall be interpreted as implying any right to engage in any activity or perform any act contrary to the fundamental principles of international law and in particular of the sovereign equality, territorial integrity and political independence of States.

Article 22

Nothing in the present framework Convention shall be construed as limiting or derogating from any of the human rights and fundamental freedoms which may be ensured under the laws of any Contracting Party or under any other agreement to which it is a Party.

Article 23

The rights and freedoms flowing from the principles enshrined in the present framework Convention, in so far as they are the subject of a corresponding provision in the Convention for the Protection of Human Rights and Fundamental Freedoms or in the Protocols thereto, shall be understood so as to conform to the latter provisions.

Section IV

Article 24

1. The Committee of Ministers of the Council of Europe shall monitor the implementation of this framework Convention by the Contracting Parties.

2. The Parties which are not members of the Council of Europe shall participate in the implementation mechanism, according to modalities to be determined.

Article 25

1. Within a period of one year following the entry into force of this framework Convention in respect of a Contracting Party, the latter shall transmit to the Secretary General of the Council of Europe full information on the legislative and other measures taken to give effect to the principles set out in this framework Convention.

2. Thereafter, each Party shall transmit to the Secretary General on a periodical basis and whenever the Committee of Ministers so requests any further information of relevance to the implementation of this framework Convention.

3. The Secretary General shall forward to the Committee of Ministers the information transmitted under the terms of this Article.

Article 26

1. In evaluating the adequacy of the measures taken by the Parties to give effect to the principles set out in this framework Convention the Committee of Ministers shall be assisted by an advisory committee, the members of which shall have recognised expertise in the field of the protection of national minorities.

2. The composition of this advisory committee and its procedure shall be determined by the Committee of Ministers within a period of one year following the entry into force of this framework Convention.

Section V

Article 27

This framework Convention shall be open for signature by the member States of the Council of Europe. Up until the date when the Convention enters into force, it shall also be open for signature by any other State so invited by the Committee of Ministers. It is subject to ratification, acceptance or approval. Instruments of ratification, acceptance or approval shall be deposited with the Secretary General of the Council of Europe.

Article 28

1. This framework Convention shall enter into force on the first day of the month following the expiration of a period of three months after the date on which twelve member States of the Council of Europe have expressed their consent to be bound by the Convention in accordance with the provisions of Article 27.

2. In respect of any member State which subsequently expresses its consent to be bound by it, the framework Convention shall enter into force on the first day of the month following the expiration of a period of three months after the date of the deposit of the instrument of ratification, acceptance or approval.

Article 29

1. After the entry into force of this framework Convention and after consulting the Contracting States, the Committee of Ministers of the Council of Europe may invite to accede to the Convention, by a decision taken by the majority provided for in Article 20.d of the Statute of the Council of Europe, any non-member State of the Council of Europe which, invited to sign in accordance with the provisions of Article 27, has not yet done so, and any other non-member State.

2. In respect of any acceding State, the framework Convention shall enter into force on the first day of the month following the expiration of a period of three months after the date of the deposit of the instrument of accession with the Secretary General of the Council of Europe.

Article 30

1. Any State may at the time of signature or when depositing its instrument of ratification, acceptance, approval or accession, specify the territory or territories for whose international relations it is responsible to which this framework Convention shall apply.

2. Any State may at any later date, by a declaration addressed to the Secretary General of the Council of Europe, extend the application of this framework Convention to any other territory over specified in the declaration. In respect of such territory the framework Convention shall enter into force on the first day of the month following the expiration of a period of three months after the date of receipt of such declaration by the Secretary General.

3. Any declaration made under the two preceding paragraphs may, in respect of any territory specified in such declaration, be withdrawn by a notification addressed to the Secretary General. The withdrawal shall become effective on the first day of the month following the expiration of a period of three months after the date of receipt of such notification by the Secretary General.

Article 31

1. Any Party may at any time denounce this framework Convention by means of a notification addressed to the Secretary General of the Council of Europe.

2. Such denunciation shall become effective on the first day of the month following the expiration of a period of six months after the date of receipt of the notification by the Secretary General.

Article 32

The Secretary General of the Council of Europe shall notify the member States of the Council, other signatory States and any State which has acceded to this framework Convention, of:

    (a) any signature;

    (b) the deposit of any instrument of ratification, acceptance, approval or accession;

    (c) any date of entry into force of this framework Convention in accordance with Articles 28, 29 and 30;

    (d) any other act, notification or communication relating to this framework Convention.

In witness whereof the undersigned, being duly authorised thereto, have signed this framework Convention.

Done at Strasbourg, this 1st day of February 1995, in English and French, both texts being equally authentic, in a single copy which shall be deposited in the archives of the Council of Europe. The Secretary General of the Council of Europe shall transmit certified copies to each member State of the Council of Europe and to any State invited to sign or accede to this framework Convention.

B. EUROPEAN UNION

Charter of Fundamental Rights of the European Union (2007)*

PREAMBLE

The peoples of Europe, in creating an ever closer union among them, are resolved to share a peaceful future based on common values.

Conscious of its spiritual and moral heritage, the Union is founded on the indivisible, universal values of human dignity, freedom, equality and solidarity; it is based on the principles of democracy and the rule of law. It places the individual at the heart of its activities, by establishing the citizenship of the Union and by creating an area of freedom, security and justice.

The Union contributes to the preservation and to the development of these common values while respecting the diversity of the cultures and traditions of the peoples of Europe as well as the national identities of the Member States and the organisation of their public authorities at national, regional and local levels; it seeks to promote balanced and sustainable development and ensures free movement of persons, goods, services and capital, and the freedom of establishment.

To this end, it is necessary to strengthen the protection of fundamental rights in the light of changes in society, social progress and scientific and technological developments by making those rights more visible in a Charter.

This Charter reaffirms, with due regard for the powers and tasks of the Union and for the principle of subsidiarity, the rights as they result, in particular, from the constitutional traditions and international obligations common to the Member States, the European Convention for the Protection of Human Rights and Fundamental Freedoms, the Social Charters adopted by the Union and by the Council of Europe and the case-law of the Court of Justice of the European Union and of the European Court of Human Rights. In this context the Charter will be interpreted by the courts of the Union and the Member States with due regard to the explanations prepared under the authority of the Praesidium of the Convention which drafted the Charter and updated under the responsibility of the Praesidium of the European Convention.

Enjoyment of these rights entails responsibilities and duties with regard to other persons, to the human community and to future generations.

The Union therefore recognises the rights, freedoms and principles set out hereafter.

Title I   Dignity

Article 1 Human dignity
Human dignity is inviolable. It must be respected and protected.

Article 2 Right to life
   1. Everyone has the right to life.
   2. No one shall be condemned to the death penalty, or executed.

Article 3   Right to the integrity of the person
   1. Everyone has the right to respect for his or her physical and mental integrity.
   2. In the fields of medicine and biology, the following must be respected in particular:
      (a) the free and informed consent of the person concerned, according to the procedures laid down by law,
      (b) the prohibition of eugenic practices, in particular those aiming at the selection of persons,

---

* http://eur-lex.europa.eu, © European Union, 1995–2020.

    (c) the prohibition on making the human body and its parts as such a source of financial gain,

    (d) the prohibition of the reproductive cloning of human beings.

Article 4   Prohibition of torture and inhuman or degrading treatment or punishment

No one shall be subjected to torture or to inhuman or degrading treatment or punishment.

Article 5   Prohibition of slavery and forced labour

1. No one shall be held in slavery or servitude.
2. No one shall be required to perform forced or compulsory labour.
3. Trafficking in human beings is prohibited.

Title II Freedoms

Article 6   Right to liberty and security

Everyone has the right to liberty and security of person.

Article 7   Respect for private and family life

Everyone has the right to respect for his or her private and family life, home and communications.

Article 8   Protection of personal data

1. Everyone has the right to the protection of personal data concerning him or her.

2. Such data must be processed fairly for specified purposes and on the basis of the consent of the person concerned or some other legitimate basis laid down by law. Everyone has the right of access to data which has been collected concerning him or her, and the right to have it rectified.

3. Compliance with these rules shall be subject to control by an independent authority.

Article 9   Right to marry and right to found a family

The right to marry and the right to found a family shall be guaranteed in accordance with the national laws governing the exercise of these rights.

Article 10   Freedom of thought, conscience and religion

1. Everyone has the right to freedom of thought, conscience and religion. This right includes freedom to change religion or belief and freedom, either alone or in community with others and in public or in private, to manifest religion or belief, in worship, teaching, practice and observance.

2. The right to conscientious objection is recognised, in accordance with the national laws governing the exercise of this right.

Article 11   Freedom of expression and information

1. Everyone has the right to freedom of expression. This right shall include freedom to hold opinions and to receive and impart information and ideas without interference by public authority and regardless of frontiers.

2. The freedom and pluralism of the media shall be respected.

Article 12   Freedom of assembly and of association

1. Everyone has the right to freedom of peaceful assembly and to freedom of association at all levels, in particular in political, trade union and civic matters, which implies the right of everyone to form and to join trade unions for the protection of his or her interests.

2. Political parties at Union level contribute to expressing the political will of the citizens of the Union.

Article 13   Freedom of the arts and sciences

The arts and scientific research shall be free of constraint. Academic freedom shall be respected.

Article 14   Right to education

1. Everyone has the right to education and to have access to vocational and continuing training.

2. This right includes the possibility to receive free compulsory education.

3. The freedom to found educational establishments with due respect for democratic principles and the right of parents to ensure the education and teaching of their children in conformity with their religious, philosophical and pedagogical convictions shall be respected, in accordance with the national laws governing the exercise of such freedom and right.

Article 15   Freedom to choose an occupation and right to engage in work

1. Everyone has the right to engage in work and to pursue a freely chosen or accepted occupation.

2. Every citizen of the Union has the freedom to seek employment, to work, to exercise the right of establishment and to provide services in any Member State.

3. Nationals of third countries who are authorised to work in the territories of the Member States are entitled to working conditions equivalent to those of citizens of the Union.

Article 16   Freedom to conduct a business

The freedom to conduct a business in accordance with Union law and national laws and practices is recognised.

Article 17   Right to property

1. Everyone has the right to own, use, dispose of and bequeath his or her lawfully acquired possessions. No one may be deprived of his or her possessions, except in the public interest and in the cases and under the conditions provided for by law, subject to fair compensation being paid in good time for their loss. The use of property may be regulated by law in so far as is necessary for the general interest.

2. Intellectual property shall be protected.

Article 18   Right to asylum

The right to asylum shall be guaranteed with due respect for the rules of the Geneva Convention of 28 July 1951 and the Protocol of 31 January 1967 relating to the status of refugees and in accordance with the Treaty on European Union and the Treaty on the Functioning of the European Union (hereinafter referred to as 'the Treaties').

Article 19   Protection in the event of removal, expulsion or extradition

1. Collective expulsions are prohibited.

2. No one may be removed, expelled or extradited to a State where there is a serious risk that he or she would be subjected to the death penalty, torture or other inhuman or degrading treatment or punishment.

Title III Equality

Article 20   Equality before the law

Everyone is equal before the law.

Article 21   Non-discrimination

1. Any discrimination based on any ground such as sex, race, colour, ethnic or social origin, genetic features, language, religion or belief, political or any other opinion, membership of a national minority, property, birth, disability, age or sexual orientation shall be prohibited.

2. Within the scope of application of the Treaties and without prejudice to any of their specific provisions, any discrimination on grounds of nationality shall be prohibited.

Article 22   Cultural, religious and linguistic diversity

The Union shall respect cultural, religious and linguistic diversity.

Article 23   Equality between women and men

Equality between women and men must be ensured in all areas, including employment, work and pay.

The principle of equality shall not prevent the maintenance or adoption of measures providing for specific advantages in favour of the under-represented sex.

Article 24   The rights of the child

1. Children shall have the right to such protection and care as is necessary for their well-being. They may express their views freely. Such views shall be taken into consideration on matters which concern them in accordance with their age and maturity.

2. In all actions relating to children, whether taken by public authorities or private institutions, the child's best interests must be a primary consideration.

3. Every child shall have the right to maintain on a regular basis a personal relationship and direct contact with both his or her parents, unless that is contrary to his or her interests.

Article 25   The rights of the elderly

The Union recognises and respects the rights of the elderly to lead a life of dignity and independence and to participate in social and cultural life.

Article 26   Integration of persons with disabilities

The Union recognises and respects the right of persons with disabilities to benefit from measures designed to ensure their independence, social and occupational integration and participation in the life of the community.

Title IV Solidarity

Article 27   Workers' right to information and consultation within the undertaking

Workers or their representatives must, at the appropriate levels, be guaranteed information and consultation in good time in the cases and under the conditions provided for by Union law and national laws and practices.

Article 28   Right of collective bargaining and action

Workers and employers, or their respective organisations, have, in accordance with Union law and national laws and practices, the right to negotiate and conclude collective agreements at the appropriate levels and, in cases of conflicts of interest, to take collective action to defend their interests, including strike action.

Article 29   Right of access to placement services

Everyone has the right of access to a free placement service.

Article 30   Protection in the event of unjustified dismissal

Every worker has the right to protection against unjustified dismissal, in accordance with Union law and national laws and practices.

Article 31   Fair and just working conditions

1. Every worker has the right to working conditions which respect his or her health, safety and dignity.

2. Every worker has the right to limitation of maximum working hours, to daily and weekly rest periods and to an annual period of paid leave.

Article 32   Prohibition of child labour and protection of young people at work

The employment of children is prohibited. The minimum age of admission to employment may not be lower than the minimum school-leaving age, without prejudice to such rules as may be more favourable to young people and except for limited derogations.

Young people admitted to work must have working conditions appropriate to their age and be protected against economic exploitation and any work likely to harm their safety, health or physical, mental, moral or social development or to interfere with their education.

Article 33   Family and professional life

1. The family shall enjoy legal, economic and social protection.

2. To reconcile family and professional life, everyone shall have the right to protection from dismissal for a reason connected with maternity and the right to paid maternity leave and to parental leave following the birth or adoption of a child.

Article 34   Social security and social assistance

1. The Union recognises and respects the entitlement to social security benefits and social services providing protection in cases such as maternity, illness, industrial accidents, dependency or old age, and in the case of loss of employment, in accordance with the rules laid down by Union law and national laws and practices.

2. Everyone residing and moving legally within the European Union is entitled to social security benefits and social advantages in accordance with Union law and national laws and practices.

3. In order to combat social exclusion and poverty, the Union recognises and respects the right to social and housing assistance so as to ensure a decent existence for all those who lack sufficient resources, in accordance with the rules laid down by Union law and national laws and practices.

Article 35   Health care

Everyone has the right of access to preventive health care and the right to benefit from medical treatment under the conditions established by national laws and practices. A high level of human health protection shall be ensured in the definition and implementation of all Union policies and activities.

Article 36   Access to services of general economic interest

The Union recognises and respects access to services of general economic interest as provided for in national laws and practices, in accordance with the Treaties, in order to promote the social and territorial cohesion of the Union.

Article 37   Environmental protection

A high level of environmental protection and the improvement of the quality of the environment must be integrated into the policies of the Union and ensured in accordance with the principle of sustainable development.

Article 38   Consumer protection

Union policies shall ensure a high level of consumer protection.

Title V Citizens' Rights

Article 39   Right to vote and to stand as a candidate at elections to the European Parliament

1. Every citizen of the Union has the right to vote and to stand as a candidate at elections to the European Parliament in the Member State in which he or she resides, under the same conditions as nationals of that State.

2. Members of the European Parliament shall be elected by direct universal suffrage in a free and secret ballot.

Article 40   Right to vote and to stand as a candidate at municipal elections

Every citizen of the Union has the right to vote and to stand as a candidate at municipal elections in the Member State in which he or she resides under the same conditions as nationals of that State.

Article 41   Right to good administration

1. Every person has the right to have his or her affairs handled impartially, fairly and within a reasonable time by the institutions, bodies, offices and agencies of the Union.

2. This right includes:

(a) the right of every person to be heard, before any individual measure which would affect him or her adversely is taken;

(b) the right of every person to have access to his or her file, while respecting the legitimate interests of confidentiality and of professional and business secrecy;

(c) the obligation of the administration to give reasons for its decisions.

3. Every person has the right to have the Union make good any damage caused by its institutions or by its servants in the performance of their duties, in accordance with the general principles common to the laws of the Member States.

4. Every person may write to the institutions of the Union in one of the languages of the Treaties and must have an answer in the same language.

Article 42   Right of access to documents

Any citizen of the Union, and any natural or legal person residing or having its registered office in a Member State, has a right of access to documents of the institutions, bodies, offices and agencies of the Union, whatever their medium.

Article 43   European Ombudsman

Any citizen of the Union and any natural or legal person residing or having its registered office in a Member State has the right to refer to the European Ombudsman cases of maladministration in the activities of the institutions, bodies, offices or agencies of the Union, with the exception of the Court of Justice of the European Union acting in its judicial role.

Article 44   Right to petition

Any citizen of the Union and any natural or legal person residing or having its registered office in a Member State has the right to petition the European Parliament.

Article 45   Freedom of movement and of residence

1. Every citizen of the Union has the right to move and reside freely within the territory of the Member States.

2. Freedom of movement and residence may be granted, in accordance with the Treaties, to nationals of third countries legally resident in the territory of a Member State.

Article 46   Diplomatic and consular protection

Every citizen of the Union shall, in the territory of a third country in which the Member State of which he or she is a national is not represented, be entitled to protection by the diplomatic or consular authorities of any Member State, on the same conditions as the nationals of that Member State.

Title VI Justice

Article 47   Right to an effective remedy and to a fair trial

Everyone whose rights and freedoms guaranteed by the law of the Union are violated has the right to an effective remedy before a tribunal in compliance with the conditions laid down in this Article.

Everyone is entitled to a fair and public hearing within a reasonable time by an independent and impartial tribunal previously established by law. Everyone shall have the possibility of being advised, defended and represented.

Legal aid shall be made available to those who lack sufficient resources in so far as such aid is necessary to ensure effective access to justice.

Article 48   Presumption of innocence and right of defence

1. Everyone who has been charged shall be presumed innocent until proved guilty according to law.

2. Respect for the rights of the defence of anyone who has been charged shall be guaranteed.

Article 49   Principles of legality and proportionality of criminal offences and penalties

1. No one shall be held guilty of any criminal offence on account of any act or omission which did not constitute a criminal offence under national law or international law at the time when it was

committed. Nor shall a heavier penalty be imposed than that which was applicable at the time the criminal offence was committed. If, subsequent to the commission of a criminal offence, the law provides for a lighter penalty, that penalty shall be applicable.

2. This Article shall not prejudice the trial and punishment of any person for any act or omission which, at the time when it was committed, was criminal according to the general principles recognised by the community of nations.

3. The severity of penalties must not be disproportionate to the criminal offence.

Article 50   Right not to be tried or punished twice in criminal proceedings for the same criminal offence

No one shall be liable to be tried or punished again in criminal proceedings for an offence for which he or she has already been finally acquitted or convicted within the Union in accordance with the law.

Title VII   General Provisions Governing the Interpretation and Application of the Charter

Article 51   Field of application

1. The provisions of this Charter are addressed to the institutions, bodies, offices and agencies of the Union with due regard for the principle of subsidiarity and to the Member States only when they are implementing Union law. They shall therefore respect the rights, observe the principles and promote the application thereof in accordance with their respective powers and respecting the limits of the powers of the Union as conferred on it in the Treaties.

2. The Charter does not extend the field of application of Union law beyond the powers of the Union or establish any new power or task for the Union, or modify powers and tasks as defined in the Treaties.

Article 52   Scope and interpretation of rights and principles

1. Any limitation on the exercise of the rights and freedoms recognised by this Charter must be provided for by law and respect the essence of those rights and freedoms. Subject to the principle of proportionality, limitations may be made only if they are necessary and genuinely meet objectives of general interest recognised by the Union or the need to protect the rights and freedoms of others.

2. Rights recognized by this Charter for which provision is made in the Treaties shall be exercised under the conditions and within the limits defined by those Treaties.

3. In so far as this Charter contains rights which correspond to rights guaranteed by the Convention for the Protection of Human Rights and Fundamental Freedoms, the meaning and scope of those rights shall be the same as those laid down by the said Convention. This provision shall not prevent Union law providing more extensive protection.

4. In so far as this Charter recognises fundamental rights as they result from the constitutional traditions common to the Member States, those rights shall be interpreted in harmony with those traditions.

5. The provisions of this Charter which contain principles may be implemented by legislative and executive acts taken by institutions, bodies, offices and agencies of the Union, and by acts of Member States when they are implementing Union law, in the exercise of their respective powers. They shall be judicially cognisable only in the interpretation of such acts and in the ruling on their legality.

6. Full account shall be taken of national laws and practices as specified in this Charter.

7. The explanations drawn up as a way of providing guidance in the interpretation of this Charter shall be given due regard by the courts of the Union and of the Member States.

Article 53   Level of protection

Nothing in this Charter shall be interpreted as restricting or adversely affecting human rights and fundamental freedoms as recognised, in their respective fields of application, by Union law and international law and by international agreements to which the Union or all the Member States are party, including the European Convention for the Protection of Human Rights and Fundamental Freedoms, and by the Member States' constitutions.

Article 54   Prohibition of abuse of rights

Nothing in this Charter shall be interpreted as implying any right to engage in any activity or to perform any act aimed at the destruction of any of the rights and freedoms recognised in this Charter or at their limitation to a greater extent than is provided for herein.

C. AMERICA

American Declaration of the Rights and Duties of Man (1948)*

WHEREAS:

The American peoples have acknowledged the dignity of the individual, and their national constitutions recognize that juridical and political institutions, which regulate life in human society, have as their principal aim the protection of the essential rights of man and the creation of circumstances that will permit him to achieve spiritual and material progress and attain happiness;

The American States have on repeated occasions recognized that the essential rights of man are not derived from the fact that he is a national of a certain state, but are based upon attributes of his human personality;

The international protection of the rights of man should be the principal guide of an evolving American law;

The affirmation of essential human rights by the American States together with the guarantees given by the internal regimes of the states establish the initial system of protection considered by the American States as being suited to the present social and juridical conditions, not without a recognition on their part that they should increasingly strengthen that system in the international field as conditions become more favorable,

The Ninth International Conference of American States

AGREES:

To adopt the following

Preamble

All men are born free and equal, in dignity and in rights, and, being endowed by nature with reason and conscience, they should conduct themselves as brothers one to another.

The fulfillment of duty by each individual is a prerequisite to the rights of all. Rights and duties are interrelated in every social and political activity of man. While rights exalt individual liberty, duties express the dignity of that liberty.

Duties of a juridical nature presuppose others of a moral nature which support them in principle and constitute their basis.

Inasmuch as spiritual development is the supreme end of human existence and the highest expression thereof, it is the duty of man to serve that end with all his strength and resources.

Since culture is the highest social and historical expression of that spiritual development, it is the duty of man to preserve, practice and foster culture by every means within his power.

And, since moral conduct constitutes the noblest flowering of culture, it is the duty of every man always to hold it in high respect.

* Reproduced by permission of the General Secretariat of the Organization of American States. https://www.cidh.oas.org/basicos/english/basic2.american%20declaration.htm.

CHAPTER ONE

Rights

Article I Right to life, liberty and personal security.

Every human being has the right to life, liberty and the security of his person.

Article II Right to equality before law.

All persons are equal before the law and have the rights and duties established in this Declaration, without distinction as to race, sex, language, creed or any other factor.

Article III Right to religious freedom and worship.

Every person has the right freely to profess a religious faith, and to manifest and practice it both in public and in private.

Article IV Right to freedom of investigation, opinion, expression and dissemination.

Every person has the right to freedom of investigation, of opinion, and of the expression and dissemination of ideas, by any medium whatsoever.

Article V Right to protection of honor, personal reputation, and private and family life.

Every person has the right to the protection of the law against abusive attacks upon his honor, his reputation, and his private and family life.

Article VI Right to a family and protection thereof.

Every person has the right to establish a family, the basic element of society, and to receive protection thereof.

Article VII Right to protection for mothers and children.

All women, during pregnancy and the nursing period, and all children have the right to special protection, care and aid.

Article VIII Right to residence and movement.

Every person has the right to fix his residence within the territory of the state of which he is a national, to move about freely within such territory, and not to leave it except by his own will.

Article IX Right to inviolability of the home.

Every person has the right to the inviolability of his home.

Article X Right to the inviolability and transmission of correspondence.

Every person has the right to the inviolability and transmission of his correspondence.

Article XI Right to the preservation of health and to well-being.

Every person has the right to the preservation of his health through sanitary and social measures relating to food, clothing, housing and medical care, to the extent permitted by public and community resources.

Article XII Right to education.

Every person has the right to an education, which should be based on the principles of liberty, morality and human solidarity.

Likewise every person has the right to an education that will prepare him to attain a decent life, to raise his standard of living, and to be a useful member of society.

The right to an education includes the right to equality of opportunity in every case, in accordance with natural talents, merit and the desire to utilize the resources that the state or the community is in a position to provide.

Every person has the right to receive, free, at least a primary education.

Article XIII   Right to the benefits of culture.

Every person has the right to take part in the cultural life of the community, to enjoy the arts, and to participate in the benefits that result from intellectual progress, especially scientific discoveries.

He likewise has the right to the protection of his moral and material interests as regards his inventions or any literary, scientific or artistic works of which he is the author.

Article XIV   Right to work and to fair remuneration.

Every person has the right to work, under proper conditions, and to follow his vocation freely, insofar as existing conditions of employment permit.

Every person who works has the right to receive such remuneration as will, in proportion to his capacity and skill, assure him a standard of living suitable for himself and for his family.

Article XV   Right to leisure time and to the use thereof.

Every person has the right to leisure time, to wholesome recreation, and to the opportunity for advantageous use of his free time to his spiritual, cultural and physical benefit.

Article XVI   Right to social security.

Every person has the right to social security which will protect him from the consequences of unemployment, old age, and any disabilities arising from causes beyond his control that make it physically or mentally impossible for him to earn a living.

Article XVII   Right to recognition of juridical personality and civil rights.

Every person has the right to be recognized everywhere as a person having rights and obligations, and to enjoy the basic civil rights.

Article XVIII   Right to a fair trial.

Every person may resort to the courts to ensure respect for his legal rights. There should likewise be available to him a simple, brief procedure whereby the courts will protect him from acts of authority that, to his prejudice, violate any fundamental constitutional rights.

Article XIX   Right to nationality.

Every person has the right to the nationality to which he is entitled by law and to change it, if he so wishes, for the nationality of any other country that is willing to grant it to him.

Article XX   Right to vote and to participate in government.

Every person having legal capacity is entitled to participate in the government of his country, directly or through his representatives, and to take part in popular elections, which shall be by secret ballot, and shall be honest, periodic and free.

Article XXI   Right of assembly.

Every person has the right to assemble peaceably with others in a formal public meeting or an informal gathering, in connection with matters of common interest of any nature.

Article XXII   Right of association.

Every person has the right to associate with others to promote, exercise and protect his legitimate interests of a political, economic, religious, social, cultural, professional, labor union or other nature.

Article XXIII   Right to property.

Every person has a right to own such private property as meets the essential needs of decent living and helps to maintain the dignity of the individual and of the home.

Article XXIV   Right of petition.

Every person has the right to submit respectful petitions to any competent authority, for reasons of either general or private interest, and the right to obtain a prompt decision thereon.

Article XXV   Right of protection from arbitrary arrest.

No person may be deprived of his liberty except in the cases and according to the procedures established by pre-existing law.

No person may be deprived of liberty for nonfulfillment of obligations of a purely civil character.

Every individual who has been deprived of his liberty has the right to have the legality of his detention ascertained without delay by a court, and the right to be tried without undue delay or, otherwise, to be released. He also has the right to humane treatment during the time he is in custody.

Article XXVI   Right to due process of law.

Every accused person is presumed to be innocent until proved guilty.

Every person accused of an offense has the right to be given an impartial and public hearing, and to be tried by courts previously established in accordance with pre-existing laws, and not to receive cruel, infamous or unusual punishment.

Article XXVII   Right of asylum.

Every person has the right, in case of pursuit not resulting from ordinary crimes, to seek and receive asylum in foreign territory, in accordance with the laws of each country and with international agreements.

Article XXVIII   Scope of the rights of man.

The rights of man are limited by the rights of others, by the security of all, and by the just demands of the general welfare and the advancement of democracy.

CHAPTER TWO

Duties

Article XXIX   Duties to society.

It is the duty of the individual so to conduct himself in relation to others that each and every one may fully form and develop his personality.

Article XXX   Duties toward children and parents.

It is the duty of every person to aid, support, educate and protect his minor children, and it is the duty of children to honor their parents always and to aid, support and protect them when they need it.

Article XXXI   Duty to receive instruction.

It is the duty of every person to acquire at least an elementary education.

Article XXXII   Duty to vote.

It is the duty of every person to vote in the popular elections of the country of which he is a national, when he is legally capable of doing so.

Article XXXIII   Duty to obey the law.

It is the duty of every person to obey the law and other legitimate commands of the authorities of his country and those of the country in which he may be.

Article XXXIV   Duty to serve the community and the nation.

It is the duty of every able-bodied person to render whatever civil and military service his country may require for its defense and preservation, and, in case of public disaster, to render such services as may be in his power.

It is likewise his duty to hold any public office to which he may be elected by popular vote in the state of which he is a national.

Article XXXV   Duty with respect to social security and welfare.

It is the duty of every person to cooperate with the state and the community with respect to social security and welfare, in accordance with his ability and with existing circumstances.

Article XXXVI   Duty to pay taxes.

It is the duty of every person to pay the taxes established by law for the support of public services.

Article XXXVII   Duty to work.

It is the duty of every person to work, as far as his capacity and possibilities permit, in order to obtain the means of livelihood or to benefit his community.

Article XXXVIII   Duty to refrain from political activities in a foreign country.

It is the duty of every person to refrain from taking part in political activities that, according to law, are reserved exclusively to the citizens of the state in which he is an alien.

American Convention on Human Rights ('Pact of San José, Costa Rica') (1969)*

PREAMBLE

The American States signatory to the present Convention

   Reaffirming their intention to consolidate in this hemisphere, within the framework of democratic institutions, a system of personal liberty and social justice based on respect for the essential rights of man;

   Recognizing that the essential rights of man are not derived from one's being a national of a certain state, but are based upon attributes of the human personality, and that they therefore justify international protection in the form of a convention reinforcing or complementing the protection provided by the domestic law of the American states;

   Considering that these principles have been set forth in the Charter of the Organization of American States, in the American Declaration of the Rights and Duties of Man, and in the Universal Declaration of Human Rights, and that they have been reaffirmed and refined in other international instruments, worldwide as well as regional in scope;

   Reiterating that, in accordance with the Universal Declaration of Human Rights, the ideal of free men enjoying freedom from fear and want can be achieved only if conditions are created whereby everyone may enjoy his economic, social, and cultural rights, as well as his civil and political rights; and

   Considering that the Third Special Inter-American Conference (Buenos Aires, 1967) approved the incorporation into the Charter of the Organization itself of broader standards with respect to economic, social, and educational rights and resolved that an inter-American convention on human rights should determine the structure, competence, and procedure of the organs responsible for these matters,

   Have agreed upon the following:

PART I STATE OBLIGATIONS AND RIGHTS PROTECTED

Chapter I General Obligations

Article 1   Obligation to respect rights

   1. The States Parties to this Convention undertake to respect the rights and freedoms recognized herein and to ensure to all persons subject to their jurisdiction the free and full exercise of those rights and freedoms, without any discrimination for reasons of race, color, sex, language, religion, political or other opinion, national or social origin, economic status, birth, or any other social condition.

   2. For the purposes of this Convention, 'person' means every human being.

Article 2   Domestic legal effects

Where the exercise of any of the rights or freedoms referred to in Article 1 is not already ensured by legislative or other provisions, the States Parties undertake to adopt, in accordance with their

  * Reproduced by permission of the General Secretariat of the Organization of American States. http://www.oas.org/dil/treaties_B-32_American_Convention_on_Human_Rights.htm

constitutional processes and the provisions of this Convention, such legislative or other measures as may be necessary to give effect to those rights or freedoms.

Chapter II Civil and Political Rights

Article 3   Right to juridical personality
Every person has the right to recognition as a person before the law.

Article 4   Right to life
1. Every person has the right to have his life respected. This right shall be protected by law, and, in general, from the moment of conception. No one shall be arbitrarily deprived of his life.

2. In countries that have not abolished the death penalty, it may be imposed only for the most serious crimes and pursuant to a final judgment rendered by a competent court and in accordance with a law establishing such punishment, enacted prior to the commission of the crime. The application of such punishment shall not be extended to crimes to which it does not presently apply.

3. The death penalty shall not be reestablished in states that have abolished it.

4. In no case shall capital punishment be inflicted for political offenses or related common crimes.

5. Capital punishment shall not be imposed upon persons who, at the time the crime was committed, were under 18 years of age or over 70 years of age; nor shall it be applied to pregnant women.

6. Every person condemned to death shall have the right to apply for amnesty, pardon, or commutation of sentence, which may be granted in all cases. Capital punishment shall not be imposed while such a petition is pending decision by the competent authority.

Article 5   Right to humane treatment
1. Every person has the right to have his physical, mental, and moral integrity respected.

2. No one shall be subjected to torture or to cruel, inhuman, or degrading punishment or treatment. All persons deprived of their liberty shall be treated with respect for the inherent dignity of the human person.

3. Punishment shall not be extended to any person other than the criminal.

4. Accused persons shall, save in exceptional circumstances, be segregated from convicted persons, and shall be subject to separate treatment appropriate to their status as unconvicted persons.

5. Minors while subject to criminal proceedings shall be separated from adults and brought before specialized tribunals, as speedily as possible, so that they may be treated in accordance with their status as minors.

6. Punishments consisting of deprivation of liberty shall have as an essential aim the reform and social readaptation of the prisoners.

Article 6   Freedom from slavery
1. No one shall be subject to slavery or to involuntary servitude, which are prohibited in all their forms, as are the slave trade and traffic in women.

2. No one shall be required to perform forced or compulsory labor. This provision shall not be interpreted to mean that, in those countries in which the penalty established for certain crimes is deprivation of liberty at forced labor, the carrying out of such a sentence imposed by a competent court is prohibited. Forced labor shall not adversely affect the dignity or the physical or intellectual capacity of the prisoner.

3. For the purposes of this article the following do not constitute forced or compulsory labor:
   (a) work or service normally required of a person imprisoned in execution of a sentence or formal decision passed by the competent judicial authority. Such work or service shall be carried out under the supervision and control of public authorities, and any persons performing such work or service shall not be placed at the disposal of any private party, company, or juridical person;
   (b) military service and, in countries in which conscientious objectors are recognized, national service that the law may provide for in lieu of military service;

(c) service exacted in time of danger or calamity that threatens the existence or the well-being of the community;

(d) work or service that forms part of normal civic obligations.

Article 7   Right to personal liberty

1. Every person has the right to personal liberty and security.

2. No one shall be deprived of his physical liberty except for the reasons and under the conditions established beforehand by the constitution of the State Party concerned or by a law established pursuant thereto.

3. No one shall be subject to arbitrary arrest or imprisonment.

4. Anyone who is detained shall be informed of the reasons for his detention and shall be promptly notified of the charge or charges against him.

5. Any person detained shall be brought promptly before a judge or other officer authorized by law to exercise judicial power and shall be entitled to trial within a reasonable time or to be released without prejudice to the continuation of the proceedings. His release may be subject to guarantees to assure his appearance for trial.

6. Anyone who is deprived of his liberty shall be entitled to recourse to a competent court, in order that the court may decide without delay on the lawfulness of his arrest or detention and order his release if the arrest or detention is unlawful. In States Parties whose laws provide that anyone who believes himself to be threatened with deprivation of his liberty is entitled to recourse to a competent court in order that it may decide on the lawfulness of such threat, this remedy may not be restricted or abolished. The interested party or another person in his behalf is entitled to seek these remedies.

7. No one shall be detained for debt. This principle shall not limit the orders of a competent judicial authority issued for nonfulfillment of duties of support.

Article 8   Right to a fair trial

1. Every person has the right to a hearing, with due guarantees and within a reasonable time, by a competent, independent, and impartial tribunal, previously established by law, in the substantiation of any accusation of a criminal nature made against him or for the determination of his rights and obligations of a civil, labor, fiscal, or any other nature.

2. Every person accused of a criminal offense has the right to be presumed innocent so long as his guilt has not been proven according to law. During the proceedings, every person is entitled, with full equality, to the following minimum guarantees:

(a) the right of the accused to be assisted without charge by a translator or interpreter, if he does not understand or does not speak the language of the tribunal or court;

(b) prior notification in detail to the accused of the charges against him;

(c) adequate time and means for the preparation of his defense;

(d) the right of the accused to defend himself personally or to be assisted by legal counsel of his own choosing, and to communicate freely and privately with his counsel;

(e) the inalienable right to be assisted by counsel provided by the state, paid or not as the domestic law provides, if the accused does not defend himself personally or engage his own counsel within the time period established by law;

(f) the right of the defense to examine witnesses present in the court and to obtain the appearance, as witnesses, of experts or other persons who may throw light on the facts;

(g) the right not to be compelled to be a witness against himself or to plead guilty; and

(h) the right to appeal the judgment to a higher court.

3. A confession of guilt by the accused shall be valid only if it is made without coercion of any kind.

4. An accused person acquitted by a non-appealable judgment shall not be subjected to a new trial for the same cause.

5. Criminal proceedings shall be public, except insofar as may be necessary to protect the interests of justice.

Article 9 Freedom from *ex post facto* laws

No one shall be convicted of any act or omission that did not constitute a criminal offense, under the applicable law, at the time it was committed. A heavier penalty shall not be imposed than the one that was applicable at the time the criminal offense was committed. If subsequent to the commission of the offense the law provides for the imposition of a lighter punishment, the guilty person shall benefit therefrom.

Article 10 Right to compensation

Every person has the right to be compensated in accordance with the law in the event he has been sentenced by a final judgment through a miscarriage of justice.

Article 11 Right to privacy

1. Everyone has the right to have his honor respected and his dignity recognized.
2. No one may be the object of arbitrary or abusive interference with his private life, his family, his home, or his correspondence, or of unlawful attacks on his honor or reputation.
3. Everyone has the right to the protection of the law against such interference or attacks.

Article 12 Freedom of conscience and religion

1. Everyone has the right to freedom of conscience and of religion. This includes freedom to maintain or to change one's religion or beliefs, and freedom to profess or disseminate one's religion or beliefs either individually or together with others, in public or in private.
2. No one shall be subject to restrictions that might impair his freedom to maintain or to change his religion or beliefs.
3. Freedom to manifest one's religion and beliefs may be subject only to the limitations prescribed by law that are necessary to protect public safety, order, health, or morals, or the rights or freedoms of others.
4. Parents or guardians, as the case may be, have the right to provide for the religious and moral education of their children or wards that is in accord with their own convictions.

Article 13 Freedom of thought and expression

1. Everyone shall have the right to freedom of thought and expression. This right shall include freedom to seek, receive, and impart information and ideas of all kinds, regardless of frontiers, either orally, in writing, in print, in the form of art, or through any other medium of one's choice.
2. The exercise of the right provided for in the foregoing paragraph shall not be subject to prior censorship but shall be subject to subsequent imposition of liability, which shall be expressly established by law to the extent necessary in order to ensure:
    (a) respect for the rights or reputations of others; or
    (b) the protection of national security, public order, or public health or morals.
3. The right of expression may not be restricted by indirect methods or means, such as the abuse of government or private controls over newsprint, radio broadcasting frequencies, or equipment used in the dissemination of information, or by any other means tending to impede the communication and circulation of ideas and opinions.
4. Notwithstanding the provisions of paragraph 2 above, public entertainments may be subject by law to prior censorship for the sole purpose of regulating access to them for the moral protection of childhood and adolescence.
5. Any propaganda for war and any advocacy of national, racial, or religious hatred that constitute incitements to lawless violence or to any other similar illegal action against any person or group of persons on any grounds including those of race, color, religion, language, or national origin shall be considered as offenses punishable by law.

Article 14 Right of reply

1. Anyone injured by inaccurate or offensive statements or ideas disseminated to the public in general by a legally regulated medium of communication has the right to reply or make a correction using the same communications outlet, under such conditions as the law may establish.

2. The correction or reply shall not in any case remit other legal liabilities that may have been incurred.

3. For the effective protection of honor and reputation, every publisher, and every newspaper, motion picture, radio, and television company, shall have a person responsible, who is not protected by immunities or special privileges.

Article 15   Right of assembly
The right of peaceful assembly, without arms, is recognized. No restrictions may be placed on the exercise of this right other than those imposed in conformity with the law and necessary in a democratic society in the interest of national security, public safety or public order, or to protect public health or morals or the rights or freedoms of others.

Article 16   Freedom of association
1. Everyone has the right to associate freely for ideological, religious, political, economic, labor, social, cultural, sports, or other purposes.

2. The exercise of this right shall be subject only to such restrictions established by law as may be necessary in a democratic society, in the interest of national security, public safety or public order, or to protect public health or morals or the rights and freedoms of others.

3. The provisions of this article do not bar the imposition of legal restrictions, including even deprivation of the exercise of the right of association, on members of the armed forces and the police.

Article 17   Rights of the family
1. The family is the natural and fundamental group unit of society and is entitled to protection by society and the state.

2. The right of men and women of marriageable age to marry and to raise a family shall be recognized, if they meet the conditions required by domestic laws, insofar as such conditions do not affect the principle of nondiscrimination established in this Convention.

3. No marriage shall be entered into without the free and full consent of the intending spouses.

4. The States Parties shall take appropriate steps to ensure the equality of rights and the adequate balancing of responsibilities of the spouses as to marriage, during marriage, and in the event of its dissolution. In case of dissolution, provision shall be made for the necessary protection of any children solely on the basis of their own best interests.

5. The law shall recognize equal rights for children born out of wedlock and those born in wedlock.

Article 18   Right to a name
Every person has the right to a given name and to the surnames of his parents or that of one of them. The law shall regulate the manner in which this right shall be ensured for all, by the use of assumed names if necessary.

Article 19   Rights of the child
Every minor child has the right to the measures of protection required by his condition as a minor on the part of his family, society, and the state.

Article 20   Right to nationality
1. Every person has the right to a nationality.

2. Every person has the right to the nationality of the state in whose territory he was born if he does not have the right to any other nationality.

3. No one shall be arbitrarily deprived of his nationality or of the right to change it.

Article 21   Right to property
1. Everyone has the right to the use and enjoyment of his property. The law may subordinate such use and enjoyment to the interest of society.

2. No one shall be deprived of his property except upon payment of just compensation, for reasons of public utility or social interest, and in the cases and according to the forms established by law.

3. Usury and any other form of exploitation of man by man shall be prohibited by law.

Article 22   Freedom of movement and residence

1. Every person lawfully in the territory of a State Party has the right to move about in it and to reside in it subject to the provisions of the law.

2. Every person has the right to leave any country freely, including his own.

3. The exercise of the foregoing rights may be restricted only pursuant to a law to the extent necessary in a democratic society to prevent crime or to protect national security, public safety, public order, public morals, public health, or the rights or freedoms of others.

4. The exercise of the rights recognized in paragraph 1 may also be restricted by law in designated zones for reasons of public interest.

5. No one can be expelled from the territory of the state of which he is a national or be deprived of the right to enter it.

6. An alien lawfully in the territory of a State Party to this Convention may be expelled from it only pursuant to a decision reached in accordance with law.

7. Every person has the right to seek and be granted asylum in a foreign territory, in accordance with the legislation of the state and international conventions, in the event he is being pursued for political offenses or related common crimes.

8. In no case may an alien be deported or returned to a country, regardless of whether or not it is his country of origin, if in that country his right to life or personal freedom is in danger of being violated because of his race, nationality, religion, social status, or political opinions.

9. The collective expulsion of aliens is prohibited.

Article 23   Right to participate in government

1. Every citizen shall enjoy the following rights and opportunities:
    (a) to take part in the conduct of public affairs, directly or through freely chosen representatives;
    (b) to vote and to be elected in genuine periodic elections, which shall be by universal and equal suffrage and by secret ballot that guarantees the free expression of the will of the voters; and
    (c) to have access, under general conditions of equality, to the public service of his country.

2. The law may regulate the exercise of the rights and opportunities referred to in the preceding paragraph only on the basis of age, nationality, residence, language, education, civil and mental capacity, or sentencing by a competent court in criminal proceedings.

Article 24   Right to equal protection

All persons are equal before the law. Consequently, they are entitled, without discrimination, to equal protection of the law.

Article 25   Right to judicial protection

1. Everyone has the right to simple and prompt recourse, or any other effective recourse, to a competent court or tribunal for protection against acts that violate his fundamental rights recognized by the constitution or laws of the state concerned or by this Convention, even though such violation may have been committed by persons acting in the course of their official duties.

2. The States Parties undertake:
    (a) to ensure that any person claiming such remedy shall have his rights determined by the competent authority provided for by the legal system of the state;
    (b) to develop the possibilities of judicial remedy; and
    (c) to ensure that the competent authorities shall enforce such remedies when granted.

Chapter III Economic, Social, and Cultural Rights

Article 26 Progressive development

The States Parties undertake to adopt measures, both internally and through international co-operation, especially those of an economic and technical nature, with a view to achieving progressively, by legislation or other appropriate means, the full realization of the rights implicit in the economic, social, educational, scientific, and cultural standards set forth in the Charter of the Organization of American States as amended by the Protocol of Buenos Aires.

Chapter IV Suspension of Guarantees, Interpretation, and Application

Article 27 Suspension of guarantes

1. In time of war, public danger, or other emergency that threatens the independence or security of a State Party, it may take measures derogating from its obligations under the present Convention to the extent and for the period of time strictly required by the exigencies of the situation, provided that such measures are not inconsistent with its other obligations under international law and do not involve discrimination on the ground of race, color, sex, language, religion, or social origin.

2. The foregoing provision does not authorize any suspension of the following articles: Article 3 (Right to juridical Personality), Article 4 (Right to Life), Article 5 (Right to Humane Treatment), Article 6 (Freedom from Slavery), Article 9 (Freedom from *Ex Post Facto* Laws), Article 12 (Freedom of Conscience and Religion), Article 17 (Rights of the Family), Article 18 (Right to a Name), Article 19 (Rights of the Child), Article 20 (Right to Nationality), and Article 23 (Right to Participate in Government), or of the judicial guarantees essential for the protection of such rights.

3. Any State Party availing itself of the right of suspension shall immediately inform the other States Parties, through the Secretary-General of the Organization of American States, of the provisions the application of which it has suspended, the reasons that gave rise to the suspension, and the date set for the termination of such suspension.

Article 28 Federal clause

1. Where a State Party is constituted as a federal state, the national government of such State Party shall implement all the provisions of the Convention over whose subject matter it exercises legislative and judicial jurisdiction.

2. With respect to the provisions over whose subject matter the constituent units of the federal state have jurisdiction, the national government shall immediately take suitable measures, in accordance with its constitution and its laws, to the end that the competent authorities of the constituent units may adopt appropriate provisions for the fulfillment of this Convention.

3. Whenever two or more States Parties agree to form a federation or other type of association they shall take care that the resulting federal or other compact contains the provisions necessary for continuing and rendering effective the standards of this Convention in the new state that is organized.

Article 29 Restrictions regarding interpretation

No provision of this Convention shall be interpreted as:

(a) permitting any State Party, group, or person to suppress the enjoyment or exercise of the rights and freedoms recognized in this Convention or to restrict them to a greater extent than is provided for herein;

(b) restricting the enjoyment or exercise of any right or freedom recognized by virtue of the laws of any State Party or by virtue of another convention to which one of the said states is a party;

(c) precluding other rights or guarantees that are inherent in the human personality or derived from representative democracy as a form of government; or

(d) excluding or limiting the effect that the American Declaration of the Rights and Duties of Man and other international acts of the same nature may have.

Article 30   Scope of restrictions

The restrictions that, pursuant to this Convention, may be placed on the enjoyment or exercise of the rights or freedoms recognized herein may not be applied except in accordance with the laws enacted for reasons of general interest and in accordance with the purpose for which such restrictions have been established.

Article 31   Recognition of other rights

Other rights and freedoms recognized in accordance with the procedures established in Articles 76 and 77 may be included in the system of protection of this Convention.

Chapter V Personal Responsibilities

Article 32   Relationship between duties and rights

1. Every person has responsibilities to his family, his community, and mankind.
2. The rights of each person are limited by the rights of others, by the security of all, and by the just demands of the general welfare, in a democratic society.

PART II MEANS OF PROTECTION

Chapter VI Competent Organs

Article 33

The following organs shall have competence with respect to matters relating to the fulfillment of the commitments made by the States Parties to this Convention:

> (a) the Inter-American Commission on Human Rights, referred to as 'The Commission'; and
> (b) the Inter-American Court of Human Rights, referred to as 'The Court'.

Chapter VII Inter-American Commission on Human Rights

Section 1 Organization

Article 34

The Inter-American Commission on Human Rights shall be composed of seven members, who shall be persons of high moral character and recognized competence in the field of human rights.

Article 35

The Commission shall represent all the member countries of the Organization of American States.

Article 36

1. The members of the Commission shall be elected in a personal capacity by the General Assembly of the Organization from a list of candidates proposed by the governments of the member states.

2. Each of those governments may propose up to three candidates, who may be nationals of the states proposing them or of any other member state of the Organization of American States. When a slate of three is proposed, at least one of the candidates shall be a national of a state other than the one proposing the slate.

Article 37

1. The members of the Commission shall be elected for a term of four years and may be reelected only once, but the terms of three of the members chosen in the first election shall expire at the end of two years. Immediately following that election the General Assembly shall determine the names of those three members by lot.

2. No two nationals of the same state may be members of the Commission.

Article 38
Vacancies that may occur on the Commission for reasons other than the normal expiration of a term shall be filled by the Permanent Council of the Organization in accordance with the provisions of the Statute of the Commission.

Article 39
The Commission shall prepare its Statute; which it shall submit to the General Assembly for approval. It shall establish its own Regulations.

Article 40
Secretariat services for the Commission shall be furnished by the appropriate specialized unit of the General Secretariat of the Organization. This unit shall be provided with the resources required to accomplish the tasks assigned to it by the Commission.

Section 2 Functions

Article 41
The main functions of the Commission shall be to promote respect for and defense of human rights. In the exercise of its mandate, it shall have the following functions and powers:

(a) to develop an awareness of human rights among the peoples of America;

(b) to make recommendations to the governments of the member states, when it considers such action advisable, for the adoption of progressive measures in favor of human rights within the framework of their domestic law and constitutional provisions as well as appropriate measures to further the observance of those rights;

(c) to prepare such studies or reports as it considers advisable in the performance of its duties;

(d) to request the governments of the member states to supply it with information on the measures adopted by them in matters of human rights;

(e) to respond, through the General Secretariat of the Organization of American States, to inquiries made by the member states on matters related to human rights and, within the limits of its possibilities, to provide those states with the advisory services they request;

(f) to take action on petitions and other communications pursuant to its authority, under the provisions of Articles 44 through 51 of this Convention; and

(g) to submit an annual report to the General Assembly of the Organization of American States.

Article 42
The States Parties shall transmit to the Commission a copy of each of the reports and studies that they submit annually to the Executive Committees of the Inter-American Economic and Social Council and the Inter-American Council for Education, Science, and Culture, in their respective fields, so that the Commission may watch over the promotion of the rights implicit in the economic, social, educational, scientific, and cultural standards set forth in the Charter of the Organization of American States as amended by the Protocol of Buenos Aires.

Article 43
The States Parties undertake to provide the Commission with such information as it may request of them as to the manner in which their domestic law ensures the effective application of any provisions of this Convention.

Section 3 Competence

Article 44
Any person or group of persons, or any nongovernmental entity legally recognized in one or more member states of the Organization, may lodge petitions with the Commission containing denunciations or complaints of violation of this Convention by a State Party.

Article 45

1. Any State Party may, when it deposits its instrument of ratification of or adherence to this Convention, or at any later time, declare that it recognizes the competence of the Commission to receive and examine communications in which a State Party alleges that another State Party has committed a violation of a human right set forth in this Convention.

2. Communications presented by virtue of this article may be admitted and examined only if they are presented by a State Party that has made a declaration recognizing the aforementioned competence of the Commission. The Commission shall not admit any communication against a State Party that has not made such a declaration.

3. A declaration concerning recognition of competence may be made to be valid for an indefinite time, for a specified period, or for a specific case.

4. Declarations shall be deposited with the General Secretariat of the Organization of American States, which shall transmit copies thereof to the member states of that Organization.

Article 46

1. Admission by the Commission of a petition or communication lodged in accordance with Articles 44 or 45 shall be subject to the following requirements:
    (a) that the remedies under domestic law have been pursued and exhausted in accordance with generally recognized principles of international law;
    (b) that the petition or communication is lodged within a period of six months from the date on which the party alleging violation of his rights was notified of the final judgment;
    (c) that the subject of the petition or communication is not pending before another international procedure for settlement; and
    (d) that, in the case of Article 44, the petition contains the name, nationality, profession, domicile, and signature of the person or persons or of the legal representative of the entity lodging the petition.

2. The provisions of paragraphs 1(a) and 1(b) of this article shall not be applicable when:
    (a) the domestic legislation of the state concerned does not afford due process of law for the protection of the right or rights that have allegedly been violated;
    (b) the party alleging violation of his rights has been denied access to the remedies under domestic law or has been prevented from exhausting them; or
    (c) there has been unwarranted delay in rendering a final judgment under the aforementioned remedies.

Article 47

The Commission shall consider inadmissible any petition or communication submitted under Articles 44 or 45 if:
    (a) any of the requirements indicated in Article 46 has not been met;
    (b) the petition or communication does not state facts that tend to establish a violation of the rights guaranteed by this Convention;
    (c) the statements of the petitioner or of the state indicate that the petition or communication is manifestly groundless or obviously out of order; or
    (d) the petition or communication is substantially the same as one previously studied by the Commission or by another international organization.

Section 4 Procedure

Article 48

1. When the Commission receives a petition or communication alleging violation of any of the rights protected by this Convention, it shall proceed as follows:
    (a) If it considers the petition or communication admissible, it shall request information from the government of the state indicated as being responsible for the alleged violations and

shall furnish that government a transcript of the pertinent portions of the petition or communication. This information shall be submitted within a reasonable period to be determined by the Commission in accordance with the circumstances of each case.

(b) After the information has been received, or after the period established has elapsed and the information has not been received, the Commission shall ascertain whether the grounds for the petition or communication still exist. If they do not, the Commission shall order the record to be closed.

(c) The Commission may also declare the petition or communication inadmissible or out of order on the basis of information or evidence subsequently received.

(d) If the record has not been closed, the Commission shall, with the knowledge of the parties, examine the matter set forth in the petition or communication in order to verify the facts. If necessary and advisable, the Commission shall carry out an investigation, for the effective conduct of which it shall request, and the states concerned shall furnish to it, all necessary facilities.

(e) The Commission may request the states concerned to furnish any pertinent information and, if so requested, shall hear oral statements or receive written statements from the parties concerned.

(f) The Commission shall place itself at the disposal of the parties concerned with a view to reaching a friendly settlement of the matter on the basis of respect for the human rights recognized in this Convention.

2. However, in serious and urgent cases, only the presentation of a petition or communication that fulfills all the formal requirements of admissibility shall be necessary in order for the Commission to conduct an investigation with the prior consent of the state in whose territory a violation has allegedly been committed.

Article 49

If a friendly settlement has been reached in accordance with paragraph 1(f) of Article 48, the Commission shall draw up a report, which shall be transmitted to the petitioner and to the States Parties to this Convention, and shall then be communicated to the Secretary-General of the Organization of American States for publication. This report shall contain a brief statement of the facts and of the solution reached. If any party in the case so requests, the fullest possible information shall be provided to it.

Article 50

1. If a settlement is not reached, the Commission shall, within the time limit established by its Statute, draw up a report setting forth the facts and stating its conclusions. If the report, in whole or in part, does not represent the unanimous agreement of the members of the Commission, any member may attach to it a separate opinion. The written and oral statements made by the parties in accordance with paragraph 1(e) of Article 48 shall also be attached to the report.

2. The report shall be transmitted to the states concerned, which shall not be at liberty to publish it.

3. In transmitting the report, the Committee may make such proposals and recommendations as it sees fit.

Article 51

1. If, within a period of three months from the date of the transmittal of the report of the Commission to the states concerned, the matter has not either been settled or submitted by the Commission or by the state concerned to the Court and its jurisdiction accepted, the Commission may, by the vote of an absolute majority of its members, set forth its opinion and conclusions concerning the question submitted for its consideration.

2. Where appropriate, the Commission shall make pertinent recommendations and shall prescribe a period within which the state is to take the measures that are incumbent upon it to remedy the situation examined.

3. When the prescribed period has expired, the Commission shall decide by the vote of an absolute majority of its members whether the state has taken adequate measures and whether to publish its report.

Chapter VIII Inter-American Court of Human Rights

Section 1 Organization

Article 52

1. The Court shall consist of seven judges, nationals of the member states of the Organization, elected in an individual capacity from among jurists of the highest moral authority and of recognized competence in the field of human rights, who possess the qualifications required for the exercise of the highest judicial functions in conformity with the law of the state of which they are nationals or of the state that proposes them as candidates.

2. No two judges may be nationals of the same state.

Article 53

1. The judges of the Court shall be elected by secret ballot by an absolute majority vote of the States Parties to the Convention in the General Assembly of the Organization, from a panel of candidates proposed by those states.

2. Each of the States Parties may propose up to three candidates, nationals of the state that proposes them or of any other member state of the Organization of American States. When a slate of three is proposed, at least one of the candidates shall be a national of a state other than the one proposing the slate.

Article 54

1. The judges of the Court shall be elected for a term of six years and may be reelected only once. The term of three of the judges chosen in the first election shall expire at the end of three years. Immediately after the election, the names of the three judges shall be determined by lot in the General Assembly.

2. A judge elected to replace a judge whose term has not expired shall complete the term of the latter.

3. The judges shall continue in office until the expiration of their term. However, they shall continue to serve with regard to cases that they have begun to hear and that are still pending, for which purposes they shall not be replaced by the newly elected judges.

Article 55

1. If a judge is a national of any of the States Parties to a case submitted to the Court, he shall retain his right to hear that case.

2. If one of the judges called upon to hear a case should be a national of one the States Parties to the case, any other State Party in the case may appoint a person of its choice to serve on the Court as an *ad hoc* judge.

3. If among the judges called upon to hear a case none is a national of any of the States Parties to the case, each of the latter may appoint an *ad hoc* judge.

4. An *ad hoc* judge shall possess the qualifications indicated in Article 52.

5. If several States Parties to the Convention should have the same interest in a case, they shall be considered as a single party for purposes of the above provisions. In case of doubt, the Court shall decide.

Article 56

Five judges shall constitute a quorum for the transaction of business by the Court.

Article 57

The Commission shall appear in all cases before the Court.

Article 58

1. The Court shall have its seat at the place determined by the States Parties to the Convention in the General Assembly of the Organization; however, it may convene in the territory of any member state of the Organization of American States when a majority of the Court consider it desirable, and with the prior consent of the state concerned.

The seat of the Court may be changed by the States Parties to the Convention in the General Assembly by a two thirds vote.

2. The Court shall appoint its own Secretary.

3. The Secretary shall have his office at the place where the Court has its seat and shall attend the meetings that the Court may hold away from its seat.

Article 59

The Court shall establish its Secretariat, which shall function under the direction of the Secretary of the Court, in accordance with the administrative standards of the General Secretariat of the Organization in all respects not incompatible with the independence of the Court. The staff of the Court's Secretariat shall be appointed by the Secretary-General of the Organization, in consultation with the Secretary of the Court.

Article 60

The Court shall draw up its Statute, which it shall submit to the General Assembly for approval. It shall adopt its own Rules of Procedure.

Section 2 Jurisdiction and Functions

Article 61

1. Only the States Parties and the Commission shall have the right to submit a case to the Court.

2. In order for the Court to hear a case, it is necessary that the procedures set forth in Articles 48 to 50 shall have been completed.

Article 62

1. A State Party may, upon depositing its instrument of ratification or adherence to this Convention, or at any subsequent time, declare that it recognizes as binding, *ipso facto*, and not re-quiring special agreement, the jurisdiction of the Court on all matters relating to the interpretation or application of this Convention.

2. Such declaration maybe made unconditionally, on the condition of reciprocity, for a specified period, or for specific cases. It shall be presented to the Secretary-General of the Organization, who shall transmit copies thereof to the other member states of the Organization and to the Secretary of the Court.

3. The jurisdiction of the Court shall comprise all cases concerning the interpretation and application of the provisions of this Convention that are submitted to it, provided that the States Parties to the case recognize or have recognized such jurisdiction, whether by special declaration pursuant to the preceding paragraphs, or by a special agreement.

Article 63

1. If the Court finds that there has been a violation of a right or freedom protected by this Convention, the Court shall rule that the injured party be ensured the enjoyment of his right or freedom that was violated. It shall also rule, if appropriate, that the consequences of the measure or situation that constituted the breach of such right or freedom be remedied and that fair compensation be paid to the injured party.

2. In cases of extreme gravity and urgency, and when necessary to avoid irreparable damage to persons, the Court shall adopt such provisional measures as it deems pertinent in matters it has under consideration. With respect to a case not yet submitted to the Court, it may act at the request of the Commission.

Article 64

1. The member states of the Organization may consult the Court regarding the interpretation of this Convention or of other treaties concerning the protection of human rights in the American states. Within their spheres of competence, the organs listed in Chapter X of the Charter of the Organization of American States, as amended by the Protocol of Buenos Aires, may in like manner consult the Court.

2. The Court, at the request of a member state of the Organization, may provide that state with opinions regarding the compatibility of any of its domestic laws with the aforesaid international instruments.

Article 65

To each regular session of the General Assembly of the Organization of American States the Court shall submit, for the Assembly's consideration, a report on its work during the previous year. It shall specify, in particular, the cases in which a state has not complied with its judgments, making any pertinent recommendations.

Section 3 Procedure

Article 66

1. Reasons shall be given for the judgment of the Court.

2. If the judgment does not represent in whole or in part the unanimous opinion of the judges, any judge shall be entitled to have his dissenting or separate opinion attached to the judgment.

Article 67

The judgment of the Court shall be final and not subject to appeal. In case of disagreement as to the meaning or scope of the judgment, the Court shall interpret it at the request of any of the parties, provided the request is made within ninety days from the date of notification of the judgment.

Article 68

1. The States Parties to the Convention undertake to comply with the judgment of the Court in any case to which they are parties.

2. That part of a judgment that stipulates compensatory damages may be executed in the country concerned in accordance with domestic procedure governing the execution of judgments against the state.

Article 69

The parties to the case shall be notified of the judgment of the Court and it shall be transmitted to the States Parties to the Convention.

Chapter IX Common Provisions

Article 70

1. The judges of the Court and the members of the Commission shall enjoy, from the moment of their election and throughout their term of office, the immunities extended to diplomatic agents in accordance with international law. During the exercise of their official function they shall, in addition, enjoy the diplomatic privileges necessary for the performance of their duties.

2. At no time shall the judges of the Court or the members of the Commission be held liable for any decisions or opinions issued in the exercise of their functions.

Article 71

The position of judge of the Court or member of the Commission is incompatible with any other activity that might affect the independence or impartiality of such judge or member, as determined in the respective statutes.

Article 72

The judges of the Court and the members of the Commission shall receive emoluments and travel allowances in the form and under the conditions set forth in their statutes, with due regard for the importance and independence of their office. Such emoluments and travel allowances shall be determined in the budget of the Organization of American States, which shall also include the expenses of the Court and its Secretariat. To this end, the Court shall draw up its own budget and submit it for approval to the General Assembly through the General Secretariat. The latter may not introduce any changes in it.

Article 73

The General Assembly may, only at the request of the Commission or the Court, as the case may be, determine sanctions to be applied against members of the Commission or judges of the Court when there are justifiable grounds for such action as set forth in the respective statutes. A vote of a two-thirds majority of the member states of the Organization shall be required for a decision in the case of members of the Commission and, in the case of judges of the Court, a two-thirds majority vote of the States Parties to the Convention shall also be required.

PART III GENERAL AND TRANSITORY PROVISIONS

Chapter X Signature, Ratification, Reservations, Amendments, Protocols, and Denunciation

Article 74

1. This Convention shall be open for signature and ratification by or adherence of any member state of the Organization of American States.

2. Ratification of or adherence to this Convention shall be made by the deposit of an instrument of ratification or adherence with the General Secretariat of the Organization of American States. As soon as eleven states have deposited their instruments of ratification or adherence, the Convention shall enter into force. With respect to any state that ratifies or adheres thereafter, the Convention shall enter into force on the date of the deposit of its instrument of ratification or adherence.

3. The Secretary-General shall inform all member states of the Organization of the entry into force of the Convention.

Article 75

This Convention shall be subject to reservations only in conformity with the provisions of the Vienna Convention on the Law of Treaties signed on May 23, 1969.

Article 76

1. Proposals to amend this Convention may be submitted to the General Assembly for the action it deems appropriate by any State Party directly, and by the Commission or the Court through the Secretary-General.

2. Amendments shall enter into force for the states ratifying them on the date when two thirds of the States Parties to this Convention have deposited their respective instruments of ratification. With respect to the other States Parties, amendments shall enter into force on the dates on which they deposit their respective instruments of ratification.

Article 77

1. In accordance with Article 31, any State Party and the Commission may submit proposed protocols to this Convention for consideration by the States Parties at the General Assembly with a view to gradually including other rights and freedoms within its system of protection.

2. Each Protocol shall determine the manner of its entry into force and shall be applied only among the States Parties to it.

Article 78

1. The States Parties may denounce this Convention at the expiration of a five-year period starting from the date of its entry into force and by means of notice given one year in advance. Notice of the denunciation shall be addressed to the Secretary-General of the Organization, who shall inform the other States Parties.

2. Such a denunciation shall not have the effect of releasing the State Party concerned from the obligations contained in this Convention with respect to any act that may constitute a violation of those obligations and that has been taken by that state prior to the effective date of denunciation.

Chapter XI Transitory Provisions

Section 1 Inter-American Commission on Human Rights

Article 79

Upon the entry into force of this Convention, the Secretary-General shall, in writing, request each member state of the Organization to present, within ninety days, its candidates for membership on the Inter-American Commission on Human Rights. The Secretary-General shall prepare a list in alphabetical order of the candidates presented, and transmit it to the member states of the Organization at least thirty days prior to the next session of the General Assembly.

Article 80

The members of the Commission shall be elected by secret ballot of the General Assembly from the list of candidates referred to in Article 79. The candidates who obtain the largest number of votes and an absolute majority of the votes of the representatives of the member states shall be declared elected. Should it become necessary to have several ballots in order to elect all the members of the Commission, the candidates who receive the smallest number of votes shall be eliminated successively, in the manner determined by the General Assembly.

Section 2   Inter-American Court of Human Rights

Article 81

Upon the entry into force of this Convention, the Secretary-General shall, in writing, request each State Party to present, within ninety days, its candidates for membership on the Inter-American Court of Human Rights. The Secretary-General shall prepare a list in alphabetical order of the candidates presented and transmit it to the States Parties at least thirty days prior to the next session of the General Assembly.

Article 82

The judges of the Court shall be elected from the list of candidates referred to in Article 81, by secret ballot of the States Parties to the Convention in the General Assembly. The candidates who obtain the largest number of votes and an absolute majority of the votes of the representatives of the States Parties shall be declared elected. Should it become necessary to have several ballots in order to elect all the judges of the Court, the candidates who receive the smallest number of votes shall be eliminated successively, in the manner determined by the States Parties.

In witness whereof, the undersigned Plenipotentiaries, whose full powers were found in good and due form, sign this Convention, which shall be called '*Pact of San José, Costa Rica*', (in the city of San José, Costa Rica, this twenty-second day of November, nineteen hundred and sixty-nine).

Additional Protocol to the American Convention on Human Rights in the Area of Economic, Social and Cultural Rights ('Protocol of San Salvador') (1988)*

PREAMBLE

The States Parties to the American Convention on Human Rights 'Pact of San José, Costa Rica,'

Reaffirming their intention to consolidate in this hemisphere, within the framework of democratic institutions, a system of personal liberty and social justice based on respect for the essential rights of man;

* Reproduced by permission of the General Secretariat of the Organization of American States. http://www.oas.org/juridico/english/treaties/a-52.html

Recognizing that the essential rights of man are not derived from one's being a national of a certain State, but are based upon attributes of the human person, for which reason they merit international protection in the form of a convention reinforcing or complementing the protection provided by the domestic law of the American States;

Considering the close relationship that exists between economic, social and cultural rights, and civil and political rights, in that the different categories of rights constitute an indivisible whole based on the recognition of the dignity of the human person, for which reason both require permanent protection and promotion if they are to be fully realized, and the violation of some rights in favor of the realization of others can never be justified;

Recognizing the benefits that stem from the promotion and development of cooperation among States and international relations;

Recalling that, in accordance with the Universal Declaration of Human Rights and the American Convention on Human Rights, the ideal of free human beings enjoying freedom from fear and want can only be achieved if conditions are created whereby everyone may enjoy his economic, social and cultural rights as well as his civil and political rights;

Bearing in mind that, although fundamental economic, social and cultural rights have been recognized in earlier international instruments of both world and regional scope, it is essential that those rights be reaffirmed, developed, perfected and protected in order to consolidate in America, on the basis of full respect for the rights of the individual, the democratic representative form of government as well as the right of its peoples to development, self-determination, and the free disposal of their wealth and natural resources, and

Considering that the American Convention on Human Rights provides that draft additional protocols to that Convention may be submitted for consideration to the States Parties, meeting together on the occasion of the General Assembly of the Organization of American States, for the purpose of gradually incorporating other rights and freedoms into the protective system thereof,

Have agreed upon the following Additional Protocol to the American Convention on Human Rights 'Protocol of San Salvador':

Article 1   Obligation to adopt measures

The States Parties to this Additional Protocol to the American Convention on Human Rights undertake to adopt the necessary measures, both domestically and through international cooperation, especially economic and technical, to the extent allowed by their available resources, and taking into account their degree of development, for the purpose of achieving progressively and pursuant to their internal legislations, the full observance of the rights recognized in this Protocol.

Article 2   Obligation to enact domestic legislation

If the exercise of the rights set forth in this Protocol is not already guaranteed by legislative or other provisions, the States Parties undertake to adopt, in accordance with their constitutional processes and the provisions of this Protocol, such legislative or other measures as may be necessary for making those rights a reality.

Article 3   Obligation of nondiscrimination

The States Parties to this Protocol undertake to guarantee the exercise of the rights set forth herein without discrimination of any kind for reasons related to race, color, sex, language, religion, political or other opinions, national or social origin, economic status, birth or any other social condition.

Article 4   Inadmissibility of restrictions

A right which is recognized or in effect in a State by virtue of its internal legislation or international conventions may not be restricted or curtailed on the pretext that this Protocol does not recognize the right or recognizes it to a lesser degree.

Article 5   Scope of restrictions and limitations

The States Parties may establish restrictions and limitations on the enjoyment and exercise of the rights established herein by means of laws promulgated for the purpose of preserving the general welfare in a democratic society only to the extent that they are not incompatible with the purpose and reason underlying those rights.

Article 6   Right to work

1. Everyone has the right to work, which includes the opportunity to secure the means for living a dignified and decent existence by performing a freely elected or accepted lawful activity.

2. The States Parties undertake to adopt measures that will make the right to work fully effective, especially with regard to the achievement of full employment, vocational guidance, and the development of technical and vocational training projects, in particular those directed to the disabled. The States Parties also undertake to implement and strengthen programs that help to ensure suitable family care, so that women may enjoy a real opportunity to exercise the right to work.

Article 7   Just, equitable, and satisfactory conditions of work

The States Parties to this Protocol recognize that the right to work to which the foregoing article refers presupposes that everyone shall enjoy that right under just, equitable, and satisfactory conditions, which the States Parties undertake to guarantee in their internal legislation, particularly with respect to:

(a) Remuneration which guarantees, as a minimum, to all workers dignified and decent living conditions for them and their families and fair and equal wages for equal work, without distinction;

(b) The right of every worker to follow his vocation and to devote himself to the activity that best fulfills his expectations and to change employment in accordance with the pertinent national regulations;

(c) The right of every worker to promotion or upward mobility in his employment, for which purpose account shall be taken of his qualifications, competence, integrity and seniority;

(d) Stability of employment, subject to the nature of each industry and occupation and the causes for just separation. In cases of unjustified dismissal, the worker shall have the right to indemnity or to reinstatement on the job or any other benefits provided by domestic legislation;

(e) Safety and hygiene at work;

(f) The prohibition of night work or unhealthy or dangerous working conditions and, in general, of all work which jeopardizes health, safety, or morals, for persons under 18 years of age. As regards minors under the age of 16, the work day shall be subordinated to the provisions regarding compulsory education and in no case shall work constitute an impediment to school attendance or a limitation on benefiting from education received;

(g) A reasonable limitation of working hours, both daily and weekly. The days shall be shorter in the case of dangerous or unhealthy work or of night work;

(h) Rest, leisure and paid vacations as well as remuneration for national holidays.

Article 8   Trade union rights

1. The States Parties shall ensure:

(a) The right of workers to organize trade unions and to join the union of their choice for the purpose of protecting and promoting their interests. As an extension of that right, the States Parties shall permit trade unions to establish national federations or confederations, or to affiliate with those that already exist, as well as to form international trade union organizations and to affiliate with that of their choice. The States Parties shall also permit trade unions, federations and confederations to function freely;

(b) The right to strike.

2. The exercise of the rights set forth above may be subject only to restrictions established by law, provided that such restrictions are characteristic of a democratic society and necessary for

safeguarding public order or for protecting public health or morals or the rights and freedoms of others. Members of the armed forces and the police and of other essential public services shall be subject to limitations and restrictions established by law.

3. No one may be compelled to belong to a trade union.

Article 9   Right to social security

1. Everyone shall have the right to social security protecting him from the consequences of old age and of disability which prevents him, physically or mentally, from securing the means for a dignified and decent existence. In the event of the death of a beneficiary, social security benefits shall be applied to his dependents.

2. In the case of persons who are employed, the right to social security shall cover at least medical care and an allowance or retirement benefit in the case of work accidents or occupational disease and, in the case of women, paid maternity leave before and after childbirth.

Article 10   Right to health

1. Everyone shall have the right to health, understood to mean the enjoyment of the highest level of physical, mental and social well-being.

2. In order to ensure the exercise of the right to health, the States Parties agree to recognize health as a public good and, particularly, to adopt the following measures to ensure that right:

    (a) Primary health care, that is, essential health care made available to all individuals and families in the community;

    (b) Extension of the benefits of health services to all individuals subject to the State's jurisdiction;

    (c) Universal immunization against the principal infectious diseases;

    (d) Prevention and treatment of endemic, occupational and other diseases;

    (e) Education of the population on the prevention and treatment of health problems, and

    (f) Satisfaction of the health needs of the highest risk groups and of those whose poverty makes them the most vulnerable.

Article 11   Right to a healthy environment

1. Everyone shall have the right to live in a healthy environment and to have access to basic public services.

2. The States Parties shall promote the protection, preservation, and improvement of the environment.

Article 12   Right to food

1. Everyone has the right to adequate nutrition which guarantees the possibility of enjoying the highest level of physical, emotional and intellectual development.

2. In order to promote the exercise of this right and eradicate malnutrition, the States Parties undertake to improve methods of production, supply and distribution of food, and to this end, agree to promote greater international cooperation in support of the relevant national policies.

Article 13   Right to education

1. Everyone has the right to education.

2. The States Parties to this Protocol agree that education should be directed towards the full development of the human personality and human dignity and should strengthen respect for human rights, ideological pluralism, fundamental freedoms, justice and peace. They further agree that education ought to enable everyone to participate effectively in a democratic and pluralistic society and achieve a decent existence and should foster understanding, tolerance and friendship among all nations and all racial, ethnic or religious groups and promote activities for the maintenance of peace.

3. The States Parties to this Protocol recognize that in order to achieve the full exercise of the right to education:

(a) Primary education should be compulsory and accessible to all without cost;

(b) Secondary education in its different forms, including technical and vocational secondary education, should be made generally available and accessible to all by every appropriate means, and in particular, by the progressive introduction of free education;

(c) Higher education should be made equally accessible to all, on the basis of individual capacity, by every appropriate means, and in particular, by the progressive introduction of free education;

(d) Basic education should be encouraged or intensified as far as possible for those persons who have not received or completed the whole cycle of primary instruction;

(e) Programs of special education should be established for the handicapped, so as to provide special instruction and training to persons with physical disabilities or mental deficiencies.

4. In conformity with the domestic legislation of the States Parties, parents should have the right to select the type of education to be given to their children, provided that it conforms to the principles set forth above.

5. Nothing in this Protocol shall be interpreted as a restriction of the freedom of individuals and entities to establish and direct educational institutions in accordance with the domestic legislation of the States Parties.

Article 14   Right to the benefits of culture

1. The States Parties to this Protocol recognize the right of everyone:

(a) To take part in the cultural and artistic life of the community;

(b) To enjoy the benefits of scientific and technological progress;

(c) To benefit from the protection of moral and material interests deriving from any scientific, literary or artistic production of which he is the author.

2. The steps to be taken by the States Parties to this Protocol to ensure the full exercise of this right shall include those necessary for the conservation, development and dissemination of science, culture and art.

3. The States Parties to this Protocol undertake to respect the freedom indispensable for scientific research and creative activity.

4. The States Parties to this Protocol recognize the benefits to be derived from the encouragement and development of international cooperation and relations in the fields of science, arts and culture, and accordingly agree to foster greater international cooperation in these fields.

Article 15   Right to the formation and the protection of families

1. The family is the natural and fundamental element of society and ought to be protected by the State, which should see to the improvement of its spiritual and material conditions.

2. Everyone has the right to form a family, which shall be exercised in accordance with the provisions of the pertinent domestic legislation.

3. The States Parties hereby undertake to accord adequate protection to the family unit and in particular:

(a) To provide special care and assistance to mothers during a reasonable period before and after childbirth;

(b) To guarantee adequate nutrition for children at the nursing stage and during school attendance years;

(c) To adopt special measures for the protection of adolescents in order to ensure the full development of their physical, intellectual and moral capacities;

(d) To undertake special programs of family training so as to help create a stable and positive environment in which children will receive and develop the values of understanding, solidarity, respect and responsibility.

Article 16   Rights of children

Every child, whatever his parentage, has the right to the protection that his status as a minor requires from his family, society and the State. Every child has the right to grow under the protection and responsibility of his parents; save in exceptional, judicially recognized circumstances, a child of young age ought not to be separated from his mother. Every child has the right to free and compulsory education, at least in the elementary phase, and to continue his training at higher levels of the educational system.

Article 17   Protection of the elderly

Everyone has the right to special protection in old age. With this in view the States Parties agree to take progressively the necessary steps to make this right a reality and, particularly, to:

(a) Provide suitable facilities, as well as food and specialized medical care, for elderly individuals who lack them and are unable to provide them for themselves;

(b) Undertake work programs specifically designed to give the elderly the opportunity to engage in a productive activity suited to their abilities and consistent with their vocations or desires;

(c) Foster the establishment of social organizations aimed at improving the quality of life for the elderly.

Article 18   Protection of the handicapped

Everyone affected by a diminution of his physical or mental capacities is entitled to receive special attention designed to help him achieve the greatest possible development of his personality. The States Parties agree to adopt such measures as may be necessary for this purpose and, especially, to:

(a) Undertake programs specifically aimed at providing the handicapped with the resources and environment needed for attaining this goal, including work programs consistent with their possibilities and freely accepted by them or their legal representatives, as the case may be;

(b) Provide special training to the families of the handicapped in order to help them solve the problems of coexistence and convert them into active agents in the physical, mental and emotional development of the latter;

(c) Include the consideration of solutions to specific requirements arising from needs of this group as a priority component of their urban development plans;

(d) Encourage the establishment of social groups in which the handicapped can be helped to enjoy a fuller life.

Article 19   Means of protection

1. Pursuant to the provisions of this article and the corresponding rules to be formulated for this purpose by the General Assembly of the Organization of American States, the States Parties to this Protocol undertake to submit periodic reports on the progressive measures they have taken to ensure due respect for the rights set forth in this Protocol.

2. All reports shall be submitted to the Secretary General of the OAS, who shall transmit them to the Inter-American Economic and Social Council and the Inter-American Council for Education, Science and Culture so that they may examine them in accordance with the provisions of this article. The Secretary General shall send a copy of such reports to the Inter-American Commission on Human Rights.

3. The Secretary General of the Organization of American States shall also transmit to the specialized organizations of the inter-American system of which the States Parties to the present Protocol are members, copies or pertinent portions of the reports submitted, insofar as they relate to matters within the purview of those organizations, as established by their constituent instruments.

4. The specialized organizations of the inter-American system may submit reports to the Inter-American Economic and Social Council and the Inter-American Council for Education, Science and Culture relative to compliance with the provisions of the present Protocol in their fields of activity.

5. The annual reports submitted to the General Assembly by the Inter-American Economic and Social Council and the Inter-American Council for Education, Science and Culture shall contain a summary of the information received from the States Parties to the present Protocol and the specialized

organizations concerning the progressive measures adopted in order to ensure respect for the rights acknowledged in the Protocol itself and the general recommendations they consider to be appropriate in this respect.

6. Any instance in which the rights established in paragraph a) of Article 8 and in Article 13 are violated by action directly attributable to a State Party to this Protocol may give rise, through participation of the Inter-American Commission on Human Rights and, when applicable, of the Inter-American Court of Human Rights, to application of the system of individual petitions governed by Article 44 through 51 and 61 through 69 of the American Convention on Human Rights.

7. Without prejudice to the provisions of the preceding paragraph, the Inter-American Commission on Human Rights may formulate such observations and recommendations as it deems pertinent concerning the status of the economic, social and cultural rights established in the present Protocol in all or some of the States Parties, which it may include in its Annual Report to the General Assembly or in a special report, whichever it considers more appropriate.

8. The Councils and the Inter-American Commission on Human Rights, in discharging the functions conferred upon them in this article, shall take into account the progressive nature of the observance of the rights subject to protection by this Protocol.

Article 20   Reservations
The States Parties may, at the time of approval, signature, ratification or accession, make reservations to one or more specific provisions of this Protocol, provided that such reservations are not incompatible with the object and purpose of the Protocol.

Article 21   Signature, ratification or accession. Entry into effect
1. This Protocol shall remain open to signature and ratification or accession by any State Party to the American Convention on Human Rights.

2. Ratification of or accession to this Protocol shall be effected by depositing an instrument of ratification or accession with the General Secretariat of the Organization of American States.

3. The Protocol shall enter into effect when eleven States have deposited their respective instruments of ratification or accession.

4. The Secretary General shall notify all the member states of the Organization of American States of the entry of the Protocol into effect.

Article 22   Inclusion of other rights and expansion of those recognized
1. Any State Party and the Inter-American Commission on Human Rights may submit for the consideration of the States Parties meeting on the occasion of the General Assembly proposed amendments to include the recognition of other rights or freedoms or to extend or expand rights or freedoms recognized in this Protocol.

2. Such amendments shall enter into effect for the States that ratify them on the date of deposit of the instrument of ratification corresponding to the number representing two thirds of the States Parties to this Protocol. For all other States Parties they shall enter into effect on the date on which they deposit their respective instrument of ratification.

Protocol to the American Convention on Human Rights to Abolish the Death Penalty (1990)*

PREAMBLE

The States Parties to this Protocol,
   Considering:
   That Article 4 of the American Convention on Human Rights recognizes the right to life and restricts the application of the death penalty;

---

* Reproduced by permission of the General Secretariat of the Organization of American States. http://www.oas.org/juridico/english/treaties/a-53.html

That everyone has the inalienable right to respect for his life, a right that cannot be suspended for any reason;

That the tendency among the American States is to be in favor of abolition of the death penalty;

That application of the death penalty has irrevocable consequences, forecloses the correction of judicial error, and precludes any possibility of changing or rehabilitating those convicted;

That the abolition of the death penalty helps to ensure more effective protection of the right to life;

That an international agreement must be arrived at that will entail a progressive development of the American Convention on Human Rights; and

That States Parties to the American Convention on Human Rights have expressed their intention to adopt an international agreement with a view to consolidating the practice of not applying the death penalty in the Americas,

Have agreed to sign the following Protocol to the American Convention on Human Rights to Abolish the Death Penalty.

Article 1

The States Parties to this Protocol shall not apply the death penalty in their territory to any person subject to their jurisdiction.

Article 2

1. No reservations may be made to this Protocol. However, at the time of ratification or accession, the States Parties to this instrument may declare that they reserve the right to apply the death penalty in wartime in accordance with international law, for extremely serious crimes of a military nature.

2. The State Party making this reservation shall, upon ratification or accession, inform the Secretary General of the Organization of American States of the pertinent provisions of its national legislation applicable in wartime, as referred to in the preceding paragraph.

3. Said State Party shall notify the Secretary General of the Organization of American States of the beginning or end of any state of war in effect in its territory.

Article 3

1. This Protocol shall be open for signature and ratification or accession by any State Party to the American Convention on Human Rights.

2. Ratification of this Protocol or accession thereto shall be made through the deposit of an instrument of ratification or accession with the General Secretariat of the Organization of American States.

Article 4

This Protocol shall enter into force among the States that ratify or accede to it when they deposit their respective instruments of ratification or accession with the General Secretariat of the Organization of American States.

Cartagena Declaration on Refugees (1984)*

I

Recalling the conclusions and recommendations adopted by the Colloquium held in Mexico in 1981 on Asylum and International Protection of Refugees in Latin America, which established important landmarks for the analysis and consideration of this matter;

Recognizing that the refugee situation in Central America has evolved in recent years to the point at which it deserves special attention;

Appreciating the generous efforts which have been made by countries receiving Central American refugees, notwithstanding the great difficulties they have had to face, particularly in the current economic crisis;

Emphasizing the admirable humanitarian and non-political task which UNHCR has been called upon to carry out in the Central American countries, Mexico and Panama in accordance with the provisions of the 1951 United Nations Convention and the 1967 Protocol, as well as those of resolution 428 (V) of the United Nations General Assembly, by which the mandate of the United Nations High Commissioner for Refugees is applicable to all States whether or not parties to the said Convention and/or Protocol;

Bearing in mind also the function performed by the Inter-American Commission on Human Rights with regard to the protection of the rights of refugees in the continent;

Strongly supporting the efforts of the Contadora Group to find an effective and lasting solution to the problem of Central American refugees, which constitute a significant step in the negotiation of effective agreements in favour of peace in the region;

Expressing its conviction that many of the legal and humanitarian problems relating to refugees which have arisen in the Central American region, Mexico and Panama can only be tackled in the light of the necessary co-ordination and harmonization of universal and regional systems and national efforts;

II

Having acknowledged with appreciation the commitments with regard to refugees included in the Contadora Act on Peace and Co-operation in Central America, the bases of which the Colloquium fully shares and which are reproduced below:

(a) 'To carry out, if they have not yet done so, the constitutional procedures for accession to the 1951 Convention and the 1967 Protocol relating to the Status of Refugees.'

(b) 'To adopt the terminology established in the Convention and Protocol referred to in the foregoing paragraph with a view to distinguishing refugees from other categories of migrants.'

(c) 'To establish the internal machinery necessary for the implementation, upon accession, of the provisions of the Convention and Protocol referred to above.'

(d) 'To ensure the establishment of machinery for consultation between the Central American countries and representatives of the Government offices responsible for dealing with the problem of refugees in each State.'

(e) 'To support the work performed by the United Nations High Commissioner for Refugees (UNHCR) in Central America and to establish direct co-ordination machinery to facilitate the fulfillment of his mandate.'

(f) 'To ensure that any repatriation of refugees is voluntary, and is declared to be so on an individual basis, and is carried out with the co-operation of UNHCR.'

(g) 'To ensure the establishment of tripartite commissions, composed of representatives of the State of origin, of the receiving State and of UNHCR with a view to facilitating the repatriation of refugees.'

(h) 'To reinforce programmes for protection of and assistance to refugees, particularly in the areas of health, education, labour and safety.'

(i) 'To ensure that programmes and projects are set up with a view to ensuring the self-sufficiency of refugees.'

(j) 'To train the officials responsible in each State for protection of and assistance to refugees, with the co-operation of UNHCR and other international agencies.'

(k) 'To request immediate assistance from the international community for Central American refugees, to be provided either directly, through bilateral or multilateral agreements, or through UNHCR and other organizations and agencies.'

(l) 'To identify, with the co-operation of UNHCR, other countries which might receive Central American refugees. In no case shall a refugee be transferred to a third country against his will.'

(m) 'To ensure that the Governments of the area make the necessary efforts to eradicate the causes of the refugee problem.'

(n) 'To ensure that, once agreement has been reached on the bases for voluntary and individual repatriation, with full guarantees for the refugees, the receiving countries permit official delegations of the country of origin, accompanied by representatives of UNHCR and the receiving country, to visit the refugee camps.'

(o) 'To ensure that the receiving countries facilitate, in co-ordination with UNHCR, the departure procedure for refugees in instances of voluntary and individual repatriation.'

(p) 'To institute appropriate measures in the receiving countries to prevent the participation of refugees in activities directed against the country of origin, while at all times respecting the human rights of the refugees.'

III

The Colloquium adopted the following conclusions:

1. To promote within the countries of the region the adoption of national laws and regulations facilitating the application of the Convention and the Protocol and, if necessary, establishing internal procedures and mechanisms for the protection of refugees. In addition, to ensure that the national laws and regulations adopted reflect the principles and criteria of the Convention and the Protocol, thus fostering the necessary process of systematic harmonization of national legislation on refugees.

2. To ensure that ratification of or accession to the 1951 Convention and the 1967 Protocol by States which have not yet taken these steps is unaccompanied by reservations limiting the scope of those instruments, and to invite countries having formulated such reservations to consider withdrawing them as soon as possible.

3. To reiterate that, in view of the experience gained from the massive flows of refugees in the Central American area, it is necessary to consider enlarging the concept of a refugee, bearing in mind, as far as appropriate and in the light of the situation prevailing in the region, the precedent of the OAU Convention (article 1, paragraph 2) and the doctrine employed in the reports of the Inter-American Commission on Human Rights. Hence the definition or concept of a refugee to be recommended for use in the region is one which, in addition to containing the elements of the 1951 Convention and the 1967 Protocol, includes among refugees persons who have fled their country because their lives, safety or freedom have been threatened by generalized violence, foreign aggression, internal conflicts, massive violation of human rights or other circumstances which have seriously disturbed public order.

4. To confirm the peaceful, non-political and exclusively humanitarian nature of grant of asylum or recognition of the status of refugee and to underline the importance of the internationally accepted principle that nothing in either shall be interpreted as an unfriendly act towards the country of origin of refugees.

5. To reiterate the importance and meaning of the principle of non-refoulement (including the prohibition of rejection at the frontier) as a corner-stone of the international protection of refugees. This principle is imperative in regard to refugees and in the present state of international law should be acknowledged and observed as a rule of jus cogens.

6. To reiterate to countries of asylum that refugee camps and settlements located in frontier areas should be set up inland at a reasonable distance from the frontier with a view to improving the protection afforded to refugees, safeguarding their human rights and implementing projects aimed at their self-sufficiency and integration into the host society.

7. To express its concern at the problem raised by military attacks on refugee camps and settlements which have occurred in different parts of the world and to propose to the Governments of the Central American countries, Mexico and Panama that they lend their support to the measures on this matter which have been proposed by the High Commissioner to the UNHCR Executive Committee.

8. To ensure that the countries of the region establish a minimum standard of treatment for refugees, on the basis of the provisions of the 1951 Convention and 1967 Protocol and of the American Convention on Human Rights, taking into consideration the conclusions of the UNHCR Executive Committee, particularly No. 22 on the Protection of Asylum Seekers in Situations of Large-Scale Influx.

9. To express its concern at the situation of displaced persons within their own countries. In this connection, the Colloquium calls on national authorities and the competent international organizations to offer protection and assistance to those persons and to help relieve the hardship which many of them face.

10. To call on States parties to the 1969 American Convention on Human Rights to apply this instrument in dealing with asilados and refugees who are in their territories.

11. To make a study, in countries in the area which have a large number of refugees, of the possibilities of integrating them into the productive life of the country by allocating to the creation or generation of employment the resources made available by the international community through UNHCR, thus making it possible for refugees to enjoy their economic, social and cultural rights.

12. To reiterate the voluntary and individual character of repatriation of refugees and the need for it to be carried out under conditions of absolute safety, preferably to the place of residence of the refugee in his country of origin.

13. To acknowledge that reunification of families constitutes a fundamental principle in regard to refugees and one which should be the basis for the regime of humanitarian treatment in the country of asylum, as well as for facilities granted in cases of voluntary repatriation.

14. To urge non-governmental, international and national organizations to continue their worthy task, co-ordinating their activities with UNHCR and the national authorities of the country of asylum, in accordance with the guidelines laid down by the authorities in question.

15. To promote greater use of the competent organizations of the inter-American system, in particular the Inter-American Commission on Human Rights, with a view to enhancing the international protection of asilados and refugees. Accordingly, for the performance of this task, the Colloquium considers that the close co-ordination and co-operation existing between the Commission and UNHCR should be strengthened.

16. To acknowledge the importance of the OAS/UNHCR Programme of Co-operation and the activities so far carried out and to propose that the next stage should focus on the problem raised by massive refugee flows in Central America, Mexico and Panama.

17. To ensure that in the countries of Central America and the Contadora Group the international norms and national legislation relating to the protection of refugees, and of human rights in general, are disseminated at all possible levels. In particular, the Colloquium believes it especially important that such dissemination should be undertaken with the valuable co-operation of the appropriate universities and centres of higher education.

IV

The Cartagena Colloquium therefore
Recommends:

- That the commitments with regard to refugees included in the Contadora Act should constitute norms for the 10 States participating in the Colloquium and be unfailingly and scrupulously observed in determining the conduct to be adopted in regard to refugees in the Central American area.
- That the conclusions reached by the Colloquium (III) should receive adequate attention in the search for solutions to the grave problems raised by the present massive flows of refugees in Central America, Mexico and Panama.
- That a volume should be published containing the working document and the proposals and reports, as well as the conclusions and recommendations of the Colloquium and other pertinent documents, and that the Colombian Government, UNHCR and the competent bodies of OAS should be requested to take the necessary steps to secure the widest possible circulation of the volume in question.
- That the present document should be proclaimed the 'Cartagena Declaration on Refugees'.
- That the United Nations High Commissioner for Refugees should be requested to transmit the contents of the present declaration officially to the heads of State of the Central American countries, of Belize and of the countries forming the Contadora Group.

Finally, the Colloquium expressed its deep appreciation to the Colombian authorities, and in particular to the President of the Republic, Mr. Belisario Betancur, the Minister for Foreign Affairs, Mr. Augusto Ramírez Ocampo, and the United Nations High Commissioner for Refugees, Mr. Poul Hartling, who honoured the Colloquium with their presence, as well as to the University of Cartagena de Indias and the Regional Centre for Third World Studies for their initiative and for the realization of this important event. The Colloquium expressed its special recognition of the support and hospitality offered by the authorities of the Department of Bolivar and the City of Cartagena. It also thanked the people of Cartagena, rightly known as the 'Heroic City', for their warm welcome.

   In conclusion, the Colloquium recorded its acknowledgement of the generous tradition of asylum and refuge practised by the Colombian people and authorities.

Cartagena de Indias, 22 November 1984

Inter-American Convention to Prevent and Punish Torture (1985)*

The American States signatory to the present Convention,

   Aware of the provision of the American Convention on Human Rights that no one shall be subjected to torture or to cruel, inhuman, or degrading punishment or treatment;

   Reaffirming that all acts of torture or any other cruel, inhuman, or degrading treatment or punishment constitute an offense against human dignity and a denial of the principles set forth in the Charter of the Organization of American States and in the Charter of the United Nations and are violations of the fundamental human rights and freedoms proclaimed in the American Declaration of the Rights and Duties of Man and the Universal Declaration of Human Rights;

   Noting that, in order for the pertinent rules contained in the aforementioned global and regional instruments to take effect, it is necessary to draft an Inter-American Convention that prevents and punishes torture;

---

* Reproduced by permission of the General Secretariat of the Organization of American States. http://www.oas.org/juridico/english/treaties/a-51.html

Reaffirming their purpose of consolidating in this hemisphere the conditions that make for recognition of and respect for the inherent dignity of man, and ensure the full exercise of his fundamental rights and freedoms,

Have agreed upon the following:

Article 1

The State Parties undertake to prevent and punish torture in accordance with the terms of this Convention.

Article 2

For the purposes of this Convention, torture shall be understood to be any act intentionally performed whereby physical or mental pain or suffering is inflicted on a person for purposes of criminal investigation, as a means of intimidation, as personal punishment, as a preventive measure, as a penalty, or for any other purpose. Torture shall also be understood to be the use of methods upon a person intended to obliterate the personality of the victim or to diminish his physical or mental capacities, even if they do not cause physical pain or mental anguish.

The concept of torture shall not include physical or mental pain or suffering that is inherent in or solely the consequence of lawful measures, provided that they do not include the performance of the acts or use of the methods referred to in this article.

Article 3

The following shall be held guilty of the crime of torture:
- (a) A public servant or employee who acting in that capacity orders, instigates or induces the use of torture, or who directly commits it or who, being able to prevent it, fails to do so.
- (b) A person who at the instigation of a public servant or employee mentioned in subparagraph (a) orders, instigates or induces the use of torture, directly commits it or is an accomplice thereto.

Article 4

The fact of having acted under orders of a superior shall not provide exemption from the corresponding criminal liability.

Article 5

The existence of circumstances such as a state of war, threat of war, state of siege or of emergency, domestic disturbance or strife, suspension of constitutional guarantees, domestic political instability, or other public emergencies or disasters shall not be invoked or admitted as justification for the crime of torture.

Neither the dangerous character of the detainee or prisoner, nor the lack of security of the prison establishment or penitentiary shall justify torture.

Article 6

In accordance with the terms of Article 1, the States Parties shall take effective measures to prevent and punish torture within their jurisdiction.

The States Parties shall ensure that all acts of torture and attempts to commit torture are offenses under their criminal law and shall make such acts punishable by severe penalties that take into account their serious nature.

The States Parties likewise shall take effective measures to prevent and punish other cruel, inhuman, or degrading treatment or punishment within their jurisdiction.

Article 7

The States Parties shall take measures so that, in the training of police officers and other public officials responsible for the custody of persons temporarily or definitively deprived of their freedom, special emphasis shall be put on the prohibition of the use of torture in interrogation, detention, or arrest.

The States Parties likewise shall take similar measures to prevent other cruel, inhuman, or degrading treatment or punishment.

Article 8

The States Parties shall guarantee that any person making an accusation of having been subjected to torture within their jurisdiction shall have the right to an impartial examination of his case.

Likewise, if there is an accusation or well-grounded reason to believe that an act of torture has been committed within their jurisdiction, the States Parties shall guarantee that their respective authorities will proceed properly and immediately to conduct an investigation into the case and to initiate, whenever appropriate, the corresponding criminal process.

After all the domestic legal procedures of the respective State and the corresponding appeals have been exhausted, the case may be submitted to the international fora whose competence has been recognized by that State.

Article 9

The States Parties undertake to incorporate into their national laws regulations guaranteeing suitable compensation for victims of torture.

None of the provisions of this article shall affect the right to receive compensation that the victim or other persons may have by virtue of existing national legislation.

Article 10

No statement that is verified as having been obtained through torture shall be admissible as evidence in a legal proceeding, except in a legal action taken against a person or persons accused of having elicited it through acts of torture, and only as evidence that the accused obtained such statement by such means.

Article 11

The States Parties shall take the necessary steps to extradite anyone accused of having committed the crime of torture or sentenced for commission of that crime, in accordance with their respective national laws on extradition and their international commitments on this matter.

Article 12

Every State Party shall take the necessary measures to establish its jurisdiction over the crime described in this Convention in the following cases:

    (a) When torture has been committed within its jurisdiction;

    (b) When the alleged criminal is a national of that State; or

    (c) When the victim is a national of that State and it so deems appropriate.

Every State Party shall also take the necessary measures to establish its jurisdiction over the crime described in this Convention when the alleged criminal is within the area under its jurisdiction and it is not appropriate to extradite him in accordance with Article 11.

This Convention does not exclude criminal jurisdiction exercised in accordance with domestic law.

Article 13

The crime referred to in Article 2 shall be deemed to be included among the extraditable crimes in every extradition treaty entered into between States Parties. The States Parties undertake to include the crime of torture as an extraditable offence in every extradition treaty to be concluded between them.

Every State Party that makes extradition conditional on the existence of a treaty may, if it receives a request for extradition from another State Party with which it has no extradition treaty, consider this Convention as the legal basis for extradition in respect of the crime of torture. Extradition shall be subject to the other conditions that may be required by the law of the requested State.

States Parties which do not make extradition conditional on the existence of a treaty shall recognize such crimes as extraditable offences between themselves, subject to the conditions required by the law of the requested State.

Extradition shall not be granted nor shall the person sought be returned when there are grounds to believe that his life is in danger, that he will be subjected to torture or to cruel, inhuman or degrading treatment, or that he will be tried by special or ad hoc courts in the requesting State.

Article 14

When a State Party does not grant the extradition, the case shall be submitted to its competent authorities as if the crime had been committed within its jurisdiction, for the purposes of investigation, and when appropriate, for criminal action, in accordance with its national law. Any decision adopted by these authorities shall be communicated to the State that has requested the extradition.

Article 15

No provision of this Convention may be interpreted as limiting the right of asylum, when appropriate, nor as altering the obligations of the States Parties in the matter of extradition.

Article 16

This Convention shall not limit the provisions of the American Convention on Human Rights, other conventions on the subject, or the Statutes of the Inter-American Commission on Human Rights, with respect to the crime of torture.

Article 17

The States Parties undertake to inform the Inter-American Commission on Human Rights of any legislative, judicial, administrative, or other measures they adopt in application of this Convention.

In keeping with its duties and responsibilities, the Inter-American Commission on Human Rights will endeavor in its annual report to analyze the existing situation in the member states of the Organization of American States in regard to the prevention and elimination of torture.

Article 18

This Convention is open to signature by the member states of the Organization of American States.

Article 19

This Convention is subject to ratification. The instruments of ratification shall be deposited with the General Secretariat of the Organization of American States.

Article 20

This Convention is open to accession by any other American state. The instruments of accession shall be deposited with the General Secretariat of the Organization of American States.

Article 21

The States Parties may, at the time of approval, signature, ratification, or accession, make reservations to this Convention, provided that such reservations are not incompatible with the object and purpose of the Convention and concern one or more specific provisions.

Article 22

This Convention shall enter into force on the thirtieth day following the date on which the second instrument of ratification is deposited. For each State ratifying or acceding to the Convention after the second instrument of ratification has been deposited, the Convention shall enter into force on the thirtieth day following the date on which that State deposits its instrument of ratification or accession.

Article 23

This Convention shall remain in force indefinitely, but may be denounced by any State Party. The instrument of denunciation shall be deposited with the General Secretariat of the Organization of American States. After one year from the date of deposit of the instrument of denunciation, this

Convention shall cease to be in effect for the denouncing State but shall remain in force for the remaining States Parties.

Article 24

The original instrument of this Convention, the English, French, Portuguese, and Spanish texts of which are equally authentic, shall be deposited with the General Secretariat of the Organization of American States, which shall send a certified copy to the Secretariat of the United Nations for registration and publication, in accordance with the provisions of Article 102 of the United Nations Charter. The General Secretariat of the Organization of American States shall notify the member states of the Organization and the States that have acceded to the Convention of signatures and of deposits of instruments of ratification, accession, and denunciation, as well as reservations, if any.

Inter-American Convention on the Forced Disappearance of Persons (1994)*

The member States of the Organization of American States,

Disturbed by the persistence of the forced disappearance of persons;

Reaffirming that the true meaning of American solidarity and good neighborliness can be none other than that of consolidating in this Hemisphere, in the framework of democratic institutions, a system of individual freedom and social justice based on respect for essential human rights;

Considering that the forced disappearance of persons is an affront to the conscience of the Hemisphere and a grave and abominable offense against the inherent dignity of the human being, and one that contradicts the principles and purposes enshrined in the Charter of the Organization of American States;

Considering that the forced disappearance of persons violates numerous non-derogable and essential human rights enshrined in the American Convention on Human Rights, in the American Declaration of the Rights and Duties of Man, and in the Universal Declaration of Human Rights;

Recalling that the international protection of human rights is in the form of a convention reinforcing or complementing the protection provided by domestic law and is based upon the attributes of the human personality;

Reaffirming that the systematic practice of the forced disappearance of persons constitutes a crime against humanity;

Hoping that this Convention may help to prevent, punish, and eliminate the forced disappearance of persons in the Hemisphere and make a decisive contribution to the protection of human rights and the rule of law,

Resolve to adopt the following Inter-American Convention on the Forced Disappearance of Persons:

Article I

The States Parties to this Convention undertake:

    (a) Not to practice, permit, or tolerate the forced disappearance of persons, even in states of emergency or suspension of individual guarantees;

    (b) To punish within their jurisdictions those persons who commit or attempt to commit the crime of forced disappearance of persons and their accomplices and accessories;

    (c) To cooperate with one another in helping to prevent, punish and eliminate the forced disappearance of persons;

    (d) To take legislative, administrative, judicial, and any other measures necessary to comply with the commitments undertaken in this Convention.

Article II

For the purposes of this Convention, forced disappearance is considered to be the act of depriving a person or persons of his or their freedom, in whatever way, perpetrated by agents of the state or by persons or groups of persons acting with the authorization, support, or acquiescence of the state, followed by an absence of information or a refusal to acknowledge that deprivation of freedom or to give information on the whereabouts of that person, thereby impeding his or her recourse to the applicable legal remedies and procedural guarantees.

Article III

The States Parties undertake to adopt, in accordance with their constitutional procedures, the legislative measures that may be needed to define the forced disappearance of persons as an offense and to impose an appropriate punishment commensurate with its extreme gravity. This offense shall be deemed continuous or permanent as long as the fate or whereabouts of the victim has not been determined.

The States Parties may establish mitigating circumstances for persons who have participated in acts constituting forced disappearance when they help to cause the victim to reappear alive or provide information that sheds light on the force disappearance of a person.

Article IV

The acts constituting the forced disappearance of persons shall be considered offenses in every State Party. Consequently, each State Party shall take measures to establish its jurisdiction over such cases in the following instances:

    (a) When the forced disappearance of persons or any act constituting such offense was committed within its jurisdiction;

    (b) When the accused is a national of that state;

    (c) When the victim is a national of that state and that state sees fit to do so.

Every State Party shall, moreover, take the necessary measures to establish its jurisdiction over the crime described in this Convention when the alleged criminal is within its territory and it does not proceed to extradite him.

This Convention does not authorize any State Party to undertake, in the territory of another State Party, the exercise of jurisdiction or the performance of functions that are placed within the exclusive purview of the authorities of that other Party by its domestic law.

Article V

The forced disappearance of persons shall not be considered a political offense for purposes of extradition.

The forced disappearance of persons shall be deemed to be included among the extraditable offenses in every extradition treaty entered into between States Parties.

The States Parties undertake to include the offense of forced disappearance alone which is extraditable in every extradition treaty to be concluded between them in the future.

Every State Party that makes extradition conditional on the existence of a treaty and receives a request for extradition from another State Party with which it has no extradition treaty may consider this Convention as the necessary legal basis for extradition with respect to the offense of forced disappearance

State Parties which do not make extradition conditional on the existence of a treaty shall recognize such offense as extraditable, subject to the conditions imposed by the law of the requested state.

Extradition shall be subject to the provisions set forth in the constitution and other laws of the requested state.

Article VI

When a State Party does not grant the extradition, the case shall be submitted to its competent authorities as if the offense had been committed within its jurisdiction for the purposes of investigation and when appropriate, for criminal action, in accordance with its national law. Any decision adopted by these authorities shall be communicated to the state that has requested the extradition.

Article VII

Criminal prosecution for the forced disappearance of persons and the penalty judicially imposed on its perpetrator shall not be subject to statutes of limitations.

However, if there should be a norm of a fundamental character preventing application of the stipulation contained in the previous paragraph, the period of limitation shall be equal to that which applies to the gravest crime in the domestic laws of the corresponding State Party.

Article VIII

The defense of due obedience to superior orders or instructions that stipulate, authorize, or encourage forced disappearance shall not be admitted. All persons who receive such orders have the right and duty not to obey them.

The States Parties shall ensure that the training of public law-enforcement personnel or officials includes the necessary education on the offense of forced disappearance of persons.

Article IX

Persons alleged to be responsible for the acts constituting the offense of forced disappearance of persons may be tried only on the competent jurisdictions of ordinary law in each state, to the exclusion of all other special jurisdictions, particularly military jurisdictions.

The acts constituting forced disappearance shall not be deemed to have been committed in the course of military duties.

Privileges, immunities, or special dispensations shall not be admitted in such trials, without prejudice to the provisions set forth in the Vienna Convention on Diplomatic Relations.

Article X

In no case may exceptional circumstances such as a state of war, the threat of war, internal political instability, or any other public emergency be invoked to justify the forced disappearance of persons. In such cases, the right to expeditious and effective judicial procedures and recourse shall be retained as a means of determining the whereabouts or state of health of a person who has been deprived of freedom, or of identifying the official who ordered or carried out such deprivation of freedom.

In pursuing such procedures or recourse, and in keeping with applicable domestic law, the competent judicial authorities shall have free and immediate access to all detention centers and to each of their units, and to all places where there is reason to believe the disappeared person might be found, including places that are subject to military jurisdiction.

Article XI

Every person deprived of liberty shall be held in an officially recognized place of detention and be brought before a competent judicial authority without delay, in accordance with applicable domestic law.

The States Parties shall establish and maintain official up-to-date registries of their detainees and, in accordance with their domestic law, shall make them available to relatives, judges, attorneys, any other person having a legitimate interest, and other authorities.

Article XII

The States Parties shall give each other mutual assistance in the search for, identification, location, and return of minors who have been removed to another state or detained therein as a consequence of the forced disappearance of their parents or guardians.

Article XIII

For the purposes of this Convention, the processing of petitions or communications presented to the Inter-American Commission on Human Rights alleging the forced disappearance of persons shall be subject to the procedures established in the American Convention on Human Rights and to the Statute and Regulations of the Inter-American Commission on Human Rights and to the Statute and Rules of Procedure of the Inter-American Court of Human Rights, including the provisions on precautionary measures.

Article XIV

Without prejudice to the provisions of the preceding article, when the Inter-American Commission on Human Rights receives a petition or communication regarding an alleged forced disappearance, its Executive Secretariat shall urgently and confidentially address the respective government and shall request that government to provide as soon as possible information as to the whereabouts of the allegedly disappeared person together with any other information it considers pertinent, and such request shall be without prejudice as to the admissibility of the petition.

Article XV

None of the provisions of this Convention shall be interpreted as limiting other bilateral or multilateral treaties or other agreements signed by the Parties.

This Convention shall not apply to the international armed conflicts governed by the 1949 Geneva Convention and its Protocol concerning protection of wounded, sick, and shipwrecked members of the armed forces; and prisoners of war and civilians in time of war.

Article XVI

This Convention is open for signature by the member states of the Organization of American States.

Article XVII

This Convention is subject to ratification. The instruments of ratification shall be deposited with the General Secretariat of the Organization of American States.

Article XVIII

This Convention shall be open to accession by any other state. The instruments of accession shall be deposited with the General Secretariat of the Organization of American States.

Article XIX

The states may make reservations with respect to this Convention when signing, ratifying or acceding to it, unless such reservations are incompatible with the object and purpose of the Convention and as long as they refer to one or more specific provisions.

Article XX

This Convention shall enter into force for the ratifying states on the thirtieth day from the date of deposit of the second instrument of ratification.

For each state ratifying or acceding to the Convention after the second instrument of ratification has been deposited, the Convention shall enter into force on the thirtieth day from the date on which that state deposited its instrument of ratification or accession.

Article XXI

This Convention shall remain in force indefinitely, but may be denounced by any State Party. The instrument of denunciation shall be deposited with the General Secretariat of the Organization of American States. The Convention shall cease to be in effect for the denouncing state and shall remain in force for the other States Parties one year from the date of deposit of the instrument of denunciation.

Article XXII

The original instrument of this Convention, the Spanish, English, Portuguese and French texts of which are equally authentic, shall be deposited with the General Secretariat of the Organization of American States, which shall forward certified copies thereof to the United Nations Secretariat, for registration and publication, in accordance with Article 102 of the Charter of the United Nations. The General Secretariat of the Organization of American States shall notify member States of the Organization and States acceding to the Convention of the signatures and deposit of instruments of ratification, accession or denunciation, as well as of any reservations that may be expressed.

In witness whereof the undersigned Plenipotentiaries, being duly authorized thereto by their respective governments, have signed this Convention, which shall be called the 'Inter-American Convention on the Forced Disappearance of Persons.'

Done in the city of Belém, Brazil, the ninth of June in the year one thousand nine hundred ninety-four.

Inter-American Convention on the Prevention, Punishment and Eradication of Violence against Women ('Convention of Belém Do Para') (1994)*

The States Parties to this Convention,

Recognizing that full respect for human rights has been enshrined in the American Declaration of the Rights and Duties of Man and the Universal Declaration of Human Rights, and reaffirmed in other international and regional instruments;

Affirming that violence against women constitutes a violation of their human rights and fundamental freedoms, and impairs or nullifies the observance, enjoyment and exercise of such rights and freedoms;

Concerned that violence against women is an offense against human dignity and a manifestation of the historically unequal power relations between women and men;

Recalling the Declaration on the Elimination of Violence against Women, adopted by the Twenty-fifth Assembly of Delegates of the Inter-American Commission of Women, and affirming that violence against women pervades every sector of society regardless of class, race or ethnic group, income, culture, level of education, age or religion and strikes at its very foundations;

Convinced that the elimination of violence against women is essential for their individual and social development and their full and equal participation in all walks of life; and

Convinced that the adoption of a convention on the prevention, punishment and eradication of all forms of violence against women within the framework of the Organization of American States is a positive contribution to protecting the rights of women and eliminating violence against them,

Have agreed to the following:

Chapter I Definition and Scope of Application

Article 1
For the purposes of this Convention, violence against women shall be understood as any act or conduct, based on gender, which causes death or physical, sexual or psychological harm or suffering to women, whether in the public or the private sphere.

Article 2
Violence against women shall be understood to include physical, sexual and psychological violence:

    (a) that occurs within the family or domestic unit or within any other interpersonal relationship, whether or not the perpetrator shares or has shared the same residence with the woman, including, among others, rape, battery and sexual abuse;

    (b) that occurs in the community and is perpetrated by any person, including, among others, rape, sexual abuse, torture, trafficking in persons, forced prostitution, kidnapping and sexual harassment in the workplace, as well as in educational institutions, health facilities or any other place; and

    (c) that is perpetrated or condoned by the state or its agents regardless of where it occurs.

* Reproduced by permission of the General Secretariat of the Organization of American States. https://www.oas.org/juridico/english/treaties/a-61.html

Chapter II Rights Protected

Article 3
Every woman has the right to be free from violence in both the public and private spheres.

Article 4
Every woman has the right to the recognition, enjoyment, exercise and protection of all human rights and freedoms embodied in regional and international human rights instruments. These rights include, among others:

  (a) The right to have her life respected;
  (b) The right to have her physical, mental and moral integrity respected;
  (c) The right to personal liberty and security;
  (d) The right not to be subjected to torture;
  (e) The right to have the inherent dignity of her person respected and her family protected;
  (f) The right to equal protection before the law and of the law;
  (g) The right to simple and prompt recourse to a competent court for protection against acts that violate her rights;
  (h) The right to associate freely;
  (i) The right of freedom to profess her religion and beliefs within the law; and
  (j) The right to have equal access to the public service of her country and to take part in the conduct of public affairs, including decision-making.

Articles 5
Every woman is entitled to the free and full exercise of her civil, political, economic, social and cultural rights, and may rely on the full protection of those rights as embodied in regional and international instruments on human rights. The States Parties recognize that violence against women prevents and nullifies the exercise of these rights.

Article 6
The right of every woman to be free from violence includes, among others:

  (a) The right of women to be free from all forms of discrimination; and
  (b) The right of women to be valued and educated free of stereotyped patterns of behavior and social and cultural practices based on concepts of inferiority or subordination.

Chapter III Duties of the States

Article 7
The States Parties condemn all forms of violence against women and agree to pursue, by all appropriate means and without delay, policies to prevent, punish and eradicate such violence and undertake to:

  (a) refrain from engaging in any act or practice of violence against women and to ensure that their authorities, officials, personnel, agents, and institutions act in conformity with this obligation;
  (b) apply due diligence to prevent, investigate and impose penalties for violence against women;
  (c) include in their domestic legislation penal, civil, administrative and any other type of provisions that may be needed to prevent, punish and eradicate violence against women and to adopt appropriate administrative measures where necessary;
  (d) adopt legal measures to require the perpetrator to refrain from harassing, intimidating or threatening the woman or using any method that harms or endangers her life or integrity, or damages her property;

(e) take all appropriate measures, including legislative measures, to amend or repeal existing laws and regulations or to modify legal or customary practices which sustain the persistence and tolerance of violence against women;

(f) establish fair and effective legal procedures for women who have been subjected to violence which include, among others, protective measures, a timely hearing and effective access to such procedures;

(g) establish the necessary legal and administrative mechanisms to ensure that women subjected to violence have effective access to restitution, reparations or other just and effective remedies; and

(h) adopt such legislative or other measures as may be necessary to give effect to this Convention.

Article 8

The States Parties agree to undertake progressively specific measures, including programs:

(a) to promote awareness and observance of the right of women to be free from violence, and the right of women to have their human rights respected and protected;

(b) to modify social and cultural patterns of conduct of men and women, including the development of formal and informal educational programs appropriate to every level of the educational process, to counteract prejudices, customs and all other practices which are based on the idea of the inferiority or superiority of either of the sexes or on the stereotyped roles for men and women which legitimize or exacerbate violence against women;

(c) to promote the education and training of all those involved in the administration of justice, police and other law enforcement officers as well as other personnel responsible for implementing policies for the prevention, punishment and eradication of violence against women;

(d) to provide appropriate specialized services for women who have been subjected to violence, through public and private sector agencies, including shelters, counseling services for all family members where appropriate, and care and custody of the affected children;

(e) to promote and support governmental and private sector education designed to raise the awareness of the public with respect to the problems of and remedies for violence against women;

(f) to provide women who are subjected to violence access to effective readjustment and training programs to enable them to fully participate in public, private and social life;

(g) to encourage the communications media to develop appropriate media guidelines in order to contribute to the eradication of violence against women in all its forms, and to enhance respect for the dignity of women;

(h) to ensure research and the gathering of statistics and other relevant information relating to the causes, consequences and frequency of violence against women, in order to assess the effectiveness of measures to prevent, punish and eradicate violence against women and to formulate and implement the necessary changes; and

(i) to foster international cooperation for the exchange of ideas and experiences and the execution of programs aimed at protecting women who are subjected to violence.

Article 9

With respect to the adoption of the measures in this Chapter, the States Parties shall take special account of the vulnerability of women to violence by reason of, among others, their race or ethnic background or their status as migrants, refugees or displaced persons. Similar consideration shall be given to women subjected to violence while pregnant or who are disabled, of minor age, elderly, socioeconomically disadvantaged, affected by armed conflict or deprived of their freedom.

Chapter IV Inter-American Mechanisms of Protection

Article 10

In order to protect the right of every woman to be free from violence, the States Parties shall include in their national reports to the Inter-American Commission of Women information on measures adopted to prevent and prohibit violence against women, and to assist women affected by violence, as well as on any difficulties they observe in applying those measures, and the factors that contribute to violence against women.

Article 11

The States Parties to this Convention and the Inter-American Commission of Women may request of the Inter-American Court of Human Rights advisory opinions on the interpretation of this Convention.

Article 12

Any person or groups of persons, or any non-governmental entity legally recognized in one or more member states of the Organization, may lodge petitions with the Inter-American Commission on Human Rights containing denunciations or complaints of violations of Article 7 of this Convention by a State Party, and the Commission shall consider such claims in accordance with the norms and pro-cedures established by the American Convention on Human Rights and the Statutes and Regulations of the Inter-American Commission on Human Rights for lodging and considering petitions.

Chapter V General Provisions

Article 13

No part of this Convention shall be understood to restrict or limit the domestic law of any State Party that affords equal or greater protection and guarantees of the rights of women and appropriate safeguards to prevent and eradicate violence against women.

Article 14

No part of this Convention shall be understood to restrict or limit the American Convention on Human Rights or any other international convention on the subject that provides for equal or greater protection in this area.

Article 15

This Convention is open to signature by all member States of the Organization of American States.

Article 16

This Convention is subject to ratification. The instruments of ratification shall be deposited with the General Secretariat of the Organization of American States.

Article 17

This Convention is open to accession by any other state. Instruments of accession shall be deposited with the General Secretariat of the Organization of American States.

Article 18

Any State may, at the time of approval, signature, ratification, or accession, make reservations to this Convention provided that such reservations are:

    (a) not incompatible with the object and purpose of the Convention, and

    (b) not of a general nature and relate to one or more specific provisions.

Article 19

Any State Party may submit to the General Assembly, through the Inter-American Commission of Women, proposals for the amendment of this Convention.

Amendments shall enter into force for the states ratifying them on the date when two-thirds of the States Parties to this Convention have deposited their respective instruments of ratification. With respect to the other States Parties, the amendments shall enter into force on the dates on which they deposit their respective instruments of ratification.

Article 20

If a State Party has two or more territorial units in which the matters dealt with in this Convention are governed by different systems of law, it may, at the time of signature, ratification or accession, declare that this Convention shall extend to all its territorial units or to only one or more of them.

Such a declaration may be amended at any time by subsequent declarations, which shall expressly specify the territorial unit or units to which this Convention applies. Such subsequent declarations shall be transmitted to the General Secretariat of the Organization of American States, and shall enter into force thirty days after the date of their receipt.

Article 21

This Convention shall enter into force on the thirtieth day after the date of deposit of the second instrument of ratification. For each State that ratifies or accedes to the Convention after the second instrument of ratification is deposited, it shall enter into force thirty days after the date on which that State deposited its instrument of ratification or accession.

Article 22

The Secretary General shall inform all member states of the Organization of American States of the entry into force of this Convention.

Article 23

The Secretary General of the Organization of American States shall present an annual report to the member states of the Organization on the status of this Convention, including the signatures, deposits of instruments of ratification and accession, and declarations, and any reservations that may have been presented by the States Parties, accompanied by a report thereon if needed.

Article 24

This Convention shall remain in force indefinitely, but any of the States Parties may denounce it by depositing an instrument to that effect with the General Secretariat of the Organization of American States. One year after the date of deposit of the instrument of denunciation, this Convention shall cease to be in effect for the denouncing State but shall remain in force for the remaining States Parties.

Article 25

The original instrument of this Convention, the English, French, Portuguese and Spanish texts of which are equally authentic, shall be deposited with the General Secretariat of the Organization of American States, which shall send a certified copy to the Secretariat of the United Nations for registration and publication in accordance with the provisions of Article 102 of the United Nations Charter.

In witness whereof the undersigned Plenipotentiaries, being duly authorized thereto by their respective governments, have signed this Convention, which shall be called the American Convention on the Prevention, Punishment and Eradication of Violence against Women 'Convention of Belém do Pará.'

Done in the city of Belém do Pará, Brazil, the ninth of June in the year one thousand nine hundred ninety-four.

D. AFRICA

OAU Convention Governing the Specific Aspects of Refugee Problems in Africa (1969)*

PREAMBLE

We, the Heads of State and Government, assembled in the city of Addis Ababa,

1. *Noting with concern* the constantly increasing numbers of refugees in Africa and desirous of finding ways and means of alleviating their misery and suffering as well as providing them with a better life and future,

2. *Recognizing* the need for an essentially humanitarian approach towards solving the problems of refugees,

3. *Aware*, however, that refugee problems are a source of friction among many Member States, and desirous of eliminating the source of such discord,

4. *Anxious* to make a distinction between a refugee who seeks a peaceful and normal life and a person fleeing his country for the sole purpose of fomenting subversion from outside,

5. *Determined* that the activities of such subversive elements should be discouraged, in accordance with the Declaration on the Problem of Subversion and Resolution on the Problem of Refugees adopted at Accra in 1965,

6. *Bearing* in mind that the Charter of the United Nations and the Universal Declaration of Human Rights have affirmed the principle that human beings shall enjoy fundamental rights and freedoms without discrimination,

7. *Recalling Resolution* 2312 (XXII) of 14 December 1967 of the United Nations General Assembly, relating to the Declaration on Territorial Asylum,

8. *Convinced* that all the problems of our continent must be solved in the spirit of the Charter of the Organization of African Unity and in the African context,

9. *Recognizing* that the United Nations Convention of 28 July 1951, as modified by the Protocol of 31 January 1967, constitutes the basic and universal instrument relating to the status of refugees and reflects the deep concern of States for refugees and their desire to establish common standards for their treatment,

10. *Recalling* Resolutions 26 and 104 of the OAU Assemblies of Heads of State and Government, calling upon Member States of the Organization who had not already done so to accede to the United Nations Convention of 1951 and to the Protocol of 1967 relating to the Status of Refugees, and meanwhile to apply their provisions to refugees in Africa,

11. *Convinced* that the efficiency of the measures recommended by the present Convention to solve the problem of refugees in Africa necessitates close and continuous collaboration between the Organization of African Unity and the Office of the United Nations High Commissioner for Refugees,

Have agreed as follows:

Article I   Definition of the term 'refugee'

1. For the purposes of this Convention, the term 'refugee' shall mean every person who, owing to well-founded fear of being persecuted for reasons of race, religion, nationality, membership of a particular social group or political opinion, is outside the country of his nationality and is unable or, owing to such fear, is unwilling to avail himself of the protection of that country, or who, not having a nationality and being outside the country of his former habitual residence as a result of such events, is unable or, owing to such fear, is unwilling to return to it.

2. The term 'refugee' shall also apply to every person who, owing to external aggression, occupation, foreign domination or events seriously disturbing public order in either part or the whole of his country of origin or nationality, is compelled to leave his place of habitual residence in order to seek refuge in another place outside his country of origin or nationality.

* © The African Union Commission

3. In the case of a person who has several nationalities, the term 'a country of which he is a national' shall mean each of the countries of which he is a national, and a person shall not be deemed to be lacking the protection of the country of which he is a national if, without any valid reason based on well-founded fear, he has not availed himself of the protection of one of the countries of which he is a national.

4. This Convention shall cease to apply to any refugee if:

    (a) he has voluntarily re-availed himself of the protection of the country of his nationality, or

    (b) having lost his nationality, he has voluntarily re-acquired it, or

    (c) he has acquired a new nationality, and enjoys the protection of the country of his new nationality, or

    (d) he has voluntarily re-established himself in the country which he left or outside which he remained owing to fear of persecution, or

    (e) he can no longer, because the circumstances in connection with which he was recognized as a refugee have ceased to exist, continue to refuse to avail himself of the protection of the country of his nationality, or

    (f) he has committed a serious non-political crime outside his country of refuge after his admission to that country as a refugee, or

    (g) he has seriously infringed the purposes and objectives of this Convention.

5. The provisions of this Convention shall not apply to any person with respect to whom the country of asylum has serious reasons for considering that:

    (a) he has committed a crime against peace, a war crime, or a crime against humanity, as defined in the international instruments drawn up to make provision in respect of such crimes,

    (b) he committed a serious non-political crime outside the country of refuge prior to his admission to that country as a refugee,

    (c) he has been guilty of acts contrary to the purposes and principles of the Organization of African Unity,

    (d) he has been guilty of acts contrary to the purposes and principles of the United Nations.

6. For the purposes of this Convention, the Contracting State of asylum shall determine whether an applicant is a refugee.

Article II   Asylum

1. Member States of the OAU shall use their best endeavours consistent with their respective legislations to receive refugees and to secure the settlement of those refugees who, for well-founded reasons, are unable or unwilling to return to their country of origin or nationality.

2. The grant of asylum to refugees is a peaceful and humanitarian act and shall not be regarded as an unfriendly act by any Member State.

3. No person shall be subjected by a Member State to measures such as rejection at the frontier, return or expulsion, which would compel him to return to or remain in a territory where his life, physical integrity or liberty would be threatened for the reasons set out in Article I, paragraphs 1 and 2.

4. Where a Member State finds difficulty in continuing to grant asylum to refugees, such Member State may appeal directly to other Member States and through the OAU, and such other Member States shall in the spirit of African solidarity and international co-operation take appropriate measures to lighten the burden of the Member State granting asylum.

5. Where a refugee has not received the right to reside in any country of asylum, he may be granted temporary residence in any country of asylum in which he first presented himself as a refugee pending arrangement for his re-settlement in accordance with the preceding paragraph.

6. For reasons of security, countries of asylum shall, as far as possible, settle refugees at a reasonable distance from the frontier of their country of origin.

Article III   Prohibition of subversive activities

1. Every refugee has duties to the country in which he finds himself, which require in particular that he conforms with its laws and regulations as well as with measures taken for the maintenance of public order. He shall also abstain from any subversive activities against any Member State of the OAU.

2. Signatory States undertake to prohibit refugees residing in their respective territories from attacking any State Member of the OAU, by any activity likely to cause tension between Member States, and in particular by use of arms, through the press, or by radio.

Article IV   Non-discrimination

Member States undertake to apply the provisions of this Convention to all refugees without discrimination as to race, religion, nationality, membership of a particular social group or political opinions.

Article V   Voluntary repatriation

1. The essentially voluntary character of repatriation shall be respected in all cases and no refugee shall be repatriated against his will.

2. The country of asylum, in collaboration with the country of origin, shall make adequate arrangements for the safe return of refugees who request repatriation.

3. The country of origin, on receiving back refugees, shall facilitate their resettlement and grant them the full rights and privileges of nationals of the country, and subject them to the same obligations.

4. Refugees who voluntarily return to their country shall in no way be penalized for having left it for any of the reasons giving rise to refugee situations. Whenever necessary, an appeal shall be made through national information media and through the Administrative Secretary-General of the OAU, inviting refugees to return home and giving assurance that the new circumstances prevailing in their country of origin will enable them to return without risk and to take up a normal and peaceful life without fear of being disturbed or punished, and that the text of such appeal should be given to refugees and clearly explained to them by their country of asylum.

5. Refugees who freely decide to return to their homeland, as a result of such assurances or on their own initiative, shall be given every possible assistance by the country of asylum, the country of origin, voluntary agencies and international and intergovernmental organizations to facilitate their return.

Article VI   Travel documents

1. Subject to Article III, Member States shall issue to refugees lawfully staying in their territories travel documents in accordance with the United Nations Convention relating to the Status of Refugees and the Schedule and Annex thereto, for the purpose of travel outside their territory, unless compelling reasons of national security or public order otherwise require. Member States may issue such a travel document to any other refugee in their territory.

2. Where an African country of second asylum accepts a refugee from a country of first asylum, the country of first asylum may be dispensed from issuing a document with a return clause.

3. Travel documents issued to refugees under previous international agreements by States Parties thereto shall be recognized and treated by Member States in the same way as if they had been issued to refugees pursuant to this Article.

Article VII   Co-operation of the national authorities with the Organization of African Unity

In order to enable the Administrative Secretary-General of the Organization of African Unity to make reports to the competent organs of the Organization of African Unity, Member States undertake to provide the Secretariat in the appropriate form with information and statistical data requested concerning:

    (a) the condition of refugees,

    (b) the implementation of this Convention, and

    (c) laws, regulations and decrees which are, or may hereafter be, in force relating to refugees.

Article VIII   Co-operation with the Office of the United Nations High Commissioner for Refugees

1. Member States shall co-operate with the Office of the United Nations High Commissioner for Refugees.

2. The present Convention shall be the effective regional complement in Africa of the 1951 United Nations Convention on the Status of Refugees.

Article IX   Settlement of disputes

Any dispute between States signatories to this Convention relating to its interpretation or application, which cannot be settled by other means, shall be referred to the Commission for Mediation, Conciliation and Arbitration of the Organization of African Unity, at the request of any one of the parties to the dispute.

Article X   Signature and ratification

1. This Convention is open for signature and accession by all Member States of the Organization of African Unity and shall be ratified by signatory States in accordance with their respective constitutional processes. The instruments of ratification shall be deposited with the Administrative Secretary-General of the Organization of African Unity.

2. The original instrument, done if possible in African languages, and in English and French, all texts being equally authentic, shall be deposited with the Administrative Secretary-General of the Organization of African Unity.

3. Any independent African State, Member of the Organization of African Unity, may at any time notify the Administrative Secretary-General of the Organization of African Unity of its accession to this Convention.

Article XI   Entry into force

This Convention shall come into force upon deposit of instruments of ratification by one-third of the Member States of the Organization of African Unity.

Article XII   Amendment

This Convention may be amended or revised if any Member State makes a written request to the Administrative Secretary-General to that effect, provided however that the proposed amendment shall not be submitted to the Assembly of Heads of State and Government for consideration until all Member States have been duly notified of it and a period of one year has elapsed. Such an amendment shall not be effective unless approved by at least two-thirds of the Member States Parties to the present Convention.

Article XIII   Denunciation

1. Any Member State Party to this Convention may denounce its provisions by a written notification to the Administrative Secretary-General.

2. At the end of one year from the date of such notification, if not withdrawn, the Convention shall cease to apply with respect to the denouncing State.

Article XIV

Upon entry into force of this Convention, the Administrative Secretary-General of the OAU shall register it with the Secretary-General of the United Nations, in accordance with Article 102 of the Charter of the United Nations.

Article XV   Notifications by the Administrative Secretary-General of the Organization of African Unity

The Administrative Secretary-General of the Organization of African Unity shall inform all Members of the Organization:

    (a) of signatures, ratifications and accessions in accordance with Article X,

    (b) of entry into force, in accordance with Article XI,

    (c) of requests for amendments submitted under the terms of Article XII,

    (d) of denunciations, in accordance with Article XIII.

IN WITNESS WHEREOF we, the Heads of African State and Government, have signed this Convention.

African Charter on Human and Peoples' Rights (1981)*

PREAMBLE

The African States members of the Organization of African Unity, parties to the present convention entitled 'African Charter on Human and Peoples' Rights';

Recalling Decision 115 (XVI) of the Assembly of Heads of State and Government at its Sixteenth Ordinary Session held in Monrovia, Liberia, from 17 to 20 July 1979 on the preparation of 'a preliminary draft on an African Charter on Human and Peoples' Rights providing *inter alia* for the establishment of bodies to promote and protect human and peoples' rights';

Considering the Charter of the Organization of African Unity, which stipulates that 'freedom, equality, justice and dignity are essential objectives for the achievement of the legitimate aspirations of the African peoples';

Reaffirming the pledge they solemnly made in Article 2 of the said Charter to eradicate all forms of colonialism from Africa, to co-ordinate and intensify their co-operation and efforts to achieve a better life for the peoples of Africa and to promote international co-operation, having due regard to the Charter of the United Nations and the Universal Declaration of Human Rights;

Taking into consideration the virtues of their historical tradition and the values of African civilization which should inspire and characterize their reflection on the concept of human and peoples' rights;

Recognizing on the one hand, that fundamental human rights stem from the attributes of human beings, which justifies their international protection and on the other hand, that the reality and respect of peoples' rights should necessarily guarantee human rights;

Considering that the enjoyment of rights and freedoms also implies the performance of duties on the part of everyone;

Convinced that it is henceforth essential to pay particular attention to the right to development and that civil and political rights cannot be dissociated from economic, social and cultural rights in their conception as well as universality and that the satisfaction of economic, social and cultural rights is a guarantee for the enjoyment of civil and political rights;

Conscious of their duty to achieve the total liberation of Africa, the peoples of which are still struggling for their dignity and genuine independence, and undertaking to eliminate colonialism, neo-colonialism, apartheid, zionism, and to dismantle aggressive foreign military bases and all forms of discrimination, particularly those based on race, ethnic group, colour, sex, language, religion or political opinion;

Reaffirming their adherence to the principles of human and peoples' rights and freedoms contained in the declarations, conventions and other instruments adopted by the Organization of African Unity, the Movement of Non-Aligned Countries and the United Nations;

Firmly convinced of their duty to promote and protect human and peoples' rights and freedoms taking into account the importance traditionally attached to these rights and freedoms in Africa;

Have agreed as follows:

PART I RIGHTS AND DUTIES

Chapter I Human and Peoples' Rights

Article 1

The Member States of the Organization of African Unity parties to the present Charter shall recognize the rights, duties and freedoms enshrined in this Charter and shall undertake to adopt legislative or other measures to give effect to them.

Article 2

Every individual shall be entitled to the enjoyment of the rights and freedoms recognized and guaranteed in the present Charter without distinction of any kind such as race, ethnic group, colour, sex, language, religion, political or any other opinion, national and social origin, fortune, birth or other status.

Article 3

1. Every individual shall be equal before the law.
2. Every individual shall be entitled to equal protection of the law.

Article 4

Human beings are inviolable. Every human being shall be entitled to respect for his life and the integrity of his person. No one may be arbitrarily deprived of this right.

Article 5

Every individual shall have the right to the respect of the dignity inherent in a human being and to the recognition of his legal status. All forms of exploitation and degradation of man particularly slavery, slave trade, torture, cruel, inhuman or degrading punishment and treatment shall be prohibited.

Article 6

Every individual shall have the right to liberty and to the security of his person. No one may be deprived of his freedom except for reasons and conditions previously laid down by law. In particular, no one may be arbitrarily arrested or detained.

Article 7

1. Every individual shall have the right to have his cause heard. This comprises:
    (a) the right to an appeal to competent national organs against acts violating his fundamental rights as recognized and guaranteed by conventions, laws, regulations and customs in force;
    (b) the right to be presumed innocent until proved guilty by a competent court or tribunal;
    (c) the right to defence, including the right to be defended by counsel of his choice;
    (d) the right to be tried within a reasonable time by an impartial court or tribunal.
2. No one may be condemned for an act or omission which did not constitute a legally punishable offence at the time it was committed. No penalty may be inflicted for an offence for which no provision was made at the time it was committed. Punishment is personal and can be imposed only on the offender.

Article 8

Freedom of conscience, the profession and free practice of religion shall be guaranteed. No one may, subject to law and order, be submitted to measures restricting the exercise of these freedoms.

Article 9

1. Every individual shall have the right to receive information.
2. Every individual shall have the right to express and disseminate his opinions within the law.

Article 10

1. Every individual shall have the right to free association provided that he abides by the law.
2. Subject to the obligation of solidarity provided for in Article 29 no one may be compelled to join an association.

Article 11

Every individual shall have the right to assemble freely with others. The exercise of this right shall be subject only to necessary restrictions provided for by law in particular those enacted in the interest of national security, the safety, health, ethics and rights and freedoms of others.

Article 12

1. Every individual shall have the right to freedom of movement and residence within the borders of a State provided he abides by the law.

2. Every individual shall have the right to leave any country including his own, and to return to his country. This right may only be subject to restrictions, provided for by law for the protection of national security, law and order, public health or morality.

3. Every individual shall have the right, when persecuted, to seek and obtain asylum in other countries in accordance with the laws of those countries and international conventions.

4. A non-national legally admitted in a territory of a State party to the present Charter, may only be expelled from it by virtue of a decision taken in accordance with the law.

5. The mass expulsion of non-nationals shall be prohibited. Mass expulsion shall be that which is aimed at national, racial, ethnic or religious groups.

Article 13

1. Every citizen shall have the right to participate freely in the government of his country, either directly or through freely chosen representatives in accordance with the provisions of the law.

2. Every citizen shall have the right of equal access to the public service of his country.

3. Every individual shall have the right of access to public property and services in strict equality of all persons before the law.

Article 14

The right to property shall be guaranteed. It may only be encroached upon in the interest of public need or in the general interest of the community and in accordance with the provisions of appropriate laws.

Article 15

Every individual shall have the right to work under equitable and satisfactory conditions, and shall receive equal pay for equal work.

Article 16

1. Every individual shall have the right to enjoy the best attainable state of physical and mental health.

2. States parties to the present Charter shall take the necessary measures to protect the health of their people and to ensure that they receive medical attention when they are sick.

Article 17

1. Every individual shall have the right to education.

2. Every individual may freely take part in the cultural life of his community.

3. The promotion and protection of morals and traditional values recognized by the community shall be the duty of the State.

Article 18

1. The family shall be the natural unit and basis of society. It shall be protected by the State which shall take care of its physical and moral health.

2. The State shall have the duty to assist the family which is the custodian of morals and traditional values recognized by the community.

3. The State shall ensure the elimination of every discrimination against women and also ensure the protection of the rights of the woman and the child as stipulated in international declarations and conventions.

4. The aged and the disabled shall also have the right to special measures of protection in keeping with their physical or moral needs.

Article 19

All peoples shall be equal; they shall enjoy the same respect and shall have the same rights. Nothing shall justify the domination of a people by another.

Article 20

1. All peoples shall have right to existence. They shall have the unquestionable and inalienable right to self-determination. They shall freely determine their political status and shall pursue their economic and social development according to the policy they have freely chosen.

2. Colonized or oppressed peoples shall have the right to free themselves from the bonds of domination by resorting to any means recognized by the international community.

3. All peoples shall have the right to the assistance of the States parties to the present Charter in their liberation struggle against foreign domination, be it political, economic or cultural.

Article 21

1. All peoples shall freely dispose of their wealth and natural resources. This right shall be exercised in the exclusive interest of the people. In no case shall a people be deprived of it.

2. In case of spoliation the dispossessed people shall have the right to the lawful recovery of its property as well as to an adequate compensation.

3. The free disposal of wealth and natural resources shall be exercised without prejudice to the obligation of promoting international economic co-operation based on mutual respect, equitable exchange and the principles of international law.

4. States parties to the present Charter shall individually and collectively exercise the right to free disposal of their wealth and natural resources with a view to strengthening African unity and solidarity.

5. States parties to the present Charter shall undertake to eliminate all forms of foreign economic exploitation particularly that practised by international monopolies so as to enable their peoples to fully benefit from the advantages derived from their national resources.

Article 22

1. All peoples shall have the right to their economic, social and cultural development with due regard to their freedom and identity and in the equal enjoyment of the common heritage of mankind.

2. States shall have the duty, individually or collectively, to ensure the exercise of the right to development.

Article 23

1. All peoples shall have the right to national and international peace and security. The principles of solidarity and friendly relations implicitly affirmed by the Charter of the United Nations and reaffirmed by that of the Organization of African Unity shall govern relations between States.

2. For the purpose of strengthening peace, solidarity and friendly relations, States parties to the present Charter shall ensure that:
   (a) any individual enjoying the right of asylum under Article 12 of the present Charter shall not engage in subversive activities against his country of origin or any other State party to the present Charter;
   (b) their territories shall not be used as bases for subversive or terrorist activities against the people of any other State party to the present Charter.

Article 24

All people shall have the right to a general satisfactory environment favourable to their development.

Article 25

States parties to the present Charter shall have the duty to promote and ensure through teaching, education and publication, the respect of the rights and freedoms contained in the present Charter and to see to it that these freedoms and rights as well as corresponding obligations and duties are understood.

Article 26

States parties to the present Charter shall have the duty to guarantee the independence of the Courts and shall allow the establishment and improvement of appropriate national institutions entrusted with the promotion and protection of the rights and freedoms guaranteed by the present Charter.

Chapter II Duties

Article 27

1. Every individual shall have duties towards his family and society, the State and other legally recognized communities and the international community.

2. The rights and freedoms of each individual shall be exercised with due regard to the rights of others, collective security, morality and common interest.

Article 28

Every individual shall have the duty to respect and consider his fellow beings without discrimination, and to maintain relations aimed at promoting, safeguarding and reinforcing mutual respect and tolerance.

Article 29

The individual shall also have the duty:

1. To preserve the harmonious development of the family and to work for the cohesion and respect of the family; to respect his parents at all times, to maintain them in case of need;

2. To serve his national community by placing his physical and intellectual abilities at its service;

3. Not to compromise the security of the State whose national or resident he is;

4. To preserve and strengthen social and national solidarity, particularly when the latter is threatened;

5. To preserve and strengthen the national independence and the territorial integrity of his country and to contribute to its defence in accordance with the law;

6. To work to the best of his abilities and competence, and to pay taxes imposed by law in the interest of the society;

7. To preserve and strengthen positive African cultural values in his relations with other members of the society, in the spirit of tolerance, dialogue and consultation and, in general, to contribute to the promotion of the moral well-being of society;

8. To contribute to the best of his abilities, at all times and at all levels, to the promotion and achievement of African unity.

PART II MEASURES OF SAFEGUARD

Chapter I Establishment and Organization of the African Commission on Human and Peoples' Rights

Article 30

An African Commission on Human and Peoples' Rights, hereinafter called 'the Commission', shall be established within the Organization of African Unity to promote human and peoples' rights and ensure their protection in Africa.

Article 31

1. The Commission shall consist of eleven members chosen from amongst African personalities of the highest reputation, known for their high morality, integrity, impartiality and competence in

matters of human and peoples' rights; particular consideration being given to persons having legal experience.

2. The members of the Commission shall serve in their personal capacity.

Article 32
The Commission shall not include more than one national of the same State.

Article 33
The members of the Commission shall be elected by secret ballot by the Assembly of Heads of State and Government, from a list of persons nominated by the States parties to the present Charter.

Article 34
Each State party to the present Charter may not nominate more than two candidates. The candidates must have the nationality of one of the States parties of the present Charter. When two candidates are nominated by a State, one of them may not be a national of that State.

Article 35
1. The Secretary-General of the Organization of African Unity shall invite States parties to the present Charter at least four months before the elections to nominate candidates.

2. The Secretary-General of the Organization of African Unity shall make an alphabetical list of the persons thus nominated and communicate it to the Heads of State and Government at least one month before the elections.

Article 36
The members of the Commission shall be elected for a six-year period and shall be eligible for re-election. However, the term of office of four of the members elected at the first election shall terminate after two years and the term of office of three others, at the end of four years.

Article 37
Immediately after the first election, the Chairman of the Assembly of Heads of State and Government of the Organization of African Unity shall draw lots to decide the names of those members referred to in Article 36.

Article 38
After their election, the members of the Commission shall make a solemn declaration to discharge their duties impartially and faithfully.

Article 39
1. In case of death or resignation of a member of the Commission, the Chairman of the Commission shall immediately inform the Secretary-General of the Organization of African Unity, who shall declare the seat vacant from the date of death or from the date on which the resignation takes effect.

2. If, in the unanimous opinion of other members of the Commission, a member has stopped discharging his duties for any reason other than a temporary absence, the Chairman of the Commission shall inform the Secretary-General of the Organization of African Unity, who shall then declare the seat vacant.

3. In each of the cases anticipated above, the Assembly of Heads of State and Government shall replace the member whose seat became vacant for the remaining period of his term unless the period is less than six months.

Article 40
Every member of the Commission shall be in office until the date his successor assumes office.

Article 41
The Secretary-General of the Organization of African Unity shall appoint the Secretary of the Commission. He shall also provide the staff and services necessary for the effective discharge of

the duties of the Commission. The Organization of African Unity shall bear the cost of the staff and services.

Article 42

1. The Commission shall elect its Chairman and Vice-Chairman for a two-year period. They shall be eligible for re-election.

2. The Commission shall lay down its rules of procedure.

3. Seven members shall form the quorum.

4. In case of an equality of votes, the Chairman shall have a casting vote.

5. The Secretary-General may attend the meetings of the Commission. He shall neither participate in deliberations nor shall he be entitled to vote. The Chairman of the Commission may, however, invite him to speak.

Article 43

In discharging their duties, members of the Commission shall enjoy diplomatic privileges and immunities provided for in the General Convention on the Privileges and Immunities of the Organization of African Unity.

Article 44

Provision shall be made for the emoluments and allowances of the members of the Commission in the Regular Budget of the Organization of African Unity.

Chapter II Mandate of the Commission

Article 45

The functions of the Commission shall be:

1. To promote Human and Peoples' Rights and in particular:

    (a) to collect documents, undertake studies and researches on African problems in the field of human and peoples' rights, organize seminars, symposia and conferences, disseminate information, encourage national and local institutions concerned with human and peoples' rights and, should the case arise, give its views or make recommendations to Governments;

    (b) to formulate and lay down, principles and rules aimed at solving legal problems relating to human and peoples' rights and fundamental freedoms upon which African Governments may base their legislations;

    (c) co-operate with other African and international institutions concerned with the promotion and protection of human and peoples' rights.

2. Ensure the protection of human and peoples' rights under conditions laid down by the present Charter.

3. Interpret all the provisions of the present Charter at the request of a State party, an institution of the Organization of African Unity or an African organization recognized by the Organization of African Unity.

4. Perform any other tasks which may be entrusted to it by the Assembly of Heads of State and Government.

Chapter III Procedure of the Commission

Article 46

The Commission may resort to any appropriate method of investigation; it may hear from the Secretary-General of the Organization of African Unity or any other person capable of enlightening it.

Communication From States

Article 47

If a State Party to the present Charter has good reasons to believe that another State party to this Charter has violated the provisions of the Charter, it may draw, by written communication, the attention of that State to the matter. This communication shall also be addressed to the Secretary-General of the Organization of African Unity and to the Chairman of the Commission. Within three months of the receipt of the communication the State to which the communication is addressed shall give the enquiring State, written explanation or statement elucidating the matter. This should include as much as possible relevant information relating to the laws and rules of procedure applied and applicable and the redress already given or course of action available.

Article 48

If within three months from the date on which the original communication is received by the State to which it is addressed, the issue is not settled to the satisfaction of the two States involved through bilateral negotiation or by any other peaceful procedure, either State shall have the right to submit the matter to the Commission through the Chairman and shall notify the other State involved.

Article 49

Notwithstanding the provisions of Article 47, if a State party to the present Charter considers that another State party has violated the provisions of the Charter, it may refer the matter directly to the Commission by addressing a communication to the Chairman, to the Secretary-General of the Organization of African Unity and the State concerned.

Article 50

The Commission can only deal with a matter submitted to it after making sure that all local remedies, if they exist, have been exhausted, unless it is obvious to the Commission that the procedure of achieving these remedies would be unduly prolonged.

Article 51

1. The Commission may ask the States concerned to provide it with all relevant information.

2. When the Commission is considering the matter, States concerned may be represented before it and submit written or oral representations.

Article 52

After having obtained from the States concerned and from other sources all the information it deems necessary and after having tried all appropriate means to reach an amicable solution based on the respect of human and peoples' rights, the Commission shall prepare, within a reasonable period of time from the notification referred to in Article 48, a report stating the facts and its findings. This report shall be sent to the States concerned and communicated to the Assembly of Heads of State and Government.

Article 53

While transmitting its report, the Commission may make to the Assembly of Heads of State and Government such recommendations as it deems useful.

Article 54

The Commission shall submit to each Ordinary Session of the Assembly of Heads of State and Government a report on its activities.

Other Communications

Article 55

1. Before each session, the Secretary of the Commission shall make a list of the communications other than those of States parties to the present Charter and transmit them to the members

of the Commission, who shall indicate which communications should be considered by the Commission.

2. A communication shall be considered by the Commission if a simple majority of its members so decide.

Article 56

Communications relating to human and peoples' rights referred to in Article 55 received by the Commission, shall be considered if they:

1. Indicate their authors even if the latter request anonymity;

2. Are compatible with the Charter of the Organization of African Unity or with the present Charter;

3. Are not written in disparaging or insulting language directed against the State concerned and its institutions or to the Organization of African Unity;

4. Are not based exclusively on news disseminated through the mass media;

5. Are sent after exhausting local remedies, if any, unless it is obvious that this procedure is unduly prolonged;

6. Are submitted within a reasonable period from the time local remedies are exhausted or from the date the Commission is seized of the matter; and

7. Do not deal with cases which have been settled by these States involved in accordance with the principles of the Charter of the United Nations, or the Charter of the Organization of African Unity or the provisions of the present Charter.

Article 57

Prior to any substantive consideration, all communications shall be brought to the knowledge of the State concerned by the Chairman of the Commission.

Article 58

1. When it appears after deliberations of the Commission that one or more communications apparently relate to special cases which reveal the existence of a series of serious or massive violations of human and peoples' rights, the Commission shall draw the attention of the Assembly of Heads of State and Government to these special cases.

2. The Assembly of Heads of State and Government may then request the Commission to undertake an in-depth study of these cases and make a factual report, accompanied by its finding and recommendations.

3. A case of emergency duly noticed by the Commission shall be submitted by the latter to the Chairman of the Assembly of Heads of State and Government who may request an in-depth study.

Article 59

1. All measures taken within the provisions of the present Charter shall remain confidential until such a time as the Assembly of Heads of State and Government shall otherwise decide.

2. However, the report shall be published by the Chairman of the Commission upon the decision of the Assembly of Heads of State and Government.

3. The report on the activities of the Commission shall be published by its Chairman after it has been considered by the Assembly of Heads of State and Government.

Chapter IV Applicable Principles

Article 60

The Commission shall draw inspiration from international law on human and peoples' rights, particularly from the provisions of various African instruments on human and peoples' rights, the Charter of the United Nations, the Charter of the Organization of African Unity, the Universal Declaration of Human Rights, other instruments adopted by the United Nations and by African countries in the field of human and peoples' rights as well as from the provisions of various instruments adopted within the Specialised Agencies of the United Nations of which the parties to the present Charter are members.

Article 61

The Commission shall also take into consideration, as subsidiary measures to determine the principles of law, other general or special international conventions, laying down rules expressly recognized by Member States of the Organization of African Unity, African practices consistent with international norms on human and peoples' rights, customs generally accepted as law, general principles of law recognized by African States as well as legal precedents and doctrine.

Article 62

Each State party shall undertake to submit every two years, from the date the present Charter comes into force, a report on the legislative or other measures taken with a view to giving effect to the rights and freedoms recognized and guaranteed by the present Charter.

Article 63

   1. The present Charter shall be open to signature, ratification or adherence of the Member States of the Organization of African Unity.

   2. The instruments of ratification or adherence to the present Charter shall be deposited with the Secretary-General of the Organization of African Unity.

   3. The present Charter shall come into force three months after the reception by the Secretary-General of the instruments of ratification or adherence of a simple majority of the Member States of the Organization of African Unity.

PART III GENERAL PROVISIONS

Article 64

   1. After the coming into force of the present Charter, members of the Commission shall be elected in accordance with the relevant Articles of the present Charter.

   2. The Secretary-General of the Organization of African Unity shall convene the first meeting of the Commission at the Headquarters of the Organization within three months of the constitution of the Commission. Thereafter, the Commission shall be convened by its Chairman whenever necessary but at least once a year.

Article 65

For each of the States that will ratify or adhere to the present Charter after its coming into force, the Charter shall take effect three months after the date of the deposit by that State of its instrument of ratification or adherence.

Article 66

Special protocols or agreements may, if necessary, supplement the provisions of the present Charter.

Article 67

The Secretary-General of the Organization of African Unity shall inform Member States of the Organization of the deposit of each instrument of ratification or adherence.

Article 68

The present Charter may be amended if a State party makes a written request to that effect to the Secretary-General of the Organization of African Unity. The Assembly of Heads of State and Government may only consider the draft amendment after all the States parties have been duly informed of it and the Commission has given its opinion on it at the request of the sponsoring State. The amendment shall be approved by a simple majority of the States parties. It shall come into force for each State which has accepted it in accordance with its constitutional procedure three months after the Secretary-General has received notice of the acceptance.

Protocol to the African Charter on Human and Peoples' Rights on the Rights of Women in Africa (2003)*

The States Parties to this Protocol,

Considering that Article 66 of the African Charter on Human and Peoples' Rights provides for special protocols or agreements, if necessary, to supplement the provisions of the African Charter, and that the Assembly of Heads of State and Government of the Organization of African Unity meeting in its Thirty-first Ordinary Session in Addis Ababa, Ethiopia, in June 1995, endorsed by resolution AHG/Res.240 (XXXI) the recommendation of the African Commission on Human and Peoples' Rights to elaborate a Protocol on the Rights of Women in Africa;

Considering that Article 2 of the African Charter on Human and Peoples' Rights enshrines the principle of non-discrimination on the grounds of race, ethnic group, colour, sex, language, religion, political or any other opinion, national and social origin, fortune, birth or other status;

Further considering that Article 18 of the African Charter on Human and Peoples' Rights calls on all States Parties to eliminate every discrimination against women and to ensure the protection of the rights of women as stipulated in international declarations and conventions;

Noting that Articles 60 and 61 of the African Charter on Human and Peoples' Rights recognise regional and international human rights instruments and African practices consistent with international norms on human and peoples' rights as being important reference points for the application and interpretation of the African Charter;

Recalling that women's rights have been recognised and guaranteed in all international human rights instruments, notably the Universal Declaration of Human Rights, the International Covenant on Civil and Political Rights, the International Covenant on Economic, Social and Cultural Rights, the Convention on the Elimination of All Forms of Discrimination Against Women and its Optional Protocol, the African Charter on the Rights and Welfare of the Child, and all other international and regional conventions and covenants relating to the rights of women as being inalienable, interdependent and indivisible human rights;

Noting that women's rights and women's essential role in development, have been reaffirmed in the United Nations Plans of Action on the Environment and Development in 1992, on Human Rights in 1993, on Population and Development in 1994 and on Social Development in 1995;

Recalling also United Nations Security Council's Resolution 1325 (2000) on the role of women in promoting peace and security;

Reaffirming the principle of promoting gender equality as enshrined in the Constitutive Act of the African Union as well as the New Partnership for Africa's Development, relevant Declarations, Resolutions and Decisions, which underline the commitment of the African States to ensure the full participation of African women as equal partners in Africa's development;

Further noting that the African Platform for Action and the Dakar Declaration of 1994 and the Beijing Platform for Action of 1995 call on all Member States of the United Nations, which have made a solemn commitment to implement them, to take concrete steps to give greater attention to the human rights of women in order to eliminate all forms of discrimination and of gender-based violence against women;

Recognising the crucial role of women in the preservation of African values based on the principles of equality, peace, freedom, dignity, justice, solidarity and democracy;

Bearing in mind related Resolutions, Declarations, Recommendations, Decisions, Conventions and other Regional and Sub-Regional Instruments aimed at eliminating all forms of discrimination and at promoting equality between women and men;

Concerned that despite the ratification of the African Charter on Human and Peoples' Rights and other international human rights instruments by the majority of States Parties, and their solemn commitment to eliminate all forms of discrimination and harmful practices against women, women in Africa still continue to be victims of discrimination and harmful practices;

* © The African Union Commission

Firmly convinced that any practice that hinders or endangers the normal growth and affects the physical and psychological development of women and girls should be condemned and eliminated;

Determined to ensure that the rights of women are promoted, realised and protected in order to enable them to enjoy fully all their human rights;

Have agreed as follows:

Article 1   Definitions

For the purpose of the present Protocol:
(a) 'African Charter' means the African Charter on Human and Peoples' Rights;
(b) 'African Commission' means the African Commission on Human and Peoples' Rights;
(c) 'Assembly' means the Assembly of Heads of State and Government of the African Union;
(d) 'AU' means the African Union;
(e) 'Constitutive Act' means the Constitutive Act of the African Union;
(f) 'Discrimination against women' means any distinction, exclusion or restriction or any differential treatment based on sex and whose objectives or effects compromise or destroy the recognition, enjoyment or the exercise by women, regardless of their marital status, of human rights and fundamental freedoms in all spheres of life;
(g) 'Harmful Practices' means all behaviour, attitudes and/or practices which negatively affect the fundamental rights of women and girls, such as their right to life, health, dignity, education and physical integrity;
(h) 'NEPAD' means the New Partnership for Africa's Development established by the Assembly;
(i) 'States Parties' means the States Parties to this Protocol;
(j) 'Violence against women' means all acts perpetrated against women which cause or could cause them physical, sexual, psychological, and economic harm, including the threat to take such acts; or to undertake the imposition of arbitrary restrictions on or deprivation of fundamental freedoms in private or public life in peace time and during situations of armed conflicts or of war;
(k) 'Women' means persons of female gender, including girls;

Article 2   Elimination of Discrimination Against Women

1. States Parties shall combat all forms of discrimination against women through appropriate legislative, institutional and other measures. In this regard they shall:
(a) include in their national constitutions and other legislative instruments, if not already done, the principle of equality between women and men and ensure its effective application;
(b) enact and effectively implement appropriate legislative or regulatory measures, including those prohibiting and curbing all forms of discrimination particularly those harmful practices which endanger the health and general well-being of women;
(c) integrate a gender perspective in their policy decisions, legislation, development plans, programmes and activities and in all other spheres of life;
(d) take corrective and positive action in those areas where discrimination against women in law and in fact continues to exist;
(e) support the local, national, regional and continental initiatives directed at eradicating all forms of discrimination against women.

2. States Parties shall commit themselves to modify the social and cultural patterns of conduct of women and men through public education, information, education and communication strategies, with a view to achieving the elimination of harmful cultural and traditional practices and all other practices which are based on the idea of the inferiority or the superiority of either of the sexes, or on stereotyped roles for women and men.

Article 3   Right to Dignity

1. Every woman shall have the right to dignity inherent in a human being and to the recognition and protection of her human and legal rights;

2. Every woman shall have the right to respect as a person and to the free development of her personality;

3. States Parties shall adopt and implement appropriate measures to prohibit any exploitation or degradation of women;

4. States Parties shall adopt and implement appropriate measures to ensure the protection of every woman's right to respect for her dignity and protection of women from all forms of violence, particularly sexual and verbal violence.

Article 4   The Rights to Life, Integrity and Security of the Person

1. Every woman shall be entitled to respect for her life and the integrity and security of her person. All forms of exploitation, cruel, inhuman or degrading punishment and treatment shall be prohibited.

2. States Parties shall take appropriate and effective measures to:

    (a) enact and enforce laws to prohibit all forms of violence against women including unwanted or forced sex whether the violence takes place in private or public;

    (b) adopt such other legislative, administrative, social and economic measures as may be necessary to ensure the prevention, punishment and eradication of all forms of violence against women;

    (c) identify the causes and consequences of violence against women and take appropriate measures to prevent and eliminate such violence;

    (d) actively promote peace education through curricula and social communication in order to eradicate elements in traditional and cultural beliefs, practices and stereotypes which legitimise and exacerbate the persistence and tolerance of violence against women;

    (e) punish the perpetrators of violence against women and implement programmes for the rehabilitation of women victims;

    (f) establish mechanisms and accessible services for effective information, rehabilitation and reparation for victims of violence against women;

    (g) prevent and condemn trafficking in women, prosecute the perpetrators of such trafficking and protect those women most at risk;

    (h) prohibit all medical or scientific experiments on women without their informed consent;

    (i) provide adequate budgetary and other resources for the implementation and monitoring of actions aimed at preventing and eradicating violence against women;

    (j) ensure that, in those countries where the death penalty still exists, not to carry out death sentences on pregnant or nursing women.

    (k) ensure that women and men enjoy equal rights in terms of access to refugee status, determination procedures and that women refugees are accorded the full protection and benefits guaranteed under international refugee law, including their own identity and other documents;

Article 5   Elimination of Harmful Practices

States Parties shall prohibit and condemn all forms of harmful practices which negatively affect the human rights of women and which are contrary to recognised international standards. States Parties shall take all necessary legislative and other measures to eliminate such practices, including:

    (a) creation of public awareness in all sectors of society regarding harmful practices through information, formal and informal education and outreach programmes;

(b) prohibition, through legislative measures backed by sanctions, of all forms of female genital mutilation, scarification, medicalisation and para-medicalisation of female genital mutilation and all other practices in order to eradicate them;

(c) provision of necessary support to victims of harmful practices through basic services such as health services, legal and judicial support, emotional and psychological counselling as well as vocational training to make them self-supporting;

(d) protection of women who are at risk of being subjected to harmful practices or all other forms of violence, abuse and intolerance.

Article 6   Marriage

States Parties shall ensure that women and men enjoy equal rights and are regarded as equal partners in marriage. They shall enact appropriate national legislative measures to guarantee that:

(a) no marriage shall take place without the free and full consent of both parties;

(b) the minimum age of marriage for women shall be 18 years;

(c) monogamy is encouraged as the preferred form of marriage and that the rights of women in marriage and family, including in polygamous marital relationships are promoted and protected;

(d) every marriage shall be recorded in writing and registered in accordance with national laws, in order to be legally recognised;

(e) the husband and wife shall, by mutual agreement, choose their matrimonial regime and place of residence;

(f) a married woman shall have the right to retain her maiden name, to use it as she pleases, jointly or separately with her husband's surname;

(g) a woman shall have the right to retain her nationality or to acquire the nationality of her husband;

(h) a woman and a man shall have equal rights, with respect to the nationality of their children except where this is contrary to a provision in national legislation or is contrary to national security interests;

(i) a woman and a man shall jointly contribute to safeguarding the interests of the family, protecting and educating their children;

(j) during her marriage, a woman shall have the right to acquire her own property and to administer and manage it freely.

Article 7   Separation, Divorce and Annulment of Marriage

States Parties shall enact appropriate legislation to ensure that women and men enjoy the same rights in case of separation, divorce or annulment of marriage. In this regard, they shall ensure that:

(a) separation, divorce or annulment of a marriage shall be effected by judicial order;

(b) women and men shall have the same rights to seek separation, divorce or annulment of a marriage;

(c) in case of separation, divorce or annulment of marriage, women and men shall have reciprocal rights and responsibilities towards their children. In any case, the interests of the children shall be given paramount importance;

(d) in case of separation, divorce or annulment of marriage, women and men shall have the right to an equitable sharing of the joint property deriving from the marriage.

Article 8   Access to Justice and Equal Protection before the Law

Women and men are equal before the law and shall have the right to equal protection and benefit of the law. States Parties shall take all appropriate measures to ensure:

(a) effective access by women to judicial and legal services, including legal aid;

(b) support to local, national, regional and continental initiatives directed at providing women access to legal services, including legal aid;

(c) the establishment of adequate educational and other appropriate structures with particular attention to women and to sensitise everyone to the rights of women;

    (d) that law enforcement organs at all levels are equipped to effectively interpret and enforce gender equality rights;
    (e) that women are represented equally in the judiciary and law enforcement organs;
    (f) reform of existing discriminatory laws and practices in order to promote and protect the rights of women.

Article 9   Right to Participation in the Political and Decision-Making Process

1. States Parties shall take specific positive action to promote participative governance and the equal participation of women in the political life of their countries through affirmative action, enabling national legislation and other measures to ensure that:
    (a) women participate without any discrimination in all elections;
    (b) women are represented equally at all levels with men in all electoral processes;
    (c) women are equal partners with men at all levels of development and implementation of State policies and development programmes.
2. States Parties shall ensure increased and effective representation and participation of women at all levels of decision-making.

Article 10   Right to Peace

1. Women have the right to a peaceful existence and the right to participate in the promotion and maintenance of peace.
2. States Parties shall take all appropriate measures to ensure the increased participation of women:
    (a) in programmes of education for peace and a culture of peace;
    (b) in the structures and processes for conflict prevention, management and resolution at local, national, regional, continental and international levels;
    (c) in the local, national, regional, continental and international decision making structures to ensure physical, psychological, social and legal protection of asylum seekers, refugees, returnees and displaced persons, in particular women;
    (d) in all levels of the structures established for the management of camps and settlements for asylum seekers, refugees, returnees and displaced persons, in particular, women;
    (e) in all aspects of planning, formulation and implementation of post conflict reconstruction and rehabilitation.
3. States Parties shall take the necessary measures to reduce military expenditure significantly in favour of spending on social development in general, and the promotion of women in particular.

Article 11   Protection of Women in Armed Conflicts

1. States Parties undertake to respect and ensure respect for the rules of international humanitarian law applicable in armed conflict situations which affect the population, particularly women.
2. States Parties shall, in accordance with the obligations incumbent upon them under the international humanitarian law, protect civilians including women, irrespective of the population to which they belong, in the event of armed conflict.
3. States Parties undertake to protect asylum seeking women, refugees, returnees and internally displaced persons, against all forms of violence, rape and other forms of sexual exploitation, and to ensure that such acts are considered war crimes, genocide and/or crimes against humanity and that their perpetrators are brought to justice before a competent criminal jurisdiction.
4. States Parties shall take all necessary measures to ensure that no child, especially girls under 18 years of age, take a direct part in hostilities and that no child is recruited as a soldier.

Article 12   Right to Education and Training

1. States Parties shall take all appropriate measures to:
    (a) eliminate all forms of discrimination against women and guarantee equal opportunity and access in the sphere of education and training;

  (b) eliminate all stereotypes in textbooks, syllabuses and the media, that perpetuate such discrimination;
  (c) protect women, especially the girl-child from all forms of abuse, including sexual harassment in schools and other educational institutions and provide for sanctions against the perpetrators of such practices;
  (d) provide access to counselling and rehabilitation services to women who suffer abuses and sexual harassment;
  (e) integrate gender sensitisation and human rights education at all levels of education curricula including teacher training.
  2. States Parties shall take specific positive action to:
  (a) promote literacy among women;
  (b) promote education and training for women at all levels and in all disciplines, particularly in the fields of science and technology;
  (c) promote the enrolment and retention of girls in schools and other training institutions and the organisation of programmes for women who leave school prematurely.

Article 13   Economic and Social Welfare Rights

States Parties shall adopt and enforce legislative and other measures to guarantee women equal opportunities in work and career advancement and other economic opportunities. In this respect, they shall:

  (a) promote equality of access to employment;
  (b) promote the right to equal remuneration for jobs of equal value for women and men;
  (c) ensure transparency in recruitment, promotion and dismissal of women and combat and punish sexual harassment in the workplace;
  (d) guarantee women the freedom to choose their occupation, and protect them from exploitation by their employers violating and exploiting their fundamental rights as recognised and guaranteed by conventions, laws and regulations in force;
  (e) create conditions to promote and support the occupations and economic activities of women, in particular, within the informal sector;
  (f) establish a system of protection and social insurance for women working in the informal sector and sensitise them to adhere to it;
  (g) introduce a minimum age for work and prohibit the employment of children below that age, and prohibit, combat and punish all forms of exploitation of children, especially the girl-child;
  (h) take the necessary measures to recognise the economic value of the work of women in the home;
  (i) guarantee adequate and paid pre and post-natal maternity leave in both the private and public sectors;
  (j) ensure the equal application of taxation laws to women and men;
  (k) recognise and enforce the right of salaried women to the same allowances and entitlements as those granted to salaried men for their spouses and children;
  (l) recognise that both parents bear the primary responsibility for the upbringing and development of children and that this is a social function for which the State and the private sector have secondary responsibility;
  (m) take effective legislative and administrative measures to prevent the exploitation and abuse of women in advertising and pornography.

Article 14   Health and Reproductive Rights

  1. States Parties shall ensure that the right to health of women, including sexual and reproductive health is respected and promoted. This includes:
  (a) the right to control their fertility;
  (b) the right to decide whether to have children, the number of children and the spacing of children;

(c) the right to choose any method of contraception;

(d) the right to self protection and to be protected against sexually transmitted infections, including HIV/AIDS;

(e) the right to be informed on one's health status and on the health status of one's partner, particularly if affected with sexually transmitted infections, including HIV/AIDS, in accordance with internationally recognised standards and best practices;

(f) the right to have family planning education.

2. States Parties shall take all appropriate measures to:

(a) provide adequate, affordable and accessible health services, including information, education and communication programmes to women especially those in rural areas;

(b) establish and strengthen existing pre-natal, delivery and post-natal health and nutritional services for women during pregnancy and while they are breast-feeding;

(c) protect the reproductive rights of women by authorising medical abortion in cases of sexual assault, rape, incest, and where the continued pregnancy endangers the mental and physical health of the mother or the life of the mother or the foetus.

Article 15   Right to Food Security

States Parties shall ensure that women have the right to nutritious and adequate food. In this regard, they shall take appropriate measures to:

(a) provide women with access to clean drinking water, sources of domestic fuel, land, and the means of producing nutritious food;

(b) establish adequate systems of supply and storage to ensure food security.

Article 16   Right to Adequate Housing

Women shall have the right to equal access to housing and to acceptable living conditions in a healthy environment. To ensure this right, States Parties shall grant to women, whatever their marital status, access to adequate housing.

Article 17   Right to Positive Cultural Context

1. Women shall have the right to live in a positive cultural context and to participate at all levels in the determination of cultural policies.

2. States Parties shall take all appropriate measures to enhance the participation of women in the formulation of cultural policies at all levels.

Article 18   Right to a Healthy and Sustainable Environment

1. Women shall have the right to live in a healthy and sustainable environment.

2. States Parties shall take all appropriate measures to:

(a) ensure greater participation of women in the planning, management and preservation of the environment and the sustainable use of natural resources at all levels;

(b) promote research and investment in new and renewable energy sources and appropriate technologies, including information technologies and facilitate women's access to, and participation in their control;

(c) protect and enable the development of women's indigenous knowledge systems;

(d) regulate the management, processing, storage and disposal of domestic waste;

(e) ensure that proper standards are followed for the storage, transportation and disposal of toxic waste.

Article 19   Right to Sustainable Development

Women shall have the right to fully enjoy their right to sustainable development. In this connection, the States Parties shall take all appropriate measures to:

(a) introduce the gender perspective in the national development planning procedures;

(b) ensure participation of women at all levels in the conceptualisation, decision-making, implementation and evaluation of development policies and programmes;

(c) promote women's access to and control over productive resources such as land and guarantee their right to property;

(d) promote women's access to credit, training, skills development and extension services at rural and urban levels in order to provide women with a higher quality of life and reduce the level of poverty among women;

(e) take into account indicators of human development specifically relating to women in the elaboration of development policies and programmes; and

(f) ensure that the negative effects of globalisation and any adverse effects of the implementation of trade and economic policies and programmes are reduced to the minimum for women.

Article 20   Widows' Rights

States Parties shall take appropriate legal measures to ensure that widows enjoy all human rights through the implementation of the following provisions:

(a) that widows are not subjected to inhuman, humiliating or degrading treatment;

(b) a widow shall automatically become the guardian and custodian of her children, after the death of her husband, unless this is contrary to the interests and the welfare of the children;

(c) a widow shall have the right to remarry, and in that event, to marry the person of her choice.

Article 21   Right to Inheritance

1. A widow shall have the right to an equitable share in the inheritance of the property of her husband. A widow shall have the right to continue to live in the matrimonial house. In case of remarriage, she shall retain this right if the house belongs to her or she has inherited it.

2. Women and men shall have the right to inherit, in equitable shares, their parents' properties.

Article 22   Special Protection of Elderly Women

The States Parties undertake to:

(a) provide protection to elderly women and take specific measures commensurate with their physical, economic and social needs as well as their access to employment and professional training;

(b) ensure the right of elderly women to freedom from violence, including sexual abuse, discrimination based on age and the right to be treated with dignity.

Article 23   Special Protection of Women with Disabilities

The States Parties undertake to:

(a) ensure the protection of women with disabilities and take specific measures commensurate with their physical, economic and social needs to facilitate their access to employment, professional and vocational training as well as their participation in decision-making;

(b) ensure the right of women with disabilities to freedom from violence, including sexual abuse, discrimination based on disability and the right to be treated with dignity.

Article 24   Special Protection of Women in Distress

The States Parties undertake to:

(a) ensure the protection of poor women and women heads of families including women from marginalized population groups and provide the an environment suitable to their condition and their special physical, economic and social needs;

(b) ensure the right of pregnant or nursing women or women in detention by providing them with an environment which is suitable to their condition and the right to be treated with dignity.

Article 25   Remedies

States Parties shall undertake to:

    (a) provide for appropriate remedies to any woman whose rights or freedoms, as herein recognised, have been violated;

    (b) ensure that such remedies are determined by competent judicial, administrative or legislative authorities, or by any other competent authority provided for by law.

Article 26   Implementation and Monitoring

1. States Parties shall ensure the implementation of this Protocol at national level, and in their periodic reports submitted in accordance with Article 62 of the African Charter, indicate the legislative and other measures undertaken for the full realisation of the rights herein recognised.

2. States Parties undertake to adopt all necessary measures and in particular shall provide budgetary and other resources for the full and effective implementation of the rights herein recognised.

Article 27   Interpretation

The African Court on Human and Peoples' Rights shall be seized with matters of interpretation arising from the application or implementation of this Protocol.

Article 28   Signature, Ratification and Accession

1. This Protocol shall be open for signature, ratification and accession by the States Parties, in accordance with their respective constitutional procedures.

2. The instruments of ratification or accession shall be deposited with the Chairperson of the Commission of the AU.

Article 29   Entry into Force

1. This Protocol shall enter into force thirty (30) days after the deposit of the fifteenth (15) instrument of ratification.

2. For each State Party that accedes to this Protocol after its coming into force, the Protocol shall come into force on the date of deposit of the instrument of accession.

3. The Chairperson of the Commission of the AU shall notify all Member States of the coming into force of this Protocol.

Article 30   Amendment and Revision

1. Any State Party may submit proposals for the amendment or revision of this Protocol.

2. Proposals for amendment or revision shall be submitted, in writing, to the Chairperson of the Commission of the AU who shall transmit the same to the States Parties within thirty (30) days of receipt thereof.

3. The Assembly, upon advice of the African Commission, shall examine these proposals within a period of one (1) year following notification of States Parties, in accordance with the provisions of paragraph 2 of this article.

4. Amendments or revision shall be adopted by the Assembly by a simple majority.

5. The amendment shall come into force for each State Party, which has accepted it thirty (30) days after the Chairperson of the Commission of the AU has received notice of the acceptance.

Article 31   Status of the Present Protocol

None of the provisions of the present Protocol shall affect more favourable provisions for the realisation of the rights of women contained in the national legislation of States Parties or in any other regional, continental or international conventions, treaties or agreements applicable in these States Parties.

Article 32   Transitional Provisions

Pending the establishment of the African Court on Human and Peoples' Rights, the African Commission on Human and Peoples' Rights shall be the seized with matters of interpretation arising from the application and implementation of this Protocol.

Adopted by the 2nd Ordinary Session of the Assembly of the Union, Maputo, 11 July 2003.

Protocol on the Statute of the African Court of Justice and Human Rights (2008)*

The Member States of the African Union, Parties to this Protocol,

Recalling the objectives and principles enunciated in the Constitutive Act of the African Union, adopted on 11 July 2000 in Lomé, Togo, in particular the commitment to settle their disputes through peaceful means;

Bearing in mind their commitment to promote peace, security and stability on the Continent and to protect human and peoples' rights in accordance with the African Charter on Human and Peoples' Rights and other relevant instruments relating to human rights;

Considering that the Constitutive Act of the African Union provides for the establishment of a Court of Justice charged with hearing, among other things, all cases relating to interpretation or application of the said Act or of all other Treaties adopted within the framework of the Union;

Further considering Decisions Assembly/AU/Dec.45 (III) and Assembly/AU/Dec.83 (V) of the Assembly of the Union, adopted respectively at its Third (6–8 July 2004, Addis Ababa, Ethiopia) and Fifth (4–5 July 2005, Sirte, Libya), Ordinary Sessions, to merge the African Court on Human and Peoples' Rights and the Court of Justice of the African Union into a single Court,

Firmly convinced that the establishment of an African Court of Justice and Human Rights shall assist in the achievement of the goals pursued by the African Union and that the attainment of the objectives of the African Charter on Human and Peoples' Rights requires the establishment of a judicial organ to supplement and strengthen the mission of the African Commission on Human and Peoples' Rights as well as the African Committee of Experts on the Rights and Welfare of the Child;

Taking due account of the Protocol to the African Charter on Human and Peoples' Rights on the Establishment an African Court on Human and Peoples' Rights, adopted by the Assembly of Heads of States and Governments of the Organization of African Unity on 10 June 1998 at Ouagadougou, Burkina Faso, and which entered into force on 25 January 2004;

Taking due account also of the Protocol of the Court of Justice of the African Union, adopted by the Assembly of the Union on 11 July 2003 in Maputo Mozambique;

Recalling their commitment to take all necessary measures to strengthen their common institutions and to endow them with the necessary powers and resources to carry out their missions effectively;

Cognizant of the Protocol to the African Charter on Human and Peoples' Rights on the Rights of Women in Africa, and the commitments contained in the Solemn Declaration on the gender equality in Africa (Assembly/AU/Decl.12 (III) adopted by the Assembly of the Union respectively at its Second and Third ordinary sessions held in July 2003 and 2004, in Maputo, Mozambique and in Addis Ababa, Ethiopia);

Convinced that that the present Protocol shall supplement the mandate and efforts of other continental treaty bodies as well as national institutions in protecting human rights:

Have agreed as follows:

Chapter I Merger of the African Court on Human and Peoples' Rights and the Court of Justice of the African Union

Article 1   Replacement of the 1998 and 2003 Protocols

The Protocol to the African Charter on Human and Peoples' Rights on the Establishment of an African Court on Human and Peoples' Rights, adopted on 10 June 1998 in Ouagadougou, Burkina Faso and which entered into force on 25 January 2004, and the Protocol of the Court of Justice of the African Union, adopted on 11 July 2003 in Maputo, Mozambique, are hereby replaced by the present Protocol and Statute annexed as its integral part hereto, subject to the provisions of Article 5, 7 and 9 of this Protocol.

Article 2   Establishment of a single Court

The African Court on Human and Peoples' Rights established by the Protocol to the African Charter on Human and Peoples' Rights on the Establishment of an African Court on Human and Peoples' Rights and the Court of Justice of the African Union established by the Constitutive Act of the African Union, are hereby merged into a single Court and established as 'The African Court of Justice and Human Rights'.

Article 3   Reference to the single Court in the Constitutive Act

References made to the 'Court of Justice' in the Constitutive Act of the African Union shall be read as references to the 'African Court of Justice and Human Rights' established under Article 2 of this Protocol.

Chapter II Transitional Provisions

Article 4   Term of Office of the Judges of the African Court on Human and Peoples' Rights

The term of office of the Judges of the African Court on Human and Peoples' Rights shall end following the election of the Judges of the African Court of Justice and Human Rights. However, the Judges shall remain in office until the newly elected Judges of the African Court of Justice and Human Rights are sworn in.

Article 5   Cases Pending before the African Court on Human and Peoples' Rights

Cases pending before the African Court on Human and Peoples' Rights, that have not been concluded before the entry into force of the present Protocol, shall be transferred to the Human Rights Section of the African Court of Justice and Human Rights on the understanding that such cases shall be dealt with in accordance with the protocol to the ACHPR on the establishment of the African Court on Human and Peoples' Rights.

Article 6   Registry of the Court

The Registrar of the African Court on Human and Peoples' Rights shall remain in office until the appointment of a new Registrar for the African Court of Justice and Human Rights.

Article 7   Provisional validity of the 1998 Protocol

The Protocol to the African Charter on Human and Peoples' Rights on the Establishment of an African Court on Human and Peoples' Rights shall remain in force for a transitional period not exceeding one (1) year or any other period determined by the Assembly, after entry into force of the present Protocol, to enable the African Court on Human and Peoples' Rights to take the necessary measures for the transfer of its prerogatives, assets, rights and obligations to the African Court of Justice and Human Rights.

Chapter III Final Provisions

Article 8   Signature, Ratification and Accession

1. The present Protocol shall be open for signature, ratification or accession by Member States, in accordance with their respective constitutional procedures.

2. The instruments of ratification or accession to the present Protocol shall be deposited with the Chairperson of the Commission of the African Union.

3. Any Member State may, at the time of signature or when depositing its instrument of ratification or accession, or at any time thereafter, make a declaration accepting the competence of the Court to receive cases under Article 30 (f) involving a State which has not made such a declaration.

Article 9   Entry into force

1. The present Protocol and the Statute annexed to it shall enter into force thirty (30) days after the deposit of the instruments of ratification by fifteen (15) Member States.

2. For each Member State which shall ratify or accede to it subsequently, the present Protocol shall enter into force on the date on which the instruments of ratification or accession are deposited,

3. The Chairperson of the Commission shall inform all Member States of the entry into force of the present Protocol.

Adopted by the eleventh Ordinary Session of the Assembly of the Union, Held in Sharm El-Sheikh, Egypt, 1st July 2008

Annex Statute of the African Court of Justice and Human Rights

Chapter I General Provisions

Article 1   Definitions
In this Statute, except otherwise indicated, the following shall mean:

'**African Charter**' means the African Charter on Human and Peoples' Rights;

'**African Commission**' means the African Commission on Human and Peoples' Rights;

'**African Committee of Experts**' means the African Committee of Experts on the Rights and Welfare of the Child;

'**African Intergovernmental Organisations**' means an organisation that has been established with the aim of ensuring socio-economic integration, and to which some Member States have ceded certain competences to act on their behalf, as well as other sub-regional, regional or inter-African Organisations;

'**African Non-Governmental Organizations**' means Non-Governmental Organizations at the sub-regional, regional or inter-African levels as well as those in the Diaspora as may be defined by the Executive Council;

'**Agent**' means a person mandated in writing to represent a party in a case before the Court;

'**Assembly**' means the Assembly of Heads of State and Government of the Union;

'**Chamber(s)**' means a Chamber established in accordance with Article 19 of the Statute.

'**Constitutive Act**' means the Constitutive Act of the African Union;

'**Commission**' means the Commission of the Union;

'**Court**' means the African Court of Justice and Human Rights as well as its sections and chambers;

'**Executive Council**' means the Executive Council of Ministers of the Union;

'**Full Court**' means joint sitting of the General Affairs and Human Rights Sections of the Court;

'**Human Rights Section**' means the Human and Peoples' Rights Section of the Court;

'**Judge**' means a judge of the Court;

'**Member State**' means a Member State of the Union;

'**National Human Rights Institutions**' means public institutions established by a state to promote and protect human rights;

'**President**' means the President of the Court elected in accordance with Article 22(1) of the Statute;

'**Protocol**' means the Protocol to the Statute of the African Court of Justice and Human Rights;

'**Registrar**' means the person appointed as such in accordance with Article 22(4) of the Statute;

'**Rules**' means the Rules of the Court;

'**Section**' means the General Affairs or the Human Rights Section of the Court;

'**Senior Judge**' means the person defined as such in the Rules of Court;

'**States Parties**' means Member States, which have ratified or acceded to this Protocol;

'**Statute**' means the present Statute;

'**Union**' means the African Union established by the Constitutive Act;

'**Vice President**' means the Vice President of the Court elected in accordance with Article 22(1) of the Statute.

Article 2   Functions of the Court

1. The African Court of Justice and Human Rights shall be the main judicial organ of the African Union.

2. The Court shall be constituted and function in accordance with the provisions of the present Statute.

Chapter II Organization of the Court

Article 3   Composition

1. The Court shall consist of sixteen (16) Judges who are nationals of States Parties. Upon recommendation of the Court, the Assembly, may, review the number of Judges.

2. The Court shall not, at any one time, have more than one judge from a single Member State.

3. Each geographical region of the Continent, as determined by the Decisions of the Assembly shall, where possible, be represented by three (3) Judges except the Western Region which shall have four (4) Judges.

Article 4   Qualifications of Judges

The Court shall be composed of impartial and independent Judges elected from among persons of high moral character, who possess the qualifications required in their respective countries for appointment to the highest judicial offices, or are juris-consults of recognized competence and experience in international law and/or, human rights law.

Article 5   Presentation of Candidates

1. As soon as the Protocol to this Statute enters into force, the Chairperson of the Commission shall invite each State Party to submit, in writing, within a period of ninety (90) days, candidatures to the post of judge of the Court.

2. Each State Party may present up to two (2) candidates and shall take into account equitable gender representation in the nomination process.

Article 6   List of candidates

1. For the purpose of election, the Chairperson of the Commission shall establish two alphabetical lists of candidates presented as follows:

   i)   List A containing the names of candidates having recognized competence and experience in International law; and

   ii) List B containing the names of candidates possessing recognized competence and experience in Human Rights law.

2. States Parties that nominate candidates possessing the competences required on the two lists shall choose the list on which their candidates may be placed.

3. At the first election, eight (8) Judges shall be elected from amongst the candidates of list A and eight (8) from among the candidates of list B. The elections shall be organized in a way as to maintain the same proportion of judges elected on the two lists.

4. The Chairperson of the Commission shall communicate the two lists to Member States, at least thirty (30) days before the Ordinary Session of the Assembly or of the Council, during which the elections shall take place.

Article 7   Election of judges

1. The Judges shall be elected by the Executive Council, and appointed by the Assembly.

2. They shall be elected through secret ballot by a two-thirds majority of Member States with voting rights, from among the candidates provided for in Article 6 of this Statute.

3. Candidates who obtain the two-thirds majority and the highest number of votes shall be elected. However, if several rounds of election are required, the candidates with the least number of votes shall withdraw.

4. The Assembly shall ensure that in the Court as a whole there is equitable representation of the regions and the principal legal traditions of the Continent.

5. In the election of the Judges, the Assembly shall ensure that there is equitable gender representation.

Article 8   Term of Office

1. The Judges shall be elected for a period of six (6) years and may be re-elected only once. However, the term of office of eight (8) judges, four (4) from each section, elected during the first election shall end after four (4) years.

2. The Judges, whose term of office shall end after the initial period of four (4) years, shall be determined for each section, by lot drawn by the Chairperson of the Assembly or the Executive Council, immediately after the first election.

3. A Judge, elected to replace another whose term of office has not expired, shall complete the term of office of his predecessor.

4. All the Judges except the President and the Vice-President, shall perform their functions on a part-time basis.

Article 9   Resignation, Suspension and Removal from Office

1. A Judge may resign his/her position in writing addressed to the President for transmission to the Chairperson of the Assembly through the Chairperson of the Commission.

2. A Judge shall not be suspended or removed from office save, where, on the recommendation of two-thirds majority of the other members, he/she no longer meets the requisite conditions to be a Judge.

3. The President shall communicate the recommendation for the suspension or removal of a Judge to the Chairperson of the Assembly through the Chairperson of the Commission.

4. Such a recommendation of the Court shall become final upon its adoption by the Assembly.

Article 10   Vacancies

1. A vacancy shall arise in the Court under the following circumstances:
   a. Death;
   b. Resignation;
   c. Removal from office.

2. In the case of death or resignation of a Judge, the President shall immediately inform the Chairperson of the Assembly through the Chairperson of the Commission in writing, who shall declare the seat vacant.

3. The same procedure and consideration for the election of a Judge shall also be followed in filling the vacancies.

Article 11   Solemn Declaration

1. After the first election, the Judges shall, at the first session of the Court and in the presence of the Chairperson of the Assembly, make a Solemn Declaration as follows:

'I. . . . ., Do solemnly swear (or affirm or declare) that I shall faithfully exercise the duties of my office as Judge of the African Court of Justice and Human Rights of the African Union impartially and conscientiously, without fear or favour, affection or ill will and that I will preserve the integrity of the Court.

2. The Chairperson of the Assembly or his/her duly authorized representative shall administer the Solemn Declaration.

3. Subsequently, the Solemn Declaration shall be made before the President of the Court.

Article 12   Independence

1. The independence of the judges shall be fully ensured in accordance with international law.

2. The Court shall act impartially, fairly and justly.

3. In performance of the judicial functions and duties, the Court and its Judges shall not be subject to the direction or control of any person or body.

Article 13   Conflict of Interest

1. Functions of a Judge are incompatible with all other activities, which might infringe on the need for independence or impartiality of the judicial profession. In case of doubt, the Court shall decide.

2. A Judge shall not exercise the function of agent, or counsel, or lawyer in any case before the Court.

Article 14   Conditions Governing the Participation of Members in the Settlement of a Specific Case

1. Where a particular judge feels he/she has a conflicting interest in a particular case, he/she shall so declare. In any event, he/she shall not participate in the settlement of a case for which he/she was previously involved as agent, counsel or lawyer of one of the parties, or as a member of a national or international Court or Tribunal, or a Commission of enquiry or in any other capacity.

2. If the President considers that a Judge should not participate in a particular case, he/she shall notify the judge concerned. Such notification from the President shall, after agreement by the Court, exclude that Judge from participating in that particular case.

3. A Judge of the nationality of a State Party to a case before the full Court or one of its Sections shall not have the right to sit on the case.

4. Where there is doubt on these points, the Court shall decide.

Article 15   Privileges and Immunities

1. The Judges shall enjoy, from the time of their election and throughout their term of office, the full privileges and immunities extended to diplomatic agents in accordance with international law.

2. The Judges shall be immune from legal proceedings for any act or omission committed in the discharge of their judicial functions.

3. The Judges shall continue, after they have ceased to hold office, to enjoy immunity in respect of acts performed by them when engaged in their official capacity.

Article 16   Sections of the Court

The Court shall have two (2) Sections; a General Affairs Section composed of eight (8) Judges and a Human Rights Section composed of eight (8) Judges.

Article 17   Assignment of matters to Sections

1. The General Affairs Section shall be competent to hear all cases submitted under Article 28 of this Statute save those concerning human and/or peoples' rights issues.

2. The Human Rights Section shall be competent to hear all cases relating to human and/or peoples' rights.

Article 18   Referral of matters to the Full Court

When a Section of the Court is seized with a case, it may, if it deems it necessary refer that case to the Full Court for consideration.

Article 19   Chambers

1. The General Affairs Section and the Human Rights Section may, at any time, constitute one or several chambers. The quorum required to constitute such chambers shall be determined in the Rules of Court.

2. A judgment given by any Section or Chamber shall be considered as rendered by the Court.

Article 20   Sessions

1. The Court shall hold ordinary and extraordinary sessions.

2. The Court shall decide each year on the periods of its ordinary sessions.

3. Extraordinary sessions shall be convened by the President or at the request of the majority of the Judges.

Article 21   Quorum

1. A quorum of nine (9) Judges shall be required for deliberations of the Full Court.

2. A quorum of six (6) Judges shall be required for the deliberations of the General Affairs Section.

3. A quorum of six (6) Judges shall be required for the deliberations of the Human and Peoples' Rights Section.

Article 22   Presidency, Vice-Presidency and Registry

1. At its first ordinary session after the election of the judges, the full Court shall elect its President as well as the Vice-President from the different lists for a period of three (3) years. The President and the Vice-President may be re-elected once.

2. The President shall preside over all sessions of the full Court and those of the Section to which he/she belongs; in the event of being unable to sit, the President shall be replaced by the Vice president for the full Court and by the most Senior Judge for the sessions of his/her Section.

3. The Vice-President shall preside over all sessions of the section to which he/she belongs. In the event of being unable to sit, the Vice-President shall be replaced by the most Senior Judge of that Section.

4. The Court shall appoint a Registrar and may provide for the appointment of such other officers as may be necessary.

5. The President, the Vice-President and the Registrar shall reside at the seat of the Court.

Article 23   Remuneration of Judges

1. The President and the Vice-President shall receive an annual salary and other benefits.

2. The other Judges shall receive a sitting allowance for each day on which he/she exercises his/her functions.

3. These salaries, allowances and compensation shall be determined by the Assembly, on the proposal of the Executive Council. They may not be decreased during the term of office of the Judges.

4. Regulations adopted by the Assembly on the proposal of the Executive Council shall determine the conditions under which retirement pensions shall be given to the Judges as well as the conditions under which their travel expenses shall be paid.

5. The above-mentioned salaries, allowances and compensation shall be free from all taxation.

Article 24   Conditions of Service of the Registrar and Members of the Registry

The salaries and conditions of service of the Registrar and other Court Officials shall be determined by the Assembly on the proposal of the Court, through the Executive Council.

Article 25   Seat and Seal of the Court

1. The Seat of the Court shall be same as the Seat of the African Court on Human and Peoples' Rights. However, the Court may sit in any other Member State, if circumstances warrant, and with the consent of the Member State concerned. The Assembly may change the seat of the Court after due consultations with the Court.

2. The Court shall have a seal bearing the inscription 'The African Court of Justice and Human Rights'.

Article 26   Budget

1. The Court shall prepare its draft annual budget and shall submit it to the Assembly through the Executive Council.

2. The budget of the Court shall be borne by the African Union.

3. The Court shall be accountable for the execution of its budget and shall submit report thereon to the Executive Council in conformity with the Financial Rules and Regulations of the African Union.

Article 27   Rules of Court

1. The Court shall adopt rules for carrying out its functions and the implementation of the present Statute. In particular, it shall lay down its own Rules.

2. In elaborating its Rules, the Court shall bear in mind the complementarity it maintains with the African Commission and the African Committee of Experts.

Chapter III Competence of the Court

Article 28   Jurisdiction of the Court

The Court shall have jurisdiction over all cases and all legal disputes submitted to it in accordance with the present Statute which relate to:

- a) the interpretation and application of the Constitutive Act;
- b) the interpretation, application or validity of other Union Treaties and all subsidiary legal instruments adopted within the framework of the Union or the Organization of African Unity;
- c) the interpretation and the application of the African Charter, the Charter on the Rights and Welfare of the Child, the Protocol to the African Charter on Human and Peoples' Rights on the Rights of Women in Africa, or any other legal instrument relating to human rights, ratified by the States Parties concerned;
- d) any question of international law;
- e) all acts, decisions, regulations and directives of the organs of the Union;
- f) all matters specifically provided for in any other agreements that States Parties may conclude among themselves, or with the Union and which confer jurisdiction on the Court;
- g) the existence of any fact which, if established, would constitute a breach of an obligation owed to a State Party or to the Union;
- h) the nature or extent of the reparation to be made for the breach of an international obligation.

Article 29   Entities Eligible to Submit Cases to the Court

1. The following entities shall be entitled to submit cases to the Court on any issue or dispute provided for in Article 28:

- a) State Parties to the present Protocol;
- b) The Assembly, the Parliament and other organs of the Union authorized by the Assembly;
- c) A staff member of the African Union on appeal, in a dispute and within the limits and under the terms and conditions laid down in the Staff Rules and Regulations of the Union;

2. The Court shall not be open to States, which are not members of the Union. The Court shall also have no jurisdiction to deal with a dispute involving a Member State that has not ratified the Protocol.

Article 30   Other Entities Eligible to Submit Cases to the Court

The following entities shall also be entitled to submit cases to the Court on any violation of a right guaranteed by the African Charter, by the Charter on the Rights and Welfare of the Child, the Protocol to the African Charter on Human and Peoples' Rights on the Rights of Women in Africa, or any other legal instrument relevant to human rights ratified by the States Parties concerned:

- a) State Parties to the present Protocol;
- b) the African Commission on Human and Peoples' Rights;
- c) the African Committee of Experts on the Rights and Welfare of the Child;

d) African Intergovernmental Organizations accredited to the Union or its organs;
e) African National Human Rights Institutions;
f) Individuals or relevant Non-Governmental Organizations accredited to the African Union or to its organs, subject to the provisions of Article 8 of the Protocol.

Article 31   Applicable Law

1. In carrying out its functions, the Court shall have regard to:
   a) The Constitutive Act;
   b) International treaties, whether general or particular, ratified by the contesting States;
   c) International custom, as evidence of a general practice accepted as law;
   d) The general principles of law recognized universally or by African States;
   e) Subject to the provisions of paragraph 1, of Article 46 of the present Statute, judicial decisions and writings of the most highly qualified publicists of various nations as well as the regulations, directives and decisions of the Union, as subsidiary means for the determination of the rules of law;
   f) Any other law relevant to the determination of the case.
2. This Article shall not prejudice the power of the Court to decide a case *ex aequo et bono*, if the parties agree thereto.

Chapter IV Procedure

Article 32   Official Languages

The official and working languages of the Court shall be those of the Union.

Article 33   Institution of Proceedings before the General Affairs Section

1. Cases brought before the Court by virtue of Article 29 of the present Statute shall be submitted by written application addressed to the Registrar. The subject of the dispute, the applicable law and basis of jurisdiction shall be indicated.
2. The Registrar shall forthwith give notice of the application to the Parties concerned.
3. The Registrar shall also notify, through the Chairperson of the Commission, all Member States and, if necessary, the organs of the Union whose decisions are in dispute.

Article 34   Institution of Proceedings before the Human Rights Section

1. Cases brought before the Court relating to an alleged violation of a human or peoples' right shall be submitted by a written application to the Registrar. The application shall indicate the right (s) alleged to have been violated, and, insofar as it is possible, the provision or provisions of the African Charter on Human and Peoples' Rights, the Charter on the Rights and Welfare of the Child, Protocol to the African Charter on Human and Peoples' Rights on the Rights of Women in Africa or any other relevant human rights instrument, ratified by the State concerned, on which it is based.
2. The Registrar shall forthwith give notice of the application to all parties concerned, as well as the Chairperson of the Commission.

Article 35   Provisional Measures

1. The Court shall have the power, on its own motion or on application by the parties, to indicate, if it considers that circumstances so require any provisional measures which ought to be taken to preserve the respective rights of the parties.
2. Pending the final decision, notice of the provisional measures shall forthwith be given to the parties and the Chairperson of the Commission, who shall inform the Assembly.

Article 36   Representation of Parties

1. The States, parties to a case, shall be represented by agents.
2. They may, if necessary, have the assistance of counsel or advocates before the Court.

3. The organs of the Union entitled to appear before the Court shall be represented by the Chairperson of the Commission or his /her representative.

4. The African Commission, the African Committee of Experts, African Inter-Governmental Organizations accredited to the Union or its organs and African National Human Rights Institutions entitled to appear before the Court shall be represented by any person they choose for that purpose.

5. Individuals and Non-Governmental Organizations accredited to the Union or its organs may be represented or assisted by a person of their choice.

6. The agents and other representatives of parties before the Court, their counsel or advocates, witnesses, and any other persons whose presence is required at the Court shall enjoy the privileges and immunities necessary to the independent exercise of their duties or the smooth functioning of the Court.

Article 37   Communications and Notices

1. Communications and notices addressed to agents or counsel of parties to a case shall be considered as addressed to the parties.

2. For the service of all communications or notices upon persons other than the agents, counsel or advocates of parties concerned, the Court shall direct its request to the government of the State upon whose territory the communication or notice has to be served.

3. The same provision shall apply whenever steps are to be taken to procure evidence on the spot.

Article 38   Procedure Before the Court

The procedures before the Court shall be laid out in the Rules of Court, taking into account the complementarity between the Court and other treaty bodies of the Union.

Article 39   Public Hearing

The hearing shall be public, unless the Court, on its own motion or upon application by the parties, decides that the session shall be closed.

Article 40   Record of Proceedings

1. A record of proceedings shall be made at each hearing and shall be signed by the Registrar and the presiding Judge of the session.

2. This record alone shall be authentic.

Article 41   Default Judgment

1. Whenever one of the parties does not appear before the Court, or fails to defend the case against it, the Court shall proceed to consider the case and to give its judgment.

2. The Court shall before doing so, satisfy itself, not only that it has jurisdiction in accordance with Articles 28, 29 and 30 of the present Statute, but also that the claim is well founded in fact and law, and that the other party had due notice.

3. An objection by the party concerned may be lodged against the judgment within ninety (90) days of it being notified of the default judgment. Unless there is a decision to the contrary by the Court, the objection shall not have effect of staying the enforcement of the default judgment.

Article 42   Majority Required for Decision of the Court

1. Without prejudice to the provisions of Article 50(4) of the present Statute, the decisions of the Court shall be decided by a majority of the Judges present.

2. In the event of an equality of votes, the presiding Judge shall have a casting vote.

Article 43   Judgments and Decisions

1. The Court shall render its judgment within ninety (90) days of having completed its deliberations.

2. All judgments shall state the reasons on which they are based.

3. The judgment shall contain the names of the Judges who have taken part in the decision.

4. The judgment shall be signed by all the Judges and certified by the Presiding Judge and the Registrar. It shall be read in open session, due notice having been given to the agents.

5. The Parties to the case shall be notified of the judgment of the Court and it shall be transmitted to the Member States and the Commission.

6. The Executive Council shall also be notified of the judgment and shall monitor its execution on behalf of the Assembly.

Article 44   Dissenting Opinion

If the judgment does not represent in whole or in part the unanimous opinion of the Judges, any Judge shall be entitled to deliver a separate or dissenting opinion.

Article 45   Compensation

Without prejudice to its competence to rule on issues of compensation at the request of a party by virtue of paragraph 1(h), of Article 28 of the present Statute, the Court may, if it considers that there was a violation of a human or peoples' right, order any appropriate measures in order to remedy the situation, including granting fair compensation.

Article 46   Binding Force and Execution of Judgments

1. The decision of the Court shall be binding on the parties.

2. Subject to the provisions of paragraph 3, Article 41 of the present Statute, the judgment of the Court is final.

3. The parties shall comply with the judgment made by the Court in any dispute to which they are parties within the time stipulated by the Court and shall guarantee its execution.

4. Where a party has failed to comply with a judgment, the Court shall refer the matter to the Assembly, which shall decide upon measures to be taken to give effect to that judgment.

5. The Assembly may impose sanctions by virtue of paragraph 2 of Article 23 of the Constitutive Act.

Article 47   Interpretation

In the event of any dispute as to the meaning or scope of a judgment, the Court shall construe it upon the request of any party.

Article 48   Revision

1. An application for revision of a judgment may be made to the Court only when it is based upon discovery of a new fact of such nature as to be a decisive factor, which fact was, when the judgment was given, unknown to the Court and also to the party claiming revision, provided that such ignorance was not due to negligence.

2. The proceedings for revision shall be opened by a ruling of the Court expressly recording the existence of the new fact, recognizing that it has such a character as to lay the case open to revision, and declaring the revision admissible on this ground.

3. The Court may require prior compliance with the terms of the judgment before it admits proceedings in revision.

4. The application for revision shall be made within six (6) months of the discovery of the new fact.

5. No application may be made after the lapse of ten (10) years from the date of the judgment.

Article 49   Intervention

1. Should a Member State or organ of the Union consider that it has an interest of a legal nature which may be affected by the decision in the case, it may submit a request to the Court to be permitted to intervene. It shall be for the Court to decide upon this request.

2. If a Member State or organ of the Union should exercise the option offered under paragraph 1 of the present Article, the interpretation contained in the decision shall be equally binding upon it.

3. In the interest of the effective administration of justice, the Court may invite any Member State that is not a party to the case, any organ of the Union or any person concerned other than the claimant, to present written observations or take part in hearings.

Article 50   Intervention in a Case Concerning the Interpretation of the Constitutive Act

1. Whenever the question of interpretation of the Constitutive Act arises, in a case in which Member States other than the parties to the dispute have expressed an interest, the Registrar shall notify all such States and organs of the Union forthwith.

2. Every State Party and organ of the Union so notified has the right to intervene in the proceedings.

3. The decisions of the Court concerning the interpretation and application of the Constitutive Act shall be binding on Member States and organs of the Union, notwithstanding the provisions of paragraph 1, of Article 46 of this Statute.

4. Any decision made by virtue of this Article shall be made by a qualified majority of at least two (2) votes and in the presence of at least two-thirds of the Judges.

Article 51   Intervention in a Case concerning the Interpretation of Other Treaties

1. Whenever the question is that of interpretation of other treaties ratified by Member States other than the parties to a dispute, the Registrar shall notify all such States and the organs of the Union forthwith.

2. Every State Party and organ of the Union so notified has the right to intervene in the proceedings, and if it exercises this right, the interpretation given by the judgment shall be equally binding upon it.

3. This Article shall not be applicable to cases relating to alleged violations of a human or peoples' right, submitted by virtue of Articles 29 or 30 of the present Statute.

Article 52   Costs

1. Unless otherwise decided by the Court, each party shall bear its own costs.

2. Should it be required in the interest of justice, free legal aid may be provided for the person presenting an individual communication, under conditions to be set out in the Rules of Court.

Chapter V Advisory Opinion

Article 53 Request for Advisory Opinion

1. The Court may give an advisory opinion on any legal question at the request of the Assembly, the Parliament, the Executive Council, the Peace and Security Council, the Economic, Social and Cultural Council (ECOSOCC), the Financial Institutions or any other organ of the Union as may be authorized by the Assembly.

2. A request for an advisory opinion shall be in writing and shall contain an exact statement of the question upon which the opinion is required and shall be accompanied by all relevant documents.

3. A request for an advisory opinion must not be related to a pending application before the African Commission or the African Committee of Experts.

Article 54 Service of Notice

1. The Registrar shall forthwith give notice of the request for an advisory opinion to all States or organs entitled to appear before the Court by virtue of Article 30 of the present Statute.

2. The Registrar shall also, by means of a special and direct communication, notify any State entitled to appear before the Court or any Intergovernmental Organization considered by the Court, or should it not be sitting, by the President, as likely to be able to furnish information on the question, that the Court will be prepared to receive, within a time limit to be fixed by the President, written statements, or to hear, at a public sitting to be held for the purpose, oral statements relating to the question.

3. Should any such State entitled to appear before the Court have failed to receive the special communication referred to in paragraph 2 of this Article, such State may express the desire to submit a written statement or to be heard, and the Court shall decide.

4. States and organizations having presented written or oral statements or both shall be permitted to comment on the statements made by other States or organizations in the form, to the extent, and within the time limits which the Court, or should it not be sitting, the President, shall decide in each particular case. Accordingly, the Registrar shall in due course communicate any such written statements to States and organizations having submitted similar statements.

Article 55   Delivery of Advisory Opinion
The Court shall deliver its advisory opinion in open court, notice having been given to the Chairperson of the Commission and Member States, and other International Organizations directly concerned.

Article 56   Application by Analogy of the Provisions of the Statute Applicable to Contentious Cases
In the exercise of its advisory functions, the Court shall further be guided by the provisions of the present Statute which apply in contentious cases to the extent to which it recognizes them to be applicable.

Chapter VI Report to the Assembly

Article 57   Annual Activity Report
The Court shall submit to the Assembly, an annual report on its work during the previous year. The report shall specify, in particular, the cases in which a party has not complied with the judgment of the Court.

Chapter VII Procedure for Amendments

Article 58   Proposed Amendments from a State Party
1. The present Statute may be amended if a State Party makes a written request to that effect to the Chairperson of the Commission, who shall transmit same to Member States within thirty (30) days of receipt thereof.

2. The Assembly may adopt by a simple majority, the proposed amendment after the Court has given its opinion on it.

Article 59   Proposed Amendments from the Court
The Court may propose such amendments to the present Statute as it may deem necessary, to the Assembly through written communication to the Chairperson of the Commission, for consideration in conformity with the provisions of Article 58 of the present Statute.

Article 60   Entry into Force of Amendments
The amendment shall enter into force for every State which has accepted it in conformity with its Constitutional laws thirty (30) days after the Chairperson of the Commission is notified of this acceptance.

African Charter on the Rights and Welfare of the Child (1990)*

PREAMBLE

The African Member States of the Organization of African Unity, Parties to the present Charter entitled 'African Charter on the Rights and Welfare of the Child',

Considering that the Charter of the Organization of African Unity recognizes the paramountcy of human rights and the African Charter on Human and Peoples' Rights proclaimed and agreed that everyone is entitled to all the rights and freedoms recognized and guaranteed therein, without distinction of any kind such as race, ethnic group, colour, sex, language, religion, political or any other opinion, national and social origin, fortune, birth or other status,

Recalling the Declaration on the Rights and Welfare of the African Child (AHG/ ST.4 (XVI) Rev. 1) adopted by the Assembly of Heads of State and Government of the Organization of African Unity at its Sixteenth Ordinary Session in Monrovia, Liberia, from 17 to 20 July 1979, which recognized the need to take all appropriate measures to promote and protect the rights and welfare of the African Child,

Noting with concern that the situation of most African children remains critical due to the unique factors of their socio-economic, cultural, traditional and developmental circumstances, natural disasters, armed conflicts, exploitation and hunger, and on account of the child's physical and mental immaturity he/she needs special safeguards and care,

Recognizing that the child occupies a unique and privileged position in the African society and that for the full and harmonious development of his personality the child should grow up in a family environment in an atmosphere of happiness, love and understanding,

Recognizing that the child, due to the needs of his physical and mental development, requires particular care with regard to health, physical, mental, moral and social development, and requires legal protection in conditions of freedom, dignity and security,

Taking into consideration the virtues of their cultural heritage, historical background and the values of the African civilization which should inspire and characterize their reflection on the concept of the rights and welfare of the child,

Considering that the promotion and protection of the rights and welfare of the child also implies the performance of duties on the part of everyone,

Reaffirming adherence to the principles of the rights and welfare of the child contained in the declarations, conventions and other instruments of the Organization of African Unity and of the United Nations and in particular the United Nations Convention on the Rights of the Child and the OAU Heads of State and Governments' Declaration on the Rights and Welfare of the African Child,

Have agreed as follows:

PART I RIGHTS AND DUTIES

Chapter One Rights and Welfare of the Child

Article 1   Obligation of States Parties

1. The Member States of the Organization of African Unity Parties to the present Charter shall recognize the rights, freedoms and duties enshrined in this Charter and shall undertake to take the necessary steps, in accordance with their constitutional processes and with the provisions of the present Charter, to adopt such legislative or other measures as may be necessary to give effect to the provisions of this Charter.

---

* © The African Union Commission

2. Nothing in this Charter shall affect any provisions that are more conducive to the realization of the rights and welfare of the child contained in the law of a State Party or in any other international convention or agreement in force in that State.

3. Any custom, tradition, or cultural or religious practice that is inconsistent with the rights, duties and obligations contained in the present Charter shall to the extent of such inconsistency be discouraged.

Article 2   Definition of a child
For the purposes of this Charter, a child means every human being below the age of 18 years.

Article 3   Non-discrimination
Every child shall be entitled to the enjoyment of the rights and freedoms recognized and guaranteed in this Charter irrespective of the child's or his/her parents' or legal guardians' race, ethnic group, colour, sex, language, religion, political or other opinion, national and social origin, fortune, birth or other status.

Article 4   Best interests of the child
1. In all actions concerning the child undertaken by any person or authority the best interests of the child shall be the primary consideration.

2. In all judicial or administrative proceedings affecting a child who is capable of communicating his/her own views, an opportunity shall be provided for the views of the child to be heard either directly or through an impartial representative as a party to the proceedings, and those views shall be taken into consideration by the relevant authority in accordance with the provisions of appropriate law.

Article 5   Survival and development
1. Every child has an inherent right to life. This right shall be protected by law.

2. States Parties to the present Charter shall ensure, to the maximum extent possible, the survival, protection and development of the child.

3. The death sentence shall not be pronounced for crimes committed by children.

Article 6   Name and nationality
1. Every child shall have the right from his birth to a name.

2. Every child shall be registered immediately after birth.

3. Every child has the right to acquire a nationality.

4. States Parties to the present Charter shall undertake to ensure that their constitutional legislation recognizes the principles according to which a child shall acquire the nationality of the State in the territory of which he has been born if, at the time of the child's birth, he is not granted nationality by any other State in accordance with its laws.

Article 7   Freedom of expression
Every child who is capable of communicating his or her own views shall be assured the rights to express his opinions freely in all matters and to disseminate his opinions subject to such restrictions as are prescribed by laws.

Article 8   Freedom of association
Every child shall have the right to free association and freedom of peaceful assembly in conformity with the law.

Article 9   Freedom of thought, conscience and religion
1. Every child shall have the right to freedom of thought, conscience and religion.

2. Parents and, where applicable, legal guardians shall have a duty to provide guidance and direction in the exercise of these rights having regard to the evolving capacities and best interests of the child.

3. States Parties shall respect the duty of parents and, where applicable, legal guardians to provide guidance and direction in the enjoyment of these rights subject to the national laws and policies.

Article 10   Protection of privacy

No child shall be subject to arbitrary or unlawful interference with his privacy, family, home or correspondence, or to attacks upon his honour or reputation, provided that parents or legal guardians shall have the right to exercise reasonable supervision over the conduct of their children. The child has the right to the protection of the law against such interference or attacks.

Article 11   Education

1. Every child shall have the right to education.
2. The education of the child shall be directed to:
    (a) the promotion and development of the child's personality, talents and mental and physical abilities to their fullest potential;
    (b) fostering respect for human rights and fundamental freedoms with particular reference to those set out in the provisions of various African instruments on human and peoples' rights and international human rights declarations and conventions;
    (c) the preservation and strengthening of positive African morals, traditional values and cultures;
    (d) the preparation of the child for responsible life in a free society, in the spirit of understanding, tolerance, dialogue, mutual respect and friendship among all peoples and ethnic, tribal and religious groups;
    (e) the preservation of national independence and territorial integrity;
    (f) the promotion and achievement of African unity and solidarity;
    (g) the development of respect for the environment and natural resources;
    (h) the promotion of the child's understanding of primary health care.
3. States Parties to the present Charter shall take all appropriate measures with a view to achieving the full realization of this right and shall in particular:
    (a) provide free and compulsory basic education;
    (b) encourage the development of secondary education in its different forms and to progressively make it free and accessible to all;
    (c) make higher education accessible to all on the basis of capacity and ability by every appropriate means;
    (d) take measures to encourage regular attendance at schools and the reduction of the drop-out rate;
    (e) take special measures in respect of female, gifted and disadvantaged children, to ensure equal access to education for all sections of the community.
4. States Parties to the present Charter shall respect the rights and duties of parents and, where applicable, of legal guardians to choose for their children schools other than those established by public authorities, which conform to such minimum standards as may be approved by the State, to ensure the religious and moral education of the child in a manner consistent with the evolving capacities of the child.
5. States Parties to the present Charter shall take all appropriate measures to ensure that a child who is subjected to school or parental discipline shall be treated with humanity and with respect for the inherent dignity of the child and in conformity with the present Charter.
6. States Parties to the present Charter shall take all appropriate measures to ensure that children who become pregnant before completing their education shall have an opportunity to continue with their education on the basis of their individual ability.
7. No part of this Article shall be construed as to interfere with the liberty of individuals and bodies to establish and direct educational institutions subject to the observance of the principles set out in paragraph 2 of this Article and the requirement that the education given in such institutions shall conform to such minimum standards as may be laid down by the State.

Article 12   Leisure, recreation and cultural activities

1. States Parties recognize the right of the child to rest and leisure, to engage in play and recreational activities appropriate to the age of the child and to participate freely in cultural life and the arts.

2. States Parties shall respect and promote the right of the child to fully participate in cultural and artistic life and shall encourage the provision of appropriate and equal opportunities for cultural, artistic, recreational and leisure activity.

Article 13   Handicapped children

1. Every child who is mentally or physically disabled shall have the right to special measures of protection in keeping with his physical and moral needs and under conditions which ensure his dignity and promote his self-reliance and active participation in the community.

2. States Parties to the present Charter shall ensure, subject to available resources, to a disabled child and to those responsible for his care, assistance for which application is made and which is appropriate to the child's condition and in particular shall ensure that the disabled child has effective access to training, preparation for employment and recreation opportunities in a manner conducive to the child achieving the fullest possible social integration, individual development and his cultural and moral development.

3. States Parties to the present Charter shall use their available resources with a view to achieving progressively the full convenience of the mentally and physically disabled person to movement and access to public highway buildings and other places to which the disabled may legitimately want to have access.

Article 14   Health and health services

1. Every child shall have the right to enjoy the best attainable state of physical, mental and spiritual health.

2. States Parties to the present Charter shall undertake to pursue the full implementation of this right and in particular shall take measures:
   - (a) to reduce infant and child mortality rate;
   - (b) to ensure the provision of necessary medical assistance and health care to all children with emphasis on the development of primary health care;
   - (c) to ensure the provision of adequate nutrition and safe drinking water;
   - (d) to combat disease and malnutrition within the framework of primary health care through the application of appropriate technology;
   - (e) to ensure appropriate health care for expectant and nursing mothers;
   - (f) to develop preventive health care and family life education and provision of service;
   - (g) to integrate basic health service programmes in national development plans;
   - (h) to ensure that all sectors of the society, in particular parents, children, community leaders and community workers, are informed and supported in the use of basic knowledge of child health and nutrition, the advantages of breast-feeding, hygiene and environmental sanitation and the prevention of domestic and other accidents;
   - (i) to ensure the meaningful participation of non-governmental organizations, local communities and the beneficiary population in the planning and management of a basic service programme for children;
   - (j) to support through technical and financial means the mobilization of local community resources in the development of primary health care for children.

Article 15   Child labour

1. Every child shall be protected from all forms of economic exploitation and from performing any work that is likely to be hazardous or to interfere with the child's physical, mental, spiritual, moral, or social development.

2. States Parties to the present Charter shall take all appropriate legislative and administrative measures to ensure the full implementation of this Article which covers both the formal and informal

sectors of employment and, having regard to the relevant provisions of the International Labour Organisation's instruments relating to children, States Parties shall in particular:

    (a) provide, through legislation, minimum ages for admission to every employment;

    (b) provide for appropriate regulation of hours and conditions of employment;

    (c) provide for appropriate penalties or other sanctions to ensure the effective enforcement of this Article;

    (d) promote the dissemination of information on the hazards of child labour to all sectors of the community.

Article 16   Protection against child abuse and torture

1. States Parties to the present Charter shall take specific legislative, administrative, social and educational measures to protect the child from all forms of torture, inhuman or degrading treatment and especially physical or mental injury or abuse, neglect or maltreatment including sexual abuse, while in the care of a parent, legal guardian or school authority or any other person who has the care of the child.

2. Protective measures under this Article shall include effective procedures for the establishment of special monitoring units to provide necessary support for the child and for those who have the care of the child, as well as other forms of prevention, and for identification, reporting, referral, investigation, treatment and follow-up of instances of child abuse and neglect.

Article 17 Administration of juvenile justice

1. Every child accused or found guilty of having infringed penal law shall have the right to special treatment in a manner consistent with the child's sense of dignity and worth and which reinforces the child's respect for human rights and fundamental freedoms of others.

2. States Parties to the present Charter shall in particular:

    (a) ensure that no child who is detained or imprisoned or otherwise deprived of his/her liberty is subjected to torture or inhuman or degrading treatment or punishment;

    (b) ensure that children are separated from adults in their place of detention or imprisonment;

    (c) ensure that every child accused of infringing the penal law:

        (i)   shall be presumed innocent until duly recognized guilty;

        (ii) shall be informed promptly in a language that he understands and in detail of the charge against him, and shall be entitled to the assistance of an interpreter if he or she cannot understand the language used;

        (iii) shall be afforded legal and other appropriate assistance in the preparation and presentation of his defence;

        (iv) shall have the matter determined as speedily as possible by an impartial tribunal and, if found guilty, be entitled to an appeal to a higher tribunal;

        (v) shall not be compelled to give testimony or confess guilt;

    (d) prohibit the press and the public from the trial.

3. The essential aim of treatment of every child during the trial and also if found guilty of infringing the penal law shall be his or her reformation, re-integration into his or her family and social rehabilitation.

4. There shall be a minimum age below which children shall be presumed not to have the capacity to infringe the penal law.

Article 18   Protection of the family

1. The family shall be the natural unit and basis of society. It shall enjoy the protection and support of the State for its establishment and development.

2. States Parties to the present Charter shall take appropriate steps to ensure equality of rights and responsibilities of spouses with regard to children during marriage and in the event of its dissolution. In case of dissolution, provision shall be made for the necessary protection of the child.

3. No child shall be deprived of maintenance by reference to the parents' marital status.

Article 19   Parental care and protection

1. Every child shall be entitled to the enjoyment of parental care and protection and shall, whenever possible, have the right to reside with his or her parents. No child shall be separated from his parents against his will, except when a judicial authority determines, in accordance with the appropriate law, that such separation is in the best interest of the child.

2. Every child who is separated from one or both parents shall have the right to maintain personal relations and direct contact with both parents on a regular basis.

3. Where separation results from the action of a State Party, the State Party shall provide the child or, if appropriate, another member of the family with essential information concerning the whereabouts of the absent member or members of the family. States Parties shall also ensure that the submission of such a request shall not entail any adverse consequences for the person or persons in whose respect it is made.

4. Where a child is apprehended by a State Party, his parents or guardians shall, as soon as possible, be notified of such apprehension by that State Party.

Article 20   Parental responsibilities

1. Parents or other persons responsible for the child shall have the primary responsibility for the upbringing and development of the child and shall have the duty:
    (a) to ensure that the best interests of the child are their basic concern at all times;
    (b) to secure, within their abilities and financial capacities, conditions of living necessary to the child's development; and
    (c) to ensure that domestic discipline is administered with humanity and in a manner consistent with the inherent dignity of the child.

2. States Parties to the present Charter shall in accordance with their means and national conditions take all appropriate measures:
    (a) to assist parents and other persons responsible for the child and in case of need provide material assistance and support programmes particularly with regard to nutrition, health, education, clothing and housing;
    (b) to assist parents and others responsible for the child in the performance of child-rearing and ensure the development of institutions responsible for providing care of children; and
    (c) to ensure that the children of working parents are provided with care services and facilities.

Article 21   Protection against harmful social and cultural practices

1. States Parties to the present Charter shall take all appropriate measures to eliminate harmful social and cultural practices affecting the welfare, dignity, normal growth and development of the child and in particular:
    (a) those customs and practices prejudicial to the health or life of the child; and
    (b) those customs and practices discriminatory to the child on the grounds of sex or other status.

2. Child marriage and the betrothal of girls and boys shall be prohibited and effective action, including legislation, shall be taken to specify the minimum age of marriage to be eighteen years and make registration of all marriages in an official registry compulsory.

Article 22   Armed conflicts

1. States Parties to this Charter shall undertake to respect and ensure respect for rules of international humanitarian law applicable in armed conflicts which affect the child.

2. States Parties to the present Charter shall take all necessary measures to ensure that no child shall take a direct part in hostilities and refrain, in particular, from recruiting any child.

3. States Parties to the present Charter shall, in accordance with their obligations under international humanitarian law, protect the civilian population in armed conflicts and shall take all feasible measures to ensure the protection and care of children who are affected by armed conflicts. Such rules shall also apply to children in situations of internal armed conflicts, tension and strife.

Article 23   Refugee children

1. States Parties to the present Charter shall take all appropriate measures to ensure that a child who is seeking refugee status or who is considered a refugee in accordance with applicable international or domestic law shall, whether unaccompanied or accompanied by parents, legal guardians or close relatives, receive appropriate protection and humanitarian assistance in the enjoyment of the rights set out in this Charter and other international human rights and humanitarian instruments to which the States are parties.

2. States Parties shall undertake to cooperate with existing international organizations which protect and assist refugees in their efforts to protect and assist such a child and to trace the parents or other close relatives of an unaccompanied refugee child in order to obtain information necessary for reunification with the family.

3. Where no parents, legal guardians or close relatives can be found, the child shall be accorded the same protection as any other child permanently or temporarily deprived of his family environment for any reason.

4. The provisions of this Article apply *mutatis mutandis* to internally displaced children whether through natural disaster, internal armed conflicts, civil strife, breakdown of economic and social order or howsoever caused.

Article 24   Adoption

States Parties which recognize the system of adoption shall ensure that the best interest of the child shall he the paramount consideration and they shall:

(a) establish competent authorities to determine matters of adoption and ensure that the adoption is carried out in conformity with applicable laws and procedures and on the basis of all relevant and reliable information, that the adoption is permissible in view of the child's status concerning parents, relatives and guardians and that, if necessary, the appropriate persons concerned have given their informed consent to the adoption on the basis of appropriate counselling;

(b) recognize that inter-country adoption in those States which have ratified or adhered to the Convention on the Rights of the Child or this Charter may, as the last resort, be considered as an alternative means of child's care, if the child cannot be placed in a foster or an adoptive family or cannot in any suitable manner be cared for in the child's country of origin;

(c) ensure that the child affected by inter-country adoption enjoys safeguards and standards equivalent to those existing in the case of national adoption;

(d) take all appropriate measures to ensure that, in inter-country adoption, the placement does not result in trafficking or improper financial gain for those who try to adopt a child;

(e) promote, where appropriate, the objectives of this Article by concluding bilateral or multilateral arrangements or agreements, and endeavour within this framework to ensure that the placement of the child in another country is carried out by competent authorities or organs;

(f) establish a machinery to monitor the well-being of the adopted child.

Article 25   Separation from parents

1. Any child who is permanently or temporarily deprived of his family environment for any reason shall be entitled to special protection and assistance.

2. States Parties to the present Charter:

(a) shall ensure that a child who is parentless, or who is temporarily or permanently deprived of his or her family environment, or who in his or her best interest cannot be brought up or allowed to remain in that environment, shall be provided with alternative family care, which could include, among others, foster placement, or placement in suitable institutions for the care of children;

(b) shall take all necessary measures to trace and re-unite children with parents or relatives where separation is caused by internal and external displacement arising from armed conflicts or natural disasters.

3. When considering alternative family care of the child and the best interests of the child, due regard shall be paid to the desirability of continuity in a child's upbringing and to the child's ethnic, religious or linguistic background.

Article 26　Protection against *Apartheid* and discrimination

1. States Parties to the present Charter shall individually and collectively undertake to accord the highest priority to the special needs of children living under *Apartheid* and in States subject to military destabilization by the *Apartheid* regime.

2. States Parties to the present Charter shall individually and collectively undertake to accord the highest priority to the special needs of children living under regimes practising racial, ethnic, religious or other forms of discrimination as well as in States subject to military destabilization.

3. States Parties shall undertake to provide, whenever possible, material assistance to such children and to direct their efforts towards the elimination of all forms of discrimination and *Apartheid* on the African continent.

Article 27　Sexual exploitation

States Parties to the present Charter shall undertake to protect the child from all forms of sexual exploitation and sexual abuse and shall in particular take measures to prevent:

    (a)　the inducement, coercion or encouragement of a child to engage in any sexual activity;

    (b)　the use of children in prostitution or other sexual practices;

    (c)　the use of children in pornographic activities, performances and materials.

Article 28　Drug abuse

States Parties to the present Charter shall take all appropriate measures to protect the child from the use of narcotics and illicit use of psychotropic substances as defined in the relevant international treaties, and to prevent the use of children in the production and trafficking of such substances.

Article 29　Sale, trafficking and abduction

States Parties to the present Charter shall take appropriate measures to prevent:

    (a)　the abduction, the sale of, or traffic in children for any purpose or in any form, by any person including parents or legal guardians of the child;

    (b)　the use of children in all forms of begging.

Article 30　Children of imprisoned mothers

States Parties to the present Charter shall undertake to provide special treatment to expectant mothers and to mothers of infants and young children who have been accused or found guilty of infringing the penal law and shall in particular:

    (a)　ensure that a non-custodial sentence will always be first considered when sentencing such mothers;

    (b)　establish and promote measures alternative to institutional confinement for the treatment of such mothers;

    (c)　establish special alternative institutions for holding such mothers;

    (d)　ensure that a mother shall not be imprisoned with her child;

    (e)　ensure that a death sentence shall not be imposed on such mothers;

    (f)　ensure that the essential aim of the penitentiary system will be reformation, the integration of the mother to the family and social rehabilitation.

Article 31　Responsibilities of the child

Every child shall have responsibilities towards his family and society, the State and other legally recognized communities and the international community. The child, subject to his age and ability, and such limitations as may be contained in the present Charter, shall have the duty:

    (a)　to work for the cohesion of the family, to respect his parents, superiors and elders at all times and to assist them in case of need;

(b) to serve his national community by placing his physical and intellectual abilities at its service;

(c) to preserve and strengthen social and national solidarity;

(d) to preserve and strengthen African cultural values in his relations with other members of the society, in the spirit of tolerance, dialogue and consultation and to contribute to the moral well-being of society;

(e) to preserve and strengthen the independence and the integrity of his country;

(f) to contribute to the best of his abilities, at all times and at all levels, to the promotion and achievement of African unity.

PART II

Chapter Two   Establishment and Organization of the Committee on the Rights and Welfare of the Child

Article 32   The Committee

An African Committee of Experts on the Rights and Welfare of the Child hereinafter called 'the Committee' shall be established within the Organization of African Unity to promote and protect the rights and welfare of the child.

Article 33   Composition

1. The Committee shall consist of 11 members of high moral standing, integrity, impartiality and competence in matters of the rights and welfare of the child.

2. The members of the Committee shall serve in their personal capacity.

3. The Committee shall not include more than one national of the same State.

Article 34   Election

As soon as this Charter shall enter into force the members of the Committee shall be elected by secret ballot by the Assembly of Heads of State and Government from a list of persons nominated by the States Parties to the present Charter.

Article 35   Candidates

Each State Party to the present Charter may nominate not more than two candidates. The candidates must have one of the nationalities of the States Parties to the present Charter. When two candidates are nominated by a State, one of them shall not be a national of that State.

Article 36

1. The Secretary-General of the Organization of African Unity shall invite States Parties to the present Charter to nominate candidates at least six months before the elections.

2. The Secretary-General of the Organization of African Unity shall draw up in alphabetical order a list of persons nominated and communicate it to the Heads of State and Government at least two months before the elections.

Article 37   Term of office

1. The members of the Committee shall be elected for a term of five years and may not be re-elected; however, the term of four of the members elected at the first election shall expire after two years and the term of six others, after four years.

2. Immediately after the first election, the Chairman of the Assembly of Heads of State and Government of the Organization of African Unity shall draw lots to determine the names of those members referred to in paragraph 1 of this Article.

3. The Secretary-General of the Organization of African Unity shall convene the first meeting of the Committee at the Headquarters of the Organization within six months of the election of the members of the Committee, and thereafter the Committee shall be convened by its Chairman whenever necessary, at least once a year.

Article 38   Bureau

1. The Committee shall establish its own Rules of Procedure.
2. The Committee shall elect its officers for a period of two years.
3. Seven Committee members shall form the quorum.
4. In case of an equality of votes, the Chairman shall have a casting vote.
5. The working languages of the Committee shall be the official languages of the OAU.

Article 39   Vacancy

If a member of the Committee vacates his office for any reason other than the normal expiration of a term, the State which nominated that member shall appoint another member from among its nationals to serve for the remainder of the term—subject to the approval of the Assembly.

Article 40   Secretariat

The Secretary-General of the Organization of African Unity shall appoint a Secretary for the Committee.

Article 41   Privileges and immunities

In discharging their duties, members of the Committee shall enjoy the privileges and immunities provided for in the General Convention on the Privileges and Immunities of the Organization of African Unity.

Chapter Three   Mandate and Procedure of the Committee

Article 42   Mandate

The functions of the Committee shall be:

(a) To promote and protect the rights enshrined in this Charter and in particular to:

    (i)   collect and document information, commission inter-disciplinary assessment of situations on African problems in the fields of the rights and welfare of the child, organize meetings, encourage national and local institutions concerned with the rights and welfare of the child, and where necessary give its views and make recommendations to Governments;

    (ii) formulate and lay down principles and rules aimed at protecting the rights and welfare of children in Africa;

    (iii) cooperate with other African, international and regional institutions and organizations concerned with the promotion and protection of the rights and welfare of the child;

(b) To monitor the implementation and ensure protection of the rights enshrined in this Charter;

(c) To interpret the provisions of the present Charter at the request of a State Party, an institution of the Organization of African Unity or any other person or institution recognized by the Organization of African Unity or any State Party;

(d) To perform such other tasks as may be entrusted to it by the Assembly of Heads of State and Government, the Secretary-General of the OAU and any other organs of the OAU, or the United Nations.

Article 43   Reporting procedure

1. Every State Party to the present Charter shall undertake to submit to the Committee, through the Secretary-General of the Organization of African Unity, reports on the measures they have adopted which give effect to the provisions of this Charter and on the progress made in the enjoyment of these rights:

(a) within two years of the entry into force of the Charter for the State Party concerned; and

(b) thereafter, every three years.

2. Every report made under this Article shall:
  (a) contain sufficient information on the implementation of the present Charter to provide the Committee with comprehensive understanding of the implementation of the Charter in the relevant country; and
  (b) indicate factors and difficulties, if any, affecting the fulfilment of the obligations contained in the Charter.

3. A State Party which has submitted a comprehensive first report to the Committee need not, in its subsequent reports submitted in accordance with paragraph 1(b) of this Article, repeat the basic information previously provided.

Article 44   Communications

1. The Committee may receive communications from any person, group or non-governmental organization recognized by the Organization of African Unity, by a Member State or by the United Nations relating to any matter covered by this Charter.

2. Every communication to the Committee shall contain the name and address of the author and shall be treated in confidence.

Article 45   Investigations by the Committee

1. The Committee may resort to any appropriate method of investigating any matter falling within the ambit of the present Charter, request from the States Parties any information relevant to the implementation of the Charter and may also resort to any appropriate method of investigating the measures a State Party has adopted to implement the Charter.

2. The Committee shall submit to each Ordinary Session of the Assembly of Heads of State and Government, every two years, a report on its activities and on any communication made under Article 44 of this Charter.

3. The Committee shall publish its report after it has been considered by the Assembly of Heads of State and Government.

4. States Parties shall make the Committee's reports widely available to the public in their own countries.

Chapter Four   Miscellaneous Provisions

Article 46   Sources of inspiration

The Committee shall draw inspiration from international law on human rights, particularly from the provisions of the African Charter on Human and Peoples' Rights, the Charter of the Organization of African Unity, the Universal Declaration of Human Rights, the Convention on the Rights of the Child and other instruments adopted by the United Nations and by African countries in the field of human rights, and from African values and traditions.

Article 47   Signature, ratification or adherence

1. The present Charter shall be open to signature by all the Member States of the Organization of African Unity.

2. The present Charter shall be subject to ratification or adherence by Member States of the Organization of African Unity. The instruments of ratification or adherence to the present Charter shall be deposited with the Secretary-General of the Organization of African Unity.

3. The present Charter shall come into force 30 days after the reception by the Secretary-General of the Organization of African Unity of the instruments of ratification or adherence of 15 Member States of the Organization of African Unity.

Article 48   Amendment and revision of the Charter

1. The present Charter may be amended or revised if any State Party makes a written request to that effect to the Secretary-General of the Organization of African Unity, provided that the proposed

amendment is not submitted to the Assembly of Heads of State and Government for consideration until all the States Parties have been duly notified of it and the Committee has given its opinion on the amendment.

    2. An amendment shall be approved by a simple majority of the States Parties.

E. ARAB STATES

Arab Charter on Human Rights (2004)*

Based on the faith of the Arab nation in the dignity of the human person whom God has exalted ever since the beginning of creation and in the fact that the Arab homeland is the cradle of religions and civilizations whose lofty human values affirm the human right to a decent life based on freedom, justice and equality,

    In furtherance of the eternal principles of fraternity, equality and tolerance among human beings consecrated by the noble Islamic religion and the other divinely-revealed religions,

    Being proud of the humanitarian values and principles that the Arab nation has established throughout its long history, which have played a major role in spreading knowledge between East and West, so making the region a point of reference for the whole world and a destination for seekers of knowledge and wisdom,

    Believing in the unity of the Arab nation, which struggles for its freedom and defends the right of nations to self-determination, to the preservation of their wealth and to development; believing in the sovereignty of the law and its contribution to the protection of universal and interrelated human rights and convinced that the human person's enjoyment of freedom, justice and equality of opportunity is a fundamental measure of the value of any society,

    Rejecting all forms of racism and Zionism, which constitute a violation of human rights and a threat to international peace and security, recognizing the close link that exists between human rights and international peace and security, reaffirming the principles of the Charter of the United Nations, the Universal Declaration of Human Rights and the provisions of the International Covenant on Civil and Political Rights and the International Covenant on Economic, Social and Cultural Rights, and having regard to the Cairo Declaration on Human Rights in Islam,

    The States parties to the Charter have agreed as follows:

Article 1

The present Charter seeks, within the context of the national identity of the Arab States and their sense of belonging to a common civilization, to achieve the following aims:

    1. To place human rights at the centre of the key national concerns of Arab States, making them lofty and fundamental ideals that shape the will of the individual in Arab States and enable him to improve his life in accordance with noble human values.

    2. To teach the human person in the Arab States pride in his identity, loyalty to his country, attachment to his land, history and common interests and to instill in him a culture of human brotherhood, tolerance and openness towards others, in accordance with universal principles and values and with those proclaimed in international human rights instruments.

    3. To prepare the new generations in Arab States for a free and responsible life in a civil society that is characterized by solidarity, founded on a balance between awareness of rights and respect for obligations, and governed by the values of equality, tolerance and moderation.

    4. To entrench the principle that all human rights are universal, indivisible, interdependent and interrelated.

Article 2

1. All peoples have the right of self-determination and to control over their natural wealth and resources, and the right to freely choose their political system and to freely pursue their economic, social and cultural development.

2. All peoples have the right to national sovereignty and territorial integrity.

3. All forms of racism, Zionism and foreign occupation and domination constitute an impediment to human dignity and a major barrier to the exercise of the fundamental rights of peoples; all such practices must be condemned and efforts must be deployed for their elimination.

4. All peoples have the right to resist foreign occupation.

Article 3

1. Each State party to the present Charter undertakes to ensure to all individuals subject to its jurisdiction the right to enjoy the rights and freedoms set forth herein, without distinction on grounds of race, colour, sex, language, religious belief, opinion, thought, national or social origin, wealth, birth or physical or mental disability.

2. The States parties to the present Charter shall take the requisite measures to guarantee effective equality in the enjoyment of all the rights and freedoms enshrined in the present Charter in order to ensure protection against all forms of discrimination based on any of the grounds mentioned in the preceding paragraph.

3. Men and women are equal in respect of human dignity, rights and obligations within the framework of the positive discrimination established in favour of women by the Islamic Shariah, other divine laws and by applicable laws and legal instruments. Accordingly, each State party pledges to take all the requisite measures to guarantee equal opportunities and effective equality between men and women in the enjoyment of all the rights set out in this Charter.

Article 4

1. In exceptional situations of emergency which threaten the life of the nation and the existence of which is officially proclaimed, the States parties to the present Charter may take measures derogating from their obligations under the present Charter, to the extent strictly required by the exigencies of the situation, provided that such measures are not inconsistent with their other obligations under international law and do not involve discrimination solely on the grounds of race, colour, sex, language, religion or social origin.

2. In exceptional situations of emergency, no derogation shall be made from the following articles: article 5, article 8, article 9, article 10, article 13, article 14, paragraph 6, article 15, article 18, article 19, article 20, article 22, article 27, article 28, article 29 and article 30. In addition, the judicial guarantees required for the protection of the aforementioned rights may not be suspended.

3. Any State party to the present Charter availing itself of the right of derogation shall immediately inform the other States parties, through the intermediary of the Secretary-General of the League of Arab States, of the provisions from which it has derogated and of the reasons by which it was actuated. A further communication shall be made, through the same intermediary, on the date on which it terminates such derogation.

Article 5

1. Every human being has the inherent right to life.

2. This right shall be protected by law. No one shall be arbitrarily deprived of his life.

Article 6

Sentence of death may be imposed only for the most serious crimes in accordance with the laws in force at the time of commission of the crime and pursuant to a final judgment rendered by a competent court. Anyone sentenced to death shall have the right to seek pardon or commutation of the sentence.

Article 7

1. Sentence of death shall not be imposed on persons under 18 years of age, unless otherwise stipulated in the laws in force at the time of the commission of the crime.

2. The death penalty shall not be inflicted on a pregnant woman prior to her delivery or on a nursing mother within two years from the date of her delivery; in all cases, the best interests of the infant shall be the primary consideration.

Article 8

1. No one shall be subjected to physical or psychological torture or to cruel, degrading, humiliating or inhuman treatment.

2. Each State party shall protect every individual subject to its jurisdiction from such practices and shall take effective measures to prevent them. The commission of, or participation in, such acts shall be regarded as crimes that are punishable by law and not subject to any statute of limitations. Each State party shall guarantee in its legal system redress for any victim of torture and the right to rehabilitation and compensation.

Article 9

No one shall be subjected to medical or scientific experimentation or to the use of his organs without his free consent and full awareness of the consequences and provided that ethical, humanitarian and professional rules are followed and medical procedures are observed to ensure his personal safety pursuant to the relevant domestic laws in force in each State party. Trafficking in human organs is prohibited in all circumstances.

Article 10

1. All forms of slavery and trafficking in human beings are prohibited and are punishable by law. No one shall be held in slavery and servitude under any circumstances.

2. Forced labour, trafficking in human beings for the purposes of prostitution or sexual exploitation, the exploitation of the prostitution of others or any other form of exploitation or the exploitation of children in armed conflict are prohibited.

Article 11

All persons are equal before the law and have the right to enjoy its protection without discrimination.

Article 12

All persons are equal before the courts and tribunals. The States parties shall guarantee the independence of the judiciary and protect magistrates against any interference, pressure or threats. They shall also guarantee every person subject to their jurisdiction the right to seek a legal remedy before courts of all levels.

Article 13

1. Everyone has the right to a fair trial that affords adequate guarantees before a competent, independent and impartial court that has been constituted by law to hear any criminal charge against him or to decide on his rights or his obligations. Each State party shall guarantee to those without the requisite financial resources legal aid to enable them to defend their rights.

2. Trials shall be public, except in exceptional cases that may be warranted by the interests of justice in a society that respects human freedoms and rights.

Article 14

1. Everyone has the right to liberty and security of person. No one shall be subjected to arbitrary arrest, search or detention without a legal warrant.

2. No one shall be deprived of his liberty except on such grounds and in such circumstances as are determined by law and in accordance with such procedure as is established thereby.

3. Anyone who is arrested shall be informed, at the time of arrest, in a language that he understands, of the reasons for his arrest and shall be promptly informed of any charges against him. He shall be entitled to contact his family members.

4. Anyone who is deprived of his liberty by arrest or detention shall have the right to request a medical examination and must be informed of that right.

5. Anyone arrested or detained on a criminal charge shall be brought promptly before a judge or other officer authorized by law to exercise judicial power and shall be entitled to trial within a reasonable time or to release. His release may be subject to guarantees to appear for trial. Pre-trial detention shall in no case be the general rule.

6. Anyone who is deprived of his liberty by arrest or detention shall be entitled to petition a competent court in order that it may decide without delay on the lawfulness of his arrest or detention and order his release if the arrest or detention is unlawful.

7. Anyone who has been the victim of arbitrary or unlawful arrest or detention shall be entitled to compensation.

Article 15

No crime and no penalty can be established without a prior provision of the law. In all circumstances, the law most favourable to the defendant shall be applied.

Article 16

Everyone charged with a criminal offence shall be presumed innocent until proved guilty by a final judgment rendered according to law and, in the course of the investigation and trial, he shall enjoy the following minimum guarantees:

1. The right to be informed promptly, in detail and in a language which he understands, of the charges against him.

2. The right to have adequate time and facilities for the preparation of his defence and to be allowed to communicate with his family.

3. The right to be tried in his presence before an ordinary court and to defend himself in person or through a lawyer of his own choosing with whom he can communicate freely and confidentially.

4. The right to the free assistance of a lawyer who will defend him if he cannot defend himself or if the interests of justice so require, and the right to the free assistance of an interpreter if he cannot understand or does not speak the language used in court.

5. The right to examine or have his lawyer examine the prosecution witnesses and to on defence according to the conditions applied to the prosecution witnesses.

6. The right not to be compelled to testify against himself or to confess guilt.

7. The right, if convicted of the crime, to file an appeal in accordance with the law before a higher tribunal.

8. The right to respect for his security of person and his privacy in all circumstances.

Article 17

Each State party shall ensure in particular to any child at risk or any delinquent charged with an offence the right to a special legal system for minors in all stages of investigation, trial and enforcement of sentence, as well as to special treatment that takes account of his age, protects his dignity, facilitates his rehabilitation and reintegration and enables him to play a constructive role in society.

Article 18

No one who is shown by a court to be unable to pay a debt arising from a contractual obligation shall be imprisoned.

Article 19

1. No one may be tried twice for the same offence. Anyone against whom such proceedings are brought shall have the right to challenge their legality and to demand his release.

2. Anyone whose innocence is established by a final judgment shall be entitled to compensation for the damage suffered.

Article 20

1. All persons deprived of their liberty shall be treated with humanity and with respect for the inherent dignity of the human person.

2. Persons in pre-trial detention shall be separated from convicted persons and shall be treated in a manner consistent with their status as unconvicted persons.

3. The aim of the penitentiary system shall be to reform prisoners and effect their social rehabilitation.

Article 21

1. No one shall be subjected to arbitrary or unlawful interference with regard to his privacy, family, home or correspondence, nor to unlawful attacks on his honour or his reputation.

2. Everyone has the right to the protection of the law against such interference or attacks.

Article 22

Everyone shall have the right to recognition as a person before the law.

Article 23

Each State party to the present Charter undertakes to ensure that any person whose rights or freedoms as herein recognized are violated shall have an effective remedy, notwithstanding that the violation has been committed by persons acting in an official capacity.

Article 24

Every citizen has the right:

1. To freely pursue a political activity.

2. To take part in the conduct of public affairs, directly or through freely chosen representatives.

3. To stand for election or choose his representatives in free and impartial elections, in conditions of equality among all citizens that guarantee the free expression of his will.

4. To the opportunity to gain access, on an equal footing with others, to public office in his country in accordance with the principle of equality of opportunity.

5. To freely form and join associations with others.

6. To freedom of association and peaceful assembly.

7. No restrictions may be placed on the exercise of these rights other than those which are prescribed by law and which are necessary in a democratic society in the interests of national security or public safety, public health or morals or the protection of the rights and freedoms of others.

Article 25

Persons belonging to minorities shall not be denied the right to enjoy their own culture, to use their own language and to practice their own religion. The exercise of these rights shall be governed by law.

Article 26

1. Everyone lawfully within the territory of a State party shall, within that territory, have the right to freedom of movement and to freely choose his residence in any part of that territory in conformity with the laws in force.

2. No State party may expel a person who does not hold its nationality but is lawfully in its territory, other than in pursuance of a decision reached in accordance with law and after that person has been allowed to submit a petition to the competent authority, unless compelling reasons of national security preclude it. Collective expulsion is prohibited under all circumstances.

Article 27

1. No one may be arbitrarily or unlawfully prevented from leaving any country, including his own, nor prohibited from residing, or compelled to reside, in any part of that country.

2. No one may be exiled from his country or prohibited from returning thereto.

Article 28

Everyone has the right to seek political asylum in another country in order to escape persecution. This right may not be invoked by persons facing prosecution for an offence under ordinary law. Political refugees may not be extradited.

Article 29

1. Everyone has the right to nationality. No one shall be arbitrarily or unlawfully deprived of his nationality.

2. States parties shall take such measures as they deem appropriate, in accordance with their domestic laws on nationality, to allow a child to acquire the mother's nationality, having due regard, in all cases, to the best interests of the child.

3. Non one shall be denied the right to acquire another nationality, having due regard for the domestic legal procedures in his country.

Article 30

1. Everyone has the right to freedom of thought, conscience and religion and no restrictions may be imposed on the exercise of such freedoms except as provided for by law.

2. The freedom to manifest one's religion or beliefs or to perform religious observances, either alone or in community with others, shall be subject only to such limitations as are prescribed by law and are necessary in a tolerant society that respects human rights and freedoms for the protection of public safety, public order, public health or morals or the fundamental rights and freedoms of others.

3. Parents or guardians have the freedom to provide for the religious and moral education of their children.

Article 31

Everyone has a guaranteed right to own private property, and shall not under any circumstances be arbitrarily or unlawfully divested of all or any part of his property.

Article 32

1. The present Charter guarantees the right to information and to freedom of opinion and expression, as well as the right to seek, receive and impart information and ideas through any medium, regardless of geographical boundaries.

2. Such rights and freedoms shall be exercised in conformity with the fundamental values of society and shall be subject only to such limitations as are required to ensure respect for the rights or reputation of others or the protection of national security, public order and public health or morals.

Article 33

1. The family is the natural and fundamental group unit of society; it is based on marriage between a man and a woman. Men and women of marrying age have the right to marry and to found a family according to the rules and conditions of marriage. No marriage can take place without the full and free consent of both parties. The laws in force regulate the rights and duties of the man and woman as to marriage, during marriage and at its dissolution.

2. The State and society shall ensure the protection of the family, the strengthening of family ties, the protection of its members and the prohibition of all forms of violence or abuse in the relations among its members, and particularly against women and children. They shall also ensure the necessary protection and care for mothers, children, older persons and persons with special needs and shall provide adolescents and young persons with the best opportunities for physical and mental development.

3. The States parties shall take all necessary legislative, administrative and judicial measures to guarantee the protection, survival, development and well-being of the child in an atmosphere

of freedom and dignity and shall ensure, in all cases, that the child's best interests are the basic criterion for all measures taken in his regard, whether the child is at risk of delinquency or is a juvenile offender.

4. The States parties shall take all the necessary measures to guarantee, particularly to young persons, the right to pursue a sporting activity.

Article 34

1. The right to work is a natural right of every citizen. The State shall endeavour to provide, to the extent possible, a job for the largest number of those willing to work, while ensuring production, the freedom to choose one's work and equality of opportunity without discrimination of any kind on grounds of race, colour, sex, religion, language, political opinion, membership in a union, national origin, social origin, disability or any other situation.

2. Every worker has the right to the enjoyment of just and favourable conditions of work which ensure appropriate remuneration to meet his essential needs and those of his family and regulate working hours, rest and holidays with pay, as well as the rules for the preservation of occupational health and safety and the protection of women, children and disabled persons in the place of work.

3. The States parties recognize the right of the child to be protected from economic exploitation and from being forced to perform any work that is likely to be hazardous or to interfere with the child's education or to be harmful to the child's health or physical, mental, spiritual, moral or social development. To this end, and having regard to the relevant provisions of other international instruments, States parties shall in particular:

    (a) Define a minimum age for admission to employment;
    (b) Establish appropriate regulation of working hours and conditions;
    (c) Establish appropriate penalties or other sanctions to ensure the effective endorsement of these provisions.

4. There shall be no discrimination between men and women in their enjoyment of the right to effectively benefit from training, employment and job protection and the right to receive equal remuneration for equal work.

5. Each State party shall ensure to workers who migrate to its territory the requisite protection in accordance with the laws in force.

Article 35

1. Every individual has the right to freely form trade unions or to join trade unions and to freely pursue trade union activity for the protection of his interests.

2. No restrictions shall be placed on the exercise of these rights and freedoms except such as are prescribed by the laws in force and that are necessary for the maintenance of national security, public safety or order or for the protection of public health or morals or the rights and freedoms of others.

3. Every State party to the present Charter guarantees the right to strike within the limits laid down by the laws in force.

Article 36

The States parties shall ensure the right of every citizen to social security, including social insurance.

Article 37

The right to development is a fundamental human right and all States are required to establish the development policies and to take the measures needed to guarantee this right. They have a duty to give effect to the values of solidarity and cooperation among them and at the international level with a view to eradicating poverty and achieving economic, social, cultural and political development. By virtue of this right, every citizen has the right to participate in the realization of development and to enjoy the benefits and fruits thereof.

Article 38

Every person has the right to an adequate standard of living for himself and his family, which ensures their well-being and a decent life, including food, clothing, housing, services and the right to a healthy environment. The States parties shall take the necessary measures commensurate with their resources to guarantee these rights.

Article 39

1. The States parties recognize the right of every member of society to the enjoyment of the highest attainable standard of physical and mental health and the right of the citizen to free basic health-care services and to have access to medical facilities without discrimination of any kind.

2. The measures taken by States parties shall include the following:

(a) Development of basic health-care services and the guaranteeing of free and easy access to the centres that provide these services, regardless of geographical location or economic status.

(b) Efforts to control disease by means of prevention and cure in order to reduce the morality rate.

(c) Promotion of health awareness and health education.

(d) Suppression of traditional practices which are harmful to the health of the individual.

(e) Provision of the basic nutrition and safe drinking water for all.

(f) Combating environmental pollution and providing proper sanitation systems;

(g) Combating drugs, psychotropic substances, smoking and substances that are damaging to health.

Article 40

1. The States parties undertake to ensure to persons with mental or physical disabilities a decent life that guarantees their dignity, and to enhance their self-reliance and facilitate their active participation in society.

2. The States parties shall provide social services free of charge for all persons with disabilities, shall provide the material support needed by those persons, their families or the families caring for them, and shall also do whatever is needed to avoid placing those persons in institutions. They shall in all cases take account of the best interests of the disabled person.

3. The States parties shall take all necessary measures to curtail the incidence of disabilities by all possible means, including preventive health programmes, awareness raising and education.

4. The States parties shall provide full educational services suited to persons with disabilities, taking into account the importance of integrating these persons in the educational system and the importance of vocational training and apprenticeship and the creation of suitable job opportunities in the public or private sectors.

5. The States parties shall provide all health services appropriate for persons with disabilities, including the rehabilitation of these persons with a view to integrating them into society.

6. The States parties shall enable persons with disabilities to make use of all public and private services.

Article 41

1. The eradication of illiteracy is a binding obligation upon the State and everyone has the right to education.

2. The States parties shall guarantee their citizens free education at least throughout the primary and basic levels. All forms and levels of primary education shall be compulsory and accessible to all without discrimination of any kind.

3. The States parties shall take appropriate measures in all domains to ensure partnership between men and women with a view to achieving national development goals.

4. The States parties shall guarantee to provide education directed to the full development of the human person and to strengthening respect for human rights and fundamental freedoms.

5. The States parties shall endeavour to incorporate the principles of human rights and fundamental freedoms into formal and informal education curricula and educational and training programmes.

6. The States parties shall guarantee the establishment of the mechanisms necessary to provide ongoing education for every citizen and shall develop national plans for adult education.

Article 42

1. Every person has the right to take part in cultural life and to enjoy the benefits of scientific progress and its application.

2. The States parties undertake to respect the freedom of scientific research and creative activity and to ensure the protection of moral and material interests resulting from scientific, literary and artistic production.

3. The state parties shall work together and enhance cooperation among them at all levels, with the full participation of intellectuals and inventors and their organizations, in order to develop and implement recreational, cultural, artistic and scientific programmes.

Article 43

Nothing in this Charter may be construed or interpreted as impairing the rights and freedoms protected by the domestic laws of the States parties or those set force in the international and regional human rights instruments which the states parties have adopted or ratified, including the rights of women, the rights of the child and the rights of persons belonging to minorities.

Article 44

The states parties undertake to adopt, in conformity with their constitutional procedures and with the provisions of the present Charter, whatever legislative or non-legislative measures that may be necessary to give effect to the rights set forth herein.

Article 45

1. Pursuant to this Charter, an 'Arab Human Rights Committee', hereinafter referred to as 'the Committee' shall be established. This Committee shall consist of seven members who shall be elected by secret ballot by the states parties to this Charter.

2. The Committee shall consist of nationals of the states parties to the present Charter, who must be highly experienced and competent in the Committee's field of work. The members of the Committee shall serve in their personal capacity and shall be fully independent and impartial.

3. The Committee shall include among its members not more than one national of a State party; such member may be re-elected only once. Due regard shall be given to the rotation principle.

4. The members of the Committee shall be elected for a four-year term, although the mandate of three of the members elected during the first election shall be for two years and shall be renewed by lot.

5. Six months prior to the date of the election, the Secretary-General of the League of Arab States shall invite the States parties to submit their nominations within the following three months. He shall transmit the list of candidates to the States parties two months prior to the date the election. The candidates who obtain the largest number of votes cast shall be elected to membership of the Committee. If, because two or more candidates have an equal number of votes, the number of candidates with the largest number of votes exceeds the number required, a second ballot will be held between the persons with equal numbers of votes. If the votes are again equal, the member or members shall be selected by lottery. The first election for membership of the Committee shall be held at least six months after the Charter enters into force.

6. The Secretary-General shall invite the States parties to a meeting at the headquarters the League of Arab States in order to elect the member of the Committee. The presence of the majority

of the States parties shall constitute a quorum. If there is no quorum, the secretary-General shall call another meeting at which at least two thirds of the States parties must be present. If there is still no quorum, the Secretary-General shall call a third meeting, which will be held regardless of the number of States parties present.

7. The Secretary-General shall convene the first meeting of the Committee, during the course of which the Committee shall elect its Chairman from among its members, for a two-year in which may be renewed only once and for an identical period. The Committee shall establish its own rules of procedure and methods of work and shall determine how often it shall meet. The Committee shall hold its meetings at the headquarters of the League of Arab States. It may also meet in any other State party to the present Charter at that party's invitation.

Article 46

1. The Secretary-General shall declare a seat vacant after being notified by the Chairman of a member's:

   (a) Death;
   (b) Resignation; or
   (c) If, in the unanimous, opinion of the other members, a member of the Committee has ceased to perform his functions without offering an acceptable justification or for any reason other than a temporary absence.

2. If a member's seat is declared vacant pursuant to the provisions of paragraph 1 and the term of office of the member to be replaced does not expire within six months from the date on which the vacancy was declared, the Secretary-General of the League of Arab States shall refer the matter to the States parties to the present Charter, which may, within two months, submit nominations, pursuant to article 45, in order to fill the vacant seat.

3. The Secretary-General of the League of Arab States shall draw up an alphabetical list of all the duly nominated candidates, which he shall transmit to the States parties to the present Charter. The elections to fill the vacant seat shall be held in accordance with the relevant provisions.

4. Any member of the Committee elected to fill a seat declared vacant in accordance with the provisions of paragraph 1 shall remain a member of the Committee until the expiry of the remainder of the term of the member whose seat was declared vacant pursuant to the provisions of that paragraph.

5. The Secretary-General of the League of Arab States shall make provision within the budget of the League of Arab States for all the necessary financial and human resources and facilities that the Committee needs to discharge its functions effectively. The Committee's experts shall be afforded the same treatment with respect to remuneration and reimbursement of expenses as experts of the secretariat of the League of Arab States.

Article 47

The States parties undertake to ensure that members of the Committee shall enjoy the immunities necessary for their protection against any form of harassment or moral or material pressure or prosecution on account of the positions they take or statements they make while carrying out their functions as members of the Committee.

Article 48

1. The States parties undertake to submit reports to the Secretary-General of the League of Arab States on the measures they have taken to give effect to the rights and freedoms recognized in this Charter and on the progress made towards the enjoyment thereof. The Secretary-General shall transmit these reports to the Committee for its consideration.

2. Each State party shall submit an initial report to the Committee within one year from the date on which the Charter enters into force and a periodic report every three years thereafter. The Committee may request the States parties to supply it with additional information relating to the implementation of the Charter.

3. The Committee shall consider the reports submitted by the States parties under paragraph 2 of this article in the presence of the representative of the State party whose report is being considered.

4. The Committee shall discuss the report, comment thereon and make the necessary recommendations in accordance with the aims of the Charter.

5. The Committee shall submit an annual report containing its comments and recommendations to the Council of the League, through the intermediary of the Secretary-General.

6. The Committee's reports, concluding observations and recommendations shall be public documents which the Committee shall disseminate widely.

Article 49

1. The Secretary-General of the League of Arab States shall submit the present Charter, once it has been approved by the Council of the League, to the States members for signature, ratification or accession.

2. The present Charter shall enter into effect two months from the date on which the seventh instrument of ratification is deposited with the secretariat of the League of Arab States.

3. After its entry into force, the present Charter shall become effective for each State two months after the State in question has deposited its instrument of ratification or accession with the secretariat.

4. The Secretary-General shall notify the States members of the deposit of each instrument of ratification or accession.

Article 50

Any State party may submit written proposals, though the Secretary-General, for the amendment of the present Charter. After these amendments have been circulated among the States members, the Secretary-General shall invite the States parties to consider the proposed amendments before submitting them to the Council of the League for adoption.

Article 51

The amendments shall take effect, with regard to the States parties that have approved them, once they have been approved by two thirds of the States parties.

Article 52

Any State party may propose additional optional protocols to the present Charter and they shall be adopted in accordance with the procedures used for the adoption of amendments to the Charter.

Article 53

1. Any State party, when signing this Charter, depositing the instruments of ratification or acceding hereto, may make a reservation to any article of the Charter, provided that such reservation does not conflict with the aims and fundamental purposes of the Charter.

2. Any State party that has made a reservation pursuant to paragraph 1 of this article may withdraw it at any time by addressing a notification to the Secretary-General of the League of Arab States.

3. The Secretary-General shall notify the States parties of reservations and of requests for their withdrawal.

Gulf Cooperation Council Human Rights Declaration (2014)*

The Member States of the Cooperation Council for the Arab States of the Gulf (GCC),

Inspired by their deep belief in the dignity of the human being, respect for his rights and their commitment to the protection of those rights that are ensured by the Islamic *Sharia* law which embody the firm and noble values and principles in the conscience of their communities and constitute the basic constants of their policies at all levels, and

---

* © Cooperation Council for the Arab States of the Gulf, 2014.

Pursuant to the GCC Charter which provides for the common destiny and the unity of aim which link their peoples, and which calls for coordination, integration and interconnection between them in all fields, as well as the deepening and strengthening of bonds, ties and cooperation between their peoples in various fields, and

Reaffirming that their achievements in various areas are ascribed to the great importance and care that the GCC States attach to the issues of human rights, and

Expressing their appreciation and gratitude to the joint efforts made at the various levels with the international and regional community, which have efficiently and effectively contributed to the reinforcement of human rights issues promoting them to the level of the desired goals in an international community where these rights are given their due position, and

Stressing their commitment to the Charter of the United Nations, the Universal Declaration of Human Rights, the Arab Charter on Human Rights, the Cairo Declaration on Human Rights in Islam, and relevant international and regional conventions and charters, and

Interacting with those efforts with a view to achieving more gains for humanity.

Now, Therefore proclaims as follows:

Article 1
Every person has the right to life and must be protected from any assault thereon. No one may be killed unlawfully. The bodies of the dead must be respected, buried and protected.

Article 2
People are equal in human dignity, in rights and in freedoms, and are equal before the regulation (law). There is no distinction between them for reasons of origin, gender, religion, language, color, or any other form of distinction.

Article 3
Slavery, servitude and human trafficking shall be prohibited in all their forms, particularly those involving women and children.

Article 4
Human organs trade, shall be prohibited, and shall be considered as a violation of human rights, and a crime to be penalized by the regulation (law).

Article 5
No medical or scientific experiment may be conducted on any human being, nor may his organs be exploited without his consent and without being fully aware of the subsequent complications that may result.

Article 6
The Freedom of belief and the practice of religious rites is a right of every person according to the regulation (law) without disruption of the public order and public morals.

Article 7
The respect for the heavenly religions, the absence of contempt or disdain for them or insulting their prophets or symbols, and the respect for the cultural diversity of other nations are guaranteed according to the regulation (law).

Article 8
The state and society shall disseminate and promote the principles of goodness, love, fraternity, tolerance and other noble principles and values. They shall also reject all feelings of hatred, grudge and extremism, as well as any other forms thereof that might undermine the fundamental principles of the community or endanger them.

Article 9
Everyone has the right to freedom of opinion and expression, and exercising such freedom is guaranteed insofar as it accords with Islamic *Sharia* law, public order and the regulations (laws) regulating this area.

Article 10

Freedom of movement, residence and departure is a right of every human being according to the regulations (law).

Article 11

No one shall be deported from his country or prevented from entering it.

Article 12

Legal personality is a right of every human being.

Article 13

Nationality is a right of every human being, and is granted by the regulation (law) and shall not be withdrawn except by it.

Article 14

The family is the natural and fundamental group unit of society, originally composed of a man and a woman, governed by religion, morals and patriotism; its entity and bonds are maintained and reinforced by religion. Motherhood, childhood and members of the family are protected by religion as well as the State and society against all forms of abuse and domestic violence.

Article 15

Men and women have the right to marry and found a family. Marriage shall only be entered into with the free will and consent of the intending spouses according to the provisions of Islamic *sharia* Law and regulation (law).

Article 16

Private life, is guaranteed for every human being, and may not be infringed, nor can a person's family affairs, residence, correspondences or communications be interfered with, and he has the right to seek protection thereof.

Article 17

Every human being has the right to a standard of living adequate for the well-being of himself and his family. The government shall ensure such standard of living within the means available.

Article 18

Every child has the right to survival, development, protection and welfare in a family setting where he is raised in the spirit of peace, dignity, freedom, equality and brotherhood.

Article 19

Every child has the right to protection against economic exploitation and the performance of any work that is likely to be dangerous, to impede his education or to cause harm to his, physical, mental health, or his spiritual, moral or social growth, in accordance with the provisions of the Islamic *Sharia* law and relevant international conventions and agreements.

Article 20

Everyone has the right to live in a clean environment free of pollution which the State and society shall conserve and protect.

Article 21

Every person has the right to healthcare, which the State and civil community institutions shall provide.

Article 22

All people with special needs have the right to comprehensive care and shall be rehabilitated and consolidate into the community.

Article 23

Every person has the right to education. Education shall be directed towards the full development of the human personality, while enhancing his dignity and the culture of human rights. Primary education shall be free and compulsory. Technical and higher education shall be made generally available, with a respect towards the right of guardians and caregivers to choose the kind of education they deem best for their children.

Article 24
Every person, who has the capacity of doing so, has the right to work and has the right to free choice of employment according to the requirements of dignity and public interest, while just and favorable employment conditions, as well as employees' and employers' rights, are ensured.

Article 25
The elderly and Infirm have the right to protection and welfare.

Article 26
Every citizen has the right to social security and insurance according to the regulation (law), while ensuring protection and welfare for the elderly and infirm people.

Article 27
Private property is inviolable and no one shall be prevented from the disposition of his property except by the regulation (law), and it may not be expropriated unless for public interest with fair compensation.

Article 28
Every citizen has the right to enjoy national property and resources, and everyone is entitled to benefit from public services according to the regulation (law).

Article 29
Every person has the right to participate in cultural life, to enjoy scientific advancement and its benefits, and to benefit from the moral and material rights of his scientific, literary or artistic production that contribute to the advancement of human civilization.

Article 30
Every citizen has the right to political participation, as well as the right to take part in the government of his country, and to have equal access to public services in his country according to the provisions of the regulation (law). A country shall provide employment opportunities for its citizens.

Article 31
Every person has the freedom to form associations, assemblies and unions, subject to the provisions of the regulation (law), and no one may be compelled to belong to an association.

Article 32
All people are equal before the courts and every person has a right to access to litigate with full independence of the judiciary.

Article 33
Punishment is personal, no crime and no penalty can be established without a prior provision of the law and, the accused shall benefit from the provision that is most favorable to him.

Article 34
No one shall be subjected to arbitrary arrest or detention or confinement or restriction of his freedom, and he has the right to humane treatment while in custody. Accused people shall be separated from convicted ones, and shall be treated in such manner consistent with their status.

Article 35
The accused is innocent until proven guilty in a fair trial which provides all legal guarantees for his defense.

Article 36
Torture is prohibited whether physically or psychologically as is cruel, inhuman or degrading treatment.

Article 37
Sentenced people who are deprived of their liberty must receive humane treatment with respect towards their dignity, and takes into account the international standards applicable by penal or corrective institutions.

Article 38
No one shall be imprisoned for a debt that is judicially proven to unable to be paid back.

Article 39
Consequences (burdens) of disasters and emergencies shall be the common responsibility of both the government and the community.

Article 40
Terrorism is a violation of human rights; it is prohibited and criminalized, in all its forms, under Islamic *Sharia* law and International conventions and shall be combatted and eliminated without infringement of the respect for human rights.

Article 41
Rules of International humanitarian law shall apply in armed conflicts with accordance to all prevailing International conventions and practices, subject to ensuring the rights of the elderly, disabled, patients, women, children, captives and civilians.

Article 42
Every person has the right to seek asylum in another country according to the regulation (law) applicable therein. An expatriate, who has legally entered a country, may not be deported without legal justification, nor may asylum seekers be handed over.

Article 43
A juvenile delinquent has the right to be treated under juvenile judicial law and to treatment appropriate to his age that maintains his rights and dignity and contributes to his rehabilitation and reinstatement in society.

Article 44
Without prejudice to the provisions of Islamic *Sharia* law and the regulation (law), the exercise and enjoyment of the rights and freedoms set out in this Declaration are the right of everyone.

Article 45
Every person, whose rights and freedoms set forth in this Declaration have been violated, has the right to appeal according to the regulation (law).

Article 46
Every person has obligations towards society. However, in the exercise of the rights and freedoms set out in this declaration, he shall be subject only to the restrictions that are determined by the regulation (law) for securing and respecting the rights and freedoms of others and public order.

Article 47
This Declaration may not be interpreted or modified in such a way that might limit the rights and freedoms that are ensured by the national legislations of the GCC States or the international and regional conventions of human rights which the GCC States have ratified or acceded to.

Part IV

United Nations World Conferences on Human Rights

Proclamation of Teheran (1968)*

The International Conference on Human Rights

Having met at Teheran from April 22 to May 13, 1968 to review the progress made in the twenty years since the adoption of the Universal Declaration of Human Rights and to formulate a programme for the future,

Having considered the problems relating to the activities of the United Nations for the promotion and encouragement of respect for human rights and fundamental freedoms,

Bearing in mind the resolutions adopted by the Conference,

Noting that the observance of the International Year for Human Rights takes place at a time when the world is undergoing a process of unprecedented change,

Having regard to the new opportunities made available by the rapid progress of science and technology,

Believing that, in an age when conflict and violence prevail in many parts of the world, the fact of human interdependence and the need for human solidarity are more evident than ever before,

Recognizing that peace is the universal aspiration of mankind and that peace and justice are indispensable to the full realization of human rights and fundamental freedoms,

Solemnly proclaims that:

1. It is imperative that the members of the international community fulfil their solemn obligations to promote and encourage respect for human rights and fundamental freedoms for all without distinctions of any kind such as race, colour, sex, language, religion, political or other opinions;

2. The Universal Declaration of Human Rights states a common understanding of the peoples of the world concerning the inalienable and inviolable rights of all members of the human family and constitutes an obligation for the members of the international community;

3. The International Covenant on Civil and Political Rights, the International Covenant on Economic, Social and Cultural Rights, the Declaration on the Granting of Independence to Colonial Countries and Peoples, the International Convention on the Elimination of All Forms of Racial Discrimination as well as other conventions and declarations in the field of human rights adopted under the auspices of the United Nations, the specialized agencies and the regional intergovernmental organizations, have created new standards and obligations to which States should conform;

4. Since the adoption of the Universal Declaration of Human Rights the United Nations has made substantial progress in defining standards for the enjoyment and protection of human rights and fundamental freedoms. During this period many important international instruments were adopted but much remains to be done in regard to the implementation of those rights and freedoms;

5. The primary aim of the United Nations in the sphere of human rights is the achievement by each individual of the maximum freedom and dignity. For the realization of this objective, the laws of every country should grant each individual, irrespective of race, language, religion or political belief, freedom of expression, of information, of conscience and of religion, as well as the right to participate in the political, economic, cultural and social life of his country;

6. States should reaffirm their determination effectively to enforce the principles enshrined in the Charter of the United Nations and in other international instruments that concern human rights and fundamental freedoms;

7. Gross denials of human rights under the repugnant policy of *apartheid* is a matter of the gravest concern to the international community. This policy of *apartheid*, condemned as a crime against humanity, continues seriously to disturb international peace and security. It is therefore imperative for the international community to use every possible means to eradicate this evil. The struggle against *apartheid* is recognized as legitimate;

8. The peoples of the world must be made fully aware of the evils of racial discrimination and must join in combating them. The implementation of this principle of non-discrimination, embodied in the Charter of the United Nations, the Universal Declaration of Human Rights, and other international instruments in the field of human rights, constitutes a most urgent task of mankind at the international as well as at the national level. All ideologies based on racial superiority and intolerance must be condemned and resisted;

9. Eight years after the General Assembly's Declaration on the Granting of Independence to Colonial Countries and Peoples the problems of colonialism continue to preoccupy the international community. It is a matter of urgency that all Member States should cooperate with the appropriate organs of the United Nations so that effective measures can be taken to ensure that the Declaration is fully implemented;

10. Massive denials of human rights, arising out of aggression or any armed conflict with their tragic consequences, and resulting in untold human misery, engender reactions which could engulf the world in ever growing hostilities. It is the obligation of the international community to co-operate in eradicating such scourges;

11. Gross denials of human rights arising from discrimination on grounds of race, religion, belief or expressions of opinion outrage the conscience of mankind and endanger the foundations of freedom, justice and peace in the world;

12. The widening gap between the economically developed and developing countries impedes the realization of human rights in the international community. The failure of the Development Decade to reach its modest objectives makes it all the more imperative for every nation, according to its capacities, to make the maximum possible effort to close this gap;

13. Since human rights and fundamental freedoms are indivisible, the full realization of civil and political rights without the enjoyment of economic, social and cultural rights is impossible. The achievement of lasting progress in the implementation of human rights is dependent upon sound and effective national and international policies of economic and social development;

14. The existence of over seven hundred million illiterates throughout the world is an enormous obstacle to all efforts at realizing the aims and purposes of the Charter of the United Nations and the provisions of the Universal Declaration of Human Rights. International action aimed at eradicating illiteracy from the face of the earth and promoting education at all levels requires urgent attention;

15. The discrimination of which women are still victims in various regions of the world must be eliminated. An inferior status for women is contrary to the Charter of the United Nations as well as the provisions of the Universal Declaration of Human Rights. The full implementation of the Declaration on the Elimination of Discrimination against Women is a necessity for the progress of mankind;

16. The protection of the family and of the child remains the concern of the international community. Parents have a basic human right to determine freely and responsibly the number and the spacing of their children;

17. The aspirations of the younger generation for a better world, in which human rights and fundamental freedoms are fully implemented, must be given the highest encouragement. It is imperative that youth participate in shaping the future of mankind;

18. While recent scientific discoveries and technological advances have opened vast prospects for economic, social and cultural progress, such developments may nevertheless endanger the rights and freedoms of individuals and will require continuing attention;

19. Disarmament would release immense human and material resources now devoted to military purposes. These resources should be used for the promotion of human rights and fundamental freedoms. General and complete disarmament is one of the highest aspirations of all peoples;

Therefore,

The International Conference on Human Rights

1. *Affirming* its faith in the principles of the Universal Declaration of Human Rights and other international instruments in this field,

2. *Urges* all peoples and governments to dedicate themselves to the principles enshrined in the Universal Declaration of Human Rights and to redouble their efforts to provide for all human beings a life consonant with freedom and dignity and conductive to physical, mental, social and spiritual welfare.

Vienna Declaration and Programme of Action (1993)*

The World Conference on Human Rights

Considering that the promotion and protection of human rights is a matter of priority for the international community, and that the Conference affords a unique opportunity to carry out a comprehensive analysis of the international human rights system and of the machinery for the protection of human rights, in order to enhance and thus promote a fuller observance of those rights, in a just and balanced manner,

Recognizing and affirming that all human rights derive from the dignity and worth inherent in the human person, and that the human person is the central subject of human rights and fundamental freedoms, and consequently should be the principal beneficiary and should participate actively in the realization of these rights and freedoms,

Reaffirming their commitment to the purposes and principles contained in the Charter of the United Nations and the Universal Declaration of Human Rights,

Reaffirming the commitment contained in Article 56 of the Charter of the United Nations to take joint and separate action, placing proper emphasis on developing effective international cooperation for the realization of the purposes set out in Article 55, including universal respect for, and observance of, human rights and fundamental freedoms for all,

Emphasizing the responsibilities of all States, in conformity with the Charter of the United Nations, to develop and encourage respect for human rights and fundamental freedoms for all, without distinction as to race, sex, language or religion,

Recalling the Preamble to the Charter of the United Nations, in particular the determination to re-affirm faith in fundamental human rights, in the dignity and worth of the human person, and in the equal rights of men and women and of nations large and small,

Recalling also the determination expressed in the Preamble of the Charter of the United Nations to save succeeding generations from the scourge of war, to establish conditions under which justice and respect for obligations arising from treaties and other sources of international law can be maintained, to promote social progress and better standards of life in larger freedom, to practice tolerance and good neighbourliness, and to employ international machinery for the promotion of the economic and social advancement of all peoples,

Emphasizing that the Universal Declaration of Human Rights, which constitutes a common standard of achievement for all peoples and all nations, is the source of inspiration and has been the basis for the United Nations in making advances in standard setting as contained in the existing international human rights instruments, in particular the International Covenant on Civil and Political Rights and the International Covenant on Economic, Social and Cultural Rights,

Considering the major changes taking place on the international scene and the aspirations of all the peoples for an international order based on the principles enshrined in the Charter of the United

Nations, including promoting and encouraging respect for human rights and fundamental freedoms for all and respect for the principle of equal rights and self-determination of peoples, peace, democracy, justice, equality, rule of law, pluralism, development, better standards of living and solidarity,

Deeply concerned by various forms of discrimination and violence, to which women continue to be exposed all over the world,

Recognizing that the activities of the United Nations in the field of human rights should be rationalized and enhanced in order to strengthen the United Nations machinery in this field and to further the objectives of universal respect for observance of international human rights standards,

Having taken into account the Declarations adopted by the three regional meetings at Tunis, San José and Bangkok and the contributions made by Governments, and bearing in mind the suggestions made by intergovernmental and non-governmental organizations, as well as the studies prepared by independent experts during the preparatory process leading to the World Conference on Human Rights,

Welcoming the International Year of the World's Indigenous People 1993 as a reaffirmation of the commitment of the international community to ensure their enjoyment of all human rights and fundamental freedoms and to respect the value and diversity of their cultures and identities,

Recognizing also that the international community should devise ways and means to remove the current obstacles and meet challenges to the full realization of all human rights and to prevent the continuation of human rights violations resulting thereof throughout the world,

Invoking the spirit of our age and the realities of our time which call upon the peoples of the world and all States Members of the United Nations to rededicate themselves to the global task of promoting and protecting all human rights and fundamental freedoms so as to secure full and universal enjoyment of these rights,

Determined to take new steps forward in the commitment of the international community with a view to achieving substantial progress in human rights endeavours by an increased and sustained effort of international cooperation and solidarity,

Solemnly adopts the Vienna Declaration and Programme of Action.

I

1. The World Conference on Human Rights reaffirms the solemn commitment of all States to fulfil their obligations to promote universal respect for, and observance and protection of, all human rights and fundamental freedoms for all in accordance with the Charter of the United Nations, other instruments relating to human rights, and international law. The universal nature of these rights and freedoms is beyond question.

In this framework, enhancement of international cooperation in the field of human rights is essential for the full achievement of the purposes of the United Nations.

Human rights and fundamental freedoms are the birthright of all human beings; their protection and promotion is the first responsibility of Governments.

2. All peoples have the right of self-determination. By virtue of that right they freely determine their political status, and freely pursue their economic, social and cultural development.

Taking into account the particular situation of peoples under colonial or other forms of alien domination or foreign occupation, the World Conference on Human Rights recognizes the right of peoples to take any legitimate action, in accordance with the Charter of the United Nations, to realize their inalienable right of self-determination. The World Conference on Human Rights considers the denial of the right of self-determination as a violation of human rights and underlines the importance of the effective realization of this right.

In accordance with the Declaration on Principles of International Law concerning Friendly Relations and Cooperation Among States in accordance with the Charter of the United Nations, this shall not be construed as authorising or encouraging any action which would dismember or impair, totally or in part, the territorial integrity or political unity of sovereign and independent States conducting themselves in compliance with the principle of equal rights and self-determination of peoples and thus possessed of a Government representing the whole people belonging to the territory without distinction of any kind.

3. Effective international measures to guarantee and monitor the implementation of human rights standards should be taken in respect of people under foreign occupation, and effective legal protection against the violation of their human rights should be provided, in accordance with human rights norms and international law, particularly the Geneva Convention relative to the Protection of Civilian Persons in Time of War, of 14 August 1949, and other applicable norms of humanitarian law.

4. The promotion and protection of all human rights and fundamental freedoms must be considered as a priority objective of the United Nations in accordance with its purposes and principles, in particular the purpose of international cooperation. In the framework of these purposes and principles, the promotion and protection of all human rights is a legitimate concern of the international community. The organs and specialized agencies related to human rights should therefore further enhance the coordination of their activities based on the consistent and objective application of international human rights instruments.

5. All human rights are universal, indivisible and interdependent and interrelated. The international community must treat human rights globally in a fair and equal manner, on the same footing, and with the same emphasis. While the significance of national and regional particularities and various historical, cultural and religious backgrounds must be borne in mind, it is the duty of States, regardless of their political, economic and cultural systems, to promote and protect all human rights and fundamental freedoms.

6. The efforts of the United Nations system towards the universal respect for, and observance of, human rights and fundamental freedoms for all, contribute to the stability and well-being necessary for peaceful and friendly relations among nations, and to improved conditions for peace and security as well as social and economic development, in conformity with the Charter of the United Nations.

7. The processes of promoting and protecting human rights should be conducted in conformity with the purposes and principles of the Charter of the United Nations, and international law.

8. Democracy, development and respect for human rights and fundamental freedoms are interdependent and mutually reinforcing. Democracy is based on the freely expressed will of the people to determine their own political, economic, social and cultural systems and their full participation in all aspects of their lives. In the context of the above, the promotion and protection of human rights and fundamental freedoms at the national and international levels should be universal and conducted without conditions attached. The international community should support the strengthening and promoting of democracy, development and respect for human rights and fundamental freedoms in the entire world.

9. The World Conference on Human Rights reaffirms that least developed countries committed to the process of democratization and economic reforms, many of which are in Africa, should be supported by the international community in order to succeed in their transition to democracy and economic development.

10. The World Conference on Human Rights reaffirms the right to development, as established in the Declaration on the Right to Development, as a universal and inalienable right and an integral part of fundamental human rights.

As stated in the Declaration on the Right to Development, the human person is the central subject of development.

While development facilitates the enjoyment of all human rights, the lack of development may not be invoked to justify the abridgement of internationally recognized human rights.

States should cooperate with each other in ensuring development and eliminating obstacles to development. The international community should promote an effective international cooperation for the realization of the right to development and the elimination of obstacles to development.

Lasting progress towards the implementation of the right to development requires effective development policies at the national level, as well as equitable economic relations and a favourable economic environment at the international level.

11. The right to development should be fulfilled so as to meet equitably the developmental and environmental needs of present and future generations. The World Conference on Human Rights recognizes that illicit dumping of toxic and dangerous substances and waste potentially constitutes a serious threat to the human rights to life and health of everyone.

Consequently, the World Conference on Human Rights calls on all States to adopt and vigorously implement existing conventions relating to the dumping of toxic and dangerous products and waste and to cooperate in the prevention of illicit dumping.

Everyone has the right to enjoy the benefits of scientific progress and its applications. The World Conference on Human Rights notes that certain advances, notably in the biomedical and life sciences as well as in information technology, may have potentially adverse consequences for the integrity, dignity and human rights of the individual, and calls for international cooperation to ensure that human rights and dignity are fully respected in this area of universal concern.

12. The World Conference on Human Rights calls upon the international community to make all efforts to help alleviate the external debt burden of developing countries, in order to supplement the efforts of the Governments of such countries to attain the full realization of the economic, social and cultural rights of their people.

13. There is a need for States and international organizations, in cooperation with non-governmental organizations, to create favourable conditions at the national, regional and international levels to ensure the full and effective enjoyment of human rights. States should eliminate all violations of human rights and their causes, as well as obstacles to the enjoyment of these rights.

14. The existence of widespread extreme poverty inhibits the full and effective enjoyment of human rights; its immediate alleviation and eventual elimination must remain a high priority for the international community.

15. Respect for human rights and for fundamental freedoms without distinction of any kind is a fundamental rule of international human rights law. The speedy and comprehensive elimination of all forms of racism and racial discrimination, xenophobia and related intolerance is a priority task for the international community. Governments should take effective measures to prevent and combat them. Groups, institutions, intergovernmental and non-governmental organizations and individuals are urged to intensify their efforts in cooperating and coordinating their activities against these evils.

16. The World Conference on Human Rights welcomes the progress made in dismantling apartheid and calls upon the international community and the United Nations system to assist in this process.

The World Conference on Human Rights also deplores the continuing acts of violence aimed at undermining the quest for a peaceful dismantling of apartheid.

17. The acts, methods and practices of terrorism in all its forms and manifestations as well as linkage in some countries to drug trafficking are activities aimed at the destruction of human rights, fundamental freedoms and democracy, threatening territorial integrity, security of States and destabilizing legitimately constituted Governments. The international community should take the necessary steps to enhance cooperation to prevent and combat terrorism.

18. The human rights of women and of the girl-child are an inalienable, integral and indivisible part of universal human rights. The full and equal participation of women in political, civil, economic, social and cultural life, at the national, regional and international levels, and the eradication of all forms of discrimination on grounds of sex are priority objectives of the international community.

Gender-based violence and all forms of sexual harassment and exploitation, including those resulting from cultural prejudice and international trafficking, are incompatible with the dignity and worth of the human person, and must be eliminated. This can be achieved by legal measures and through national action and international cooperation in such fields as economic and social development, education, safe maternity and health care, and social support.

The human rights of women should form an integral part of the United Nations human rights activities, including the promotion of all human rights instruments relating to women.

The World Conference on Human Rights urges Governments, institutions, intergovernmental and non-governmental organizations to intensify their efforts for the protection and promotion of human rights of women and the girl-child.

19. Considering the importance of the promotion and protection of the rights of persons belonging to minorities and the contribution of such promotion and protection to the political and social stability of the States in which such persons live, the World Conference on Human Rights reaffirms the obligation of States to ensure that persons belonging to minorities may exercise fully and effectively all human rights and fundamental freedoms without any discrimination and in full equality before the law in accordance with the Declaration on the Rights of Persons Belonging to National or Ethnic, Religious and Linguistic Minorities.

The persons belonging to minorities have the right to enjoy their own culture, to profess and practise their own religion and to use their own language in private and in public, freely and without interference or any form of discrimination.

20. The World Conference on Human Rights recognizes the inherent dignity and the unique contribution of indigenous people to the development and plurality of society and strongly reaffirms the commitment of the international community to their economic, social and cultural well-being and their enjoyment of the fruits of sustainable development. States should ensure the full and free participation of indigenous people in all aspects of society, in particular in matters of concern to them. Considering the importance of the promotion and protection of the rights of indigenous people, and the contribution of such promotion and protection to the political and social stability of the States in which such people live, States should, in accordance with international law, take concerted positive steps to ensure respect for all human rights and fundamental freedoms of indigenous people, on the basis of equality and non-discrimination, and recognize the value and diversity of their distinct identities, cultures and social organization.

21. The World Conference on Human Rights, welcoming the early ratification of the Convention on the Rights of the Child by a large number of States and noting the recognition of the human rights of children in the World Declaration on the Survival, Protection and Development of Children and Plan of Action adopted by the World Summit for Children, urges universal ratification of the Convention by 1995 and its effective implementation by States parties through the adoption of all the necessary legislative, administrative and other measures and the allocation to the maximum extent of the available resources. In all actions concerning children, non-discrimination and the best interest of the child should be primary considerations and the views of the child given due weight. National and international mechanisms and programmes should be strengthened for the defence and protection of children, in particular, the girl-child, abandoned children, street children, economically and sexually exploited children, including through child pornography, child prostitution or sale of organs, children victims of diseases including acquired immunodeficiency syndrome, refugee and displaced children, children in detention, children in armed conflict, as well as children victims of famine and drought and, other emergencies. International cooperation and solidarity should be promoted to support the implementation of the Convention and the rights of the child should be a priority in the United Nations system-wide action on human rights.

The World Conference on Human Rights also stresses that the child for the full and harmonious development of his or her personality should grow up in a family environment which accordingly merits broader protection.

22. Special attention needs to be paid to ensuring non-discrimination, and the equal enjoyment of all human rights and fundamental freedoms by disabled persons, including their active participation in all aspects of society.

23. The World Conference on Human Rights reaffirms that everyone, without distinction of any kind, is entitled to the right to seek and to enjoy in other countries asylum from persecution, as well as the right to return to one's own country. In this respect it stresses the importance of the Universal Declaration of Human Rights, the 1951 Convention relating to the Status of Refugees, its 1967 Protocol and regional instruments. It expresses its appreciation to States that continue to admit and host large numbers of refugees in their territories, and to the Office of the United Nations High

Commissioner for Refugees for its dedication to its task. It also expresses its appreciation to the United Nations Relief and Works Agency for Palestine Refugees in the Near East.

The World Conference on Human Rights recognizes that gross violations of human rights, including in armed conflicts, are among the multiple and complex factors leading to displacement of people.

The World Conference on Human Rights recognizes that, in view of the complexities of the global refugee crisis and in accordance with the Charter of the United Nations, relevant international instruments and international solidarity and in the spirit of burden-sharing, a comprehensive approach by the international community is needed in coordination and cooperation with the countries concerned and relevant organizations, bearing in mind the mandate of the United Nations High Commissioner for Refugees. This should include the development of strategies to address the root causes and effects of movements of refugees and other displaced persons, the strengthening of emergency preparedness and response mechanisms, the provision of effective protection and assistance; bearing in mind the special needs of women and children, as well as the achievement of durable solutions, primarily through the preferred solution of dignified and safe voluntary repatriation, including solutions such as those adopted by the international refugee conferences. The World Conference on Human Rights underlines the responsibilities of States, particularly as they relate to the countries of origin.

In the light of the comprehensive approach, the World Conference on Human Rights emphasizes the importance of giving special attention including through intergovernmental and humanitarian organizations and finding lasting solutions to questions related to internally displaced persons including their voluntary and safe return and rehabilitation.

In accordance with the Charter of the United Nations and the principles of humanitarian law, the World Conference on Human Rights further emphasizes the importance of and the need for humanitarian assistance to victims of all natural and man-made disasters.

24. Great importance must be given to the promotion and protection of the human rights of persons belonging to groups which have been rendered vulnerable, including migrant workers, the elimination of all forms of discrimination against them, and the strengthening and more effective implementation of existing human rights instruments. States have an obligation to create and maintain adequate measures at the national level, in particular in the fields of education, health and social support, for the promotion and protection of the rights of persons in vulnerable sectors of their populations and to ensure the participation of those among them who are interested in finding a solution to their own problems.

25. The World Conference on Human Rights affirms that extreme poverty and social exclusion constitute a violation of human dignity and that urgent steps are necessary to achieve better knowledge of extreme poverty and its causes, including those related to the problem of development, in order to promote the human rights of the poorest, and to put an end to extreme poverty and social exclusion and to promote the enjoyment of the fruits of social progress. It is essential for States to foster participation by the poorest people in the decision-making process by the community in which they live, the promotion of human rights and efforts to combat extreme poverty.

26. The World Conference on Human Rights welcomes the progress made in the codification of human rights instruments, which is a dynamic and evolving process, and urges the universal ratification of human rights treaties. All States are encouraged to accede to these international instruments; all States are encouraged to avoid, as far as possible, the resort to reservations.

27. Every State should provide an effective framework of remedies to redress human rights grievances or violations. The administration of justice, including law enforcement and prosecutorial agencies and, especially, an independent judiciary and legal profession in full conformity with applicable standards contained in international human rights instruments, are essential to the full and non-discriminatory realization of human rights and indispensable to the processes of democracy and sustainable development. In this context, institutions concerned with the administration of justice should be properly funded, and an increased level of both technical and financial assistance should be provided by the international community. It is incumbent upon the United Nations to make use

of special programmes of advisory services on a priority basis for the achievement of a strong and independent administration of justice.

28. The World Conference on Human Rights expresses its dismay at massive violations of human rights especially in the form of genocide, 'ethnic cleansing' and systematic rape of women in war situations, creating mass exodus of refugees and displaced persons. While strongly condemning such abhorrent practices it reiterates the call that perpetrators of such crimes be punished and such practices immediately stopped.

29. The World Conference on Human Rights expresses grave concern about continuing human rights violations in all parts of the world in disregard of standards as contained in international human rights instruments and international humanitarian law and about the lack of sufficient and effective remedies for the victims.

The World Conference on Human Rights is deeply concerned about violations of human rights during armed conflicts, affecting the civilian population, especially women, children, the elderly and the disabled. The Conference therefore calls upon States and all parties to armed conflicts strictly to observe international humanitarian law, as set forth in the Geneva Conventions of 1949 and other rules and principles of international law, as well as minimum standards for protection of human rights, as laid down in international conventions.

The World Conference on Human Rights reaffirms the right of the victims to be assisted by humanitarian organizations, as set forth in the Geneva Conventions of 1949 and other relevant instruments of international humanitarian law, and calls for the safe and timely access for such assistance.

30. The World Conference on Human Rights also expresses its dismay and condemnation that gross and systematic violations and situations that constitute serious obstacles to the full enjoyment of all human rights continue to occur in different parts of the world. Such violations and obstacles include, as well as torture and cruel, inhuman and degrading treatment or punishment, summary and arbitrary executions, disappearances, arbitrary detentions, all forms of racism, racial discrimination and apartheid, foreign occupation and alien domination, xenophobia, poverty, hunger and other denials of economic, social and cultural rights, religious intolerance, terrorism, discrimination against women and lack of the rule of law.

31. The World Conference on Human Rights calls upon States to refrain from any unilateral measure not in accordance with international law and the Charter of the United Nations that creates obstacles to trade relations among States and impedes the full realization of the human rights set forth in the Universal Declaration of Human Rights and international human rights instruments, in particular the rights of everyone to a standard of living adequate for their health and well-being, including food and medical care, housing and the necessary social services. The World Conference on Human Rights affirms that food should not be used as a tool for political pressure.

32. The World Conference on Human Rights reaffirms the importance of ensuring the universality, objectivity and non-selectivity of the consideration of human rights issues.

33. The World Conference on Human Rights reaffirms that States are duty-bound, as stipulated in the Universal Declaration of Human Rights and the International Covenant on Economic, Social and Cultural Rights and in other international human rights instruments, to ensure that education is aimed at strengthening the respect of human rights and fundamental freedoms. The World Conference on Human Rights emphasizes the importance of incorporating the subject of human rights education programmes and calls upon States to do so. Education should promote understanding, tolerance, peace and friendly relations between the nations and all racial or religious groups and encourage the development of United Nations activities in pursuance of these objectives. Therefore, education on human rights and the dissemination of proper information, both theoretical and practical, play an important role in the promotion and respect of human rights with regard to all individuals without distinction of any kind such as race, sex, language or religion, and this should be integrated in the education policies at the national as well as international levels. The World Conference on Human Rights notes that resource constraints and institutional inadequacies may impede the immediate realization of these objectives.

34. Increased efforts should be made to assist countries which so request to create the conditions whereby each individual can enjoy universal human rights and fundamental freedoms. Governments and the United Nations system as well as other multilateral organizations are urged to increase considerably the resources allocated to programmes aiming at the establishment and strengthening of national legislation, national institutions and related infrastructures which uphold the rule of law and democracy, electoral assistance, human rights awareness through training, teaching and education, popular participation and civil society.

The programmes of advisory services and technical cooperation under the Centre for Human Rights should be strengthened as well as made more efficient and transparent and thus become a major contribution to improving respect for human rights. States are called upon to increase their contributions to these programmes, both through promoting a larger allocation from the United Nations regular budget and through voluntary contributions.

35. The full and effective implementation of United Nations activities to promote and protect human rights must reflect the high importance accorded to human rights by the Charter of the United Nations and the demands of the United Nations human rights activities, as mandated by Member States. To this end, United Nations human rights activities should be provided with increased resources.

36. The World Conference on Human Rights reaffirms the important and constructive role played by national institutions for the promotion and protection of human rights, in particular in their advisory capacity to the competent authorities, their role in remedying human rights violations, in the dissemination of human rights information, and education in human rights.

The World Conference on Human Rights encourages the establishment and strengthening of national institutions, having regard to the 'Principles relating to the status of national institutions' and recognizing that it is the right of each State to choose the framework which is best suited to its particular needs at the national level.

37. Regional arrangements play a fundamental role in promoting and protecting human rights. They should reinforce universal human rights standards, as contained in international human rights instruments, and their protection. The World Conference on Human Rights endorses efforts under way to strengthen these arrangements and to increase their effectiveness, while at the same time stressing the importance of cooperation with the United Nations human rights activities.

The World Conference on Human Rights reiterates the need to consider the possibility of establishing regional and sub-regional arrangements for the promotion and protection of human rights where they do not already exist.

38. The World Conference on Human Rights recognizes the important role of non-governmental organizations in the promotion of all human rights and in humanitarian activities at national, regional and international levels. The World Conference on Human Rights appreciates their contribution to increasing public awareness of human rights issues, to the conduct of education, training and research in this field, and to the promotion and protection of all human rights and fundamental freedoms. While recognizing that the primary responsibility for standard-setting lies with States, the Conference also appreciates the contribution of non-governmental organizations to this process. In this respect, the World Conference on Human Rights emphasizes the importance of continued dialogue and cooperation between Governments and non-governmental organizations. Non-governmental organizations and their members genuinely involved in the field of human rights should enjoy the rights and freedoms recognized in the Universal Declaration of Human Rights, and the protection of the national law. These rights and freedoms may not be exercised contrary to the purposes and principles of the United Nations. Non-governmental organizations should be free to carry out their human rights activities, without interference, within the framework of national law and the Universal Declaration of Human Rights.

39. Underlining the importance of objective, responsible and impartial information about human rights and humanitarian issues, the World Conference on Human Rights encourages the increased involvement of the media, for whom freedom and protection should be guaranteed within the framework of national law.

II

A. INCREASED COORDINATION ON HUMAN RIGHTS WITHIN THE UNITED NATIONS SYSTEM

1. The World Conference on Human Rights recommends increased coordination in support of human rights and fundamental freedoms within the United Nations system. To this end, the World Conference on Human Rights urges all United Nations organs, bodies and the specialized agencies whose activities deal with human rights to cooperate in order to strengthen, rationalize and streamline their activities, taking into account the need to avoid unnecessary duplication. The World Conference on Human Rights also recommends to the Secretary-General that high-level officials of relevant United Nations bodies and specialized agencies at their annual meeting, besides coordinating their activities, also assess the impact of their strategies and policies on the enjoyment of all human rights.

2. Furthermore, the World Conference on Human Rights calls on regional organizations and prominent international and regional finance and development institutions to assess also the impact of their policies and programmes on the enjoyment of human rights.

3. The World Conference on Human Rights recognizes that relevant specialized agencies and bodies and institutions of the United Nations system as well as other relevant inter-governmental organizations whose activities deal with human rights play a vital role in the formulation, promotion and implementation of human rights standards, within their respective mandates, and should take into account the outcome of the World Conference on Human Rights within their fields of competence.

4. The World Conference on Human Rights strongly recommends that a concerted effort be made to encourage and facilitate the ratification of and accession or succession to international human rights treaties and protocols adopted within the framework of the United Nations system with the aim of universal acceptance. The Secretary-General, in consultation with treaty bodies, should consider opening a dialogue with States not having acceded to these human rights treaties, in order to identify obstacles and to seek ways of overcoming them.

5. The World Conference on Human Rights encourages States to consider limiting the extent of any reservations they lodge to international human rights instruments, formulate any reservations as precisely and narrowly as possible, ensure that none is incompatible with the object and purpose of the relevant treaty and regularly review any reservations with a view to withdrawing them.

6. The World Conference on Human Rights, recognizing the need to maintain consistency with the high quality of existing international standards and to avoid proliferation of human rights instruments, reaffirms the guidelines relating to the elaboration of new international instruments contained in General Assembly resolution 41/120 of 4 December 1986 and calls on the United Nations human rights bodies, when considering the elaboration of new international standards, to keep those guidelines in mind, to consult with human rights treaty bodies on the necessity for drafting new standards and to request the Secretariat to carry out technical reviews of proposed new instruments.

7. The World Conference on Human Rights recommends that human rights officers be assigned if and when necessary to regional offices of the United Nations Organization with the purpose of disseminating information and offering training and other technical assistance in the field of human rights upon the request of concerned Member States. Human rights training for international civil servants who are assigned to work relating to human rights should be organized.

8. The World Conference on Human Rights welcomes the convening of emergency sessions of the Commission on Human Rights as a positive initiative and that other ways of responding to acute violations of human rights be considered by the relevant organs of the United Nations system.

Resources

9. The World Conference on Human Rights, concerned by the growing disparity between the activities of the Centre for Human Rights and the human, financial and other resources available to carry them out, and bearing in mind the resources needed for other important United Nations programmes, requests the Secretary-General and the General Assembly to take immediate steps to

increase substantially the resources for the human rights programme from within the existing and future regular budgets of the United Nations, and to take urgent steps to seek increased extrabudgetary resources.

10. Within this framework, an increased proportion of the regular budget should be allocated directly to the Centre for Human Rights to cover its costs and all other costs borne by the Centre for Human Rights, including those related to the United Nations human rights bodies. Voluntary funding of the Centre's technical cooperation activities should reinforce this enhanced budget; the World Conference on Human Rights calls for generous contributions to the existing trust funds.

11. The World Conference on Human Rights requests the Secretary-General and the General Assembly to provide sufficient human, financial and other resources to the Centre for Human Rights to enable it effectively, efficiently and expeditiously to carry out its activities.

12. The World Conference on Human Rights, noting the need to ensure that human and financial resources are available to carry out the human rights activities, as mandated by intergovernmental bodies, urges the Secretary-General, in accordance with Article 101 of the Charter of the United Nations, and Member States to adopt a coherent approach aimed at securing that resources commensurate to the increased mandates are allocated to the Secretariat. The World Conference on Human Rights invites the Secretary-General to consider whether adjustments to procedures in the programme budget cycle would be necessary or helpful to ensure the timely and effective implementation of human rights activities as mandated by Member States.

Centre for Human Rights

13. The World Conference on Human Rights stresses the importance of strengthening the United Nations Centre for Human Rights.

14. The Centre for Human Rights should play an important role in coordinating system-wide attention for human rights. The focal role of the Centre can best be realized if it is enabled to cooperate fully with other United Nations bodies and organs. The coordinating role of the Centre for Human Rights also implies that the office of the Centre for Human Rights in New York is strengthened.

15. The Centre for Human Rights should be assured adequate means for the system of thematic and country rapporteurs, experts, working groups and treaty bodies. Follow-up on recommendations should become a priority matter for consideration by the Commission on Human Rights.

16. The Centre for Human Rights should assume a larger role in the promotion of human rights. This role could be given shape through cooperation with Member States and by an enhanced programme of advisory services and technical assistance. The existing voluntary funds will have to be expanded substantially for these purposes and should be managed in a more efficient and coordinated way. All activities should follow strict and transparent project management rules and regular programme and project evaluations should be held periodically. To this end, the results of such evaluation exercises and other relevant information should be made available regularly. The Centre should, in particular, organize at least once a year information meetings open to all Member States and organizations directly involved in these projects and programmes.

Adaptation and strengthening of the United Nations machinery for human rights, including the question of the establishment of a United Nations High Commissioner for Human Rights

17. The World Conference on Human Rights recognizes the necessity for a continuing adaptation of the United Nations human rights machinery to the current and future needs in the promotion and protection of human rights, as reflected in the present Declaration and within the framework of a balanced and sustainable development for all people. In particular, the United Nations human rights organs should improve their coordination, efficiency and effectiveness.

18. The World Conference on Human Rights recommends to the General Assembly that, when examining the report of the Conference at its forty-eighth session, it begin, as a matter of priority, consideration of the question of the establishment of a High Commissioner for Human Rights for the promotion and protection of all human rights.

B. EQUALITY, DIGNITY AND TOLERANCE

1. Racism, racial discrimination, xenophobia and other forms of intolerance

19. The World Conference on Human Rights considers the elimination of racism and racial discrimination, in particular in their institutionalized forms such as apartheid or resulting from doctrines of racial superiority or exclusivity or contemporary forms and manifestations of racism, as a primary objective for the international community and a worldwide promotion programme in the field of human rights. United Nations organs and agencies should strengthen their efforts to implement such a programme of action related to the third decade to combat racism and racial discrimination as well as subsequent mandates to the same end. The World Conference on Human Rights strongly appeals to the international community to contribute generously to the Trust Fund for the Programme for the Decade for Action to Combat Racism and Racial Discrimination.

20. The World Conference on Human Rights urges all Governments to take immediate measures and to develop strong policies to prevent and combat all forms and manifestations of racism, xenophobia or related intolerance, where necessary by enactment of appropriate legislation, including penal measures, and by the establishment of national institutions to combat such phenomena.

21. The World Conference on Human Rights welcomes the decision of the Commission on Human Rights to appoint a Special Rapporteur on contemporary forms of racism, racial discrimination, xenophobia and related intolerance. The World Conference on Human Rights also appeals to all States parties to the International Convention on the Elimination of All Forms of Racial Discrimination to consider making the declaration under article 14 of the Convention.

22. The World Conference on Human Rights calls upon all Governments to take all appropriate measures in compliance with their international obligations and with due regard to their respective legal systems to counter intolerance and related violence based on religion or belief, including practices of discrimination against women and including the desecration of religious sites, recognizing that every individual has the right to freedom of thought, conscience, expression and religion. The Conference also invites all States to put into practice the provisions of the Declaration on the Elimination of All Forms of Intolerance and of Discrimination Based on Religion or Belief.

23. The World Conference on Human Rights stresses that all persons who perpetrate or authorize criminal acts associated with ethnic cleansing are individually responsible and accountable for such human rights violations, and that the international community should exert every effort to bring those legally responsible for such violations to justice.

24. The World Conference on Human Rights calls on all States to take immediate measures, individually and collectively, to combat the practice of ethnic cleansing to bring it quickly to an end. Victims of the abhorrent practice of ethnic cleansing are entitled to appropriate and effective remedies.

2. Persons belonging to national or ethnic, religious and linguistic minorities

25. The World Conference on Human Rights calls on the Commission on Human Rights to examine ways and means to promote and protect effectively the rights of persons belonging to minorities as set out in the Declaration on the Rights of Persons belonging to National or Ethnic, Religious and Linguistic Minorities. In this context, the World Conference on Human Rights calls upon the Centre for Human Rights to provide, at the request of Governments concerned and as part of its programme of advisory services and technical assistance, qualified expertise on minority issues and human rights, as well as on the prevention and resolution of disputes, to assist in existing or potential situations involving minorities.

26. The World Conference on Human Rights urges States and the international community to promote and protect the rights of persons belonging to national or ethnic, religious and linguistic minorities in accordance with the Declaration on the Rights of Persons belonging to National or Ethnic, Religious and Linguistic Minorities.

27. Measures to be taken, where appropriate, should include facilitation of their full participation in all aspects of the political, economic, social, religious and cultural life of society and in the economic progress and development in their country.

Indigenous people

28. The World Conference on Human Rights calls on the Working Group on Indigenous Populations of the Sub-commission on Prevention of Discrimination and Protection of Minorities to complete the drafting of a declaration on the rights of indigenous people at its eleventh session.

29. The World Conference on Human Rights recommends that the Commission on Human Rights consider the renewal and updating of the mandate of the Working Group on Indigenous Populations upon completion of the drafting of a declaration on the rights of indigenous people.

30. The World Conference on Human Rights also recommends that advisory services and technical assistance programmes within the United Nations system respond positively to requests by States for assistance which would be of direct benefit to indigenous people. The World Conference on Human Rights further recommends that adequate human and financial resources be made available to the Centre for Human Rights within the overall framework of strengthening the Centre's activities as envisaged by this document.

31. The World Conference on Human Rights urges States to ensure the full and free participation of indigenous people in all aspects of society, in particular in matters of concern to them.

32. The World Conference on Human Rights recommends that the General Assembly proclaim an international decade of the world's indigenous people, to begin from January 1994, including action-orientated programmes, to be decided upon in partnership with indigenous people. An appropriate voluntary trust fund should be set up for this purpose. In the framework of such a decade, the establishment of a permanent forum for indigenous people in the United Nations system should be considered.

Migrant workers

33. The World Conference on Human Rights urges all States to guarantee the protection of the human rights of all migrant workers and their families.

34. The World Conference on Human Rights considers that the creation of conditions to foster greater harmony and tolerance between migrant workers and the rest of the society of the State in which they reside is of particular importance.

35. The World Conference on Human Rights invites States to consider the possibility of signing and ratifying, at the earliest possible time, the International Convention on the Rights of All Migrant Workers and Members of Their Families.

3. The equal status and human rights of women

36. The World Conference on Human Rights urges the full and equal enjoyment by women of all human rights and that this be a priority for Governments and for the United Nations. The World Conference on Human Rights also underlines the importance of the integration and full participation of women as both agents and beneficiaries in the development process, and reiterates the objectives established on global action for women towards sustainable and equitable development set forth in the Rio Declaration on Environment and Development and chapter 24 of Agenda 21, adopted by the United Nations Conference on Environment and Development (Rio de Janeiro, Brazil, 3–14 June 1992).

37. The equal status of women and the human rights of women should be integrated into the mainstream of United Nations system-wide activity. These issues should be regularly and systematically addressed throughout relevant United Nations bodies and mechanisms. In particular, steps should be taken to increase cooperation and promote further integration of objectives and goals between the Commission on the Status of Women, the Commission on Human Rights, the Committee for the Elimination of Discrimination against Women, the United Nations Development Fund for Women, the United Nations Development Programme and other United Nations agencies. In this context, cooperation and coordination should be strengthened between the Centre for Human Rights and the Division for the Advancement of Women.

38. In particular, the World Conference on Human Rights stresses the importance of working towards the elimination of violence against women in public and private life, the elimination of all forms of sexual harassment, exploitation and trafficking in women, the elimination of gender bias in

the administration of justice and the eradication of any conflicts which may arise between the rights of women and the harmful effects of certain traditional or customary practices, cultural prejudices and religious extremism. The World Conference on Human Rights calls upon the General Assembly to adopt the draft declaration on violence against women and urges States to combat violence against women in accordance with its provisions. Violations of the human rights of women in situations of armed conflict are violations of the fundamental principles of international human rights and humanitarian law. All violations of this kind, including in particular murder, systematic rape, sexual slavery, and forced pregnancy, require a particularly effective response.

39. The World Conference on Human Rights urges the eradication of all forms of discrimination against women, both hidden and overt. The United Nations should encourage the goal of universal ratification by all States of the Convention on the Elimination of All Forms of Discrimination against Women by the year 2000. Ways and means of addressing the particularly large number of reservations to the Convention should be encouraged. *Inter alia*, the Committee on the Elimination of Discrimination against Women should continue its review of reservations to the Convention. States are urged to withdraw reservations that are contrary to the object and purpose of the Convention or which are otherwise incompatible with international treaty law.

40. Treaty monitoring bodies should disseminate necessary information to enable women to make more effective use of existing implementation procedures in their pursuits of full and equal enjoyment of human rights and non-discrimination. New procedures should also be adopted to strengthen implementation of the commitment to women's equality and the human rights of women. The Commission on the Status of Women and the Committee on the Elimination of Discrimination against Women should quickly examine the possibility of introducing the right of petition through the preparation of an optional protocol to the Convention on the Elimination of All Forms of Discrimination against Women. The World Conference on Human Rights welcomes the decision of the Commission on Human Rights to consider the appointment of a special rapporteur on violence against women at its fiftieth session.

41. The World Conference on Human Rights recognizes the importance of the enjoyment by women of the highest standard of physical and mental health throughout their life-span. In the context of the World Conference on Women and the Convention on the Elimination of All Forms of Discrimination against Women, as well as the Proclamation of Tehran of 1968, the World Conference on Human Rights reaffirms, on the basis of equality between women and men, a woman's right to accessible and adequate health care and the widest range of family planning services, as well as equal access to education at all levels.

42. Treaty monitoring bodies should include the status of women and the human rights of women in their deliberations and findings, making use of gender-specific data. States should be encouraged to supply information on the situation of women *de jure* and *de facto* in their reports to treaty monitoring bodies. The World Conference on Human Rights notes with satisfaction that the Commission on Human Rights adopted at its forty-ninth session resolution 1993/46 of 8 March 1993 stating that rapporteurs and working groups in the field of human rights should also be encouraged to do so. Steps should also be taken by the Division for the Advancement of Women in cooperation with other United Nations bodies, specifically the Centre for Human Rights, to ensure that the human rights activities of the United Nations regularly address violations of women's human rights, including gender-specific abuses. Training for United Nations human rights and humanitarian relief personnel to assist them to recognize and deal with human rights abuses particular to women and to carry out their work without gender bias should be encouraged.

43. The World Conference on Human Rights urges Governments and regional and international organizations to facilitate the access of women to decision-making posts and their greater participation in the decision-making process. It encourages further steps within the United Nations Secretariat to appoint and promote women staff members in accordance with the Charter of the United Nations, and encourages other principal and subsidiary organs of the United Nations to guarantee the participation of women under conditions of equality.

44. The World Conference on Human Rights welcomes the World Conference on Women to be held in Beijing in 1995 and urges that human rights of women should play an important role in its deliberations, in accordance with the priority themes of the World Conference on Women of equality, development and peace.

4. The rights of the child

45. The World Conference on Human Rights reiterates the principle of 'First Call for Children' and, in this respect, underlines the importance of major national and international efforts, especially those of the United Nations Children's Fund, for promoting respect for the rights of the child to survival, protection, development and participation.

46. Measures should be taken to achieve universal ratification of the Convention on the Rights of the Child by 1995 and the universal signing of the World Declaration on the Survival, Protection and Development of Children and Plan of Action adopted by the World Summit for Children, as well as their effective implementation. The World Conference on Human Rights urges States to withdraw reservations to the Convention on the Rights of the Child contrary to the object and purpose of the Convention or otherwise contrary to international treaty law.

47. The World Conference on Human Rights urges all nations to undertake measures to the maximum extent of their available resources, with the support of international cooperation, to achieve the goals in the World Summit Plan of Action. The Conference calls on States to integrate the Convention on the Rights of the Child into their national action plans. By means of these national action plans and through international efforts, particular priority should be placed on reducing infant and maternal mortality rates, reducing malnutrition and illiteracy rates and providing access to safe drinking-water and to basic education. When ever so called for, national plans of action should be devised to combat devastating emergencies resulting from natural disasters and armed conflicts and the equally grave problem of children in extreme poverty.

48. The World Conference on Human Rights urges all States, with the support of international cooperation, to address the acute problem of children under especially difficult circumstances. Exploitation and abuse of children should be actively combated, including by addressing their root causes. Effective measures are required against female infanticide, harmful child labour, sale of children and organs, child prostitution, child pornography, as well as other forms of sexual abuse.

49. The World Conference on Human Rights supports all measures by the United Nations and its specialized agencies to ensure the effective protection and promotion of human rights of the girl child. The World Conference on Human Rights urges States to repeal existing laws and regulations and remove customs and practices which discriminate against and cause harm to the girl child.

50. The World Conference on Human Rights strongly supports the proposal that the Secretary-General initiate a study into means of improving the protection of children in armed conflicts. Humanitarian norms should be implemented and measures taken in order to protect and facilitate assistance to children in war zones. Measures should include protection for children against indiscriminate use of all weapons of war, especially antipersonnel mines. The need for after-care and rehabilitation of children traumatized by war must be addressed urgently. The Conference calls on the Committee on the Rights of the Child to study the question of raising the minimum age of recruitment into armed forces.

51. The World Conference on Human Rights recommends that matters relating to human rights and the situation of children be regularly reviewed and monitored by all relevant organs and mechanisms of the United Nations system and by the supervisory bodies of the specialized agencies in accordance with their mandates.

52. The World Conference on Human Rights recognizes the important role played by non-governmental organizations in the effective implementation of all human rights instruments and, in particular, the Convention on the Rights of the Child.

53. The World Conference on Human Rights recommends that the Committee on the Rights of the Child, with the assistance of the Centre for Human Rights, be enabled expeditiously and effectively

to meet its mandate, especially in view of the unprecedented extent of ratification and subsequent submission of country reports.

5. *Freedom from torture*

54. The World Conference on Human Rights welcomes the ratification by many Member States of the Convention against Torture and Other Cruel, Inhuman or Degrading Treatment or Punishment and encourages its speedy ratification by all other Member States.

55. The World Conference on Human Rights emphasizes that one of the most atrocious violations against human dignity is the act of torture, the result of which destroys the dignity and impairs the capability of victims to continue their lives and their activities.

56. The World Conference on Human Rights reaffirms that under human rights law and international humanitarian law, freedom from torture is a right which must be protected under all circumstances, including in times of internal or international disturbance or armed conflicts.

57. The World Conference on Human Rights therefore urges all States to put an immediate end to the practice of torture and eradicate this evil for ever through full implementation of the Universal Declaration of Human Rights as well as the relevant conventions and, where necessary, strengthening of existing mechanisms. The World Conference on Human Rights calls on all States to cooperate fully with the Special Rapporteur on the question of torture in the fulfilment of his mandate.

58. Special attention should be given to ensure universal respect for, and effective implementation of, the Principles of Medical Ethics relevant to the Role of Health Personnel, particularly Physicians, in the Protection of Prisoners and Detainees against Torture and other Cruel, Inhuman or Degrading Treatment or Punishment adopted by the General Assembly of the United Nations.

59. The World Conference on Human Rights stresses the importance of further concrete action within the framework of the United Nations with the view to providing assistance to victims of torture and ensuring more effective remedies for their physical, psychological and social rehabilitation. Providing the necessary resources for this purpose should be given high priority, *inter alia*, by additional contributions to the United Nations Voluntary Fund for the Victims of Torture.

60. States should abrogate legislation leading to impunity for those responsible for grave violations of human rights such as torture and prosecute such violations, thereby providing a firm basis for the rule of law.

61. The World Conference on Human Rights reaffirms that efforts to eradicate torture should, first and foremost, be concentrated on prevention and, therefore, calls for the early adoption of an optional protocol to the Convention against Torture and Other Cruel, Inhuman and Degrading Treatment or Punishment, which is intended to establish a preventive system of regular visits to places of detention.

Enforced disappearances

62. The World Conference on Human Rights, welcoming the adoption by the General Assembly of the Declaration on the Protection of All Persons from Enforced Disappearance, calls upon all States to take effective legislative, administrative, judicial or other measures to prevent, terminate and punish acts of enforced disappearances. The World Conference on Human Rights reaffirms that it is the duty of all States, under any circumstances, to make investigations whenever there is reason to believe that an enforced disappearance has taken place on a territory under their jurisdiction and, if allegations are confirmed, to prosecute its perpetrators.

6. *The rights of the disabled person*

63. The World Conference on Human Rights reaffirms that all human rights and fundamental freedoms are universal and thus unreservedly include persons with disabilities. Every person is born equal and has the same rights to life and welfare, education and work, living independently and active participation in all aspects of society. Any direct discrimination or other negative discriminatory treatment of a disabled person is therefore a violation of his or her rights. The World Conference on Human Rights calls on Governments, where necessary, to adopt or adjust legislation to assure access to these and other rights for disabled persons.

64. The place of disabled persons is everywhere. Persons with disabilities should be guaranteed equal opportunity through the elimination of all socially determined barriers, be they physical, financial, social or psychological, which exclude or restrict full participation in society.

65. Recalling the World Programme of Action concerning Disabled Persons, adopted by the General Assembly at its thirty-seventh session, the World Conference on Human Rights calls upon the General Assembly and the Economic and Social Council to adopt the draft standard rules on the equalization of opportunities for persons with disabilities, at their meetings in 1993.

C. CO-OPERATION, DEVELOPMENT AND STRENGTHENING OF HUMAN RIGHTS

66. The World Conference on Human Rights recommends that priority be given to national and international action to promote democracy, development and human rights.

67. Special emphasis should be given to measures to assist in the strengthening and building of institutions relating to human rights, strengthening of a pluralistic civil society and the protection of groups which have been rendered vulnerable. In this context, assistance provided upon the request of Governments for the conduct of free and fair elections, including assistance in the human rights aspects of elections and public information about elections, is of particular importance. Equally important is the assistance to be given to the strengthening of the rule of law, the promotion of freedom of expression and the administration of justice, and to the real and effective participation of the people in the decision-making processes.

68. The World Conference on Human Rights stresses the need for the implementation of strengthened advisory services and technical assistance activities by the Centre for Human Rights. The Centre should make available to States upon request assistance on specific human rights issues, including the preparation of reports under human rights treaties as well as for the implementation of coherent and comprehensive plans of action for the promotion and protection of human rights. Strengthening the institutions of human rights and democracy, the legal protection of human rights, training of officials and others, broad-based education and public information aimed at promoting respect for human rights should all be available as components of these programmes.

69. The World Conference on Human Rights strongly recommends that a comprehensive programme be established within the United Nations in order to help States in the task of building and strengthening adequate national structures which have a direct impact on the overall observance of human rights and the maintenance of the rule of law. Such a programme, to be coordinated by the Centre for Human Rights, should be able to provide, upon the request of the interested Government, technical and financial assistance to national projects in reforming penal and correctional establishments, education and training of lawyers, judges and security forces in human rights, and any other sphere of activity relevant to the good functioning of the rule of law. That programme should make available to States assistance for the implementation of plans of action for the promotion and protection of human rights.

70. The World Conference on Human Rights requests the Secretary-General of the United Nations to submit proposals to the United Nations General Assembly, containing alternatives for the establishment, structure, operational modalities and funding of the proposed programme.

71. The World Conference on Human Rights recommends that each State consider the desirability of drawing up a national action plan identifying steps whereby that State would improve the promotion and protection of human rights.

72. The World Conference on Human Rights reaffirms that the universal and inalienable right to development, as established in the Declaration on the Right to Development, must be implemented and realized. In this context, the World Conference on Human Rights welcomes the appointment by the Commission on Human Rights of a thematic working group on the right to development and urges that the Working Group, in consultation and co-operation with other organs and agencies of the United Nations system, promptly formulate, for early consideration by the United Nations General Assembly, comprehensive and effective measures to eliminate obstacles to the implementation and

realization of the Declaration on the Right to Development and recommending ways and means towards the realization of the right to development by all States.

73. The World Conference on Human Rights recommends that non-governmental and other grass-roots organizations active in development and/or human rights should be enabled to play a major role on the national and international levels in the debate, activities and implementation relating to the right to development and, in co-operation with Governments, in all relevant aspects of development co-operation.

74. The World Conference on Human Rights appeals to Governments, competent agencies and institutions to increase considerably the resources devoted to building well-functioning legal systems able to protect human rights, and to national institutions working in this area. Actors in the field of development co-operation should bear in mind the mutually reinforcing inter-relationship between development, democracy and human rights. Cooperation should be based on dialogue and transparency. The World Conference on Human Rights also calls for the establishment of comprehensive programmes, including resource banks of information and personnel with expertise relating to the strengthening of the rule of law and of democratic institutions.

75. The World Conference on Human Rights encourages the Commission on Human Rights, in co-operation with the Committee on Economic, Social and Cultural Rights, to continue the examination of optional protocols to the International Covenant on Economic, Social and Cultural Rights.

76. The World Conference on Human Rights recommends that more resources be made available for the strengthening or the establishment of regional arrangements for the promotion and protection of human rights under the programmes of advisory services and technical assistance of the Centre for Human Rights. States are encouraged to request assistance for such purposes as regional and subregional workshops, seminars and information exchanges designed to strengthen regional arrangement for the promotion and protection of human rights in accord with universal human rights standards as contained in international human rights instruments.

77. The World Conference on Human Rights supports all measures by the United Nations and its relevant specialized agencies to ensure the effective promotion and protection of trade union rights, as stipulated in the International Covenant on Economic, Social and Cultural Rights and other relevant international instruments. It calls on all States to abide fully by their obligations in this regard contained in international instruments.

D. HUMAN RIGHTS EDUCATION

78. The World Conference on Human Rights considers human rights education, training and public information essential for the promotion and achievement of stable and harmonious relations among communities and for fostering mutual understanding, tolerance and peace.

79. States should strive to eradicate illiteracy and should direct education towards the full development of the human personality and to the strengthening of respect for human rights and fundamental freedoms. The World Conference on Human Rights calls on all States and institutions to include human rights, humanitarian law, democracy and rule of law as subjects in the curricula of all learning institutions in formal and non-formal settings.

80. Human rights education should include peace, democracy, development and social justice, as set forth in international and regional human rights instruments, in order to achieve common understanding and awareness with a view to strengthening universal commitment to human rights.

81. Taking into account the World Plan of Action on Education for Human Rights and Democracy, adopted in March 1993 by the International Congress on Education for Human Rights and Democracy of the United Nations Educational, Scientific and Cultural Organization, and other human rights instruments, the World Conference on Human Rights recommends that States develop specific programmes and strategies for ensuring the widest human rights education and the dissemination of public information, taking particular account of the human rights needs of women.

82. Governments, with the assistance of intergovernmental organizations, national institutions and non-governmental organizations, should promote an increased awareness of human

rights and mutual tolerance. The World Conference on Human Rights underlines the importance of strengthening the World Public Information Campaign for Human Rights carried out by the United Nations. They should initiate and support education in human rights and undertake effective dissemination of public information in this field. The advisory services and technical assistance programmes of the United Nations system should be able to respond immediately to requests from States for educational and training activities in the field of human rights as well as for special education concerning standards as contained in international human rights instruments and in humanitarian law and their application to special groups such as military forces, law enforcement personnel, police and the health profession. The proclamation of a United Nations decade for human rights education in order to promote, encourage and focus these educational activities should be considered.

E. IMPLEMENTATION AND MONITORING METHODS

83. The World Conference on Human Rights urges Governments to incorporate standards as contained in international human rights instruments in domestic legislation and to strengthen national structures, institutions and organs of society which play a role in promoting and safeguarding human rights.

84. The World Conference on Human Rights recommends the strengthening of United Nations activities and programmes to meet requests for assistance by States which want to establish or strengthen their own national institutions for the promotion and protection of human rights.

85. The World Conference on Human Rights also encourages the strengthening of co-operation between national institutions for the promotion and protection of human rights, particularly through exchanges of information and experience, as well as co-operation with regional organizations and the United Nations.

86. The World Conference on Human Rights strongly recommends in this regard that representatives of national institutions for the promotion and protection of human rights convene periodic meetings under the auspices of the Centre for Human Rights to examine ways and means of improving their mechanisms and sharing experiences.

87. The World Conference on Human Rights recommends to the human rights treaty bodies, to the meetings of chairpersons of the treaty bodies and to the meetings of States parties that they continue to take steps aimed at coordinating the multiple reporting requirements and guidelines for preparing State reports under the respective human rights conventions and study the suggestion that the submission of one overall report on treaty obligations undertaken by each State would make these procedures more effective and increase their impact.

88. The World Conference on Human Rights recommends that the States parties to international human rights instruments, the General Assembly and the Economic and Social Council should consider studying the existing human rights treaty bodies and the various thematic mechanisms and procedures with a view to promoting greater efficiency and effectiveness through better coordination of the various bodies, mechanisms and procedures, taking into account the need to avoid unnecessary duplication and overlapping of their mandates and tasks.

89. The World Conference on Human Rights recommends continued work on the improvement of the functioning, including the monitoring tasks, of the treaty bodies, taking into account multiple proposals made in this respect, in particular those made by the treaty bodies themselves and by the meetings of the chairpersons of the treaty bodies. The comprehensive national approach taken by the Committee on the Rights of the Child should also be encouraged.

90. The World Conference on Human Rights recommends that States parties to human rights treaties consider accepting all the available optional communication procedures.

91. The World Conference on Human Rights views with concern the issue of impunity of perpetrators of human rights violations, and supports the efforts of the Commission on Human Rights and the Subcommission on Prevention of Discrimination and Protection of Minorities to examine all aspects of the issue.

92. The World Conference on Human Rights recommends that the Commission on Human Rights examine the possibility for better implementation of existing human rights instruments at the international and regional levels and encourages the International Law Commission to continue its work on an international criminal court.

93. The World Conference on Human Rights appeals to States which have not yet done so to accede to the Geneva Conventions of 12 August 1949 and the Protocols thereto, and to take all appropriate national measures, including legislative ones, for their full implementation.

94. The World Conference on Human Rights recommends the speedy completion and adoption of the draft declaration on the right and responsibility of individuals, groups and organs of society to promote and protect universally recognized human rights and fundamental freedoms.

95. The World Conference on Human Rights underlines the importance of preserving and strengthening the system of special procedures, rapporteurs, representatives, experts and working groups of the Commission on Human Rights and the Subcommission on the Prevention of Discrimination and Protection of Minorities, in order to enable them to carry out their mandates in all countries throughout the world, providing them with the necessary human and financial resources. The procedures and mechanisms should be enabled to harmonize and rationalize their work through periodic meetings. All States are asked to co-operate fully with these procedures and mechanisms.

96. The World Conference on Human Rights recommends that the United Nations assume a more active role in the promotion and protection of human rights in ensuring full respect for international humanitarian law in all situations of armed conflict, in accordance with the purposes and principles of the Charter of the United Nations.

97. The World Conference on Human Rights, recognizing the important role of human rights components in specific arrangements concerning some peace-keeping operations by the United Nations, recommends that the Secretary-General take into account the reporting, experience and capabilities of the Centre for Human Rights and human rights mechanisms, in conformity with the Charter of the United Nations.

98. To strengthen the enjoyment of economic, social and cultural rights, additional approaches should be examined, such as a system of indicators to measure progress in the realization of the rights set forth in the International Covenant on Economic, Social and Cultural Rights. There must be a concerted effort to ensure recognition of economic, social and cultural rights at the national, regional and international levels.

F. FOLLOW-UP TO THE WORLD CONFERENCE ON HUMAN RIGHTS

99. The World Conference on Human Rights recommends that the General Assembly, the Commission on Human Rights and other organs and agencies of the United Nations system related to human rights consider ways and means for the full implementation, without delay, of the recommendations contained in the present Declaration, including the possibility of proclaiming a United Nations decade for human rights. The World Conference on Human Rights further recommends that the Commission on Human Rights annually review the progress towards this end.

100. The World Conference on Human Rights requests the Secretary-General of the United Nations to invite on the occasion of the fiftieth anniversary of the Universal Declaration of Human Rights all States, all organs and agencies of the United Nations system related to human rights, to report to him on the progress made in the implementation of the present Declaration and to submit a report to the General Assembly at its fifty-third session, through the Commission on Human Rights and the Economic and Social Council. Likewise, regional and, as appropriate, national human rights institutions, as well as nongovernmental organizations, may present their views to the Secretary-General on the progress made in the implementation of the present Declaration. Special attention should be paid to assessing the progress towards the goal of universal ratification of international human rights treaties and protocols adopted within the framework of the United Nations system.

Index

NB: Documents are indexed under their principal subject matter

C

Children
  African Charter on Rights and Welfare
      1990 *422–31*
  Convention on Rights of the Child 1989 *95–108*
    Protocols
      Communications Procedure *117–22*
      Involvement in Armed Conflict 2000 *108–11*
      Sale, Prostitution and Pornography
        2000 *111–17*
Civil and Political Rights
  International Covenant on Civil and Political
      Rights 1966 *33–45*
    Protocols
      Abolition of Death Penalty 1990 *400–1*
      Communications from Victims 1966 *45–7*

D

Development
  Declaration on the Right to, 1986 *92–5*
Disabilities
  Convention on Rights 2006 *198–215*
    Protocol 2006 *215–18*

E

Economic, Social and Cultural Rights
  International Covenant on Economic,
      Social and Cultural Rights 1966 *49–56*
    Protocol 2008 *56–61*
Employment
  European Social Charter 1961 *306–16*
  European Social Charter
      (Revised) 1996 *328–46*
    Protocols
      Additional 1988 *317–22*
      Amending 1991 *322–5*
      Collective Complaints 1995 *325–8*
  International Convention on Migrant
      Workers 1990 *122–46*
Enforced Disappearance
  Inter-American Convention 1994 *409–13*
  International Convention 2006 *218–30*

G

Genocide
  Convention on Prevention and
      Punishment 1948 *7–9*

H

Human Rights
  see also Civil and Political Rights
  African Charter 1981 *422–31*
    Protocol Establishing a Single Court
      2008 *441–53*

Protocol on Women's Rights 2003 *432–40*
American Convention 1969 *379–94*
  Protocols
    Abolition of the Death Penalty 1990 *400–1*
    Economic, Social and Cultural Rights (San
      Salvador) 1988 *394–400*
American Declaration of the Rights and Duties of
    Man 1948 *375–9*
Arab Charter 2004 *465–75*
European Charter of Fundamental Rights
    2007 *368–75*
European Convention
    (as amended) 1950 *285–95*
  First Protocol *295–6*
  Fourth Protocol *296–7*
  Sixth Protocol *298–9*
  Seventh Protocol *299–301*
  Twelfth Protocol *301–2*
  Thirteenth Protocol *302–3*
  Sixteenth Protocol *304–5*
Gulf Cooperation Council Declaration *475–9*
Teheran Proclamation 1968 *480–2*
UN Complaints Procedure
  Resolution 60/251 Human Rights Council
    2006 *265–6*
  Resolution 5/1 Human Rights Council
    2007 *267–84*
UN Guiding Principles on Business and Human
    Rights 2011 *237–43*
Universal Declaration 1948 *10–13*
Vienna Declaration 1993 *482–500*

I

Indigenous Peoples
  United Nations Declaration 2007 *230–7*
Internal Displacement
  Guiding Principles 1998 *149–55*
International Courts
  Protocol to the African Charter 2008 *441–53*
  Rome Statute 1998 (as amended 2010) *155–98*
International Crimes
  Convention on Prevention and Punishment
    1948 *7–9*
  Prevention and Punishment of Crimes Against
    Humanity 2019 *255–63*

L

League of Nations, Covenant 1919 *1–2*

M

Minorities
  Declaration on Ethnic, Religious and Linguistic
    Rights 1992 *147–9*

European Charter for Regional or Minority
    Languages 1992 *352–62*
Framework Convention for National Minorities
    1995 *362–67*

R
Racial Discrimination
    International Convention 1965 *25–33*
Refugees
    Cartagena Declaration on
        Refugees 1984 *401–5*
    Convention on Status 1951 *13–23*
    OAU Convention on African Aspects 1969 *418–21*
    Protocol 1967 *23–5*
Religious Discrimination
    Declaration 1981 *73–5*

T
Torture
    Convention 1984 *75–84*
        Protocol 2002 *84–92*

European Convention 1987 *346–50*
    First Protocol 1999 *350–1*
    Second Protocol 1993 *351*
Inter-American Convention 1985 *405–9*

U
United Nations Charter 1945 *2–7*

W
Women
    Convention on Discrimination 1979 *61–9*
        Protocol 1999 *69–73*
    Inter-American Convention on Violence
        1994 *413–7*
    Protocol to African Charter 2003 *432–41*
Workers
    see also Employment
    United Nations Declaration on the Rights of
        Peasants and Other People Working in Rural
        Areas *243–55*